The Humanities
in the
Western Tradition

A Reader

EDITED BY
MICHAEL GRAHAM
MICHAEL LEVIN
CONSTANCE BOUCHARD
STEPHEN HARP and
SHELLEY BARANOWSKI

Houghton Mifflin Company
Boston   New York

Ignatius of Loyola: THE SPIRITUAL EXERCISES AND SELECTED WORKS, George Ganss, ed, (Paulist Press, 1991), pp. 121-45

Excerpts from CLASSICS OF WESTERN THOUGHT: Volume III, The Modern World, Fourth Edition by Edgar E. Knoebel, copyright © 1988 by Harcourt, Inc., reprinted by permission of the publisher.

"The Starry Messenger" from DISCOVERIES AND OPINIONS OF GALILEO by Galileo Galilei, translated by Stillman Drake, copyright © 1957 by Stillman Drake. Used by permission of Doubleday, a division of Random House, Inc.

The Declaration of Independence, July 4, 1776.

Keith Baker, ed, READINGS IN WESTERN CIVILIZATION, VOL. 7: THE OLD REGIME AND THE FRENCH REVOLUTION. Copyright © 1987 by the University of Chicago Press. Reprinted with permission.

Wordsworth, William, Tables Turned, 1798.

Wordsworth, William, Tintern Abbey, 1798.

"The Gay Science" from THE GAY SCIENCE by Friedrich Nietzsche, translated by Walter Kaufmann, copyright © 1974 by Random House, Inc. Translated & edited, with commentary by Walter Kaufmann. Used by permission of Random House, Inc.

"Beyond Good and Evil" from BEYOND GOOD AND EVIL by Friedrich Nietzsche, translated by Walter Kaufmann, copyright © 1966 by Random House, Inc. Used by permission of Random House, Inc.

"With a Great Price" from THE SEVEN STOREY MOUNTAIN by Thomas Merton, copyright © 1948 by Harcourt, Inc. and renewed 1976 by the Trustees of The Merton Legacy Trust, reprinted by permission of the publisher.

"The Guest" from EXILE AND THE KINGDOM by Albert Camus, translated by Justin O'Brien, copyright © 1957, 1958 by Alfred A. Knopf, Inc., a division of Random House, Inc. Used by permission of Alfred A. Knopf, a division of Random House, Inc.

Discipline and Punish: The Birth of the Prison, by Michel Foucault (New York: Pantheon, 1977). Originally published in French as Surveiller et Punir; Naissance de la Prison. Copyright C 1975 by Les Editions Gallimard. Reprinted by permission of Georges Borchardt, Inc.

This work was produced by Houghton Mifflin Custom Publishing and contains material not subject to Houghton Mifflin Company editorial review. The author is responsible for editing, accuracy, and content.

Cover Designer: Joel Gendron
Cover Photograph: Photodisc, Inc.

Custom Publishing Editor: Jan Scipio
Custom Publishing Production Manager: Christina Battista
Project Coordinator: Georgia Young

This book contains select works from existing Houghton Mifflin Company resources and was produced by Houghton Mifflin Custom Publishing for collegiate use. As such, those adopting and/or contributing to this work are responsible for editorial content, accuracy, continuity and completeness.

ISBN-13:978-0-618-81246-2
ISBN-10: 0-618-81246-6
N-06786

2 3 4 5 6 7 8 9 - CCI - 08

Houghton Mifflin
Custom Publishing

222 Berkeley Street • Boston, MA 02116

Address all correspondence and order information to the above address.

CONTENTS

Introduction

Michael Graham

General education courses, such as the one for which this reader has been prepared, are often controversial—with students, with faculty, and with the wider public which higher education in part serves. Students may wonder why they are "forced" to take courses which do not on the surface seem directly relevant to their professional preparation. Why do accountants, or engineers, or nurses (just to name three non-humanities professional fields) need to learn about Plato, Thomas Hobbes or the Qu'ran? Faculty are often dissatisfied with what is included in general education curricula compared to what is left out. How can general surveys covering such a broad range of material be expected to give students any depth of understanding of critical issues? Some see them as inherently biased. For example, the limited educational, political and social opportunities given women throughout western (or for that matter, human) history has meant that relatively few words written by women in the first 5,000 years of writing have survived. Do courses like this, which stress what has been written by our human ancestors, merely perpetuate that disenfranchisement? Some members of the general public are suspicious of the ways traditional core beliefs are subject to scrutiny in this type of course. For example, does encouraging students to examine the evolution of Christian beliefs and their relationship to other religious and philosophical systems undermine the foundations of a religion to which so many adhere, providing yet another example of an academy funded in part through tax dollars which is "out of touch" with public opinion?

We are probably guilty as charged on most counts, and that is precisely why courses like this remain, and should remain, part of a strong general education curriculum. A significant proportion of a traditional university education involves preparation for life and responsible citizenship, not just professional training or the upholding of tradition. Preparation for life and responsible citizenship requires the development and honing of skills—in critical reading, in sifting through unfamiliar and sometimes contradictory information, in argumentation and in written and oral communication—as well as the inculcation of a bit of what has been termed "cultural literacy." Such skills take a long time to develop, and their possession is difficult to measure, but those who gain them are empowered for a life of learning, aesthetic appreciation, empathy and adaptability, all of which are very practical attributes in our rapidly—changing and increasingly interconnected world. These attributes are every bit as valuable to the future speech therapist, township trustee or investment banker as they are to the future novelist or theologian. The Humanities in the Western Tradition is aimed at helping students attain them.

The "western" focus of courses like this has also been questioned. Many people around the world have an ambivalent or hostile view of western civilization, seeing it as embodying a legacy of putative cultural superiority coupled with exploitation and a disinclination to value other cultures. Others embrace it, seeing it as representing a tradition which has fostered political representation and concepts of individual rights along with certain kinds of rationality and technological progress. Love it or hate it, what is undeniable is that we live in the midst of it, in a world on which it has left its indelible imprint, from the classically-influenced buildings of Washington, D.C., to Japanese string quartets playing European art music, to the mosques of Istanbul and the Nike sneakers sold in Calcutta or Dakar (and manufactured elsewhere in the developing world). We are better off learning about it, whether we would like to celebrate it, destroy it, or simply make sense of our world and the roots of so many assumptions, beliefs and conflicts.

Plato quoted his mentor and hero Socrates as saying "the unexamined life is not worth living." The sources in this book help us to examine the past lives of the culture that surrounds us. One of the first things that astute readers will notice is that the western tradition is not monolithic. Rather, it is full of contradictions. It is a long-running argument between many voices about the origins of the universe, our place within it, the nature (or existence) of God, the nature of humanity, proper relationships between humans, how we can best govern ourselves and whether our lives ultimately have any meaning. If, in reading through the sources in this book you do not find some things with which you disagree, you are not paying close enough attention. One of our fundamental goals is to give students an understanding, or even appreciation, of views which they may not share. You may be put off by Homer's celebration of masculine violence or his tendency to explain so many things, good or evil, as the results of the interventions of the gods in human affairs. You might think Socrates in the *Phaedo* is far too eager to embrace death. You might not share Ovid's cynicism about love, and you may be offended by the low regard he seems to have had for the female intellect. You might find the account of the creation of the world in the Book of Genesis self-contradictory. In reading Matthew's account of Jesus' teachings, you might find yourself with the Pharisees, searching for consistency in what seemed to be confusing doctrine. You might conclude that Augustine was far too hard on his youthful self. By the time you read the "Conquest of Orange" epic, you will probably be appalled at the author's lack of understanding of Islamic beliefs. You may find it harsh that Dante places Plato in the first circle of Hell, and you might be depressed by the hellish picture Thomas Hobbes presents of humanity in a state of nature (conversely, you may find his portrayal depressingly accurate).

So you will end up reading a seeming cacophony of diverse voices, some pushing ideas you embrace and others ideas you cannot accept. In some cases, you will probably wonder what all the fuss is about. The point is not for you to be improved or seduced by the "great minds" of the past. Rather, it is for you to understand the context from which particular views have emerged, and the ways in which they have been influential. Our world is full of people who do not share our views on any manner of subjects. So is our past. A better understanding of the latter will leave us much better prepared to deal with the former. You will probably find that you have more in common with the people purchasing those Nike shoes in Calcutta today than you do with Homer, Thomas Aquinas or any number of quintessentially "western" figures.

But do not write off our strange cultural ancestors. Sometimes we can learn the most about the past when we focus on what seems at first most odd. If something seems weird to us, but apparently made sense to them, we need to figure out why—what is it that has caused our attitudes to change? Further, you will discover that we take many of our common assumptions, expressions, symbols and even cliches from these people of the distant past. There are things that we think we know as well as behavioral patterns and habits of speech which we take for granted, rarely considering the fact that most aspects of our lives have been shaped by our cultural past, in a process of evolution which is ongoing. Our own distant descendants will probably look on us as strange also, even as they re-enact the patterns of life which we have shaped.

It is appropriate here to define two critical terms found in the title of this reader. "Western" as a cultural label is difficult to pin down. The approach of this reader and the course for which it is intended is to interpret the term broadly, taking it as referring to cultures whose origins can be located in the area of the world where the three major continents of Africa, Asia and Europe meet—today's Middle East, Asia Minor and southeastern Europe. Later, due to the geographic spread of the Roman Empire, the borders of the "west" expanded to include much of Europe. Later still, European exploration and colonial expansion would bring the Americas into the "western" orbit, while today western culture is in many ways global, due to movements in peoples and technologies, as well as the imperial practices of traditionally western societies, in the last few centuries. "Western" in this sense defines more the borders of a long cultural conversation than it does a geographic area, although it certainly has geographic roots. Furthermore, the conversational borders have rarely been impermeable, often taking in voices from outside and in turn influencing those outsiders.

By "humanities" we refer to subjects studied in several academic disciplines, including literature, history, philosophy, religion, art, architecture and music. Certainly, western culture has left behind many artifacts which are studied outside of those disciplines (the Mesopotamian pottery fragments analyzed by archaeologists come to mind), but our approach here is to concentrate on the western past as seen in written works and the fine arts. There are many ways of getting at the past, and ours is but one. The approaches taken by the social sciences and even the physical sciences are also valid and very useful, but this course will focus more on the qualitative analysis of written sources and artistic works; it is in these that the past speaks most eloquently, if imprecisely.

A term which is not part of the book's title, but is also worth pondering here is "civilization." This word comes from Latin roots having to do with cities and citizenship. To the Latin-speaking Romans, a *civitas* was a city or commonwealth, a union of citizens, and an individual citizen was a *civis*. They had a word for the science of politics: *civilitas*, which had the additional meaning of "politeness" or "civility." At first glance, this would seem to suggest that civilization has generally been an urban thing, and the derogative term *pagani*, used by the Romans to refer to the residents of rural villages (from which we get the word "pagan"), reinforces the notion that city life was regarded as more "civilized." But was this always the case? Is "civilization" possible without cities? And does it make us more polite or "civil" to each other? The value of civilization is one of the things you will ponder in this course.

Our general approach with this reader has been to give students substantial excerpts of a few works, rather than short snippets of many. We have resisted the common tendency of primary source collections to abridge texts by removing parts deemed less significant. This is because we believe that authors write things a certain way for their own good reasons, and parts of a work which our modern sensibilities might rate as less important or even unnecessary might have been regarded as critical by an author. If we are to meet the past on its own terms, we must let it speak freely, without us filtering out the parts that do not seem to relate to us. We also feel that this more prolonged exposure to particular writers will allow students a more substantial engagement with the works in question, resulting in more thoughtful and provocative classroom discussions, as well as better retention of the material. We do not want *The Humanities in the Western Tradition* to offer the intellectual equivalent of a fast food meal. Rather, we aim for something more nutritious and long-lasting, even if its preparation takes more time and expense.

With the development of critical reading skills as one of our primary objectives, we hope that students and their instructors engage in some fundamental source criticism as they approach these texts. In assessing everyday information we often caution others to "consider the source," and this is of paramount importance in the text-based study of the past. With every one of the sources in this book, students and instructors should ponder the following questions: who is the author of the work and what was their likely intent in writing it? In what format was the work initially intended to be presented (e.g. oral performance, written down, or—a post-1460s option, publication)? For what audience was it intended? If events are described, are they events that the author is likely to have witnessed? How far removed in time was the writing of the work from the events described? What issues seem to be particularly important for the author? There are many other questions which can also be asked in reference to particular sources. But knowing (or making an educated guess at) the answers to these sorts of questions will put a reader in a much better position to understand why a text is written the way it is and how it can be used to give us a better understanding of the past.

Finally, we are well aware that some of the sources included here are difficult to read and interpret, even in the modern translations which we have used. Styles of writing today are much different than they were a mere century ago, not to mention 2,800 years ago, at the time Homer was composing the *Iliad*. Students may be frustrated that these authors take a long time to "get to the point." In the face of this, we counsel patience. Sifting through material like this can take time. More importantly, what we consider to be "the point" might be something very different from what the author considered it to be. While some of them were writing for posterity, they were not necessarily writing for us. We have just stepped into their long-running conversation. In a situation like that, the best thing to do is to pay close attention to what people are saying to help yourself get up to speed, rather than interrupting the flow of things by rudely demanding an update on what they are talking about! Good things come to those who wait, and listen, and study, and think.

Homer

THE ILIAD

Introduction by Michael Graham

The Iliad is one of the earliest works in western literature. It is an epic poem attributed to an author named Homer, said to have been blind, who lived somewhere in Greece around 800–750 B.C. The Iliad takes its name from Ilium, the Greek word for Troy, a city in Asia Minor (modern-day Turkey). It describes the efforts of the Greeks (referred to in the poem as "Achaeans") to capture the city of Troy. The site of Troy was excavated by archaeologists in the nineteenth century, and there is evidence that a city on the site was destroyed by fire between about 1250 and 1225 B.C., suggesting that Homer's poem may be based on actual events. But the precise details will never be known, and we must treat the Iliad more as a work of literature than history. It may not offer us a documentary history of the Trojan War, but it does offer us substantial insights into the mentality of the Greeks of Homer's time—their values, their beliefs, their ethical codes and how they thought the world operated.

Even in translation (which can almost never do full justice to an original work), the *Iliad* is a feast of language. We must keep in mind that it was intended to be recited aloud. The vast majority of the Greeks of Homer's time were illiterate, so they would have heard this poem, rather than reading it. And while written copies of the poem circulated for centuries, it was not actually published for the first time until 1488, at which point the poem was already more than 2200 years old. Therefore, we should see this poem as part of a Greek oral tradition; indeed, much of the education of a Greek boy in the Classical era would have involved memorizing Homer's poetry for recitation, and it is quite possible, even likely, that details would have been modified as the work was passed on. So when you are reading this section of the *Iliad* (which includes the first two "books" out of a total of twenty-four), take some time to read aloud, and imagine yourself as a listener rather than a reader.

When the poem begins, the Achaeans have been battling the Trojans for ten years. Troy has not fallen, but there has been a falling-out within the ranks of the Achaeans. Achilles, one of the Achaean commanders, is angry at Agamemnon, king of Mycenae and general of all the Achaean forces. As you read it will become clear what the disagreement is about. What caused it, and what does this say about the values of these men? Are either of them presented in a way which makes them seem heroic? What makes someone a hero in this story? The first two books raise other issues as well. In book two you will meet Helen of Troy. What role does she play in this conflict between the Achaeans and the Trojans? What sort of character is she? You might extend this question to all the female characters who appear in the poem. What does this tell you about gender relations in ancient Greek society? You will also notice that the gods seem to take an active interest in the various conflicts presented in the story. For example, Achilles' mother is the sea-goddess Thetis, and she tries to help him out. How does she go about doing this, and what does this tell us about Greek perceptions of the gods? How would you compare the behavior of Zeus, king of the gods, with the behavior of the Judeo-Christian God as presented in the Bible? Do these gods seem trustworthy? What ethical values do these Greeks seem to have held dear? Did they value mercy or compassion? Parts of book two may seem to you like an endless recitation of names. Why do you think the poet thought it was important to include all this information?

We hope that after reading books one and two, you will have become absorbed enough in the story to want to know how it turned out, so we won't spoil things by giving away the outcome here. But even if you find the *Iliad* not to your taste, you will have received a crash course in Greek values the same way that many ancient Greeks learned them: through the poetry of Homer.

The Iliad

BOOK ONE

The Rage of Achilles

Rage—Goddess, sing the rage of Peleus' son Achilles,
murderous, doomed, that cost the Achaeans countless losses,
hurling down to the House of Death so many sturdy souls,
great fighters' souls, but made their bodies carrion,
feasts for the dogs and birds,
and the will of Zeus was moving toward its end.
Begin, Muse, when the two first broke and clashed,
Agamemnon lord of men and brilliant Achilles.

    What god drove them to fight with such a fury?
Apollo the son of Zeus and Leto. Incensed at the king   10
he swept a fatal plague through the army—men were dying
and all because Agamemnon spurned Apollo's priest.
Yes, Chryses approached the Achaeans' fast ships
to win his daughter back, bringing a priceless ransom
and bearing high in hand, wound on a golden staff,
the wreaths of the god, the distant deadly Archer.
He begged the whole Achaean army but most of all
the two supreme commanders, Atreus' two sons,
"Agamemnon, Menelaus—all Argives geared for war!
May the gods who hold the halls of Olympus give you   20
Priam's city to plunder, then safe passage home.
Just set my daughter free, my dear one . . . here,
accept these gifts, this ransom. Honor the god
who strikes from worlds away—the son of Zeus, Apollo!"

Homer, *The Iliad* (Robert Fagles, trans.), Penguin, 1990 (ISBN 0-14-044592-7), original pp. 77–127.

And all ranks of Achaeans cried out their assent:
"Respect the priest, accept the shining ransom!"
But it brought no joy to the heart of Agamemnon.
The king dismissed the priest with a brutal order
ringing in his ears: "Never again, old man,   30
let me catch sight of you by the hollow ships!
Not loitering now, not slinking back tomorrow.
The staff and the wreaths of god will never save you then.
The girl—I won't give up the girl. Long before that,
old age will overtake her in *my* house, in Argos,
far from her fatherland, slaving back and forth
at the loom, forced to share my bed!
                                   Now go,
don't tempt my wrath—and you may depart alive."

The old man was terrified. He obeyed the order,
turning, trailing away in silence down the shore
where the battle lines of breakers crash and drag.   40
And moving off to a safe distance, over and over
the old priest prayed to the son of sleek-haired Leto,
lord Apollo, "Hear me, Apollo! God of the silver bow
who strides the walls of Chryse and Cilla sacrosanct—
lord in power of Tenedos—Smintheus, god of the plague!
If I ever roofed a shrine to please your heart,
ever burned the long rich bones of bulls and goats
on your holy altar, now, now bring my prayer to pass.
Pay the Danaans back—your arrows for my tears!"

His prayer went up and Phoebus Apollo heard him.   50
Down he strode from Olympus' peaks, storming at heart
with his bow and hooded quiver slung across his shoulders.
The arrows clanged at his back as the god quaked with rage,
the god himself on the march and down he came like night.
Over against the ships he dropped to a knee, let fly a shaft
and a terrifying clash rang out from the great silver bow.
First he went for the mules and circling dogs but then,
launching a piercing shaft at the men themselves,
he cut them down in droves—
and the corpse-fires burned on, night and day, no end in sight.   60

Nine days the arrows of god swept through the army.
On the tenth Achilles called all ranks to muster—
the impulse seized him, sent by white-armed Hera
grieving to see Achaean fighters drop and die.
Once they'd gathered, crowding the meeting grounds,
the swift runner Achilles rose and spoke among them:
"Son of Atreus, now we are beaten back, I fear,

the long campaign is lost. So home we sail . . .
if we can escape our death—if war and plague
are joining forces now to crush the Argives.   70
But wait: let us question a holy man,
a prophet, even a man skilled with dreams—
dreams as well can come our way from Zeus—
come, someone to tell us why Apollo rages so,
whether he blames us for a vow we failed, or sacrifice.
If only the god would share the smoky savor of lambs
and full-grown goats, Apollo might be willing, still,
somehow, to save us from this plague."
                          So he proposed
and down he sat again as Calchas rose among them,
Thester's son, the clearest by far of all the seers   80
who scan the flight of birds. He knew all things that are,
all things that are past and all that are to come,
the seer who had led the Argive ships to Troy
with the second sight that god Apollo gave him.
For the armies' good the seer began to speak:
"Achilles, dear to Zeus . . .
you order me to explain Apollo's anger,
the distant deadly Archer? I will tell it all.
But strike a pact with me, swear you will defend me
with all your heart, with words and strength of hand.   90
For there is a man I will enrage—I see it now—
a powerful man who lords it over all the Argives,
one the Achaeans must obey . . . A mighty king,
raging against an inferior, is too strong.
Even if he can swallow down his wrath today,
still he will nurse the burning in his chest
until, sooner or later, he sends it bursting forth.
Consider it closely, Achilles. Will you save me?"

    And the matchless runner reassured him: "Courage!
Out with it now, Calchas. Reveal the will of god,   100
whatever you may know. And I swear by Apollo
dear to Zeus, the power you pray to, Calchas,
when you reveal god's will to the Argives—no one,
not while I am alive and see the light on earth, no one
will lay his heavy hands on you by the hollow ships.
None among all the armies. Not even if you mean
Agamemnon here who now claims to be, by far,
the best of the Achaeans."
                  The seer took heart
and this time he spoke out, bravely: "Beware—
he casts no blame for a vow we failed, a sacrifice.   110
The god's enraged because Agamemnon spurned his priest,

he refused to free his daughter, he refused the ransom.
That's why the Archer sends us pains and he will send us more
and never drive this shameful destruction from the Argives,
not till we give back the girl with sparkling eyes
to her loving father—no price, no ransom paid—
and carry a sacred hundred bulls to Chryse town.
Then we can calm the god, and only then appease him."

So he declared and sat down. But among them rose   120
the fighting son of Atreus, lord of the far-flung kingdoms,
Agamemnon—furious, his dark heart filled to the brim,
blazing with anger now, his eyes like searing fire.
With a sudden, killing look he wheeled on Calchas first:
"Seer of misery! Never a word that works to my advantage!
Always misery warms your heart, your prophecies—
never a word of profit said or brought to pass.
Now, again, you divine god's will for the armies,
bruit it about, as fact, why the deadly Archer
multiplies our pains: because I, I refused
that glittering price for the young girl Chryseis.   130
Indeed, I prefer *her* by far, the girl herself,
I want her mine in my own house! I rank her higher
than Clytemnestra, my wedded wife—she's nothing less
in build or breeding, in mind or works of hand.
But I am willing to give her back, even so,
if that is best for all. What I really want
is to keep my people safe, not see them dying.
But fetch me another prize, and straight off too,
else I alone of the Argives go without my honor.
That would be a disgrace. You are all witness,   140
look—*my* prize is snatched away!"
                                    But the swift runner
Achilles answered him at once, "Just how, Agamemnon,
great field marshal . . . most grasping man alive,
how can the generous Argives give you prizes now?
I know of no troves of treasure, piled, lying idle,
anywhere. Whatever we dragged from towns we plundered,
all's been portioned out. But collect it, call it back
from the rank and file? *That* would be the disgrace.
So return the girl to the god, at least for now.
We Achaeans will pay you back, three, four times over,   150
if Zeus will grant us the gift, somehow, someday,
to raze Troy's massive ramparts to the ground."

But King Agamemnon countered, "Not so quickly,
brave as you are, godlike Achilles—trying to cheat *me*.
Oh no, you won't get past me, take me in that way!

What do you want? To cling to your own prize
while I sit calmly by—empty-handed here?
No—if our generous Argives *will* give me a prize,
a match for my desires, equal to what I've lost,   160
well and good. But if they give me nothing
I will take a prize myself—your own, or Ajax'
or Odysseus' prize—I'll commandeer her myself
and let that man I go to visit choke with rage!
Enough. We'll deal with all this later, in due time.
Now come, we haul a black ship down to the bright sea,
gather a decent number of oarsmen along her locks
and put abroad a sacrifice, and Chryseis herself,
in all her beauty . . . we embark her too.
Let one of the leading captains take command.   170
Ajax, Idomeneus, trusty Odysseus or you, Achilles,
you—the most violent man alive—so you can perform
the rites for us and calm the god yourself."
                              A dark glance
and the headstrong runner answered him in kind: "Shameless—
armored in shamelessness—always shrewd with greed!
How could an Argive soldier obey your orders,
freely and gladly do your sailing for you
or fight your enemies, full force? Not I, no.
It wasn't Trojan spearmen who brought me here to fight.
The Trojans never did *me* damage, not in the least,   180
they never stole my cattle or my horses, never
in Phthia where the rich soil breeds strong men
did they lay waste my crops. How could they?
Look at the endless miles that lie between us . . .
shadowy mountain ranges, seas that surge and thunder.
No, you colossal, shameless—we all followed you,
to please you, to fight for you, to win your honor
back from the Trojans—Menelaus and you, you dog-face!
What do *you* care? Nothing. You don't look right or left.
And now you threaten to strip me of my prize in person—   190
the one I fought for long and hard, and sons of Achaea
handed her to me.
                    My honors never equal yours,
whenever we sack some wealthy Trojan stronghold—
my arms bear the brunt of the raw, savage fighting,
true, but when it comes to dividing up the plunder
the lion's share is yours, and back I go to my ships,
clutching some scrap, some pittance that I love,
when I have fought to exhaustion.
                            No more now—
back I go to Phthia. Better that way by far,
to journey home in the beaked ships of war.   200

I have no mind to linger here disgraced,
brimming your cup and piling up your plunder."

But the lord of men Agamemnon shot back,
"*Desert,* by all means—if the spirit drives you home!
I will never beg you to stay, not on *my* account.
Never—others will take my side and do me honor,
Zeus above all, whose wisdom rules the world.
You—I hate you most of all the warlords
loved by the gods. Always dear to your heart,
strife, yes, and battles, the bloody grind of war.   210
What if you are a great soldier? That's just a gift of god.
Go home with your ships and comrades, lord it over your Myrmidons!
You *are* nothing to me—you and your overweening anger!
But let this be my warning on your way:
since Apollo insists on taking my Chryseis,
I'll send her back in my own ships with *my* crew.
But I, I will be there in person at your tents
to take *Briseis* in all her beauty, your own prize—
so you can learn just how much greater I am than you
and the next man up may shrink from matching words with me,   220
from hoping to rival Agamemnon strength for strength!"

He broke off and anguish gripped Achilles.
The heart in his rugged chest was pounding, torn . . .
Should he draw the long sharp sword slung at his hip,
thrust through the ranks and kill Agamemnon now?—
or check his rage and beat his fury down?
As his racing spirit veered back and forth,
just as he drew his huge blade from its sheath,
down from the vaulting heavens swept Athena,
the white-armed goddess Hera sped her down: 230
Hera loved both men and cared for both alike.
Rearing behind him Pallas seized his fiery hair—
only Achilles saw her, none of the other fighters—
struck with wonder he spun around, he knew her at once,
Pallas Athena! the terrible blazing of those eyes,
and his winged words went flying: "Why, why now?
Child of Zeus with the shield of thunder, why come now?
To witness the outrage Agamemnon just committed?
I tell you this, and so help me it's the truth—
he'll soon pay for his arrogance with his life!"   240

Her gray eyes clear, the goddess Athena answered,
"Down from the skies I come to check your rage
if only you will yield.
The white-armed goddess Hera sped me down:

she loves you both, she cares for you both alike.
Stop this fighting, now. Don't lay hand to sword.
Lash him with threats of the price that he will face.
And I tell you this—and I *know* it is the truth—
one day glittering gifts will lie before you,
three times over to pay for all his outrage.   250
Hold back now. Obey us both."

moderation   So she urged
and the swift runner complied at once: "I must—
when the two of you hand down commands, Goddess,
a man submits though his heart breaks with fury.
Better for him by far. If a man obeys the gods
they're quick to hear his prayers."

                                        And with that
Achilles stayed his burly hand on the silver hilt
and slid the huge blade back in its sheath.
He would not fight the orders of Athena.
Soaring home to Olympus, she rejoined the gods   260
aloft in the halls of Zeus whose shield is thunder.

   But Achilles rounded on Agamemnon once again,
lashing out at him, not relaxing his anger for a moment:
"Staggering drunk, with your dog's eyes, your fawn's heart!
Never once did you arm with the troops and go to battle
or risk an ambush packed with Achaea's picked men—
you lack the courage, you can see death coming.
Safer by far, you find, to foray all through camp,
commandeering the prize of any man who speaks against you.
King who devours his people! Worthless husks, the men you rule—   270
if not, Atrides, this outrage would have been your last.
I tell you this, and I swear a mighty oath upon it . . .
by this, this scepter, look,
that never again will put forth crown and branches,
now it's left its stump on the mountain ridge forever,
nor will it sprout new green again, now the brazen ax
has stripped its bark and leaves, and now the sons of Achaea
pass it back and forth as they hand their judgments down,
upholding the honored customs whenever Zeus commands—
This scepter will be the mighty force behind my oath: 280
someday, I swear, a yearning for Achilles will strike
Achaea's sons and all your armies! But then, Atrides,
harrowed as you will be, *nothing* you do can save you—
not when your hordes of fighters drop and die,
cut down by the hands of man-killing Hector! Then—
then you will tear your heart out, desperate, raging
that you disgraced the best of the Achaeans!"

                                        Down on the ground

he dashed the scepter studded bright with golden nails,
then took his seat again. The son of Atreus smoldered,
glaring across at him, but Nestor rose between them,   290
the man of winning words, the clear speaker of Pylos . . .
Sweeter than honey from his tongue the voice flowed on and on.
Two generations of mortal men he had seen go down by now,
those who were born and bred with him in the old days,
in Pylos' holy realm, and now he ruled the third.
He pleaded with both kings, with clear good will,
"No more—or enormous sorrow comes to all Achaea!
How they would exult, Priam and Priam's sons
and all the Trojans. Oh they'd leap for joy   300
to hear the two of you battling on this way,
you who excel us all, first in Achaean councils,
first in the ways of war.
                         Stop. Please.
Listen to Nestor. You are both younger than I,
and in my time I struck up with better men than you,
even you, but never once did they make light of me.
I've never seen such men, I never will again . . .
men like Pirithous, Dryas, that fine captain,
Caeneus and Exadius, and Polyphemus, royal prince,
and Theseus, Aegeus' boy, a match for the immortals.
They were the strongest mortals ever bred on earth,   310
the strongest, and they fought against the strongest too,
shaggy Centaurs, wild brutes of the mountains—
they hacked them down, terrible, deadly work.
And I was in their ranks, fresh out of Pylos,
far away from home—they enlisted me themselves
and I fought on my own, a free lance, single-handed.
And none of the men who walk the earth these days
could battle with those fighters, none, but they,
they took to heart my counsels, marked my words.
So now you listen too. Yielding is far better . . .   320
Don't seize the girl, Agamemnon, powerful as you are—
leave her, just as the sons of Achaea gave her,
his prize from the very first.
And you, Achilles, never hope to fight it out
with your king, pitting force against his force:
no one can match the honors dealt a king, you know,
a sceptered king to whom great Zeus gives glory.
Strong as you are—a goddess was your mother—
he has more power because he rules more men.
Atrides, end your anger—look, it's Nestor!   330
I beg you, cool your fury against Achilles.
Here the man stands over all Achaea's armies,
our rugged bulwark braced for shocks of war."

But King Agamemnon answered him in haste,
"True, old man—all you say is fit and proper—
but this soldier wants to tower over the armies,
he wants to rule over all, to lord it over all,
give out orders to every man in sight. Well,
there's one, I trust, who will never yield to *him*!
What if the everlasting gods have made a spearman of him?   340
Have they entitled him to hurl abuse at *me*?"

    "Yes!"—blazing Achilles broke in quickly—
"What a worthless, burnt-out coward I'd be called
if I would submit to you and all your orders,
whatever you blurt out. Fling them at others,
don't give me commands!
Never again, *I* trust, will Achilles yield to *you*.
And I tell you this—take it to heart, I warn you—
my hand will never do battle for that girl,
neither with you, King, nor any man alive.   350
You Achaeans gave her, now you've snatched her back.
But all the rest I possess beside my fast black ship—
not one bit of it can you seize against my will, Atrides.
Come, try it! So the men can see, that instant,
your black blood gush and spurt around my spear!"

    Once the two had fought it out with words,
battling face-to-face, both sprang to their feet
and broke up the muster beside the Argive squadrons.
Achilles strode off to his trim ships and shelters,
back to his friend Patroclus and their comrades.   360
Agamemnon had a vessel hauled down to the sea,
he picked out twenty oarsmen to man her locks,
put aboard the cattle for sacrifice to the god
and led Chryseis in all her beauty amidships.
Versatile Odysseus took the helm as captain.
                                        All embarked,
the party launched out on the sea's foaming lanes
while the son of Atreus told his troops to wash,
to purify themselves from the filth of plague.
They scoured it off, threw scourings in the surf
and sacrificed to Apollo full-grown bulls and goats   370
along the beaten shore of the fallow barren sea
and savory smoke went swirling up the skies.

    So the men were engaged throughout the camp.
But King Agamemnon would not stop the quarrel,
the first threat he hurled against Achilles.
He called Talthybius and Eurybates briskly,

his two heralds, ready, willing aides:
"Go to Achilles' lodge. Take Briseis at once,
his beauty Briseis by the hand and bring her here.
But if he will not surrender her, I'll go myself,   380
I'll seize her myself, with an army at my back—
and all the worse for him!"
                                   He sent them off
with the strict order ringing in their ears.
Against their will the two men made their way
along the breaking surf of the barren salt sea
and reached the Myrmidon shelters and their ships.
They found him beside his lodge and black hull,
seated grimly—and Achilles took no joy
when he saw the two approaching.
They were afraid, they held the king in awe   390
and stood there, silent. Not a word to Achilles,
not a question. But he sensed it all in his heart,
their fear, their charge, and broke the silence for them:
"Welcome, couriers! Good heralds of Zeus and men,
here, come closer. You have done nothing to me.
You are not to blame. No one but Agamemnon—
he is the one who sent you for Briseis.
Go, Patroclus, Prince, bring out the girl
and hand her to them so they can take her back.
But let them both bear witness to my loss . . .
in the face of blissful gods and mortal men,
in the face of that unbending, ruthless king—
if the day should come when the armies need *me*
to save their ranks from ignominious, stark defeat.
The man is raving—with all the murderous fury in his heart.
He lacks the sense to see a day behind, a day ahead,
and safeguard the Achaeans battling by the ships."

    Patroclus obeyed his great friend's command.
He led Briseis in all her beauty from the lodge
and handed her over to the men to take away.   410
And the two walked back along the Argive ships
while she trailed on behind, reluctant, every step.
But Achilles wept, and slipping away from his companions,
far apart, sat down on the beach of the heaving gray sea
and scanned the endless ocean. Reaching out his arms,
again and again he prayed to his dear mother: "Mother!
You gave me life, short as that life will be,
so at least Olympian Zeus, thundering up on high,
should give he honor—but now he gives me nothing.
Atreus' son Agamemnon, for all his far-flung kingdoms—   420

the man disgraces me, seizes and keeps my prize,
he tears her away himself!"
                              So he wept and prayed
and his noble mother heard him, seated near her father,
the Old Man of the Sea in the salt green depths.
Suddenly up she rose from the churning surf
like mist and settling down beside him as he wept,
stroked Achilles gently, whispering his name, "My child—
why in tears? What sorrow has touched your heart?
Tell me, please. Don't harbor it deep inside you.
We must share it all."
                              And now from his depths   430
the proud runner groaned: "You know, you know,
why labor through it all? You know it all so well . . .
We raided Thebe once, Eetion's sacred citadel,
we ravaged the place, hauled all the plunder here
and the armies passed it round, share and share alike,
and they chose the beauty Chryseis for Agamemnon.
But soon her father, the holy priest of Apollo
the distant deadly Archer, Chryses approached
the fast trim ships of the Argives armed in bronze
to win his daughter back, bringing a priceless ransom   440
and bearing high in hand, wound on a golden staff,
the wreaths of the god who strikes from worlds away.
He begged the whole Achaean army but most of all
the two supreme commanders, Atreus' two sons,
and all ranks of Achaeans cried out their assent,
'Respect the priest, accept the shining ransom!'
But it brought no joy to the heart of Agamemnon,
our high and mighty king dismissed the priest
with a brutal order ringing in his ears.
And shattered with anger, the old man withdrew   450
but Apollo heard his prayer—he loved him, deeply—
he loosed his shaft at the Argives, withering plague,
and now the troops began to drop and die in droves,
the arrows of god went showering left and right,
whipping through the Achaeans' vast encampment.
But the old seer who knew the cause full well
revealed the will of the archer god Apollo.
And I was the first, mother, I urged them all,
'Appease the god at once!' That's when the fury
gripped the son of Atreus. Agamemnon leapt to his feet   460
and hurled his threat—his threat's been driven home.
One girl, Chryseis, the fiery-eyed Achaeans
ferry out in a fast trim ship to Chryse Island,
laden with presents for the god. The other girl,

just now the heralds came and led her away from camp,
Briseus' daughter, the prize the armies gave me.
But you, mother, if you have any power at all,
protect your son! Go to Olympus, plead with Zeus,
if you ever warmed his heart with a word or any action . . .

Time and again I heard your claims in father's halls,   470
boasting how you and you alone of all the immortals
rescued Zeus, the lord of the dark storm cloud,
from ignominious, stark defeat . . .
That day the Olympians tried to chain him down,
Hera, Poseidon lord of the sea, and Pallas Athena—
you rushed to Zeus, dear Goddess, broke those chains,
quickly ordered the hundred-hander to steep Olympus,
that monster whom the immortals call Briareus
but every mortal calls the Sea-god's son, Aegaeon,
though he's stronger than his father. Down he sat,   480
flanking Cronus' son, gargantuan in the glory of it all,
and the blessed gods were struck with terror then,
they stopped shackling Zeus.
                              Remind him of that,
now, go and sit beside him, grasp his knees . . .
persuade him, somehow, to help the Trojan cause,
to pin the Achaeans back against their ships,
trap them round the bay and mow them down.
So all can reap the benefits of their king—
so even mighty Atrides can see how mad he was
to disgrace Achilles, the best of the Achaeans!"   490

And Thetis answered, bursting into tears,
"O my son, my sorrow, why did I ever bear you?
All I bore was doom . . .
Would to god you could linger by your ships
without a grief in the world, without a torment!
Doomed to a short life, you have so little time.
And not only short, now, but filled with heartbreak too,
more than all other men alive—doomed twice over.
Ah to a cruel fate I bore you in our halls!
Still, I shall go to Olympus crowned with snow   500
and repeat your prayer to Zeus who loves the lightning.
Perhaps he will be persuaded.
                              But you, my child,
stay here by the fast ships, rage on at the Achaeans,
just keep clear of every foray in the fighting.
Only yesterday Zeus went off to the Ocean River
to feast with the Aethiopians, loyal, lordly men,
and all the gods went with him. But in twelve days

the Father returns to Olympus. Then, for your sake,
up I go to the bronze floor, the royal house of Zeus—
I'll grasp his knees, I think I'll win him over."
                                    With that vow   510
his mother went away and left him there, alone,
his heart inflamed for the sashed and lovely girl
they'd wrenched away from him against his will.
Meanwhile Odysseus drew in close to Chryse Island,
bearing the splendid sacrifice in the vessel's hold.
And once they had entered the harbor deep in bays
they furled and stowed the sail in the black ship,
they lowered the mast by the forestays, smoothly,
quickly let it down on the forked mast-crutch
and rowed her into a mooring under oars.   520
Out went the bow-stones—cables fast astern—
and the crew themselves swung out in the breaking surf,
leading out the sacrifice for the archer god Apollo,
and out of the deep-sea ship Chryseis stepped too.
Then tactful Odysseus led her up to the altar,
placing her in her loving father's arms, and said,
"Chryses, the lord of men Agamemnon sent me here
to bring your daughter back and perform a sacrifice,
a grand sacrifice to Apollo—for all Achaea's sake—
so we can appease the god   530
who's loosed such grief and torment on the Argives."

   With those words he left her in Chryses' arms
and the priest embraced the child he loved, exultant.
At once the men arranged the sacrifice for Apollo,
making the cattle ring his well-built altar,
then they rinsed their hands and took up barley.
Rising among them Chryses stretched his arms to the sky
and prayed in a high resounding voice, "Hear me, Apollo!
God of the silver bow who strides the walls of Chryse
and Cilla sacrosanct—lord in power of Tenedos!   540
If you honored me last time and heard my prayer
and rained destruction down on all Achaea's ranks,
now bring my prayer to pass once more. Now, at last,
drive this killing plague from the armies of Achaea!"

   His prayer went up and Phoebus Apollo heard him.
And soon as the men had prayed and flung the barley,
first they lifted back the heads of the victims,
slit their throats, skinned them and carved away
the meat from the thighbones and wrapped them in fat,
a double fold sliced clean and topped with strips of flesh.   550
And the old man burned these over dried split wood

and over the quarters poured out glistening wine
while young men at his side held five-pronged forks.
Once they had burned the bones and tasted the organs
they cut the rest into pieces, pierced them with spits,
roasted them to a turn and pulled them off the fire.
The work done, the feast laid out, they ate well
and no man's hunger lacked a share of the banquet.
When they had put aside desire for food and drink,
the young men brimmed the mixing bowls with wine   560
and tipping first drops for the god in every cup
they poured full rounds for all. And all day long
they appeased the god with song, raising a ringing hymn
to the distant archer god who drives away the plague,
those young Achaean warriors singing out his power,
and Apollo listened, his great heart warm with joy.

    Then when the sun went down and night came on
they made their beds and slept by the stern-cables . . .
When young Dawn with her rose-red fingers shone once more,
they set sail for the main encampment of Achaea.   570
The Archer sent them a bracing following wind,
they stepped the mast, spread white sails wide,
the wind hit full and the canvas bellied out
and a dark blue wave, foaming up at the bow,
sang out loud and strong as the ship made way,
skimming the whitecaps, cutting toward her goal.
And once offshore of Achaea's vast encampment
they eased her in and hauled the black ship high,
far up on the sand, and shored her up with timbers.
Then they scattered, each to his own ship and shelter.   580

    But *he* raged on, grimly camped by his fast fleet,
the royal son of Peleus, the swift runner Achilles.
Now he no longer haunted the meeting grounds
where men win glory, now he no longer went to war
but day after day he ground his heart out, waiting there,
yearning, always yearning for battle cries and combat.

    But now as the twelfth dawn after this shone clear
the gods who live forever marched home to Olympus,
all in a long cortege, and Zeus led them on.
And Thetis did not forget her son's appeals.   590
She broke from a cresting wave at first light
and soaring up to the broad sky and Mount Olympus,
found the son of Cronus gazing down on the world,
peaks apart from the other gods and seated high
on the topmost crown of rugged ridged Olympus.

And crouching down at his feet,
quickly grasping his knees with her left hand,
her right hand holding him underneath the chin,
she prayed to the lord god Zeus, the son of Cronus:
"Zeus, Father Zeus! If I ever served you well   600
among the deathless gods with a word or action,
bring this prayer to pass: honor my son Achilles!—
doomed to the shortest life of any man on earth.
And now the lord of men Agamemnon has disgraced him,
seizes and keeps his prize, tears her away himself. But you—
exalt him, Olympian Zeus: your urgings rule the world!
Come, grant the Trojans victory after victory
till the Achaen armies pay my dear son back,
building higher the honor he deserves!"

                                     She paused
but Zeus who commands the storm clouds answered nothing.   610
The Father sat there, silent. It seemed an eternity . . .
But Thetis, clasping his knees, held on, clinging,
pressing her question once again: "Grant my prayer,
once and for all, Father, bow your head in assent!
Or deny me outright. What have *you* to fear?
So I may know, too well, just how cruelly
I am the most dishonored goddess of them all."

                               Filled with anger
Zeus who marshals the storm clouds answered her at last:
"Disaster. You will drive me into war with Hera.
She will provoke me, she with her shrill abuse.   620
Even now in the face of all the immortal gods
she harries me perpetually, Hera charges *me*
that I always go to battle for the Trojans.
Away with you now. Hera might catch us here.
I will see to this. I will bring it all to pass.
Look, I will bow my head if that will satisfy you.
That, I remind you, that among the immortal gods
is the strongest, truest sign that I can give.
No word or work of mine—nothing can be revoked,
there is no treachery, nothing left unfinished   630
once I bow my head to say it shall be done."

   So he decreed. And Zeus the son of Cronus bowed
his craggy dark brows and the deathless locks came pouring
down from the thunderhead of the great immortal king
and giant shock waves spread through all Olympus.

   So the two of them made their pact and parted.
Deep in the sea she drove from radiant Mount Olympus.
Zeus went back to his own halls, and all the gods

in full assembly rose from their seats at once
to meet the Father striding toward them now.   640
None dared remain at rest as Zeus advanced,
they all sprang up to greet him face-to-face
as he took his place before them on his throne.
But Hera knew it all. She had seen how Thetis,
the Old Man of the Sea's daughter, Thetis quick
on her glistening feet was hatching plans with Zeus.
And suddenly Hera taunted the Father, son of Cronus:
"So, who of the gods this time, my treacherous one,
was hatching plans with you?
Always your pleasure, whenever my back is turned,   650
to settle things in your grand clandestine way.
You never deign, do you, freely and frankly,
to share your plots with me—never, not a word!"

     The father of men and gods replied sharply,
"Hera—stop hoping to fathom all my thoughts.
You will find them a trial, though you are my wife.
Whatever is right for you to hear, no one, trust me,
will know of it before you, neither god nor man.
Whatever I choose to plan apart from all the gods—
no more of your everlasting questions, probe and pry no more."   660

     And Hera the Queen, her dark eyes wide, exclaimed,
"Dread majesty, son of Cronus, what are you saying?
Now surely I've never probed or pried in the past.
Why, you can scheme to your heart's content
without a qualm in the world for me. But now
I have a terrible fear that she has won you over,
Thetis, the Old Man of the Sea's daughter, Thetis
with her glistening feet. I know it. Just at dawn
she knelt down beside you and grasped your knees
and I suspect you bowed your head in assent to her—   670
you granted once and for all to exalt Achilles now
and slaughter hordes of Achaeans pinned against their ships."

     And Zeus who marshals the thunderheads returned,
"Maddening one . . . you and your eternal suspicions—
I can never escape you. Ah but tell me, Hera,
just what can you *do* about all this? Nothing.
Only estrange yourself from me a little more—
and all the worse for you.
If what you say is true, that must be my pleasure.
Now go sit down. Be quiet now. Obey my orders,   680
for fear the gods, however many Olympus holds,

are powerless to protect you when I come
to throttle you with my irresistible hands."

                       He subsided
but Hera the Queen, her eyes wider, was terrified.
She sat in silence. She wrenched her will to his.
And throughout the halls of Zeus the gods of heaven
quaked with fear. Hephaestus the Master Craftsman
rose up first to harangue them all, trying now
to bring his loving mother a little comfort,
the white-armed goddess Hera: "Oh disaster . . .
that's what it is, and it will be unbearable
if the two of you must come to blows this way,
flinging the gods in chaos just for mortal men.
No more joy for us in the sumptuous feast
when riot rules the day.
I urge you, mother—you know that I am right—
work back into his good graces, so the Father,
our beloved Father will never wheel on us again,
send our banquets crashing! The Olympian lord of lightning—
what if he would like to blast us from our seats?   700
He is far too strong. Go back to him, mother,
stroke the Father with soft, winning words—
at once the Olympian will turn kind to us again."

    Pleading, springing up with a two-handled cup,
he reached it toward his loving mother's hands
with his own winning words: "Patience, mother!
Grieved as you are, bear up, or dear as you are,
I have to see you beaten right before my eyes.
I would be shattered—what could I do to save you?
It's hard to fight the Olympian strength for strength.   710
You remember the last time I rushed to your defense?
He seized my foot, he hurled me off the tremendous threshold
and all day long I dropped, I was dead weight and then,
when the sun went down, down I plunged on Lemnos,
little breath left in me. But the mortals there
soon nursed a fallen immortal back to life."

    At that the white-armed goddess Hera smiled
and smiling, took the cup from her child's hands.
Then dipping sweet nectar up from the mixing bowl
he poured it round to all the immortals, left to right.   720
And uncontrollable laughter broke from the happy gods
as they watched the god of fire breathing hard
and bustling through the halls.
                      That hour then

and all day long till the sun went down they feasted
and no god's hunger lacked a share of the handsome banquet
or the gorgeous lyre Apollo struck or the Muses singing
voice to voice in choirs, their vibrant music rising.

At last, when the sun's fiery light had set,
each immortal went to rest in his own house,
the splendid high halls Hephaestus built for each   730
with all his craft and cunning, the famous crippled Smith.
And Olympian Zeus the lord of lightning went to his own bed
where he had always lain when welcome sleep came on him.
There he climbed and there he slept and by his side
lay Hera the Queen, the goddess of the golden throne.

BOOK TWO

The Great Gathering of Armies

Now the great array of gods and chariot-driving men
slept all night long, but the peaceful grip of sleep
could not hold Zeus, turning it over in his mind . . .
how to exalt Achilles?—how to slaughter
hordes of Achaeans pinned against their ships?
As his spirit churned, at last one plan seemed best:
he would send a murderous dream to Agamemnon.
Calling out to the vision, Zeus winged it on:
"Go, murderous Dream, to the fast Achaean ships
and once you reach Agamemnon's shelter rouse him,   10
order him, word-for-word, exactly as I command.
Tell Atrides to arm his long-haired Achaeans,
to attack at once, full force—
now he can take the broad streets of Troy.
The immortal gods who hold Olympus clash no more,
Hera's appeals have brought them round and all agree:
griefs are about to crush the men of Troy."
                                        At that command
the dream went winging off, and passing quickly
along the fast trim ships, made for the king
and found him soon, sound asleep in his tent   20
with refreshing godsent slumber drifted round him.
Hovering at his head the vision rose like Nestor,
Neleus' son, the chief Agamemnon honored most.
Inspired with Nestor's voice and sent by Zeus,

the dream cried out, "Still asleep, Agamemnon?
The son of Atreus, that skilled breaker of horses?
How can you sleep all night, a man weighed down with duties?
Your armies turning over their lives to your command—
responsibilities so heavy. Listen to me, quickly!
I bring you a message sent by Zeus, a world away   30
but he has you in his heart, he pities you now . . .
Zeus commands you to arm your long-haired Achaeans,
to attack at once, full force—
now you can take the broad streets of Troy!
The immortal gods who hold Olympus clash no more,
Hera's appeals have brought them round and all agree:
griefs from Zeus are about to crush the men of Troy!
But keep this message firmly in your mind.
Remember—let no loss of memory overcome you
when the sweet grip of slumber sets you free."   40

　　With that the dream departed, leaving him there,
his heart racing with hopes that would not come to pass.
He thought he would take the city of Priam then,
that very day, the fool. How could he know
what work the Father had in mind? The Father,
still bent on plaguing the Argives and Trojans both
with wounds and groans in the bloody press of battle.
But rousing himself from sleep, the divine voice
swirling round him, Atrides sat up, bolt awake,
pulled on a soft tunic, linen never worn,   50
and over it threw his flaring battle-cape,
under his smooth feet he fastened supple sandals,
across his shoulder slung his silver-studded sword.
Then he seized the royal scepter of his fathers—
its power can never die—and grasping it tightly
off he strode to the ships of Argives armed in bronze.

　　Now the goddess Dawn climbed up to Olympus heights,
declaring the light of day to Zeus and the deathless gods
as the king commanded heralds to cry out loud and clear
and muster the long-haired Achaeans to full assembly.   60
Their cries rang out. Battalions gathered quickly.

　　But first he called his ranking chiefs to council
beside the ship of Nestor, the warlord born in Pylos.
Summoning them together there Atrides set forth
his cunning, foolproof plan: "Hear me, friends—
a dream sent by the gods has come to me in sleep.
Down through the bracing godsent night it came
like good Nestor in features, height and build,

the old king himself, and hovering at my head
the dream called me on: 'Still asleep, Agamemnon?   70
The son of Atreus, that skilled breaker of horses?
How can you sleep all night, a man weighed down with duties?
Your armies turning over their lives to your command—
responsibilities so heavy. Listen to me, quickly!
I bring you a message sent by Zeus, a world away
but he has you in his heart, he pities you now . . .
Zeus commands you to arm your long-haired Achaeans,
to attack at once, full force—
now you can take the broad streets of Troy!
The immortal gods who hold Olympus clash no more,   80
Hera's appeals have brought them round and all agree:
griefs from Zeus are about to crush the men of Troy!
But keep this message firmly in your mind.'
                                With that
the dream went winging off and soothing sleep released me.
Come—see if we can arm the Achaeans for assault.
But first, according to time-honored custom,
I will test the men with a challenge, tell them all
to crowd the oarlocks, cut and run in their ships.
But you take up your battle-stations at every point,
command them, hold them back."
                            So much for his plan.   90
Agamemnon took his seat and Nestor rose among them.
Noble Nestor the king of Pylos' sandy harbor
spoke and urged them on with all good will:
"Friends, lords of the Argives, O my captains!
If any other Achaean had told us of this dream
we'd call it false and turn our backs upon it.
But look, the man who saw it has every claim
to be the best, the bravest Achaean we can field.
Come—see if we can arm the Achaeans for assault."

    And out he marched, leading the way from council.   100
The rest sprang to their feet, the sceptered kings
obeyed the great field marshal. Rank and file
streamed behind and rushed like swarms of bees
pouring out of a rocky hollow, burst on endless burst,
bunched in clusters seething over the first spring blooms,
dark hordes swirling into the air, this way, that way—
so the many armed platoons from the ships and tents
came marching on, close-file, along the deep wide beach
to crowd the meeting grounds, and Rumor, Zeus's crier,
like wildfire blazing among them, whipped them on.   110
The troops assembled. The meeting grounds shook.
The earth groaned and rumbled under the huge weight

as soldiers took positions—the whole place in uproar.
Nine heralds shouted out, trying to keep some order,
"Quiet, battalions, silence! Hear your royal kings!"
The men were forced to their seats, marshaled into ranks,
the shouting died away . . . silence.
                                        King Agamemnon
rose to his feet, raising high in hand the scepter
Hephaestus made with all his strength and skill.
Hephaestus gave it to Cronus' son, Father Zeus,   120
and Zeus gave it to Hermes, the giant-killing Guide
and Hermes gave it to Pelops, that fine charioteer,
Pelops gave it to Atreus, marshal of fighting men,
who died and passed it on to Thyestes rich in flocks
and he in turn bestowed it on Agamemnon, to bear on high
as he ruled his many islands and lorded mainland Argos.
Now, leaning his weight upon that kingly scepter,
Atrides declared his will to all Achaea's armies:
"Friends—fighting Danaans, aides-in-arms of Ares!
Cronus' son has trapped me in madness, blinding ruin—   130
Zeus is a harsh, cruel god. He vowed to me long ago,
he bowed his head that I should never embark for home
till I had brought the walls of Ilium crashing down.
But now, I see, he only plotted brutal treachery:
now he commands me back to Argos in disgrace,
whole regiments of my men destroyed in battle.
So it must please his overweening heart, who knows?
Father Zeus has lopped the crowns of a thousand cities,
true, and Zeus will lop still more—his power is too great.
What humiliation! Even for generations still to come,   140
to learn that Achaean armies so strong, so vast,
fought a futile war . . . We are still fighting it,
no end in sight, and battling forces we outnumber—
by far. Say that Trojans and Argives both agreed
to swear a truce, to seal their oaths in blood,
and opposing sides were tallied out in full:
count one by one the Trojans who live in Troy
but count our Achaeans out by ten-man squads
and each squad pick a Trojan to pour its wine—
many Achaean tens would lack their steward then!   150
That's how far we outnumber them, I'd say—Achaeans
to Trojans—the men who hail from Troy at least.
But they have allies called from countless cities,
fighters brandishing spears who block my way,
who throw me far off course,
thwarting my will to plunder Ilium's rugged walls.
And now nine years of almighty Zeus have marched by,
our ship timbers rot and the cables snap and fray

and across the sea our wives and helpless children
wait in the halls, wait for our return . . . And we?—   160
Our work drags on, unfinished as always, hopeless—
the labor of war that brought us here to Troy.
So come, follow my orders. All obey me now.
Cut and run! Sail home to the fatherland we love!
We'll never take the broad streets of Troy."

                                    Testing his men
but he only made the spirit race inside their chests,
all the rank and file who'd never heard his plan.
And the whole assembly surged like big waves at sea,
the Icarian Sea when East and South Winds drive it on,   170
blasting down in force from the clouds of Father Zeus,
or when the West Wind shakes the deep standing grain
with hurricane gusts that flatten down the stalks—
so the massed assembly of troops was shaken now.
They cried in alarm and charged toward the ships
and the dust went whirling up from under rushing feet
as the men jostled back and forth, shouting orders—
"Grapple the ships! Drag them down to the bright sea!
Clean out the launching-channels!" Shrill shouts
hitting the heavens, fighters racing for home,
knocking the blocks out underneath the hulls.   180

    And now they might have won their journey home,
the men of Argos fighting the will of fate, yes,
if Hera had not alerted Athena: "Inconceivable!
Child of Zeus whose battle-shield is thunder,
tireless one, Athena—what, is *this* the way?
All the Argives flying home to their fatherland,
sailing over the sea's broad back? Leaving Priam
and all the men of Troy a trophy to glory over,
Helen of Argos, Helen for whom so many Argives
lost their lives in Troy, far from native land.   190
Go, range the ranks of Achaeans armed in bronze.
With your winning words hold back each man you find—
don't let them haul their rolling ships to sea!"

    The bright-eyed goddess Pallas lost no time.
Down she flashed from the peaks of Mount Olympus,
quickly reached the ships and found Odysseus first,
a mastermind like Zeus, still standing fast.
He had not laid a hand on his black benched hull,
such anguish racked his heart and fighting spirit.
Now close beside him the bright-eyed goddess stood   200
and urged him on: "Royal son of Laertes, Odysseus,
great tactician—what, is *this* the way?

All you Argives flying home to your fatherland,
tumbling into your oar-swept ships? Leaving Priam
and all the men of Troy a trophy to glory over,
Helen of Argos, Helen for whom so many Argives
lost their lives in Troy, far from native land!
No, don't give up now. Range the Achaean ranks,
with your winning words hold back each man you find—
don't let them haul their rolling ships to sea!"   210

    He knew the goddess' voice—he went on the run,
flinging off his cape as Eurybates picked it up,
the herald of Ithaca always at his side.
Coming face-to-face with Atrides Agamemnon,
he relieved him of his fathers' royal scepter—
its power can never die—and grasping it tightly
off he strode to the ships of Argives armed in bronze.

    Whenever Odysseus met some man of rank, a king,
he'd halt and hold him back with winning words:
"My *friend*—it's wrong to threaten you like a coward,   220
but you stand fast, you keep your men in check!
It's too soon to see Agamemnon's purpose clearly.
Now he's only testing us, soon he'll bear down hard.
Didn't we all hear his plan in secret council?
God forbid his anger destroy the army he commands.
The rage of kings is strong, they're nursed by the gods,
their honor comes from Zeus—
they're dear to Zeus, the god who rules the world."

    When he caught some common soldier shouting out,
he'd beat him with the scepter, dress him down: 230
"You *fool*—sit still! Obey the commands of others,
your superiors—you, you deserter, rank coward,
you count for nothing, neither in war nor council.
How can all Achaeans be masters here in Troy?
Too many kings can ruin an army—mob rule!
Let there be one commander, one master only,
endowed by the son of crooked-minded Cronus
with kingly scepter and royal rights of custom:
whatever one man needs to lead his people well."

    So he ranged the ranks, commanding men to order—   240
and back again they surged from ships and shelters,
back to the meeting grounds with a deep pounding din,
thundering out as battle lines of breakers crash and drag
along some endless beach, and the rough sea roars.

The armies took their seats, marshaled into ranks.
But one man, Thersites, still railed on, nonstop.
His head was full of obscenities, teeming with rant,
all for no good reason, insubordinate, baiting the kings—
anything to provoke some laughter from the troops.
Here was the ugliest man who ever came to Troy.   250
Bandy-legged he was, with one foot clubbed,
both shoulders humped together, curving over
his caved-in chest, and bobbing above them
his skull warped to a point,
sprouting clumps of scraggly, woolly hair.
Achilles despised him most, Odysseus too—
he was always abusing both chiefs, but now
he went for majestic Agamemnon, hollering out,
taunting the king with strings of cutting insults.
The Achaeans were furious with him, deeply offended.   260
But he kept shouting at Agamemnon, spewing his abuse:
"Still moaning and groaning, mighty Atrides—why now?
What are you panting after now? Your shelters packed
with the lion's share of bronze, plenty of women too,
crowding your lodges. Best of the lot, the beauties
we hand you first, whenever we take some stronghold.
Or still more gold you're wanting? More ransom a son
of the stallion-breaking Trojans might just fetch from Troy?—
though I or another hero drags him back in chains . . .
Or a young woman, is it?—to spread and couple,   270
to bed down for yourself apart from all the troops?
How shameful for you, the high and mighty commander,
to lead the sons of Achaea into bloody slaughter!
Sons? No, my soft friends, wretched excuses—
women, not men of Achaea! Home we go in our ships!
Abandon him here in Troy to wallow in all his prizes—
he'll see if the likes of us have propped him up or not.
Look—now it's Achilles, a greater man he disgraces,
seizes and keeps his prize, tears her away himself.
But no gall in Achilles. Achilles lets it go.   280
If not, Atrides, that outrage would have been your last!"

So Thersites taunted the famous field marshal.
But Odysseus stepped in quickly, faced him down
with a dark glance and threats to break his nerve:
"What a flood of abuse, Thersites! Even for you,
fluent and flowing as you are. Keep quiet.
Who are *you* to wrangle with kings, you alone?
No one, I say—no one alive less soldierly than you,
none in the ranks that came to Troy with Agamemnon.

So stop your babbling, mouthing the names of kings,   290
flinging indecencies in their teeth, your eyes
peeled for a chance to cut and run for home.
We can have no idea, no clear idea at all
how the long campaign will end . . .
whether Achaea's sons will make it home unharmed
or slink back in disgrace.
                              But there you sit,
hurling abuse at the son of Atreus, Agamemnon,
marshal of armies, simply because our fighters
give Atrides the lion's share of all our plunder.
You and your ranting slander—*you*'re the outrage.   300
I tell you this, so help me it's the truth:
if I catch you again, blithering on this way,
let Odysseus' head be wrenched off his shoulders,
never again call me the father of Telemachus
if I don't grab you, strip the clothing off you,
cloak, tunic and rags that wrap your private parts,
and whip you howling naked back to the fast ships,
out of the armies' muster—whip you like a cur!"

   And he cracked the scepter across his back and shoulders.
The rascal doubled over, tears streaking his face   310
and a bloody welt bulged up between his blades,
under the stroke of the golden scepter's studs.
He squatted low, cringing, stunned with pain,
blinking like some idiot . . .
rubbing his tears off dumbly with a fist.
Their morale was low but the men laughed now,
good hearty laughter breaking over Thersites' head—
glancing at neighbors they would shout, "A terrific stroke!
A thousand terrific strokes he's carried off—Odysseus,
taking the lead in tactics, mapping battle-plans.   320
But here's the best thing yet he's done for the men—
he's put a stop to this babbling, foulmouthed fool!
Never again, I'd say, will our gallant comrade
risk his skin to attack the kings with insults."

   So the soldiers bantered but not Odysseus.
The raider of cities stood there, scepter in hand,
and close beside him the great gray-eyed Athena
rose like a herald, ordering men to silence. All,
from the first to lowest ranks of Achaea's troops,
should hear his words and mark his counsel well.   330
For the good of all he urged them: "Agamemnon!
Now, my king, the Achaeans are bent on making you

a disgrace in the eyes of every man alive. Yes,
they fail to fulfill their promise sworn that day
they sailed here from the stallion-land of Argos:
that not until you had razed the rugged walls of Troy
would they sail home again. But look at them now,
like green, defenseless boys or widowed women
whimpering to each other, wailing to journey back.
True, they've labored long—they're desperate for home.   340
Any fighter, cut off from his wife for one month,
would chafe at the benches, moaning in his ship,
pinned down by gales and heavy, raging seas.
A month—but look at *us*.
This is the ninth year come round, the ninth
we've hung on here. Who could blame the Achaeans
for chafing, bridling beside the beaked ships?
Ah but still—what a humiliation it would be
to hold out so long, then sail home empty-handed.
Courage, my friends, hold out a little longer.   350
Till we see if Calchas divined the truth or not.
We all recall that moment—who could forget it?
We were all witnesses then. All, at least,
the deadly spirits have not dragged away . . .
                                               Why,
it seems like only yesterday or the day before
when our vast armada gathered, moored at Aulis,
freighted with slaughter bound for Priam's Troy.
We were all busy then, milling round a spring
and offering victims up on the holy altars,
full sacrifice to the gods to guarantee success,   360
under a spreading plane tree where the water splashed,
glittering in the sun—when a great omen appeared.
A snake, and his back streaked red with blood,
a thing of terror! Olympian Zeus himself
had launched him into the clean light of day . . .
He slid from under the altar, glided up the tree
and there the brood of a sparrow, helpless young ones,
teetered high on the topmost branch-tips, cowering
under the leaves there, eight they were all told
and the mother made the ninth, she'd borne them all—   370
chirping to break the heart but the snake gulped them down
and the mother cried out for her babies, fluttering over him . . .
he coiled, struck, fanging her wing—a high thin shriek!
But once he'd swallowed down the sparrow with her brood,
the son of crooked Cronus who sent the serpent forth
turned him into a sign, a monument clear to see—
Zeus struck him to stone! And we stood by,

amazed that such a marvel came to light.
                                        So then,
when those terrible, monstrous omens burst in
on the victims we were offering to the gods,   380
Calchas swiftly revealed the will of Zeus:
'Why struck dumb now, my long-haired Achaeans?
Zeus who rules the world has shown us an awesome sign,
an event long in the future, late to come to birth
but the fame of that great work will never die.
As the snake devoured the sparrow with her brood,
eight and the mother made the ninth, she'd borne them all,
so *we* will fight in Troy that many years and then,
then in the tenth we'll take her broad streets.'
So that day the prophet revealed the future—   390
and now, look, by god, it all comes to pass!
Up with you, all you Argives geared for combat,
stand your ground, right here,
until we take the mighty walls of Priam!"
                                        He fired them so
the armies roared and the ships resounded round them,
shattering echoes ringing from their shouts
as Argives cried assent to King Odysseus' words.
And Nestor the noble horseman spurred them more:
"What disgrace! Look at you, carrying on
in the armies' muster just like boys—fools!   400
Not a thought in your heads for works of battle.
What becomes of them now, the pacts and oaths we swore?
Into the flames with councils, all the plans of men,
the vows sealed with the strong, unmixed wine,
the firm clasp of the right hand we trusted!
We battle on in words, as always, mere words,
and what's the cure? We cannot find a thing.
No matter how many years we wrangle here.
                                        Agamemnon—
never swerve, hold to your first plan of action,
lead your armies headlong into war!   410
The rest of them? Let them rot, the one or two
who hatch their plans apart from all the troops—
what good can they win from that? Nothing at all.
Why, they'd scuttle home before they can even learn
if the vows of Zeus with his dark cloudy shield
are false or not. Zeus the son of almighty Cronus,
I remind you, bowed his head that day we boarded ship,
all the Argives laden with blood and death for Troy—
his lightning bolts on the right, good omens blazing forth.
So now let no man hurry to sail for home, not yet . . .   420

not till he beds down with a faithful Trojan wife,
payment in full for the groans and shocks of war
we have all borne for Helen.
                              But any soldier
wild with desire to reach his home at once—
just let him lay a hand on his black benched ship
and right in front of the rest he'll reach his death!
But you, my King, be on your guard yourself. Come,
listen well to another man. Here's some advice,
not to be tossed aside, and I will tell it clearly.
Range your men by tribes, even by clans, Agamemnon,   430
so clan fights by the side of clan, tribe by tribe.
Fight this way, if the Argives still obey you,
then you can see which captain is a coward,
which contingent too, and which is loyal, brave,
since they will fight in separate formations of their own.
Then, what's more, if you fail to sack the city,
you will know if the will of god's to blame
or the cowardice of your men—inept in battle."

    And King Agamemnon took his lead, saluting:
"Again, old man, you outfight the Argives in debate!   440
Father Zeus, Athena, Apollo, if only I had ten men
like Nestor to plan with me among Achaea's armies—
then we could topple Priam's citadel in a day,
throttle it in our hands and gut Troy to nothing.
But Cronus' son, Zeus with his shield of storm
insists on embroiling me in painful struggles,
futile wars of words . . .
Imagine—I and Achilles, wrangling over a girl,
battling man-to-man. And I, I was the first
to let my anger flare. Ah if the two of us   450
could ever think as one, Troy could delay
her day of death no longer, not one moment.
Go now, take your meal—the sooner to bring on war.
Quickly—let each fighter sharpen his spear well,
balance his shield well, feed his horses well
with plenty of grain to build their racing speed—
each man look well to his chariot's running order,
nerve himself for combat now, so all day long
we can last out the grueling duels of Ares!
No breathing space, no letup, not a moment, not   460
till the night comes on to part the fighters' fury!
Now sweat will soak the shield-strap round your chest,
your fist gripping the spear will ache with tensing,
now the lather will drench your war-team's flanks,
hauling your sturdy chariot.

But any man I catch,
trying to skulk behind his long beaked ships,
hanging back from battle—he is finished.
No way for *him* to escape the dogs and birds!"

So he commanded
and the armies gave a deep resounding roar like waves
crashing against a cliff when the South Wind whips it,   470
bearing down, some craggy headland jutting out to sea—
the waves will never leave it in peace, thrashed by gales
that hit from every quarter, breakers left and right.
The troops sprang up, scattered back to the ships,
lit fires beside their tents and took their meal.
Each sacrificed to one or another deathless god,
each man praying to flee death and the grind of war.
But the lord of men Agamemnon sacrificed a fat rich ox,
five years old, to the son of mighty Cronus, Zeus,
and called the chiefs of all the Argive forces: 480
Nestor first and foremost, then King Idomeneus,
the Great and Little Ajax, Tydeus' son Diomedes
and Odysseus sixth, a mastermind like Zeus.
The lord of the war cry Menelaus came uncalled,
he knew at heart what weighed his brother down.
They stood in a ring around the ox, took up barley
and then, rising among them, King Agamemnon
raised his voice in prayer: "Zeus, Zeus,
god of greatness, god of glory, lord god
of the dark clouds who lives in the bright sky,   490
don't let the sun go down or the night descend on us!
Not till I hurl the smoke-black halls of Priam headlong—
torch his gates to blazing rubble—rip the tunic of Hector
and slash his heroic chest to ribbons with my bronze—
and a ruck of comrades round him, groveling facedown,
gnaw their own earth!"

And so Agamemnon prayed
but the son of Cronus would not bring his prayer to pass,
not yet . . . the Father accepted the sacrifices, true,
but doubled the weight of thankless, ruthless war.
Once the men had prayed and flung the barley,   500
first they lifted back the heads of the victims,
slit their throats, skinned them and carved away
the meat from the thighbones and wrapped them in fat,
a double fold sliced clean and topped with strips of flesh.
And they burned these on a cleft stick, peeled and dry,
spitted the vitals, held them over Hephaestus' flames
and once they'd charred the thighs and tasted the organs
they cut the rest into pieces, pierced them with spits,
roasted them to a turn and pulled them off the fire.

The work done, the feast laid out, they ate well   510
and no man's hunger lacked a share of the banquet.
When they had put aside desire for food and drink,
Nestor the noble old horseman spoke out first:
"Marshal Atrides, lord of men Agamemnon,
no more trading speeches now. No more delay,
putting off the work the god puts in our hands.
Come, let the heralds cry out to all contingents,
full battle-armor, muster the men along the ships.
Now down we go, united—review them as we pass.
Down through the vast encampment of Achaea,   520
the faster to rouse the slashing god of war!"

    Agamemnon the lord of men did not resist.
He commanded heralds to cry out loud and clear
and summon the long-haired Achaean troops to battle.
Their cries rang out. The battalions gathered quickly.
The warlords dear to the gods and flanking Agamemnon
strode on ahead, marshaling men-at-arms in files,
and down their ranks the fiery-eyed Athena bore
her awesome shield of storm, ageless, deathless—
a hundred golden tassels, all of them braided tight   530
and each worth a hundred oxen, float along the front.
Her shield of lightning dazzling, swirling around her,
headlong on Athena swept through the Argive armies,
driving soldiers harder, lashing the fighting-fury
in each Achaean's heart—no stopping them now,
mad for war and struggle. Now, suddenly,
battle thrilled them more than the journey home,
than sailing hollow ships to their dear native land.

    As ravening fire rips through big stands of timber
high on a mountain ridge and the blaze flares miles away,   540
so from the marching troops the blaze of bronze armor,
splendid and superhuman, flared across the earth,
flashing into the air to hit the skies.
                                        Armies gathering now
as the huge flocks on flocks of winging birds; geese or cranes
or swans with their long lancing necks—circling Asian marshes
round the Cayster outflow, wheeling in all directions,
glorying in their wings—keep on landing, advancing,
wave on shrieking wave and the tidal flats resound.
So tribe on tribe, pouring out of the ships and shelters,
marched across the Scamander plain and the earth shook,   550
tremendous thunder from under trampling men and horses
drawing into position down the Scamander meadow flats

breaking into flower—men by the thousands, numberless
as the leaves and spears that flower forth in spring.

The armies massing . . . crowding thick-and-fast
as the swarms of flies seething over the shepherds' stalls
in the first spring days when the buckets flood with milk—
so many long-haired Achaeans swarmed across the plain
to confront the Trojans, fired to smash their lines.

The armies grouping now—as seasoned goatherds   560
split their wide-ranging flocks into packs with ease
when herds have mixed together down the pasture:
so the captains formed their tight platoons,
detaching right and left, moving up for action—
and there in the midst strode powerful Agamemnon,
eyes and head like Zeus who loves the lightning,
great in the girth like Ares, god of battles,
broad through the chest like sea lord Poseidon.
Like a bull rising head and shoulders over the herds,
a royal bull rearing over his flocks of driven cattle—   570
so imposing was Atreus' son, so Zeus made him that day,
towering over fighters, looming over armies.

Sing to me now, you Muses who hold the halls of Olympus!
You are goddesses, you are everywhere, you know all things—
all we hear is the distant ring of glory, we know nothing—
who were the captains of Achaea? Who were the kings?
The mass of troops I could never tally, never name,
not even if I had ten tongues and ten mouths,
a tireless voice and the heart inside me bronze,
never unless you Muses of Olympus, daughter of Zeus   580
whose shield is rolling thunder, sing, sing in memory
all who gathered under Troy. Now I can only tell
the lords of the ships, the ships in all their numbers!

First came the Boeotian units led by Leitus and Peneleos:
Arcesilaus and Prothoënor and Clonius shared command
of the armed men who lived in Hyria, rocky Aulis,
Schoenus, Scolus and Eteonus spurred with hills,
Thespia and Graea, the dancing rings of Mycalessus,
men who lived round Harma, Ilesion and Erythrae
and those who settled Eleon, Hyle and Peteon,   590
Ocalea, Medeon's fortress walled and strong,
Copae, Eutresis and Thisbe thronged with doves,
fighters from Coronea, Haliartus deep in meadows,
and the men who held Plataea and lived in Glisas,

men who held the rough-hewn gates of Lower Thebes,
Onchestus the holy, Poseidon's sun-filled grove,
men from the town of Arne green with vineyards,
Midea and sacred Nisa, Anthedon-on-the-marches.
Fifty ships came freighted with these contingents,
one hundred and twenty young Boeotians manning each.   600

Then men who lived in Aspledon, Orchomenos of the Minyans,
fighters led by Ascalaphus and Ialmenus, sons of Ares
whom Astyoche bore in Actor son of Azeus' halls
when the shy young girl, climbing into the upper rooms,
made love with the god of war in secret, shared his strength.
In her two sons' command sailed thirty long curved ships.

Then Schedius and Epistrophus led the men of Phocis—
two sons of Iphitus, that great heart, Naubolus' son—
the men who held Cyparissus and Pytho's high crags,
the hallowed earth of Crisa, Daulis and Panopeus,   610
men who dwelled round Anemoria, round Hyampolis,
men who lived along the Cephisus' glinting waters,
men who held Lilaea close to the river's wellsprings.
Laden with all their ranks came forty long black ships
and Phocian captains ranged them column by column,
manning stations along the Boeotians' left flank.

Next the Locrians led by racing Ajax, son of Oileus,
Little Ajax—a far cry from the size of Telamonian Ajax—
a smaller man but trim in his skintight linen corslet,
he outthrew all Hellenes, all Achaeans with his spear.   620
He led the men who lived in Opois, Cynus, Calliarus,
Bessa and Scarphe, the delightful town of Augeae,
Tarphe and Thronion down the Boagrius River.
In Oilean Ajax' charge came forty long black ships,
Locrians living across the straits from sacrosanct Euboea.

And the men who held Euboea, Abantes breathing fury,
Chalcis and Eretria, Histiaea covered with vineyards,
Cerinthus along the shore and Dion's hilltop streets,
the men who held Carystus and men who settled Styra.
Elephenor, comrade of Ares, led the whole contingent,   630
Chalcodon's son, a lord of the fierce Abantes.
The sprinting Abantes followed hard at his heels,
their forelocks cropped, hair grown long at the back,
troops nerved to lunge with their tough ashen spears
and slash the enemies' breastplates round their chests.
In Elephenor's command sailed forty long black ships.

Next the men who held the strong-built city of Athens,
realm of high-hearted Erechtheus. Zeus's daughter Athena
tended him once the grain-giving fields had borne him,
long ago, and then she settled the king in Athens,   640
in her own rich shrine, where sons of Athens worship him
with bulls and goats as the years wheel round in season.
Athenians all, and Peteos' son Menestheus led them on,
and no one born on the earth could match that man
in arraying teams of horse and shielded fighters—
Nestor his only rival, thanks to Nestor's age.
And in his command sailed fifty long black ships.

Out of Salamis Great Telamonian Ajax led twelve ships
drawn up where Athenian forces formed their line of battle.

Then men of Argos and Tiryns with her tremendous walls   650
and Hermione and Asine commanding the deep wide gulf,
Troezen, Eionae and Epidaurus green with vines
and Achaea's warrior sons who held Aegina and Mases—
Diomedes lord of the war cry led their crack contingents
flanked by Sthenelus, far-famed Capaneus' favorite son.
Third in the vanguard marched Euryalus strong as a god,
son of King Mecisteus son of Talaus, but over them all,
with cries to marshal men Diomedes led the whole force
and his Argives sailed in eighty long black ships.

Next the men who held Mycenae's huge walled citadel,   660
Corinth in all her wealth and sturdy, strong Cleonae,
men of Orniae, lovely Araethyrea and Sicyon,
Adrastus' domain before he ruled Mycenae,
men of Hyperesia, Gonoëssa perched on hills,
men who held Pellene and those who circled Aegion,
men of the coastal strip and Helice's broad headland.
They came in a hundred ships and Agamemnon led them on,
Atreus' royal son, and marching in his companies
came the most and bravest fighting men by far.
And there in the midst, armed in gleaming bronze,   670
in all his glory, he towered high over all his fighters—
he was the greatest warlord, he led by far the largest army.

Next those who held Lacedaemon's hollows deep with gorges,
Pharis, Sparta and Messe, crowded haunt of the wild doves,
men who lived in Brysiae and Augeae's gracious country,
men who held Amyclae, Helos the seaboard fortress,
men who settled Laas and lived near Oetylus:
Agamemnon's brother, Menelaus lord of the war cry

led their sixty ships, armed them apart, downshore,
and amidst their ranks he marched, ablaze with valor,   680
priming men for attack. And his own heart blazed the most
to avenge the groans and shocks of war they'd borne for Helen.

Next the men who lived in Pylos and handsome Arene,
Thryon, the Alpheus ford and finely-masoned Aepy,
men who lived in Cyparisseis and Amphigenia,
Pteleos, Helos and Dorion where the Muses met
the Thracian Thamyris, stopped the minstrel's song.
From Oechalia he came, from Oechalia's King Eurytus,
boasting to high heaven that he could outsing the very Muses,
the daughters of Zeus whose shield resounds with thunder.   690
They were enraged, they maimed him, they ripped away
his voice, the rousing immortal wonder of his song
and wiped all arts of harping from his mind.
Nestor the noble old horseman led those troops
in ninety sweeping ships lined up along the shore.

And those who held Arcadia under Cyllene's peak,
near Aepytus' ancient tomb where men fight hand-to-hand,
men who lived in Pheneos and Orchomenos rife with sheep,
Stratia, Rhipe and Enispe whipped by the sudden winds,
men who settled Tegea, Mantinea's inviting country,   700
men who held Stymphalus, men who ruled Parrhasia—
the son of Ancaeus led them, powerful Agapenor
with sixty ships in all, and aboard each vessel
crowded full Arcadian companies skilled in war.
Agamemnon himself, the lord of men had given them
those well-benched ships to plow the wine-dark sea,
since works of the sea meant nothing to those landsmen.

Then the men who lived in Buprasion, brilliant Elis,
all the realm as far as Hyrmine and Myrsinus, frontier towns
and Olenian Rock and Alesion bound within their borders.   710
Four warlords led their ranks, ten-ship flotillas each,
and filling the decks came bands of Epean fighters,
two companies under Thalpius and Amphimachus, sons
of the line of Actor, one of Eurytus, one of Cteatus.
Strong Diores the son of Amarynceus led the third
and the princely Polyxinus led the fourth,
the son of King Agasthenes, Augeas' noble stock.

Then ocean men from Dulichion and the Holy Islands,
the Echinades rising over the sea across from Elis—
Meges a match for Ares led their troops to war,   720
a son of the rider Phyleus dear to Zeus who once,

enraged at his father, fled and settled Dulichion.
In his son's command sailed forty long black ships.

Next Odysseus led his Cephallonian companies,
gallant-hearted fighters, the island men of Ithaca,
of Mount Neriton's leafy ridges shimmering in the wind,
and men who lived in Crocylia and rugged Aegilips,
men who held Zacynthus and men who dwelled near Samos
and mainland men who grazed their flocks across the channel.
That mastermind like Zeus, Odyssus led those fighters on.   730
In his command sailed twelve ships, prows flashing crimson.

And Thoas son of Andraemon led Aetolia's units,
soldiers who lived in Pleuron, Pylene and Olenus,
Chalcis along the shore and Calydon's rocky heights
where the sons of wellborn Oeneus were no more
and the king himself was dead
and Meleager with his golden hair was gone.
So the rule of all Aetolian men had passed to Thoas.
In Thoas' command sailed forty long black ships.

And the great spearman Idomeneus led his Cretans,   740
the men who held Cnossos and Gortyn ringed in walls,
Lyctos, Miletus, Lycastus' bright chalk bluffs,
Phaestos and Rhytion, cities a joy to live in—
the men who peopled Crete, a hundred cities strong.
The renowned spearman Idomeneus led them all in force
with Meriones who butchered men like the god of war himself.
And in their command sailed eighty long black ships.

And Heracles' son Tlepolemus tall and staunch
led nine ships of the proud Rhodians out of Rhodes,
the men who lived on Rhodes in three island divisions,   750
Lindos and Ialysus and Camirus' white escarpment,
armies led by the famous spearman Tlepolemus
whom Astyochea bore to Heracles filled with power.
He swept her up from Ephyra, from the Selleis River
after he'd ravaged many towns of brave young warlords
bred by the gods. But soon as his son Tlepolemus
came of age in Heracles' well-built palace walls
the youngster abruptly killed his father's uncle—
the good soldier Licymnius, already up in years—
and quickly fitting ships, gathering partisans,   760
he fled across the sea with threats of the sons
and the sons' sons of Heracles breaking at his back.
But he reached Rhodes at last, a wanderer rocked by storms,
and there they settled in three divisions, all by tribes,

loved by Zeus himself the king of gods and mortals
showering wondrous gold on all their heads.

Nireus led his three trim ships from Syme,
Nireus the son of Aglaea and King Charopus,
Nireus the handsomest man who ever came to Troy,
of all the Achaeans after Peleus' fearless son.   770
But he was a lightweight, trailed by a tiny band.

And men who held Nisyrus, Casus and Crapathus,
Cos, Eurypylus' town, and the islands called Calydnae—
combat troops, and Antiphus and Phidippus led them on,
the two sons of the warlord Thessalus, Heracles' son.
In their command sailed thirty long curved ships.
                                    And now, Muse,
sing all those fighting men who lived in Pelasgian Argos,
the big contingents out of Alus and Alope and Trachis,
men of Phthia and Hellas where the women are a wonder,
all the fighters called Achaeans, Hellenes and Myrmidons   780
ranked in fifty ships, and Achilles was their leader.
But they had no lust for the grind of battle now—
where was the man who marched their lines to war?
The brilliant runner Achilles lay among his ships,
raging over Briseis, the girl with lustrous hair,
the prize he seized from Lyrnessus—
after he had fought to exhaustion at Lyrnessus,
storming the heights, and breached the walls of Thebes
and toppled the vaunting spearmen Epistrophus and Mynes,
sons of King Euenus, Selepius' son. All for Briseis   790
his heart was breaking now . . . Achilles lay there now
but he would soon rise up in all his power.

Then men of Phylace, Pyrasus banked in flowers,
Demeter's closed and holy grove and Iton mother of flocks,
Antron along the shore and Pteleos deep in meadows.
The veteran Protesilaus had led those troops
while he still lived, but now for many years
the arms of the black earth had held him fast
and his wife was left behind, alone in Phylace,
both cheeks torn in grief, their house half-built.   800
Just as he vaulted off his ship a Dardan killed him,
first by far of the Argives slaughtered on the beaches.
But not even then were his men without a captain,
yearn as they did for their lost leader. No,
Podarces a fresh campaigner ranged their units—
a son of Iphiclus son of Phylacus rich in flocks—

Podarces, gallant Protesilaus' blood brother,
younger-born, but the older man proved braver too,
an iron man of war. Yet not for a moment did his army
lack a leader, yearn as they did for the braver dead.   810
Under Podarces sailed their forty long black ships.

And the men who lived in Pherae fronting Lake Boebeis,
in Boebe and Glaphyrae and Iolcos' sturdy ramparts:
their eleven ships were led by Admetus' favored son,
Eumelus, born to Admetus by Alcestis, queen of women,
the most radiant daughter Pelias ever fathered.

Then men who lived in Methone and Thaumacia,
men who held Meliboea and rugged ridged Olizon:
Philoctetes the master archer had led them on
in seven ships with fifty oarsmen aboard each,   820
superbly skilled with the bow in lethal combat.
But their captain lay on an island, racked with pain,
on Lemnos' holy shores where the armies had marooned him,
agonized by his wound, the bite of a deadly water-viper.
There he writhed in pain but soon, encamped by the ships,
the Argives would recall Philoctetes, their great king.
But not even then were his men without a captain,
yearn as they did for their lost leader. No,
Medon formed them up, Oileus' bastard son
whom Rhene bore to Oileus, grim raider of cities.   830

And men who settled Tricca, rocky Ithome terraced high
and men who held Oechalia, Oechalian Eurytus' city:
the two sons of Asclepius led their units now,
both skilled healers, Podalirius and Machaon.
In their command sailed forty curved black ships.

And men who held Ormenion and the Hyperian Spring,
men who held Asterion, Titanos' chalk-white cliffs:
Eurypylus marched them on, Euaemon's shining son.
In his command sailed forty long black ships.

And the men who settled Argissa and Gyrtone,   840
Orthe, Elone, the gleaming citadel Oloosson:
Polypoetes braced for battle led them on,
the son of Pirithous, son of deathless Zeus.
Famous Hippodamia bore the warrior to Pirithous
that day he wreaked revenge on the shaggy Centaurs,
routed them out of Pelion, drove them to the Aethices.
Polypoetes was not alone, Leonteus shared the helm,

companion of Ares, Caeneus' grandson, proud Coronus' son.
And in his command sailed forty long black ships.

And Guneus out of Cyphus led on two and twenty ships   850
and in his platoons came Enienes and battle-tried Peraebians
who pitched homes in the teeth of Dodona's bitter winters,
who held the tilled acres along the lovely Titaressus
that runs her pure crystal currents into Peneus—
never mixed with Peneus' eddies glistening silt
but gliding over the surface smooth as olive oil,
branching, breaking away from the river Styx,
the dark and terrible oath-stream of the gods.

And Prothous son of Tenthredon led the Magnesians,
men who lived around the Peneus, up along Mount Pelion   860
sloped in wind-whipped leaves. Racing Prothous led them on
and in his command sailed forty long black ships.

These, these were the captains of Achaea and the kings.
Now tell me, Muse, who were the bravest of them all,
of the men and chariot-teams that came with Atreus' sons?

The best by far of the teams were Eumelus' mares
and Pheres' grandson drove them—swift as birds,
matched in age and their glossy coats and matched
to a builder's level flat across their backs.
Phoebus Apollo lord of the silver bow   870
had bred them both in Perea, a brace of mares
that raced the War-god's panic through the lines.
But best by far of the men was Telamonian Ajax
while Achilles raged apart. The famed Achilles
towered over them all, he and the battle-team
that bore the peerless son of Peleus into war.
But off in his beaked seagoing ships he lay,
raging away at Atrides Agamemnon, king of armies,
while his men sported along the surf, marking time,
hurling the discus, throwing spears and testing bows.   880
And the horses, each beside its chariot, champing clover
and parsley from the marshes, waited, pawing idly.
Their masters' chariots stood under blankets now,
stored away in the tents while the rank and file,
yearning for their leader, the great man of war,
drifting here and there throughout the encampment,
hung back from the fighting.
                                    But on the armies came
as if the whole earth were devoured by wildfire, yes,
and the ground thundered under them, deep as it does

for Zeus who loves the lightning, Zeus in all his rage   890
when he lashes the ground around Typhoeus in Arima,
there where they say the monster makes his bed of pain—
so the earth thundered under their feet, armies trampling,
sweeping through the plain at blazing speed.
                                             Now the Trojans.
Iris the wind-quick messenger hurried down to Ilium,
bearing her painful message, sent by storming Zeus.
The Trojans assembled hard by Priam's gates,
gathered together there, young men and old,
and rushing closer, racing Iris addressed them,
keying her voice to that of Priam's son Polites.   900
He had kept a watch for the Trojans, posted atop
old Aesyetes' tomb and poised to sprint for home
at the first sign of Argives charging from the ships.
Like him to the life, the racing Iris urged, "Old Priam,
words, endless words—that is your passion, always,
as once in the days of peace. But ceaseless war's upon us!
Time and again I've gone to battle, fought with men
but I've never seen an army great as this. Too much—
like piling leaves or sand, and on and on they come,
advancing across the plain to fight before our gates.   910
Hector, I urge you first of all—do as I tell you.
Armies of allies crowd the mighty city of Priam,
true, but they speak a thousand different tongues,
fighters gathered here from all ends of the realm.
Let each chief give commands to the tribe he leads,
move them out, marshal his own contingents—now!"

    Hector missed nothing—that was a goddess' call.
He broke up the assembly at once. They rushed to arms
and all the gates flung wide and the Trojan mass surged out,
horses, chariots, men on foot—a tremendous roar went up.   920

    Now a sharp ridge rises out in front of Troy,
all on its own and far across the plain
with running-room around it, all sides clear.
Men call it Thicket Ridge, the immortals call it
the leaping Amazon Myrine's mounded tomb, and there
the Trojans and allies ranged their troops for battle.

    First, tall Hector with helmet flashing led the Trojans—
Priam's son and in his command by far the greatest, bravest army,
divisions harnessed in armor, veterans bristling spears.

    And the noble son of Anchises led the Dardanians—   930
Aeneas whom the radiant Aphrodite bore Anchises

down the folds of Ida, a goddess bedded with a man.
Not Aeneas alone but flanked by Antenor's two sons,
Acamas and Archelochus, trained for every foray.

And men who lived in Zelea under the foot of Ida,
a wealthy clan that drank the Aesepus' dark waters—
Trojans all, and the shining son of Lycaon led them on,
Pandarus, with the bow that came from Apollo's own hands.

And the men who held the land of Apaesus and Adrestia,
men who held Pityea, Terea's steep peaks—the units led   940
by Adrestus joined by Amphius trim in linen corslet,
the two good sons of Merops out of Percote harbor,
Merops adept beyond all men in the *mantic arts*.
He refused to let his two boys march to war,
this man-killing war, but the young ones fought him
all the way—the forces of black death drove them on.

And the men who lived around Percote and Practios,
men who settled Sestos, Abydos and gleaming Arisbe:
Asius son of Hyrtacus led them on, captain of armies,
Hyrtacus' offspring Asius—hulking, fiery stallions   950
bore him in from Arisbe, from the Selleis River.

Hippothous led the Pelasgian tribes of spearmen,
fighters who worked Larissa's dark rich plowland.
Hippothous and Pylaeus, tested soldier, led them on,
both sons of Pelasgian Lethus, Teutamus' scion.

Acamas and the old hero Pirous led the Thracians,
all the Hellespont bounds within her riptide straits.

Euphemus led the Cicones, fighters armed with spears,
son of Troezenus, Ceas' son, a warlord bred by the gods.

Pyraechmes led the Paeonians, reflex bows in hand,   960
hailing from Amydon far west and the broad river Axius,
Axius, clearest stream that flows across the earth.

That burly heart Pylaemenes led his Paphlagonians
out of Enetian country, land where the wild mules breed:
the men who held Cytorus and lived in range of Sesamus,
building their storied halls along the Parthenius River,
at Cromna, Aegialus and the highland fortress Erythini.

Odius and Epistrophus led the Halizonians out of Alybe
miles east where the mother lode of silver came to birth.

Chromis led the Mysian men with Ennomus seer of birds—   970
but none of his winged signs could beat off black death.
Down he went, crushed by racing Achilles' hands, destroyed
in the river where he slaughtered other Trojans too.

Ascanius strong as a god and Phorcys led the Phrygians
in from Ascania due east, primed for the clash of combat.

Mesthles and Antiphus led Maeonia's proud contingent,
Talaemenes' two sons sprung from the nymph of Gyge Lake
led on Maeonian units born and bred under Mount Tmolus.

Nastes led the Carians wild with barbarous tongues,
men who held Miletus, Phthires' ridges thick with timber,   980
Maeander's currents and Mount Mycale's craggy peaks.
Amphimachus and Nastes led their formations on,
Nastes and Amphimachus, Nomion's flamboyant sons.
Nastes strolled to battle decked in gold like a girl,
the fool! None of his trappings kept off grisly death—
down he went, crushed by racing Achilles' hands, destroyed
at the ford where battle-hard Achilles stripped his gold away.

And last, Sarpedon and valiant Glaucus marched the Lycians on
from Lycia far south, from the Xanthus' swirling rapids.

Plato

THE PHAEDO

Introduction by James Eichler

Plato (circa 427–347 B.C.), a student of Socrates, established the basis for a major strand of Western philosophy called idealism. Like his teacher, he opposed the relativism of the Sophists and sought to define absolute standards of justice, beauty, good, etc. This, coupled with the influences of the Pythagoreans, and of Heraclitus and Parmenides, led him to develop a synthesis that addressed most of the philosophical problems of his day.

Plato is said to have been of aristocratic birth, and a critic of the democratic form of government so highly esteemed in Athens during its "golden age." Because, in 399 B.C., a restored Athenian democracy made Socrates a scapegoat for its ill fortunes in the Peloponnesian War, and because Plato was personally associated with Socrates, and related to members of the short-lived but infamous Thirty Tyrant Regime imposed by the victorious Spartans at the end of that war, he left Athens following Socrates' execution, returning in 387 B.C. to establish a school (The Academy) in which he taught until his death. He also wrote a series of dialogues—among them the *Apology,* the *Crito,* the *Republic,* and the *Laws.* These dialogues preserved his thought for succeeding generations of philosophers.

One theme which permeates these writings is the nature of virtue and the need to live the "good life." In the dialogue entitled the *Phaedo,* which recounts Socrates' death, Plato describes the good life and the key role philosophy plays in its attainment. In reading the *Phaedo,* it will be helpful to keep several questions in mind. How does Plato define reality or truth (ontology)? What are its qualities? How does he think one can know that reality or truth (epistemology)? Given his definition of truth, how then should one apply it to his or her life (ethics)? What will be the reward for doing so and how does this imply order and justice in the universe? What does Plato have to say about God? What about human nature, the soul, or death? What did Socrates mean in the dialogue when he said he had no fear of death, because he had "practiced dying" his entire life? How do Plato's views of reality, humanity, and the afterlife inspire religious and philosophical systems of thought we follow today? Do we define a virtuous life in similar ways? Finally, consider why Plato chose to write in the form of conversations and make Socrates his chief spokesman. What purposes might this have served for him?

In reading this, note that Plato equates the intellect with the soul, and that for him, the improvement of one translates into the improvement of the other. On moral grounds then, Plato makes a strong case for rationalism as a guide to "the good life." His emphasis on the importance of spirit and idea shapes his answers to the questions listed above, and has influenced Western thought so pervasively that philosophers and theologians of the twentieth century still acknowledge their debt to him.

Phaedo

CHARACTERS OF THE DIALOGUE

PHAEDO	APOLLODORUS
The Narrator	CEBES
ECHECRATES	CRITO
SOCRATES	SIMMIAS

THE SERVANT OF THE ELEVEN

SCENE—*The Prison of Socrates*

Echecrates.   Were you with Socrates yourself, Phaedo, on that day when he drank the poison in the prison, or did you hear the story from someone else?

Phaedo.   I was there myself, Echecrates.

Ech.   Then what was it that our master said before his death, and how did he die? I should be very glad if you would tell me. None of our citizens go very much to Athens now; and no stranger has come from there for a long time who could give us any definite account of these things, except that he drank the poison and died. We could learn nothing beyond that.

Phaedo.   Then have you not heard about the trial either, how that went?

Ech.   Yes, we were told of that, and we were rather surprised to find that he did not die till so long after the trial. Why was that, Phaedo?

Phaedo.   It was an accident, Echecrates. The stern of the ship, which the Athenians send to Delos, happened to have been crowned on the day before the trial.

Ech.   And what is this ship?

Phaedo.   It is the ship, as the Athenians say, in which Theseus took the seven youths and the seven maidens to Crete, and saved them from death, and himself was saved. The Athenians made a vow then to Apollo, the story goes, to send a sacred mission to Delos every year, if they should be saved; and from that time to this they have always sent it to the god, every year. They have a law to keep the city pure as soon as the mission begins, and not to execute any sentence of death until the ship has returned from Delos; and sometimes, when it is detained by contrary winds, that is a long while. The sacred mission begins when the priest of Apollo crowns the

Plato, *Phaedo* (F.J. Church, trans.), Bobbs–Merrill, 1951, original pp. 1–33 (through "deliverance and purification.")

stern of the ship; and as I said, this happened to have been done on the day before the trial. That was why Socrates lay so long in prison between his trial and his death.

Ech.   But tell me about his death, Phaedo. What was said and done, and which of   II his friends were with our master? Or would not the authorities let them be there? Did he die alone?

Phaedo.   Oh, no; some of them were there, indeed several.

Ech.   It would be very good of you, if you are not busy, to tell us the whole story as exactly as you can.

Phaedo.   No, I have nothing to do, and I will try to relate it. Nothing is more pleasant to me than to recall Socrates to my mind, whether by speaking of him myself or by listening to others.

Ech.   Indeed, Phaedo, you will have an audience like yourself. But try to tell us everything that happened as precisely as you can.

Phaedo.   Well, I myself was strangely moved on that day. I did not feel that I was being present at the death of a dear friend; I did not pity him, for he seemed to me happy, Echecrates, both in his bearing and in his words, so fearlessly and nobly did he die. I could not help thinking that the gods would watch over him still on his journey to the other world, and that when he arrived there it would be well with him, if it was ever   59 well with any man. Therefore I had scarcely any feeling of pity, as you would expect at such a mournful time. Neither did I feel the pleasure which I usually felt at our philosophical discussions; for our talk was of philosophy. A very singular feeling came over me, a strange mixture of pleasure and pain when I remembered that he was presently to die. All of us who were there were in much the same state, laughing and crying by turns; particularly Apollodorus. I think you know the man and his ways.

Ech.   Of course I do.

Phaedo.   Well, he did not restrain himself at all and I myself and the others were greatly agitated too.

Ech.   Who were there, Phaedo?

Phaedo.   Of native Athenians, there was this Apollodorus, and Critobulus, and his father Crito, and Hermogenes, and Epigenes, and Aeschines, and Antisthenes. Then there was Ctesippus the Paeanian, and Menexenus, and some other Athenians. Plato I believe was ill.

Ech.   Were any strangers there?

Phaedo.   Yes, there was Simmias of Thebes, and Cebes, and Phaedondes; and Eucleides and Terpsion from Megara.

Ech.   But Aristippus and Cleombrotus, were they present?

Phaedo.   No, they were not. They were said to be in Aegina.

Ech.   Was anyone else there?

Phaedo.   No, I think that these were all.

Ech.   Then tell us about your conversation.

Phaedo.   I will try to relate the whole story to you from the beginning. On the pre-   III vious days I and the others had always met in the morning at the court where the trial was held, which was close to the prison; and then we had gone in to Socrates. We used to wait each morning until the prison was opened, conversing, for it was not opened early. When it was opened we used to go in to Socrates, and we generally spent the whole day with him. But on that morning we met earlier than usual; for the evening before we had learned, on leaving the prison, that the ship had arrived from Delos. So we arranged to be at the usual place as early as possible. When we reached the prison, the porter, who generally let us in, came out to us and bade us wait a little, and not to go in until he summoned us himself: "For the Eleven," he said, "are releasing Socrates from his fetters and giving directions for his death today." In no great while he returned and bade us enter. So we went in and found Socrates just released, and Xanthippe—you know her—sitting by him, holding his child in her arms. When Xanthippe saw us, she wailed aloud, and cried, in her woman's way, "This is the last time, Socrates, that you will talk with your friends, or they with you." And Socrates glanced at Crito, and said, "Crito, let her be taken home." So some of Crito's servants led her away weeping bitterly and beating her breast. But Socrates sat up on the bed, and bent his leg and rubbed it with his hand, and while he was rubbing it said to us, How strange a thing is what men call pleasure! How wonderful is its relation to pain, which seems to be the opposite of it! They will not come to a man together; but if he pursues the one and gains it, he is almost forced to take the other also, as if they were two distinct things united at one end. And I think, said he, that if Aesop had noticed them he would have composed a fable about them, to the effect that God had wished to reconcile them when they were quarreling, and that, when he could not do that, he joined their ends together; and that therefore whenever the one comes to a man, the other is sure to follow. That is just the case with me. There was pain in my leg caused by the chains, and now, it seems, pleasure is come following the pain.

Cebes interrupted him and said, By the bye, Socrates, I am glad that you reminded me. Several people have been inquiring about your poems, the hymn to Apollo, and Aesop's fables which you have put into meter, and only a day or two ago Evenus asked me what was your reason for writing poetry on coming here, when you had never written a line before. So if you wish me to be able to answer him when he asks me again, as I know that he will, tell me what to say.

Then tell him the truth, Cebes, he said. Say that it was from no wish to pose as a rival to him, or to his poems. I knew that it would not be easy to do that. I was only testing the meaning of certain dreams and acquitting my conscience about them, in case they should be bidding me make this kind of music. The fact is this. The same dream used often to come to me in my past life, appearing in different forms at different times, but always saying the same words, "Socrates, work at music and compose it." Formerly I used to think that the dream was encouraging me and cheering me on in what was already the work of my life, just as the spectators cheer on different runners in a race. I supposed that the dream was encouraging me to create the music at which I was working already, for I thought that philosophy was the highest music, and my life was spent in philosophy. But then, after the trial, when the feast of the god delayed my death, it occurred to me that the dream might possibly be bidding me create music in the popular sense, and that in that case I ought to do so, and not to disobey. I thought that it would be safer to acquit my conscience by creating poetry in obedience to the dream before I departed. So first I composed a hymn to the god whose feast it was. And then I turned such fables of Aesop as I knew, and had ready to my hand, into verse, taking those which came first; for I reflected that a man who means to be a poet has to use fiction and not facts for his poems; and I could not invent fiction myself.

Tell Evenus this, Cebes, and bid him farewell from me; and tell him to follow me as quickly as he can, if he is wise. I, it seems, shall depart today, for that is the will of the Athenians.

IV

61

V

And Simmias said, What strange advice to give Evenus, Socrates! I have often met him, and from what I have seen of him I think that he is certainly not at all the man to take it, if he can help it.

What, he said, is not Evenus a philosopher?

Yes, I suppose so, replied Simmias.

Then Evenus will wish to die, he said, and so will every man who is worthy of having any part in this study. But he will not lay violent hands on himself; for that, they say, is wrong. And as he spoke he put his legs off the bed on to the ground, and remained sitting thus for the rest of the conversation.

Then Cebes asked him, What do you mean, Socrates, by saying that it is wrong for a man to lay violent hands on himself, but that the philosopher will wish to follow the dying man?

What, Cebes? Have you and Simmias been with Philolaus, and not heard about these things?

Nothing very definite, Socrates.

Well, I myself only speak of them from hearsay, yet there is no reason why I should not tell you what I have heard. Indeed, as I am setting out on a journey to the other world, what could be more fitting for me than to talk about my journey and to consider what we imagine to be its nature? How could we better employ the interval between this and sunset?

Then what is their reason for saying that it is wrong for a man to kill himself, Socrates? It is quite true that I have heard Philolaus say, when he was living at Thebes, that it is not right; and I have heard the same thing from others, too, but I never heard anything definite on the subject from any of them.   VI

You must be of good cheer, said he, possibly you will hear something some day. But perhaps you will be surprised if I say that this law, unlike every other law to which mankind is subject, is absolute and without exception; and that it is not true that death is better than life only for some persons and at some times. And perhaps you will be surprised if I tell you that these men, for whom it would be better to die, may not do themselves a service, but that they must await a benefactor from without.   62

Oh indeed, said Cebes, laughing quietly, and speaking in his native dialect.

Indeed, said Socrates, so stated it may seem strange, and yet perhaps a reason may be given for it. The reason which the secret teaching[1] gives, that man is in a kind of prison, and that he may not set himself free, nor escape from it, seems to me rather profound and not easy to fathom. But I do think, Cebes, that it is true that the gods are our guardians, and that we men are a part of their property. Do you not think so?

I do, said Cebes.

Well then, said he, if one of your possessions were to kill itself, though you had not signified that you wished it to die, should you not be angry with it? Should you not punish it, if punishment were possible?

Certainly, he replied.

Then in this way perhaps it is not unreasonable to hold that no man has a right to take his own life, but that he must wait until God sends some necessity upon him, as has now been sent upon me.

---

[1] The Esoteric system of the Pythagoreans.

Yes, said Cebes, that does seem natural. But you were saying just now that the   VII
philosopher will desire to die. Is not that a paradox, Socrates, if what we have just been
saying, that God is our guardian and that we are his property, be true? It is not reasonable to say that the wise man will be content to depart from this service, in which the
gods, who are the best of all rulers, rule him. He will hardly think that when he becomes
free he will take better care of himself than the gods take of him. A fool perhaps might
think so, and say that he would do well to run away from his master; he might not consider that he ought not to run away from a good master, but that he ought to remain with
him as long as possible, and so in his thoughtlessness he might run away. But the wise
man will surely desire to remain always with one who is better than himself. But if this
be true, Socrates, the reverse of what you said just now seems to follow. The wise man
should grieve to die, and the fool should rejoice.

I thought Socrates was pleased with Cebes' insistence. He looked at us, and said,   63
Cebes is always examining arguments. He will not be convinced at once by anything
that one says.

Yes, Socrates, said Simmias, but I do think that now there is something in what
Cebes says. Why should really wise men want to run away from masters who are better
than themselves, and lightly quit their service? And I think Cebes is aiming his argument at you, because you are so ready to leave us, and the gods, who are good rulers, as
you yourself admit.

You are right, he said. I suppose you mean that I must defend myself against your
charge, as if I were in a court of justice.

That is just our meaning, said Simmias.

Well then, he replied, let me try to make a more successful defense to you than I did   VIII
to the judges at my trial. I should be wrong, Cebes and Simmias, he went on, not to
grieve at death, if I did not think that I was going to live both with other gods who are
good and wise, and with men who have died and who are better than the men of this
world. But you must know that I hope that I am going to live among good men, though I
am not quite sure of that. But I am so sure as I can be in such matters that I am going to
live with gods who are very good masters. And therefore I am not so much grieved at
death; I am confident that the dead have some kind of existence, and, as has been said of
old, an existence that is far better for the good than for the wicked.

Well, Socrates, said Simmias, do you mean to go away and keep this belief to yourself, or will you let us share it with you? It seems to me that we too have an interest in
this good. And it will also serve as your defense, if you can convince us of what you say.

Only, Socrates, said Crito, that the man who is going to give you the poison has
been telling me to warn you not to talk much. He says that talking heats people, and that
the action of the poison must not be counteracted by heat. Those who excite themselves
sometimes have to drink it two or three times.

Let him be, said Socrates; let him mind his own business, and be prepared to give
me the poison twice, or, if need be, thrice.

I knew that would be your answer, said Crito, but the man has been importunate.

Never mind him, he replied. But I wish not to explain to you, my judges, why it
seems to me that a man who has really spent his life in philosophy has reason to be of
good cheer when he is about to die, and may well hope after death to gain in the other   64
world the greatest good. I will try to show you, Simmias and Cebes, how this may be.

The world, perhaps, does not see that those who rightly engage in philosophy study   IX
only dying and death. And, if this be true, it would be surely strange for a man all
through his life to desire only death, and then, when death comes to him, to be vexed at
it, when it has been his study and his desire for so long.

Simmias laughed, and said: Indeed, Socrates, you make me laugh, though I am
scarcely in a laughing humor now. If the multitude heard that, I fancy they would think
that what you say of philosophers is quite true; and my countrymen would entirely
agree with you that philosophers are indeed eager to die, and they would say that they
know full well that philosophers deserve to be put to death.

And they would be right, Simmias, except in saying that they know it. They do not
know in what sense the true philosopher is eager to die, or what kind of death he
deserves, or in what sense he deserves it. Let us dismiss them from our thoughts, and
converse by ourselves. Do we believe death to be anything?

We do, replied Simmias.

And do we not believe it to be the separation of the soul from the body? Does not
death mean that the body comes to exist by itself, separated from the soul, and that the
soul exists by herself, separated from the body? What is death but that?

It is that, he said.

Now consider, my good friend, if you and I are agreed on another point which I
think will help us to understand the question better. Do you think that a philosopher will
care very much about what are called pleasures, such as the pleasures of eating and
drinking?

Certainly not, Socrates, said Simmias.

Or about the pleasures of sexual passion?

Indeed, no.

And, do you think that he holds the remaining cares of the body in high esteem?
Will he think much of getting fine clothes, and sandals, and other bodily adornments, or
will he despise them, except so far as he is absolutely forced to meddle with them?

The real philosopher, I think, will despise them, he replied.

In short, said he, you think that his studies are not concerned with the body? He
stands aloof from it, as far as he can, and turns toward the soul?

I do.

Well then, in these matters, first, it is clear that the philosopher releases his soul   65
from communion with the body, so far as he can, beyond all other men?

It is.

And does not the world think, Simmias, that if a man has no pleasure in such
things, and does not take his share in them, his life is not worth living? Do not they hold
that he who thinks nothing of bodily pleasures is almost as good as dead?

Indeed you are right.

But what about the actual acquisition of wisdom? If the body is taken as a compan-   X
ion in the search for wisdom, is it a hindrance or not? For example, do sight and hearing
convey any real truth to men? Are not the very poets forever telling us that we neither
hear nor see anything accurately? But if these senses of the body are not accurate or
clear, the others will hardly be so, for they are all less perfect than these, are they not?

Yes, I think so, certainly, he said.

Then when does the soul attain truth? he asked. We see that, as often as she seeks to
investigate anything in company with the body, the body leads her astray.

True.

Is it not by reasoning, if at all, that any real truth becomes manifest to her?

Yes.

And she reasons best, I suppose, when none of the senses, whether hearing, or sight, or pain, or pleasure, harasses her; when she has dismissed the body, and released herself as far as she can from all intercourse or contact with it, and so, coming to be as much alone with herself as is possible, strives after real truth.

That is so.

And here too the soul of the philosopher very greatly despises the body, and flies from it, and seeks to be alone by herself, does she not?

Clearly.

And what do you say to the next point, Simmias? Do we say that there is such a thing as absolute justice, or not?

Indeed we do.

And absolute beauty, and absolute good?

Of course.

Have you ever seen any of them with your eyes?

Indeed I have not, he replied.

Did you ever grasp them with any bodily sense? I am speaking of all absolutes, whether size, or health, or strength; in a word, of the essence or real being of everything. Is the very truth of things contemplated by the body? Is it not rather the case that the man who prepares himself most carefully to apprehend by his intellect the essence of each thing which he examines will come nearest to the knowledge of it?

Certainly.

And will not a man attain to this pure thought most completely if he goes to each thing, as far as he can, with his mind alone, taking neither sight nor any other sense along with his reason in the process of thought, to be an encumbrance? In every case he will pursue pure and absolute being, with his pure intellect alone. He will be set free as far as possible from the eye and the ear and, in short, from the whole body, because intercourse with the body troubles the soul, and hinders her from gaining truth and wisdom. Is it not he who will attain the knowledge of real being, if any man will?

Your words are admirably true, Socrates, said Simmias.

And, he said, must not all this cause real philosophers to reflect, and make them say to each other, It seems that there is a narrow path which will bring us safely to our journey's end, with reason as our guide. As long as we have this body, and an evil of that sort is mingled with our souls, we shall never fully gain what we desire; and that is truth. For the body is forever taking up our time with the care which it needs; and, besides, whenever diseases attack it, they hinder us in our pursuit of real being. It fills us with passions, and desires, and fears, and all manner of phantoms, and much foolishness; and so, as the saying goes, in very truth we can never think at all for it. It alone and its desires cause wars and factions and battles; for the origin of all wars is the pursuit of wealth,[2] and we are forced to pursue wealth because we live in slavery to the cares of the body. And therefore, for all these reasons, we have no leisure for philosophy. And last of all, if we ever are free from the body for a time, and then turn to examine some

66

XI

---

[2] Cf. *Republic* 373d.

matter, it falls in our way at every step of the inquiry, and causes confusion and trouble and panic, so that we cannot see the truth for it. Verily we have learned that if we are to have any pure knowledge at all, we must be freed from the body; the soul by herself must behold things as they are. Then, it seems, after we are dead, we shall gain the wisdom which we desire, and for which we say we have a passion, but not while we are alive, as the argument shows. For if it be not possible to have pure knowledge while the body is with us, one of two things must be true: either we cannot gain knowledge at all, or we can gain it only after death. For then, and not till then, will the soul exist by herself, separate from the body. And while we live, we shall come nearest to knowledge, if we have no communion or intercourse with the body beyond what is absolutely necessary, and if we are not defiled with its nature. We must live pure from it until God himself releases us. And when we are thus pure and released from its follies, we shall dwell, I suppose, with others who are pure like ourselves, and we shall of ourselves know all that is pure; and that may be the truth. For I think that the impure is not allowed to attain to the pure. Such, Simmias, I fancy must needs be the language and the reflection of the true lovers of knowledge. Do you not agree with me?

67

Most assuredly I do, Socrates.

And, my friend, said Socrates, if this be true, I have good hope that, when I reach the place whither I am going, I shall there, if anywhere, gain fully that which we have sought so earnestly in the past. And so I shall set forth cheerfully on the journey that is appointed me today, and so may every man who thinks that his mind is prepared and purified.

XII

That is quite true, said Simmias.

And does not the purification consist, as we have said, in separating the soul from the body, as far as is possible, and in accustoming her to collect and rally herself as much as she can, both now and hereafter, released from the bondage of the body?

Yes, certainly, he said.

Is not what we call death a release and separation of the soul from the body?

Undoubtedly, he replied.

And the true philosopher, we hold, is alone in his constant desire to set his soul free? His study is simply the release and separation of the soul from the body, is it not?

Clearly.

Would it not be absurd then, as I began by saying for a man to complain at death coming to him, when in his life he has been preparing himself to live as nearly in a state of death as he could? Would not that be absurd?

Yes, indeed.

In truth, then, Simmias, he said, the true philosopher studies to die, and to him of all men is death least terrible. Now look at the matter in this way. In everything he is at enmity with his body, and he longs to possess his soul alone. Would it not then be most unreasonable if he were to fear and complain when he has his desire, instead of rejoicing to go to the place where he hopes to gain the wisdom that he has passionately longed for all his life, and to be released from the company of his enemy? Many a man has willingly gone to the other world, when a human love or wife or son has died, in the hope of seeing there those whom he longed for, and of being with them: and will a man who has a real passion for wisdom, and a firm hope of really finding wisdom in the other world and nowhere else, grieve at death, and not depart rejoicing? Nay, my friend, you ought not to think that, if he be truly a philosopher. He will be firmly convinced that

68

there and nowhere else will he meet with wisdom in its purity. And if this be so, would it not, I repeat, be very unreasonable for such a man to fear death?

Yes, indeed, he replied, it would.

Does not this show clearly, he said, that any man whom you see grieving at the approach of death is after all no lover of wisdom, but a lover of his body? He is also, most likely, a lover either of wealth, or of honor, or, it may be, of both.

XIII

Yes, he said, it is as you say.

Well then, Simmias, he went on, does not what is called courage belong especially to the philosopher?

Certainly I think so, he replied.

And does not temperance, the quality which even the world calls temperance, and which means to despise and control and govern the passions—does not temperance belong only to such men as most despise the body, and pass their lives in philosophy?

Of necessity, he replied.

For if you will consider the courage and the temperance of other men, said he, you will find that they are strange things.

How so, Socrates?

You know, he replied, that all other men regard death as one of the great evils to which mankind is subject?

Indeed they do, he said.

And when the brave men of them submit to death, do not they do so from a fear of still greater evils?

Yes.

Then all men but the philosopher are brave from fear and because they are afraid. Yet it is rather a strange thing for a man to be brave out of fear and cowardice.

Indeed it is.

And are not the orderly men of them in exactly the same case? Are not they temperate from a kind of intemperance? We should say that this cannot be; but in them this state of foolish temperance comes to that. They desire certain pleasures, and fear to lose them; and so they abstain from other pleasures because they are mastered by these. Intemperance is defined to mean being under the dominion of pleasure, yet they only master certain pleasures because they are mastered by others. But that is exactly what I said just now—that, in a way, they are made temperate from intemperance.

69

It seems to be so.

My dear Simmias, I fear that virtue is not really to be bought in this way, by bartering pleasure for pleasure, and pain for pain, and fear for fear, and the greater for the less, like coins. There is only one sterling coin for which all these things ought to be exchanged, and that is wisdom. All that is bought and sold for this and with this, whether courage, or temperance, or justice, is real; in one word, true virtue cannot be without wisdom, and it matters nothing whether pleasure, and fear, and all other such things are present or absent. But I think that the virtue which is composed of pleasures and fears bartered with one another, and severed from wisdom, is only a shadow of true virtue, and that it has no freedom, nor health, nor truth. True virtue in reality is a kind of purifying from all these things; and temperance, and justice, and courage, and wisdom itself are the purification. And I fancy that the men who established our mysteries had a very real meaning: in truth they have been telling us in parables all the time that whosoever comes to Hades uninitiated and profane will lie in the mire, while he that has been purified and initiated shall dwell with the gods. For "the thyrsus-bearers are many," as they say in the mysteries, "but the inspired few." And by these last, I believe, are meant only the true philosophers. And I in my life have striven as hard as I was able, and have left nothing undone, that I might become one of them. Whether I have striven in the right way, and whether I have succeeded or not, I suppose that I shall learn in a little while, when I reach the other world, if it be the will of God.

That is my defense, Simmias and Cebes, to show that I have reason for not being angry or grieved at leaving you and my masters here. I believe that in the next world, no less than in this, I shall meet with good masters and friends, though the multitude are incredulous of it. And if I have been more successful with you in my defense than I was with my Athenian judges, it is well.

When Socrates had finished, Cebes replied to him, and said, I think that for the most part you are right, Socrates. But men are very incredulous of what you have said of the soul. They fear that she will no longer exist anywhere when she has left the body, but that she will be destroyed and perish on the very day of death. They think that the moment that she is released and leaves the body, she will be dissolved and vanish away like breath or smoke, and thenceforward cease to exist at all. If she were to exist somewhere as a whole, released from the evils which you enumerated just now, we should have good reason to hope, Socrates, that what you say is true. But it will need no little persuasion and assurance to show that the soul exists after death, and continues to possess any power or wisdom. **XIV** **70**

True, Cebes, said Socrates; but what are we to do? Do you wish to converse about these matters and see if what I say is probable?

I for one, said Cebes, should gladly hear your opinion about them.

I think, said Socrates, that no one who heard me now, even if he were a comic poet, would say that I am an idle talker about things which do not concern me. So, if you wish it, let us examine this question.

Let us consider whether or not the souls of men exist in the next world after death, thus. There is an ancient belief, which we remember, that on leaving this world they exist there, and that they return hither and are born again from the dead. But if it be true that the living are born from the dead, our souls must exist in the other world; otherwise they could not be born again. It will be a sufficient proof that this is so if we can really prove that the living are born only from the dead. But if this is not so, we shall have to find some other argument. **XV**

Exactly, said Cebes.

Well, said he, the easiest way of answering the question will be to consider it not in relation to men only, but also in relation to all animals and plants, and in short to all things that are generated. Is it the case that everything which has an opposite is generated only from its opposite? By opposites I mean the honorable and the base, the just and the unjust, and so on in a thousand other instances. Let us consider then whether it is necessary for everything that has an opposite to be generated only from its own opposite. For instance, when anything becomes greater, I suppose it must have been less and then become greater?

Yes.

And if a thing becomes less, it must have been greater, and afterward become less? **71**
That is so, said he.

And further, the weaker is generated from the stronger, and the swifter from the slower?

Certainly.

And the worse is generated from the better, and the more just from the more unjust?

Of course.

Then it is sufficiently clear to us that all things are generated in this way, opposites from opposites?

Quite so.

And in every pair of opposites, are there not two generations between the two members of the pair, from the one to the other, and then back again from the other to the first? Between the greater and the less are growth and diminution, and we say that the one grows and the other diminishes, do we not?

Yes, he said.

And there is division and composition, and cold and hot, and so on. In fact, is it not a universal law, even though we do not always express it in so many words, that opposites are generated always from one another, and that there is a process of generation from one to the other?

It is, he replied.

Well, said he, is there an opposite to life, in the same way that sleep is the opposite   XVI
of being awake?

Certainly, he answered.

What is it?

Death, he replied.

Then if life and death are opposites, they are generated the one from the other: they are two, and between them there are two generations. Is it not so?

Of course.

Now, said Socrates, I will explain to you one of the two pairs of opposites of which I spoke just now, and its generations, and you shall explain to me the other. Sleep is the opposite of waking. From sleep is produced the state of waking, and from the state of waking is produced sleep. Their generations are, first, to fall asleep; secondly, to awake. Is that clear? he asked.

Yes, quite.

Now then, said he, do you tell me about life and death. Death is the opposite of life, is it not?

It is.

And they are generated the one from the other?

Yes.

Then what is that which is generated from the living?

The dead, he replied.

And what is generated from the dead?

I must admit that it is the living.

Then living things and living men are generated from the dead, Cebes?

Clearly, said he.

Then our souls exist in the other world? he said.

Apparently.

Now of these two generations the one is certain? Death I suppose is certain enough, is it not?

Yes, quite, he replied.

What then shall we do? said he. Shall we not assign an opposite generation to correspond? Or is nature imperfect here? Must we not assign some opposite generation to dying?

I think so, certainly, he said.

And what must it be?

To come to life again.

And if there be such a thing as a return to life, he said, it will be a generation from the dead to the living, will it not?   72

It will, certainly.

Then we are agreed on this point: namely, that the living are generated from the dead no less than the dead from the living. But we agreed that, if this be so, it is sufficient proof that the souls of the dead must exist somewhere, whence they come into being again.

I think, Socrates, that that is the necessary result of our premises.

And I think, Cebes, said he, that our conclusion has not been an unfair one. For if   XVII
opposites did not always correspond with opposites as they are generated, moving as it were round in a circle, and there was generation in a straight line forward from one opposite only, with no turning or return to the other, then, you know, all things would come at length to have the same form and be in the same state, and would cease to be generated at all.

What do you mean? he asked.

It is not at all hard to understand my meaning, he replied. If, for example, the one opposite, to go to sleep, existed without the corresponding opposite, to wake up, which is generated from the first, then all nature would at last make the tale of Endymion meaningless, and he would no longer be conspicuous; for everything else would be in the same state of sleep that he was in. And if all things were compounded together and never separated, the Chaos of Anaxagoras would soon be realized. Just in the same way, my dear Cebes, if all things in which there is any life were to die, and when they were dead were to remain in that form and not come to life again, would not the necessary result be that everything at last would be dead, and nothing alive? For if living things were generated from other sources than death, and were to die, the result is inevitable that all things would be consumed by death. Is it not so?

It is indeed, I think, Socrates, said Cebes; I think that what you say is perfectly true.

Yes, Cebes, he said, I think it is certainly so. We are not misled into this conclusion. The dead do come to life again, and the living are generated from them, and the souls of the dead exist; and with the souls of the good it is well, and with the souls of the evil it is evil.   XVIII

And besides, Socrates, rejoined Cebes, if the doctrine which you are fond of stating, that our learning is only a process of recollection, be true, then I suppose we must have learned at some former time what we recollect now. And that would be impossible   73
unless our souls had existed somewhere before they came into this human form. So that is another reason for believing the soul immortal.

But, Cebes, interrupted Simmias, what are the proofs of that? Recall them to me; I am not very clear about them at present.

One argument, answered Cebes, and the strongest of all, is that if you question men about anything in the right way, they will answer you correctly of themselves. But they would not have been able to do that unless they had had within themselves knowledge and right reason. Again, show them such things as geometrical diagrams, and the proof of the doctrine is complete.[3]

And if that does not convince you, Simmias, said Socrates, look at the matter in another way and see if you agree then. You have doubts, I know, how what is called knowledge can be recollection.

Nay, replied Simmias, I do not doubt. But I want to recollect the argument about recollection. What Cebes undertook to explain has nearly brought your theory back to me and convinced me. But I am nonetheless ready to hear you undertake to explain it.

In this way, he returned. We are agreed, I suppose, that if a man remembers anything, he must have known it at some previous time.

Certainly, he said.

And are we agreed that when knowledge comes in the following way, it is recollection? When a man has seen or heard anything, or has perceived it by some other sense, and then knows not that thing only, but has also in his mind an impression of some other thing, of which the knowledge is quite different, are we not right in saying that he remembers the thing of which he has an impression in his mind?

What do you mean?

I mean this. The knowledge of a man is different from the knowledge of a lyre, is it not?

Certainly.

And you know that when lovers see a lyre, or a garment, or anything that their favorites are wont to use, they have this feeling. They know the lyre, and in their mind they receive the image of the youth whose the lyre was. That is recollection. For instance, someone seeing Simmias often is reminded of Cebes; and there are endless examples of the same thing.

Indeed there are, said Simmias.

Is not that a kind of recollection, he said; and more especially when a man has this feeling with reference to things which the lapse of time and inattention have made him forget?

Yes, certainly, he replied.

Well, he went on, is it possible to recollect a man on seeing the picture of a horse, or the picture of a lyre? Or to recall Simmias on seeing a picture of Cebes?

Certainly.

And it is possible to recollect Simmias himself on seeing a picture of Simmias?

No doubt, he said.

74

Then in all these cases there is recollection caused by similar objects, and also by dissimilar objects?

XIX

There is.

But when a man has a recollection caused by similar objects, will he not have a further feeling and consider whether the likeness to that which he recollects is defective in any way or not?

---

[3] For an example of this see *Meno* 82a ff., where, as here, Socrates proves the doctrine of Reminiscence, and therefore the Immortality of the Soul, by putting judicious questions about geometry to a slave who was quite ignorant of geometry, and, with the help of diagrams, obtaining from him correct answers.

He will, he said.

Now see if this is true, he went on. Do we not believe in the existence of equality—not the equality of pieces of wood or of stones, but something beyond that—equality in the abstract? Shall we say that there is such a thing, or not?

Yes indeed, said Simmias, most emphatically we will.

And do we know what this abstract equality is?

Certainly, he replied.

Where did we get the knowledge of it? Was it not from seeing the equal pieces of wood, and stones, and the like, which we were speaking of just now? Did we not form from them the idea of abstract equality, which is different from them? Or do you think that is it not different? Consider the question in this way. Do not equal pieces of wood and stones appear to us sometimes equal and sometimes unequal, though in fact they remain the same all the time?

Certainly they do.

But did absolute equals ever seem to you to be unequal, or abstract equality to be inequality?

No, never, Socrates.

Then equal things, he said, are not the same as abstract equality?

No, certainly not, Socrates.

Yet is was from these equal things, he said, which are different from abstract equality, that you have conceived and got your knowledge of abstract equality?

That is quite true, he replied.

And that whether it is like them or unlike them?

Certainly.

But that makes no difference, he said. As long as the sight of one thing brings another thing to your mind, there must be recollection, whether or not the two things are like.

That is so.

Well then, said he, do the equal pieces of wood, and other similar equal things, of which we have been speaking, affect us at all this way? Do they seem to us to be equal, in the way that abstract equality is equal? Do they come short of being like abstract equality, or not?

Indeed, they come very short of it, he replied.

Are we agreed about this? A man sees something and thinks to himself, "This thing that I see aims at being like some other thing, but it comes short and cannot be like that other thing; it is inferior"; must not the man who thinks that have known at some previous time that other thing, which he says that it resembles, and to which it is inferior?

He must.

Well, have we ourselves had the same sort of feeling with reference to equal things, and to abstract equality?

Yes, certainly.

Then we must have had knowledge of equality before we first saw equal things, and perceived that they all strive to be like equality, and all come short of it.

That is so.

And we are agreed also that we have not, nor could we have, obtained the idea of equality except from sight or touch or some other sense; the same is true of all the senses.

Yes, Socrates, for the purposes of the argument that is so.

At any rate it is by the senses that we must perceive that all sensible objects strive to resemble absolute equality, and are inferior to it. Is not that so?

Yes.

Then before we began to see, and to hear, and to use the other senses, we must have received the knowledge of the nature of abstract and real equality; otherwise we could not have compared equal sensible objects with abstract equality, and seen that the former in all cases strive to be like the latter, though they are always inferior to it?

That is the necessary consequence of what we have been saying, Socrates.

Did we not see, and hear, and possess the other senses as soon as we were born?

Yes, certainly.

And we must have received the knowledge of abstract equality before we had these senses?

Yes.

Then, it seems, we must have received that knowledge before we were born?

It does.

Now if we received this knowledge before our birth, and were born with it, we knew, both before and at the moment of our birth, not only the equal, and the greater, and the less, but also everything of the same kind, did we not? Our present reasoning does not refer only to equality. It refers just as much to absolute good, and absolute beauty, and absolute justice, and absolute holiness; in short, I repeat, to everything which we mark with the name of the real, in the questions and answers of our dialectic. So we must have received our knowledge of all realities before we were born.

That is so.

And we must always be born with this knowledge, and must always retain it throughout life, if we have not each time forgotten it, after having received it. For to know means to receive and retain knowledge, and not to have lost it. Do not we mean by forgetting, the loss of knowledge, Simmias?

Yes, certainly, Socrates, he said.

But, I suppose, if it be the case that we lost at birth the knowledge which we received before we were born, and then afterward, by using our senses on the objects of sense, recovered the knowledge which we had previously possessed, then what we call learning is the recovering of knowledge which is already ours. And are we not right in calling that recollection?

Certainly.

For we have found it possible to perceive a thing by sight, or hearing, or any other sense, and thence to form a notion of some other thing, like or unlike, which had been forgotten, but with which this thing was associated. And therefore, I say, one of two things must be true. Either we are all born with this knowledge and retain it all our life; or, after birth, those whom we say are learning are only recollecting, and our knowledge is recollection.

Yes indeed, that is undoubtedly true, Socrates.

Then which do you choose, Simmias? Are we born with knowledge or do we recollect the things of which we have received knowledge before our birth?

I cannot say at present, Socrates.

Well, have you an opinion about this question? Can a man who knows give an account of what he knows, or not? What do you think about that?

XX

76

XXI

Yes, of course he can, Socrates.

And do you think that everyone can give an account of the ideas of which we have been speaking?

I wish I did, indeed, said Simmias, but I am very much afraid that by this time tomorrow there will no longer be any man living able to do so as it should be done.

Then, Simmias, he said, you do not think that all men know these things?

Certainly not.

Then they recollect what they once learned?

Necessarily.

And when did our souls gain this knowledge? It cannot have been after we were born men.

No, certainly not.

Then it was before?

Yes.

Then, Simmias, our souls existed formerly, apart from our bodies, and possessed intelligence before they came into man's shape.[4]

Unless we receive this knowledge at the moment of birth, Socrates. That time still remains.

Well, my friend, and at what other time do we lose it? We agreed just now that we are not born with it; do we lose it at the same moment that we gain it, or can you suggest any other time?

I cannot, Socrates. I did not see that I was talking nonsense.

Then, Simmias, he said, is not this the truth? If, as we are forever repeating, beauty,   XXII
and good, and the other ideas[5] really exist, and if we refer all the objects of sensible perception to these ideas which were formerly ours, and which we find to be ours still, our souls must have existed before ever we were born. But if they do exist, then our reasoning will have been thrown away. Is it so? If these ideas exist, does it not at once follow that our souls must have existed before we were born, and if they do not exist, then neither did our souls?

Admirably put, Socrates, said Simmias. I think that the necessity is the same for the
one as for the other. The reasoning has reached a place of safety in the common proof of   77
the existence of our souls before we were born and of the existence of the ideas of which you spoke. Nothing is so evident to me as that beauty, and good, and the other ideas which you spoke of just now have a very real existence indeed. Your proof is quite sufficient for me.

But what of Cebes? said Socrates. I must convince Cebes too.

I think that he is satisfied, said Simmias, though he is the most skeptical of men in argument. But I think that he is perfectly convinced that our souls existed before we were born.

But I do not think myself, Socrates, he continued, that you have proved that the soul   XXIII
will continue to exist when we are dead. The common fear which Cebes spoke of, that she may be scattered to the winds at death, and that death may be the end of her exis-

---

[4] Cf. Wordworth's famous *Ode on Intimations of Immortality*. It must be noticed that in one respect Wordsworth exactly reverses Plato's theory. With Wordsworth "Heaven lies about us in our infancy," and as we grow to manhood we gradually forget it. With Plato, we lose the knowledge which we possessed in a prior state of existence, at birth, and recover it, as we grow up.

[5] For a fuller account of the ideas, see 100b ff.

tence, still stands in the way. Assuming that the soul is generated and comes together from some other elements, and exists before she ever enters the human body, why should she not come to an end and be destroyed, after she has entered into the body, when she is released from it?

You are right, Simmias, said Cebes. I think that only half the required proof has been given. It has been shown that our souls existed before we were born; but it must also be shown that our souls will continue to exist after we are dead, no less than that they existed before we were born, if the proof is to be complete.

That has been shown already, Simmias and Cebes, said Socrates, if you will combine this reasoning with our previous conclusion, that all life is generated from death. For if the soul exists in a previous state and if, when she comes into life and is born, she can only be born from death, and from a state of death, must she not exist after death too, since she has to be born again? So the point which you speak of has been already proved.

Still I think that you and Simmias would be glad to discuss this question further. XXIV Like children, you are afraid that the wind will really blow the soul away and disperse her when she leaves the body, especially if a man happens to die in a storm and not in a calm.

Cebes laughed and said, Try and convince us as if we were afraid, Socrates; or rather, do not think that we are afraid ourselves. Perhaps there is a child within us who has these fears. Let us try and persuade him not to be afraid of death, as if it were a bugbear.

You must charm him every day, until you have charmed him away, said Socrates.

And where shall we find a good charmer, Socrates, he asked, now that you are leaving us? 78

Hellas is a large country, Cebes, he replied, and good men may doubtless be found in it; and the nations of the Barbarians are many. You must search them all through for such a charmer, sparing neither money nor labor; for there is nothing on which you could spend money more profitably. And you must search for him among yourselves too, for you will hardly find a better charmer than yourselves.

That shall be done, said Cebes. But let us return to the point where we left off, if you will.

Yes, I will: why not?

Very good, he replied.

Well, said Socrates, must we not ask ourselves this question? What kind of thing is XXV liable to suffer dispersion, and for what kind of thing have we to fear dispersion? And then we must see whether the soul belongs to that kind or not, and be confident or afraid about our own souls accordingly.

That is true, he answered.

Now is it not the compound and composite which is naturally liable to be dissolved in the same way in which it was compounded? And is not what is uncompounded alone not liable to dissolution, if anything is not?

I think that that is so, said Cebes.

And what always remains in the same state and unchanging is most likely to be uncompounded, and what is always changing and never the same is most likely to be compounded, I suppose?

Yes, I think so.

Now let us return to what we were speaking of before in the discussion, he said. Does the being, which in our dialectic we define as meaning absolute existence, remain always in exactly the same state, or does it change? Do absolute equality, absolute beauty, and every other absolute existence, admit of any change at all? Or does absolute existence in each case, being essentially uniform, remain the same and unchanging, and never in any case admit of any sort or kind of change whatsoever?

It must remain the same and unchanging, Socrates, said Cebes.

And what of the many beautiful things, such as men, and horses, and garments, and the like, and of all which bears the names of the ideas, whether equal, or beautiful, or anything else? Do they remain the same or is it exactly the opposite with them? In short, do they never remain the same at all, either in themselves or in their relations?

These things, said Cebes, never remain the same.

You can touch them, and see them, and perceive them with the other senses, while   79 you can grasp the unchanging only by the reasoning of the intellect. These latter are invisible and not seen. Is it not so?

That is perfectly true, he said.

Let us assume then, he said, if you will, that there are two kinds of existence, the   XXVI one visible, the other invisible.

Yes, he said.

And the invisible is unchanging, while the visible is always changing.

Yes, he said again.

Are not we men made up of body and soul?

There is nothing else, he replied.

And which of these kinds of existence should we say that the body is most like, and most akin to?

The visible, he replied; that is quite obvious.

And the soul? Is that visible or invisible?

It is invisible to man, Socrates, he said.

But we mean by visible and invisible, visible and invisible to man; do we not?

Yes; that is what we mean.

Then what do we say of the soul? Is it visible or not visible?

It is not visible.

Then is it invisible?

Yes.

Then the soul is more like the invisible than the body; and the body is like the visible.

That is necessarily so, Socrates.

Have we not also said that, when the soul employs the body in any inquiry, and   XXVII makes use of sight, or hearing, or any other sense—for inquiry with the body means inquiry with the senses—she is dragged away by it to the things which never remain the same, and wanders about blindly, and becomes confused and dizzy, like a drunken man, from dealing with things that are ever changing?

Certainly.

But when she investigates any question by herself, she goes away to the pure, and eternal, and immortal, and unchangeable, to which she is akin, and so she comes to be ever with it, as soon as she is by herself, and can be so; and then she rests from her wanderings and dwells with it unchangingly, for she is dealing with what is unchanging. And is not this state of the soul called wisdom?

Indeed, Socrates, you speak well and truly, he replied.

Which kind of existence do you think from our former and our present arguments that the soul is more like and more akin to?

I think, Socrates, he replied, that after this inquiry the very dullest man would agree that the soul is infinitely more like the unchangeable than the changeable.

And the body?

That is like the changeable.

Consider the matter in yet another way. When the soul and the body are united, XXVIII nature ordains the one to be a slave and to be ruled, and the other to be master and to   80 rule. Tell me once again, which do you think is like the divine, and which is like the mortal? Do you not think that the divine naturally rules and has authority, and that the mortal naturally is ruled and is a slave?

I do.

Then which is the soul like?

That is quite plain, Socrates. The soul is like the divine, and the body is like the mortal.

Now tell me, Cebes, is the result of all that we have said that the soul is most like the divine, and the immortal, and the intelligible, and the uniform, and the indissoluble, and the unchangeable; while the body is most like the human, and the mortal, and the unintelligible, and the multiform, and the dissoluble, and the changeable? Have we any other argument to show that this is not so, my dear Cebes?

We have not.

Then if this is so, is it not the nature of the body to be dissolved quickly, and of the   XXIX soul to be wholly or very nearly indissoluble?[6]

Certainly.

You observe, he said, that after a man is dead, the visible part of him, his body, which lies in the visible world and which we call the corpse, which is subject to dissolution and decomposition, is not dissolved and decomposed at once? It remains as it was for a considerable time, and even for a long time, if a man dies with his body in good condition and in the vigor of his life. And when the body falls in and is embalmed, like the mummies of Egypt, it remains nearly entire for an immense time. And should it decay, yet some parts of it, such as the bones and muscles, may almost be said to be immortal. Is it not so?

Yes.

And shall we believe that the soul, which is invisible, and which goes hence to a place that is like herself, glorious, and pure, and invisible, to Hades, which is rightly called the unseen world, to dwell with the good and wise God, whither, if it be the will of God, my soul too must shortly go—shall we believe that the soul, whose nature is so glorious, and pure, and invisible, is blown away by the winds and perishes as soon as she leaves the body, as the world says? Nay, dear Cebes and Simmias, it is not so. I will tell you what happens to a soul which is pure at her departure, and which in her life has had no intercourse that she could avoid with the body, and so draws after her, when she dies, no taint of the body, but has shunned it, and gathered herself into herself, for such

---

[6] Compare Bishop Butler's *Analogy,* Pt. I, Ch. I, where a similar argument is used: the soul being indiscerptible is immortal. The argument based on the "divine" nature of the soul is, of course, also a modern one. See *e.g.* Lord Tennyson, *In Memoriam,* LIV-LVI.

has been her constant study—and that only means that she has loved wisdom rightly,   81
and has truly practiced how to die. Is not this the practice of death?

Yes, certainly.

Does not the soul, then, which is in that state, go away to the invisible that is like
herself, and to the divine, and the immortal, and the wise, where she is released from
error, and folly, and fear, and fierce passions, and all the other evils that fall to the lot of
men, and is happy, and for the rest of time lives in very truth with the gods, as they say
that the initiated do? Shall we affirm this, Cebes?

Yes, certainly, said Cebes.

But if she be defiled and impure when she leaves the body, from being ever with it,   XXX
and serving it and loving it, and from being besotted by it and by its desires and pleasures, so that she thinks nothing true but what is bodily and can be touched, and seen,
and eaten, and drunk, and used for men's lusts; if she has learned to hate, and tremble at,
and fly from what is dark and invisible to the eye, and intelligible and apprehended by
philosophy—do you think that a soul which is in that state will be pure and without
alloy at her departure?

No, indeed, he replied.

She is penetrated, I suppose, by the corporeal, which the unceasing intercourse and
company and care of the body has made a part of her nature.

Yes.

And, my dear friend, the corporeal must be burdensome, and heavy, and earthy,
and visible; and it is by this that such a soul is weighed down and dragged back to the
visible world, because she is afraid of the invisible world of Hades, and haunts, it is
said, the graves and tombs, where shadowy forms of souls have been seen, which are
the phantoms of souls which were impure at their release and still cling to the visible;
which is the reason why they are seen.[7]

That is likely enough, Socrates.

That is likely, certainly, Cebes; and these are not the souls of the good, but of the
evil, which are compelled to wander in such places as a punishment for the wicked lives
that they had lived; and their wanderings continue until, from the desire for the corporeal that clings to them, they are again imprisoned in a body.

And, he continued, they are imprisoned, probably, in the bodies of animals with   XXXI
habits similar to the habits which were theirs in their lifetime.

What do you mean by that, Socrates?

I mean that men who have practiced unbridled gluttony, and wantonness, and
drunkenness probably enter the bodies of asses and suchlike animals. Do you not   82
think so?

Certainly that is very likely.

And those who have chosen injustice, and tyranny, and robbery enter the bodies of
wolves, and hawks, and kites. Where else should we say that such souls go?

No doubt, said Cebes, they go into such animals.

In short, it is quite plain, he said, whither each soul goes; each enters an animal
with habits like its own.

Certainly, he replied, that is so.

---

[7] Professor Jowett compares Milton, *Comus*, 463 ff.

And of these, he said, the happiest, who go to the best place, are those who have practiced the popular and social virtues which are called temperance and justice, and which come from habit and practice, without philosophy or reason.

And why are they the happiest?

Because it is probable that they return into a mild and social nature like their own, such as that of bees, or wasps, or ants; or, it may be, into the bodies of men, and that from them are made worthy citizens.

Very likely.

But none but the philosopher or the lover of knowledge, who is wholly pure when he goes hence, is permitted to go to the race of the gods; and therefore, my friends, Simmias and Cebes, the true philosopher is temperate and refrains from all the pleasures of the body, and does not give himself up to them. It is not squandering his substance and poverty that he fears, as the multitude and the lovers of wealth do; nor again does he dread the dishonor and disgrace of wickedness, like the lovers of power and honor. It is not for these reasons that he is temperate. XXXII

No, it would be unseemly in him if he were, Socrates, said Cebes.

Indeed it would, he replied, and therefore all those who have any care for their souls, and who do not spend their lives in forming and molding their bodies, bid farewell to such persons, and do not walk in their ways, thinking that they know not whither they are going. They themselves turn and follow whithersoever philosophy leads them, for they believe that they ought not to resist philosophy, or its deliverance and purification.

Ovid

THE ART OF LOVE

Introduction by Michael Graham

Ovid (whose full name was Publius Ovidus Naso) was a Roman poet, born in 43 B.C. His family was prominent, and he was trained as a lawyer. Despite his legal talent, however, he fell in love with poetry and decided to devote all his energies to writing it, and he became one of the leading lights in the literary culture of Augustan Rome—that is, among those writers who were active during the reign of the emperor Augustus (27 B.C.–14 A.D.), a group which also included the poet Virgil and the historian Livy.

Ovid's subject matter was wide-ranging, from tragedy to imaginary love letters to a poem on artificial aids to beauty, but he often returned to what seems to have been his favorite topic— love, or perhaps to be more specific, seduction. We cannot gauge his real expertise in this field, but he was certainly willing to offer advice, and did so in what is generally regarded as his masterpiece, the *Ars Amatoria,* or *Art of Love,* which appeared about 1 B.C. This long poem has been widely-read through the ages, enjoying, for instance, some popularity in the high middle ages as part of the inspiration behind the literary movement which has been labeled "courtly love." The subject is one which continues to fascinate, although today's readers might be disturbed, or even shocked, by some of Ovid's basic assumptions about relations between the sexes.

In order to better understand Ovid as his original audience may have understood him, it is helpful to know a bit about social relations and literary culture in Augustan Rome. First of all, advice literature was a popular form during the period—with works available on fighting, farming and courting, just to name a few popular subjects. The "ars" in the poem's title, which is usually translated as "art," might be better rendered as "technique." Earlier love poets such as Catullus (84–54 B.C.) had offered readers flowery verses overflowing with passion, whereas Ovid adopted a much more businesslike approach; he would dispense cool advice rather than romantic rhapsodies.

Augustan Rome was a city of one million inhabitants, and it often seemed a rowdy, ungovernable place, full of young men with time on their hands. Well-born girls were usually married early in their teenage years, typically to men of similar social standing who were in their mid-twenties. Once married, wealthy women enjoyed a high degree of social freedom, and could control their own property. This left them much freer than the women of classical Athens, for instance. Fearful that Roman society was becoming too decadent, and that the family was breaking down, Augustus issued morality legislation designed to reinforce traditional family and marital ties and to promote childbearing, particularly among upper-class Romans. In 18 B.C., he issued a law against adultery. To prove that he was serious, Augustus in 2 B.C. had to force Julia, his daughter and only child, into exile on a barren island due to her well-known extramarital affairs. It may be significant that Ovid wrote this poem in the year after Julia's banishment. Was it intended to offer ironic commentary on the times? Interestingly, Ovid himself was exiled in 8 A.D., but we do not know why. He died on the Black Sea, having never returned to Rome, in 17 A.D.

The *Art of Love* raises other questions as well. First of all, who do you think Ovid was writing for? Who would be in a position to take his advice? What references did he make to other works which you have read? What picture of Augustan Rome does this poem give you? Who were the women Ovid was writing about, and what basic assumptions about them did he make? Does the poem raise issues of relations between classes as well as genders? Do you think Ovid's advice is still useful today? Why or why not?

The Art of Love

BOOK 1

Should anyone here in Rome lack finesse at love-making, let him
    Try me—read my book, and results are guaranteed!
Technique is the secret. Charioteer, sailor, oarsman,
    All need it. Technique can control
Love himself. As Automedon was charioteer to Achilles,   5
    And Tiphys Jason's steersman, so I,
By Venus' appointment, am made Love's artificer, shall be known as
    The Tiphys, the very Automedon of Love.
He's a wild handful, will often rebel against me,
    But still just a child—   10
Malleable, easily disciplined. Chiron made young Achilles
    A fine musician, hammered that fierce heart
On the anvil of peaceful artistry. So this future terror
    To friend and foe alike went in awe, it's said,
Of his elderly teacher, at whose bidding the hand that in after-   15
    Time bore down Hector was held out for the tawse.
As Chiron taught Achilles, so I am Love's preceptor:
    Wild boys both, both goddess-born—and yet
Even bulls can be broken to plough, or spirited horses
    Subdued with bridle and bit.   20
So Love shall likewise own my mastery, though his bowshots
    Skewer my breast, though his torch
Flicker and sear me. The worse the wounds, the deeper the branding,
    That much keener I to avenge
Such outrage. Nor shall I falsely ascribe my arts to Apollo: 25
    No airy bird comes twittering advice

Ovid, *The Erotic Poems* (Peter Green, trans.), Penguin, 1983 (ISBN 0-140-44360-6), original pp. 166–213. (Books one and two of "The Art of Love")

Into *my* ear, *I* never had a vision of the Muses
    Herding sheep in Ascra's valleys. This work is based
On experience: what I write, believe me, I have practised.
    My poem will deal in truth.   30

Aid my enterprise, Venus! Respectable ladies, the kind who
    Wear hairbands and ankle-length skirts,
Are hereby warned off. Safe love, legitimate liaisons
    Will be my theme. This poem breaks no taboos.
First, then, you fledgling troopers in passion's service,   35
    Comes the task of finding an object for your love.
Next, you must labour to woo and win your lady;
    Thirdly, ensure that the affair will last.
Such are my limitations, such the ground I will cover,
    The race I propose to run.   40

While you are fancy-free still, and can drive at leisure,
    Pick a girl, tell her, 'You're the one I love.
And only you.' But this search means using your eyes: a mistress
    Won't drop out of the sky at your feet.
A hunter's skilled where to spread his nets for the stag, senses   45
    In which glen the wild boar lurks.
A fowler's familiar with copses, an expert angler
    Knows the richest shoaling-grounds for fish.
You too, so keen to establish some long-term relationship,
    Must learn, first, where girl is to be found.   50
Your search need not take you—believe me—on an overseas voyage:
    A short enough trek will bring you to your goal.
True, Perseus fetched home Andromeda from the coloured Indies,
    While Phrygian Paris abducted Helen in Greece,
But Rome can boast of so many and such dazzling beauties   55
    You'd swear the whole world's talent was gathered here.
The girls of your city outnumber Gargara's wheatsheaves,
    Methymna's grape-clusters, all
Birds on the bough, stars in the sky, fish in the ocean:
    Venus indeed still haunts   60
Her son Aeneas' foundation. If you like budding adolescents
    Any number of (guaranteed) maidens are here to delight
Your roving eye. You prefer young women? They'll charm you
    By the thousand, you won't know which to choose.
And if you happen to fancy a more mature, experienced   65
    Age-group, believe me, *they* show up in droves.

Here's what to do. When the sun's on the back of Hercules'
    Lion, stroll down some shady colonnade,

Pompey's, say, or Octavia's (for her dead son Marcellus:
    Extravagant marble facings, R.I.P.),   70
Or Livia's, with its gallery of genuine Old Masters,
    Or the Danaids' Portico (note
The artwork: Danaus' daughters plotting mischief for their cousins,
    Father attitudinizing with drawn sword).
Don't miss the shrine of Adonis, mourned by Venus,   75
    Or the synagogue—Syrian Jews
Worship there each Sabbath—or the linen-clad heifer-goddess's
    Memphian temple: Io makes many a maid what *she*
Was to Jove. The very courts are hunting-grounds for passion;
    Amid lawyers' rebuttals love will often be found.   80
Here, where under Venus' marble temple the Appian
    Fountain pulses its jets high in the air,
Your jurisconsult's entrapped by Love's beguilements—
    Counsel to others, he cannot advise himself.
Here, all too often, words fail the most eloquent pleader,   85
    And a new sort of case comes on—his own. He must
Defend *himself* for a change, while Venus in her nearby
    Temple snickers at this reversal of roles.

But the theatre's curving tiers should form your favourite
    Hunting-ground: here you are sure to find
The richest returns, be your wish for lover or playmate,
    A one-night stand or a permanent affair.
As ants hurry to and fro in column, mandibles
    Clutching grains of wheat
(Their regular diet), as bees haunt fragrant pastures   95
    And meadows, hovering over the thyme,
Flitting from flower to flower, so our fashionable ladies
    Swarm to the games in such crowds, I often can't
Decide which I like. As spectators they come, come to be inspected:
    Chaste modesty doesn't stand a chance.   100
Such incidents at the games go back to Romulus—
    Men without women, Sabine rape.
No marble theatre then, no awnings, no perfumed saffron
    To spray the stage red:
The Palatine woods supplied a leafy backdrop (nature's   105
    Scenery, untouched by art),
While the tiers of seats were plain turf, and spectators shaded
    Their shaggy heads with leaves.
Urgently brooding in silence, the men kept glancing
    About them, each marking his choice   110
Among the girls. To the skirl of Etruscan flutes' rough triple
    Rhythm, the dancers stamped

And turned. Amid cheers (applause then lacked discrimination)
    The king gave the sign for which
They'd so eagerly watched. Project Rape was on. Up they sprang then   115
    With a lusty roar, laid hot hands on the girls.
As timorous doves flee eagles, as a lambkin
    Runs when it sees the hated wolf,
So this wild charge of men left the girls all panic-stricken,
    Not one had the same colour in her cheeks as before—   120
The same nightmare for all, though terror's features varied:
    Some tore their hair, some just froze
Where they sat; some, dismayed, kept silence, others vainly
    Yelled for Mamma; some wailed; some gaped;
Some fled, some just stood there. So they were carried off as   125
    Marriage-bed plunder; even so, many contrived
To make panic look fetching. Any girl who resisted her pursuer
    Too vigorously would find herself picked up
And borne off regardless. 'Why spoil those pretty eyes with weeping?'
    She'd hear, 'I'll be all to you   130
That your Dad ever was to your Mum.' (You alone found the proper
    Bounty for soldiers, Romulus: give me that,
And I'll join up myself!) Ever since that day, by hallowed custom,
    Our theatres have always held dangers for pretty girls.

Don't forget the races, either: the spacious Circus offers   135
    Chances galore. No need,
Here, of private finger-talk, or secret signals,
    Nods conveying messages: you'll sit
Right beside your mistress, without let or hindrance,
    So be sure to press against her wherever you can—   140
An easy task: the seating-divisions restrict her,
    Regulations facilitate contact. Now find
Some excuse to engage in friendly conversation,
    Casual small-talk at first—
Ask, with a show of interest, whose are those horses   145
    Just coming past: find out
Her favourite, back it yourself. When the long procession of ivory
    Deities approaches, be sure you give
A big hand to Lady Venus. If some dust should settle
    In your girl's lap, flick it away   150
With your fingers; and if there's no dust, still flick away—nothing:
    Let any excuse serve to prove your zeal.
If her cloak's trailing, gather it up, make a great business
    Of rescuing it from the dirt—
Instant reward for your gallantry, a licensed peep at   155
    Delectable ankles, and more.

Keep an eye on whoever may be sitting behind you,
    Don't let him rub his knee
Against her smooth back. Light minds are captivated by trifles:
    Plumping out a cushion can often help,   160
Or fanning the lady, or slipping a little footstool
    Under her dainty feet.

Such approaches will the Circus afford to a new courtship,
    Such, too, the crowded forum with its grim
Sanded arena, where Cupid's a regular contestant,   165
    Where the blood-and-guts fancier gets bloodied himself:
While he's chatting, and touching her hand, and checking the programme,
    And anxious (once he's placed his bet) to know
Which contestant will win, the winged steel has transfixed him,
    He groans at the wound, becomes part   170
Of the show he was watching. When Caesar lately staged that
    Naval mock-battle between Persians and Greeks,
Young men and girls converged from east coast and west, the whole wide
    World was packed into Rome—
With such a throng, who could fail to find what caught his fancy?   175
    Many a man was singed by some foreign flame!

Now Caesar is planning to fill in the final gaps of
    Empire: now the furthest East will be ours,
Revenge fall on Parthia, joy lighten the grave of Crassus,
    Redeem the standards profaned   180
By barbarian hands! The avenger's prepared, proclaims his
    Captaincy, though of green years: embraces a war
No boy—no other boy—could direct. Why cravenly reckon
    The age of a god? These Caesars come to courage young,
The surge of heavenly spirit outstrips mere calendars,   185
    Takes mean delays ill. A mere babe
Was Hercules when he strangled those two serpents: even
    In the cradle he proved worthy of Jove.
And you, Bacchus, still a youth, what age were *you* when conquered
    India bowed before your rod?   190
With the years—and luck—of your father, boy, you'll fight this
    Campaign: with his years—and luck—you'll win.
Such a debut befits so great a name: today prince of
    The youths, tomorrow of their seniors! Since
You have brothers, avenge these brothers' insults; since a   195
    Father is yours, uphold a father's rights.
Your father, your country's father, has armed you for battle;
    Your enemy has wrested *his* kingdom from
A reluctant sire. Your righteous javelins shall match his

Treacherous arrows. Justice and right shall march   200
     Before your banners. May these lost-cause Parthians likewise
          Lose every fight, may my prince bring the wealth of the East
Back home! Mars and Caesar—one god, one god-to-be—endow him
          With your paternal powers as he sets forth!
I prophesy victory for you, vow a song in your honour,   205
          Will extol you with loud praise:
You'll stand and exhort your troops in words I have written—
          May my words, I pray, not fall short
Of your valour! I'll speak of Parthian backs, of Roman courage,
          Of the shafts discharged by the foe   210
As he retreats on horseback. If a Parthian flees to conquer
          What's left him for defeat? That's a bad
Omen for warfare already. The day will come, most splendid
          Of beings, when you'll ride in gold behind
Four snow-white steeds, preceded by captive chieftains, fetters   215
          About their necks to prevent the flight that brought
Them safety before. Cheering youths will look on, and girls beside them,
          A day to make every heart run wild for joy;
And when some girl inquires the names of the monarchs,
          Or the towns, rivers, hills portrayed
On the floats, answer all her questions (and don't draw the line at
          Questions only): pretend
You know even when you don't. *Here comes Euphrates*, tell her,
          With reed-fringed brow; those dark
Blue tresses belong to Tigris, I fancy; there go Armenians,   225
          That's Persia, and that, h'r'm, is some
Upland Achaemenid city. Both those men there are generals—
          Give the names if you know them; if not, invent.

Banquets, too, give you an *entrée,* offer
          More to the palate than wine: 230
There flushed Love has often clasped the horns of reclining
          Bacchus in a seductive embrace,
And when wine has sodden Cupid's bibulous pinions
          He's grounded, too sluggish for the sport he's begun.
Still, it takes *him* no time to shake out his damp plumage—   235
          But if Love merely brushes the breast
You're wounded, it hurts. Wine rouses the heart, inclines to passion:
          Heavy drinking dilutes and banishes care
In a sea of laughter, gives the poor man self-confidence,
          Smooths out wrinkles, puts paid   240
To pain and sorrow. Then our age's rarest endowment,
          Simplicity, opens all hearts, as the god
Dissipates guile. Men's minds have often been enchanted
          By girls at such times: ah, Venus in the wine
Is fire within fire! Night and drink can impair your eye for beauty: 245

Don't trust the lamplight too much,
    It's deceptive. When Paris examined those goddesses, when he said, 'You
        Beat them both, Venus,' he did it in broad
Daylight. But darkness hides faults, each blemish is forgiven:
    Any woman you name will pass   250
As a beauty at night. Judge jewels or fine fabrics,
    A face or a figure, *by day*.

How list every female resort with prospects for the hunter?
    Sand-grains are fewer. Why tell of Baiae with
Its yacht-fringed beaches and hot sulphurous thermal   255
    Baths? I met one tourist who came back
Home from there with a nasty hole in his heart, said the waters
    Weren't half as healthy as report made out.
Then there's Diana's woodland shrine, not far from the city,
    With its murderous slave-priest—   260
Diana's a virgin, detests the shafts of Cupid: that's why
    People who go in the woods
Always get hurt, always will.
                        So far my elegiacs
    Have taught you which coverts to draw, where to spread
Your erotic nets. What follows is more subtly artistic—   265
    How to snare the girl of your choice.
All you gallants, mark and attend now; and you, the common
    People, encourage my task with a thumbs-up!

The first thing to get in your head is that every single
    Girl can be caught—and that you'll catch her if   270
You set your toils right. Birds will sooner fall dumb in springtime,
    Cicadas in summer, or a hunting-dog
Turn his back on a hare, than a lover's bland inducements
    Can fail with a woman. Even one you suppose
Reluctant will want it. Like men, girls love stolen passion,   275
    But are better at camouflaging their desires:
If masculine custom precluded courtship of women
    You'd find each besotted girl
Taking the lead herself. A heifer amid lush pastures
    Lows to the bull, a mare   280
Whinnies at stallions; but our male libido's milder,
    Less rabid: man's sex has bounds
Imposed by convention. Incest is out. Think of wretched Byblis—
    Burned up by her brother, expiating her crime
With a suicide's noose. Myrrha loved her father (but hardly   285
    As a daughter should), and now she's straitjacketed
Behind tree-bark, oozing those fragrant tears we use for
    Perfume, named after her: myrrh.
Once in the shady valleys of woodland Ida

There roamed a milk-white bull,   290
Pride of the herd, spotless save for one single
   Black mark between his horns:
The heifers of Crete all yearned to sustain that burden
   On their backs; but Pasiphaë
Proudly rejoiced in her role as bull's mistress, eyed his   295
   Cows with envious hate.
What I say is well-known: not even Crete of the hundred
   Cities, for all her mendacious ways,
Can deny it. With unpractised hands—they say—the lady
   Plucked leaves and lush grass   300
For this bull, went off with the herds, unrestrained by concern for
   Her husband. A bull won out
Over Minos himself. Why dress richly, Pasiphaë?
   Your lover's blind to your wealth.
Why bother with mirrors when the company you're seeking   305
   Is upland cattle? Why keep fixing your hair,
You silly girl? You're no heifer (on *that* you can trust your mirror)—
   But oh, how you wish you could sprout horns!
If you love Minos, steer clear of *all* adulterers; if you
   Choose to cuckold your man, then at least   310
Cuckold him with a man!
                   See the queen desert her bower
   For woods and glens, like some god—
Frenzied maenad: ah, the times she eyed a cow in fury,
   Crying, 'What can my lord ever see
In *that*? Just watch the silly creature frisking before him   315
   Down there at pasture—I suppose *she* thinks
She's a raving beauty.' With that, she would have the wretched
   Cow dragged from the herd to be yoked to the plough
Or poleaxed at the altar in a bogus sacrifice, just to
   Let her—a rare pleasure—get her hands   320
On her rival's entrails. The times she slaughtered such heifers
   To appease the gods, and cried, as she held out
Their guts, 'Go see how he likes you *now*!' Now she craves to be Io,
   Now Europa: bovine, or bull-borne.
Yet the herd-leader, taken in by a wooden cow, contrived to   325
   Fill her: their offspring betrayed
Its paternity. Had Aerope restrained her love for Thyestes
   (And to forego even one man
Is a serious matter), Phoebus would never have turned backwards
   In mid-flight, have driven his steeds   330
And chariot Dawnwards. From Nisus his daughter stole that purple
   Lock—and now fights down
The mad dogs that swarm from her groin. Agamemnon lived through battles
   On land, and great storms by sea,
To become his wife's victim. Who's not wept for flame-racked   335

Creüsa, for the children whose bloody death
Stained Medea's hands? Amyntor's son Phoenix wept tears
    From sightless orbs; fright-maddened horses tore
Hippolytus limb from limb. Ah Phineus, why blind your
    Innocent sons? On your own head the same   340
Horror will fall. Each one of these crimes was prompted
    By woman's lust—lust that far
Outstrips ours in keenness and frenzy. Why doubt that you can conquer
    Any girl in sight? Few indeed
Will turn you down—and (willing or not) a male proposition   345
    Is something they all enjoy. Draw a blank,
Rejection brings no danger. But why should you be rejected
    When new thrills delight, when what's not ours
Has more allure than what is? The harvest's always richer
    In another man's fields, the herd   350
Of our neighbour has fuller udders.

                    But first you must get acquainted
    With your quarry's maid—she can help
In the early stages. Make sure she enjoys the full confidence
    Of her mistress: make sure you can trust
Her with your secret liaison. Corrupt her with promises,   355
    Corrupt her with prayers. If
She's willing, you'll get what you want. She'll await the propitious
    Time (like a doctor) when her mistress is in
A receptive, seducible mood, when she's bursting out all over
    With cheerfulness, like a wheat-crop in rich soil.   360
When hearts are rejoicing, and have no sorrow to constrict them,
    They're wide open, Venus can steal
In by persuasive guile. Grim Troy long faced her besiegers,
    But a light-hearted change of mood
Fell for that troop-gravid horse.
                 Another time to try her   365
    Is when she's been miffed by a rival. Make it your job
To ensure she gets her revenge. Prime her maid to egg her on while
    Combing her hair each morning, put an oar in
To boost Ma'am's plain sailing, sigh to herself, and murmur:
    'What a pity it is you can't just pay him out   370
With a tit-for-tat,' then talk about *you* in persuasive
    Language, swear you're dying of mad
Passion. But lose no time, don't let the wind subside or
    The sails drop slack. Fury, like brittle ice,
Melts with delay. You may ask, does it pay to seduce the   375
    Maid herself? Such a gambit involves great risk.
Bed makes one girl jealous, takes the edge off another: will she
    Want you for her mistress—or for *her*?
It can go either way. Though the situation calls for

Bold risks, my advice is, *Don't.* I'm not the sort   380
　To climb precipitous paths, sharp peaks. With me for leader
　　No young man will be caught. But if,
While she carries your letters back and forth, it's not just
　Her zeal but her figure that tickles your fancy, then make
Mistress first, maid second. Never *begin* your wooing   385
　With the lady's companion. And here's one piece of advice
(If you trust in my skill at all, if the greedy winds don't
　Blow my words out to sea):
Lay off—*or make sure of her.* Once she's involved, and guilty,
　There's no longer any fear   390
That she'll turn informer against you. What's the use of liming
　A bird's wings if it escapes? A loose-netted boar
That breaks free is no good. Play your fish on the hook she's taken,
　Press home your assault, don't give up till victory's won.*

But keep such relationships secret: with a secret informer   397
　You'll always know every move your mistress makes.

It's wrong to suppose that only shipmen and toiling farmers
　Must observe due season. Grain   400
Cannot always be trusted to the treacherous furrow, nor curving
　Hulls to the green deep; likewise
It's not always safe to pursue young girls: the occasion
　Will often condition success. Thus, avoid
Her birthday; and April the First (the feast of Venus   405
　In conjunction with Mars); and when
The Circus is decorated, not, as before, with gew-gaws
　But with the wealth of kings: never make
Your attempt at such times—then storms are roughest, the Pleiads
　Sinking horizonwards, or the Kid washed down   410
Under the waves. Best to sit tight: those who venture
　On the high seas now, limp home
With a dismembered vessel. Begin on a day of mourning:
　The anniversary of Rome's bloody defeat
At the Allia—or perhaps on the Jewish sabbath: many   415
　Shops will be shut then. Regard
Your mistress's birthday with superstitious horror,
　Set a black mark against
Any day when you have to buy presents. Yet avoid it as you may, she'll
　Collect all the same. Every woman knows just how   420
To fleece her panting lover. When she's got a spending mood on,

---

* Lines 395–6 do not appear in two of the better MSS, and are omitted as spurious by some editors. I am in two minds about this verdict, so translate them here:

Then guilty complicity will keep her from betraying you,
　And you will learn of all your mistress says or does.

Some loose-garbed pedlar will come and spread out his wares
With you sitting by. She'll ask you to look at the stuff, show off your
    Expert knowledge. Kisses will follow. Then
She'll insist that you buy it, swear it'll satisfy her   425
    For years, say she needs it now, now's a good
Time to buy it. Tell her you haven't the cash in the house, she'll
    Ask for a note-of-hand—just to make
You sorry you learnt how to write. There's the birthday-cake gambit,
    A broad hint for presents: she's born x times a year   430
As the occasion demands. Or she'll come up weeping, pretend she's
    Lost one of her ear-bobs. Such girls
Are always borrowing things that, once they've had loaned them,
    They never return. Your loss in this sort of case
Isn't even offset by gratitude. To list the tricks such gold-digging   435
    Tarts employ, I'd require ten mouths, ten tongues.

Let wax pave the way for you, spread out on smooth tablets,
    Let wax go before as witness to your mind—
Bring her your flattering words, words that ape the lover:
    And remember, whoever you are, to throw in some good   440
Entreaties. Entreaties are what made Achilles give back Hector's
    Body to Priam; even an angry god
Is moved by the voice of prayer. Make promises, what's the harm in
    Promising? Here's where anyone can play rich.
Hope, once entertained, is enduring: a deceptive   445
    Goddess—but useful. Your gift
Once made, you can be abandoned, and with good reason:
    She'll have fleeced you, past tense, at no
Loss to herself. But a present withheld breeds expectations:
    That's how farmers, so often, are fooled by a barren field,   450
That's why the inveterate gambler doubles his losses
    To stave off loss, why the dice-box beckons his hand
Back again and again. *This the task, this the labour,* to win her
    Gift-free: she'll continue to give
Lest she lose what she's given already. A persuasive letter's   455
    The thing to lead off with, explore her mind,
Reconnoitre the landscape. A message scratched on an apple
    Betrayed Cydippe: she was snared by her own words.
My advice, then, young men of Rome, is to learn the noble
    Advocate's arts—not only to let you defend   460
Some trembling client: a woman, no less than the populace,
    Elite senator, or grave judge,
Will surrender to eloquence. Nevertheless, dissemble
    Your powers, avoid long words,
Don't look too highbrow. Who but a mindless ninny   465
    Declaims to his mistress? An over-lettered style
Repels girls as often as not. Use ordinary language,

Familiar yet coaxing words—as though
You were there, in her presence. If she refuses your letter,
   Sends it back unread, persist: 470
Say you hope she'll read it later. Time breaks stubborn oxen
   To the plough, time teaches a horse
To accept the bridle. An iron ring's worn by constant
   Friction, the furrowed soil
Rubs away the curved ploughshare. What is softer than water,   475
   What harder than stone? Yet the soft
Water-drip hollows hard rock. In time, with persistence,
   You'll conquer Penelope. Troy fell late,
But fall it did. Suppose she reads your notes, but won't answer?
   Don't press her, just keep up   480
Your flattering *billets-doux*. The girl who reads letters
   Will reply to them in the end: affairs like these
Go by degrees and stages. First you may get an angry
   Note saying 'Don't pester me, please.'
She's really afraid you'll stop: what she wants (but says she doesn't)   485
   Is for you to go on. Press hard, you'll win through in the end.

What else? If she's out, reclining in her litter,
   Make your approach discreet,
And—just to fox the sharp ears of those around you—
   Cleverly riddle each phrase   490
With ambiguous subtleties. If she's taking a leisurely
   Stroll down the colonnade, then you stroll there too—
Vary your pace to hers, march ahead, drop behind her,
   Dawdling and brisk by turns. Be bold,
Dodge in round the columns between you, brush your person   495
   Lingeringly past hers. You must never fail
To attend the theatre when she does, gaze at her beauty—
   From the shoulders up she's time
Most delectably spent, a feast for adoring glances,
   For the eloquence of eyebrows, the speaking sign.   500
Applaud when some male dancer struts on as the heroine,
   Cheer for each lover's role.
When she leaves, leave too—but sit there as long as she does:
   Waste time at your mistress's whim.

Don't torture your hair, though, with curling-irons: don't pumice   505
   Your legs into smoothness. Leave *that*
To Mother Cybele's votaries, ululating in chorus
   With their Phrygian modes. Real men
Shouldn't primp their good looks. When Theseus abducted Ariadne
   No pins held up *his* locks;   510
Hippolytus was no dandy, yet Phaedra loved him; Adonis,
   That creature of woodland, allured

A goddess. Keep pleasantly clean, take exercise, work up an outdoor
    Tan; make quite sure that your toga fits
And doesn't show spots; don't lace your shoes too tightly   515
    Or ignore any rusty buckles, or slop
Around in too large a fitting. Don't let some incompetent barber
    Ruin your looks: both hair and beard demand
Expert attention. Keep your nails pared, and dirt-free;
    Don't let those long hairs sprout   520
In your nostrils, make sure your breath is never offensive,
    Avoid the rank male stench
That wrinkles noses. Beyond this is for wanton women—
    Or any half-man who wants to attract men.

Lo! Bacchus calls to his poet: Bacchus too helps lovers,   525
    Fosters that flame with which he burns himself—
As Ariadne discovered, ranging the unfamiliar
    Sea-strand of Naxos, crazed
Out of her mind, fresh-roused from sleep, in an ungirt
    Robe, blonde hair streaming loose, barefoot,   530
Calling 'Ah cruel Theseus!' to the deaf waves, tears coursing
    Down her innocent-tender cheeks.
She wept, she besought, yet contrived to remain appealing
    Despite all: not even those tears
Could imperil such beauty. Hands beating her soft bosom,   535
    'He's gone,' she cried, 'he's betrayed me: what, ah what
Will become of me now?' Then, presto, the whole shore echoed
    With frenzied drumming, the clash
Of cymbals. She broke off, speechless, fainted
    In terror, the blood fled   540
From her pale inert limbs, as wild-tressed Bacchanals, wanton
    Satyrs, the god's forerunners, appeared,
With drunken old Silenus, scarce fit to ride his swaybacked
    Ass, hands clutching its mane
As he chased the Maenads—the Maenads would flee and rally—   545
    A dizzy rider, whipping his steed ahead
Till he pitched off the long-eared ass on his head, and the satyrs
    All shouted: 'Up with you, Dad!
Come on up there!' And then came the god, his chariot grape-clustered,
    Paired tigers padding on as he shook   550
The golden reins. Poor girl: lost voice, lost colour—lost Theseus.
    Thrice she tried to run, thrice stood frozen with fear,
Shivering, like the thin breeze-rustled cornstalk,
    Or osiers in a marsh. 'I am here
For you,' the god told her. '*My* love will prove more faithful.   555
    No need for fear. You shall be
Wife to Bacchus, take the sky as your dowry, be seen there
    As a star, the Cretan Crown, a familiar guide

To wandering vessels.' Down he sprang from his chariot, lest the
    Girl take fright at the tigers; set his foot   560
On the shore, then gathered her up in his arms—no resistance—
    And bore her away. No trouble for gods to do
Whatever they please. Loud cheers, a riotous wedding: Bacchus
    And his bride were soon bedded down.
So when the blessings of Bacchus are set out before you   565
    At dinner, with a lady to share your couch,
Then pray the Lord of Darkness and Nocturnal Orgies
    To stop the wine going to your head!
Here double-talk is the vogue: lace your conversation
    With ambiguous phrases designed to make the girl   570
Feel they're specially meant for her. Write flatteries on the table
    In wine, let her read herself your heart's
Mistress: gaze deep in her eyes with open passion—
    One silent glance can speak
Whole volumes. Make sure you're the first to snatch the cup that   575
    Her lips have touched: drink from where she has drunk;
And if there's some piece of food she's fingered, take it,
    Brushing her hand as you reach out.
Let it be your concern, too, to please your lady's escort—
    He'll be more use to you as a friend.   580
When you're dicing to settle the drinking-order, let him take your
    Place, give him the garland off your head,
Never mind if he's placed below you or with you, still let him
    Be served first every time, defer to his words.*
I'll give you specific advice, now, on just what limits
    You should set to your drinking. Keep mind and feet   590
Steady. Above all, avoid drunken quarrels, don't get
    Into a fight too fast.
His stupid swilling killed off Eurytion the Centaur;
    Wine over dinner was rather meant to promote
Fun and games. So if you've a voice, then sing; or if your movements 595
    Are graceful, dance. Please with whatever gifts
You possess to give pleasure. And though real drunkenness can harm you,
    To feign it may prove useful. Let your devious tongue
Stutter and slur: then, however licentious your words or
    Actions, they'll be blamed on the wine. 'A health   600
To the lady,' you'll cry, 'a health to the man she sleeps with!'
    —While silently wishing her present partner in hell.
But when the tables are cleared, and the guests departing,
    And in the confusion you perceive your chance

---

* Lines 585–8 are a spurious (and moralizing) insertion by some post-Ovidian hand:

    It's a safe, well-trodden path to deceive in friendship's name: safe
    And well-trodden perhaps, but still
The path of guilt. That way a collector collects more
    Than is due him, looks to care for more than his charge.

To make contact, then join the crowd, discreetly approach her   605
    On the way out, let your fingers brush against
Her side, touch her foot with yours. Now's the time for chatting
    Her up, no clodhopping bashfulness—the bold
Are favoured by Chance and Venus. Don't think that your eloquence
    Must conform to poetic canons. Just pitch in   610
And you'll find yourself fluent enough. You must play the lover,
    Ape heartache with words, use every subtle device
To compel her belief. It's not hard—what woman doesn't believe she's
    A natural object for love, or, however plain,
Isn't thrilled by her own appearance? Besides, very often   615
    That passion a gallant feigns in his opening round
Will become the real thing. (So, girls, show more kindness to pretenders:
    True love may spring tomorrow from today's
False declaration.) Press on, undermine them with devious
    Flatteries: so a stream will eat away   620
Its overhanging bank. Never weary of praising
    Her face, her hair, her slim fingers, her tiny feet.
Even the chaste like having their good looks published,
    Even virgins are taken up with their own
Cute figures. Why does it still bother Juno and Pallas   625
    That they didn't win first prize in the Phrygian woods?
When it's praised, then Juno's peacock displays its plumage;
    If you stare without comment—no show.
Even racehorses, back in the paddock, respond with pleasure
    To a combed mane, a pat on the neck.   630

Don't be shy about promising: it's promises girls are undone by;
    Invoke any gods you please
To endorse your performance. Jupiter smiles from heaven
    On foresworn lovers, lets all their perjuries blow
Away unrequited. (*He* used to swear falsely, by Styx, to Juno—   635
    So looks now with favour on others who do the same.)
The existence of gods is expedient: let us therefore assume it,
    With gifts of incense and wine on their antique hearths—
No carefree repose, like a drowsy siesta, keeps them
    Remote after all. So, lead an innocent life: 640
Divinity's nigh. Honour bonds, don't embezzle deposits,
    Avoid murder and fraud. If you're wise
Gull only girls, they're no danger. In this one deception
    It's good faith that ought to make you blush.
They're cheats, so cheat *them:* most are dumb and unscrupulous: let them   645
    Fall into the traps they've set themselves.
Egypt had drought for nine years once, no rain to quicken
    Her harvest-fields. Then Thrasius the sage
Told King Busiris the gods could be propitiated
    With a stranger's spilt blood.   650

Busiris replied: '*You* shall be the gods' first victim, you the
    Stranger who brings water to Egypt's soil.'
So Perillus, the inventor of Phalaris' brazen bull, was
    The first, unlucky man, to roast in his own
Cruel contrivance. Both kings did right. No fairer statute   655
    Than that which condemns the artificer of death
To perish by his art. So let perjuries gull the perjured,
    Let Woman smart from the wounds she first dealt out!

Tears, too, will help: with tears you'll shift adamant. Flaunt wet
    Cheeks—if you can—for *her* to see: 660
But if tears won't come (and they sometimes fail in a crisis)
    Just wipe a moist hand across your eyes!
What sensible man will not intersperse his coaxing
    With kisses? Even if she doesn't kiss back,
Still force on regardless! She may struggle, cry 'Naughty!',   665
    Yet she wants to be overcome. Just take care
Not to bruise her tender lips with such hard-snatched kisses,
    Don't give her a chance to protest
You're too rough. Those who grab their kisses, but not what follows,
    Deserve to lose all they've gained. How short were you   670
Of the ultimate goal after all your kissing? That was
    Gaucheness, not modesty, I'm afraid . . .

It's all right to use force—force of *that* sort goes down well with
    The girls: what in fact they love to yield
They'd often rather have stolen. Rough seduction   675
    Delights them, the audacity of near-rape
Is a compliment—so the girl who *could* have been forced, yet somehow
    Got away unscathed, may feign delight, but in fact
Feels sadly let down. Hilaira and Phoebe, both ravished,
    Both fell for their ravishers. Then there's another tale,   680
Well-known, but well worth retelling, which recounts how Achilles
    Made a girl on Scyros his:
It was after the goddess had won that beauty-competition
    Against her peers on Ida, and had given her own
Reward to Paris; after Priam had welcomed his foreign   685
    Daughter-in-law, and a Greek wife came to dwell
Within Troy's walls. All swore allegiance to the injured
    Husband. So one man's hurt became
A national cause. But Achilles—to his shame, were the act not prompted
    By a mother's prayers—concealed his manhood beneath   690
A girl's long robe. What's this? Wool-spinning's not your business.
    Achilles: it's quite another of Pallas' arts
Through which you'll find fame. What have you to do with baskets?
    Your arm should support a shield. Why does the hand
That will one day slay Hector carry a skein? Cast aside your spindle   695

With its laborious threading: the Pelian spear
Is what *you* should wield.
                                    The king's daughter, Deidamia,
    Who shared his room soon proved
That manhood through rape. Her seduction must have been forceful,
    But to *be* forced was what she desired.   700
'Don't go,' she cried, when Achilles was hastening from her,
    Distaff forgotten, a warrior under arms.
Where's that violence now? Why coax the perpetrator
    Of your rape to remain, Deidamia? If you take
The initiative, it's true, you may feel some embarrassment: better   705
    Tò let *him*—and more fun when you submit.
Any lover who waits for his girl to make the running
    Has too much faith in his own
Irresistible charms. The first approaches, the pleading,
    Are the man's concern: *her* place   710
Is to hear his smooth line with kindness. To win her, ask her:
    She's dying to be asked. Just provide a good excuse
For her to fulfil your wishes. Jupiter wooed those antique
    Heroines as a suppliant. No girl seduced
The Almighty. But if you find that your pleading induces   715
    Puffed-up disdain, then ease off,
Take a step back. Many women adore the elusive,
    Hate over-eagerness. So, play hard to get,
Stop boredom developing. And don't let your entreaties
    Sound too confident of possession. Insinuate sex   720
Camouflaged as friendship. I've seen ultra-stubborn creatures
    Fooled by this gambit, the switch from companion to stud.

For sailors a pale complexion is inappropriate,
    They should be tanned and dark,
Fetchingly weatherbeaten; so should husbandmen   725
    Who spend their time out of doors
With plough and harrow; so should the champion athlete—
    If *they're* white, it looks all wrong.
But let every lover be pale: here's the proper complexion
    For lovers; this gambit, please note,   730
Has worked on every occasion. Pale was Orion, roaming
    The woodlands, pining for Side; pale
Daphnis (ah, unkind Naiad!). Look lean and haggard
    As proof of your passion, don't baulk
At hooding your lustrous curls. Sleepless nights, the pangs and worry 735
    Of consuming love—these will reduce young men
To a thin nothing. If you mean to achieve your purpose
    Be an object of pity, so that the passers-by
Will say at once, 'He's in love'.

Now should I complain, or warn you,
   That no one now distinguishes right from wrong?   740
Friendship and honour are empty words, it's not safe to praise your
   Girl to a friend—if he believes what you say
He'll be in there himself. You may ask, 'Did Patroclus cuckold
   Achilles? Wasn't Phaedra perfectly chaste
With Pirithoüs? Didn't Pylades love Hermione as Apollo   745
   Loved Pallas, or Castor his twin?'
If anyone nurses *that* hope, he'll believe that apples grow on
   Tamarisks, that honey's to be found in midstream.
The base alone gives pleasure; men seek only their own enjoyment,
   And find that sweet when it springs from another's pain.   750
How outrageous, when it's not their enemies that lovers
   Most need to fear! Nowadays you'll be safe enough
If you shun those you trust. Cousins, brothers, loyal comrades—
   Here's where your real trouble lies.
One word more before I stop. The characters of women   755
   All differ. To capture a thousand hearts demands
A thousand devices. Some soils are better for olives,
   Some for vines, or for wheat: you can't
Raise them all in one field. Hearts have as many changing
   Moods as the face has expressions. A wise man   760
Will adapt to countless fashions, will resolve himself, like Proteus,
   Into water, now lion, now tree,
Now bristling boar. Some fish are trawled, some netted,
   Some caught with line and hook:
And don't try the same technique on every age-group,   765
   An old doe will spot the trap
From much further off. If a simpleton finds you too highbrow
   Or a prude over-coarse, they'll feel
Self-distrust and dismay. That's how the girl who shies off decent
   Lovers will cheapen herself by giving in   770
To some low cad.
      This concludes the first part of my venture—
   Now throw out the anchor, let my craft ride secure!

BOOK 2

Cry hurrah, and hurrah again, for a splendid triumph—
   The quarry I sought has fallen into my toils.
Each happy lover now rates my verses higher
   Than Homer's or Hesiod's, awards them the palm
Of victory. He's as cheerful as Paris was, sailing away from   5
   Warlike Sparta, the guest who stole a bride,
Or Pelops, the stranger, the winner of Hippodameia
   After that chariot-race.

Why hurry, young man? Your ship's still in mid-passage,
    And the harbour I seek is far away.   10
Through my verses, it's true, you may have *acquired* a mistress,
    But that's not enough. If my art
Caught her, my art must keep her. To guard a conquest's
    As tricky as making it. There was luck in the chase,
But *this* task will call for skill. If ever I needed support from   15
    Venus and Son, and Erato—the Muse
Erotic by name—it's now, for my too-ambitious project
    To relate some techniques that might restrain
That fickle young globetrotter, Love. He's winged and flighty,
    Hard to pin down. Just so   20
Minos might block every line of escape, yet his guest still found a
    Daring way out—by air.
When Daedalus had built his labyrinth to imprison
    The bull-man, man-bull, conceived through a queen's guilt,
He said: 'Most just Minos, put a term, now, to my exile,   25
    Let my native soil receive
My ashes. Since unkind fate would not let me live there,
    Grant me at least to die
In my own country. Release the boy, if you hold his father's
    Services cheap; spare me if you will not spare   30
My son.' So much he said—but might have gone on pleading
    For ever in vain: the king
Would not grant his request. When Daedalus perceived this,
    Now, now is the time, he told himself, *to deploy*
All your skill and craft. Minos rules earth, rules ocean: 35
    No escape by sea or land. All that remains
Is the sky. So, through the sky we'll seek our passage—
    God in high heaven, forgive
Such a project! I do not aspire to touch your starry dwellings:
    This is the only way I have to escape   40
My master. Were there a way by Styx, through Stygian waters
    We'd swim to freedom. I must devise new laws
For human nature. Necessity often mothers invention.
    Who would have believed man could ever fly?
But Daedalus fashioned birds' oarage, trimmed it with feathers   45
    Bonded the flimsy fabric with linen thread,
Melted wax to glue wings in place. Very soon his novel
    Craftsman's task was achieved:
Excitedly the boy studied wings and wax, not guessing   50
    The gear had been made for his own
Shoulders and arms, till his father said: 'These are the craft which
    Must bear us home, with their aid
We must escape from Minos. Though he's blocked all other
    Routes to us, he cannot master the air—as you   55
Can do, through my device. But take care, don't go stargazing

At belted Orion or the Bear:
Take these pinions, fly behind me: I'll go ahead, you
    Follow my lead. That way
You'll be safe. If we fly too close to the sun, through the upper   60
    Air, then the wax will be softened by the heat;
If we stoop too low seaward, then our thrashing pinions
    Will grow waterlogged from the spray.
So, my son, set a middle course—and watch out for turbulent
    Air-currents: spread your wings
To the steady breeze, go with it.' While he talked, he was fitting   65
    The boy's gear, showing him how to move
Like a mother bird with her fledglings. Then he fixed his own harness
    To his shoulders, nervously poised himself for this strange
New journey; paused on the brink of take-off, embraced his
    Son, couldn't fight back his tears.   70
They'd found a hilltop—above the plain, but no mountain—
    And from this they took off
On their hapless flight. Daedalus flexed his wings, glanced back at
    His son's, held a steady course. The new
Element bred delight. Fear forgotten, Icarus flew more   75
    Boldly, with daring skill. The pair
Were glimpsed by an angler, line bobbing, who at the sight of them
    Dropped his rod in surprise. They left
Naxos and Paros behind them, skirted Delos, beloved of
    Apollo, flew on east: to the north   80
Lay Samos, southward Lebynthos, Calýmne with its shady
    Forests, and Astypálaea, set amid fish-rich shoals.
Then the boy, made over-reckless by youthful daring, abandoned
    His father, soared aloft
Too close to the sun: the wax melted, the ligatures   85
    Flew apart, his flailing arms had no hold
On the thin air. From dizzy heaven he gazed down seaward
    In terror. Fright made the scene go black
Before his eyes. No wax, wings gone, a thrash of naked
    Arms, a shuddering plunge   90
Down through the void, a scream—'Father, father, I'm falling—'
    Cut off as he hit the waves.
His unhappy father, a father no longer, cried: 'Icarus!
    Icarus, where are you? In what part of the sky
Do you fly now?'—then saw wings littering the water.   95
    Earth holds his bones; the Icarian Sea, his name.
So Minos failed to clip the wings of a mortal—yet here am
    I now, planning to pin down the winged god.
Delusions abound. Don't mess with Thessalian witchcraft—
    That love-charm torn from the brow   100
Of a foal is no good. Not all Medea's herbs, not every
    Spell and magical cantrip will suffice

To keep love alive—else Circe had held Ulysses,
  And Medea her Jason, by their arts alone.
Giving girls aphrodisiac drugs, too, is useless—and dangerous: 105
  Drugs can affect the brain, induce madness. Avoid
All such nasty tricks. To be loved you must show yourself lovable—
  Something good looks alone
Can never achieve. You may be handsome as Homer's Nireus,
  Or young Hylas, snatched by those bad   110
Naiads; but all the same, to avoid a surprise desertion
  And to keep your girl, it's best you have gifts of mind
In addition to physical charms. Beauty's fragile, the passing
  Years diminish its substance, eat it away.
Violets and bell-mouthed lilies do not bloom for ever,   115
  Hard thorns are all that's left of the blown rose.
So with you, my handsome youth: soon wrinkles will furrow
  Your body; soon, too soon, your hair turn grey.
Then build an enduring mind, add that to your beauty:
  It alone will last till the flames   120
Consume you. Keep your wits sharp, explore the liberal
  Arts, win a mastery over Greek
As well as Latin. Ulysses was eloquent, not handsome—
  Yet he filled sea-goddesses' hearts
With aching passion. How often Calypso lamented   125
  His haste to be off, swore the sea
Was too rough for rowing! Again and again she'd beg him
  To recount Troy's fate, made him find fresh words
For the same old tale. They'd pace the shore; pretty Calypso
  Would say: 'Now tell me how King Rhesus met   130
His bloody end.' Then Ulysses would take the stick he was holding
  And sketch in the wet sand whatever scene
She'd demanded. 'Here's Troy,' he'd say, making walls of shingle.
  'And here's the river. Let's call this bit my camp.
This was the plain—' he levelled it—'where we butchered Dolon,   135
  The spy-by-night, as he dreamed
Of Achilles' horses. There stood the tents of Rhesus;
  I rode back home that night
On the King's captured steeds—'As he spoke, a sudden breaker
  Washed away Rhesus, his camp, and Troy itself.   140
Then the goddess exclaimed: 'You'd trust *these* waves for your voyage?
  Look at the great names they've destroyed!'
So don't rely too much on looks, they can prove deceptive
  Whoever you are: have something more than physique!

Nothing works on a mood like tactful tolerance: harshness   145
  Provokes hatred, makes nasty rows.
We detest the hawk and the wolf, those natural hunters,
  Always preying on timid flocks;

But the gentle swallow goes safe from man's snares, we fashion
    Little turreted houses for doves.   150
Keep clear of all quarrels, sharp-tongued recriminations—
    Love's sensitive, needs to be fed
With gentle words. Leave nagging to wives and husbands,
    Let *them,* if they want, think it a natural law,
A permanent state of feud. Wives thrive on wrangling,   155
    That's their dowry. A mistress should always hear
What she wants to be told. You don't share one bed by legal
    Fiat, with you love substitutes for law.
Use tender blandishments, language that caresses
    The ear, make her glad you came.   160
I'm not here as preceptor of loving to the wealthy; a suitor
    With gifts doesn't need my skills—
Anyone attractive who says 'Here's something for you,'
    Has genius of his own. To such a one
I give place: he's got my tricks beat. I'm the poor man's poet,   165
    Was poor myself as a lover, couldn't afford
Gifts, so spun words. Poor suitors must woo with caution,
    Watch their tongues, bear much that the rich
Would never put up with. I recall how once in anger
    I pulled my girl's hair. The days I lost through that   170
Little outburst! I don't think I tore her dress, I wasn't conscious
    Of doing so—but *she* said I did, and the bill
Was paid for at my expense. Avoid (if you're wise) your teacher's
    Errors, shun what may cost you dear.
Fight Parthians, but keep peace with a civilized mistress,   175
    Have fun together, do all that induces love.

If the girl's curt and unreceptive to your wooing,
    Persist, be obdurate: the time will come
When she's more welcoming. Go with the bough, you'll bend it;
    Use brute force, it'll snap.   180
Go with the current: that's how to swim across rivers—
    Fighting upstream's no good.
Go easy with lions or tigers if you aim to tame them;
    The bull gets inured to the plough by slow degrees.
Was there ever a girl more prickly than Atalanta?   185
    Yet tough as she was, she went down
Before a man's prowess, Milanion, roaming the forest,
    Kept bewailing his lot, and the girl's
Unkindness. She made him hump hunting-nets on his back, he
    Was for ever spearing wild boars;   190
His wounded flesh learnt the strength of Hylaeus the Centaur's
    Taut bow—yet his keener pangs
Came from another bow, Cupid's. I'm not suggesting
    You have to go lugging nets up mountain glens

Or play the hunter, or bare your breast to flying arrows—   195
    A cautious lover will find the rules of my art
Undemanding enough. So, yield if she shows resistance:
    That way you'll win in the end. Just be sure to play
The part she allots you. Censure the things she censures,
    Endorse her endorsements, echo her every word,   200
Pro or con, and laugh whenever she laughs; remember,
    If she weeps, to weep too: take your cue
From her every expression. Suppose she's playing a board-game,
    Then throw the dice carelessly, move
Your pieces all wrong. At knucklebones, when you beat her,   205
    Exact no forfeit, roll low throws yourself
As often as you can manage. If you're playing halma, permit her
    Glass piece to take yours. Open up
Her parasol, hold it over her when she's out walking,
    Clear her a path through the crowd.   210
When she's on her chaise-lounge, make haste to find a footstool
    For those dainty feet of hers, help her on and off
With her slippers. At times she'll feel cold: then (though you're shivering
    Yourself) warm her tiny hand
In your bosom. Don't jib at a slavish task like holding   215
    Her mirror: slavish or not, such attentions please.
When his stepmother Hera tired of sending him monsters
    To vanquish, then the hero who won a place
In the sky he'd formerly shouldered took to the distaff
    And basket, spun wool among Ionian girls.   220
If Hercules, then, obeyed *his* mistress's orders, will you
    Flinch from enduring what he endured?
She says you've a date in town? Be sure you always get there
    Ahead of time: don't give her up
Till it's *really* late. If she asks you to meet her somewhere,   225
    Put everything off, elbow your way through the crowd
At the double. When she comes home, late at night, from a party,
    You still must attend, like her slave,
If she summons you. It's the same when she's in the country:
    Love detests laggards. You've no transport? Walk.   230
Don't be put off by bad weather, or a heatwave,
    Or snowdrifts blocking your road.

Love is a species of warfare. Slack troopers, go elsewhere!
    It takes more than cowards to guard
These standards. Night-duty in winter, long route-marches, every   235
    Hardship, all forms of suffering: these await
The recruit who expects a soft option. You'll often be out in
    Cloudbursts, and bivouack on the bare
Ground. We know how Apollo pastured Admetus' cattle,
    Dossed down in a herdsman's hut. What mere   240

Mortal's too good for conditions a god accepted? Is lasting
    Love your ambition? Then put away all pride.
The simple, straightforward way in may be denied you,
    Doors bolted, shut in your face—
So be ready to slip down from the roof through a lightwell,   245
    Or sneak in by an upper-floor window. She'll be glad
To know you're risking your neck, and for her sake: that will offer
    Any mistress sure proof of your love.
Leander might, often enough, have endured Hero's absence—
    But swam over to show her how he felt.   250
Don't think it beneath you to cultivate madam's houseboys
    And her more important maids:
Greet each one by name (the gesture costs you nothing),
    Clasp their coarse hands in yours—all part of the game.

On Good Luck Day, if you're asked for a present, even   255
    By a slave, then give: the expense
Will be minimal. See that the maids, too, get a handout
    On *their* day (the day those Gauls
Were figged by some dressed-up slaveys). It pays, believe me,
    To keep in with the servants—especially those who watch   260
Her front-door or bedroom entrance.
                                 Don't give your mistress costly
    Presents: let them be small, but chosen with skill
And discretion. At harvest-time, when fields are full, boughs heavy,
    Send round a basket of fruit—
Say it came from your country estate (though you really bought it   265
    At some smart city shop). Give her grapes,
Or the chestnuts to which Amaryllis was so devoted—
    No, not chestnuts, she's off them these days:
Much too cheap. Why not try a poulterer's hoop of thrushes
    By way of remembrance? (It's shameful to use such gifts   270
In the hope of a death, to bribe the elderly or barren:
    I've not time for those who give presents a bad name.)
Would you be well advised to send her love-poems?
    Poetry, I fear, is held in small esteem.
Girls praise a poem, but go for expensive presents: 275
    Any illiterate oaf can catch their eye
Provided he's rich. Today is truly the Golden
    Age: gold buys honours, gold
Procures love. If Homer dropped by—with all the Muses,
    But empty-handed—he'd be shown the door.   280
There *are* a few cultured girls (not many, it's true), and others
    Who'd like to be cultured, but aren't;
Flatter any of these with poems: a bravura declamation
    Even of trash—this will suffice to win

Their approval. Clever or stupid, they'll take a poem fashioned   285
    In the small hours, for *them,* as a cute little gift.

Make your mistress ask as a favour for what you intended,
    All along, to do yourself
In the way of self-interest. You've promised manumission
    To one slave? See that he begs it, first, from her.   290
You plan to spare another in his flogging, or the chain-gang?
    Then put her in your debt for a 'change of heart'
That never existed. The benefit's yours, give her the credit,
    Waste not want not, while she
Plays the Lady Bountiful. You're anxious to keep your mistress?   295
    Convince her she's knocked you all of a heap
With her stunning looks. If it's purple she's wearing, praise purple;
    When she's in a silk dress, say silk
Suits her best of all; if her mantle's gold-embroidered
    Say she's dearer than gold to you; if tweeds   300
Take her fancy, back tweeds. She's in her slip? She inflames you
    (Tell her) with passion—but ask, at the same time,
Very shyly, 'Aren't you cold?' Compliment the way she's parted
    Or curled her hair. Admire
Her singing voice, her gestures as she dances,   305
    Cry 'Encore!' when she stops. You can even praise
Her performance in bed, her talent for love-making—
    Spell out what turned you on.
Though she may show fiercer in action than any Medusa,
    Her lover will always describe her as kind   310
And gentle. But take care not to give yourself away while
    Making such tongue-in-cheek compliments, don't allow
Your expression to ruin the message. Art's most effective
    When concealed. Detection discredits you for good.

Often in early autumn, when the year's at its sweetest,   315
    When grapes glow purple and full,
One day we'll be chilled to the bone, the next get heat-exhaustion,
    Our bodies made listless by the changing air.
Let's hope your girl keeps well—but if this unhealthy
    Season turns her sickly, sends her to bed,   320
Then let her see, beyond doubt, how she's loved and cherished,
    Then sow your seed: you'll reap a bumper crop
When the time is ripe. Bear with her fretful sickness,
    Attend in person to all she'll let you do;
Let her see you weeping, comfort her with kisses   325
    Day in, day out; let her parched
Lips drink your tears. Invent cheerful dreams to tell her,
    Make vows galore—and all of them aloud.

Bring round some old crone to purify bed and bedroom,
    Eggs and sulphur clutched in her tremulous hands.   330
All this will be proof of your willing care: such tactics
    Have often led to a legacy. But don't
Let your services risk incurring the invalid's displeasure—
    Sedulous zeal should know its proper bounds.
Never restrict her diet, never make her drink unpleasant   335
    Medicines: leave your rival to deal with such things.

Remember, the wind you spread your sails to when leaving
    Harbour should not be used out on the high
Seas: let your young love, fancy free, gather strength through
    Experience. Nourish it well, in time   340
It will grow steadfast. The bull you now fear began as
    The calf you stroked; the tree
Beneath which you recline was once a sapling. A river's
    Small beginnings swell with progression, embrace
Many confluent waters. Get her accustomed to you: 345
    Habit's the key, spare no pains till that's achieved.
Let her always see you around, always hear you talking,
    Show her your face night and day.
When you're confident you'll be missed, when your absence
    Seems sure to cause her regret,   350
Then give her some respite: a field improves when fallow,
    Parched soil soaks up the rain.
Demophoön's presence gave Phyllis no more than mild excitement;
    It was his sailing caused arson in her heart.
Penelope was racked by crafty Ulysses' absence,   355
    Protesilaus, abroad, made Laodameia burn.
Short partings do best, though: time wears out affections,
    The absent love fades, a new one takes its place.
With Menelaus away, Helen's disinclination for sleeping
    Alone led her into her guest's   360
Warm bed at night. Were you crazy, Menelaus?
    Why go off leaving your wife
With a stranger in the house? Do you trust doves to falcons,
    Full sheepfolds to mountain wolves?
Here Helen's not at fault, the adulterer's blameless—   365
    He did no more than you, or any man else,
Would do yourself. By providing place and occasion
    You precipitated the act. What else did she do
But act on your clear advice? Husband gone; this stylish stranger
    Here on the spot; too scared to sleep alone—   370
Oh, Helen wins my acquittal, the blame's her husband's:
    All *she* did was take advantage of a man's
Human complaisance. And yet, more savage than the tawny
    Boar in his rage, as he tosses the maddened dogs

On lightning tusks, or a lioness suckling her unweaned 375
    Cubs, or the tiny adder crushed
By some careless foot, is a woman's wrath, when some rival
    Is caught in the bed *she* shares. Her feelings show
On her face. Decorum's flung to the wind, a maenadic
    Frenzy grips her, she rushes headlong off 380
After fire and steel. Deserted, barbarian Medea
    Avenged her marital wrongs
On Jason by killing their children—like Procne the swallow,
    Another ruthless mother, breast stained red
With blood. Such acts destroy the most strongly bonded 385
    Passions: all prudent men should avoid
Set-tos of this sort. Such a ruling, though, won't condemn you
    (God forbid!) to one girl alone. No bride can expect
That degree of devotion. Have fun, but play it discreetly—
    Don't broadcast your intrigues 390
As a boost for your ego. Don't make regular assignations,
    Don't give X presents that Y might recognize.
Don't always meet in the same place: the lady may catch you
    If you haunt the milieux that she knows—
And whenever you write, make sure all previous letters 395
    Have been erased from your tablets: many girls read
More than was ever sent them. Venus, when affronted,
    Hits back, inflicts on you
All that she suffered. So long as Agamemnon was faithful,
    Clytemnestra stayed chaste. It was her husband's crimes 400
Turned her to the bad. She'd heard how Chryses, sacerdotal
    Fillet on head and laurel in hand, had failed
To win back his daughter. She'd heard the sad tale of abducted
    Briseis, knew how shameful delay
Had prolonged the war. Yet all this was mere hearsay: Priam's daughter 405
    Cassandra she'd *seen,* the conqueror shamefully caught
By his own captive. It was then she welcomed Thyestes' son to
    Her heart and bed, avenged her husband's ill deed.

Should your carefully camouflaged actions he brought not notwithstanding
    To light, then deny them still, through thick and thin; 410
Don't be over-subservient, don't flatter her more than usual—
    Such traits are clear proof of guilt.
Go to it in bed: that's the one way you'll get round her,
    With cocksmanship so fine it *has* to disprove
Any earlier peccadillo. Some advise taking aphrodisiac 415
    Herbal concoctions—they're poison, believe you me.
Some crush up pepper with nettleseed, an urticant mixture,
    Or blend yellow camomile in vintage wine;
But the goddess worshipped high on Eryx's leafy mountain
    Won't let her joys be forced this way— 420

Try white Megarian onions, and salacious colewort
 Picked from your kitchen-garden; eat eggs;
Enrich your diet with Hymettus honey, with the needled
 Pine-tree's delectable nuts.
Why digress on such hocus-pocus, Muse? I must guide my chariot   425
 Straight down the innermost lane,
Grazing the rail. Just now, at my urging, you were ready
 To keep your affairs a secret. Now change tack
—At my urging—and publish them. Don't chide me for fickle
 Impulses: no ship is always blown   430
By the same prevailing wind. We veer to every quarter
 As the breeze fills our sails. Watch how
A charioteer will handle his horses, first letting them gallop,
 Then skilfully reining them in.
Some women just don't react well to timid complaisance: 435
 If there's no competition in sight
Their love wanes. Success will often breed presumption,
 It's hard to keep your head
Through a run of good luck. You've seen the fire that smoulders
 Down to nothing, grows a crown of pale ash   440
Over its hidden embers (yet a sprinkling of sulphur
 Will suffice to rekindle the flame)?
So with the heart. It grows torpid from lack of worry,
 Needs a sharp stimulus to elicit love.
Get her anxious about you, reheat her tepid passions,   445
 Tell her your guilty secrets, watch her blanch.
Thrice fortunate that man, lucky past calculation,
 Who can make some poor injured girl
Torture herself over him, lose voice, go pale, pass out when
 The unwelcome news reaches her. Ah, may I   450
Be the one whose hair she tears out in her fury, the one whose
 Soft cheeks she rips with her nails,
Whom she sees, eyes glaring, through a rain of tears; without whom,
 Try as she will, she cannot live!
How long (you may ask) should you leave her lamenting her wrong? A little   455
 While only, lest rage gather strength
Through procrastination. By then you should have her sobbing
 All over your chest, your arms tight round her neck.
You want peace? Give her kisses, make love to the girl while she's crying—
 That's the only way to melt her angry mood.   460

When she's been raging at you, when she seems utterly hostile,
 Then is the time to try
An alliance in bed. She'll come through. Bed's where harmony dwells when
 The fighting's done: that's the place
Where loving-kindness was born. The doves that lately fought now   465
 Call softly, bill and coo.

The world at first was mere mass, confused and patternless, one great
    Mingled vista: stars, earth, sea. But soon
Heaven was set above earth, land ringed with water,
    And the void withdrew to its own place.   470
Birds made their home in the air, beasts in the forest:
    Deep underwater, fish lurked.
Mankind was nomadic then, went wandering through an empty
    Landscape, mere muscular brutes
Whose home was the woodland, who ate grass, used leaves for bedding,   475
    Went solitary, long avoided their own kind.
What softened those fierce hearts? Voluptuous pleasure
    When a man and a woman stopped
In the same place. They found what to do by themselves. No teacher
    Was needed. Venus saw the sweet game through   480
Without subtle trimmings. The bird has his mate, the fish will
    Find a partner out in the deep,
Hind follows stag, serpent tangles with serpent,
    Dog mounts random dog, the ewe
Thrills to be covered, bulls rouse their heifers, the snub-nosed   485
    She-goat's back sustains
Her rank male partner. Mares are driven to frenzy,
    Cross rivers in hot pursuit
Of their stallions. So get moving with this potent medicine
    When your lady's angry: nothing else will relieve   490
Her fierce distress, this dose surpasses even Machaon's
    Drugs: if you've been unfaithful, this will make your peace.

As I was reciting these lines, Apollo abruptly
    Materialized beside me, thrumming a chord
On his gilded lyre, bay in hand, bay wreathed about his sacred   495
    Hair (to poets he will sometimes appear
In visible form). 'Preceptor,' he told me, 'of wanton
    Love, come, lead your disciples to my shrine,
Show them the world-famous sign, that brief commandment:
    Know yourself. Only with true   500
Self-knowledge will a man love wisely, pursue the matter
    By exploiting the gifts he's got.
If nature's made him handsome, let him flash his best profile;
    If smooth-skinned, he should recline
Bare-shouldered. The brilliant talker can fill in those awkward   505
    Silences; the good singer should sing,
The good drinker—drink. But brilliant declamations
    And highflown poetic recitals are out of place
In common-or-garden discourse.' Such was Apollo's counsel,
    Counsel to be obeyed: this god speaks truth.   510
Back to my theme, then. Any intelligent lover
    Will win in the end: my techniques

Are sure to bring him fulfilment. Not every sown furrow
 Repays its investment with interest, not every wind
Blows your wandering ship on course. Lovers get less pleasure   515
 Than pain: let them steel their hearts
To endless hardship. As thick as Sicily's swarming
 Bees, or hares on Athos, or the grey
Olive-tree's clustering yield, or shells on the shore, so many
 Are the pains of love: there's gall for us in those pricks.   520

She's out, they'll announce, although you well may glimpse her
 Somewhere inside. So, she's out,
You were seeing visions. Suppose she locks the door against you
 Come the promised night? Then doss down
On the bare ground. It's dirty? Too bad. Even when some lying   525
 And snotty maid asks, 'What's this
Fellow hanging around for?' still coax door and cruel mistress,
 Take off your wreath of roses, hang it up
On the knocker. When she's willing, move in; when she avoids you,
 Take yourself off: no gentleman should become   530
An importunate bore. Why force your mistress to say, 'You
 Just can't get rid of old so-and-so'? She won't
Always be set against you. And don't think it demeaning
 To endure a girl's blows or curses, to kiss her feet.

Why waste time over trifles? My mind's on greater matters,   535
 Great themes will I tackle—your full
Attention, please, reader! The task will be arduous—but no credit
 Otherwise: hard and exacting the toil
My art demands. Bear patiently with a rival, and victory
 Will be yours, you'll triumph in the end.   540
Take this not as mere human opinion, believe it rather
 Prophetic utterance: nothing in my art
Is of greater importance. Put up with her flirtations,
 Leave her billets-doux alone, let her come or go
As she pleases. Husbands allow this latitude to lawful   545
 Wives—they nod off, let sleep assist the fun.
At this game, I must confess, I fall short of perfection,
 But what to do? I just can't follow my own
Instructions. What, sit by while someone's making passes
 At my girl? Let that go, not blow my top?   550
Her own incumbent, as I remember, had kissed her: I resented
 The kisses: my love abounds with wild
Uncivilized instincts (a fault that has caused me trouble
 On more than one occasion). Wiser the man
Who oils doors for his rivals. But it's best to know nothing,   555
 Let guilty secrets be hidden; don't make her confess,
Spare her blushes. Observe, you young blades, don't catch out your girls: no,

Let them cheat you—and while they're cheating, believe
They've eluded discovery. Passion's fanned by detection,
    A guilty pair revealed will always persist   560
In the love that undid them. Take one famous example—
    Vulcan's crafty snaring of Mars
And Venus. Driven wild by a frantic passion
    For the goddess, Mars was transformed
From grim captain to lover. Nor did Venus play the rustic   565
    And hold out against his entreaties: there's no
Goddess more willing. Ah, the times she mocked her husband's
    Limp, the wanton, or his hands, made hard
By toil at the forge and bellows! To ape him in Mars' presence
    Lent her chic, gave added charm   570
To her beauty. At first they concealed their adulterous
    Meetings: guilt blushed, shame kept
The affair quite dark. But who could deceive the Sun? He
    Saw all—and told Vulcan what acts
His wife was performing. Sun, that's a bad example   575
    You set there. Just ask, she'll oblige
You too in return for your silence. So Vulcan set hidden
    Snares round and over the bed (no eye
Could detect them), then put about he was off to Lemnos. The lovers
    Met as arranged, were trapped   580
In the toils, lay naked: tableau. Then Vulcan invited
    All the gods round. Venus came close to tears—
She and Mars couldn't cover their faces, couldn't even
    Move a hand to their private parts.
Someone laughed and said: 'If you find your chains a burden,   585
    Brave Mars, transfer them to me!'
At Neptune's urging, reluctantly, Vulcan released them:
    Venus ran off to Paphos, Mars to Thrace.
So much for Vulcan's plotting: once their shameful
    Secret was out, the lovers did as they pleased   590
Without thought for concealment. Later Vulcan admitted
    His folly, they say, and would curse the fatal skill
He'd deployed to catch them. So, be warned by the fate of Venus,
    Don't set up the kind of snare
She had to endure. Don't organize traps for your rivals,   595
    Don't intercept secret letters—that's a job
More proper to husbands (if they reckon such correspondence
    Worth interception). Once more, let me repeat,
There's no sport here that isn't legitimate, no long-skirted
    Respectable ladies figure in *my* fun.   600

Who'd dare to profane the rites of Ceres, who would publish
    The high mysteries held on Samothrace? To keep
Silence is no great virtue, but blurting out religious

Secrets—that's a most heinous crime.
Garrulous Tantalus, vainly reaching up for apples,   605
    In water, yet parched with thirst,
Deserved his fate: Venus expressly commands that her holy
    Rites be kept private. I'm warning you, let no
Kiss-and-tell gossip come near them. These mysteries may not
    Lurk in a box, may not echo to the wild   610
Clash of bronze cymbals; yet, though so popular among us,
    Among us they still insist
On concealment. Venus herself, when she poses naked,
    Bends down, places one hand
Over her mons. Brute beasts may couple in public,   615
    Promiscuously, a sight to make girls blush
And avert their eyes; but our more furtive passions call for
    Locked doors and bedrooms, we hide
Our private parts under the bedclothes, and prefer, if not darkness,
    At least something less than bright   620
Noonday, a touch of shadow. In the old days, when sun and weather
    Weren't yet kept off by roof-tiles, when oaks
Provided both food and shelter, love-making was restricted
    To caves or woods. Even these simple folk
Would have blushed to be seen in the act. But now we flaunt our prowess   625
    At such nocturnal pursuits, pay a high price
Just for the kick of bragging. Will you give every girl in town the
    Treatment, just to be able to tell your friends
'I had her, too?' Will you find some circumstantial scandal
    To repeat about each as she's mentioned, never lack   630
For a victim to point at? That's mild, though: some fabricate stories
    They'd deny if true, claim there's no
Woman they haven't slept with. If they cannot touch girls'
    Bodies, they'll smear their names: though the flesh escape
Defilement, repute is tarnished. So, bar the lady's chamber,   635
    You crabby old doorkeeper, fix on a hundred bolts—
What's left secure when her name's fair game for 'adulterers'
    Who work to convince the world of what never took place?
Myself, I remain discreet about my erotic encounters
    Even when they're true: keep such secrets under seal.   640

Take care not to criticize girls for their shortcomings: many
    Have found it advantageous to pretend
Such things didn't exist. Andromeda's dusky complexion
    Left wing-footed Perseus silent. Although
Everyone else thought Andromache too large a woman,   645
    To Hector alone she looked
Just the right size. Habit breeds tolerance: a long-established
    Love will condone much, whereas
At first it's all-sensitive. While a new graft's growing

In the green cortex, a light   650
Breeze can detach it; but soon, time-strengthened, the tree will
    Outface all winds, hold firm,
Bear adopted fruit. Time heals each physical blemish,
    The erstwhile flaw will fade:
Young nostrils cannot abide the stink of tanning leather,   655
    But age inures them to it, after a while
They don't even notice the smell. Labels minimize feelings—
    She's blacker than pitch? Try 'brunette'.
If she squints, compare her to Venus. She croaks? She's Minerva!
    A living skeleton? 'Svelte' is the word. Call her 'trim'   660
When she's minuscule, or 'plumpish' when she's a Fat Lady—
    Use proximate virtues to camouflage each fault.

Don't ask her age, don't inquire under just which consul
    She was born—leave that kind of chore
To the Censor's office, especially if she's past her girlish   665
    Prime, and already plucking those first
White hairs. Such ladies, in this (or even a higher) age-group
    Are good value, a field worth sowing, ready to bear.*
Besides, they possess a wider range of knowledge   675
    And experience, the sole source
Of true skill: they make up for their years with sophistication,
    Camouflaging their age through art; they know
A thousand postures—name yours—for making love in,
    More ways than any pillow-book could reveal.   680
They need no stimuli to warm up their passions—
    Men and women should share the same
Pleasures. I hate it unless both lovers reach a climax:
    That's why I don't much go for boys.
I can't stand a woman who puts out because she has to,   685
    Who lies there dry as a bone
With her mind on her knitting. Pleasure by way of duty
    Holds no charm for me, I don't want
Any dutiful martyrs. I love the sighs that betray their rapture,
    That beg me to go slow, to keep it up   690
Just a little longer. It's great when my mistress comes, eyes swooning,
    Then collapses, can't take any more
For a long while. Such joys attend you in your thirties:
    Nature does not bestow them on green youth.
For the hasty, new-bottled wine; for me, a vintage   695
    Laid down long years before.
Only an ageing plane-tree can block the sunlight,

---

*Editors have often remarked that lines 669–74 are out of place here, but no truly satisfactory place was found for them until it was shown that they properly belong at the *end* of Book 2, between lines 732 and 733. I have therefore transposed them in the present version.

Bare feet are crippled by a new-grown field.
Would you rate Helen's daughter Hermione over Helen? Was Medusa
    An improvement on *her* mother? Any man   700
Willing to get involved with mature passions,
    And to stay the course, will win a worthwhile prize.

So the bed, as though consciously, has received its two lovers.
    And the door is shut. Muse, you must wait outside:
They don't need you, now, to prompt their whispered endearments,   705
    Their hands won't be idle, fingers will learn
What to do in those hidden parts where Love's unnoticed
    Darts transfix the flesh.
Andromache got this treatment from most valiant Hector—
    His talents extended beyond war: 710
Captive Briseis was handled thus by the great Achilles,
    Who came, battle-weary, to her soft bed.
Those hands, Briseis, you let those bloody hands caress you
    Though daily they claimed their stint
Of Phrygian dead. Or was that just what you found so exciting—   715
    The hands of a conqueror on your limbs?
Believe me, love's acme of pleasure must not be hurried,
    But drawn insensibly on—and when you've found
Those places a woman adores to have touched up, don't let any
    Feeling of shame prevent you, go right in.   720
You'll see that tremulous glint in her eyes, like the dazzle
    Of sunlight on a lake;
She'll moan and gasp, murmur words of sweet endearment
    Well matched to the sport you're playing, heave soft sighs.
But take care not to cram on sail and outrace your mistress,   725
    Or let *her* overtake *you;* both should pass
The winning-post neck and neck—that's the height of pleasure,
    When man and woman lie knocked out at once.
This is the pace you should keep when time's no object,
    And your stolen pleasures take no prick from fear;   730
When delay isn't safe, though, it helps to press on regardless,
    Step up the strike-rate, spur that galloping horse.
While strength and age permit it, keep at such labours: 669
    Bent age will come soon enough   670
On stealthy feet. Cleave the sea with oars, the soil with a ploughshare,   671
    Turn your fierce hands to war—   672
Or expend your strength and toil and vigour on women: 673
    This too is military service, this too needs sweat.   674

My task is ended: give me the palm, you grateful   733
    Young lovers, wreathe myrtle in my scented hair!
As great as Podalirius was among the Achaeans   735
    For his healing arts, or Achilles for his strength,

Or Nestor in counsel, or Calchas as prophet, or Ajax
    In arms, or Automedon as charioteer,
So great am I at the love-game. Sing my praises, declare me
    Your prophet and poet, young men: let my name   740
Be broadcast world-wide. As Vulcan made arms for Achilles,
    So have I done for you: then use
My gift, as he did, to conquer! And when you've brought down your
    Amazon, write on the trophy *Ovid was my guide*.

Now the girls (hullo there!) are begging me for lessons: 745
    The next part of this poem will be yours.

The Bible

THE OLD TESTAMENT

Introduction by Michael Levin

The Bible is arguably the single most important work of Western literature; it has had a pro-found effect on the culture, philosophy, and even the languages of Western civilization. It is also perhaps the most controversial work you will find in this sourcebook, precisely because it is so important to so many people. For all these reasons, no course on the Humanities in the Western Tradition would be complete without a close look at the Bible. Our ideas about human nature, human society, the role of religion — in short, most of the themes of this course — have all been shaped by this one work.

More specifically, the first half of the Bible, or the Hebrew Scriptures (referred to as the Old Testament after the development of Christianity) is at the heart of the Jewish religion and people. The various individual books of the Hebrew Scriptures, written by different people over the course of many centuries, collectively tell the story of the Israelites. We can follow the development of this particular group of people, from their origins (or Genesis), through their first encounters with God, who tells the Israelites that they are his Chosen People. Eventually the Israelites become a people of Law, guided by divine wisdom as revealed to them by God. But the Israelites are very human — they often doubt, and they sometimes fail to live up to God's expectations, leading to divine punishment. When reading these stories, it is important to remember that the Hebrew Scriptures are a combination of religious instruction and historical narrative. Modern day Jews regard these scriptures as both a moral guide and a record of where they came from.

Our selections from the Hebrew Scriptures begin with the beginning of everything, from the Book of Genesis (which means origin or creation). Many of the stories included in this sec-tion may be familiar to you — the Garden of Eden, Cain and Abel, Noah and Flood. But do not skip this section! Read these stories carefully — you might be surprised. Ask yourself what is really going on here. What is God's purpose in placing the Tree of the Knowledge of Good and Evil in the Garden of Eden? Why does God decide to cause the Flood? These stories are not as simple as you might think. Also, in chapter nine pay close attention to the idea of a "covenant," or a contract between God and Noah. This is a key concept in the Hebrew Scriptures, the idea that people (and in particular the Chosen People) can make agreements with God.

In the Book of Exodus, we see evidence that God honors his side of the convenant he made with the Israelites; he rescues the Israelites from slavery in Egypt. But he acts through a human agent, a reluctant hero named Moses. And initially, the Israelites are not all that grateful to be rescued. They wander through the desert for forty years, and go through several crises of faith. What message is being given here about human nature? Eventually, they arrive at Mount Sinai, where God gives Moses the Ten Commandments as well as many other laws. This section is one of the foundation stones of Western society. What do the laws emphasize? How are we supposed to live our lives?

The Book of Isaiah takes place much later in the history of the Israelites, after they have settled in the land of Canaan. By this time, the Israelites have become prosperous, but they have begun to neglect their religious duties. Isaiah is one of a series of prophets who warn the Israelites that if they do not correct the error of their ways, God will punish them. And this is exactly what happens — the Babylonians conquer Canaan and enslave the Israelites. Isaiah also predicts that one day a child will be born who will be a Messiah, or a savior. Centuries later, followers of Jesus would claim that Jesus was in fact the Messiah who Isaiah had foreseen.

Finally, in the Book of Job we have a fascinating (and perhaps troubling) story about how God sometimes tests our faith. Job is a virtuous man, who, for no apparent reason, loses everything. Eventually, even Job's famous patience begins to wear thin, and he dares to question God. How does God respond? Compare the vision of God presented here with the Greek gods you read about earlier in the semester. What makes the God of the Hebrew Scriptures different from all other gods?

THE FIRST BOOK OF MOSES COMMONLY CALLED

Genesis

IN THE BEGINNING God CREATED*[a]* the heavens and the earth. 2 The earth was without form and void, and darkness was upon the face of the deep; and the Spirit*[b]* of God was moving over the face of the waters.

3 And God said, "Let there be light"; and there was light. 4 And God saw that the light was good; and God separated the light from the darkness. 5 God called the light Day, and the darkness he called Night. And there was evening and there was morning, one day.

6 And God said, "Let there be a firmament in the midst of the waters, and let it separate the waters from the waters." 7 And God made the firmament and separated the waters which were under the firmament from the waters which were above the firmament. And it was so. 8 And God called the firmament Heaven. And there was evening and there was morning, a second day.

a Or *When God began to create*   *b* Or *wind*

1.1–2.4a: The Priestly story of creation. Out of original chaos God created an orderly world in which he assigned a preeminent place to man. **1:** Probably a preface to the whole story, though possibly introductory to v. 3: *When God began to create* (note *a*) . . . *God said* (compare 2.4b–7). The ancients believed the world originated from and was founded upon a watery chaos (*the deep;* compare Ps.24.1,2), portrayed as a dragon in various myths (Is.51.9). **3–5:** Creation by the word of God (Ps.33.6–9) expresses God's absolute lordship and prepares for the doctrine of creation out of nothing (2 Macc.7.28). Light was created first (2 Cor.4.6), even before the sun, and was *separated* from *night,* a remnant of uncreated darkness (v. 2). Since the Jewish day began with sundown, the order is *evening* and *morning.* **6–8:** A *firmament,* or solid dome (Job 37.18), separated the upper from the lower waters (Ex.20.4; Ps.148.4).

Bible, THE NEW OXFORD ANNOTATED BIBLE WITH THE APOCRYPHA Revised Standard Edition, Genesis 1–9.

9 And God said, "Let the waters under the heavens be gathered together into one place, and let the dry land appear." And it was so. [10] God called the dry land Earth, and the waters that were gathered together he called Seas. And God saw that it was good. [11] And God said, "Let the earth put forth vegetation, plants yielding seed, and fruit trees bearing fruit in which is their seed, each according to its kind, upon the earth." And it was so. [12] The earth brought forth vegetation, plants yielding seed according to their own kinds, and trees bearing fruit in which is their seed, each according to its kind. And God saw that it was good. [13] And there was evening and there was morning, a third day.

14 And God said, "Let there be lights in the firmament of the heavens to separate the day from the night; and let them be for signs and for seasons and for days and years, [15] and let them be lights in the firmament of the heavens to give light upon the earth." And it was so. [16] And God made the two great lights, the greater light to rule the day, and the lesser light to rule the night; he made the stars also. [17] And God set them in the firmament of the heavens to give light upon the earth, [18] to rule over the day and over the night, and to separate the light from the darkness. And God saw that it was good. [19] And there was evening and there was morning, a fourth day.

20 And God said, "Let the waters bring forth swarms of living creatures, and let birds fly above the earth across the firmament of the heavens." [21] So God created the great sea monsters and every living creature that moves, with which the waters swarm, according to their kinds, and every winged bird according to its kind. And God saw that it was good. [22] And God blessed them, saying, "Be fruitful and multiply and fill the waters in the seas, and let birds multiply on the earth." [23] And there was evening and there was morning, a fifth day.

24 And God said, "Let the earth bring forth living creatures according to their kinds: cattle and creeping things and beasts of the earth according to their kinds." And it was so. [25] And God made the beasts of the earth according to their kinds and the cattle according to their kinds, and everything that creeps upon the ground according to its kind. And God saw that it was good.

26 Then God said, "Let us make man in our image, after our likeness; and let them have dominion over the fish of the sea, and over the birds of the air, and over the cattle, and over all the earth, and over every creeping thing that creeps upon the earth." [27] So God created man in his own image, in the image of God he created him; male and female he created them. [28] And God blessed them, and God said to them, "Be fruitful and multiply, and fill the earth and subdue it; and have dominion over the fish of the sea and over the birds of the air and over every living thing that moves upon the earth." [29] And God said, "Behold, I have given you every plant yielding seed which is upon the face of all the earth, and every tree with seed in its fruit; you shall have them for food. [30] And to every beast of the earth, and to every bird of the air, and to

See 7.11 n. **9–10:** The *seas*, a portion of the watery chaos, were assigned boundaries at the edge of the earth (Ps.139.9; Pr.8.29), where they continue to menace God's creation (Jer.5.22; Ps.104.7–9). **11–13:** *Vegetation* was created only indirectly by God; his creative command was directed to *the earth*. **14–19:** The sun, moon, and stars are not divine powers that control man's destiny, as was believed in antiquity, but are only *lights*. Implicitly worship of the heavenly host is forbidden (Dt.4.19; Zeph.1.5). **20–23:** The creation of birds and fishes. *Sea monsters*, see Pss.74.13; 104.25–26. **24–25:** God's command for the earth to *bring forth* (compare v. 11) suggests that the animals are immediately bound to *the ground* and only indirectly related to God, in contrast with man. **26–27:** The solemn divine decision emphasizes man's supreme place at the climax of God's creative work. **26:** The plural *us, our* (3.22; 11.7; Is.6.8) probably refers to the divine beings who compose God's heavenly court (1 Kg.22.19; Job 1.6). Made in *the image of God*, man is the creature through whom God manifests his rule on earth. The language reflects "royal theology" in which, as in Egypt, the king was the "image of God." **27:** *Him, them:* man was not created to be alone but is *male and female* (2.18–24). *Man*, the Hebrew word is "adam," a collective, referring to mankind. **28:** As God's representative, man is given *dominion* (Ps.8.6–8). **29–30:** His dominion is limited, as shown by the vegetarian requirement, modified in

everything that creeps on the earth, everything that has the breath of life, I have given every green plant for food." And it was so. [31] And God saw everything that he had made, and behold, it was very good. And there was evening and there was morning, a sixth day.

2 Thus the heavens and the earth were finished, and all the host of them. [2] And on the seventh day God finished his work which he had done, and he rested on the seventh day from all his work which he had done. [3] So God blessed the seventh day and hallowed it, because on it God rested from all his work which he had done in creation.

4 These are the generations of the heavens and the earth when they were created.

In the day that the LORD God made the earth and the heavens, [5] when no plant of the field was yet in the earth and no herb of the field had yet sprung up — for the LORD God had not caused it to rain upon the earth, and there was no man to till the ground; [6] but a mist*c* went up from the earth and watered the whole face of the ground — [7] then the LORD God formed man of dust from the ground, and breathed into his nostrils the breath of life; and man became a living being. [8] And the LORD God planted a garden in Eden, in the east; and there he put the man whom he had formed. [9] And out of the ground the LORD God made to grow every tree that is pleasant to the sight and good for food, the tree of life

also in the midst of the garden, and the tree of the knowledge of good and evil.

10 A river flowed out of Eden to water the garden, and there it divided and became four rivers. [11] The name of the first is Pishon; it is the one which flows around the whole land of Hav′ilah, where there is gold; [12] and the gold of that land is good; bdellium and onyx stone are there. [13] The name of the second river is Gihon; it is the one which flows around the whole land of Cush. [14] And the name of the third river is Tigris, which flows east of Assyria. And the fourth river is the Euphra′tes.

15 The LORD God took the man and put him in the garden of Eden to till it and keep it. [16] And the LORD God commanded the man, saying, "You may freely eat of every tree of the garden; [17] but of the tree of the knowledge of good and evil you shall not eat, for in the day that you eat of it you shall die."

18 Then the LORD God said, "It is not good that the man should be alone; I will make him a helper fit for him." [19] So out of the ground the LORD God formed every beast of the field and every bird of the air, and brought them to the man to see what he would call them; and whatever the man called every living creature, that was its name. [20] The man gave names to all cattle, and to the birds of the air, and to every beast of the field; but for the man there was not found a helper fit for him.

c Or flood

Noah's time (9.2–3); it is to be benevolent and peaceful (compare Is.11.6–8). **31:** *Very good* (vv. 4,10,12. etc.), corresponding perfectly to God's purpose. **2.1–3:** The verb *rested* (Hebrew *"shabat"*) is the basis of the noun sabbath (Ex.31.12–17).

2.4b–3.24: The creation and the fall of man. This is a different tradition from that in 1.1–2.4a, as evidenced by the flowing style and the different order of events, e.g. man is created before vegetation, animals, and woman. **6:** *A mist* (or *flood*) probably refers to the water which surged up from the subterranean ocean, the source of fertility (49.25). **7:** The word-play on *man* ('adham) and *ground* ('adhamah) introduces a motif characteristic of this early tradition: man's relation to the ground from which he was *formed*, like a potter molds clay (Jer.18.6). Man is not body and soul (a Greek distinction) but is dust animated by the LORD God's *breath* or "spirit" which constitutes him *a living being* or psycho-physical self (Ps.104.29–30; Job 34.14–15). **8–9:** *Eden,* meaning "delight," is a "garden of God" (Is.51.3; Ezek.31.8–9; Jl.2.3) or divine park. **9:** The *tree of life* was believed to confer eternal life (3.22; see Pr.3.18 n.; Rev.22.2,14,19), as the *tree of the knowledge of good and evil* confers wisdom (see 2 Sam.14.17; Is.7.15). **10–14:** The rivers, springing from the subterranean ocean (v. 6), flowed out to the four corners of the known historical world. **15–17:** Man is given a task: to *till* and *keep* the garden. The prohibition against eating the forbidden fruit (3.3) stresses God's lordship and man's obedience. **18:** *To be alone* is not good, for man is social by nature (see 1.27 n.). *A helper fit for him* means a partner who is suitable for him, who completes his being. **19:** Naming the animals signifies man's

²¹ So the LORD God caused a deep sleep to fall upon the man, and while he slept took one of his ribs and closed up its place with flesh; ²² and the rib which the LORD God had taken from the man he made into a woman and brought her to the man. ²³ Then the man said,

"This at last is bone of my bones
　and flesh of my flesh;
she shall be called Woman,*d*

　because she was taken out of Man."*e*

²⁴ Therefore a man leaves his father and his mother and cleaves to his wife, and they become one flesh. ²⁵ And the man and his wife were both naked, and were not ashamed.

3 Now the serpent was more subtle than any other wild creature that the LORD God had made. He said to the woman, "Did God say, 'You shall not eat of any tree of the garden'?" ² And the woman said to the serpent, "We may eat of the fruit of the trees of the garden; ³ but God said, 'You shall not eat of the fruit of the tree which is in the midst of the garden, neither shall you touch it, lest you die.'" ⁴ But the serpent said to the woman, "You will not die. ⁵ For God knows that when you eat of it your eyes will be opened, and you will be like God, knowing good and evil." ⁶ So when the woman saw that the tree was good for food, and that it was a delight to the eyes, and that the tree was to be desired to make one wise, she took of its fruit and ate; and she also gave some to her husband, and he ate. ⁷ Then the eyes of both were opened, and they knew that they were naked; and they sewed fig leaves together and made themselves aprons.

⁸ And they heard the sound of the LORD God walking in the garden in the cool of the day, and the man and his wife hid themselves from the presence of the LORD God among the trees of the garden. ⁹ But the LORD God called to the man, and said to him, "Where are you?" ¹⁰ And he said, "I heard the sound of thee in the garden, and I was afraid, because I was naked; and I hid myself." ¹¹ He said, "Who told you that you were naked? Have you eaten of the tree of which I commanded you not to eat?" ¹² The man said, "The woman whom thou gavest to be with me, she gave me fruit of the tree, and I ate." ¹³ Then the LORD God said to the woman, "What is this that you have done?" The woman said, "The serpent beguiled me, and I ate." ¹⁴ The LORD God said to the serpent,

"Because you have done this,
　cursed are you above all cattle,
　and above all wild animals;
upon your belly you shall go,
　and dust you shall eat
　all the days of your life.
¹⁵ I will put enmity between you and the
　　woman,
　and between your seed and her seed;
he shall bruise your head,
　and you shall bruise his heel."
¹⁶ To the woman he said,
"I will greatly multiply your pain in child-
　　bearing;
　in pain you shall bring forth children,
yet your desire shall be for your husband,
　and he shall rule over you."

d Heb *ishshah*　　*e* Heb *ish*

---

dominion over them (compare 1.28). **21–23:** The deep affinity between man and woman is portrayed in the statement that God made the woman from the man's *rib.* **24–25:** Sex is not regarded as evil but as a God-given impulse which draws man and woman together so that *they become one flesh.* **25:** The two were unashamedly *naked,* a symbol of their guiltless relation to God and to one another. **3.1–7:** The temptation begins with the insinuation of doubt (vv. 1–3), increases as suspicion is cast upon God's motive (vv. 4–5), and becomes irresistible when the couple sense the possibilities of freedom (v. 6). **1:** *The serpent,* one of the wild creatures, distinguished by uncanny wisdom (Mt.10.16); there is a hint of a seductive power in man's environment, hostile to God. **5:** *Like God:* perhaps "like gods" (Septuagint), the divine beings of the heavenly court (v. 22; 1.26 n.). *Knowing good and evil,* see 2.9 n. **7:** Bodily shame (2.25) symbolizes anxiety about broken relationship with God. **8–13:** Anxiety leads to a guilty attempt to hide from God (Ps.139.7–12), described anthropomorphically as strolling in his garden. **14–15:** The curse contains an old explanation of why the serpent crawls rather than walks and why men are instinctively hostile to it. **16:** This divine judgment contains an old explanation of woman's pain in childbirth, her sexual *desire* for her husband (i.e. her motherly

¹⁷ And to Adam he said,

"Because you have listened to the voice of
    your wife,
  and have eaten of the tree
of which I commanded you,
  'You shall not eat of it,'
cursed is the ground because of you;
    in toil you shall eat of it all the days of
    your life;
¹⁸ thorns and thistles it shall bring forth to
    you;
  and you shall eat the plants of the field.
¹⁹ In the sweat of your face
    you shall eat bread
till you return to the ground,
    for out of it you were taken;
you are dust,
    and to dust you shall return."

20 The man called his wife's name Eve,^{*f*} because she was the mother of all living. ²¹ And the LORD God made for Adam and for his wife garments of skins, and clothed them.

22 Then the LORD God said, "Behold, the man has become like one of us, knowing good and evil; and now, lest he put forth his hand and take also of the tree of life, and eat, and live for ever"— ²³ therefore the LORD God sent him forth from the garden of Eden, to till the ground from which he was taken. ²⁴ He drove out the man; and at the east of the garden of Eden he placed the cherubim, and a flaming sword which turned every way, to guard the way to the tree of life.

4 Now Adam knew Eve his wife, and she conceived and bore Cain, saying, "I have gotten^g a man with the help of the LORD." ² And again, she bore his brother Abel. Now Abel was a keeper of sheep, and Cain a tiller of the ground. ³ In the course of time Cain brought to the LORD an offering of the fruit of the ground, ⁴ and Abel brought of the firstlings of his flock and of their fat portions. And the LORD had regard for Abel and his offering, ⁵ but for Cain and his offering he had no regard. So Cain was very angry, and his countenance fell. ⁶ The LORD said to Cain, "Why are you angry, and why has your countenance fallen? ⁷ If you do well, will you not be accepted? And if you do not do well, sin is couching at the door; its desire is for you, but you must master it."

8 Cain said to Abel his brother, "Let us go out to the field."^h And when they were in the field, Cain rose up against his brother Abel, and killed him. ⁹ Then the LORD said to Cain, "Where is Abel your brother?" He said, "I do not know; am I my brother's keeper?" ¹⁰ And the LORD said, "What have you done? The voice of your brother's blood is crying to me from the ground. ¹¹ And now you are cursed from the ground, which has opened its mouth to receive your brother's blood from your hand. ¹² When you till the ground, it shall no longer yield to you its strength; you shall be a

f The name in Hebrew resembles the word for *living*
g Heb *qanah*, get

---

impulse, compare 30.1), and her subordinate position to man in ancient society. **17–19:** An explanation of man's struggle to eke an existence from the soil. Work is not essentially evil (2.15) but it becomes *toil* as a result of man's broken relationship with his Creator. **17:** The Hebrew word *Adam* is usually translated "man" in this story (see 1.27 n.). Note that the curse is upon the ground, not man. **19:** *Till you return to the ground:* The mortal nature of man was implicit in the circumstances of his origin (2.7); because of man's disobedience, God now makes death an inevitable fate that haunts man throughout life. **21:** *Garments of skins,* a sign of God's protective care even in the time of judgment (4.15). **22:** *Like one of us,* see 3.5 n. *The tree of life* (2.9) does not figure in the temptation story, which explicitly speaks of only one tree in the center of the garden (3.3–6, 11–12, 17). **24:** *The cherubim,* guardians of sacred areas (1 Kg.8.6–7), were represented as winged creatures like the Sphynx of Egypt, half human and half lion (Ezek.41.18–19). *A flaming sword* (compare Jer.47.6) was placed near the cherubim to remind banished man of the impossibility of overstepping his creaturely bounds (compare Ezek.28.13–16).

    4.1–26: Cain, Abel, and Seth. 2–5: The story reflects the tension between farmers and semi-nomads, two different ways of life that are symbolized in the two types of offerings. No reason is given for the acceptance of Abel's offering (compare Ex.33.19). **7:** Perhaps the meaning is that Cain himself will be *accepted,* even though his offering is not, if his deed springs from the right motive. Sin is pictured as a predatory animal, *couching at the door.* **10–11:** Blood is sacred to God, for it is the seat of life (Dt.12.23) and cries *from the ground* for vindication. **13–14:** Cain concludes that

fugitive and a wanderer on the earth." [13] Cain said to the LORD, "My punishment is greater than I can bear. [14] Behold, thou hast driven me this day away from the ground; and from thy face I shall be hidden; and I shall be a fugitive and a wanderer on the earth, and whoever finds me will slay me." [15] Then the LORD said to him, "Not so![i] If any one slays Cain, vengeance shall be taken on him sevenfold." And the LORD put a mark on Cain, lest any who came upon him should kill him. [16] Then Cain went away from the presence of the LORD, and dwelt in the land of Nod,[j] east of Eden.

17 Cain knew his wife, and she conceived and bore Enoch; and he built a city, and called the name of the city after the name of his son, Enoch. [18] To Enoch was born Irad; and Irad was the father of Me-hu′ja-el, and Me-hu′ja-el the father of Me-thu′sha-el, and Me-thu′sha-el the father of Lamech. [19] And Lamech took two wives; the name of the one was Adah, and the name of the other Zillah. [20] Adah bore Jabal; he was the father of those who dwell in tents and have cattle. [21] His brother's name was Jubal; he was the father of all those who play the lyre and pipe. [22] Zillah bore Tubal-cain; he was the forger of all instruments of bronze and iron. The sister of Tubal-cain was Na′amah.

23 Lamech said to his wives:

"Adah and Zillah, hear my voice;
you wives of Lamech, hearken to what I say:
I have slain a man for wounding me,
a young man for striking me.

[24] If Cain is avenged sevenfold,
truly Lamech seventy-sevenfold."

25 And Adam knew his wife again, and she bore a son and called his name Seth, for she said, "God has appointed for me another child instead of Abel, for Cain slew him." [26] To Seth also a son was born, and he called his name Enosh. At that time men began to call upon the name of the LORD.

5 This is the book of the generations of Adam. When God created man, he made him in the likeness of God. [2] Male and female he created them, and he blessed them and named them Man when they were created. [3] When Adam had lived a hundred and thirty years, he became the father of a son in his own likeness, after his image, and named him Seth. [4] The days of Adam after he became the father of Seth were eight hundred years; and he had other sons and daughters. [5] Thus all the days that Adam lived were nine hundred and thirty years; and he died.

6 When Seth had lived a hundred and five years, he became the father of Enosh. [7] Seth lived after the birth of Enosh eight hundred and seven years, and had other sons and daughters. [8] Thus all the days of Seth were nine hundred and twelve years; and he died.

9 When Enosh had lived ninety years, he became the father of Kenan. [10] Enosh lived after the birth of Kenan eight hundred and fifteen years, and had other sons and daughters.

h Sam Gk Syr Compare Vg: Heb lacks *Let us go out to the field*   i Gk Syr Vg: Heb *Therefore*   j That is *Wandering*

exile from the farmland is also exile from the LORD's *face,* i.e. protective presence, exposing him to blood revenge. **15:** The "mark of Cain" was a protective mark, perhaps a tattoo, signifying divine mercy. **17:** Here Cain is not the ancestor of nomadic tribesmen (vv. 11–16) but the founder of sedentary culture. **19–22:** Cultural advance is evidenced by the three occupations of Lamech's sons: shepherds, musicians, and smiths. **23–24:** An ancient song, probably once sung in praise of Lamech, is here quoted to illustrate the development of wickedness from murder to measureless blood revenge. **25–26:** From Cain's genealogy the narrator returns to the sequel of Cain's banishment (vv. 11–16) and introduces the new line of Seth. **26b:** This tradition traces the worship of the LORD (Yahweh) back to the time of Adam's grandson, in contrast to other traditions which claim that the sacred name was introduced in Moses' time (Ex.3.13–15; 6.2–3).

5.1–32: The generations from Adam to Noah. This priestly tradition bridges the times from the creation to the flood. **1:** *The book of the generations* was evidently a separate source from which the writer drew genealogical data (6.9; 10.1; 11.10,27; etc.). **1b–2:** See 1.26–28. **3:** The divine *likeness* (v. 1; see 1.26 n.) was continued in Adam's son Seth, born *in his own likeness,* and thus was transmitted to succeeding generations without effacement (9.6). Priestly tradition makes no reference to the account of the fall of man. **4–32:** Babylonian tradition also reckons ten heroes

¹¹ Thus all the days of Enosh were nine hundred and five years; and he died.

12 When Kenan had lived seventy years, he became the father of Ma-hal′-alel. ¹³ Kenan lived after the birth of Ma-hal′alel eight hundred and forty years, and had other sons and daughters. ¹⁴ Thus all the days of Kenan were nine hundred and ten years; and he died.

15 When Ma-hal′alel had lived sixty-five years, he became the father of Jared. ¹⁶ Ma-hal′alel lived after the birth of Jared eight hundred and thirty years, and had other sons and daughters. ¹⁷ Thus all the days of Ma-hal′-alel were eight hundred and ninety-five years; and he died.

18 When Jared had lived a hundred and sixty-two years he became the father of Enoch. ¹⁹ Jared lived after the birth of Enoch eight hundred years, and had other sons and daughters. ²⁰ Thus all the days of Jared were nine hundred and sixty-two years; and he died.

21 When Enoch had lived sixty-five years, he became the father of Methu′selah. ²² Enoch walked with God after the birth of Methu′selah three hundred years, and had other sons and daughters. ²³ Thus all the days of Enoch were three hundred and sixty-five years. ²⁴ Enoch walked with God; and he was not, for God took him.

25 When Methu′selah had lived a hundred and eighty-seven years, he became the father of Lamech. ²⁶ Methu′selah lived after the birth of Lamech seven hundred and eighty-two years, and had other sons and daughters. ²⁷ Thus all the days of Methu′selah were nine hundred and sixty-nine years; and he died.

28 When Lamech had lived a hundred and eighty-two years, he became the father of a son, ²⁹ and called his name Noah, saying, "Out of the ground which the LORD has cursed this one shall bring us relief from our work and from the toil of our hands." ³⁰ Lamech lived after the birth of Noah five hundred and ninety-five years, and had other sons and daughters. ³¹ Thus all the days of Lamech were seven hundred and seventy-seven years; and he died.

32 After Noah was five hundred years old, Noah became the father of Shem, Ham, and Japheth.

6 When men began to multiply on the face of the ground, and daughters were born to them, ² the sons of God saw that the daughters of men were fair; and they took to wife such of them as they chose. ³ Then the LORD said, "My spirit shall not abide in man for ever, for he is flesh, but his days shall be a hundred and twenty years." ⁴ The Nephilim were on the earth in those days, and also afterward, when the sons of God came in to the daughters of men, and they bore children to them. These were the mighty men that were of old, the men of renown.

5 The LORD saw that the wickedness of man was great in the earth, and that every imagination of the thoughts of his heart was only evil continually. ⁶ And the LORD was sorry that he had made man on the earth, and it grieved him to his heart. ⁷ So the LORD said, "I will blot out man whom I have created from the face of the ground, man and beast and creeping things and birds of the air, for I am

before the flood but ascribes fantastically higher ages. In Hebrew tradition the ages decrease from 900–1000 (Adam to Noah), to 200–600 (Noah to Abraham), to 100–200 (the patriarchs), to the normal three-score years and ten (Ps.90.10). This list is somehow related to the genealogy of Cain (4.17–21) as shown by the resemblance of some of the names. **24:** Babylonian tradition also reports that the seventh hero before the flood was taken by God, i.e. translated (2 Kg.2.11). **29:** This verse, the only connection with the early traditions of Eden (3.17–19) and Cain and Abel, anticipates the new age inaugurated with Noah (9.20).

6.1–4: The birth of the Nephilim is related to demonstrate the increase of wickedness on the earth. **1:** This old fragment of mythology connects immediately with chs. 2–4. **2:** *The sons of God* were divine beings who belonged to the heavenly court (1.26 n.). **3:** Despite the lustful intrusion of divine beings into the human sphere, man did not become semi-divine (compare 3.22–24) but remained a mortal creature in whom the LORD's *spirit* dwells temporarily (see 2.7 n.). **4:** Originally the story accounted for *the Nephilim* (Num.13.33; Dt.2.10–11), men of gigantic stature whose superhuman power was thought to result from divine-human marriage.

sorry that I have made them." [8] But Noah found favor in the eyes of the LORD.

9 These are the generations of Noah. Noah was a righteous man, blameless in his generation; Noah walked with God. [10] And Noah had three sons, Shem, Ham, and Japheth.

11 Now the earth was corrupt in God's sight, and the earth was filled with violence. [12] And God saw the earth, and behold, it was corrupt; for all flesh had corrupted their way upon the earth. [13] And God said to Noah, "I have determined to make an end of all flesh; for the earth is filled with violence through them; behold, I will destroy them with the earth. [14] Make yourself an ark of gopher wood; make rooms in the ark, and cover it inside and out with pitch. [15] This is how you are to make it: the length of the ark three hundred cubits, its breadth fifty cubits, and its height thirty cubits. [16] Make a roof[k] for the ark, and finish it to a cubit above; and set the door of the ark in its side; make it with lower, second, and third decks. [17] For behold, I will bring a flood of waters upon the earth, to destroy all flesh in which is the breath of life from under heaven; everything that is on the earth shall die. [18] But I will establish my covenant with you; and you shall come into the ark, you, your sons, your wife, and your sons' wives with you. [19] And of every living thing of all flesh, you shall bring two of every sort into the ark, to keep them alive with you; they shall be male and female. [20] Of the birds according to their kinds, and of the animals according to their kinds, and of the animals according to their kinds, of every creeping thing of the ground according to its kind, two of every sort shall come in to you, to keep them alive. [21] Also take with you every sort of food that is eaten, and store it up; and it shall serve as food for you and for them." [22] Noah did this; he did all that God commanded him.

7 Then the LORD said to Noah, "Go into the ark, you and all your household, for I have seen that you are righteous before me in this generation. [2] Take with you seven pairs of all clean animals, the male and his mate; and a pair of the animals that are not clean, the male and his mate; [3] and seven pairs of the birds of the air also, male and female, to keep their kind alive upon the face of all the earth. [4] For in seven days I will send rain upon the earth forty days and forty nights; and every living thing that I have made I will blot out from the face of the ground." [5] And Noah did all that the LORD had commanded him.

6 Noah was six hundred years old when the flood of waters came upon the earth. [7] And Noah and his sons and his wife and his sons' wives with him went into the ark, to escape the waters of the flood. [8] Of clean animals, and of animals that are not clean, and of birds, and of everything that creeps on the ground, [9] two and two, male and female, went into the ark with Noah, as God had commanded Noah. [10] And after seven days the waters of the flood came upon the earth.

k Or window

6.5–8.22: **The great flood.** God's judgment took the form of a destructive flood, and his mercy was shown in saving a remnant with whom he made a new historical beginning. **5–8:** An introduction, belonging to the old literary tradition found in 2.4b–3.24; 4.1–26; 6.1–4. **5:** The *heart* includes the will and reason, as shown by its capacity for *imagination* of thought. **7:** The Biblical account is superficially similar to the Babylonian Gilgamesh Epic. The Biblical perspective, however, is basically different, for the flood was not the expression of polytheistic caprice but of God's judgment upon the *wickedness of man.* **9:** Noah was *a righteous man,* i.e. he stood in right relationship to God (15.6). **11–22:** A parallel version. It is generally recognized that an earlier and a later (priestly) tradition have been combined. **11:** The earth, once seen to be "good" (1.31), is called *corrupt* owing to man's *violence* or wilful, lawless deeds. **14–16:** In the Babylonian epic too, the hero is commanded to build a houseboat, sealing it with pitch. **15:** The dimensions: about 450 × 75 × 45 feet.

7.1–10: This section is essentially a continuation of the early tradition (6.5–8). **2–3:** On clean and unclean animals, see Lev. ch. 11. (The priestly version mentions two animals of every sort [v.9; 6.19], presuming that the clean-unclean distinction was introduced at Sinai.) **4:** The flood was caused by heavy rainfall, lasting *forty days and forty nights*

11 In the six hundredth year of Noah's life, in the second month, on the seventeenth day of the month, on that day all the fountains of the great deep burst forth, and the windows of the heavens were opened. [12] And rain fell upon the earth forty days and forty nights. [13] On the very same day Noah and his sons, Shem and Ham and Japheth, and Noah's wife and the three wives of his sons with them entered the ark, [14] they and every beast according to its kind, and all the cattle according to their kinds, and every creeping thing that creeps on the earth according to its kind, and every bird according to its kind, every bird of every sort. [15] They went into the ark with Noah, two and two of all flesh in which there was the breath of life. [16] And they that entered, male and female of all flesh, went in as God had commanded him; and the LORD shut him in.

17 The flood continued forty days upon the earth; and the waters increased, and bore up the ark, and it rose high above the earth. [18] The waters prevailed and increased greatly upon the earth; and the ark floated on the face of the waters. [19] And the waters prevailed so mightily upon the earth that all the high mountains under the whole heaven were covered; [20] the waters prevailed above the mountains, covering them fifteen cubits deep. [21] And all flesh died that moved upon the earth, birds, cattle, beasts, all swarming creatures that swarm upon the earth, and every man; [22] everything on the dry land in whose nostrils was the breath of life died. [23] He blotted out every living thing that was upon the face of the ground, man and animals and creeping things and birds of the air; they were blotted out from the earth. Only Noah was left, and those that were with him in the ark. [24] And the waters prevailed upon the earth a hundred and fifty days.

8 But God remembered Noah and all the beasts and all the cattle that were with him in the ark. And God made a wind blow over the earth, and the waters subsided; [2] the fountains of the deep and the windows of the heavens were closed, the rain from the heavens was restrained, [3] and the waters receded from the earth continually. At the end of a hundred and fifty days the waters had abated; [4] and in the seventh month, on the seventeenth day of the month, the ark came to rest upon the mountains of Ar'arat. [5] And the waters continued to abate until the tenth month; in the tenth month, on the first day of the month, the tops of the mountains were seen.

6 At the end of forty days Noah opened the window of the ark which he had made, [7] and sent forth a raven; and it went to and fro until the waters were dried up from the earth. [8] Then he sent forth a dove from him, to see if the waters had subsided from the face of the ground; [9] but the dove found no place to set her foot, and she returned to him to the ark, for the waters were still on the face of the whole earth. So he put forth his hand and took her and brought her into the ark with him. [10] He waited another seven days, and again he sent forth the dove out of the ark; [11] and the dove came back to him in the evening, and lo, in her mouth a freshly plucked olive leaf; so Noah knew that the waters had subsided from the earth. [12] Then he waited another seven days, and sent forth the dove; and she did not return to him any more.

(v. 12; compare the difference in the priestly version, v. 24). **11–24:** Largely from the priestly tradition. **11:** Here the flood was not caused by a rain storm but was a cosmic catastrophe resulting from opening the *windows of the heavens* (or the firmament) and the upsurging of the *fountains of the great deep* (or the subterranean watery chaos; see 1.6–8 n.). Thus the earth was threatened with a return to pre-creation chaos (1.2). **15:** The animals went in *two by two* (6.19; see 7.2 n.). **16b:** *The LORD shut him in*, a note from the early tradition, which delights in anthropomorphic touches. **18–20:** The waters covered *all the high mountains*, thus threatening a confluence of the upper and lower waters (1.6). Archaeological evidence suggests that traditions of a prehistoric flood covering the whole earth are heightened versions of local inundations, e.g. in the Tigris-Euphrates basin. **8.1–5:** In the main a continuation of the priestly tradition. Because God *remembered Noah*, he stayed the cosmic destruction by water from above and below (v. 2a). **4:** In the Babylonian epic the boat also rested on a mountain. *Ararat* (2 Kg.19.37; Jer.51.27) is the name of a region in Armenia. **6–12:** Essentially from the early tradition. In the Babylonian epic the hero sent out two birds, a dove and a swallow,

13 In the six hundred and first year, in the first month, the first day of the month, the waters were dried from off the earth; and Noah removed the covering of the ark, and looked, and behold, the face of the ground was dry. 14 In the second month, on the twenty-seventh day of the month, the earth was dry. 15 Then God said to Noah, 16 "Go forth from the ark, you and your wife, and your sons and your sons' wives with you. 17 Bring forth with you every living thing that is with you of all flesh — birds and animals and every creeping thing that creeps on the earth — that they may breed abundantly on the earth, and be fruitful and multiply upon the earth." 18 So Noah went forth, and his sons and his wife and his sons' wives with him. 19 And every beast, every creeping thing, and every bird, everything that moves upon the earth, went forth by families out of the ark.

20 Then Noah built an altar to the LORD, and took of every clean animal and of every clean bird, and offered burnt offerings on the altar. 21 And when the LORD smelled the pleasing odor, the LORD said in his heart, "I will never again curse the ground because of man, for the imagination of man's heart is evil from his youth; neither will I ever again destroy every living creature as I have done. 22 While the earth remains, seedtime and harvest, cold and heat, summer and winter, day and night, shall not cease."

9 And God blessed Noah and his sons, and said to them, "Be fruitful and multiply, and fill the earth. 2 The fear of you and the dread of you shall be upon every beast of the earth, and upon every bird of the air, upon everything that creeps on the ground and all the fish of the sea; into your hand they are delivered. 3 Every moving thing that lives shall be food for you; and as I gave you the green plants, I give you everything. 4 Only you shall not eat flesh with its life, that is, its blood. 5 For your lifeblood I will surely require a reckoning; of every beast I will require it and of man; of every man's brother I will require the life of man. 6 Whoever sheds the blood of man, by man shall his blood be shed; for God made man in his own image. 7 And you, be fruitful and multiply, bring forth abundantly on the earth and multiply in it."

8 Then God said to Noah and to his sons with him. 9 "Behold, I establish my covenant with you and your descendants after you, 10 and with every living creature that is with you, the birds, the cattle, and every beast of the earth with you, as many as came out of the ark.^{l} 11 I establish my covenant with you, that never again shall all flesh be cut off by the waters of a flood, and never again shall there be a flood to destroy the earth." 12 And God said, "This is the sign of the covenant which I make between me and you and every living creature that is with you, for all future generations: 13 I set my bow in the cloud, and it shall be a sign of the covenant between me and the earth. 14 When I bring clouds over the earth

l Gk: Heb repeats *every beast of the earth*

each of which came back; the third, a raven, did not return. **13–19:** A continuation of the priestly account. **20–22:** The early tradition relates that Noah sacrificed *burnt offerings* (Lev. ch. 1) of clean animals (see 7.2–3 n.). In the Babylonian epic the hero offered sacrifices and "the gods smelt [compare v. 21] the goodly savor." For the curse, compare 3.17. Despite the evil *imagination of man's heart* (6.5), the LORD's steadfast mercy will be expressed in the regularities of nature, *seedtime and harvest,* etc.

9.1–19: God's covenant with Noah included all mankind under divine promise and law. **1:** The new age opened with a renewal of the blessing which had been given at creation (v. 7; compare 1.28). **3–6:** The command to exercise dominion (1.28–30) is qualified by the permission to eat animal flesh but not with *its life,* i.e. *its blood* (see 4.10–11 n.). The violence which had corrupted the earth (6.11) is restrained by a very old law against murder, the validity of which is grounded in the creation: man is made in God's *image* (1.26–27). These verses set forth the laws given to Noah, binding not only on Israel but on all men (Acts 15.20; 21.25). **8–11:** The preservation of the natural order from the waters of chaos is guaranteed by a *covenant* (see 17.2 n.). Unlike later covenants (ch. 17; Ex. ch. 24), this is a universal covenant with Noah, his *descendants,* and *every living creature,* for Noah's three sons (6.10; 9.18–19) are regarded as the ancestors of all the nations (see ch. 10). **13:** Ancients imagined the rainbow as God's weapon (bow) from which the lightnings of his arrows were shot (Ps.7.12–13; Hab.3.9–11). God places his weapon in the heavens as a *sign,* or visible token, that his wrath has abated.

and the bow is seen in the clouds, [15] I will remember my covenant which is between me and you and every living creature of all flesh; and the waters shall never again become a flood to destroy all flesh. [16] When the bow is in the clouds, I will look upon it and remember the everlasting covenant between God and every living creature of all flesh that is upon the earth." [17] God said to Noah, "This is the sign of the covenant which I have established between me and all flesh that is upon the earth."

18 The sons of Noah who went forth from the ark were Shem, Ham, and Japheth. Ham was the father of Canaan. [19] These three were the sons of Noah; and from these the whole earth was peopled.

20 Noah was the first tiller of the soil. He planted a vineyard; [21] and he drank of the wine, and became drunk, and lay uncovered in his tent. [22] And Ham, the father of Canaan, saw the nakedness of his father, and told his two brothers outside. [23] Then Shem and Japheth took a garment, laid it upon both their shoulders, and walked backward and covered the nakedness of their father; their faces were turned away, and they did not see their father's nakedness. [24] When Noah awoke from his wine and knew what his youngest son had done to him, [25] he said,

> "Cursed be Canaan;
>> a slave of slaves shall he be to his
>>> brothers."

[26] He also said,

> "Blessed by the LORD my God be Shem;[m]
>> and let Canaan be his slave.

[27] God enlarge Japheth,
>> and let him dwell in the tents of Shem;
>> and let Canaan be his slave."

28 After the flood Noah lived three hundred and fifty years. [29] All the days of Noah were nine hundred and fifty years; and he died.

m Or *Blessed be the* LORD, *the God of Shem*

9.18–27: Noah's curse upon Canaan. 20: In the new age, Noah was the *first tiller of the soil.* His success in agriculture fulfilled the prophecy made at his birth (5.29). **22:** Since the curse was later put on Canaan rather than Ham (v. 25), it is likely that Canaan was the actor originally. **24:** Here Noah's *youngest son* is clearly Canaan, not Ham as in v. 22. **25:** The curse implies that Canaan's subjugation to Israel was the result of Canaanite sexual perversions (Lev.18.24–30). **26:** *Shem,* 10.21. **27:** *Japheth,* 10.2–5. The verse may refer to the Philistines, one of the sea-peoples who dwelt *in the tents of Shem,* i.e. conquered the coast of Canaan.

Exodus

12 The LORD said to Moses and Aaron in the land of Egypt, 2 "This month shall be for you the beginning of months; it shall be the first month of the year for you. 3 Tell all the congregation of Israel that on the tenth day of this month they shall take every man a lamb according to their fathers' houses, a lamb for a household; 4 and if the household is too small for a lamb, then a man and his neighbor next to his house shall take according to the number of persons; according to what each can eat you shall make your count for the lamb. 5 Your lamb shall be without blemish, a male a year old; you shall take it from the sheep or from the goats; 6 and you shall keep it until the fourteenth day of this month, when the whole assembly of the congregation of Israel shall kill their lambs in the evening.*o* 7 Then they shall take some of the blood, and put it on the two doorposts and the lintel of the houses in which they eat them. 8 They shall eat the flesh that night, roasted; with unleavened bread and bitter herbs they shall eat it. 9 Do not eat any of it raw or boiled with water, but roasted, its head with its legs and its inner parts. 10 And you shall let none of it remain until the morning, anything that remains until the morning you shall burn. 11 In this manner you shall eat it: your loins girded, your sandals on your feet, and your staff in your hand; and you shall eat it in haste. It is the LORD's passover. 12 For I will pass through the land of Egypt that night, and I will smite all the firstborn in the land of Egypt, both man and beast; and on all the gods of Egypt I will execute judgments: I am the LORD. 13 The blood shall be a sign for you, upon the houses where you are; and when I see the blood, I will pass over

o Heb *between the two evenings*

12.1–28: The feasts of passover and unleavened bread. 1–13 (and vv. 43–49): This is priestly tradition concerning the passover, an ancient nomadic spring festival which Israel reinterpreted as a memorial of the LORD's deliverance of his people from Egypt (Dt.16.1–8; Num.9.1–14; Ezek.45.21–25). **2:** *This month* refers to Nisan (March–April) which in the post-exilic ecclesiastical calendar was *the beginning of months* (see Lev.23.5,23–25 n.). According to the older agricultural calendar, the new year began in the autumn (Ex.23.16; 34.22). **3–4:** Priestly tradition assumes that Israel in Egypt was already an organized *congregation* under the leadership of tribal princes (16.22). *Fathers' houses,* see Num.1.2–4 n. The passover was a nocturnal festival, celebrated during full moon (v. 8; see Is. 30.29). **7:** Blood, regarded as the deity's portion of the sacrifice (Lev.1.5), was smeared on the doorposts and the lintel, the holy places of the house (21.6; Dt.6.9), as a protection against the destroyer (vv. 22–23; see 4.24 n.). **11:** The feast must be eaten in readiness for the march, in commemoration of Israel's hasty exodus. **12–13:** Here *passover* is

Bible, THE NEW OXFORD ANNOTATED BIBLE WITH THE APOCRYPHA Revised Standard Edition, Exodus 12–24.

you, and no plague shall fall upon you to destroy you, when I smite the land of Egypt.

14 "This day shall be for you a memorial day, and you shall keep it as a feast to the LORD; throughout your generations you shall observe it as an ordinance for ever. [15] Seven days you shall eat unleavened bread; on the first day you shall put away leaven out of your houses, for if any one eats what is leavened, from the first day until the seventh day, that person shall be cut off from Israel. [16] On the first day you shall hold a holy assembly, and on the seventh day a holy assembly; no work shall be done on those days; but what every one must eat, that only may be prepared by you. [17] And you shall observe the feast of unleavened bread, for on this very day I brought your hosts out of the land of Egypt: therefore you shall observe this day, throughout your generations, as an ordinance for ever. [18] In the first month, on the fourteenth day of the month at evening, you shall eat unleavened bread, and so until the twenty-first day of the month at evening. [19] For seven days no leaven shall be found in your houses; for if any one eats what is leavened, that person shall be cut off from the congregation of Israel, whether he is a sojourner or a native of the land. [20] You shall eat nothing leavened; in all your dwellings you shall eat unleavened bread."

21 Then Moses called all the elders of Israel, and said to them, "Select lambs for yourselves according to your families, and kill the passover lamb. [22] Take a bunch of hyssop and dip it in the blood which is in the basin, and touch the lintel and the two doorposts with the blood which is in the basin; and none of you shall go out of the door of his house until the morning. [23] For the LORD will pass through to slay the Egyptians; and when he sees the blood on the lintel and on the two doorposts, the LORD will pass over the door, and will not allow the destroyer to enter your houses to slay you. [24] You shall observe this rite as an ordinance for you and for your sons for ever. [25] And when you come to the land which the LORD will give you, as he has promised, you shall keep this service. [26] And when your children say to you, 'What do you mean by this service?' [27] you shall say, 'It is the sacrifice of the LORD's passover, for he passed over the houses of the people of Israel in Egypt, when he slew the Egyptians but spared our houses.'" And the people bowed their heads and worshiped.

28 Then the people of Israel went and did so; as the LORD had commanded Moses and Aaron, so they did.

29 At midnight the LORD smote all the first-born in the land of Egypt, from the first-born of Pharaoh who sat on his throne to the first-born of the captive who was in the dungeon, and all the first-born of the cattle. [30] And Pharaoh rose up in the night, he, and all his servants, and all the Egyptians; and there was a great cry in Egypt, for there was not a house where one was not dead. [31] And he summoned Moses and Aaron by night, and said, "Rise up, go forth from among my people, both you and the people of Israel; and

---

interpreted from a verb meaning "to pass over," referring to the LORD's passing over Israelite houses during the plague of the first-born (vv. 24–27). **14–20:** The feast of unleavened cakes, originally an agricultural festival held at the time of barley harvest, was also converted into an historical commemoration and came to be closely connected with the passover (Dt.16.1–8; Ezek.45.21–25). **14:** The passover was celebrated on the 14th of Nisan (v. 6); *this day* refers to the 15th (Lev.23.6; Num.28.17). The seven day festival is regarded as a continuation of the passover. **15:** The absence of leaven (yeast) is interpreted as due to hasty preparations for flight (vv. 34,39; Dt.16.3). Originally leaven, owing to its fermenting or corrupting power (23.18; Mt.16.6; 1 Cor.5.7), was regarded as a ritually unclean substance (compare Lev.2.11) which could contaminate the whole harvest. **18:** So closely is the festival combined with the passover that it is said to begin on the evening of the 14th, i.e. the night of the passover (see v. 14). **21–28:** An older tradition concerning the passover. **22:** See v. 7 n. *Hyssop,* the foliage of an aromatic plant. Because of its presumed magical powers, it was used for ritual purposes (Lev.14.4; Num.19.6,18; Ps.51.7). **23:** *The destroyer,* or the angel of death (2 Sam.24.16; Is.37.36), was regarded as a manifestation of the LORD's power.

12.29–50: Israel's departure from Egypt. 29–32: The conclusion of the tenth plague (11.1–10). **33–34:** See v. 15 n. **35–36:** See 3.21–22 and 11.2–3. **37:** Rameses (1.11) and Succoth (13.20) were the starting places on Israel's itinerary

go, serve the LORD, as you have said. 32 Take your flocks and your herds, as you have said, and be gone; and bless me also!"

33 And the Egyptians were urgent with the people, to send them out of the land in haste; for they said, "We are all dead men." 34 So the people took their dough before it was leavened, their kneading bowls being bound up in their mantles on their shoulders. 35 The people of Israel had also done as Moses told them, for they had asked of the Egyptians jewelry of silver and of gold, and clothing; 36 and the LORD had given the people favor in the sight of the Egyptians, so that they let them have what they asked. Thus they despoiled the Egyptians.

37 And the people of Israel journeyed from Ram'eses to Succoth, about six hundred thousand men on foot, besides women and children. 38 A mixed multitude also went up with them, and very many cattle, both flocks and herds. 39 And they baked unleavened cakes of the dough which they had brought out of Egypt, for it was not leavened, because they were thrust out of Egypt and could not tarry, neither had they prepared for themselves any provisions.

40 The time that the people of Israel dwelt in Egypt was four hundred and thirty years. 41 And at the end of four hundred and thirty years, on that very day, all the hosts of the LORD went out from the land of Egypt. 42 It was a night of watching by the LORD, to bring them out of the land of Egypt; so this same night is a night by watching kept to the LORD by all the people of Israel throughout their generations.

43 And the LORD said to Moses and Aaron, "This is the ordinance of the passover: no foreigner shall eat of it; 44 but every slave that is bought for money may eat of it after you have circumcised him. 45 No sojourner or hired servant may eat of it. 46 In one house shall it be eaten; you shall not carry forth any of the flesh outside the house; and you shall not break a bone of it. 47 All the congregation of Israel shall keep it. 48 And when a stranger shall sojourn with you and would keep the passover to the LORD, let all his males be circumcised, then he may come near and keep it; he shall be as a native of the land. But no uncircumcised person shall eat of it. 49 There shall be one law for the native and for the stranger who sojourns among you."

50 Thus did all the people of Israel; as the LORD commanded Moses and Aaron, so they did. 51 And on that very day the LORD brought the people of Israel out of the land of Egypt by their hosts.

13 The LORD said to Moses, 2 "Consecrate to me all the first-born; whatever is the first to open the womb among the people of Israel, both of man and of beast, is mine."

3 And Moses said to the people, "Remember this day, in which you came out from Egypt, out of the house of bondage, for by strength of hand the LORD brought you out from this place; no leavened bread shall be eaten. 4 This day you are to go forth, in the month of Abib. 5 And when the LORD brings you into the land of the Canaanites, the Hittites,

---

(Num.33.5). *Six hundred thousand men on foot* (Num.11.21), in addition to women and children, is an exaggeration, for neither the land of Goshen nor the southern Palestinian wilderness could have supported so large a population (at least two and a half million). The number apparently reflects the census list in Num.1.17–46. **38:** The *mixed multitude* (Num.11.4) included other "Hebrews" (see 1.15 n.) or rootless people. **40:** If the four hundred and thirty years (see Gen.15.13; Acts 7.6 n.; Gal.3.17 n.) covers the total time of the Egyptian sojourn, then the descent into Egypt coincided with the Hyksos invasion (about 1720 B.C.; see Gen.45.10 n.) and the Exodus occurred during the reign of Rameses II, about 1290 B.C. (see 1.8 n.). **42:** The *night of watching* refers to the passover. **43–49:** A supplement to the priestly tradition about the passover (12.1–13). A *foreigner* (v. 43), a visiting *sojourner,* and a *hired servant* (v. 45) are excluded on the ground that they are related to other gods; however, the purchased slave who becomes a part of the family (v. 44) and the sojourner who resides permanently within Israel may eat the passover, if the *one law* of circumcision is kept (Gen.17.9–14).

13.1–16: The consecration of the first-born. 2: According to ancient belief, the devotion of the first-born of man and beast to God, the giver of fertility, was necessary for continuing increase and well-being (22.29b–30; Lev.27.26–27; Num.3.13; 8.17–18; 18.15). **3–10:** Old tradition about the feast of unleavened bread (compare the

the Amorites, the Hivites, and the Jeb′usites, which he swore to your fathers to give you, a land flowing with milk and honey, you shall keep this service in this month. [6] Seven days you shall eat unleavened bread, and on the seventh day there shall be a feast to the LORD. [7] Unleavened bread shall be eaten for seven days; no leavened bread shall be seen with you, and no leaven shall be seen with you in all your territory. [8] And you shall tell your son on that day, 'It is because of what the LORD did for me when I came out of Egypt.' [9] And it shall be to you as a sign on your hand and as a memorial between your eyes, that the law of the LORD may be in your mouth; for with a strong hand the LORD has brought you out of Egypt. [10] You shall therefore keep this ordinance at its appointed time from year to year.

[11] "And when the LORD brings you into the land of the Canaanites, as he swore to you and your fathers, and shall give it to you, [12] you shall set apart to the LORD all that first opens the womb. All the firstlings of your cattle that are males shall be the LORD's. [13] Every firstling of an ass you shall redeem with a lamb, or if you will not redeem it you shall break its neck. Every first-born of man among your sons you shall redeem. [14] And when in time to come your son asks you, 'What does this mean?' you shall say to him, 'By strength of hand the LORD brought us out of Egypt, from the house of bondage. [15] For when Pharaoh stubbornly refused to let us go, the LORD slew all the first-born in the land of Egypt, both the first-born of man and the first-born of cattle. Therefore I sacrifice to the LORD all the males that first open the womb; but all the first-born of my sons I redeem.' [16] It shall be as a mark on your hand or frontlets between your eyes; for by a strong hand the LORD brought us out of Egypt."

[17] When Pharaoh let the people go, God did not lead them by way of the land of the Philistines, although that was near; for God said, "Lest the people repent when they see war, and return to Egypt." [18] But God led the people round by the way of the wilderness toward the Red Sea. And the people of Israel went up out of the land of Egypt equipped for battle. [19] And Moses took the bones of Joseph with him; for Joseph had solemnly sworn the people of Israel, saying, "God will visit you; then you must carry my bones with you from here." [20] And they moved on from Succoth, and encamped at Etham, on the edge of the wilderness. [21] And the LORD went before them by day in a pillar of cloud to lead them along the way, and by night in a pillar of fire to give them light, that they might travel by day and by night; [22] the pillar of cloud by day and the pillar of fire by night did not depart from before the people.

14 Then the LORD said to Moses, [2] "Tell the people of Israel to turn back and encamp in front of Pi-ha-hi′roth, between Migdol and the sea, in front of Ba′al-ze′phon; you shall encamp over against it, by the sea. [3] For Pharaoh will say of the people of Israel, 'They are entangled in the land; the wilderness has shut them in.' [4] And I will harden

---

parallel priestly version, 12.14–20). **4:** *Abib,* the older name for the month of the Exodus (23.15; see 12.2 n.). **5:** See 3.8. **8:** In later times a man could tell *what the LORD did for me when I came out of Egypt,* for in worship the redemptive event was made present (12.26–27; see Dt.5.2–3 n.). **9:** See Dt.6.8. **11–16:** An old tradition about the consecration of the first-born. **13:** Unclean animals, of which the ass is typical (Lev. ch. 11; Dt. ch. 14), may be redeemed by substituting a lamb. In early times the custom arose of substituting an animal for the human first-born (34.19–20; compare Gen.22.13), although pagan human sacrifice persisted (1 Kg.16.34; 2 Kg.16.3; Ezek.20.26; Mic.6.7). **14–15:** The practice, rooted in ancient fertility beliefs, is here reinterpreted in the light of the Exodus.
    13.17–14.22. Israel's deliverance. 17–18: *Philistines,* see Gen.21.34 n. The route mentioned was the main military road into Canaan. To avoid attack, the people were providentially led *round by the way of the wilderness.* On the *Red Sea,* see 14.2 n. **19:** See Gen.50.25–26 n. **21–22:** The *pillar of cloud* and the *pillar of fire* may reflect the ancient custom of carrying a burning brazier at the head of a marching army or caravan to indicate the line of march by day and night. Whatever the nature of the phenomenon originally, cloud and fire have become traditional ways of expressing God's presence and guidance (see 3.2 n.; 19.9; 33.9; 40.34–38; 1 Kg.8.10–11). **14.2:** The places mentioned, like Etham (13.20), were probably Egyptian frontier fortresses. Apparently the Israelites were unable to break through and

Pharaoh's heart, and he will pursue them and I will get glory over Pharaoh and all his host; and the Egyptians shall know that I am the LORD." And they did so.

5 When the king of Egypt was told that the people had fled, the mind of Pharaoh and his servants was changed toward the people, and they said, "What is this we have done, that we have let Israel go from serving us?" 6 So he made ready his chariot and took his army with him, 7 and took six hundred picked chariots and all the other chariots of Egypt with officers over all of them. 8 And the LORD hardened the heart of Pharaoh king of Egypt and he pursued the people of Israel as they went forth defiantly. 9 The Egyptians pursued them, all Pharaoh's horses and chariots and his horsemen and his army, and overtook them encamped at the sea, by Pi-ha-hi′roth, in front of Ba′al-ze′phon.

10 When Pharaoh drew near, the people of Israel lifted up their eyes, and behold, the Egyptians were marching after them; and they were in great fear. And the people of Israel cried out to the LORD; 11 and they said to Moses, "Is it because there are no graves in Egypt that you have taken us away to die in the wilderness? What have you done to us, in bringing us out of Egypt? 12 Is not this what we said to you in Egypt, 'Let us alone and let us serve the Egyptians'? For it would have been better for us to serve the Egyptians than to die in the wilderness." 13 And Moses said to the people, "Fear not, stand firm, and see the salvation of the LORD, which he will work for you today; for the Egyptians whom you see today, you shall never see again. 14 The LORD will fight for you, and you have only to be still." 15 The LORD said to Moses, "Why do you cry to me? Tell the people of Israel to go forward. 16 Lift up your rod, and stretch out your hand over the sea and divide it, that the people of Israel may go on dry ground through the sea. 17 And I will harden the hearts of the Egyptians so that they shall go in after them, and I will get glory over Pharaoh and all his host, his chariots, and his horsemen. 18 And the Egyptians shall know that I am the LORD, when I have gotten glory over Pharaoh, his chariots, and his horsemen."

19 Then the angel of God who went before the host of Israel moved and went behind them; and the pillar of cloud moved from before them and stood behind them, 20 coming between the host of Egypt and the host of Israel. And there was the cloud and the darkness; and the night passed*p* without one coming near the other all night.

21 Then Moses stretched out his hand over the sea; and the LORD drove the sea back by a strong east wind all night, and made the sea dry land, and the waters were divided. 22 And the people of Israel went into the midst of the sea on dry ground, the waters being a wall to them on their right hand and on their left. 23 The Egyptians pursued, and went in after them into the midst of the sea, all Pharaoh's horses, his chariots, and his horsemen. 24 And in the morning watch the LORD in the pillar of fire and of cloud looked down upon the host of the Egyptians, and discomfited the host of the Egyptians, 25 clogging*q* their chariot wheels so that they drove heavily; and the Egyptians said, "Let us flee from before Israel; for the LORD fights for them against the Egyptians."

p Gk: Heb *and it lit up the night*
q Or *binding*. Sam Gk Syr: Heb *removing*

had to *turn back,* with the result that they were trapped (v. 3) between the water barrier and the Egyptian forces. *The sea,* known in Hebrew as the "sea of reeds," was not the Red Sea itself but a shallow body of water farther north, perhaps in the area of Lake Timsah. **11–12:** See 15.24 n. **13–14:** Viewed in faith, the victory was a mighty act of the LORD who was fighting for his people in a contest with the powerful Pharaoh (v. 25). *Salvation,* see Gen.49.18. **19–20:** One tradition expresses the divine presence as *the angel of God* (see Gen.16.7 n.), another as the shining pillar of cloud (v. 24; see 13.21–22 n.). **21–29:** The divine victory was rooted in a natural phenomenon: during a storm the shallow waters were driven back by *a strong east wind* (v. 21), making it possible for the Israelites to cross on foot. Egyptian chariots, however, were mired in the mud and engulfed by the returning waters. Tradition heightened the miracle by

26 Then the LORD said to Moses, "Stretch out your hand over the sea, that the water may come back upon the Egyptians, upon their chariots, and upon their horsemen." 27 So Moses stretched forth his hand over the sea, and the sea returned to its wonted flow when the morning appeared; and the Egyptians fled into it, and the LORD routed[r] the Egyptians in the midst of the sea. 28 The waters returned and covered the chariots and the horsemen and all the host[s] of Pharaoh that had followed them into the sea; not so much as one of them remained. 29 But the people of Israel walked on dry ground through the sea, the waters being a wall to them on their right hand and on their left.

30 Thus the LORD saved Israel that day from the hand of the Egyptians; and Israel saw the Egyptians dead upon the seashore. 31 And Israel saw the great work which the LORD did against the Egyptians, and the people feared the LORD; and they believed in the LORD and in his servant Moses.

15 Then Moses and the people of Israel sang this song to the LORD, saying,
"I will sing to the LORD, for he has
    triumphed gloriously;
  the horse and his rider[t] he has thrown
    into the sea.
2 The LORD is my strength and my song,
    and he has become my salvation;
  this is my God, and I will praise him,
    my father's God, and I will exalt him.
3 The LORD is a man of war;
    the LORD is his name.

4 "Pharaoh's chariots and his host he cast
    into the sea;
  and his picked officers are sunk in the
    Red Sea.

5 The floods cover them;
    they went down into the depths like
      a stone.
6 Thy right hand, O LORD, glorious in
      power,
    thy right hand, O LORD, shatters the
      enemy.
7 In the greatness of thy majesty thou
      overthrowest thy adversaries;
    thou sendest forth thy fury, it consumes
      them like stubble.
8 At the blast of thy nostrils the waters
      piled up,
    the floods stood up in a heap;
    the deeps congealed in the heart of the
      sea.
9 The enemy said, 'I will pursue, I will
      overtake,
    I will divide the spoil, my desire shall
      have its fill of them.
    I will draw my sword, my hand shall
      destroy them.'
10 Thou didst blow with thy wind, the sea
      covered them;
    they sank as lead in the mighty waters.

11 "Who is like thee, O LORD, among the
      gods?
    Who is like thee, majestic in holiness,
    terrible in glorious deeds, doing
      wonders?
12 Thou didst stretch out thy right hand,
    the earth swallowed them.

13 "Thou hast led in thy steadfast love the
      people whom thou hast redeemed,
    thou hast guided them by thy strength
      to thy holy abode.

r Heb shook off   s Gk Syr: Heb to all the host
t Or its chariot

attributing it to Moses' wonder-working rod (vv. 16,21a,26–27) and by saying that the waters stood up like walls (vv. 22b,29b).
   15.1–21: Two songs of praise which celebrate the LORD's deliverance of his people. **1:** The song of Moses (vv. 1–18) is introduced by quoting the ancient song of Miriam (v. 21). **2:** See 14.13–14 n. *My father's God* refers to "the God of the fathers" (3.6). **3:** *A man of war,* i.e. Divine Warrior (Ps.24.8). In the following vv. Canaanite mythical motifs are used to confess the Lord's saving action in behalf of Israel (14.14,25). **4–10:** Recital of the Divine Warrior's victory at the Sea (Ps.78.12–13). **8–10:** The language seems influenced by the myth of a divine battle against the *sea,* the chaotic power hostile to God's rule (see Ps.77.16–19; 114.3–6; Hab. 3.8–15). **11:** The LORD's *glorious deeds* demonstrate that he is incomparable *among the gods* who compose his heavenly council (Pss.86.8; 89.7–8; Gen.1.26 n.). **13–17:** The guidance into Canaan. **13:** *Thy holy abode,* i.e. Canaan (Ps.78.54). **14:** *Philistia* was settled by the

¹⁴ The peoples have heard, they tremble;
    pangs have seized on the inhabitants
        of Philistia.
¹⁵ Now are the chiefs of Edom dismayed;
    the leaders of Moab, trembling seizes
        them;
    all the inhabitants of Canaan have
        melted away.
¹⁶ Terror and dread fall upon them;
    because of the greatness of thy arm,
        they are as still as a stone,
    till thy people, O LORD, pass by,
        till the people pass by whom thou hast
            purchased.
¹⁷ Thou wilt bring them in, and plant them on
        thy own mountain,
    the place, O LORD, which thou hast
        made for thy abode,
    the sanctuary, O LORD, which thy hands
        have established.
¹⁸ The LORD will reign for ever and ever."

19 For when the horses of Pharaoh with his chariots and his horsemen went into the sea, the LORD brought back the waters of the sea upon them; but the people of Israel walked on dry ground in the midst of the sea. ²⁰ Then Miriam, the prophetess, the sister of Aaron, took a timbrel in her hand; and all the women went out after her with timbrels and dancing. ²¹ And Miriam sang to them:

"Sing to the LORD, for he has triumphed
        gloriously;
    the horse and his rider he has thrown into
        the sea."

22 Then Moses led Israel onward from the Red Sea, and they went into the wilderness of Shur; they went three days in the wilderness and found no water. ²³ When they came to Marah, they could not drink the water of Marah because it was bitter; therefore it was named Marah.*u* ²⁴ And the people murmured against Moses, saying, "What shall we drink?" ²⁵ And he cried to the LORD; and the LORD showed him a tree, and he threw it into the water, and the water became sweet.

There the LORD*v* made for them a statute and an ordinance and there he proved them, ²⁶ saying, "If you will diligently hearken to the voice of the LORD your God, and do that which is right in his eyes, and give heed to his commandments and keep all his statutes, I will put none of the diseases upon you which I put upon the Egyptians; for I am the LORD, your healer."

27 Then they came to Elim, where there were twelve springs of water and seventy palm trees; and they encamped there by the water.

16 They set out from Elim, and all the congregation of the people of Israel came to the wilderness of Sin, which is between Elim and Sinai, on the fifteenth day of the second month after they had departed from the land of Egypt. ² And the whole congregation of the people of Israel murmured against Moses and Aaron in the wilderness, ³ and said to them, "Would that we had died

u That is *Bitterness*   *v* Heb *he*

Philistines (Gen.21.32 n.) about 1175 B.C.; hence the poem was written afterwards. **15:** See Num.20.18–21; 21.13. **16:** *Purchased,* possibly "created." **17:** Canaan is described as the mythical cosmic mountain, Zaphon, where God has his *abode* and *sanctuary* (see Ps.48.1–3 n.). **19–21:** Miriam's victory dance. Miriam (Num.26.59) is called a prophetess (compare Jg.4.4) because of her ecstatic rousing of devotion to the LORD through song and dance. Compare 1 Sam.18.6–7). **21:** The Song of Miriam, one of the oldest poetic couplets in the Old Testament, was probably composed by an eyewitness of the event.
 15.22–16.36: Crises in the wilderness. In times of need, when faith was put to the test, Israel perceived signs of the LORD's care and protection. **22:** *The Wilderness of Shur,* identified with the wilderness of Etham in Num.33.8, was on the border of Egypt. **24:** Israel's continual murmuring in the wilderness is a dominant theme of the tradition (16.2–3; 17.3; 32.1–4,25; Num.11.4–6; 12.1–2; 14.2–3; 16.13–14; 20.2–13; 21.4–5). **25:** It was believed that the leaves or bark of certain trees had magical properties for sweetening or "healing" water (2 Kg.2.21). **26:** *Diseases,* i.e. the Egyptian plagues. *Your healer,* Num.21.4–9; Dt.7.15; Ps.103.3. **16.1–36:** The provision of food in the wilderness. **1:** *The wilderness of Sin* (17.1; Num.33.11–12), probably on the Sinaitic Peninsula. **3:** The murmuring wanderers

by the hand of the LORD in the land of Egypt, when we sat by the fleshpots and ate bread to the full; for you have brought us out into this wilderness to kill this whole assembly with hunger."

4 Then the LORD said to Moses, "Behold, I will rain bread from heaven for you; and the people shall go out and gather a day's portion every day, that I may prove them, whether they will walk in my law or not. [5] On the sixth day, when they prepare what they bring in, it will be twice as much as they gather daily." [6] So Moses and Aaron said to all the people of Israel, "At evening you shall know that it was the LORD who brought you out of the land of Egypt, [7] and in the morning you shall see the glory of the LORD, because he has heard your murmurings against the LORD. For what are we, that you murmur against us?" [8] And Moses said, "When the LORD gives you in the evening flesh to eat and in the morning bread to the full, because the LORD has heard your murmurings which you murmur against him — what are we? Your murmurings are not against us but against the LORD."

9 And Moses said to Aaron, "Say to the whole congregation of the people of Israel, 'Come near before the LORD, for he has heard your murmurings.'" [10] And as Aaron spoke to the whole congregation of the people of Israel, they looked toward the wilderness, and behold, the glory of the LORD appeared in the cloud. [11] And the LORD said to Moses, [12] "I have heard the murmurings of the people of Israel; say to them, 'At twilight you shall eat flesh, and in the morning you shall be filled with bread; then you shall know that I am the LORD your God.'"

13 In the evening quails came up and covered the camp; and in the morning dew lay round about the camp. [14] And when the dew had gone up, there was on the face of the wilderness a fine, flake-like thing, fine as hoarfrost on the ground. [15] When the people of Israel saw it, they said to one another, "What is it?"[w] For they did not know what it was. And Moses said to them, "It is the bread which the LORD has given you to eat. [16] This is what the LORD has commanded: 'Gather of it, every man of you, as much as he can eat; you shall take an omer apiece, according to the number of the persons whom each of you has in his tent.'" [17] And the people of Israel did so; they gathered, some more, some less. [18] But when they measured it with an omer, he that gathered much had nothing over, and he that gathered little had no lack; each gathered according to what he could eat. [19] And Moses said to them, "Let no man leave any of it till the morning." [20] But they did not listen to Moses; some left part of it till the morning, and it bred worms and became foul; and Moses was angry with them. [21] Morning by morning they gathered it, each as much as he could eat; but when the sun grew hot, it melted.

22 On the sixth day they gathered twice as much bread, two omers apiece; and when all the leaders of the congregation came and told Moses, [23] he said to them, "This is what the LORD has commanded: 'Tomorrow is a day of solemn rest, a holy sabbath to the LORD; bake what you will bake and boil what you will boil, and all that is left over lay by to be kept till the morning.'" [24] So they laid it by till the

w Or *"It is manna."* Heb *man hu*

---

preferred the seasoned food of *the fleshpots of Egypt* to the precarious freedom of the wilderness. **4:** *Prove,* i.e. test their faith by providing only a *portion* sufficient for one day (see Dt.8.3,16; Mt.6.11). **5:** See vv. 22–30. **6–7:** *At evening* when the quails come; *in the morning* when the manna is found (vv. 8,12). In the priestly view, *the glory of the LORD* was an envelope of light (associated with the pillar of cloud and fire; see 13.21–22 n.) which veiled his being. Though men could not see God they could behold the glory which signified his presence (40.34; Num.14.10b,22; 16.19; Ezek.11.23). **9–10:** *Before the LORD,* see vv. 33–34 n. **13–21:** An early tradition concerning the provision of bread (v. 15). **13:** On the quails, see Num.11.1–35. **14:** The description here (see also v. 31 and Num.11.7–9) corresponds fairly closely to the "honey-dew" excretion of two scale-insects which feed on the twigs of the tamarisk tree. **15:** The name of the food, *manna* (v. 31), is explained by an expression meaning "What is it?" For men of faith the answer was that the natural phenomenon was *bread which the LORD has given.* **22–36:** The provision of manna

morning, as Moses bade them; and it did not become foul, and there were no worms in it. 25 Moses said, "Eat it today, for today is a sabbath to the LORD; today you will not find it in the field. 26 Six days you shall gather it; but on the seventh day, which is a sabbath, there will be none." 27 On the seventh day some of the people went out to gather, and they found none. 28 And the LORD said to Moses, "How long do you refuse to keep my commandments and my laws? 29 See! The LORD has given you the sabbath, therefore on the sixth day he gives you bread for two days; remain every man of you in his place, let no man go out of his place on the seventh day." 30 So the people rested on the seventh day.

31 Now the house of Israel called its name manna; it was like coriander seed, white, and the taste of it was like wafers made with honey. 32 And Moses said, "This is what the LORD has commanded: 'Let an omer of it be kept throughout your generations, that they may see the bread with which I fed you in the wilderness, when I brought you out of the land of Egypt.'" 33 And Moses said to Aaron, "Take a jar, and put an omer of manna in it, and place it before the LORD, to be kept throughout your generations." 34 As the LORD commanded Moses, so Aaron placed it before the testimony, to be kept. 35 And the people of Israel ate the manna forty years, till they came to a habitable land; they ate the manna, till they came to the border of the land of Canaan. 36 (An omer is the tenth part of an ephah.)

17 All the congregation of the people of Israel moved on from the wilderness of Sin by stages, according to the commandment of the LORD, and camped at Reph'idim; but there was no water for the people to drink. 2 Therefore the people found fault with Moses, and said, "Give us water to drink." And Moses said to them, "Why do you find fault with me? Why do you put the LORD to the proof?" 3 But the people thirsted there for water, and the people murmured against Moses, and said, "Why did you bring us up out of Egypt, to kill us and our children and our cattle with thirst?" 4 So Moses cried to the LORD, "What shall I do with this people? They are almost ready to stone me." 5 And the LORD said to Moses, "Pass on before the people, taking with you some of the elders of Israel; and take in your hand the rod with which you struck the Nile, and go. 6 Behold, I will stand before you there on the rock at Horeb; and you shall strike the rock, and water shall come out of it, that the people may drink." And Moses did so, in the sight of the elders of Israel. 7 And he called the name of the place Massah[x] and Mer'ibah,[y] because of the fault-finding of the children of Israel, and because they put the LORD to the proof by saying, "Is the LORD among us or not?"

8 Then came Am'alek and fought with Israel at Reph'idim. 9 And Moses said to Joshua, "Choose for us men, and go out, fight with Am'alek; tomorrow I will stand on the top of the hill with the rod of God in my hand." 10 So Joshua did as Moses told him, and fought with Am'alek; and Moses, Aaron, and Hur went up to the top of the hill. 11 Whenever Moses held up his hand, Israel prevailed; and whenever he lowered his hand, Am'alek prevailed. 12 But Moses' hands grew weary; so they took a stone and put it under

x That is *Proof*   *y* That is *Contention*

---

is the occasion for the insertion of priestly teaching concerning the sabbath, *a day of solemn rest* (31.15; 35.2). **33–34:** *Before the LORD,* i.e. before the ark. In priestly tradition the ark is sometimes designated by its chief contents, *the Testimony* or tablets of law (27.21; Lev.16.13; Num.17.4).

17.1–16: Other trying experiences in the wilderness. 1–7: Israel's thirst was quenched with water from the rock (compare Num.20.2–13). **1:** *By stages,* see Num.33.1–49. **2–3:** See 15.24 n. *Put the LORD to proof,* i.e. challenged him to show that he was in their midst (v. 7b). **6:** Water lies below the limestone surface in the region of Sinai. **7:** The place is named both *Massah* from the Hebrew verb "test" and *Meribah* from the verb "find fault"— names which became memorials of Israel's faithlessness (Dt.6.16; 9.22; 33.8; Ps.95.8). Meribah was one of the springs at Kadesh (Num.20.13; 27.14; Dt.32.51). Marah (15.23) and Massah were evidently springs at the same oasis. Some traditions in 15.23–18.27 come from this oasis south of Beer-sheba (see Num.13.26 n.). **8–15:** The battle with the Amalekites.

him, and he sat upon it, and Aaron and Hur held up his hands, one on one side, and the other on the other side; so his hands were steady until the going down of the sun. [13] And Joshua mowed down Am′alek and his people with the edge of the sword.

14 And the LORD said to Moses, "Write this as a memorial in a book and recite it in the ears of Joshua, that I will utterly blot out the remembrance of Am′alek from under heaven." [15] And Moses built an altar and called the name of it, The LORD is my banner, [16] saying, "A hand upon the banner of the LORD![z] The LORD will have war with Am′alek from generation to generation."

18 Jethro, the priest of Mid′ian, Moses' father-in-law, heard of all that God had done for Moses and for Israel his people, how the LORD had brought Israel out of Egypt. [2] Now Jethro, Moses' father-in-law, had taken Zippo′rah, Moses' wife, after he had sent her away, [3] and her two sons, of whom the name of the one was Gershom (for he said, "I have been a sojourner[a] in a foreign land"), [4] and the name of the other, Elie′zer[b] (for he said, "The God of my father was my help, and delivered me from the sword of Pharaoh"). [5] And Jethro, Moses' father-in-law, came with his sons and his wife to Moses in the wilderness where he was encamped at the mountain of God. [6] And when one told Moses, "Lo,[c] your father-in-law Jethro is coming to you with your wife and her two sons with her," [7] Moses went out to meet his father-in-law, and did obeisance and kissed him; and they asked each other of their welfare, and went into the tent. [8] Then Moses told his father-in-law all that the LORD had done to Pharaoh and to the Egyptians for Israel's sake, all the hardship that had come upon them in the way, and how the LORD had delivered them. [9] And Jethro rejoiced for all the good which the LORD had done to Israel, in that he had delivered them out of the hand of the Egyptians.

10 And Jethro said, "Blessed be the LORD, who has delivered you out of the hand of the Egyptians and out of the hand of Pharaoh. [11] Now I know that the LORD is greater than all gods, because he delivered the people from under the hand of the Egyptians,[d] when they dealt arrogantly with them." [12] And Jethro, Moses' father-in-law, offered[e] a burnt offering and sacrifices to God; and Aaron came with all the elders of Israel to eat bread with Moses' father-in-law before God.

13 On the morrow Moses sat to judge the people, and the people stood about Moses from morning till evening. [14] When Moses' father-in-law saw all that he was doing for the people, he said, "What is this that you are doing for the people? Why do you sit alone, and all the people stand about you from morning till evening?" [15] And Moses said to his father-in-law, "Because the people come to me to inquire of God; [16] when they have a dis-

z Cn: Heb obscure   *a* Heb *ger*   *b* Heb *Eli*, my God, *ezer*, help   *c* Sam Gk Syr: Heb *I*   *d* Transposing the last clause of v. 10 to v. 11   *e* Syr Tg Vg: Heb *took*

8: The Amalekites, a fierce desert tribe, claimed control of the wilderness in the region of Kadesh (Gen.14.7; Num.13.29; 14.25). **9–13:** *Choose for us men* implies holy war (v. 16) with a select group (compare Jg. ch. 7). The young warrior, Joshua, here mentioned for the first time, was at the head of the Israelite army. Moses, however, led the battle from a hilltop and ensured victory by the power of his rod and outstretched arms and perhaps by the power of the curse (Num.22.4–6). **10:** *Hur*, elsewhere mentioned only in 24.14. **14:** *Utterly blot out*, i.e. the foe will be subjected to the sacrificial ban, a practice of holy war. **16:** The bitter feud with Amalek persisted (Num.24.20; Dt.25.17–19; 1 Sam.15.7–8; 27.8; ch. 30) until the foe was exterminated during the reign of Hezekiah (1 Chr.4.41–43).

18.1–27: Jethro's visit. The priest of Midian celebrated a sacred meal and counseled Moses about the administration of law. **1:** *Jethro*, see 2.18 n. **2–4:** Zipporah and her sons (2.21–22) apparently had been sent back from Egypt to Midian. **5:** The narrative is out of order, for Israel reached *the mountain of God* later (19.2). **9–12:** This passage may imply that the priest of Midian was already a worshiper of the LORD (see 3.1 n.). As the priest of the cult, Jethro came to rejoice in the LORD's great deeds and to officiate at a cultic celebration. **12:** *Eat bread*, an allusion to a sacred meal held *before God* (24.9–11). Moses was not invited, perhaps because he had already been initiated into the cult (3.1–6). **13–27:** Jethro's plan for the reorganization of legal administration (compare Dt.1.9–18). **13:** Like a bedouin chief,

pute, they come to me and I decide between a man and his neighbor, and I make them know the statutes of God and his decisions." [17] Moses' father-in-law said to him, "What you are doing is not good. [18] You and the people with you will wear yourselves out, for the thing is too heavy for you; you are not able to perform it alone. [19] Listen now to my voice; I will give you counsel, and God be with you! You shall represent the people before God, and bring their cases to God; [20] and you shall teach them the statutes and the decisions, and make them know the way in which they must walk and what they must do. [21] Moreover choose able men from all the people, such as fear God, men who are trustworthy and who hate a bribe; and place such men over the people as rulers of thousands, of hundreds, of fifties, and of tens. [22] And let them judge the people at all times; every great matter they shall bring to you, but any small matter they shall decide themselves; so it will be easier for you, and they will bear the burden with you. [23] If you do this, and God so commands you, then you will be able to endure, and all this people also will go to their place in peace."

24 So Moses gave heed to the voice of his father-in-law and did all that he had said. [25] Moses chose able men out of all Israel, and made them heads over the people, rulers of thousands, of hundreds, of fifties, and of tens. [26] And they judged the people at all times; hard cases they brought to Moses, but any small matter they decided themselves. [27] Then

Moses let his father-in-law depart, and he went his way to his own country.

19 On the third new moon after the people of Israel had gone forth out of the land of Egypt, on that day they came into the wilderness of Sinai. [2] And when they set out from Reph'-idim and came into the wilderness of Sinai, they encamped in the wilderness; and there Israel encamped before the mountain. [3] And Moses went up to God, and the LORD called to him out of the mountain, saying, "Thus you shall say to the house of Jacob, and tell the people of Israel: [4] You have seen what I did to the Egyptians, and how I bore you on eagles' wings and brought you to myself. [5] Now therefore, if you will obey my voice and keep my covenant, you shall be my own possession among all peoples; for all the earth is mine, [6] and you shall be to me a kingdom of priests and a holy nation. These are the words which you shall speak to the children of Israel."

7 So Moses came and called the elders of the people, and set before them all these words which the LORD had commanded him. [8] And all the people answered together and said, "All that the LORD has spoken we will do." And Moses reported the words of the people to the LORD. [9] And the LORD said to Moses, "Lo, I am coming to you in a thick cloud, that the people may hear when I speak with you, and may also believe you for ever."

Then Moses told the words of the people to the LORD. [10] And the LORD said to Moses,

Moses acted as judge in the people's disputes (2 Sam.15.1–6). **15–16:** *Inquire of God,* i.e. seek a verdict by oracle (Jg.4.4–5). **21–22:** Moses was to deal with cases without legal precedent which required a special oracle (compare Dt.17.8–13); ordinary cases were to be handled by lay leaders (Num.11.16–17, 24–25) or appointed judges (compare Dt.16.18–20). *Rulers of thousands,* see Num.1.17–46 n.

    19.1–25 (20.18–21): The theophany at Sinai. At the sacred mountain the LORD offered to make a covenant with Israel. **2:** *Sinai,* see 3.1 n. **3:** The account assumes that the LORD dwells in heaven, whence he "comes down" (v. 20; 3.8) to the mountain top for meeting with men (24.9–11). Compare the similar view reflected in the Babylonian temple-tower (Gen.11.1–9). **4:** *You have seen what I did,* the background and presupposition of the *covenant* (see Gen.17.2 n.) is the LORD's mighty acts of deliverance. *On eagles' wings,* Dt.32.11–12. **5:** On Israel's side, the covenant rests upon a condition, *if you will obey my voice* — an allusion to the covenant laws to be given. *My own possession,* or "treasure," is a metaphor for Israel's special relationship to God. In freedom and grace he chose this people for his own (Dt.7.6; 14.2; 26.18), though all the earth belongs to him (Ex.9.29b). **6:** That which is holy is set apart as belonging to God; thus Israel is to be *a kingdom of priests and a holy nation,* consecrated for his service (see Is.61.6; 1 Pet.2.5,9). **7–8:** Compare 24.7. **9:** This tradition stresses Moses' role as the covenant mediator whom the people are to believe *for ever* (20.19; 24.1–2,9–11). **10–15:** In this tradition all the people are to prepare for participation in the

"Go to the people and consecrate them today and tomorrow, and let them wash their garments, [11] and be ready by the third day; for on the third day the LORD will come down upon Mount Sinai in the sight of all the people. [12] And you shall set bounds for the people round about, saying, 'Take heed that you do not go up into the mountain or touch the border of it; whoever touches the mountain shall be put to death; [13] no hand shall touch him, but he shall be stoned or shot; whether beast or man, he shall not live.' When the trumpet sounds a long blast, they shall come up to the mountain." [14] So Moses went down from the mountain to the people, and consecrated the people; and they washed their garments. [15] And he said to the people, "Be ready by the third day; do not go near a woman."

16 On the morning of the third day there were thunders and lightnings, and a thick cloud upon the mountain, and a very loud trumpet blast, so that all the people who were in the camp trembled. [17] Then Moses brought the people out of the camp to meet God; and they took their stand at the foot of the mountain. [18] And Mount Sinai was wrapped in smoke, because the LORD descended upon it in fire; and the smoke of it went up like the smoke of a kiln, and the whole mountain quaked greatly. [19] And as the sound of the trumpet grew louder and louder, Moses spoke, and God answered him in thunder. [20] And the LORD came down upon Mount Sinai, to the top of the mountain; and the LORD called Moses to the top of the mountain, and Moses went up. [21] And the LORD said to Moses, "Go down and warn the people, lest they break through to the LORD to gaze and many of them perish. [22] And also let the priests who come near to the LORD consecrate themselves, lest the LORD break out upon them." [23] And Moses said to the LORD, "The people cannot come up to Mount Sinai; for thou thyself didst charge us, saying, 'Set bounds about the mountain, and consecrate it.'" [24] And the LORD said to him, "Go down, and come up bringing Aaron with you; but do not let the priests and the people break through to come up to the LORD, lest he break out against them." [25] So Moses went down to the people and told them.

20 And God spoke all these words, saying,

2 "I am the LORD your God, who brought you out of the land of Egypt, out of the house of bondage.

3 "You shall have no other gods before[f] me.

4 "You shall not make for yourself a graven image, or any likeness of anything that is in heaven above, or that is in the earth beneath, or that is in the water under the earth; [5] you shall not bow down to them or serve them; for I the LORD your God am a jealous God, visiting the iniquity of the fathers upon the children to the third and the fourth generation of those who hate me, [6] but showing steadfast love to thousands of those who love me and keep my commandments.

f Or besides

covenant ceremony (24.3–8). **12:** The setting of bounds so that the people do not come near the mountain (v. 21) reflects the ancient view of holiness as a mysterious, threatening power with which the mountain is charged (see 3.6 n.; 2 Sam.6.6–9). No hand may touch the offender who has become affected with the contagion of holiness (Lev.6.27–28). **14–15:** Washing or changing of garments (Gen.35.2) and sexual abstinence (1 Sam.21.4–6) were forms of ceremonial purification. **16–19:** The theophany is portrayed primarily in the imagery of a violent thunderstorm (Jg.5.4–5; Pss.18.7–15; 29.3–9; etc.). This traditional language — "earthquake, wind, and fire" (1 Kg.19.11–13) — depicts the wonder and majesty of God's revelation. **16:** The trumpet (v. 13) was sounded on cultic occasions (2 Sam.6.15).

20.1–17: The Ten Commandments, the epitome of man's duties toward God and his neighbor. **1:** _These words,_ i.e. "the ten words" or the Decalogue (34.28; Dt.4.13; 10.4). Originally each commandment was a short utterance (see vv. 13,14,15), lacking the explanatory comments found, e.g. in vv. 5,6,9–11. **2:** Jewish tradition considers this to be the first commandment. Actually it is a preface which summarizes the meaning of the Exodus, thus setting law within the context of God's redemptive action. **3:** The first commandment asserts that for Israel there shall be no other gods, because the LORD is _a jealous God_ (v. 5; 34.14) who will tolerate no rivals for his people's devotion. **4–6:** Imageless worship of the LORD made Israel's faith unique in the ancient world where natural powers were personified and statues

7 "You shall not take the name of the LORD your God in vain; for the LORD will not hold him guiltless who takes his name in vain.

8 "Remember the sabbath day, to keep it holy. ⁹ Six days you shall labor, and do all your work; ¹⁰ but the seventh day is a sabbath to the LORD your God; in it you shall not do any work, you, or your son, or your daughter, your manservant, or your maidservant, or your cattle, or the sojourner who is within your gates; ¹¹ for in six days the LORD made heaven and earth, the sea, and all that is in them, and rested the seventh day; therefore the LORD blessed the sabbath day and hallowed it.

12 "Honor your father and your mother, that your days may be long in the land which the LORD your God gives you.

13 "You shall not kill.

14 "You shall not commit adultery.

15 "You shall not steal.

16 "You shall not bear false witness against your neighbor.

17 "You shall not covet your neighbor's house; you shall not covet your neighbor's wife, or his manservant, or his maidservant, or his ox, or his ass, or anything that is your neighbor's."

18 Now when all the people perceived the thunderings and the lightnings and the sound of the trumpet and the mountain smoking, the people were afraid and trembled; and they stood afar off, ¹⁹ and said to Moses, "You speak to us, and we will hear; but let not God speak to us, lest we die." ²⁰ And Moses said to the people, "Do not fear; for God has come to prove you, and that the fear of him may be before your eyes, that you may not sin."

21 And the people stood afar off, while Moses drew near to the thick darkness where God was. ²² And the LORD said to Moses, "Thus you shall say to the people of Israel: 'You have seen for yourselves that I have talked with you from heaven. ²³ You shall not make gods of silver to be with me, nor shall you make for yourselves gods of gold. ²⁴ An altar of earth you shall make for me and sacrifice on it your burnt offerings and your peace offerings, your sheep and your oxen; in every place where I cause my name to be remembered I will come to you and bless you. ²⁵ And if you make me an altar of stone, you shall not build it of hewn stones; for if you wield your tool upon it you profane it. ²⁶ And you shall not go up by steps to my altar, that your nakedness be not exposed on it.'

21 "Now these are the ordinances which you shall set before them. ² When you buy a Hebrew slave, he shall serve six years, and in the seventh he shall go out free, for nothing. ³ If he comes in single, he shall go

---

of them (animal or human) were worshiped. Some interpreters consider vv. 3–6 as one commandment and divide v. 17 into two commandments. **7:** The third commandment prohibits the misuse of the LORD's name in magic, divination, or false swearing (Lev.19.12). It reflects the ancient view that knowledge of the name could be used to exert magical control (see Gen.32.27,29 n.). **8–11:** Keeping the sabbath *holy* means to observe it as a day separated from others, a segment of time belonging especially to God. **10:** 16.22–30. **11:** Compare Dt.5.15. **12:** 21.15,17; Dt.27.16. **13:** This commandment forbids murder (see Gen.9.5,6 n.), not the forms of killing authorized for Israel, e.g. war or capital punishment. **16:** This law demands telling the truth in a law suit involving the neighbor (23.1; Dt.19.15–21; 1 Kg.21.8–14). **17:** Some regard the first sentence as a separate commandment; however, *neighbor's house* probably includes what is enumerated in the second part of the verse: wife, manservant, etc. **18–21:** The conclusion to the theophany scene (ch. 19). The people request that Moses be the covenant mediator (see 19.9 n.) so that they need not hear God's law directly (compare Dt.5.4–5).

20.22–23.33: The Covenant Code. These laws are largely neutral in regard to Israelite faith and presuppose a settled agricultural society. They reflect a situation after Israel's invasion of Canaan, when prevailing laws were borrowed and adapted to the covenant tradition. **22–26:** Cultic regulations. **23:** See 20.4–6 n. **24–26:** The Israelite altar, in contrast to pagan models, is to be the simplest kind and is to be built wherever the LORD *causes his name to be remembered,* i.e. chooses to reveal himself. Contrast the reform demanded in Dt.12.5–14. **21.1–11:** The rights of a slave (compare Dt.15.12–18). **1:** *Ordinances* refers to laws formulated (usually in the third person) to deal with various cases, in contrast to the apodictic or unconditional law of the Israelite theocracy (e.g. the Decalogue). These case laws reflect the agricultural way of life in Canaan (e.g. 22.5–6) and are similar in style and content to other legal codes of the ancient Near East. **2:** *Hebrew,* see Ex.1.15 n. An Israelite could go into servitude because of debts (Ex.22.1;

out single; if he comes in married, then his wife shall go out with him. [4] If his master gives him a wife and she bears him sons or daughters, the wife and her children shall be her master's and he shall go out alone. [5] But if the slave plainly says, 'I love my master, my wife, and my children; I will not go out free,' [6] then his master shall bring him to God, and he shall bring him to the door or the doorpost; and his master shall bore his ear through with an awl; and he shall serve him for life.

[7] "When a man sells his daughter as a slave, she shall not go out as the male slaves do. [8] If she does not please her master, who has designated her[g] for himself, then he shall let her be redeemed; he shall have no right to sell her to a foreign people, since he has dealt faithlessly with her. [9] If he designates her for his son, he shall deal with her as with a daughter. [10] If he takes another wife to himself, he shall not diminish her food, her clothing, or her marital rights. [11] And if he does not do these three things for her, she shall go out for nothing, without payment of money.

[12] "Whoever strikes a man so that he dies shall be put to death. [13] But if he did not lie in wait for him, but God let him fall into his hand, then I will appoint for you a place to which he may flee. [14] But if a man willfully attacks another to kill him treacherously, you shall take him from my altar, that he may die.

[15] "Whoever strikes his father or his mother shall be put to death.

[16] "Whoever steals a man, whether he sells him or is found in possession of him, shall be put to death.

[17] "Whoever curses his father or his mother shall be put to death.

[18] "When men quarrel and one strikes the other with a stone or with his fist and the man does not die but keeps his bed, [19] then if the man rises again and walks abroad with his staff, he that struck him shall be clear; only he shall pay for the loss of his time, and shall have him thoroughly healed.

[20] "When a man strikes his slave, male or female, with a rod and the slave dies under his hand, he shall be punished. [21] But if the slave survives a day or two, he is not to be punished; for the slave is his money.

[22] "When men strive together, and hurt a woman with child, so that there is a miscarriage, and yet no harm follows, the one who hurt her shall[h] be fined, according as the woman's husband shall lay upon him; and he shall pay as the judges determine. [23] If any harm follows, then you shall give life for life, [24] eye for eye, tooth for tooth, hand for hand, foot for foot, [25] burn for burn, wound for wound, stripe for stripe.

[26] "When a man strikes the eye of his slave, male or female, and destroys it, he shall let the slave go free for the eye's sake. [27] If he knocks out the tooth of his slave, male or female, he shall let the slave go free for the tooth's sake.

[28] "When an ox gores a man or a woman to death, the ox shall be stoned, and its flesh shall not be eaten; but the owner of the ox shall be clear. [29] But if the ox has been accustomed to gore in the past, and its owner has been warned but has not kept it in, and it kills a man or a woman, the ox shall be stoned, and its owner also shall be put to death. [30] If a

g Another reading is *so that he has not designated her*
h Heb *he shall*

Lev.25.39; 2 Kg.4.1). **6:** *To God,* i.e. the legal act had to be performed at the sacred doorpost of the house (see 12.7 n.), perhaps in the presence of the household gods (Gen.31.19). **7–11:** The rights of a female slave or concubine (compare Dt.15.12,17). **8:** *Redeemed,* i.e. by a relative or another buyer who pays the purchase price.

21.12–32: Laws protecting human beings. 12–14: A distinction is drawn between intentional and unintentional murder. As protection from the swift justice of the blood-avenger, the man-slayer is guaranteed asylum (Num.35.12; Dt.4.41–43; 19.1–13; Jos. ch. 20), so that the case may be adjudicated soberly by legal authorities. The asylum in ancient times was at the altar (1 Kg.2.28–34). **17:** The curse, according to ancient belief, released an inexorable power (Num.22.6), thus making it as serious to curse parents as to strike them. **22–25:** This lex talionis (see Lev.24.20) was not an expression of vengeance but a limitation upon measureless vengeance.

ransom is laid on him, then he shall give for the redemption of his life whatever is laid upon him. [31] If it gores a man's son or daughter, he shall be dealt with according to this same rule. [32] If the ox gores a slave, male or female, the owner shall give to their master thirty shekels of silver, and the ox shall be stoned.

33 "When a man leaves a pit open, or when a man digs a pit and does not cover it, and an ox or an ass falls into it, [34] the owner of the pit shall make it good; he shall give money to its owner, and the dead beast shall be his.

35 "When one man's ox hurts another's, so that it dies, then they shall sell the live ox and divide the price of it; and the dead beast also they shall divide. [36] Or if it is known that the ox has been accustomed to gore in the past, and its owner has not kept it in, he shall pay ox for ox, and the dead beast shall be his.

22 [i] "If a man steals an ox or a sheep, and kills it or sells it, he shall pay five oxen for an ox, and four sheep for a sheep.[j] He shall make restitution; if he has nothing, then he shall be sold for his theft. [4] If the stolen beast is found alive in his possession, whether it is an ox or an ass or a sheep, he shall pay double.

2[k] "If a thief is found breaking in, and is struck so that he dies, there shall be no bloodguilt for him; [3] but if the sun has risen upon him, there shall be bloodguilt for him.

5 "When a man causes a field or vineyard to be grazed over, or lets his beast loose and it feeds in another man's field, he shall make restitution from the best in his own field and in his own vineyard.

6 "When fire breaks out and catches in thorns so that the stacked grain or the standing grain or the field is consumed, he that kindled the fire shall make full restitution.

7 "If a man delivers to his neighbor money or goods to keep, and it is stolen out of the man's house, then, if the thief is found, he shall pay double. [8] If the thief is not found, the owner of the house shall come near to God, to show whether or not he has put his hand to his neighbor's goods.

9 "For every breach of trust, whether it is for ox, for ass, for sheep, for clothing, or for any kind of lost thing, of which one says, 'This is it,' the case of both parties shall come before God; he whom God shall condemn shall pay double to his neighbor.

10 "If a man delivers to his neighbor an ass or an ox or a sheep or any beast to keep, and it dies or is hurt or is driven away, without any one seeing it, [11] an oath by the LORD shall be between them both to see whether he has not put his hand to his neighbor's property; and the owner shall accept the oath, and he shall not make restitution. [12] But if it is stolen from him, he shall make restitution to its owner. [13] If it is torn by beasts, let him bring it as evidence; he shall not make restitution for what has been torn.

14 "If a man borrows anything of his neighbor, and it is hurt or dies, the owner not being with it, he shall make full restitution. [15] If the owner was with it, he shall not make restitution; if it was hired, it came for its hire.[l]

16 "If a man seduces a virgin who is not betrothed, and lies with her, he shall give the marriage present for her, and make her his wife. [17] If her father utterly refuses to give her to him, he shall pay money equivalent to the marriage present for virgins.

i Ch 21.37 in Heb
j Restoring the second half of verse 3 with 4 to their place immediately following verse 1
k Ch 22.1 in Heb
l Or *it is reckoned in* (Heb *comes into*) *its hire*

21.33–22.17: Laws dealing with property. 33–36: These laws establish responsibility in cases of carelessness. **22:1–4:** Case laws regulating stealing. **2–3:** These verses may mean that if the invader is caught in the act (at night) he may be slain with impunity, but if he is slain in broad daylight there is blood guilt. **5–6:** Cases of neglect. **7–15:** Cases involving trusteeship. **9:** *Before God* (v. 8), i.e. to the sanctuary (possibly to the doorpost; 21.6) for an oracular decision or the sacred oath (v. 11; 1 Kg.8.31–32). **16–17:** This law is included here because it deals with a financial matter, the *marriage present* (Dt.22.29). Laws concerning sexual relations are found in Dt.22.13–30.

18 "You shall not permit a sorceress to live.

19 "Whoever lies with a beast shall be put to death.

20 "Whoever sacrifices to any god, save to the LORD only, shall be utterly destroyed.

21 "You shall not wrong a stranger or oppress him, for you were strangers in the land of Egypt. [22] You shall not afflict any widow or orphan. [23] If you do afflict them, and they cry out to me, I will surely hear their cry; [24] and my wrath will burn, and I will kill you with the sword, and your wives shall become widows and your children fatherless.

25 "If you lend money to any of my people with you who is poor, you shall not be to him as a creditor, and you shall not exact interest from him. [26] If ever you take your neighbor's garment in pledge, you shall restore it to him before the sun goes down; [27] for that is his only covering, it is his mantle for his body; in what else shall he sleep? And if he cries to me, I will hear, for I am compassionate.

28 "You shall not revile God, nor curse a ruler of your people.

29 "You shall not delay to offer from the fulness of your harvest and from the outflow of your presses.

"The first-born of your sons you shall give to me. [30] You shall do likewise with your oxen and with your sheep: seven days it shall be with its dam; on the eighth day you shall give it to me.

31 "You shall be men consecrated to me; therefore you shall not eat any flesh that is torn by beasts in the field; you shall cast it to the dogs.

23 "You shall not utter a false report. You shall not join hands with a wicked man, to be a malicious witness. [2] You shall not follow a multitude to do evil; nor shall you bear witness in a suit, turning aside after a multitude, so as to pervert justice; [3] nor shall you be partial to a poor man in his suit.

4 "If you meet your enemy's ox or his ass going astray, you shall bring it back to him. [5] If you see the ass of one who hates you lying under its burden, you shall refrain from leaving him with it, you shall help him to lift it up.[m]

6 "You shall not pervert the justice due to your poor in his suit. [7] Keep far from a false charge, and do not slay the innocent and righteous, for I will not acquit the wicked. [8] And you shall take no bribe, for a bribe blinds the officials, and subverts the cause of those who are in the right.

9 "You shall not oppress a stranger; you know the heart of a stranger, for you were strangers in the land of Egypt.

10 "For six years you shall sow your land and gather in its yield; [11] but the seventh year you shall let it rest and lie fallow, that the poor of your people may eat; and what they leave the wild beasts may eat. You shall do likewise with your vineyard, and with your olive orchard.

12 "Six days you shall do your work, but on the seventh day you shall rest; that your ox and your ass may have rest, and the son of your bondmaid, and the alien, may be refreshed. [13] Take heed to all that I have said to you; and make no mention of the names of other gods, nor let such be heard out of your mouth.

l Or *it is reckoned in* (Heb *comes into*) *its hire*
m Gk: Heb obscure

22.18–23.9: Miscellaneous social and cultic laws. The laws of vv. 18–20 (compare 21.12,15–17) are in the unconditional style of the Decalogue. **20:** Compare 20.3; Dt.13.12–18. **21–27:** Israel's God is the protector of the legally defenseless: the stranger (sojourner), orphan, widow, and poor. **25:** Being a farming people, Israel frowned upon the mercantile way of life (Hos.12.7–8) and specifically upon the exaction of interest from a fellow-Israelite (Lev.25.35–38). **26:** A loan with a garment as security could only be for the day, lest a poor man suffer (Dt.24.12–13; Am.2.8). **28:** Lev.24.15–16; 2 Sam.16.9; 1 Kg.2.8–9; 21.10. **29–30:** See 13.2 n. **31:** Flesh torn by beasts was regarded as unclean because it was not properly drained of blood (Lev.7.24; 17.15). **23.1–9:** Laws expounding Israel's sense of justice. **4–5:** Justice extends even to helping *your enemy* (Dt.22.1–4).

23.10–19: A cultic calendar (34.18–26; Lev.23.1–44; Dt.16.1–17). **10–11:** See Lev.25.2–7. **12:** Here the observance of the sabbath is based upon humanitarian concern (compare 20.11). **14–17:** This law reflects the practice of

14 "Three times in the year you shall keep a feast to me. [15] You shall keep the feast of unleavened bread; as I commanded you, you shall eat unleavened bread for seven days at the appointed time in the month of Abib, for in it you came out of Egypt. None shall appear before me empty-handed. [16] You shall keep the feast of harvest, of the first fruits of your labor, of what you sow in the field. You shall keep the feast of ingathering at the end of the year, when you gather in from the field the fruit of your labor. [17] Three times in the year shall all your males appear before the Lord GOD.

18 "You shall not offer the blood of my sacrifice with leavened bread, or let the fat of my feast remain until the morning.

19 "The first of the first fruits of your ground you shall bring into the house of the LORD your God.

"You shall not boil a kid in its mother's milk.

20 "Behold, I send an angel before you, to guard you on the way and to bring you to the place which I have prepared. [21] Give heed to him and hearken to his voice, do not rebel against him, for he will not pardon your transgression; for my name is in him.

22 "But if you hearken attentively to his voice and do all that I say, then I will be an enemy to your enemies and an adversary to your adversaries.

23 "When my angel goes before you, and brings you in to the Amorites, and the Hittites, and the Per'izzites, and the Canaanites, the Hivites, and the Jeb'usites, and I blot them out, [24] you shall not bow down to their gods, nor serve them, nor do according to their works, but you shall utterly overthrow them and break their pillars in pieces. [25] You shall serve the LORD your God, and I[n] will bless your bread and your water; and I will take sickness away from the midst of you. [26] None shall cast her young or be barren in your land; I will fulfil the number of your days. [27] I will send my terror before you, and will throw into confusion all the people against whom you shall come, and I will make all your enemies turn their backs to you. [28] And I will send hornets before you, which shall drive out Hivite, Canaanite, and Hittite from before you. [29] I will not drive them out from before you in one year, lest the land become desolate and the wild beasts multiply against you. [30] Little by little I will drive them out from before you, until you are increased and possess the land. [31] And I will set your bounds from the Red Sea to the sea of the Philistines, and from the wilderness to the Euphra'tes; for I will deliver the inhabitants of the land into your hand, and you shall drive them out before you. [32] You shall make no covenant with them or with their gods. [33] They shall not dwell in your land, lest they make you sin against me; for if you serve their gods, it will surely be a snare to you."

24 And he said to Moses, "Come up to the LORD, you and Aaron, Nadab, and Abi'hu, and seventy of the elders of Israel, and worship afar off. [2] Moses alone shall come

n Gk Vg: Heb *he*

making a pilgrimage to the central sanctuary of the tribal confederacy (1 Sam.1.3,21). **15:** *Empty-handed,* i.e. without a gift of the first fruits of the barley harvest. **16:** The *feast of harvest,* i.e. the feast of weeks (or pentecost, see Lev.23.15–21 n.) which was celebrated at the time of the wheat harvest (June). The third feast, *the feast of ingathering,* or feast of booths, was celebrated *at the end of the year* (autumn), according to the old agricultural calendar (see 12.2 n.), when fruit, grapes, and olives were harvested. **17:** According to ancient practice, men were the chief participants in the cult (34.23; see 10.7–11 n.). **18–19:** 34.25–26. The prohibition against seething a kid in its mother's milk (Dt.14.21) is a protest against a Canaanite method of preparing a sacrifice.

23.20–33: The conclusion to the Covenant Code (beginning 20.22). **20–21:** The *angel* is the LORD himself (14.19; see Gen.16.7 n.). On *the name,* see Gen.32.27 n. **27.28:** Here the language of "holy war" is used. *Terror,* Gen.35.5 n. The term *hornets* apparently is used figuratively to portray the panic aroused in holy war (Dt.7.20; Jos.24.12 n.).

24.1–18: The ceremony of covenant ratification. 1–2: This tradition is continued in vv. 9–11. *Moses alone,* an indication of Moses' special role as covenant mediator (19.9; 20.19). **3–8:** The first version of the covenant ceremony

near to the LORD; but the others shall not come near, and the people shall not come up with him."

3 Moses came and told the people all the words of the LORD and all the ordinances; and all the people answered with one voice, and said, "All the words which the LORD has spoken we will do." [4] And Moses wrote all the words of the LORD. And he rose early in the morning, and built an altar at the foot of the mountain, and twelve pillars, according to the twelve tribes of Israel. [5] And he sent young men of the people of Israel, who offered burnt offerings and sacrificed peace offerings of oxen to the LORD. [6] And Moses took half of the blood and put it in basins, and half of the blood he threw against the altar. [7] Then he took the book of the covenant, and read it in the hearing of the people; and they said, "All that the LORD has spoken we will do, and we will be obedient." [8] And Moses took the blood and threw it upon the people, and said, "Behold the blood of the covenant which the LORD has made with you in accordance with all these words."

9 Then Moses and Aaron, Nadab, and Abi'hu, and seventy of the elders of Israel went up, [10] and they saw the God of Israel; and there was under his feet as it were a pavement of sapphire stone, like the very heaven for clearness. [11] And he did not lay his hand on the chief men of the people of Israel; they beheld God, and ate and drank.

12 The LORD said to Moses, "Come up to me on the mountain, and wait there; and I will give you the tables of stone, with the law and the commandment, which I have written for their instruction." [13] So Moses rose with his servant Joshua, and Moses went up into the mountain of God. [14] And he said to the elders, "Tarry here for us, until we come to you again; and, behold, Aaron and Hur are with you; whoever has a cause, let him go to them."

15 Then Moses went up on the mountain, and the cloud covered the mountain. [16] The glory of the LORD settled on Mount Sinai, and the cloud covered it six days; and on the seventh day he called to Moses out of the midst of the cloud. [17] Now the appearance of the glory of the LORD was like a devouring fire on the top of the mountain in the sight of the people of Israel. [18] And Moses entered the cloud, and went up on the mountain. And Moses was on the mountain forty days and forty nights.

---

stresses the people's participation (19.10–15). **3:** *The words,* i.e. the Decalogue; *the ordinances,* i.e. the laws of the Covenant Code (see 21.1 n.). **4:** The participation of all the people is symbolized by *twelve pillars,* one for each tribe. **5:** On the types of sacrifice, see Lev. chs. 1 and 3. **6–8:** The ritual dramatizes the uniting of the two parties: the LORD, whose presence is represented by the altar, and the people. Compare the ancient covenant ceremony found in Gen. ch. 15. **7:** *The book of the covenant* (Jos.24.25–26) apparently contained the covenant laws, here tacitly identified with *the words* and *the ordinances* (v. 3). **8:** *The blood of the covenant* (compare Mt.26.28; 1 Cor.11.25) reflects the ancient view that blood was efficacious in establishing community between God and man (see Lev.1.5 n.). **9–11:** The second version of the covenant ceremony (continuing vv. 1–2). **9:** The people did not take part but were represented by the seventy *elders* or *chief men.* Moses, the covenant mediator, was accompanied by the priestly family, Aaron, Nadab, and Abihu (6.14–25; Lev, 10.1–3). **10:** The leaders did not see God directly; they saw only the lower part of his heavenly throne-room — the sapphire pavement (the firmament) above which the LORD was enthroned (compare Is.6.1; Ezek.1.1,26–28). **11:** Unharmed by divine holiness (see 3.6 n.), the leaders partook of the covenant meal (18.12). **12–14:** A separate tradition about the gift of *the tables of stone* on which the Decalogue was written (32.15; 34.28; Dt.9.9,11,15). **14:** 18.16. This verse sets the stage for the episode of ch. 32. *Hur,* see 17.10 n. **15–18:** This theophany introduces the priestly material of chs. 25–31, which apparently has replaced the early tradition about Moses making the ark and putting the tables of law in it (Dt.10.1–5). *The glory,* see 16.6–7 n.

The Book of Job

THERE WAS A MAN IN THE LAND OF UZ, whose name was Job; and that man was blameless and upright, one who feared God, and turned away from evil. ² There were born to him seven sons and three daughters. ³ He had seven thousand sheep, three thousand camels, five hundred yoke of oxen, and five hundred she-asses, and very many servants; so that this man was the greatest of all the people of the east. ⁴ His sons used to go and hold a feast in the house of each on his day; and they would send and invite their three sisters to eat and drink with them. ⁵ And when the days of the feast had run their course, Job would send and sanctify them, and he would rise early in the morning and offer burnt offerings according to the number of them all; for Job said, "It may be that my sons have sinned, and cursed God in their hearts." Thus Job did continually.

6 Now there was a day when the sons of God came to present themselves before the LORD, and Satan[a] also came among them. ⁷ The LORD said to Satan, "Whence have you come?" Satan answered the LORD, "From going to and fro on the earth, and from walking up and down on it." ⁸ And the LORD said to Satan, "Have you considered my servant Job, that there is none like him on the earth, a blameless and upright man, who fears God and turns away from evil?" ⁹ Then Satan answered the LORD, "Does Job fear God for nought? ¹⁰ Hast thou not put a hedge about him and his house and all that he has, on every side? Thou hast blessed the work of his hands, and his possessions have increased in the land. ¹¹ But put forth thy hand now, and touch all that he has, and he will curse thee to thy face." ¹² And the LORD said to Satan, "Behold, all that he has is in your power; only upon him-self do not put forth your hand." So Satan went forth from the presence of the LORD.

13 Now there was a day when his sons and daughters were eating and drinking wine in their eldest brother's house; ¹⁴ and there came a messenger to Job, and said, "The oxen were plowing and the asses feeding beside them; ¹⁵ and the Sabe'ans fell upon them and took them, and slew the servants with the edge of the sword; and I alone have escaped to tell you." ¹⁶ While he was yet speaking, there came another, and said, "The fire of God fell from heaven and burned up the sheep and the servants, and consumed them; and I alone have escaped to tell you." ¹⁷ While he was yet speaking, there came another, and said, "The Chalde'-ans formed three companies, and made a raid upon the camels and took them, and slew the servants with the edge of the sword; and I alone have escaped to tell you." ¹⁸ While he was yet speaking, there came another, and said, "Your sons and daughters were eating and drinking wine in their eldest brother's house; ¹⁹ and behold, a great wind came across the wilderness, and struck the four corners of the house, and it fell upon the young people, and they are dead; and I alone have escaped to tell you."

20 Then Job arose, and rent his robe, and shaved his head, and fell upon the ground, and worshiped. ²¹ And he said, "Naked I came from my mother's womb, and naked shall I return; the LORD gave, and the LORD has taken away; blessed be the name of the LORD."

22 In all this Job did not sin or charge God with wrong.

2 Again there was a day when the sons of God came to present themselves before

a Heb the adversary

1.1–2.13: The prologue. A blameless man is deprived of wealth, posterity, and health, but keeps his faith in God. **1:** *The land of Uz* is probably Edom, although some locate it in north Transjordan. The name *Job* may mean "hostile" or "penitent." *Blameless*, i.e. healthy, whole, and socially responsible. **6–8:** *Satan* (see note a; Zech.3.1 n.) is *among the sons of God.* He is not yet the demonic personification of later Judaism (compare 1 Chr.21.1) and Christianity. **15:** *Sabeans*, nomads from Arabia. **17:** *Chaldeans*, originally from southern Mesopotamia. The folk-teller respects archaic and local color. **21:** *Naked shall I return*, Hebrew adds "there," suggesting correspondence between *mother's womb* and "mother earth." Although a foreigner, Job uses the covenant-name, Yahweh (the LORD); this is an indication of early date. In the poem, the sacred name Yahweh is never used by the speakers (except in 12.9, a proverbial quotation). **22:** The Deity is not accused of capricious malevolence. **2.4:** *Skin for skin,* a hide for a hide, a proverb probably

---

the LORD, and Satan also came among them to present himself before the LORD. [2] And the LORD said to Satan, "Whence have you come?" Satan answered the LORD, "From going to and fro on the earth, and from walking up and down on it." [3] And the LORD said to Satan, "Have you considered my servant Job, that there is none like him on the earth, a blameless and upright man, who fears God and turns away from evil? He still holds fast his integrity, although you moved me against him, to destroy him without cause." [4] Then Satan answered the LORD, "Skin for skin! All that a man has he will give for his life. [5] But put forth thy hand now, and touch his bone and his flesh, and he will curse thee to thy face." [6] And the LORD said to Satan, "Behold, he is in your power; only spare his life."

7 So Satan went forth from the presence of the LORD, and afflicted Job with loathsome sores from the sole of his foot to the crown of his head. [8] And he took a potsherd with which to scrape himself, and sat among the ashes.

9 Then his wife said to him, "Do you still hold fast your integrity? Curse God, and die." [10] But he said to her, "You speak as one of the foolish women would speak. Shall we receive good at the hand of God, and shall we not receive evil?" In all this Job did not sin with his lips.

11 Now when Job's three friends heard of all this evil that had come upon him, they came each from his own place, Eli′phaz the Te′manite, Bildad the Shuhite, and Zophar the Na′amathite. They made an appointment together to come to condole with him and comfort him. [12] And when they saw him from afar, they did not recognize him; and they raised their voices and wept; and they rent their robes and sprinkled dust upon their heads toward heaven. [13] And they sat with him on the ground seven days and seven nights, and no one spoke a word to him, for they saw that his suffering was very great.

3 After this Job opened his mouth and cursed the day of his birth. [2] And Job said:
3 "Let the day perish wherein I was born,
  and the night which said,
  'A man-child is conceived.'
4 Let that day be darkness!
  May God above not seek it,
  nor light shine upon it.
5 Let gloom and deep darkness claim it.
  Let clouds dwell upon it;
  let the blackness of the day terrify it.
6 That night — let thick darkness seize it!
  let it not rejoice among the days
    of the year,
  let it not come into the number
    of the months.
7 Yea, let that night be barren;
  let no joyful cry be heard[b] in it.
8 Let those curse it who curse the day,
  who are skilled to rouse up Leviathan.
9 Let the stars of its dawn be dark;
  let it hope for light, but have none,
  nor see the eyelids of the morning;
10 because it did not shut the doors of my
    mother's womb,
  nor hide trouble from my eyes.

11 "Why did I not die at birth,
  come forth from the womb and expire?
12 Why did the knees receive me?
  Or why the breasts, that I should suck?
13 For then I should have lain down and been
    quiet;
  I should have slept; then I should have
    been at rest,

b Heb come

---

used by tradesmen. **7:** *Loathsome sores,* not necessarily leprosy (Hansen's disease) but a skin ailment, one of many in the Near East. **9:** *Curse God, and die,* Job's wife still believed in his *integrity* (see 4.6 n.) but wished to shorten his torture. **10:** *Foolish women,* i.e. those who do not believe in divine intervention into human affairs (see Ps.14.1 n.). **11:** The friends of Job came from northwest Arabia.

3.1–26: Job's soliloquy. 8: Those *who are skilled to rouse Leviathan* are magicians, astrologers, and calendar-makers who were believed to produce as well as announce eclipses. *Leviathan,* the sea monster (7.12), like Rahab (9.13; 26.12; Is.51.9), threatens to engulf the created order and the succession of days and nights, especially during

14 with kings and counselors of the earth
   who rebuilt ruins for themselves,
15 or with princes who had gold,
   who filled their houses with silver.
16 Or why was I not as a hidden untimely
   birth,
   as infants that never see the light?
17 There the wicked cease from troubling,
   and there the weary are at rest.
18 There the prisoners are at ease together;
   they hear not the voice of the task-
   master.
19 The small and the great are there,
   and the slave is free from his master.

20 "Why is light given to him that is in
   misery,
   and life to the bitter in soul,
21 who long for death, but it comes not,
   and dig for it more than for hid
   treasures;
22 who rejoice exceedingly,
   and are glad, when they find the grave?
23 Why is light given to a man whose way
   is hid,
   whom God has hedged in?
24 For my sighing comes as*c* my bread,
   and my groanings are poured out like
   water.
25 For the thing that I fear comes upon me,
   and what I dread befalls me.
26 I am not at ease, nor am I quiet;
   I have no rest; but trouble comes."

4 Then Eli′phaz the Te′manite
  answered:
2 "If one ventures a word with you, will you
  be offended?
  Yet who can keep from speaking?
3 Behold, you have instructed many,

and you have strengthened the weak
   hands.
4 Your words have upheld him who was
   stumbling,
   and you have made firm the feeble knees.
5 But now it has come to you, and you are
   impatient;
   it touches you, and you are dismayed.
6 Is not your fear of God your confidence,
   and the integrity of your ways your
   hope?

7 "Think now, who that was innocent ever
   perished?
   Or where were the upright cut off?
8 As I have seen, those who plow iniquity
   and sow trouble reap the same.
9 By the breath of God they perish,
   and by the blast of his anger they are
   consumed.
10 The roar of the lion, the voice of the fierce
   lion,
   the teeth of the young lions, are broken.
11 The strong lion perishes for lack of prey,
   and the whelps of the lioness are
   scattered.

12 "Now a word was brought to me stealthily,
   my ear received the whisper of it.
13 Amid thoughts from visions of the night,
   when deep sleep falls on men,
14 dread came upon me, and trembling,
   which made all my bones shake.
15 A spirit glided past my face;
   the hair of my flesh stood up.
16 It stood still,
   but I could not discern its appearance.
   A form was before my eyes;
   there was silence, then I heard a voice:

c Heb *before*

---

eclipses of the sun or moon. **14:** *Ruins,* probably pyramids. The thought of a happy afterlife is not Hebraic but Egyptian. **23:** *God,* Hebrew Eloah, a name which stresses the terrible aspect of the Deity, whose omnipotence is never
doubted by Job. Job's dilemma is directly related to his theological view that God is the cause of both good and evil
(disaster, calamities, etc.); see 2.10; Is.45.7; Am.3.6.
   4.1–5.27: First discourse of Eliphaz. 1–4: The opening words are courteous. The poet insists on the sincerity
of Job's comforters. **6:** Job's *integrity* (Hebrew word related to "blameless" in 1.1; see 2.9 n.) is not yet questioned.
7: The dogma of individual, this-worldly retribution is upheld. **12–16:** Eliphaz appeals to a supranatural, almost
prophetic, source of authority. He does not speak in the name of tradition or experience, as wise men generally do.
17: Surely no *mortal man is righteous before God,* and Job should adopt an attitude of humility instead of rebelling

¹⁷ 'Can mortal man be righteous before^d God?
  Can a man be pure before^d his Maker?
¹⁸ Even in his servants he puts no trust,
  and his angels he charges with error;
¹⁹ how much more those who dwell in houses
    of clay,
  whose foundation is in the dust,
  who are crushed before the moth.
²⁰ Between morning and evening they are
    destroyed;
  they perish for ever without any
    regarding it.
²¹ If their tent-cord is plucked up within
    them,
  do they not die, and that without
    wisdom?'

5 "Call now; is there any one who will
  answer you?
  To which of the holy ones will you turn?
² Surely vexation kills the fool,
  and jealousy slays the simple.
³ I have seen the fool taking root,
  but suddenly I cursed his dwelling.
⁴ His sons are far from safety,
  they are crushed in the gate,
  and there is no one to deliver them.
⁵ His harvest the hungry eat,
  and he takes it even out of thorns;^e
  and the thirsty^f pant after his^g wealth.
⁶ For affliction does not come from the dust,
  nor does trouble sprout from the
    ground;
⁷ but man is born to trouble
  as the sparks fly upward.

⁸ "As for me, I would seek God,
  and to God would I commit my cause;
⁹ who does great things and unsearchable,
  marvelous things without number:
¹⁰ he gives rain upon the earth
  and sends waters upon the fields;

¹¹ he sets on high those who are lowly,
  and those who mourn are lifted to safety.
¹² He frustrates the devices of the crafty,
  so that their hands achieve no success.
¹³ He takes the wise in their own craftiness;
  and the schemes of the wily are brought
    to a quick end.
¹⁴ They meet with darkness in the daytime,
  and grope at noonday as in the night.
¹⁵ But he saves the fatherless from their mouth,^h
  the needy from the hand of the mighty.
¹⁶ So the poor have hope,
  and injustice shuts her mouth.

¹⁷ "Behold, happy is the man whom God
    reproves;
  therefore despise not the chastening of
    the Almighty.
¹⁸ For he wounds, but he binds up;
  he smites, but his hands heal.
¹⁹ He will deliver you from six troubles;
  in seven there shall no evil touch you.
²⁰ In famine he will redeem you from death,
  and in war from the power of the sword.
²¹ You shall be hid from the scourge of the
    tongue,
  and shall not fear destruction when it
    comes.
²² At destruction and famine you shall laugh,
  and shall not fear the beasts of the earth.
²³ For you shall be in league with the stones
    of the field,
  and the beasts of the field shall be at
    peace with you.
²⁴ You shall know that your tent is safe,
  and you shall inspect your fold and miss
    nothing.
²⁵ You shall know also that your descendants
    shall be many,

d Or *more than*   e Heb obscure   f Aquila Symmachus
Syr Vg: Heb *snare*   g Heb *their*   h Cn: Heb uncertain

against the divine will. **21:** The word translated *tent-cord* has two separate meanings; here it should be translated "pre-eminence" or "excellency"; men's pre-eminence or excellency is of no avail. They have only an illusion of *wisdom.* **5.1:** *The holy ones,* divine beings (see 15.15; Ex.15.11 n.; Ps.82.1 n.); members of the heavenly court cannot be inter-cessors. Eliphaz suspects, perhaps, that Job has attempted to justify himself by invoking other gods. **8:** *I would,* that is, were I in Job's place; if Job would only turn from his arrogance, his present misery would be ended. **17–27:** Suffering must be accepted as *the chastening of the Almighty.* The poet refers to the doctrine of *musar* (chastening or correction), which is characteristic of Jewish orthodoxy.

and your offspring as the grass of the
   earth.
26 You shall come to your grave in ripe old
   age,
      as a shock of grain comes up to the
      threshing floor in its season.
27 Lo, this we have searched out; it is true.
   Hear, and know it for your good."[i]

6 Then Job answered:
2 "O that my vexation were weighed,
   and all my calamity laid in the balances!
3 For then it would be heavier than the sand
   of the sea;
      therefore my words have been rash.
4 For the arrows of the Almighty are in me;
   my spirit drinks their poison;
      the terrors of God are arrayed against
      me.
5 Does the wild ass bray when he has grass,
   or the ox low over his fodder?
6 Can that which is tasteless be eaten
   without salt,
      or is there any taste in the slime of the
      purslane?[j]
7 My appetite refuses to touch them;
   they are as food that is loathsome to
   me.[k]

8 "O that I might have my request,
   and that God would grant my desire;
9 that it would please God to crush me,
   that he would let loose his hand and cut
   me off!
10 This would be my consolation;
   I would even exult[l] in pain unsparing;
      for I have not denied the words of the
      Holy One.
11 What is my strength, that I should wait?
   And what is my end, that I should be
   patient?

12 Is my strength the strength of stones,
   or is my flesh bronze?
13 In truth I have no help in me,
   and any resource is driven from me.
14 "He who withholds[m] kindness from a
   friend
      forsakes the fear of the Almighty.
15 My brethren are treacherous as a torrent-
   bed,
      as freshets that pass away,
16 which are dark with ice,
   and where the snow hides itself.
17 In time of heat they disappear;
   when it is hot, they vanish from their
   place.
18 The caravans turn aside from their course;
   they go up into the waste, and perish.
19 The caravans of Tema look,
   the travelers of Sheba hope.
20 They are disappointed because they were
   confident;
      they come thither and are confounded.
21 Such you have now become to me;[n]
   you see my calamity, and are afraid.
22 Have I said, 'Make me a gift'?
   Or, 'From your wealth offer a bribe for
   me'?
23 Or, 'Deliver me from the adversary's
   hand'?
   Or, 'Ransom me from the hand of
   oppressors'?

24 "Teach me, and I will be silent;
   make me understand how I have erred.
25 How forceful are honest words!
   But what does reproof from you reprove?

i Heb *for yourself*   *j* The meaning of the Hebrew word
is uncertain   *k* Heb obscure   *l* The meaning of the
Hebrew word is uncertain   *m* Syr Vg Compare Tg:
Heb obscure   *n* Cn Compare Gk Syr: Heb obscure

6.1–7.21: Reply of Job. The orthodox explanation cannot be valid in Job's case, for his *calamity* exceeds all ordinary misfortunes. **6:** *Slime of the purslane,* an insipid and repulsive food. Purslane is a potherb. **8–11:** The Egyptian
theme of desire for an early death reappears (see ch. 3). Moreover Job fears that, if his days (and hence, his tortures)
are prolonged, he may deny *the words of the Holy One* (v. 10). The poet suggests thereby the complexity of the hero's
personality; Job is an unwilling blasphemer. **14:** The test of true religion lies in human compassion for others. Another
rendering is: "A man should show kindness to a man in despair, even to one who forsakes the fear of the Almighty."
Some commentators suggest that the verse is a marginal note made by a scribe. **15–20:** Friendship fails precisely when
it is needed. **24:** Job is willing to admit that he has *erred,* if only convincing evidence is brought forward. **30:** His con-

²⁶ Do you think that you can reprove words,
when the speech of a despairing man is
wind?
²⁷ You would even cast lots over the fatherless,
and bargain over your friend.

²⁸ "But now, be pleased to look at me;
for I will not lie to your face.
²⁹ Turn, I pray, let no wrong be done.
Turn now, my vindication is at stake.
³⁰ Is there any wrong on my tongue?
Cannot my taste discern calamity?

7 "Has not man a hard service upon earth,
and are not his days like the days of a
hireling?
² Like a slave who longs for the shadow,
and like a hireling who looks for his
wages,
³ so I am allotted months of emptiness,
and nights of misery are apportioned
to me.
⁴ When I lie down I say, 'When shall I arise?'
But the night is long,
and I am full of tossing till the dawn.
⁵ My flesh is clothed with worms and dirt;
my skin hardens, then breaks out afresh.
⁶ My days are swifter than a weaver's shuttle,
and come to their end without hope.

⁷ "Remember that my life is a breath;
my eye will never again see good.
⁸ The eye of him who sees me will behold
me no more;
while thy eyes are upon me, I shall be
gone.
⁹ As the cloud fades and vanishes,
so he who goes down to Sheol does not
come up;
¹⁰ he returns no more to his house,
nor does his place know him any more.

¹¹ "Therefore I will not restrain my mouth;
I will speak in the anguish of my spirit;
I will complain in the bitterness of my
soul.
¹² Am I the sea, or a sea monster,
that thou settest a guard over me?
¹³ When I say, 'My bed will comfort me,
my couch will ease my complaint,'
¹⁴ then thou dost scare me with dreams
and terrify me with visions,
¹⁵ so that I would choose strangling
and death rather than my bones.
¹⁶ I loathe my life; I would not live for ever.
Let me alone, for my days are a breath.
¹⁷ What is man, that thou dost make so much
of him,
and that thou dost set thy mind upon him,
¹⁸ dost visit him every morning,
and test him every moment?
¹⁹ How long wilt thou not look away from
me,
nor let me alone till I swallow my
spittle?
²⁰ If I sin, what do I do to thee, thou watcher
of men?
Why hast thou made me thy mark?
Why have I become a burden to thee?
²¹ Why dost thou not pardon my transgression
and take away my iniquity?
For now I shall lie in the earth;
thou wilt seek me, but I shall not be."

---

science, however, is able to *discern* the right of his case. **7.1–6:** The life of mortal man in general is comparable to that of *a slave who longs for the shadow;* moreover, its transient nature is the source of new anguish. **7–21:** A prayer. It is at the moment of despair that man begins to pray. **7–9:** *Remember that my life is a breath.* Job appeals to divine compassion with the implied mockery that God will act when it will be too late. Job has heard of foreign speculations on the descent of men and gods to the underworld, only to deny any return from there. **12:** *Am I the sea, or a sea monster?* Again the hero alludes to the personification of evil (see 3.8 n.) in a context of sarcastic humor. Job compares himself in jest to the primeval forces which in Semitic polytheism threaten the security of the inhabited earth. His pain and his destitution are likened to the watch or *guard* which Marduk posted around the conquered dragon in the Babylonian poem on creation. **17–18:** A parody of Ps. 8. While the psalmist praised the creator who assigns to insignificant and mortal man a place of pre-eminence in nature, Job ironically prefers to receive minimal attention (see also Ps.144.3–4). **20:** Human sin cannot justify God's hostility to man. **21:** *Thou wilt seek me,* i.e. thou wilt grope in the darkness after me, *but I shall not be.* Job threatens the Almighty with his own non-being! He at once reaffirms his former trust in a loving God and sarcastically implies the frustration of that love.

40

And the LORD said to Job:

2 "Shall a faultfinder contend with the Almighty?
He who argues with God, let him answer it."

3 Then Job answered the LORD:

4 "Behold, I am of small account; what shall I answer thee?
I lay my hand on my mouth.

5 I have spoken once, and I will not answer; twice, but I will proceed no further."

6 Then the LORD answered Job out of the whirlwind:

7 "Gird up your loins like a man;
I will question you, and you declare to me.

8 Will you even put me in the wrong?
Will you condemn me that you may be justified?

9 Have you an arm like God,
and can you thunder with a voice like his?

10 "Deck yourself with majesty and dignity;
clothe yourself with glory and splendor.

11 Pour forth the overflowings of your anger,
and look on every one that is proud, and abase him.

12 Look on every one that is proud, and bring him low;
and tread down the wicked where they stand.

13 Hide them all in the dust together;
bind their faces in the world below.[n]

14 Then will I also acknowledge to you,
that your own right hand can give you victory.

15 "Behold, Be'hemoth,[o]
which I made as I made you;
he eats grass like an ox.

16 Behold, his strength in his loins,
and his power in the muscles of his belly.

17 He makes his tail stiff like a cedar;
the sinews of his thighs are knit together.

18 His bones are tubes of bronze,
his limbs like bars of iron.

19 "He is the first of the works[p] of God;
let him who made him bring near his sword!

20 For the mountains yield food for him
where all the wild beasts play.

21 Under the lotus plants he lies,
in the covert of the reeds and in the marsh.

22 For his shade the lotus trees cover him;
the willows of the brook surround him.

23 Behold, if the river is turbulent he is not frightened;
he is confident though Jordan rushes against his mouth.

24 Can one take him with hooks,[q]
or pierce his nose with a snare?

41

[r] "Can you draw out Levi'athan[s] with a fishhook,
or press down his tongue with a cord?

2 Can you put a rope in his nose,
or pierce his jaw with a hook?

3 Will he make many supplications to you?
Will he speak to you soft words?

4 Will he make a covenant with you
to take him for your servant for ever?

5 Will you play with him as with a bird,
or will you put him on leash for your maidens?

6 Will traders bargain over him?
Will they divide him up among the merchants?

7 Can you fill his skin with harpoons,
or his head with fishing spears?

8 Lay hands on him;

n Heb *hidden place*   o Or *the hippopotamus*
p Heb *ways*   q Cn: Heb *in his eyes*
r Ch 40.25 in Heb   s Or *the crocodile*

40.1–5: Job refuses the challenge to fight. **1:** *Shall a faultfinder contend with the Almighty?* Read, with some ancient versions, "Will he who disputes with the Almighty yield?" The Deity never condemns Job for moral faults but clearly implies that he has been guilty of theological insolence.

40.6–41.34: Second discourse of the LORD. 40.6–9: The divine challenge of man is renewed, apparently because Job is only silenced but not convinced. **8:** *Will you condemn me that you may be justified?* The poet indicates here the

think of the battle; you will not do it
again!

⁹ᵗ Behold, the hope of a man is disappointed;
he is laid low even at the sight of him.

¹⁰ No one is so fierce that he dares to stir
him up.
Who then is he that can stand before
me?

¹¹ Who has given to me,ᵘ that I should
repay him?
Whatever is under the whole heaven
is mine.

¹² "I will not keep silence concerning his
limbs,
or his mighty strength, or his goodly
frame.

¹³ Who can strip off his outer garment?
Who can penetrate his double coat
of mail?ᵛ

¹⁴ Who can open the doors of his face?
Round about his teeth is terror.

¹⁵ His backʷ is made of rows of shields,
shut up closely as with a seal.

¹⁶ One is so near to another
that no air can come between them.

¹⁷ They are joined one to another;
they clasp each other and cannot be
separated.

¹⁸ His sneezings flash forth light,
and his eyes are like the eyelids of the
dawn.

¹⁹ Out of his mouth go flaming torches;
sparks of fire leap forth.

²⁰ Out of his nostrils comes forth smoke,
as from a boiling pot and burning
rushes.

²¹ His breath kindles coals,
and a flame comes forth from his
mouth.

²² In his neck abides strength,
and terror dances before him.

²³ The folds of his flesh cleave together,
firmly cast upon him and immovable.

²⁴ His heart is hard as a stone,
hard as the nether millstone.

²⁵ When he raises himself up the mightyˣ are
afraid;
at the crashing they are beside
themselves.

²⁶ Though the sword reaches him, it does not
avail;
nor the spear, the dart, or the javelin.

²⁷ He counts iron as straw,
and bronze as rotten wood.

²⁸ The arrow cannot make him flee;
for him slingstones are turned to
stubble.

²⁹ Clubs are counted as stubble;
he laughs at the rattle of javelins.

³⁰ His underparts are like sharp potsherds;
he spreads himself like a threshing
sledge on the mire.

³¹ He makes the deep boil like a pot;
he makes the sea like a pot of ointment.

³² Behind him he leaves a shining wake;
one would think the deep to be hoary.

³³ Upon earth there is not his like,
a creature without fear.

³⁴ He beholds everything that is high;
he is king over all the sons of pride."

42 Then Job answered the LORD:
² "I know that thou canst do all
things,
and that no purpose of thine can be
thwarted.

t Ch 41.1 in Heb   *u* The meaning of the Hebrew is
uncertain   *v* Gk: Heb *bridle*   *w* Cn Compare Gk Vg:
Heb *pride*   *x* Or *gods*

central theme of the work. Self-righteousness leads man to condemn God. **15–24:** This portrait of *Behemoth* (like that
of Leviathan, 41.1–34) may have received literary amplification, but it plays an integral part of the poet's purpose: the
creating God is in control of all forces of evil, despite appearances to the contrary. **15:** The primeval monster (compare
v. 19) is not a mere hippopotamus, but a mythical symbol. *Which I made as I made you,* the mystery of evil is not dissolved, but the divine sway embraces all. **41.1–34:** *Leviathan,* not an ordinary crocodile, but the sea-monster (3.8;
26.13; Ps.74.14), which was associated with chaos. Like the psalmist (Ps.104.26), the poet shows that it is only a play-
thing in the eyes of God.
  42.1–6: The answer of Job. Having contemplated divine activity, the sufferer now knows the purposefulness of
God (v. 2). **3a:** A quotation from 38.2; Job acknowledges his finitude. **4:** An echo of the divine questioning (40.7),

3 'Who is this that hides counsel without
    knowledge?'
  Therefore I have uttered what I did not
    understand,
      things too wonderful for me, which I
        did not know.
4 'Hear, and I will speak;
      I will question you, and you declare
        to me.'
5 I had heard of thee by the hearing of the
    ear,
      but now my eye sees thee;
6 therefore I despise myself,
      and repent in dust and ashes."

7 After the LORD had spoken these words
to Job, the LORD said to Eli'phaz the Te'manite: "My wrath is kindled against you and
against your two friends; for you have not
spoken of me what is right, as my servant Job
has. 8 Now therefore take seven bulls and
seven rams, and go to my servant Job, and
offer up for yourselves a burnt offering; and
my servant Job shall pray for you, for I will
accept his prayer not to deal with you according to your folly; for you have not spoken of
me what is right, as my servant Job has." 9 So
Eli'phaz the Te'manite and Bildad the Shuhite
and Zophar the Na'amathite went and did
what the LORD had told them; and the LORD
accepted Job's prayer.

10 And the LORD restored the fortunes of
Job, when he had prayed for his friends; and
the LORD gave Job twice as much as he had
before. 11 Then came to him all his brothers
and sisters and all who had known him before,
and ate bread with him in his house; and they
showed him sympathy and comforted him for
all the evil that the LORD had brought upon
him; and each of them gave him a piece of
money.ʸ and a ring of gold. 12 And the LORD
blessed the latter days of Job more than his
beginning; and he had fourteen thousand
sheep, six thousand camels, a thousand yoke
of oxen, and a thousand she-asses. 13 He had
also seven sons and three daughters. 14 And he
called the name of the first Jemi'mah; and the
name of the second Kezi'ah; and the name of
the third Ker'en-hap'puch. 15 And in all the
land there were no women so fair as Job's
daughters; and their father gave them inheritance among their brothers. 16 And after this
Job lived a hundred and forty years, and saw
his sons, and his sons' sons, four generations.
17 And Job died, an old man, and full of days.

y Heb *qesitah*

---

preparing for the confession of the following lines. **5:** The contrast between belief through tradition and faith through
prophetic vision. God has not justified Job, but he has come to him personally; the upholder of the universe cares for a
lonely man so deeply that he offers him the fulness of his communion. Job is not vindicated but he has obtained far
more than a recognition of his innocence: he has been accepted by the ever-present master-worker, and intimacy with
the Creator makes vindication superfluous. The philosophical problem is not solved, but it is transfigured by the theological reality of the divine-human rapport. **6:** *I despise myself;* the Hebrew verb is obscure, but is probably related to
a root meaning "to melt into nothing." *I repent,* the Hebrew verb used here is not the usual one for repentance of sins,
but a word expressing the utmost grief and self-depreciation. Such an experience follows rather than precedes the
vision of God.
  42.7–17: The epilogue. The style, language, and situation of the folktale (1.1–2.13) reappear abruptly (see Introduction). **8:** *Burnt offering,* sacrificial ritual, absent from the poem, is a characteristic of the archaic story (1.5).
10: Job's restoration follows not his repentance but his intercession on behalf of his friends (v. 8). Intercessory power
is a feature which is in accord with the figure of the ancient legend (Ezek.14.14,20). **10–17:** Job receives a double
restitution, although no healing of his disease is explicitly mentioned. **11:** *A piece of money,* a qesitah (see note y and
Gen.33.19; Jos.24.32). **14:** The names of Job's new daughters have a flavor of folklore: *Jemimah,* Dove; *Keziah,*
Cinnamon; *Keren-happuch,* Horn of eye-shadow. **15b:** An exceptional procedure (contrast Num.27.1–11). **16–17:** A
patriarchal theme (Gen.25.8; 35.29; 50.23; see also Ps.128.6; Pr.17.6; 1 Chr.29.28).

The Book of Isaiah

THE VISION OF ISAIAH THE SON OF Amoz,
which he saw concerning Judah and
Jerusalem in the days of Uzzi'ah, Jotham,
Ahaz, and Hezeki'ah, kings of Judah.
2 Hear, O heavens, and give ear, O earth;
 for the LORD has spoken:
 "Sons have I reared and brought up,
 but they have rebelled against me.
3 The ox knows its owner,
 and the ass its master's crib;
 but Israel does not know,
 my people does not understand."

4 Ah, sinful nation,
 a people laden with iniquity,
 offspring of evildoers,
 sons who deal corruptly!
 They have forsaken the LORD,
 they have despised the Holy One of
 Israel,
 they are utterly estranged.

5 Why will you still be smitten,
 that you continue to rebel?
 The whole head is sick,
 and the whole heart faint.
4 From the sole of the foot even to the
 head,
 there is no soundness in it,
 but bruises and sores
 and bleeding wounds;
 they are not pressed out, or bound up,
 or softened with oil.

7 Your country lies desolate,
 your cities are burned with fire;
 in your very presence
 aliens devour your land;
 it is desolate, as overthrown by aliens.
8 And the daughter of Zion is left
 like a booth in a vineyard,
 like a lodge in a cucumber field,
 like a besieged city.

9 If the LORD of hosts
 had not left us a few survivors,
 we should have been like Sodom,
 and become like Gomor'rah.

1.1–5.24: Oracles against rebellious Judah. 1.1: Superscription. *Vision of Isaiah* (6.1–13; Jer. ch. 1; Ezek. chs. 1–3) identifies Is. chs. 1–39 as God's message to Judah through the prophet. The name *Isaiah* means "The LORD [Yahweh] gives salvation." The latter part of the verse beginning with "in the days of" may be an editorial expansion.
1.2–31: First series of oracles, serving as a kind of prologue. 2–3: Poetic exhortation reminiscent of God's address to the heavenly host in 40.1–2. *Sons* compare Jer.3.19–22. The Biblical word *know* implies a profound, identifying comprehension of the right relationship with God; it is a recurring prophetic theme (Jer.1.5; Hos.2.20; 4.1,6; 5.4). 4–9: An appeal to a people heedless of the significance of Judah's devastation by Tiglath-Pileser III (734–733 B.C.; 7.1–2) or Sennacherib (701 B.C.; 36.1) and Jerusalem's isolation (*daughter of Zion,* see Jer.4.29–31 n.). 4: Note the poetic parallelism: *nation, people; offspring, sons.* The expression, *Holy One of Israel* (5.19,24; 10.20; 12.6; 17.7; 29.19; 30.11,12,15; 37.23), emphasizes God's unapproachable separateness, which he has bridged by his gracious

---

¹⁰ Hear the word of the LORD,
  you rulers of Sodom!
Give ear to the teaching of our God,
  you people of Gomor′rah!
¹¹ "What to me is the multitude of your
    sacrifices?
  says the LORD;
I have had enough of burnt offerings of
    rams
  and the fat of fed beasts;
I do not delight in the blood of bulls,
  or of lambs, or of he-goats.

¹² "When you come to appear before me,
  who requires of you
  this trampling of my courts?
¹³ Bring no more vain offerings;
  incense is an abomination to me.
New moon and sabbath and the calling of
    assemblies —
  I cannot endure iniquity and solemn
    assembly.
¹⁴ Your new moons and your appointed
    feasts
  my soul hates;
they have become a burden to me,
  I am weary of bearing them.
¹⁵ When you spread forth your hands,
  I will hide my eyes from you;
even though you make many prayers,
  I will not listen;
  your hands are full of blood.
¹⁶ Wash yourselves; make yourselves clean;
  remove the evil of your doings
  from before my eyes;
cease to do evil,
¹⁷ learn to do good;
seek justice,
  correct oppression;

defend the fatherless,
  plead for the widow.

¹⁸ "Come now, let us reason together,
  says the LORD:
though your sins are like scarlet,
  they shall be as white as snow;
though they are red like crimson,
  they shall become like wool.
¹⁹ If you are willing and obedient,
  you shall eat the good of the land;
²⁰ But if you refuse and rebel,
  you shall be devoured by the sword;
  for the mouth of the LORD has spoken."

²¹ How the faithful city
  has become a harlot,
  she that was full of justice!
Righteousness lodged in her,
  but now murderers.
²² Your silver has become dross,
  your wine mixed with water,
²³ Your princes are rebels
  and companions of thieves.
Every one loves a bribe
  and runs after gifts.
They do not defend the fatherless,
  and the widow's cause does not come to
    them.

²⁴ Therefore the Lord says,
  the LORD of hosts,
  the Mighty One of Israel:
"Ah, I will vent my wrath on my enemies,
  and avenge myself on my foes.
²⁵ I will turn my hand against you
  and will smelt away your dross as with
    lye
  and remove all your alloy.

election of Israel as his people (Hos.8.1, Jer.3.20). **10–20:** God's pronouncement concerning Judah's religious superficiality (Am.5.21–24; Jer.6.20). Judah may repent and return (Jer.7.5–7); the alternative is destruction (Jer.7.22–34). **10:** *Teaching,* the Hebrew word is "torah," which is frequently translated "law." On *Sodom* and *Gomorrah* see Gen.18.16–19.28; Jer.23.14; Ezek.16.46–58. **14:** *My soul,* a Hebrew idiom which in this context means "I" (compare Lev.26.11,30). *Burden,* see Jer.23.33–40. **16–17:** Compare Ex.22.21,22; Am.5.6–7. **18:** *Reason,* as one argues a case before a judge (Job 23.7). *White* for holiness (Rev.19.8); *scarlet* for wickedness (garments of Babylon, Rev.17.4). **21–23:** Lamentation over Jerusalem. **21:** *Harlot,* Jer.3.6–10; Ezek. chs. 16 and 23. *Justice* and *righteousness* express Isaiah's ideal for the people of God. **24:** *Mighty one of Israel* recalls Israel's patriarchal traditions (49.26; Gen.49.24; Ps.132.2,5). **25:** *As with lye,* or "thoroughly." **26:** Isaiah frequently uses symbolic names (7.14; 8.1; 9.6; see also

26 And I will restore your judges as at the
first,
and your counselors as at the beginning.
Afterward you shall be called the city of
righteousness,
the faithful city."

27 Zion shall be redeemed by justice,
and those in her who repent, by
righteousness.
28 But rebels and sinners shall be destroyed
together,
and those who forsake the LORD shall
be consumed.
29 For you shall be ashamed of the oaks
in which you delighted;
and you shall blush for the gardens
which you have chosen.
30 For you shall be like an oak
whose leaf withers,
and like a garden without water.
31 And the strong shall become tow,
and his work a spark,
and both of them shall burn together,
with none to quench them.

2 The word which Isaiah the son of Amoz
saw concerning Judah and Jerusalem.
2 It shall come to pass in the latter days
that the mountain of the house of the LORD
shall be established as the highest of the
mountains,
and shall be raised above the hills;
and all the nations shall flow to it,
3 and many peoples shall come, and say:
"Come, let us go up to the mountain of the
LORD,
to the house of the God of Jacob;

that he may teach us his ways
and that we may walk in his paths."
For out of Zion shall go forth the law,
and the word of the LORD from
Jerusalem.
4 He shall judge between the nations,
and shall decide for many peoples;
and they shall beat their swords into
plowshares,
and their spears into pruning hooks;
nation shall not lift up sword against
nation,
neither shall they learn war any more.

5 O house of Jacob,
come, let us walk
in the light of the LORD.

6 For thou hast rejected thy people,
the house of Jacob,
because they are full of diviners[a] from the
east
and of soothsayers like the Philistines,
and they strike hands with foreigners.
7 Their land is filled with silver and gold,
and there is no end to their treasures;
their land is filled with horses,
and there is no end to their chariots.
8 Their land is filled with idols;
they bow down to the work of their
hands,
to what their own fingers have made.
9 So man is humbled,
and men are brought low —
forgive them not!
10 Enter into the rock,
and hide in the dust

a Cn: Heb lacks *of diviners*

Jer.33.16; Ezek.48.35 n.). There will be a new creation; compare Am.9.11; Rev.3.12; 21.1–4. **29–31:** An allegory on
Judah's faithlessness based on one of Isaiah's rare references to pagan religious practices; compare 57.5; Jer.2.27
Ezek.6.1–14.
    2.1: Second superscription, perhaps for chs. 2–4. *Word* connotes "message" (Jer.7.1; 11.1). **2–5: The new age,**
involving the elevation of Zion, the acknowledgment of the nations, and the age of peace. This oracle (vv. 2–4) is also
found in Mic.4.1–4. **3:** *Law,* i.e. "teaching" (1.10), which is more suitable to the thought of the passage. **4:** The age of
peace will follow the judgment of the LORD (compare 5.25; 30.27–28). **5:** Compare v. 3, paraphrased in Mic.4.5.
    2.4–22: The day of the LORD. This is probably to be taken as three stanzas, vv. 6–11,12–17,18–22. The first two
have a similar conclusion (compare vv. 11,17), and it is suggested that the third ended similarly, for the present v. 22 is
missing in the Septuagint and is grammatically corrupt. **6–11:** Judgment on idolatry. **6:** *Diviners* were forbidden in

from before the terror of the LORD,
and from the glory of his majesty.

[11] The haughty looks of man shall be brought
low,
and the pride of men shall be humbled;
and the LORD alone will be exalted
in that day.

[12] For the LORD of hosts has a day
against all that is proud and lofty,
against all that is lifted up and high;[b]
[13] against all the cedars of Lebanon,
lofty and lifted up;
and against all the oaks of Bashan;
[14] against all the high mountains,
and against all the lofty hills;
[15] against every high tower,
and against every fortified wall;
[16] against all the ships of Tarshish,
and against all the beautiful craft.
[17] And the haughtiness of man shall be
humbled,
and the pride of men shall be brought low;
and the LORD alone will be exalted in
that day.
[18] And the idols shall utterly pass away.
[19] And men shall enter the caves of the rocks
and the holes of the ground,
from before the terror of the LORD,
and from the glory of his majesty,
when he rises to terrify the earth.

[20] In that day men will cast forth
their idols of silver and their idols of
gold,
which they made for themselves to
worship,
to the moles and the bats,

[21] to enter the caverns of the rocks
and the clefts of the cliffs,
from before the terror of the LORD,
and from the glory of his majesty,
when he rises to terrify the earth.
[22] Turn away from man
in whose nostrils is breath,
for of what account is he?

3 For, behold, the Lord, the LORD of hosts,
is taking away from Jerusalem and from
Judah
stay and staff,
the whole stay of bread,
and the whole stay of water;
[2] the mighty man and the soldier,
the judge and the prophet,
the diviner and the elder,
[3] the captain of fifty
and the man of rank,
the counselor and the skilful magician
and the expert in charms.
[4] And I will make boys their princes,
and babes shall rule over them.
[5] And the people will oppress one another,
every man his fellow
and every man his neighbor;
the youth will be insolent to the elder,
and the base fellow to the honorable.

[6] When a man takes hold of his brother
in the house of his father, saying:
"You have a mantle;
you shall be our leader,
and this heap of ruins
shall be under your rule";
[7] in that day he will speak out, saying:

b Cn Compare Gk: Heb low

Israel (Ex.22.18; Lev.20.27; Dt.18.10–11; compare 8.19; 1 Sam.28.8–25; Ezek.13.9). The situation fits Uzziah's reign 2.Kg.15.1–7; 2 Chr. ch. 26). **7:** Judah's prosperity (Dt.17.16–17; 1 Kg.10.14–29). **11:** *In that day,* the day of the LORD, in which God judges his enemies and manifests his glory is a recurring prophetic theme (13.6; Am.5.18–20; Jer.17.16–18; Ezek.30.3; J.1.15). **12–17:** pride and punishment. **13:** *Lebanon, Bashan,* Ezek.27.5–6; Jer.22.20. **16:** *Ships of Tarshish,* the phrase may mean "refinery fleet" (see 1 Kg.10.22 n.; Jer.10.9 n.). **18–22:** Judgment on idolatry. **19:** The innumerable *caves* in Palestine's limestone hills are age-old places of refuge.

    3.1–15: Anarchy in Jerusalem. 1–7: Without key men, society breaks down. **1:** *Stay and staff,* everything which supports life, including food and drink (economic resources), and perhaps also the functionaries in vv. 2–3. **2–3:** Offices deemed necessary for the continuity and stability of the state. **4:** The inexperienced and naïve will rule. **5–6:** Civil unrest will become open violence. **8–12:** A commentary on vv. 1–7. Judah's brazen sinfulness and rejection of

"I will not be a healer;
　in my house there is neither bread nor
　　mantle;
you shall not make me
　leader of the people."
8 For Jerusalem has stumbled,
　and Judah has fallen;
because their speech and their deeds are
　　against the LORD,
　defying his glorious presence.

9 Their partiality witnesses against them;
　they proclaim their sin like Sodom,
　they do not hide it.
Woe to them!
　For they have brought evil upon
　　themselves.
10 Tell the righteous that it shall be well with
　them,
　for they shall eat the fruit of their deeds.
11 Woe to the wicked! It shall be ill with him,
　for what his hands have done shall be
　　done to him.
12 My people — children are their oppressors,
　and women rule over them.
　O my people, your leaders mislead you,
　and confuse the course of your paths.

13 The LORD has taken his place to contend,
　he stands to judge his people.*d*
14 The LORD enters into judgment
　with the elders and princes of his people:
"It is you who have devoured the vineyard,
　the spoil of the poor is in your houses.
15 What do you mean by crushing my people,
　by grinding the face of the poor?" says
　　the Lord GOD of hosts.

16 The LORD said:
Because the daughters of Zion are haughty
　and walk with outstretched necks,

glancing wantonly with their eyes,
mincing along as they go,
　tinkling with their feet;
17 the Lord will smite with a scab
　the heads of the daughters of Zion,
　and the LORD will lay bare their secret
　　parts.
18 In that day the Lord will take away the
finery of the anklets, the headbands, and the
crescents; 19 the pendants, the bracelets, and
the scarfs; 20 the headdresses, the armlets, the
sashes, the perfume boxes, and the amulets;
21 the signet rings and nose rings; 22 the festal
robes, the mantles, the cloaks, and the hand-
bags; 23 the garments of gauze, the linen garments, the turbans, and the veils.
24 Instead of perfume there will be
　　rottenness;
　and instead of a girdle, a rope;
and instead of well-set hair, baldness;
　and instead of a rich robe, a girding of
　　sackcloth;
　instead of beauty, shame.*e*
25 Your men shall fall by the sword
　and your mighty men in battle.
26 And her gates shall lament and mourn;
　ravaged, she shall sit upon the ground.

4 And seven women shall take hold of one
man in that day, saying, "We will eat our
own bread and wear our own clothes, only let
us be called by your name; take away our
reproach."
　2 In that day the branch of the LORD shall
be beautiful and glorious, and the fruit of the
land shall be the pride and glory of the survivors of Israel. 3 And he who is left in Zion
and remains in Jerusalem will be called holy,
every one who has been recorded for life in

d Gk Syr: Heb *judge peoples*
e One ancient Ms: Heb lacks *shame*

God's leadership has ruined the people. **13–15:** God will judge the corrupt judges. *Elders,* primary administrators of justice (Ex.19.7; Jos.20.4; Dt.21.19–21). *Princes,* royal appointees (1 Kg.4.2; 2 Kg.10.1; Jer.34.19). *Vineyard,* see 5.1–7.
　3.16–4.1: The humiliation of Jerusalem's women (Am.4.1–3). **18–24:** Detailed expansion of v. 17. **3.25–
4.1:** War's decimation of the male population forces the women to resort to desperate measures to preserve themselves
and their self-respect. *Our reproach* summarizes 3.16–4.1.
　4.2–6: Jerusalem's restoration. 2: *Branch,* the righteous remnant (3.10; compare the Messiah to a Branch in
11.1; Jer.23.5); *fruit of the land,* a "return to paradise." **3:** *Recorded for life,* compare Ex.32.32; Mal.3.16; Dan.12.1;

Jerusalem, ⁴ when the Lord shall have washed away the filth of the daughters of Zion and cleansed the bloodstains of Jerusalem from its midst by a spirit of judgment and by a spirit of burning. ⁵ Then the LORD will create over the whole site of Mount Zion and over her assemblies a cloud by day, and smoke and the shining of a flaming fire by night; for over all the glory there will be a canopy and a pavilion. ⁶ It will be for a shade by day from the heat, and for a refuge and a shelter from the storm and rain.

5 Let me sing for my beloved
a love song concerning his vineyard:
   My beloved had a vineyard
      on a very fertile hill.
² He digged it and cleared it of stones,
     and planted it with choice vines;
  he built a watchtower in the midst of it,
     and hewed out a wine vat in it;
  and he looked for it to yield grapes,
     but it yielded wild grapes.

³ And now, O inhabitants of Jerusalem
     and men of Judah,
  judge, I pray you, between me
     and my vineyard.
⁴ What more was there to do for my vineyard,
     that I have not done in it?
  When I looked for it to yield grapes,
     why did it yield wild grapes?

⁵ And now I will tell you
     what I will do to my vineyard.

I will remove its hedge,
     and it shall be devoured;
I will break down its wall,
     and it shall be trampled down.
⁶ I will make it a waste;
     it shall not be pruned or hoed,
     and briers and thorns shall grow up;
I will also command the clouds
     that they rain no rain upon it.

⁷ For the vineyard of the LORD of hosts
     is the house of Israel,
and the men of Judah
     are his pleasant planting;
and he looked for justice,
     but behold, bloodshed;
for righteousness,
     but behold, a cry!

⁸ Woe to those who join house to house,
     who add field to field,
until there is no more room,
     and you are made to dwell alone
     in the midst of the land.
⁹ The LORD of hosts has sworn in my hearing:
  "Surely many houses shall be desolate,
     large and beautiful houses, without
     inhabitant.
¹⁰ For ten acres of vineyard shall yield but
     one bath,
and a homer of seed shall yield but an
     ephah."

¹¹ Woe to those who rise early in the
     morning,

Rev.20.12,15. **5:** *Smoke and flaming fire,* the signs of God's presence among his people at the Exodus (Ex.13.21–22; 40.34–38).

    5.1–7: Song of the vineyard (Hos.10.1; Jer.2.21; Ezek.19.10–14), an allegory. This unique didactic poem may have been composed for a celebration of the feast of tabernacles during Jotham's reign, the prophet imitating a vintage festival song. **1a:** Introduction to the poem. **2:** *Choice vines,* the Hebrew word ("soreq") means either red grapes, or grapes native to the valley of Sorek, west of Jerusalem. **3–4:** Judah's only possible answer would be judgment against the vineyard. Judah is asked to pass judgment on herself, much as Nathan through a parable had David pass judgment on himself (2 Sam.12.1–12). **7:** *Justice,* the faithful application of God's will to daily living. *Righteousness,* the living, dynamic relationship between man and God wherein man is spiritually and morally acceptable to God (1.27; 9.7; 16.5; 28.17). Righteousness and justice are naturally coupled (1.21) and grow out of the covenant relationship, the existence of which is assumed (Ex. chs. 19–20). *A cry,* from the oppressed.

    5.8–23: Six reproaches (vv. 8,11,18,20,21,22; perhaps 10.1–4 is a seventh). Compare Am.5.7,18; 6.1; Jer.22.13. **8–10:** Against covetousness (Mic.2.1–5,8–9; Ex.20.17). *Bath, ephah,* 6.07 gallons; *homer,* 6.5 bushels (see Ezek. 45.11 n.). **11–12:** Against carousing (Am.6.4–6). **13–17:** *Knowledge,* 1.3. The severity of Judah's punishment will

that they may run after strong drink,
who tarry late into the evening
till wine inflames them!

¹² They have lyre and harp,
timbrel and flute and wine at their
feasts;
but they do not regard the deeds of the
LORD,
or see the work of his hands.

¹³ Therefore my people go into exile
for want of knowledge;
their honored men are dying of hunger,
and their multitude is parched with
thirst.

¹⁴ Therefore Sheol has enlarged its appetite
and opened its mouth beyond measure,
and the nobility of Jerusalem^f and her multitude go down,
her throng and he who exults in her.

¹⁵ Man is bowed down, and men are brought
low,
and the eyes of the haughty are
humbled.

¹⁶ But the LORD of hosts is exalted in justice,
and the Holy God shows himself holy in
righteousness.

¹⁷ Then shall the lambs graze as in their pas-
ture,
fatlings and kids^g shall feed among the
ruins.

¹⁸ Woe to those who draw iniquity with cords
of falsehood,
who draw sin as with cart ropes,

¹⁹ who say: "Let him make haste,
let him speed his work
that we may see it;
let the purpose of the Holy One of Israel
draw near,
and let it come, that we may know it!"

²⁰ Woe to those who call evil good and good
evil,

who put darkness for light and light for
darkness,
who put bitter for sweet and sweet for
bitter!

²¹ Woe to those who are wise in their own eyes,
and shrewd in their own sight!

²² Woe to those who are heroes at drinking
wine,
and valiant men in mixing strong drink,

²³ who acquit the guilty for a bribe,
and deprive the innocent of his right!

²⁴ Therefore, as the tongue of fire devours the
stubble,
and as dry grass sinks down in the
flame,
so their root will be as rottenness,
and their blossom go up like dust;
for they have rejected the law of the LORD
of hosts,
and have despised the word of the Holy
One of Israel.

²⁵ Therefore the anger of the LORD was
kindled against his people,
and he stretched out his hand against
them and smote them,
and the mountains quaked;
and their corpses were as refuse
in the midst of the streets.
For all this his anger is not turned away
and his hand is stretched out still.

²⁶ He will raise a signal for a nation afar off,
and whistle for it from the ends of the
earth;
and lo, swiftly, speedily it comes!

²⁷ None is weary, none stumbles,
none slumbers or sleeps,
not a waistcloth is loose,
not a sandal-thong broken;

²⁸ their arrows are sharp,
all their bows bent,

f Heb *her nobility*   *g* Cn Compare Gk: Heb *aliens*

require the enlargement of *Sheol* (the underworld, 14.9–18). **16:** In all he does, God is just and right. **18–19:** Against mocking God. **20:** Against moral depravity (32.5; Pr.17.15). **21:** Against conceit. **22–23:** Against bravado and bribery. **24b–30:** These verses should probably follow 10.4 (see 9.8–10.4 n.). *Law,* here also in the sense of "teaching" (see 1.10 n.). The Assyrians (*a nation afar off;* Jer.5.15, referring to Babylon) will be the executors of God's judgment.

their horses' hoofs seem like flint,
  and their wheels like the whirlwind.
²⁹ Their roaring is like a lion,
  like young lions they roar;
they growl and seize their prey,
  they carry it off, and none can rescue.
³⁰ They will growl over it on that day,
  like the roaring of the sea.
And if one look to the land,
  behold, darkness and distress;
and the light is darkened by its clouds.

6 In the year that King Uzzi'ah died I saw the Lord sitting upon a throne, high and lifted up; and his train filled the temple. ² Above him stood the seraphim; each had six wings: with two he covered his face, and with two he covered his feet, and with two he flew. ³ And one called to another and said:

"Holy, holy, holy is the LORD of hosts;
  the whole earth is full of his glory."

4 And the foundations of the thresholds shook at the voice of him who called, and the house was filled with smoke. ⁵ And I said: "Woe is me! For I am lost; for I am a man of unclean lips, and I dwell in the midst of a people of unclean lips; for my eyes have seen the King, the LORD of hosts!"

6 Then flew one of the seraphim to me, having in his hand a burning coal which he had taken with tongs from the altar. ⁷ And he touched my mouth, and said: "Behold, this has touched your lips; your guilt is taken away, and your sin forgiven." ⁸ And I heard the voice of the Lord saying, "Whom shall I send, and who will go for us?" then I said, "Here am I! Send me." ⁹ And he said, "Go, and say to this people:

'Hear and hear, but do not understand;
  see and see, but do not perceive.'
¹⁰ Make the heart of this people fat,
  and their ears heavy,
  and shut their eyes;
lest they see with their eyes,
  and hear with their ears,
and understand with their hearts,
  and turn and be healed."
¹¹ Then I said, "How long, O Lord?"
And he said:
"Until cities lie waste
  without inhabitant,
and houses without men,
  and the land is utterly desolate,
¹² and the LORD removes men far away,
  and the forsaken places are many in the
    midst of the land.
¹³ And though a tenth remain in it,
  it will be burned again,
like a terebinth or an oak,
  whose stump remains standing
  when it is felled."
The holy seed is its stump.

7 In the days of Ahaz the son of Jotham, son of Uzzi'ah, king of Judah, Rezin the king of Syria and Pekah the son of Remali'ah the king of Israel came up to Jerusalem to wage war against it, but they could not conquer it. ² When the house of David was told, "Syria is in league with E'phraim," his heart and the heart of his people shook as the trees of the forest shake before the wind.

3 And the LORD said to Isaiah, "Go forth to meet Ahaz, you and She'ar-jash'ub[h] your son, at the end of the conduit of the upper pool

h That is *A remnant shall return*

6.1–13: The call of Isaiah. God's appearance is described in the setting of the Jerusalem temple (compare the description of the enthroned deity in 1 Kg.22.19–23; Ezek.1.4–2.1). 1: *Year,* 742 B.C. *Throne,* ark of the covenant. 2: *Seraphim,* possibly griffin-like creatures; compare the cherubim, also associated with the glory of the Lord (Ezek. ch. 1). 3: Thrice-*holy* for emphasis (Jer.7.4). 5: Before the holy God, sinful man cannot stand (Ex.33.18–20). 6–8: Cleansed by God's forgiving act, Isaiah may now speak for God. 9–12: Compare Jer.1.10,13–19. Verses 9b–10 are quoted in Mt.13.10–15; compare Mk.4.12; Lk.8.10; Jn.12.39–41; Acts 28.26–27. 13: The last part of the verse is obscure and textually corrupt and perhaps should be restored to read, ". . . . like the terebinth [of the goddess] and the oak of Asherah, cast out with the pillar of the high places," that is, like the destroyed furnishings of a pagan high place.

7.1–8.15: Isaiah and the Syro-Ephraimite War (734–733 B.C.). For the historical background see 2 Kg.16.1–20. 1–9: Sign of Shear-jashub. 2: The continuation of the Davidic monarchy was threatened (see v. 6). 3: *Shear-jashub,* "A remnant shall return"; assuming the worst eventuality, God's promise to David (2 Sam.7.8–16) will be preserved in

on the highway to the Fuller's Field, [4] and say to him, 'Take heed, be quiet, do not fear, and do not let your heart be faint because of these two smoldering stumps of firebrands, at the fierce anger of Rezin and Syria and the son of Remali'ah. [5] Because Syria, with E'phraim and the son of Remali'ah, has devised evil against you, saying, [6] "Let us go up against Judah and terrify it; and let us conquer it for ourselves, and set up the son of Ta'be-el as king in the midst of it," [7] thus says the Lord GOD:

It shall not stand,
> and it shall not come to pass.
[8] For the head of Syria is Damascus,
> and the head of Damascus is Rezin.

(Within sixty-five years E'phraim will be broken to pieces so that it will no longer be a people.)
[9] And the head of E'phraim is Sama'ria,
> and the head of Sama'ria is the son of
>> Remali'ah.
If you will not believe,
> surely you shall not be established.'

10 Again the LORD spoke to Ahaz, [11] "Ask a sign of the LORD your God; let it be deep as Sheol or high as heaven." [12] But Ahaz said, "I will not ask, and I will not put the LORD to the test." [13] And he said, "Hear then, O house of David! Is it too little for you to weary men, that you weary my God also? [14] Therefore the Lord himself will give you a sign. Behold, a young woman[i] shall conceive and bear[j] a son, and shall call his name Imman'u-el.[k] [15] He shall eat curds and honey when he knows how to refuse the evil and choose the good. [16] For before the child knows how to refuse the evil and choose the good, the land before whose two kings you are in dread will be deserted. [17] The LORD will bring upon you and upon your people and upon your father's house such days as have not come since the day that E'phraim departed from Judah — the king of Assyria."

18 In that day the LORD will whistle for the fly which is at the sources of the streams of Egypt, and for the bee which is in the land of Assyria. [19] And they will all come and settle in the steep ravines, and in the clefts of the rocks, and on all the thornbushes, and on all the pastures.

20 In that day the Lord will shave with a razor which is hired beyond the River — with the king of Assyria — the head and the hair of the feet, and it will sweep away the beard also.

21 In that day a man will keep alive a young cow and two sheep; [22] and because of the abundance of milk which they give, he will eat curds; for every one that is left in the land will eat curds and honey.

23 In that day every place where there used to be a thousand vines, worth a thousand shekels of silver, will become briers and thorns. [24] With bow and arrows men will come there, for all the land will be briers and thorns; [25] and as for all the hills which used to be hoed with a hoe, you will not come there for fear of briers and thorns; but they will become a place where cattle are let loose and where sheep tread.

8 Then the LORD said to me, "Take a large tablet and write upon it in common characters, 'Belonging to Ma'her-shal'al-hash-baz.'"[l] [2] And I got reliable witnesses, Uri'ah the priest and Zechari'ah the son of Jeberechi'ah, to attest for me. [3] And I went to the prophet-

i Or *virgin* *j* Or *is with child and shall bear* *k* That is *God is with us*

---

the remnant (10.20–23). *Upper pool,* reservoir south of the Pool of Siloam. **5:** *Son of Tabeel,* perhaps a prince of Judah whose mother came from Tabeel, a region of northern Transjordan. **8–9a:** The text and meaning are unclear.

7.10–17: Sign of Immanuel. 13: This expresses Isaiah's impatience. **14:** The sign is *Immanuel,* "God with us"; a second (compare vv. 3–9) assurance to the frightened, wavering Ahaz. *Young woman,* Hebrew *'almah,* feminine of *'elem,* young man (1 Sam.17.56; 20.22); the word appears in Gen.24.43; Ex.2.8; Ps.68.25, and elsewhere, where it is translated "young woman," "girl," "maiden." **15:** *Curds, honey,* simple foods suggesting difficult times; *good and evil,* age of moral discrimination. **18–25:** Four threats amplifying v. 17. **20:** Feet, see Ex.4.25 n.

8.1–4: The sign of Maher-shalal-hash-baz, "The spoil speeds, the prey hastes"; Isaiah's third assurance to Ahaz. **1:** *Tablet,* of wood. **2:** *Uriah,* 2 Kg.16.10–16. *Zechariah,* perhaps Ahaz's father-in-law (2 Kg.18.2). **3:** *Prophetess,* Isa-

ess, and she conceived and bore a son. Then the LORD said to me, "Call his name Ma'her-shal'al-hash-baz; [4] for before the child knows how to cry 'My father' or 'My mother,' the wealth of Damascus and the spoil of Sama'ria will be carried away before the king of Assyria."

5 The LORD spoke to me again: [6] "Because this people have refused the waters of Shilo'ah that flow gently, and melt in fear before[m] Rezin and the son of Remali'ah; [7] therefore, behold, the Lord is bringing up against them the waters of the River, mighty and many, the king of Assyria and all his glory; and it will rise over all his channels and go over all its banks; [8] and it will sweep on into Judah, it will overflow and pass on, reaching even to the neck; and its outspread wings will fill the breadth of your land, O Imman'u-el."

[9] Be broken, you peoples, and be dismayed;
    give ear, all you far countries;
gird yourselves and be dismayed;
    gird yourselves and be dismayed.
[10] Take counsel together, but it will come to
        nought;
    speak a word, but it will not stand,
    for God is with us.[x]

11 For the LORD spoke thus to me with his strong hand upon me, and warned me not to walk in the way of this people, saying: [12] "Do not call conspiracy all that this people call conspiracy, and do not fear what they fear, nor be in dread. [13] But the LORD of hosts, him you shall regard as holy; let him be your fear, and let him be your dread. [14] And he will become a sanctuary, and a stone of offense, and a rock of stumbling to both houses of Israel, a trap and a snare to the inhabitants of Jerusalem. [15] And many shall stumble thereon; they shall fall and be broken; they shall be snared and taken."

16 Bind up the testimony, seal the teaching among my disciples. [17] I will wait for the LORD, who is hiding his face from the house of Jacob, and I will hope in him. [18] Behold, I and the children whom the LORD has given me are signs and portents in Israel from the LORD of hosts, who dwells on Mount Zion. [19] And when they say to you, "Consult the mediums and the wizards who chirp and mutter," should not a people consult their God? Should they consult the dead on behalf of the living? [20] To the teaching and to the testimony! Surely for this word which they speak there is no dawn. [21] They will pass through the land,[n] greatly distressed and hungry; and when they are hungry, they will be enraged and will curse[o] their king and their God, and turn their faces upward; [22] and they will look to the earth, but behold, distress and darkness, the gloom of anguish; and they will be thrust into thick darkness.

9[p] But there will be no gloom for her that was in anguish. In the former time he brought into contempt the land of Zeb'ulun and the land of Naph'tali, but in the latter time he will make glorious the way of the sea, the land beyond the Jordan, Galilee of the nations. [2q] The people who walked in darkness
    have seen a great light;

l That is *The spoil speeds, the prey hastes*
m Cn; Heb *rejoices in*   *x* Heb *immanu el*
n Heb *it*   *o* Or *curse by*   *p* Ch 8.23 in Heb

iah's wife. **5–8:** Oracle of Shiloah and the Euphrates; Judah also is included in Assyria's sweep. *Shiloah,* a conduit flanking Ophel from the spring Gihon (see 1 Kg.1.33 n.) to the reservoir (7.3), is contrasted with the *River,* the great Euphrates. Ahaz's mighty ally, Assyria, will inundate tiny Judah, God's people. **9–10:** God is with his people (see 7.14 n.) to deliver them (Ps. 46, esp. vv. 7,11).

8.11–22: The testimony and the teaching. 11–15: "Man proposes — God disposes" (Pr.16.9). **16:** *Bind, seal,* as one binds and seals a scroll (Jer.32.10). **18:** *Signs,* 7.3; 7.14; 8.1. **19–20:** Condemnation of superstition (2.6). for necromancy (consultation of the dead), see 1 Sam.28.7 n. **9.1:** Transitional verse from doom to promise. *Zebulun, Naphtali,* and Issachar constituted later *Galilee. Way of the sea,* the highway from Damascus to the sea, probable route of the Assyrian invasion in 733–732 B.C. (2 Kg.15.29).

9.2–7: The messianic king (compare 11.1–9). Filled with borrowed phrases referring to the Davidic monarchy, this passage may have originally celebrated the accession of a Judean king, perhaps Hezekiah; in its present context it

those who dwelt in a land of deep
     darkness,
   on them has light shined.
3 Thou hast multiplied the nation,
     thou hast increased its joy;
   they rejoice before thee
     as with joy at the harvest,
     as men rejoice when they divide the
       spoil.
4 For the yoke of his burden,
     and the staff for his shoulder,
     the rod of his oppressor,
     thou hast broken as on the day of
       Mid'ian.
5 For every boot of the tramping warrior in
     battle tumult
     and every garment rolled in blood
     will be burned as fuel for the fire.
6 For to us a child is born,
     to us a son is given;
   and the government will be upon his
     shoulder,
     and his name will be called
   "Wonderful Counselor, Mighty God,
     Everlasting Father, Prince of Peace."
7 Of the increase of his government and of
     peace
     there will be no end,
   upon the throne of David, and over his
     kingdom,
     to establish it, and to uphold it
   with justice and with righteousness
     from this time forth and for evermore.
   The zeal of the LORD of hosts will do this.

8 The Lord has sent a word against Jacob,
   and it will light upon Israel;
9 and all the people will know,
   E'phraim and the inhabitants of
     Sama'ria,

who say in pride and in arrogance of
     heart:
10 "The bricks have fallen,
     but we will build with dressed stones;
   the sycamores have been cut down,
     but we will put cedars in their place."
11 So the LORD raises adversaries[r] against
     them,
     and stirs up their enemies.
12 The Syrians on the east and the Philistines
     on the west
     devour Israel with open mouth.
   For all this his anger is not turned away
     and his hand is stretched out still.
13 The people did not turn to him who smote
     them,
     nor seek the LORD of hosts.
14 So the LORD cut off from Israel head and
     tail,
     palm branch and reed in one day —
15 the elder and honored man is the head,
     and the prophet who teaches lies is the
       tail;
16 for those who lead this people lead them
     astray,
     and those who are led by them are
       swallowed up.
17 Therefore the Lord does not rejoice over
     their young men,
     and has no compassion on their
       fatherless and widows;
   for every one is godless and an evildoer,
     and every mouth speaks folly.
   For all this his anger is not turned away
     and his hand is stretched out still.

18 For wickedness burns like a fire,
     it consumes briers and thorns;
     it kindles the thickets of the forest,

q Ch 9.1 in Heb   r Cn: Heb *the adversaries of Rezin*

describes the coming Messiah as the ideal king. **4:** *Midian,* Jg.7.15–25. **6:** *Government,* symbol of authority. *Mighty God,* divine in might. *Everlasting Father,* continuing fatherly love and care. *Prince of Peace,* the king who brings peace and prosperity. The king represents the best qualities of Israel's heroes (Ezek.37.25).
   9.8–10.4: Ephraim's judgment an object lesson for Judah (five stanzas, including 5.24b–30; with the same refrain, 9.12,17,21; 10.4; 5.25; compare Jer.3.6–10; Ezek.16.44–58). **8–12:** Punishment for pride and unrepented wickedness. **8:** *Word,* more than a statement; it includes the potential and fact of accomplishment (55.10–11; Jer.23.18–20). **10:** *Bricks, sycamore,* for ordinary houses; *dressed stone, cedar* for palaces (Jer.22.7,23). **13–17:** Corrupt leaders misled their people (Jer.6.14). **18–21:** Moral decay consumes like a forest fire (Hos.7.6); civil war breaks

and they roll upward in a column of
smoke.

19 Through the wrath of the LORD of hosts
the land is burned,
and the people are like fuel for the fire;
no man spares his brother.

20 They snatch on the right, but are still
hungry,
and they devour on the left, but are not
satisfied;
each devours his neighbor's[s] flesh,

21 Manas'seh E'phraim, and E'phraim
Manas'seh,
and together they are against Judah.
For all this his anger is not turned away
and his hand is stretched out still.

10 Woe to those who decree iniquitous
decrees,
and the writers who keep writing
oppression,

2 to turn aside the needy from justice
and to rob the poor of my people of
their right,
that widows may be their spoil,
and that they may make the fatherless
their prey!

3 What will you do on the day of punishment,
in the storm which will come from afar?
To whom will you flee for help,
and where will you leave your wealth?

4 Nothing remains but to crouch among the
prisoners
or fall among the slain.
For all this his anger is not turned away
and his hand is stretched out still.

5 Ah, Assyria, the rod of my anger,
the staff of my fury![t]

6 Against a godless nation I send him,

and against the people of my wrath I
command him,
to take spoil and seize plunder,
and to tread them down like the mire of
the streets.

7 But he does not so intend,
and his mind does not so think;
but it is in his mind to destroy,
and to cut off nations not a few;

8 for he says:
"Are not my commanders all kings?

9 Is not Calno like Car'chemish?
Is not Hamath like Arpad?
Is not Sama'ria like Damascus?

10 As my hand has reached to the kingdoms
of the idols
whose graven images were greater than
those of Jerusalem and Sama'ria,

11 shall I not do to Jerusalem and her idols
as I have done to Sama'ria and her
images?"

12 When the Lord has finished all his
work on Mount Zion and on Jerusalem he[u]
will punish the arrogant boasting of the king
of Assyria and his haughty pride. 12 For he
says:

"By the strength of my hand I have done it,
and by my wisdom, for I have
understanding;
I have removed the boundaries of peoples,
and have plundered their treasures;
like a bull I have brought down those
who sat on thrones.

14 My hand has found like a nest
the wealth of the peoples;
and as men gather eggs that have been
forsaken
so I have gathered all the earth;

s Tg Compare Gk: Heb *the flesh of his arm*
t Heb *a staff it is in their hand my fury*   u Heb *I*

---

out (2 Kg.15.23–31; 16.5). **20:** *His neighbor's flesh;* the Hebrew consonantal text may be read "the flesh of his off-spring" (on cannibalism, see Jer.19.9). Some treat this passage as a proverb. **10.1–4:** Justice is miscarried (3.13–15; Jer.8.8).

10.5–19: Woe, O Assyria! Unaware that he was serving as God's instrument, powerful Assyria was doomed by his pride to destruction (Jer.25.8–14; 50.23). **9:** In northern Syria, Tiglath-Pileser III captured *Calno* (742 B.C.), *Carchemish, Hamath* (738), *Arpad* (741), southern Syria, *Damascus* (732). Menahem of Israel paid him tribute (2 Kg.15.19–20). **10–11:** To Assyria, the LORD was another idol. **12:** Prose summation of vv. 5–11,13–19. **13–14:** Assyria's boast.

and there was none that moved a wing,
or opened the mouth, or chirped."

15 Shall the axe vaunt itself over him who
hews with it,
or the saw magnify itself against him
who wields it?
As if a rod should wield him who lifts it,
or as if a staff should lift him is not
wood!
16 Therefore the Lord, the LORD of hosts,
will send wasting sickness among his
stout warriors,
and under his glory a burning will be
kindled,
like the burning of fire.
17 The light of Israel will become a fire,
and his Holy One a flame;
and it will burn and devour
his thorns and briers in one day.
18 The glory of his forest and of his fruitful
land
the LORD will destroy, both soul and
body,
and it will be as when a sick man wastes
away.
19 The remnant of the trees of his forest will
be so few
that a child can write them down.

20 In that day the remnant of Israel and the
survivors of the house of Jacob will no more
lean upon him that smote them, but will lean
upon the LORD, the Holy One of Israel, in
truth. 21 A remnant will return, the remnant of
Jacob, to the mighty God. 22 For though your
people Israel be as the sand of the sea, only a
remnant of them will return. Destruction is
decreed, overflowing with righteousness.
23 For the Lord, the LORD of hosts, will make
a full end, as decreed, in the midst of all the
earth.

24 Therefore thus says the Lord, the LORD
of hosts: "O my people, who dwell in Zion, be
not afraid of the Assyrians when they smite
with the rod and lift up their staff against you
as the Egyptians did. 25 For in a very little
while my indignation will come to an end, and
my anger will be directed to their destruction.
26 And the LORD of hosts will wield against
them a scourge, as when he smote Mid′ian at
the rock of Oreb; and his rod will be over the
sea, and he will lift it as he did in Egypt.
27 And in that day his burden will depart from
your shoulder, and his yoke will be destroyed
from your neck."

He has gone up from Rommon,ᵛ
28   has come to Ai′ath;
he has passed through Migron,
at Michmash he stores his baggage;
29 they have crossed over the pass,
at Geba they lodge for the night;
Ramah trembles,
Gib′e-ah of Saul has fled.
30 Cry aloud, O daughter of Gallim!
Hearken, O La′ishah!
Answer her, O An′athoth!

v Cn: Heb *and his yoke from your neck, and a yoke will
be destroyed because of fatness*

Removed boundaries, to discourage rebellion, Assyria transplanted subject peoples. **15:** Rhetorical question recalling
v. 5 (45.9). **16–19:** Light of Israel, God's majestic glory (2.10; 29.6; Ezek.1.26–28). God will ravage Assyria like a
forest fire.
  10.20–23: Only a remnant will return. 21: *A remnant will return,* in Hebrew this is the same as the name of Isaiah's son Shear-jashub; in 7.3–4 it stands in an oracle of encouragement, but here in an oracle of doom. **22:** *Sand of the
sea* recalls God's oath to the patriarchs (Gen.22.17; compare Rom.9.27). In Isaiah (4.2–3; 6.13; 7.3; 28.5–6; 37.4;
37.31–32; compare Mic.4.7; 5.2–9; Zeph.2.7) *remnant* refers to those remaining after Judah's punishment, from
whom a great people will arise. During the Exile the remnant was the deported people (Ezek.6.8–10; Jer.23.3; 31.7),
whom God would bring back and make great. After the Exile Jewish faithlessness evoked again the pre-exilic concept
(Zech.8.11; Hag.1.12; Zech.14.2).
  10.24–27c: Oracle of promise. *Oreb,* Jg.7.25; *rod,* Ex.14.16.
  10.27d–32: The approach of the Assyrians. The invader (Tiglath-Pileser III or Sennacherib, 1.4–9 n.)
approached from the north toward the outskirts of Jerusalem (Jer.6.1–3). This may be a "traditional" description of the
northern invasion route; for a southern route, see Mic.1.10–15. **33–34:** The LORD, the forester, will cut down Assyria.

31 Madme′nah is in flight,
    the inhabitants of Gebim flee for safety.
32 This very day he will halt at Nob,
    he will shake his fist
    at the mount of the daughter of Zion,
    the hill of Jerusalem.

33 Behold, the Lord, the LORD of hosts
    will lop the boughs with terrifying
        power;
    the great in height will be hewn down,
    and the lofty will be brought low.
34 He will cut down the thickets of the forest
        with an axe,
    and Lebanon with its majestic trees[w]
        will fall.

11 There shall come forth a shoot from
    the stump of Jesse,
    and a branch shall grow out of his roots.
2 And the Spirit of the LORD shall rest upon
        him,
    the spirit of wisdom and understanding,
    the spirit of counsel and might,
    the spirit of knowledge and the fear of
        the LORD.
3 And his delight shall be in the fear of the
        LORD.

He shall not judge by what his eyes see,
    or decide by what his ears hear;
4 but with righteousness he shall judge the
        poor,
    and decide with equity for the meek of
        the earth;
    and he shall smite the earth with the rod of
        his mouth,
    and with the breath of his lips he shall
        slay the wicked.

5 Righteousness shall be the girdle of his
        waist,
    and faithfulness the girdle of his loins.

6 The wolf shall dwell with the lamb,
    and the leopard shall lie down with the
        kid,
    and the calf and the lion and the fatling
        together,
    and a little child shall lead them.
7 The cow and the bear shall feed;
    their young shall lie down together;
    and the lion shall eat straw like the ox.
8 The sucking child shall play over the hole
        of the asp,
    and the weaned child shall put his hand
        on the adder's den.
9 They shall not hurt or destroy
    in all my holy mountain;
    for the earth shall be full of the knowledge
        of the LORD
    as the waters cover the sea.

10 In that day the root of Jesse shall stand as
an ensign to the peoples; him shall the nations
seek, and his dwellings shall be glorious.

11 In that day the Lord will extend his
hand yet a second time to recover the remnant
which is left of his people, from Assyria, from
Egypt, from Pathros, from Ethiopia, from
Elam, from Shinar, from Hamath, and from
the coastlands of the sea.
12 He will raise an ensign for the nations,
    and will assemble the outcasts of Israel,
    and gather the dispersed of Judah
    from the four corners of the earth.
13 The jealousy of E′phraim shall depart,
    and those who harass Judah shall be cut
        off;

w Cn Compare Gk Vg: Heb *with a majestic one*

11.1–9: The messianic king (compare 9.2–7). For the occasion of the original oracle, see 9.2–7 n. **1–3a:** The Messiah will manifest the characteristics of Israel's great men. **1:** *Jesse,* David's father (1 Sam.16.1–20). **2:** To these six "Gifts of the Spirit" the Septuagint adds "piety." **3b–5:** Wisdom and justice (5.7) were traditionally associated in the ideal king (1 Kg. ch. 3; Ps. 72). **6–8:** His reign will be "paradise regained"; the disorder of nature will be restored to its pristine harmony (Ezek.47.1–12). **9:** *My holy mountain,* 65.25; Ezek.20.40.
11.10–16: The messianic age. 10: *Root* is a person, not the dynasty (v. 1). **11–16:** Restored and reunited Israel takes vengeance against her oppressors. The terminology and mood of vv. 11–16 indicate a post-exilic date. **11:** *Pathros,* Upper Egypt; *Shinar,* Babylonia; *coastlands,* Aegean seacoast and islands. **12:** *Ensign,* here a standard, not a person (v. 10). **15:** *The tongue of the sea,* the Red Sea (Ex. ch. 14), *River,* Euphrates.

E'phraim shall not be jealous of Judah,
and Judah shall not harass E'phraim.
[14] But they shall swoop down upon the
shoulder of the Philistines in the west,
and together they shall plunder the
people of the east.
They shall put forth their hand against
Edom and Moab,
and the Ammonites shall obey them.
[15] And the LORD will utterly destroy
the tongue of the sea of Egypt;
and will wave his hand over the River
with his scorching wind,
and smite it into seven channels
that men may cross dryshod.
[16] And there will be a highway from Assyria
for the remnant which is left of his people,
as there was for Israel
when they came up from the land of
Egypt.

12 You will say in that day: "I will give
thanks to thee, O LORD,
for though thou wast angry with me,

thy anger turned away,
and thou didst comfort me.

[2] "Behold, God is my salvation;
I will trust, and will not be afraid;
for the LORD GOD is my strength and my
song,
and he has become my salvation."
3 With joy you will draw water from the
wells of salvation. [4] And you will say in that
day:
"Give thanks to the LORD,
call upon his name;
make known his deeds among the nations,
proclaim that his name is exalted.

[5] "Sing praises to the LORD, for he has done
gloriously;
let this be known[x] in all the earth.
[6] Shout, and sing for joy, O inhabitant of
Zion,
for great in your midst is the Holy One
of Israel."

x Or *this is made known*

12.1–6: Two songs conclude Section I of the book of Isaiah. (a) **1–3:** Song of deliverance (compare Ps. 116). **1a** and **4a** are liturgical rubrics. **2b:** Ex.15.2; Ps.118.14. (b) **4–6:** Song of thanksgiving. *Shout and sing for joy,* compare Zeph.3.14. *In your midst,* God in his temple. *Holy One,* see 1.4.

THE NEW TESTAMENT

Introduction by Constance Bouchard

Because Christianity began as a sect of Judaism, the original Christian Bible was exactly the same as the Jewish Bible. However, both oral and written accounts of the life and death of Jesus soon began taking on a significance for believers equal to the teachings of the Bible they already had. Although it took close to two centuries to decide which accounts belonged in the "new" Bible, and although some people argued, unsuccessfully, that Christians needed to reject the Jewish Bible, eventually a general agreement was reached on what belonged in the "New" Testament, to put alongside the "Old" Testament they already had. The New Testament was written in Greek, the language of all educated people in the eastern parts of the Roman Empire, which in the first few centuries A.D. included the entire Mediterranean region.

The New Testament, as it was put together by the second century A.D., begins with four different accounts of Jesus and his teachings. They are generally credited with having been written by Matthew, Mark, Luke, and John, all names of apostles of Jesus; in fact, it is not known who actually wrote them, but the names are convenient labels. The four accounts, or "gospels," take quite different positions on the significance of the life of Jesus, a Jewish teacher who was put to death by the Romans, on grounds of sedition, around 30 A.D. All four gospels were written within a generation or so after 70 A.D., when the Romans cracked down on Jewish rebellion against Roman domination and destroyed the Temple in Jerusalem. The Gospel of Mark is the earliest, and that of John the last, to be written. All four gospels were written by men who thought that they, and they alone, understood the true significance of Jesus. But in the second century A.D., rather than argue about which version was the best, the Christian community decided to accept all four, putting them back to back. From then on, Christians put parts of all four gospels together for a coherent story of Jesus, ignoring or reconciling the gospels' differences.

The gospels are not, however, the oldest part of the New Testament. The oldest part is the letters of Paul. Paul was a highly-educated Jew who was also a Roman citizen (as not many Jews were in the first century A.D.). Although he never met Jesus personally, he became an early leader of the new Christian sect. He helped spread Christianity through the Roman Empire, wandering from one Christian community to another. His letters were sent to friends in these communities when he was elsewhere. His significance, however, lies in his theology. Paul was the first to apply Hellenistic philosophy, in which he was highly learned, to Christian doctrine.

Hence, from the beginning, Christianity was influenced by a combination of Jewish thought, Greek philosophy, and Roman culture, as well as the specific teachings of Jesus.

The following selections begin with the Gospel of Matthew, which was an account of the life of Jesus composed specifically for a Jewish audience. One of the earliest questions within the Christian community was whether it would continue, as it had begun, as a form of Judaism, or whether non-Jews could be admitted. This gospel was written to argue that Christianity was the culmination of Jewish prophecy. Thus it begins by invoking Abraham, the original Jewish patriarch, and by demonstrating that Jesus was descended from Abraham via King David. In this gospel the Roman governors, like Pilate, or the kings like Herod who ruled as puppets of the Romans, are the chief enemies of the Jews, but the Jewish priests are also portrayed as bitterly opposed to Jesus. Here the author is suggesting that Jews ought to realize that Christianity was the culmination of Judaism, but that many Jewish leaders wrongly refused to recognize this.

The Gospel of John begins quite differently, not with Jewish antecedents, but with a statement on the nature of the Word that incorporates Hellenistic philosophy with Christianity. Although the author indicated that Jesus had fulfilled Jewish prophecy (especially that of Isaiah), he was at pains to distinguish Judaism and Christianity. This gospel author wrote about two generations after Paul wrote his Letter to the Romans, which set out very clearly the philosophical underpinnings which he saw in Christianity, and also distinguished Jewish and Christian beliefs. Paul's discussion of sin and salvation in this letter became the basis of all later Christian theology.

The Gospel According to Matthew

THE BOOK OF THE GENEALOGY OF Jesus Christ, the son of David, the son of Abraham.

2 Abraham was the father of Isaac, and Isaac the father of Jacob, and Jacob the father of Judah and his brothers, ³ and Judah the father of Perez and Zerah by Tamar, and Perez the father of Hezron, and Hezron the father of Ram,ᵃ ⁴ and Ramᵃ the father of Ammin′adab, and Ammin′adab the father of Nahshon, and Nahshon the father of Salmon, ⁵ and Salmon the father of Bo′az by Rahab, and Bo′az the father of Obed by Ruth, and Obed the father of Jesse, ⁶ and Jesse the father of David the king.

And David was the father of Solomon by the wife of Uri′ah, ⁷ and Solomon the father of Rehobo′am, and Rehobo′am the father of Abi′jah, and Abi′jah the father of Asa,ᵇ ⁸ and Asaᵇ the father of Jehosh′aphat, and Jehosh′aphat the father of Joram, and Joram the father of Uzzi′ah, ⁹ and Uzzi′ah the father of Jotham, and Jotham the father of Ahaz, and Ahaz the father of Hezeki′ah, ¹⁰ and Hezeki′ah the father of Manas′seh, and Manas′seh the father of Amos,ᶜ and Amosᶜ the father of Josi′ah,¹¹ and Josi′ah the father of Jechoni′ah and his brothers, at the time of the deportation to Babylon.

12 And after the deportation to Babylon: Jechoni′ah was the father of She-al′ti-el,ᵈ and She-al′ti-elᵈ the father of Zerub′babel, ¹³ and Zerub′babel the father of Abi′ud, and Abi′ud the father of Eli′akim, and Eli′akim the father of Azor, ¹⁴ and Azor the father of Zadok, and Zadok the father of Achim, and Achim the father of Eli′ud, ¹⁵ and Eli′ud the father of Elea′zar, and Elea′zar the father of Matthan, and Matthan the father of Jacob, ¹⁰ and Jacob the father of Joseph the husband of Mary, of whom Jesus was born, who is called Christ.

17 So all the generations from Abraham to David were fourteen generations, and from David to the deportation to Babylon fourteen generations, and from the deportation to Babylon to the Christ fourteen generations.

18 Now the birth of Jesus Christᶠ took place in this way. When his mother Mary had been betrothed to Joseph, before they came together she was found to be with child of the Holy Spirit; ¹⁹ and her husband Joseph, being a just man and unwilling to put her to shame, resolved to divorce her quietly. ²⁰ But as he considered this, behold, an angel of the Lord appeared to him in a dream, saying, "Joseph, son of David, do not fear to take Mary your wife, for that which is conceived in her is of the Holy Spirit; ²¹ she will bear a son, and you shall call his name Jesus, for he will save his people from their sins." ²² All this took place to fulfil what the Lord had spoken by the prophet:

23 "Behold, a virgin shall conceive and bear
     a son,
   and his name shall be called Emman′u-el"
(which means, God with us). ²⁴ When Joseph woke from sleep, he did as the angel of the Lord commanded him; he took his wife, ²⁵ but knew her not until she had borne a son; and he called his name Jesus.

---

a Greek *Aram*   b Greek *Asaph*   c Other authorities read *Amon*   d Greek *Salaṭhiel*   ƒ Other ancient authorities read *of the Christ*

1.1–17: Jesus' royal descent (Lk.3.23–38) is traced through *David the king* (22.41–45; Rom. 1.3) back to Abraham the patriarch (Gal.3.16). **3–6:** Ru.4.18–22; 1 Chr.2.1–15. **11:** *The deportation,* 2 Kg.24.8–16; Jer.27.20. **12:** *Jeconiah,* or Jehoiachin (2 Kg.24.6; 1 Chr.3.16). *Shealtiel* apparently transmitted the line of legal descent from *Jeconiah* to *Zerubbabel* (Ezra 3.2; Hag.2.2; Lk.3.27), although the Chronicler traces it through Pedaiah (1 Chr.3.16–19). **13–16:** The persons from *Abiud* to *Jacob* are otherwise unknown. **16:** *Christ,* the Greek translation of the Hebrew word "Messiah," which means "anointed one" (compare Lev.4.3,5,16; 2 Sam.1.14,16).

1.18–2.23: Jesus' birth and infancy (Lk.1.26–2.40). **20:** *Angel,* see Heb.1.14 n. **21:** The Hebrew and Aramaic forms of *Jesus* and *he will save* are similar. The point could be suggested by translating, "You shall call his name 'Savior' because he will save." **22–23:** See Is.7.14 n. **25:** *Until:* According to Catholic teaching, the Semitic idiom in the use of *until* here does not imply that they had conjugal relations after the birth of Jesus.

Bible, THE NEW OXFORD ANNOTATED BIBLE WITH THE APOCRYPHA Revised Standard Edition, All of Matthew's Gospel.

2 Now when Jesus was born in Bethlehem of Judea in the days of Herod the king, behold, wise men from the East came to Jerusalem, saying [2] "Where is he who has been born king of the Jews? For we have seen his star in the East, and have come to worship him." [3] When Herod the king heard this, he was troubled, and all Jerusalem with him; [4] and assembling all the chief priests and scribes of the people, he inquired of them where the Christ was to be born. [5] They told him, "In Bethlehem of Judea; for so it is written by the prophet:

[6]   'And you, O Bethlehem, in the land of
        Judah,
      are by no means least among the rulers of
        Judah;
      for from you shall come a ruler
      who will govern my people Israel.'"

[7] Then Herod summoned the wise men secretly and ascertained from them what time the star appeared; [8] and he sent them to Bethlehem, saying, "Go and search diligently for the child, and when you have found him bring me word, that I too may come and worship him." [9] When they had heard the king they went their way; and lo, the star which they had seen in the East went before them, till it came to rest over the place where the child was. [10] When they saw the star, they rejoiced exceedingly with great joy; [11] and going into the house they saw the child with Mary his mother, and they fell down and worshiped him. Then, opening their treasures, they offered him gifts, gold and frankincense and myrrh. [12] And being warned in a dream not to return to Herod, they departed to their own country by another way.

13 Now when they had departed, behold, an angel of the Lord appeared to Joseph in a dream and said, "Rise, take the child and his mother, and flee to Egypt, and remain there till I tell you; for Herod is about to search for the child, to destroy him." [14] And he rose and took the child and his mother by night, and departed to Egypt, [15] and remained there until the death of Herod. This was to fulfil what the Lord had spoken by the prophet, "Out of Egypt have I called my son."

16 Then Herod, when he saw that he had been tricked by the wise men, was in a furious rage, and he sent and killed all the male children in Bethlehem and in all that region who were two years old or under, according to the time which he had ascertained from the wise men. [17] Then was fulfilled what was spoken by the prophet Jeremiah:

[18] "A voice was heard in Ramah,
      wailing and loud lamentation,
      Rachel weeping for her children;
      she refused to be consoled,
      because they were no more."

19 But when Herod died, behold, an angel of the Lord appeared in a dream to Joseph in Egypt, saying, [20] "Rise, take the child and his mother, and go to the land of Israel, for those who sought the child's life are dead." [21] And he rose and took the child and his mother, and went to the land of Israel. [22] But when he heard that Archela'us reigned over Judea in place of his father Herod, he was afraid to go there, and being warned in a dream he withdrew to the district of Galilee. [23] And he went and dwelt in a city called Nazareth, that what was spoken by the prophets might be fulfilled, "He shall be called a Nazarene."

2.1–12: **The wise men** (Magi). **1:** *Herod* the Great died early in 4 B.C. The *wise men,* a learned class in ancient Persia. **2:** Jer.23.5; Num.24.17. **5:** Jn.7.42. **6:** Mic.5.2. **11:** See Lk.2.7 n.

2.13–23: **Escape to Egypt and return. 15:** *Out of Egypt.* . . , a quotation from Hos.11.1, where the reference is to Israel (compare Ex.4.22). **18:** Quoted from Jer.31.15. *Rachel,* wife of Jacob, died in childbirth and according to Gen.35.16–20 was buried near Bethlehem. *Ramah,* north of Jerusalem, was the scene of national grief (Jer.40.1) inflicted by an enemy. **22:** *Archelaus* reigned from 4 B.C. to A.D. 6 and was replaced by a Roman procurator. **23:** There is a similarity in sound and possibly in meaning between the Aramaic word for *Nazareth* and the Hebrew word translated *branch* (Is.11.1).

3 In those days came John the Baptist, preaching in the wilderness of Judea, [2] "Repent, for the kingdom of heaven is at hand." [3] For this is he who was spoken of by the prophet Isaiah when he said,

"The voice of one crying in the wilderness:
Prepare the way of the Lord,
make his paths straight."

[4] Now John wore a garment of camel's hair, and a leather girdle around his waist; and his food was locusts and wild honey. [5] Then went out to him Jerusalem and all Judea and all the region about the Jordan, [6] and they were baptized by him in the river Jordan, confessing their sins.

[7] But when he saw many of the Pharisees and Sad'ducees coming for baptism, he said to them, "You brood of vipers! Who warned you to flee from the wrath to come? [8] Bear fruit that befits repentance, [9] and do not presume to say to yourselves, 'We have Abraham as our father'; for I tell you, God is able from these stones to raise up children to Abraham. [10] Even now the axe is laid to the root of the trees; every tree therefore that does not bear good fruit is cut down and thrown into the fire. [11] "I baptize you with water for repentance, but he who is coming after me is mightier than I, whose sandals I am not worthy to carry; he will baptize you with the Holy Spirit and with fire. [12] His winnowing fork is in his hand, and he will clear his threshing floor and gather his wheat into the granary, but the chaff he will burn with unquenchable fire."

[13] Then Jesus came from Galilee to the Jordan to John, to be baptized by him. [14] John would have prevented him, saying, "I need to be baptized by you, and do you come to me?" [15] But Jesus answered him, "Let it be so now; for thus it is fitting for us to fulfil all righteousness." Then he consented. [16] And when Jesus was baptized, he went up immediately from the water, and behold, the heavens were opened[g] and he saw the Spirit of God descending like a dove, and alighting on him; [17] and lo, a voice from heaven, saying, "This is my beloved Son,[h] with whom I am well pleased."

4 Then Jesus was led up by the Spirit into the wilderness to be tempted by the devil. [2] And he fasted forty days and forty nights, and afterward he was hungry. [3] And the tempter came and said to him, "If you are the Son of God, command these stones to become loaves of bread." [4] But he answered, "It is written,

'Man shall not live by bread alone,
but by every word that proceeds from the
mouth of God.'"

g Other ancient authorities add *to him*   h Or *my Son, my* (or *the*) *Beloved*

3.1–12: **Activity of John the Baptist** (Mk.1.1–8; Lk.3.1–18; Jn.1.6–8,19–28). **1:** *John* resembled the Old Testament prophets (compare v. 4 with 2 Kg.1.8; Zech.13.4). Christian faith understood him to fulfil Is.40.3; Mal.3.1; 4.5 (see 3.3; 17.10–12). His influence outside Christianity is attested by Acts 18.25; 19.1–7. *Those days*, namely, when Jesus began his public life. *The wilderness of Judea* lay east and southeast of Jerusalem. **2:** *Repent*, literally "return," meant to come back to the way of life charted by the covenant between God and Israel (Ex.19.3–6; 24.3–8; Jer.31.31–34). *The kingdom*, see 4.17 n. **3:** Is.40.3 **6:** See Mk.1.4 n. **7:** *Pharisees* and *Sadducees* formed two major divisions among the Jews (for differences between them, see 22.23 n. and Acts 23.6–10). A third Jewish sect in Palestine was the Essenes (see Josephus, *B. J.*, II, viii, 2–13); their beliefs and practices are reflected in the Dead Sea Scrolls found at Qumran (see "Survey of . . . Bible Lands," §15, end). *The wrath to come*, God's judgment (1 Th. 1.10). **8–10:** See Lk.3.7–9 n.; Jn.8.33. **11–12:** See Lk.12.49 n.; Acts 2.17–21; 19.1–7; 18.24–26.

3.13–17: **Jesus' baptism** (Mk.1.9–11; Lk.3.21–22; Jn.1.31–34). **13–15:** Jesus recognized John's authority and identified himself with those who responded in faith to John's call. **16–17:** A description of the surge of certainty and self-understanding that came to Jesus at his baptism. The language, akin to Old Testament speech, portrays a spiritual experience which words cannot adequately describe. *Beloved Son*, see Mk.1.11 n.

4.1–11: **Jesus' temptation** (Mk.1.12–13; Lk.4.1–13; Heb.2.18; 4.15). The accounts illustrate Jesus' habitual refusal to allow his sense of mission to be influenced by concern for his safety or for merely practical interests. **1:** *The devil, tempter* (v. 3), and *Satan* (v. 10) are names for evil conceived as a personal will actively hostile to God (see Lk.13.11,16 n.). **2:** *Forty*, compare Ex.34.28; 1 Kg.19.8. **3:** *If you are the Son of God*; but see the declaration in 3.17. **4:** Dt.8.3. **5:** *The holy city*, Jerusalem. **6:** Ps.91.11–12. **7:** Dt.6.16. **10:** Dt.6.13.

[5] Then the devil took him to the holy city, and set him on the pinnacle of the temple, [6] and said to him, "If you are the Son of God, throw yourself down; for it is written,

'He will give his angels charge of you,'
and
'On their hands they will bear you up,
 lest you strike your foot against a stone.'"

[7] Jesus said to him, "Again it is written, 'You shall not tempt the Lord your God.'" [8] Again, the devil took him to a very high mountain, and showed him all the kingdoms of the world and the glory of them; [9] and he said to him, "All these I will give you, if you will fall down and worship me." [10] Then Jesus said to him, "Begone, Satan! for it is written,

'You shall worship the Lord your God
 and him only shall you serve.'"

[11] Then the devil left him, and behold, angels came and ministered to him.

12 Now when he heard that John had been arrested, he withdrew into Galilee; [13] and leaving Nazareth he went and dwelt in Caper'na-um by the sea, in the territory of Zeb'ulun and Naph'tali, [14] that what was spoken by the prophet Isaiah might be fulfilled:

[15] "The land of Zeb'ulun and the land of
        Naph'tali,
    toward the sea, across the Jordan,
    Galilee of the Gentiles —
[16] the people who sat in darkness
        have seen a great light,
    and for those who sat in the region and
        shadow of death
    light has dawned."

[17] From that time Jesus began to preach, saying, "Repent, for the kingdom of heaven is at hand."

18 As he walked by the Sea of Galilee, he saw two brothers, Simon who is called Peter and Andrew his brother, casting a net into the sea; for they were fishermen. [19] And he said to them, "Follow me, and I will make you fishers of men." [20] Immediately they left their nets and followed him. [21] And going on from there he saw two other brothers, James the son of Zeb'edee and John his brother, in the boat with Zeb'edee their father, mending their nets, and he called them. [22] Immediately they left the boat and their father, and followed him.

23 And he went about all Galilee, teaching in their synagogues and preaching the gospel of the kingdom and healing every disease and every infirmity among the people. [24] So his fame spread throughout all Syria, and they brought him all the sick, those afflicted with various diseases and pains, demoniacs, epileptics, and paralytics, and he healed them. [25] And great crowds followed him from Galilee and the Decap'olis and Jerusalem and Judea and from beyond the Jordan.

5 Seeing the crowds, he went up on the mountain, and when he sat down his disciples came to him. [2] And he opened his mouth and taught them, saying:

3 "Blessed are the poor in spirit, for theirs is the kingdom of heaven.

4 "Blessed are those who mourn, for they shall be comforted.

4.12–25: Beginnings of Jesus' activity in Galilee. 12–17: Mk.1.14–15; Lk.4.14–15. **15–16:** Is.9.1–2. **17:** *From that time,* the arrest of John (v. 12). *The kingdom of heaven* is Matthew's usual way of expressing the equivalent phrase, "the kingdom of God," found in parallel accounts in the other gospels. In asserting that God's *kingdom is at hand* Jesus meant that all God's past dealings with his creation were coming to climax and fruition. Jesus taught both the present reality of God's rule (Lk.10.18; 11.20; 17.21) and its future realization (Mt.6.10). See Mk.1.15 n. **18–22:** Mk.1.16–20; Lk.5.1–11; Jn.1.35–42. **24:** *Demoniacs,* persons controlled in body or will, or in both, by evil forces (Mt.8.16,28; 9.32; 15.22; Mk.5.15; see Lk.13.11,16 n.). *Demons,* see Lk.4.33 n. **25:** *Decapolis,* see Mk.5.20 n.

5.1–7.27: The Sermon on the Mount sounds the keynote of the new age which Jesus came to introduce. Internal analysis and comparison with Luke's Gospel suggest that the Evangelist (in accord with his habit of synthesis) has inserted into this account of the Sermon portions of Jesus' teaching given on other occasions. **1:** *He sat down,* the usual position of Jewish rabbis while teaching (compare Lk.4.20–21).

5.3–12: The Beatitudes (Lk.6.17,20–23) proclaim God's favor toward those who aspire to live under his rule. **3:** *Poor in spirit,* those who feel a deep sense of spiritual poverty (Is.66.2). **4:** *Comforted,* the word implies strengthening

5 "Blessed are the meek, for they shall inherit the earth.

6 "Blessed are those who hunger and thirst for righteousness, for they shall be satisfied.

7 "Blessed are the merciful, for they shall obtain mercy.

8 "Blessed are the pure in heart, for they shall see God.

9 "Blessed are the peacemakers, for they shall be called sons of God.

10 "Blessed are those who are persecuted for righteousness' sake, for theirs is the kingdom of heaven.

11 "Blessed are you when men revile you and persecute you and utter all kinds of evil against you falsely on my account. ^{12} Rejoice and be glad, for your reward is great in heaven, for so men persecuted the prophets who were before you.

13 "You are the salt of the earth; but if salt has lost its taste, how shall its saltness be restored? It is no longer good for anything except to be thrown out and trodden under foot by men.

14 "You are the light of the world. A city set on a hill cannot be hid. ^{15} Nor do men light a lamp and put it under a bushel, but on a stand, and it gives light to all in the house. ^{16} Let your light so shine before men, that they may see your good works and give glory to your Father who is in heaven.

17 "Think not that I have come to abolish the law and the prophets; I have come not to abolish them but to fulfil them. ^{18} For truly, I say to you, till heaven and earth pass away, not

an iota, not a dot, will pass from the law until all is accomplished. ^{19} Whoever then relaxes one of the least of these commandments and teaches men so, shall be called least in the kingdom of heaven; but he who does them and teaches them shall be called great in the kingdom of heaven. ^{20} For I tell you, unless your righteousness exceeds that of the scribes and Pharisees, you will never enter the kingdom of heaven.

21 "You have heard that it was said to the men of old, 'You shall not kill; and whoever kills shall be liable to judgment.' ^{22} But I say to you that every one who is angry with his brother^i shall be liable to judgment; whoever insults^j his brother shall be liable to the council, and whoever says, 'You fool!' shall be liable to the hell^k of fire. ^{23} So if you are offering your gift at the altar, and there remember that your brother has something against you, ^{24} leave your gift there before the altar and go; first be reconciled to your brother, and then come and offer your gift. ^{25} Make friends quickly with your accuser, while you are going with him to court, lest your accuser hand you over to the judge, and the judge to the guard, and you be put in prison; ^{26} truly, I say to you, you will never get out till you have paid the last penny.

27 "You have heard that it was said, 'You shall not commit adultery.' ^{28} But I say to you that every one who looks at a woman lustfully

i Other ancient authorities insert *without cause*
j Greek *says Raca to* (an obscure term of abuse)
k Greek *Gehenna*

as well as consolation. **5:** Ps.37.11. **6:** Is.55.1–2; Jn.4.14; 6.48–51. **8:** Purity of *heart* is single-mindedness or sincerity, freedom from mixed motives; it is not synonymous with chastity, but includes it (Ps.24.4; Heb.12.14). *See God*, 1 Cor.13.12; 1 Jn.3.2; Rev. 22.4. **9:** *Peacemakers* are not merely "peaceable," but those who work earnestly to "make" peace. **10:** 1 Pet.3.14; 4.14. **12:** 2 Chr.36.15–16; Mt.23–3; Acts 7.52.

5.13–16: The witness of the disciples. 13: Mk.9.49–50; Lk.14.34–35. **14:** Phil.2.15; Jn.8.12. **15:** See Mk.4.21 n. **16:** 1 Pet.2.12.

5.17–20: The relation of Jesus' message to the Jewish law was a great concern to followers with a Jewish background. **17:** *The prophets* in the Hebrew Scriptures comprise the books of Joshua, Judges, Samuel, Kings, Isaiah, Jeremiah, Ezekiel, and the twelve minor prophets (see Lk.24.27 n., 44 n.). **18:** Mk.13.31; Lk.16.17. **19:** *Relaxes*, or "sets aside." *Teaches*, Jas.3.1. **20:** *Righteousness*, one's acceptance of God's requirements and one's being accepted by God (Lk.18.10–14).

5.21–48: Illustrations of the true understanding of the Law. 21: Ex.20.13; Dt.5.17; 16.18. **25–26:** Lk.12.57–59. **26:** *Penny*, see Lk.12.59 n. **27:** Ex.20.14; Dt.5.18. **29–30:** Mk.9.43–48; Mt.18.8–9. **31:** *It was also said,*

has already committed adultery with her in his heart. [29] If your right eye causes you to sin, pluck it out and throw it away; it is better that you lose one of your members than that your whole body be thrown into hell.[k] [30] And if your right hand causes you to sin, cut if off and throw it away; it is better that you lose one of your members than that your whole body go into hell.[k]

31 "It was also said, 'Whoever divorces his wife, let him give her a certificate of divorce.' [32] But I say to you that every one who divorces his wife, except on the ground of unchastity, makes her an adulteress; and whoever marries a divorced woman commits adultery.

33 "Again you have heard that it was said to the men of old, 'You shall not swear falsely, but shall perform to the Lord what you have sworn.' [34] But I say to you, Do not swear at all, either by heaven, for it is the throne of God, [35] or by the earth, for it is his footstool, or by Jerusalem, for it is the city of the great King. [36] And do not swear by your head, for you cannot make one hair white or black. [37] Let what you say be simply 'Yes' or 'No'; anything more than this comes from evil.[l]

38 "You have heard that it was said, 'An eye for an eye and a tooth for a tooth.' [39] But I say to you, Do not resist one who is evil. But if any one strikes you on the right cheek, turn to him the other also; [40] and if any one would sue you and take your coat, let him have your cloak as well; [41] and if any one forces you to go one mile, go with him two miles. [42] Give to him who begs from you, and do not refuse him who would borrow from you.

43 "You have heard that it was said, 'You shall love your neighbor and hate your enemy.' [44] But I say to you, Love your enemies and pray for those who persecute you, [45] so that you may be sons of your Father who is in heaven; for he makes his sun rise on the evil and on the good, and sends rain on the just and on the unjust. [46] For if you love those who love you, what reward have you? Do not even the tax collectors do the same? [47] And if you salute only your brethren, what more are you doing than others? Do not even the Gentiles do the same? [48] You, therefore, must be perfect, as your heavenly Father is perfect.

6 "Beware of practicing your piety before men in order to be seen by them; for then you will have no reward from your Father who is in heaven.

2 "Thus, when you give alms, sound no trumpet before you, as the hypocrites do in the synagogues and in the streets, that they may be praised by men. Truly, I say to you, they have received their reward. [3] But when you give alms, do not let your left hand know what your right hand is doing, [4] so that your alms may be in secret; and your Father who sees in secret will reward you.

5 "And when you pray, you must not be like the hypocrites; for they love to stand and pray in the synagogues and at the street corners, that they may be seen by men. Truly, I say to you, they have received their reward. [6] But when you pray, go into your room and shut the door and pray to your Father who is in secret; and your Father who sees in secret will reward you.

k Greek *Gehenna*   *l* Or *the evil one*

Dt.24.1–4. **32:** The expression *except . . . unchastity* occurs also in 19.9; it is absent from the accounts in Mk.10.11–12 and Lk.16.18 (compare also Rom.7.2–3; 1 Cor.7.10–11). **33–37:** Lev.19.12; Num.30.2; Dt.23.21; Mt.23.16–22; Jas.5.12. **35:** Is.66.1. **38:** Ex.21.23–24; Lev.24.19–20; Dt.19.21. Though this principle *controlled* retaliation in primitive society, it did not justify it. **39–42:** Lk.6.29–30; Rom.12.17; 1 Cor.6.7; 1 Pet.2.19; 3.9. **43–48:** Lk.6.27–28,32–36. **45:** To be *sons of* God is to pattern attitudes after God's. The words *son of* commonly mean that one shows the quality named or trait of character implied (see 23.31 n.; Lk.6.35; 10.6; Jn.8.39–47).

   6.1–34: Teachings in practical piety; Jesus emphasizes a sincere response to God that identifies oneself with his purposes. **1:** 23.5. **5:** Lk.18.10–14. **9–13:** The Lord's Prayer (compare Lk.11.2–4) falls into two parts relating to God and to man; after the opening invocation, there are three petitions concerning God's glory, followed by those concerning our needs. The phrase, *on earth as it is in heaven* (v. 10), belongs to each of the first three petitions. On the basis of

7 "And in praying do not heap up empty phrases as the Gentiles do; for they think that they will be heard for their many words. 8 Do not be like them, for your Father knows what you need before you ask him. 9 Pray then like this:

Our Father who art in heaven,
Hallowed be thy name.
10 Thy kingdom come.
Thy will be done,
On earth as it is in heaven.
11 Give us this day our daily bread;*m*
12 And forgive us our debts,
As we also have forgiven our debtors;
13 And lead us not into temptation,
But deliver us from evil.*n*

14 For if you forgive men their trespasses, your heavenly Father also will forgive you; 15 but if you do not forgive men their trespasses, neither will your Father forgive your trespasses.

16 "And when you fast, do not look dismal, like the hypocrites, for they disfigure their faces that their fasting may be seen by men. Truly, I say to you, they have received their reward. 17 But when you fast, anoint your head and wash your face, 18 that your fasting may not be seen by men but by your Father who is in secret; and your Father who sees in secret will reward you.

19 "Do not lay up for yourselves treasures on earth, where moth and rust*o* consume and where thieves break in and steal, 20 but lay up for yourselves treasures in heaven, where neither moth nor rust*o* consumes and where thieves do not break in and steal. 21 For where your treasure is, there will your heart be also.

22 "The eye is the lamp of the body. So, if your eye is sound, your whole body will be full of light; 23 but if your eye is not sound, your whole body will be full of darkness. If then the light in you is darkness, how great is the darkness!

24 "No one can serve two masters; for either he will hate the one and love the other, or he will be devoted to the one and despise the other. You cannot serve God and mammon.*x*

25 "Therefore I tell you, do not be anxious about your life, what you shall eat or what you shall drink, nor about your body, what you shall put on. Is not life more than food, and the body more than clothing? 26 Look at the birds of the air: they neither sow nor reap nor gather into barns, and yet your heavenly Father feeds them. Are you not of more value than they? 27 And which of you by being anxious can add one cubit to his span of life?*p* 28 And why are you anxious about clothing? Consider the lilies of the field, how they grow; they neither toil nor spin; 29 yet I tell you, even Solomon in all his glory was not arrayed like one of these. 30 But if God so clothes the grass of the field, which today is alive and tomorrow is thrown into the oven, will he not much more clothe you, O men of little faith? 31 Therefore do not be anxious, saying, 'What shall we eat?' or 'What shall we drink?' or 'What shall we wear?' 32 For the Gentiles seek all these things; and your heavenly Father knows that you need them all. 33 But seek first his kingdom and his righteousness, and all these things shall be yours as well.

m Or *our bread for the morrow*   *n* Or *the evil one.* Other authorities, some ancient, add, in some form, *For thine is the kingdom and the power and the glory, for ever. Amen.*   *o* Or *worm*   *x Mammon* is a Semitic word for money or riches   *p* Or *to his stature*

David's prayer (1 Chr.29.11–13) the early church added an appropriate concluding doxology (see note *n*). **9:** Is.63.16; 64.8. **13:** 2 Th.3.3; Jas.1.13. **14–15:** 18.35; Mk.11.25–26; Eph.4.32; Col.3 13. **16–18:** Acceptable fasting (Is.58.5). **19–21:** The uselessness of trusting in worldly goods (Jas.5.2–3). **22–23:** Lk.11.34–36. **24:** Lk.16.13. **25–33:** Lk.12.22–31. **25:** Lk.10.41; 12.11; Phil.4.6. **27:** A *cubit,* about 18 inches. "Cubit" may be used figuratively of length of life (see Ps.39.5 for a similar usage); or in the literal sense Jesus could note that growing in stature (see note *p*) is natural to life and beyond control by anxiety. **29:** 1 Kg.10.4–7. **30:** *Men of little faith* are unwilling to rest in the assurance that God cares about their lives (8.26; 14.31; 16.8). **33:** Mk.10.29–30; Lk.18.29–30.

34 "Therefore do not be anxious about tomorrow, for tomorrow will be anxious for itself. Let the day's own trouble be sufficient for the day.

7 "Judge not, that you be not judged. 2 For with the judgment you pronounce you will be judged, and the measure you give will be the measure you get. 3 Why do you see the speck that is in your brother's eye, but do not notice the log that is in your own eye? 4 Or how can you say to your brother, 'Let me take the speck out of your eye,' when there is the log in your own eye? 5 You hypocrite, first take the log out of your own eye, and then you will see clearly to take the speck out of your brother's eye.

6 "Do not give dogs what is holy; and do not throw your pearls before swine, lest they trample them under foot and turn to attack you.

7 "Ask, and it will be given you; seek, and you will find; knock, and it will be opened to you. 8 For every one who asks receives, and he who seeks finds, and to him who knocks it will be opened. 9 Or what man of you, if his son asks him for bread, will give him a stone? 10 Or if he asks for a fish, will give him a serpent? 11 If you then, who are evil, know how to give good gifts to your children, how much more will your Father who is in heaven give good things to those who ask him! 12 So whatever you wish that men would do to you, do so to them; for this is the law and the prophets.

13 "Enter by the narrow gate; for the gate is wide and the way is easy,[q] that leads to destruction, and those who enter by it are many. 14 For the gate is narrow and the way is hard, that leads to life, and those who find it are few.

15 "Beware of false prophets, who come to you in sheep's clothing but inwardly are ravenous wolves. 16 You will know them by their fruits. Are grapes gathered from thorns, or figs from thistles? 17 So, every sound tree bears good fruit, but the bad tree bears evil fruit. 18 A sound tree cannot bear evil fruit, nor can a bad tree bear good fruit. 19 Every tree that does not bear good fruit is cut down and thrown into the fire. 20 Thus you will know them by their fruits.

21 "Not every one who says to me, 'Lord, Lord,' shall enter the kingdom of heaven, but he who does the will of my Father who is in heaven. 22 On that day many will say to me, 'Lord, Lord, did we not prophesy in your name, and cast out demons in your name, and do many mighty works in your name?' 23 And then will I declare to them, 'I never knew you; depart from me, you evildoers.'

24 "Every one then who hears these words of mine and does them will be like a wise man who built his house upon the rock; 25 and the rain fell, and the floods came, and the winds blew and beat upon that house, but it did not fall, because it had been founded on the rock. 26 And every one who hears these words of mine and does not do them will be like a foolish man who built his house upon the sand; 27 and the rain fell, and the floods came, and the winds blew and beat against that house, and it fell; and great was the fall of it."

28 And when Jesus finished these sayings, the crowds were astonished at his teaching, 29 for he taught them as one who had authority, and not as their scribes.

q Other ancient authorities read *for the way is wide and easy*

7.1–27: Illustrations of the practical meaning of Jesus message. 1–5: Judgment of others (Lk.6.37–38,41–42; Mk.4.24; Rom.2.1; 14.10). **7–11:** Encouragement to prayer (6.8; Mk.11.23–24; Jn.15.7; 1 Jn.3.22; 5.14). **12:** Lk.6.31; Mt.22.39–40; Rom.13.8–10. **13–14:** Lk.13.23–24; Jer.21.8; Ps.1; Dt.30.19; Jn.10.7; 14.6. **15–20:** Lk.6.43–45. **15:** 24.11,24; Ezek.22.27; 1 Jn.4.1; Jn.10.12. *Sheep* often symbolize a group of followers in a religious sense (Ezek.34.1–24; Lk.12.32). **16:** 3.8; 12.33–35; Lk.6.43–45. **19:** 3.10; Lk.13.6–9; Jas.3.10–12. **22:** *That day,* the day of judgment, Jesus speaks as the divine judge. **24–27:** Lk.6.47–49; Jas.1.22–25. **28:** *When Jesus finished these sayings,* this (or a similar) formula marks the conclusion of each of the five main discourses in the gospel (see Introduction and 11.1; 13.53; 19.1; 26.1). **29:** *Unlike their scribes,* Jesus speaks on his own responsibility without appeal to traditional authority (Mk.1.22; 11.18; Lk.4.32).

8 When he came down from the mountain, great crowds followed him; ² and behold, a leper came to him and knelt before him, saying, "Lord, if you will, you can make me clean." ³ And he stretched out his hand and touched him, saying, "I will; be clean." And immediately his leprosy was cleansed. ⁴ And Jesus said to him, "See that you say nothing to any one; but go, show yourself to the priest, and offer the gift that Moses commanded, for a proof to the people."ʳ

5 As he entered Caper′na-um, a centurion came forward to him, beseeching him ⁶ and saying, "Lord, my servant is lying paralyzed at home, in terrible distress." ⁷ And he said to him, "I will come and heal him." ⁸ But the centurion answered, "Lord, I am not worthy to have you come under my roof; but only say the word, and my servant will be healed. ⁹ For I am a man under authority, with soldiers under me; and I say to one, 'Go,' and he goes, and to another, 'Come,' and he comes, and to my slave, 'Do this,' and he does it." ¹⁰ When Jesus heard him, he marveled, and said to those who followed him, "Truly, I say to you, not evenˢ in Israel have I found such faith. ¹¹ I tell you, many will come from east and west and sit at table with Abraham, Isaac, and Jacob in the kingdom of heaven, ¹² while the sons of the kingdom will be thrown into the outer darkness; there men will weep and gnash their teeth." ¹³ And to the centurion Jesus said, "Go; be it done for you as you have believed." And the servant was healed at that very moment.

14 And when Jesus entered Peter's house, he saw his mother-in-law lying sick with a fever; ¹⁵ he touched her hand, and the fever left her, and she rose and served him. ¹⁶ That evening they brought to him many who were possessed with demons; and he cast out the spirits with a word, and healed all who were sick. ¹⁷ This was to fulfil what was spoken by the prophet Isaiah, "He took our infirmities and bore our diseases."

18 Now when Jesus saw great crowds around him, he gave orders to go over to the other side. ¹⁹ And a scribe came up and said to him, "Teacher, I will follow you wherever you go." ²⁰ And Jesus said to him, "Foxes have holes, and birds of the air have nests; but the Son of man has nowhere to lay his head." ²¹ Another of the disciples said to him, "Lord, let me first go and bury my father." ²² But Jesus said to him, "Follow me, and leave the dead to bury their own dead."

23 And when he got into the boat, his disciples followed him. ²⁴ And behold, there arose a great storm on the sea, so that the boat was being swamped by the waves; but he was asleep. ²⁵ And they went and woke him, saying, "Save, Lord; we are perishing." ²⁶ And he said to them, "Why are you afraid, O men of little faith?" Then he rose and rebuked the winds and the sea; and there was a great calm. ²⁷ And the men marveled, saying, "What sort of man is this, that even winds and sea obey him?"

28 And when he came to the other side, to the country of the Gadarenes,ᵗ two demoniacs met him, coming out of the tombs, so fierce

r Greek *to them*   s Other ancient authorities read *with no one*   t Other ancient authorities read *Gergesenes;* some, *Gerasenes*   u Other ancient authorities read *seeing*

8.1–9.38: Events in Galilee. 8.2–4: Mk.1.40–44; Lk.5.12–14. *Leprosy,* a skin disorder of an uncertain nature. Several diseases were possibly referred to by this name (see Lev.13.1–59 n.; Num.5.1–4). Its presence excluded the sufferer from associating with others. *Make me clean,* the leper seeks not merely healing but the freedom to rejoin the Jewish community. **4:** Lev.14.2–32. **5–13:** Lk.7.1–10; Jn.4.46–53. The *centurion,* a non-Jewish military officer, is convinced that diseases are as obedient to Jesus as soldiers are to him. **10:** *Faith* refers to the centurion's trust and recognition of Jesus' power (v. 13; Mk.11.23 n., 24 n.). **11–12:** See Lk.14.15 n.; Is.49.12; 59.19; Mt.13.42,50; 22.13; 24.51; 25.30. **14–17:** Mk.1.29–34; Lk.4.38–41. **16:** *Demons,* see 4.24 n.; 12.22 n.; Lk.4.33 n.; 7.33 n.; 13.16 n. **17:** Is.53.4. **18–22:** Mk.4.35; Lk.8.22; 9.57–60. **18:** *The other side,* the eastern shore of the Sea of Galilee. **20:** *Son of man,* see Mk.2.10 n. **22:** *Follow me,* Jesus implies that obedience to his call must take precedence over every other duty or love (compare 10.37). *Leave the dead,* i.e. the spiritually dead, who are not alive to the greater demands of the kingdom of God. **23–27:** Mk.4.36–41; Lk.8.22–24. **25:** See Lk.8.24 n. **28–34:** Mk.5.1–20; Lk.8.26–39. **31:** See v. 16 n.

that no one could pass that way. [29] And behold, they cried out, "What have you to do with us, O Son of God? Have you come here to torment us before the time?" [30] Now a herd of many swine was feeding at some distance from them. [31] And the demons begged him, "If you cast us out, send us away into the herd of swine." [32] And he said to them, "Go." So they came out and went into the swine; and behold, the whole herd rushed down the steep bank into the sea, and perished in the waters. [33] The herdsmen fled, and going into the city they told everything, and what had happened to the demoniacs. [34] And behold, all the city came out to meet Jesus; and when they saw him, they begged him to leave their neighborhood.

9 And getting into a boat he crossed over and came to his own city. [2] And behold, they brought to him a paralytic, lying on his bed; and when Jesus saw their faith he said to the paralytic, "Take heart, my son; your sins are forgiven." [3] And behold; some of the scribes said to themselves, "This man is blaspheming." [4] But Jesus, knowing[u] their thoughts, said, "Why do you think evil in your hearts? [5] For which is easier, to say, 'Your sins are forgiven,' or to say, 'Rise and walk'? [6] But that you may know that the Son of man has authority on earth to forgive sins"— he then said to the paralytic —"Rise, take up your bed and go home." [7] And he rose and went home. [8] When the crowds saw it, they were afraid, and they glorified God, who had given such authority to men.

[9] As Jesus passed on from there, he saw a man called Matthew sitting at the tax office; and he said to him, "Follow me." And he rose and followed him.

[10] And as he sat at table[v] in the house, behold, many tax collectors and sinners came and sat down with Jesus and his disciples. [11] And when the Pharisees saw this, they said to his disciples, "Why does your teacher eat with tax collectors and sinners?" [12] But when he heard it, he said, "Those who are well have no need of a physician, but those who are sick. [13] Go and learn what this means, 'I desire mercy, and not sacrifice.' For I came not to call the righteous, but sinners."

[14] Then the disciples of John came to him, saying, "Why do we and the Pharisees fast,[w] but your disciples do not fast?" [15] And Jesus said to them, "Can the wedding guests mourn as long as the bridegroom is with them? The days will come, when the bridegroom is taken away from them, and then they will fast. [16] And no one puts a piece of unshrunk cloth on an old garment, for the patch tears away from the garment, and a worse tear is made. [17] Neither is new wine put into old wineskins; if it is, the skins burst, and the wine is spilled, and the skins are destroyed; but new wine is put into fresh wineskins, and so both are preserved."

[18] While he was thus speaking to them, behold, a ruler came in and knelt before him, saying, "My daughter has just died; but come and lay your hand on her, and she will live." [19] And Jesus rose and followed him, with his disciples. [20] And behold, a woman who had suffered from a hemorrhage for twelve years came up behind him and touched the fringe of his garment; [21] for she said to herself, "If I only touch his garment, I shall be made well." [22] Jesus turned, and seeing her he said, "Take heart, daughter; your faith has made you

v Greek *reclined*   w Other ancient authorities add *much or often*

9.1–8: Healing a paralytic (Mk.2.1–12; Lk.5.17–26). **1:** *His own city,* Capernaum. **8:** 7.28–29. **9–13:** Mk.2.13–17; Lk.5.27–32. **10:** Lk.7.34; 15.1–2. **13:** Hos.6.6; Mt.12.7; 15.2–6. Jesus uses a Biblical quotation to challenge a conventional religious idea (see Lk.5.32 n.). **14–17:** Mk.2.18–22; Lk.5.33–39. **15:** Jesus recognizes the principle of fasting, but denies that it fits the circumstances of his life. **16–17:** The two pictorial sayings defend the practices of John's disciples and the practices of his own disciples; Jesus insists that the two ways should not be joined. **18–26:** Mk.5.21–43; Lk.8.40–56. **18:** *A ruler,* a leader in a synagogue. **21:** The Greek word here translated *be made well* (also v. 22; Mk.5.23,28,34; 10.52; Lk.8.36,48,50; 17.19; 18.42) carries with it the idea of rescue from impending destruc-

well." And instantly the woman was made well. 23 And when Jesus came to the ruler's house, and saw the flute players, and the crowd making a tumult, 24 he said, "Depart; for the girl is not dead but sleeping." And they laughed at him. 25 But when the crowd had been put outside, he went in and took her by the hand, and the girl arose. 26 And the report of this went through all that district.

27 And as Jesus passed on from there, two blind men followed him, crying aloud, "Have mercy on us, Son of David." 28 When he entered the house, the blind men came to him; and Jesus said to them, "Do you believe that I am able to do this?" They said to him, "yes, Lord." 29 Then he touched their eyes, saying, "According to your faith be it done to you." 30 And their eyes were opened. And Jesus sternly charged them, "See that no one knows it." 31 But they went away and spread his fame through all that district.

32 As they were going away, behold, a dumb demoniac was brought to him. 33 And when the demon had been cast out, the dumb man spoke; and the crowds marveled, saying, "Never was anything like this seen in Israel." 34 But the Pharisees said, "He casts out demons by the prince of demons."[a]

35 And Jesus went about all the cities and villages, teaching in their synagogues and preaching the gospel of the kingdom, and healing every disease and every infirmity. 36 When he saw the crowds, he had compassion for them, because they were harassed and helpless, like sheep without a shepherd. 37 Then he said to his disciples, "The harvest is plentiful, but the laborers are few; 38 pray

therefore the Lord of the harvest to send out laborers into his harvest."

10 And he called to him his twelve disciples and gave them authority over unclean spirits, to cast them out, and to heal every disease and every infirmity. 2 The names of the twelve apostles are these: first, Simon, who is called Peter, and Andrew his brother; James the son of Zeb'edee, and John his brother; 3 Philip and Bartholomew; Thomas and Matthew the tax collector; James the son of Alphaeus, and Thaddaeus;[x] 4 Simon the Canaanean, and Judas Iscariot, who betrayed him.

5 These twelve Jesus sent out, charging them, "Go nowhere among the Gentiles, and enter no town of the Samaritans, 6 but go rather to the lost sheep of the house of Israel. 7 And preach as you go, saying, 'The kingdom of heaven is at hand.' 8 Heal the sick, raise the dead, cleanse lepers, cast out demons. You received without paying, give without pay. 9 Take no gold, nor silver, nor copper in your belts, 10 no bag for your journey, nor two tunics, nor sandals, nor a staff; for the laborer deserves his food. 11 And whatever town or village you enter, find out who is worthy in it, and stay with him until you depart. 12 As you enter the house, salute it. 13 And if the house is worthy, let your peace come upon it; but if it is not worthy, let your peace return to you. 14 And if any one will not receive you or listen to your words, shake off the dust from your feet as you leave that house or town. 15 Truly, I say to you, it shall be more

a Other ancient authorities omit this verse   *x* Other ancient authorities read *Lebbaeus* or *Lebbaeus called Thaddaeus*

tion or from a superior power. **22:** Mk.11.23 n., 24 n. **23:** Jer.9.17–18. **24:** Jesus speaks in the perspective of the kingdom of God in which physical death is not finally destructive of a person's existence but is a temporary cessation of personal activity (and analogous to sleeping). Verse 18 and the crowd's attitude clearly assert the fact of physical death. **27–31:** 20.29–34. **29:** 9.22 n. **30:** 8.4. **32–34:** 12.22–24; Lk.11.14–15. **34:** See 12.24 n.; Mk.3.22 n.; Jn.7.20. **35–38:** 4.23–25. **36:** Mk.6.34; Mt.14.14; 15.32; Num.27.17; Ezek.34.1–6; Zech.10.2.
   10.1–11.1: Commissioning and instruction of the Twelve. 10.1–4: Mk.6.7; 3.13–19; Lk.9.1; 6.12–16. **1:** *Unclean spirits,* see Mk.1.23 n. **5–15:** Mk.6.8–11; Lk.9.2–5; 10.3–12. **5:** 15.21–28; Lk.9.52; Jn.4.9. **6:** 15.24. **7:** The primary message. Through acceptance, or at least openness to this message and its bearer, healing would follow (see 4.17 n.; 4.23; 9.21,35). **9:** Lk.22.35–36. **10:** *Tunic,* a short-sleeved garment of knee-length, held in at the waist by a girdle (Mk.1.6). *Deserves,* 1 Cor.9.14. **15:** Life and death depend on man's response to God's kingdom.

tolerable on the day of judgment for the land of Sodom and Gomor'rah than for that town.

16 "Behold, I send you out as sheep in the midst of wolves; so be wise as serpents and innocent as doves. 17 Beware of men; for they will deliver you up to councils, and flog you in their synagogues, 18 and you will be dragged before governors and kings for my sake, to bear testimony before them and the Gentiles. 19 When they deliver you up, do not be anxious how you are to speak or what you are to say; for what you are to say will be given to you in that hour; 20 for it is not you who speak, but the Spirit of your Father speaking through you. 21 Brother will deliver up brother to death, and the father his child, and children will rise against parents and have them put to death; 22 and you will be hated by all for my name's sake. But he who endures to the end will be saved. 23 When they persecute you in one town, flee to the next; for truly, I say to you, you will not have gone through all the towns of Israel, before the Son of man comes.

24 "A disciple is not above his teacher, nor a servant[y] above his master; 25 it is enough for the disciple to be like his teacher, and the servant[y] like his master. If they have called the master of the house Be-el'zebul, how much more will they malign those of his household.

26 "So have no fear of them; for nothing is covered that will not be revealed, or hidden that will not be known. 27 What I tell you in the dark, utter in the light; and what you hear whispered, proclaim upon the housetops. 28 And do not fear those who kill the body but cannot kill the soul; rather fear him who can

destroy both soul and body in hell.[z] 29 Are not two sparrows sold for a penny? And not one of them will fall to the ground without your Father's will. 30 But even the hairs of your head are all numbered. 31 Fear not, therefore; you are of more value than many sparrows. 32 So every one who acknowledges me before men, also will acknowledge before my Father who is in heaven; 33 but whoever denies me before men, I also will deny before my Father who is in heaven.

34 "Do not think that I have come to bring peace on earth; I have not come to bring peace, but a sword. 35 For I have come to set a man against his father, and a daughter against her mother, and a daughter-in-law against her mother-in-law; 36 and a man's foes will be those of his own household. 37 He who loves father or mother more than me is not worthy of me; and he who loves son or daughter more than me is not worthy of me; 38 and he who does not take his cross and follow me is not worthy of me. 39 He who finds his life will lose it, and he who loses his life for my sake will find it.

40 "He who receives you receives me, and he who receives me receives him who sent me. 41 He who receives a prophet because he is a prophet shall receive a prophet's reward, and he who receives a righteous man because he is a righteous man shall receive a righteous man's reward. 42 And whoever gives to one of these little ones even a cup of cold water because he is a disciple, truly, I say to you, he shall not lose his reward."

y Or *slave*   z Greek *Gehenna*

Sodom and Gomorrah illustrate God's judgment on wickedness (Gen.18.16–33; ch. 19). **16–25:** 24.9,13; Mk.13.9–13; Lk.21.12–17,19. **20:** Jn.16.7–11. **21:** 10.35–36; Lk.12.52–53. **22:** *My name's sake,* "because of me and my cause." **23:** The words stress the urgency of the disciples' task. **25:** Lk.6.40; Jn.13.16; 15.20; Mt.9.34; 12.24; Mk.3.22. **26–33:** Lk.12.2–9. **28:** Heb.10.31. **29–33:** 6.26–33. **29:** See Lk.12.6 n. **31:** 12.12. **32–33:** Jesus claims to mediate God's will; a favorable response to him is a response to God (compare vv. 40–42). **34–36:** Lk.12.51–53. **35:** Mic.7.6. **37–39:** 16.24–25; Mk.8.34–35; Lk.9.23–24; 14.26–27; 17.33. **37:** Compare the stronger form of expression in Lk.14.26. **38:** A *cross,* a Roman means of execution, was carried by the condemned man to the scene of death. Jesus sees that the acceptance of his message with its promise also brings seeming destruction (v. 34). Only those who in faith accept the threat of destruction will find life (v. 39; 5.11–12; 16.24; Mk.8.34–35; 10.29–31; Lk.9.24–25; 14.27; 17.33; Jn.12.25). **42:** *Little ones,* see 18.6 n.

11 And when Jesus had finished instructing his twelve disciples, he went on from there to teach and preach in their cities.

2 Now when John heard in prison about the deeds of the Christ, he sent word by his disciples [3] and said to him, "Are you he who is to come, or shall we look for another?" [4] And Jesus answered them, "Go and tell John what you hear and see: [5] the blind receive their sight and the lame walk, lepers are cleansed and the deaf hear, and the dead are raised up, and the poor have good news preached to them. [6] And blessed is he who takes no offense at me."

7 As they went away, Jesus began to speak to the crowds concerning John: "What did you go out into the wilderness to behold? A reed shaken by the wind? [8] Why then did you go out? To see a man[a] clothed in soft raiment? Behold, those who wear soft raiment are in kings' houses. [9] Why then did you go out? To see a prophet?[b] Yes, I tell you, and more than a prophet. [10] This is he of whom it is written,

'Behold, I send my messenger before thy face,

who shall prepare thy way before thee.'

[11] Truly, I say to you, among those born of women there has risen no one greater than John the Baptist; yet he who is least in the kingdom of heaven is greater than he. [12] From the days of John the Baptist until now the kingdom of heaven has suffered violence,[c] and men of violence take it by force. [13] For all the prophets and the law prophesied until John; [14] and if you are willing to accept it, he is Eli'jah who is to come. [15] He who has ears to hear,[d] let him hear.

16 "But to what shall I compare this generation? It is like children sitting in the market places and calling to their playmates,

[17] 'We piped to you, and you did not dance; we wailed, and you did not mourn.'

[18] For John came neither eating nor drinking, and they say, 'He has a demon'; [19] the Son of man came eating and drinking, and they say, 'Behold, a glutton and a drunkard, a friend of tax collectors and sinners!' Yet wisdom is justified by her deeds.'[e]

20 Then he began to upbraid the cities where most of his mighty works had been done, because they did not repent. [21] "Woe to you, Chora'zin! woe to you, Beth-sa'ida! for if the mighty works done in you had been done in Tyre and Sidon, they would have repented long ago in sackcloth and ashes. [22] But I tell you, it shall be more tolerable on the day of judgment for Tyre and Sidon than for you. [23] And you, Caper'na-um, will you be exalted to heaven? You shall be brought down to Hades. For if the mighty works done in you had been done in Sodom, it would have remained until this day. [24] But I tell you that it shall be more tolerable on the day of judgment for the land of Sodom than for you."

25 At that time Jesus declared, "I thank thee, Father, Lord of heaven and earth, that thou hast hidden these things from the wise and understanding and revealed them to babes; [26] yea, Father, for such was thy gracious will.[f] [27] All things have been delivered

a Or *What then did you go out to see? A man . . .*
b Other ancient authorities read *What then did you go out to see? A prophet?* c Or *has been coming violently*
d Other ancient authorities omit *to hear* e Other ancient authorities read *children* (Lk 7.35) f Or *so it was well-pleasing before thee*

11.1: *Finished,* see 7.28 n. **11.2–12.50: Narratives illustrating the authority claimed by Jesus. 11.2–19:** Jesus and John (Lk.7.18–35; 16.16). **2–3:** *The Christ,* i.e. the Messiah who *is to come.* **4–5:** Jesus performs the works of the predicted Messiah (Is.29.18–19; 35.5–6; 61.1; compare Lk.4.18–19). **6:** Jesus invites John to answer his own question, basing his decision on what he hears of Jesus' activities interpreted in comparison with Isaiah's words (compare Lk.4.17–21. **7–15:** John was important because he introduced the new manifestation (or "coming") of God's kingdom. **10:** From Mal.3.1; compare Mk.1.2. **14:** Mal.4.5; Lk.1.17; Mk.9.11–13. Biblical prophecy depends on human acceptance of God's terms for fulfilment. If John's message were accepted, his activity would become that foretold in Elijah's name. Jesus seems not to have expected the literal return of *Elijah* (17.10–13; Mk.9.9–13). **18:** See Lk.7.33 n. **23:** Is.14.13,15. **25–30:** Lk.10.21–22. **25:** 9.13; 10.42; see 16.17 n.; Lk.10.21–22; 24.16. **27:** Jesus claimed a special

to me by my Father; and no one knows the Son except the Father, and no one knows the Father except the Son and any one to whom the Son chooses to reveal him. [28] Come to me, all who labor and are heavy laden, and I will give you rest. [29] Take my yoke upon you, and learn from me; for I am gentle and lowly in heart, and you will find rest for your souls. [30] For my yoke is easy, and my burden is light."

12 At that time Jesus went through the grainfields on the sabbath; his disciples were hungry, and they began to pluck heads of grain and to eat. [2] But when the Pharisees saw it, they said to him, "Look, your disciples are doing what is not lawful to do on the sabbath." [3] He said to them, "Have you not read what David did, when he was hungry, and those who were with him: [4] how he entered the house of God and ate the bread of the Presence, which it was not lawful for him to eat nor for those who were with him, but only for the priests? [5] Or have you not read in the law how on the sabbath the priests in the temple profane the sabbath, and are guiltless? [6] I tell you, something greater than the temple is here. [7] And if you had known what this means, 'I desire mercy, and not sacrifice,' you would not have condemned the guiltless. [8] For the Son of man is lord of the sabbath."

[9] And he went on from there, and entered their synagogue, [10] And behold, there was a man with a withered hand. And they asked him, "Is it lawful to heal on the sabbath?" so that they might accuse him. [11] He said to them, "What man of you, if he has one sheep and it falls into a pit on the sabbath, will not lay hold of it and lift it out? [12] Of how much more value is a man than a sheep! So it is lawful to do good on the sabbath." [13] Then he said to the man, "Stretch out your hand." And the man stretched it out, and it was restored, whole like the other. [14] But the Pharisees went out and took counsel against him, how to destroy him.

[15] Jesus, aware of this, withdrew from there. And many followed him, and he healed them all, [16] and ordered them not to make him known. [17] This was to fulfil what was spoken by the prophet Isaiah:

[18] "Behold, my servant whom I have chosen,
    my beloved with whom my soul is well
        pleased.
I will put my Spirit upon him,
    and he shall proclaim justice to the
        Gentiles.
[19] He will not wrangle or cry aloud,
    nor will any one hear his voice in the
        streets;
[20] he will not break a bruised reed
    or quench a smoldering wick,
till he brings justice to victory;
[21]   and in his name will the Gentiles hope."

[22] Then a blind and dumb demoniac was brought to him, and he healed him, so that the dumb man spoke and saw. [23] And all the people were amazed, and said, "Can this be the Son of David?" [24] But when the Pharisees

---

relation to God which he could share with others (Jn.3.35; 13.3). **29:** The rabbis spoke of the *yoke* of the Law. Jesus regarded his claim as more demanding and more rewarding (5.17–20).

12.1–14: Jesus and sabbath laws (Mk.2.23–3.6; Lk.6.1–11). **1:** Dt.23.25. **2:** The objection rested on the traditional interpretation that plucking grain by hand was an activity forbidden by Ex.20.8–11. **3–4:** 1 Sam.21.1–6; Lev.24.5–9. **5:** Num.28.9–10. **6:** Since no penalty was exacted from those who set aside provisions of the Law for the sake of some human need or some more significant service to God, Jesus' disciples eat because of their need and serve him who is greater than the institutions of the Law (see vv. 41–42). **7:** Hos.6.6; Mt.9.13. **8:** Jesus claims, by virtue of his mission as the Messiah, authority over man's obedience to God (11.27; Is.5.1–18). **11–12:** The rabbis agreed with the principle of attending to accidental injury and danger on the sabbath, but they thought that chronic conditions should wait (Lk.13.14). For Jesus it was important to restore a person to useful life. **12:** 10.31.

12.15–21: Work of healing (Mk.3.7–12; Lk.6.17–19; 4.40). **17–21:** Is.42.1–4.

12.22–37: Sources of Jesus' power (Mk.3.20–30; Lk.11.14–23; 12.10). **22–24:** The dumbness here said to be caused by demonic possession is said in Lk.11.14 to describe the demon itself. The Biblical writers speak either of *healing* the victim or casting out the demon (v. 24; 9.32–33; Lk.11.14–15). **23:** *Son of David*, a title of the Messiah (21.9). **24:** The issue is how to account for Jesus' manifest power. The Pharisees attribute it to evil forces hostile to

heard it they said, "It is only by Be-el'zebul, the prince of demons, that this man casts out demons." 25 Knowing their thoughts, he said to them, "Every kingdom divided against itself is laid waste, and no city or house divided against itself will stand; 26 and if Satan casts out Satan, he is divided against himself; how then will his kingdom stand? 27 And if I cast out demons by Be-el'zebul, by whom do your sons cast them out? Therefore they shall be your judges. 28 But if it is by the Spirit of God that I cast out demons, then the kingdom of God has come upon you. 29 Or how can one enter a strong man's house and plunder his goods, unless he first binds the strong man? Then indeed he may plunder his house. 30 He who is not with me is against me, and he who does not gather with me scatters. 31 Therefore I tell you, every sin and blasphemy will be forgiven men, but the blasphemy against the Spirit will not be forgiven. 32 And whoever says a word against the Son of man will be forgiven; but whoever speaks against the Holy Spirit will not be forgiven, either in this age or in the age to come.

33 "Either make the tree good, and its fruit good; or make the tree bad, and its fruit bad; for the tree is known by its fruit. 34 You brood of vipers! how can you speak good, when you are evil? For out of the abundance of the heart the mouth speaks. 35 The good man out of his good treasure brings forth good, and the evil man out of his evil treasure brings forth evil. 36 I tell you, on the day of judgment men will render account for every careless word they utter; 37 for by your words you will be justified, and by your words you will be condemned."

38 Then some of the scribes and Pharisees said to him, "Teacher, we wish to see a sign from you." 39 But he answered them, "An evil and adulterous generation seeks for a sign; but no sign shall be given to it except the sign of the prophet Jonah. 40 For as Jonah was three days and three nights in the belly of the whale, so will the Son of man be three days and three nights in the heart of the earth. 41 The men of Nin'eveh will rise at the judgment with this generation and condemn it; for they repented at the preaching of Jonah, and behold, something greater than Jonah is here. 42 The queen of the South will arise at the judgment with this generation and condemn it; for she came from the ends of the earth to hear the wisdom of Solomon, and behold, something greater than Solomon is here.

43 "When the unclean spirit has gone out of a man, he passes through waterless places seeking rest, but he finds none. 44 Then he says, 'I will return to my house from which I came.' And when he comes he finds it empty, swept, and put in order. 45 Then he goes and brings with him seven other spirits more evil than himself, and they enter and dwell there; and the last state of that man becomes worse than the first. So shall it be also with this evil generation."

46 While he was still speaking to the people, behold, his mother and his brothers stood outside, asking to speak to him.*g* 48 But he replied to the man who told him, "Who is my mother, and who are my brothers?" 49 And

---

g Other ancient authorities insert verse 47, *Some one told him, "Your mother and your brothers are standing outside, asking to speak to you"*

---

mankind (see Lk.7.33 n.). *Beelzebul*, see 2 Kg.1.2 n.; Mk.3.22 n. **27:** *Your sons*, your disciples (compare 1 Pet.5.13). Exorcising demons was not limited to Jesus and his followers (7.22–23; Mk.9.38; Acts 19.13–19). **28:** Lk.4.18–20. **31–32:** The unforgivable sin is the utter rebellion against God that denies him as the doer of his own acts (Lk.12.10). **32:** Mk.3.28–30. **33–36:** 7.16–20; Mk.7.14–23; Lk.6.43–45. **33:** *Make*, recognize that fruit and tree will be alike (Jas.3.11–12). **36:** *Careless*, useless; "barren" in Jas.2.20. **37:** Compare Rom.2.6.

12.38–42: Request for a sign (Lk.11.16,29–32). **39:** *Adulterous* was used by Old Testament prophets to describe Israel's turning away from God (Jer.3.8; Ezek.23.37; Hos.2.2–10). *Sign*, compare v. 40. **40:** *Whale*, "sea monster" (compare Jon.1.17). **41:** Jon.3.5; Mt.11.20–24; 12.6. **42:** 1 Kg.10.1–10; 2 Chr.9.1–9.

12.43–45: The return of the unclean spirit (Lk.11.24–26; see Mk.1.23 n.). **43:** Waterless places, or deserts, supposed to be the favorite abode of demons (compare Is.13.21–22; 34.14). **44:** *My house*, the man himself. *Empty*, though evil has been temporarily expelled, nothing good has been put in its place.

12.46–50: Jesus' true family (Mk.3.31–35; Lk.8.19–21). See 13.55 n.

stretching out his hand toward his disciples, he said, "Here are my mother and my brothers! [50] For whoever does the will of my Father in heaven is my brother, and sister, and mother."

13 That same day Jesus went out of the house and sat beside the sea. [2] And great crowds gathered about him, so that he got into a boat and sat there; and the whole crowd stood on the beach. [3] And he told them many things in parables, saying: "A sower went out to sow. [4] And as he sowed, some seeds fell along the path, and the birds came and devoured them. [5] Other seeds fell on rocky ground, where they had not much soil, and immediately they sprang up, since they had no depth of soil, [6] but when the sun rose they were scorched; and since they had no root they withered away. [7] Other seeds fell upon thorns, and the thorns grew up and choked them. [8] Other seeds fell on good soil and brought forth grain, some a hundredfold, some sixty, some thirty. [9] He who has ears,[h] let him hear."

10 Then the disciples came and said to him, "Why do you speak to them in parables?" [11] And he answered them, "To you it has been given to know the secrets of the kingdom of heaven, but to them it has not been given. [12] For to him who has will more be given, and he will have abundance; but from him who has not, even what he has will be taken away. [13] This is why I speak to them in parables, because seeing they do not see, and hearing they do not hear, nor do they understand. [14] With them indeed is fulfilled the prophecy of Isaiah which says:

'You shall indeed hear but never understand,
and you shall indeed see but never perceive.
[15] For this people's heart has grown dull,
and their ears are heavy of hearing,
and their eyes they have closed,
lest they should perceive with their eyes,
and hear with their ears,
and understand with their heart,
and turn for me to heal them.'

[16] But blessed are your eyes, for they see, and your ears, for they hear. [17] Truly, I say to you, many prophets and righteous men longed to see what you see, and did not see it, and to hear what you hear, and did not hear it.

18 "Hear then the parable of the sower. [19] When any one hears the word of the kingdom and does not understand it, the evil one comes and snatches away what is sown in his heart; this is what was sown along the path. [20] As for what was sown on rocky ground, this is he who hears the word and immediately receives it with joy; [21] yet he has no root in himself, but endures for a while, and when tribulation or persecution arises on account of the word, immediately he falls away.[i] [22] As for what was sown among thorns, this is he who hears the word, but the cares of the world and the delight in riches choke the word, and it proves unfruitful. [23] As for what was sown on good soil, this is he who hears the word and understands it; he indeed bears fruit, and yields, in one case a hundredfold, in another sixty, and in another thirty."

h Other ancient authorities add here and in verse 43 *to hear* i Or *stumbles*

13.1–52: Teaching in parables (Mk.4.1–34; Lk.8.4–18; 13.18–21). **1:** *The sea,* of Galilee. **3:** *Parables* are stories describing situations in everyday life which, as Jesus used them, convey a spiritual meaning. In general the teaching of each parable relates to a single point, and apart from this the details may, or may not, have a particular meaning. Jesus used this method of teaching because: (a) it gave vivid, memorable expression to his teachings; (b) it led those who heard to reflect on his words and bear responsibility for their decision to accept or oppose his claim; (c) it probably reduced specific grounds for contention by hostile listeners. **3b–8:** The sower, explained in vv. 18–23 (see Mk.4.1–9). **11:** The disciples heard and accepted the message about God's kingdom and by their faith had access to deeper understanding (see Mk.4.11 n). **12:** 25.29; Mk.4.24–25; Lk.8.18; 19.26. **13:** The parables do not obscure truth but present it; men receive the message through their physical senses but do not comprehend (see 11.25 n.). **14–15:** Is.6.9–10; Mk.8.18; see Acts 28.26 n. **16–17:** See Lk.10.23–24 n. **17:** *See . . . hear,* Jesus' message about God's kingdom. **18–23:** Response

24 Another parable he put before them, saying, "The kingdom of heaven may be compared to a man who sowed good seed in his field; [25] but while men were sleeping, his enemy came and sowed weeds among the wheat, and went away. [26] So when the planets came up and bore grain, then the weeds appeared also. [27] And the servants[j] of the householder came and said to him, 'Sir, did you not sow good seed in your field? How then has it weeds?' [28] He said to them, 'An enemy has done this.' The servants[j] said to him, 'Then do you want us to go and gather them?' [29] But he said, 'No; lest in gathering the weeds you root up the wheat along with them. [30] Let both grow together until the harvest; and at harvest time I will tell the reapers, Gather the weeds first and bind them in bundles to be burned, but gather the wheat into my barn.'"

31 Another parable he put before them, saying, "The kingdom of heaven is like a grain of mustard seed which a man took and sowed in his field; [32] it is the smallest of all seeds, but when it has grown it is the greatest of shrubs and becomes a tree, so that the birds of the air come and make nests in its branches."

33 He told them another parable. "The kingdom of heaven is like leaven which a woman took and hid in three measures of flour, till it was all leavened."

34 All this Jesus said to the crowds in parables; indeed he said nothing to them without a parable. [35] This was to fulfil what was spoken by the prophet:[k]

"I will open my mouth in parables,
I will utter what has been hidden since the
    foundation of the world."

36 Then he left the crowds and went into the house. And his disciples came to him, saying, "Explain to us the parable of the weeds of the field." [37] He answered, "He who sows the good seed is the Son of man; [38] the field is the world, and the good seed means the sons of the kingdom; the weeds are the sons of the evil one, [39] and the enemy who sowed them is the devil; the harvest is the close of the age, and the reapers are angels. [40] Just as the weeds are gathered and burned with fire, so will it be at the close of the age. [41] The Son of man will send his angels, and they will gather out of his kingdom all causes of sin and all evildoers, [42] and throw them into the furnace of fire; there men will weep and gnash their teeth. [43] Then the righteous will shine like the sun in the kingdom of their Father. He who has ears, let him hear.

44 "The kingdom of heaven is like treasure hidden in a field, which a man found and covered up; then in his joy he goes and sells all that he has and buys that field.

45 "Again, the kingdom of heaven is like a merchant in search of fine pearls, [46] who, on finding one pearl of great value, went and sold all that he had and bought it.

47 "Again, the kingdom of heaven is like a net which was thrown into the sea and gathered fish of every kind; [48] when it was full, men drew it ashore and sat down and sorted the good into vessels but threw away the bad. [49] So it will be at the close of the age. The angels will come out and separate the evil from the righteous, [50] and throw them into the furnace of fire; there men will weep and gnash their teeth.

j Or *slaves*   *k* Other ancient authorities read *the prophet Isaiah*

---

to Jesus' message affected by the circumstances of human life. **22:** 19.23. **24–30: Weeds in the wheat.** God allows good and evil to exist together until the close of human history (vv. 36–43). **31–32: The mustard seed.** (Lk.13.18–19). The beginnings of God's kingdom are small, but it has an inherent nature that will grow to its intended end, startlingly different in size from its beginning. **32:** Dan.4.12. **33: Leaven** (Lk.13.20–21). God's rule, like *leaven* working in a hidden way, will pervade man's life, giving it a new quality. **35:** *The prophet,* i.e. Asaph the seer (2 Chr.29.30), the author of Ps. 78, from which (v. 2) the quotation is taken. **42:** See Lk.12.49 n. **43:** Dan.12.3. **44–46: Hidden treasure and the pearl of great value. 44:** Some men respond in whole-hearted dedication to Jesus' message without any other thought than to have what it yields. **45–46:** Some men dedicate themselves to God's kingdom because, being able to judge the value of other claims being made on them, they value it more. **47–50: The drag-**

51 "Have you understood all this?" They said to him, "Yes." ⁵² And he said to them, "Therefore every scribe who has been trained for the kingdom of heaven is like a householder who brings out of his treasure what is new and what is old."

53 And when Jesus had finished these parables, he went away from there, ⁵⁴ and coming to his own country he taught them in their synagogue, so that they were astonished, and said, "Where did this man get this wisdom and these mighty works? ⁵⁵ Is not this the carpenter's son? Is not his mother called Mary? And are not his brothers James and Joseph and Simon and Judas? ⁵⁶ And are not all his sisters with us? Where then did this man get all this?" ⁵⁷ And they took offense at him. But Jesus said to them, "A prophet is not without honor except in his own country and in his own house." ⁵⁸ And he did not do many mighty works there, because of their unbelief.

14 At that time Herod the tetrarch heard about the fame of Jesus; ² and he said to his servants, "This is John the Baptist, he has been raised from the dead; that is why these powers are at work in him." ³ For Herod had seized John and bound him and put him in prison, for the sake of Hero′di-as, his brother Philip's wife;*ʲ* ⁴ because John said to him, "It is not lawful for you to have her." ⁵ And though he wanted to put him to death, he feared the people, because they held him to be a prophet. ⁶ But when Herod's birthday came, the daughter of Hero′di-as danced before the company, and pleased Herod, ⁷ so that he promised with an oath to give her whatever

she might ask. ⁸ Prompted by her mother, she said, "Give me the head of John the Baptist here on a platter." ⁹ And the king was sorry; but because of his oaths and his guests he commanded it to be given; ¹⁰ he sent and had John beheaded in the prison, ¹¹ and his head was brought on a platter and given to the girl, and she brought it to her mother. ¹² And his disciples came and took the body and buried it; and they went and told Jesus.

13 Now when Jesus heard this, he withdrew from there in a boat to a lonely place apart. But when the crowds heard it, they followed him on foot from the towns. ¹⁴ As he went ashore he saw a great throng; and he had compassion on them, and healed their sick. ¹⁵ When it was evening, the disciples came to him and said, "This is a lonely place, and the day is now over; send the crowds away to go into the villages and buy food for themselves." ¹⁶ Jesus said, "They need not go away; you give them something to eat." ¹⁷ They said to him, "We have only five loaves here and two fish." ¹⁸ And he said, "Bring them here to me." ¹⁹ Then he ordered the crowds to sit down on the grass; and taking the five loaves and the two fish he looked up to heaven, and blessed, and broke and gave the loaves to the disciples, and the disciples gave them to the crowds. ²⁰ And they all ate and were satisfied. And they took up twelve baskets full of the broken pieces left over. ²¹ And those who ate were about five thousand men, besides women and children.

j Or *slaves*   *k* Other ancient authorities read *the prophet Isaiah*   *l* Other ancient authorities read *his brother's wife*

---

net. 52: *Scribe,* an expert in the Mosaic law, having become a disciple of Jesus is able to preserve past insights and enlarge them.

13.53–17.27: Events of decisive acceptance or rejection of Jesus. 13.53–58: Rejection at home. 53: *Finished,* see 7.28 n. **54:** *His own country,* Nazareth (Lk.4.16,23). **55:** *Brothers,* regarded by Protestants as children of Mary, younger than Jesus. In Semitic usage, besides its ordinary meaning, the word *brothers* may also refer to persons of varying degrees of blood relationship; here (and in Mt.12.46; Mk.3.31–32; 6.3; Lk.8.19–20; Jn.2.12; 7.3,5; Acts 1.14; 1 Cor.9.5; Gal.1.19) Catholic tradition regards them as relatives of Jesus, not blood brothers (see also Mt.1.25 n.; Lk.2.7 n.). **58:** See Mk.6.5–6 n.

14.1–12: Death of John (Mk.6.14–29; Lk.9.7–9). **1:** *Herod* Antipas, son of Herod the Great *Tetrarch,* ruler of a minor political unit. **3:** *Philip,* not the tetrarch of Lk.3.1, but a half-brother of *Herod* Antipas. **4:** Lev.18.16; 20.21. **6:** *The daughter of Herodias* was Salome.

14.13–21: Five thousand fed (Mk.6.30–44; Lk.9.10–17; Jn.6.1–13). **13:** After John's death Jesus faced a new stage in his life (compare his reaction to John's imprisonment, Mk.1.14–15). **14:** 20.25–28.

22 Then he made the disciples get into the boat and go before him to the other side, while he dismissed the crowds. 23 And after he had dismissed the crowds, he went up on the mountain by himself to pray. When evening came, he was there alone, 24 but the boat by this time was many furlongs distant from the land,*m* beaten by the waves; for the wind was against them. 25 And in the fourth watch of the night he came to them, walking on the sea. 26 But when the disciples saw him walking on the sea, they were terrified, saying, "It is a ghost!" And they cried out for fear. 27 But immediately he spoke to them, saying, "Take heart, it is I; have no fear."

28 And Peter answered him, "Lord, if it is you, bid me come to you on the water." 29 He said, "Come." So Peter got out of the boat and walked on the water and came to Jesus; 30 but when he saw the wind,*n* he was afraid, and beginning to sink he cried out, "Lord, save me."31 Jesus immediately reached out his hand and caught him, saying to him, "O man of little faith, why did you doubt?" 32 And when they got into the boat, the wind ceased. 33 And those in the boat worshiped him, saying, "Truly you are the Son of God."

34 And when they had crossed over, they came to land at Gennes'aret. 35 And when the men of that place recognized him, they sent round to all that region and brought to him all that were sick, 36 and besought him that they might only touch the fringe of his garment; and as many as touched it were made well.

15 Then Pharisees and scribes came to Jesus from Jerusalem and said, 2 "Why do your disciples transgress the tradition of the elders? For they do not wash their hands when they eat." 3 He answered them, "And why do you transgress the commandment of God for the sake of your tradition? 4 For God commanded, 'Honor your father and your mother,' and, 'He who speaks evil of father or mother, let him surely die.' 5 But you say, 'If any one tells his father or his mother, What you would have gained from me is given to God,*o* he need not honor his father.' 6 So, for the sake of your tradition, you have made void the word*p* of God. 7 You hypocrites! Well did Isaiah prophesy of you, when he said:
8 'This people honors me with their lips,
    but their heart is far from me;
9 in vain do they worship me,
    teaching as doctrines the precepts of
        men.'"

10 And he called the people to him and said to them, "Hear and understand: 11 not what goes into the mouth defiles a man, but what comes out of the mouth, this defiles a man." 12 Then the disciples came and said to him, "Do you know that the Pharisees were offended when they heard this saying?" 13 He answered, "Every plant which my heavenly Father has not planted will be rooted up. 14 Let them alone; they are blind guides. And if a blind man leads a blind man, both will fall into a pit." 15 But Peter said to him, "Explain the parable to us." 16 And he said, "Are you also still without understanding? 17 Do you not see that whatever goes into the mouth passes into the stomach, and so passes on?*q* 18 But what comes out of the mouth proceeds from the heart, and this defiles a man. 19 For out of the heart come evil thoughts, murder, adultery, fornication, theft, false witness, slander. 20 These are what defile a man; but to eat with unwashed hands does not defile a man."

m Other ancient authorities read *was out on the sea*
n Other ancient authorities read *strong wind*
o Or *an offering*   *p* Other ancient authorities read *law*
q Or *is evacuated*

14.22–36: Jesus walks on water (Mk.6.45–52; Jn.6.15–21). **24:** A *furlong,* about one-eighth of a mile. **25:** *The fourth watch,* see Mk.6.48 n. **26:** Lk.24.37. **33:** Mk.6.51–52.

15.1–20: Tradition of the elders (Mk.7.1–23). **2:** *The tradition of the elders,* the rabbinical exposition of the Law of Moses. **4:** Ex.20.12; Dt.5.16; Ex.21.17; Lev.20.9. **7–9:** Is.29.13 (see Mk.7.6–7 n.). **10–20:** The teaching here depends on the principle in the Law that certain physical conditions can and do render an individual unfit to share in the worship of the community. **11:** *Defiles,* renders unfit to share in public ritual (Acts 10.14–15; 1 Tim.4.3). **13:** Is.60.21. **14:** Lk.6.39; Mt.23.16,24. **19–20:** Violations of the rights and interests of another hinder worship (5.23–24).

21 And Jesus went away from there and withdrew to the district of Tyre and Sidon. [22] And behold, a Canaanite woman from that region came out and cried, "Have mercy on me, O Lord, Son of David; my daughter is severely possessed by a demon." [23] But he did not answer her a word. And his disciples came and begged him, saying, "Send her away, for she is crying after us." [24] He answered, "I was sent only to the lost sheep of the house of Israel." [25] But she came and knelt before him, saying, "Lord, help me." [26] And he answered, "It is not fair to take the children's bread and throw it to the dogs." [27] She said, "Yes, Lord, yet even the dogs eat the crumbs that fall from their masters' table." [28] Then Jesus answered her, "O woman, great is your faith! Be it done for you as you desire." And her daughter was healed instantly.

29 And Jesus went on from there and passed along the Sea of Galilee. And he went up on the mountain, and sat down there. [30] And great crowds came to him, bringing with them the lame, the maimed, the blind, the dumb, and many others, and they put them at his feet, and he healed them, [31] so that the throng wondered, when they saw the dumb speaking, the maimed whole, the lame walking, and the blind seeing; and they glorified the God of Israel.

32 Then Jesus called his disciples to him and said, "I have compassion on the crowd, because they have been with me now three days, and have nothing to eat; and I am unwilling to send them away hungry, lest they faint on the way." [33] And the disciples said to him, "Where are we to get bread enough in the desert to feed so great a crowd?" [34] And Jesus said to them, "How many loaves have you?" They said, "Seven, and a few small fish." [35] And commanding the crowd to sit down on the ground, [36] he took the seven loaves and the fish, and having given thanks he broke them and gave them to the disciples, and the disciples gave them to the crowds. [37] And they all ate and were satisfied; and they took up seven baskets full of the broken pieces left over. [38] Those who ate were four thousand men, besides women and children. [39] And sending away the crowds, he got into the boat and went to the region of Mag'adan.

16 And the Pharisees and Sad'ducees came, and to test him they asked him to show them a sign from heaven. [2] He answered them,[r] "When it is evening, you say, 'It will be fair weather; for the sky is red.' [3] And in the morning, 'It will be stormy today, for the sky is red and threatening.' You know how to interpret the appearance of the sky, but you cannot interpret the signs of the times. [4] An evil and adulterous generation seeks for a sign, but no sign shall be given to it except the sign of Jonah." So he left them and departed.

5 When the disciples reached the other side, they had forgotten to bring any bread. [6] Jesus said to them, "Take heed and beware of the leaven of the Pharisees and Sad'ducees." [7] And they discussed it among themselves, saying, "We brought no bread." [8] But Jesus, aware of this, said, "O men of little faith, why do you discuss among yourselves the fact that you have no bread? [9] Do you not yet

r Other ancient authorities omit the following words to the end of verse 3

15.21–28: The Canaanite woman (Mk.7.24–30). **22:** The woman, though a Gentile, speaks to Jesus as the Jewish Messiah. **24:** 10.6,23. Jesus consistently said that his primary mission was to call Jews back to God. The Gentile woman's claim must be based on her own personal acceptance of his message. The distinction is between his mission and his willingness to respond to faith wherever found. **27:** The woman accepts Jesus' mission and as a Gentile asks his help.
15.29–31: Healings (Mk.7.31–37).
15.32–39: Four thousand fed (see Mk.8.1–10 n.). **39:** *Magadan* was apparently on the west side of the Sea of Galilee.
16.1–4: Demand for signs (Mk.8.11–13; Lk.11.16,29; 12.54–56). **3:** *The signs of the times* may refer to 15.29–31; compare 11.2–6. **4:** See 12.39 n., 40 n.; Jon.3.4–5.
16.5–12: Leaven of the Pharisees (Mk.8.14–21; Lk.12.1). **5:** *The other side,* the eastern shore of the Sea of Galilee. **6:** *Leaven,* see Mk.8.15 n. **9:** 14.17–21. **10:** 15.34–38.

perceive? Do you not remember the five loaves of the five thousand, and how many baskets you gathered? [10] Or the seven loaves of the four thousand, and how many baskets you gathered? [11] How is it that you fail to perceive that I did not speak about bread? Beware of the leaven of the Pharisees and Sad'ducees." [12] Then they understood that he did not tell them to beware of the leaven of bread, but of the teaching of the Pharisees and Sad'ducees.

13 Now when Jesus came into the district of Caesare'a Philip'pi, he asked his disciples, "Who do men say that the Son of man is?" [14] And they said, "Some say John the Baptist, others say Eli'jah, and others Jeremiah or one of the prophets." [15] He said to them, "But who do you say that I am?" [16] Simon Peter replied, "You are the Christ, the Son of the living God." [17] And Jesus answered him, "Blessed are you, Simon Bar-Jona! For flesh and blood has not revealed this to you, but my Father who is in heaven. [18] And I tell you, you are Peter,[s] and on this rock[t] I will build my church, and the powers of death[u] shall not prevail against it. [19] I will give you the keys of the kingdom of heaven, and whatever you bind on earth shall be bound in heaven, and whatever you loose on earth shall be loosed in heaven." [29] Then he strictly charged the disciples to tell no one that he was the Christ.

21 From that time Jesus began to show his disciples that he must go to Jerusalem and suffer many things from the elders and chief priests and scribes, and be killed, and on the third day be raised. [22] And Peter took him and began to rebuke him, saying, "God forbid, Lord! This shall never happen to you." [23] But he turned and said to Peter, "Get behind me, Satan! You are a hindrance[v] to me; for you are not on the side of God, but of men."

24 Then Jesus told his disciples, "If any man would come after me, let him deny himself and take up his cross and follow me. [25] For whoever would save his life will lose it, and whoever loses his life for my sake will find it. [26] For what will it profit a man, if he gains the whole world and forfeits his life? Or what shall a man give in return for his life? [27] For the Son of man is to come with his angels in the glory of his Father, and then he will repay every man for what he has done. [28] Truly, I say to you, there are some standing here who will not taste death before they see the Son of man coming in his kingdom."

17 And after six days Jesus took with him Peter and James and John his brother, and led them up a high mountain apart. [2] And he was transfigured before them, and his face shone like the sun, and his garments became white as light. [3] And behold, there appeared to them Moses and Eli'jah, talking with him. [4] And Peter said to Jesus, "Lord, it is well that we are here; if you wish, I will make three

s Greek *Petros*   *t* Greek *petra*   *u* Greek *the gates of Hades*   *v* Greek *stumbling block*

16.13–23: Peter's confession (Mk.8.27–33; Lk.9.18–22). **13:** See Mk.8.27 n. *Son of man* here is equivalent to "I." **16:** Peter asserts that Jesus is the Messiah, not merely one of the prophets (v. 14). He identifies Jesus with the figure of Mal.3.1–4 (compare Mk.1.2; Mt.1.16; Jn.1.49; 11.27). **17:** *Simon* was Peter's personal name. *Bar-Jona* identifies Simon as "son of John." *Flesh and blood,* human beings (1 Cor.15.50; Gal.1.16; Eph.6.12). *Revealed,* understanding spiritual realities involves God's disclosure (see 11.25 n.; Lk.24.16; 1 Cor.1.18–25; 2.6–16). **18:** The Greek text involves a play on two words, *Petros* ("Peter") and *petra* ("rock"). Palestinian Aramaic, which Jesus usually spoke, used the same word for both proper name and common noun: "You are *Kepha* [Cephas; compare 1 Cor.15.5; Gal.2.9], and on this *kepha* [rock] I will build . . ." For the view that all the apostles also form the foundation of the church, see Eph.2.20; Rev.21.14. *Church,* see Gal.1.13 n. **19:** *The keys of the kingdom* are a symbol of Peter's power as the leader of the church. *Bind* and *loose* are technical rabbinic terms meaning "forbid" and "permit" some action about which a question has arisen. Later the authority of binding and loosing was also conferred upon all the apostles (18.18). **20:** See Mk.8.30 n. **21:** See Lk.9.22 n. **22–23:** See Mk.8.32 n., 33 n.

16.24–28: On discipleship (Mk.8.34–9.1; Lk.9.23–27). **24:** See 10.38 n. **25:** See Mk.8.35 n. **26:** Here *life* is not merely physical existence, but the higher or spiritual life of man, his real self (compare Lk.9.25; 12.15). **27:** Ps.62.12; Mt.10.33; Lk.12.8–9; Rom.2.6; 1 Jn.2.28; Rev.22.12. **28:** See Mk.9.1 n.; 1 Cor.16.22; 1 Th.4.15–18; Jas.5.7; Rev.1.7.

17.1–8: The transfiguration. See notes on the parallel passages, Mk.9.2–8; Lk.9.28–36.

booths here, one for you and one for Moses and one for Eli'jah." [5] He was still speaking, when lo, a bright cloud overshadowed them, and a voice from the cloud said, "This is my beloved Son,[w] with whom I am well pleased; listen to him." [6] When the disciples heard this, they fell on their faces, and were filled with awe. [7] But Jesus came and touched them, saying, "Rise, and have no fear." [8] And when they lifted up their eyes, they saw no one but Jesus only.

[9] And as they were coming down the mountain, Jesus commanded them, "Tell no one the vision, until the Son of man is raised from the dead." [10] And the disciples asked him, "Then why do the scribes say that first Eli'jah must come?" [11] He replied, "Eli'jah does come, and he is to restore all things; [12] but I tell you that Eli'jah has already come, and they did not know him, but did to him whatever they pleased. So also the Son of man will suffer at their hands." [13] Then the disciples understood that he was speaking to them of John the Baptist.

[14] And when they came to the crowd, a man came up to him and kneeling before him said, [15] "Lord, have mercy on my son, for he is an epileptic and he suffers terribly; for often he falls into the fire, and often into the water. [16] And I brought him to your disciples, and they could not heal him." [17] And Jesus answered, "O faithless and perverse generation, how long am I to be with you? How long am I to bear with you? Bring him here to me." [18] And Jesus rebuked him, and the demon came out of him, and the boy was cured instantly. [19] Then the disciples came to Jesus privately and said, "Why could we not cast it out?" [20] He said to them, "Because of your little faith. For truly, I say to you, if you have faith as a grain of mustard seed, you will say to this mountain, 'Move from here to there,' and it will move; and nothing will be impossible to you."[x]

[22] As they were gathering[y] in Galilee, Jesus said to them, "The Son of man is to be delivered into the hands of men, [23] and they will kill him, and he will be raised on the third day." And they were greatly distressed.

[24] When they came to Caper'na-um, the collectors of the half-shekel tax went up to Peter and said, "Does not your teacher pay the tax?" [25] He said, "Yes." And when he came home, Jesus spoke to him first, saying, "What do you think, Simon? From whom do kings of the earth take toll or tribute? From their sons or from others?" [26] And when he said, "From others," Jesus said to him, "Then the sons are free. [27] However, not to give offense to them, go to the sea and cast a hook, and take the first fish that comes up, and when you open its mouth you will find a shekel; take that and give it to them for me and for yourself."

18 At that time the disciples came to Jesus, saying, "Who is the greatest in the kingdom of heaven?" [2] And calling to him a child, he put him in the midst of them, [3] and said, "Truly, I say to you, unless you turn and become like children, you will never enter the kingdom of heaven. [4] Whoever humbles him-

w Or *my Son, my* (or *the*) *Beloved*   *x* Other ancient authorities insert verse 21, *"But this kind never comes out except by prayer and fasting"*   *y* Other ancient authorities read *abode*

17.9–13: Prophecies about Elijah (Mk.9.9–13). **9:** See Mk.8.30 n. **10:** See 11.14 n. **12:** *Elijah has already come,* in the person of John the Baptist.

17.14–21: An epileptic child healed (Mk.9.14–29; Lk.9.37–42). **15:** To be *epileptic* was attributed to the baleful influences of the moon, a demonic force (compare Ps.121.6). **20:** *Little faith* as distinguished from unbelief (13.58). Jesus' saying is in figurative language; faith is concerned with God's will, not with moving mountains (compare 21.21–22; Mk.11.22–23; Lk.17.6; 1 Cor.13.2; Jas.1.6).

17.22–23: The Passion foretold a second time (Mk.9.30–32; Lk.9.43–45). Compare 16.21; 20.17–19.

17.24–27: Money for the temple tax. 24: The half-shekel tax was paid by Jewish males annually to support the temple. On the value see 26.15 n. (Ex.30.13; 38.26).

18.1–35: Sayings on humility and forgiveness. 1–5: True greatness (Mk.9.33–37; Lk.9.46–48). **3:** *Turn and become like children,* turn away from self-chosen goals and relate oneself to God as to a father. Childlike relations to a

self like this child, he is the greatest in the kingdom of heaven.

5 "Whoever receives one such child in my name receives me; [6] but whoever causes one of these little ones who believe in me to sin,[z] it would be better for him to have a great millstone fastened round his neck and to be drowned in the depth of the sea.

7 "Woe to the world for temptations to sin![a] For it is necessary that temptations come, but woe to the man by whom the temptation comes! [8] And if your hand or your foot causes you to sin,[z] cut it off and throw it away; it is better for you to enter life maimed or lame than with two hands or two feet to be thrown into the eternal fire. [9] And if your eye causes you to sin,[z] pluck it out and throw it away; it is better for you to enter life with one eye than with two eyes to be thrown into the hell[b] of fire.

10 "See that you do not despise one of these little ones; for I tell you that in heaven their angels always behold the face of my Father who is in heaven.[c] [12] What do you think? If a man has a hundred sheep, and one of them has gone astray, does he not leave the ninety-nine on the mountains and go in search of the one that went astray? [13] And if he finds it, truly, I say to you, he rejoices over it more than over the ninety-nine that never went astray. [14] So it is not the will of my[d] Father who is in heaven that one of these little ones should perish.

15 "If your brother sins against you, go and tell him his fault, between you and him alone. If he listens to you, you have gained your brother. [16] But if he does not listen, take one or two others along with you, that every word may be confirmed by the evidence of two or three witnesses. [17] If he refuses to listen to them, tell it to the church; and if he refuses to listen even to the church, let him be to you as a Gentile and a tax collector. [18] Truly, I say to you, whatever you bind on earth shall be bound in heaven, and whatever you loose on earth shall be loosed in heaven. [19] Again I say to you, if two of you agree on earth about anything they ask, it will be done for them by my Father in heaven. [20] For where two or three are gathered in my name, there am I in the midst of them."

21 Then Peter came up and said to him, "Lord, how often shall my brother sin against me, and I forgive him? As many as seven times?" [22] Jesus said to him, "I do not say to you seven times, but seventy times seven.[e]

23 "Therefore the kingdom of heaven may be compared to a king who wished to settle accounts with his servants. [24] When he began the reckoning, one was brought to him who owed him ten thousand talents;[f] [25] and as he could not pay, his lord ordered him to be sold, with his wife and children and all that he had, and payment to be made. [26] So the servant fell on his knees, imploring him, 'Lord, have patience with me, and I will pay you everything.' [27] And out of pity for him the lord of that servant released him and forgave him the debt. [28] But that same servant, as he went out, came upon one of his fellow servants who owed him a hundred denarii;[g] and seizing him

z Greek *causes . . . to stumble*   a Greek *stumbling blocks*   b Greek *Gehenna*   c Other ancient authorities add verse 11, *For the Son of man came to save the lost*   d Other ancient authorities read *your*   e Or *seventy-seven times*   f This talent was more than fifteen years' wages of a laborer   g The denarius was a day's wage for a laborer

parent, not childish behavior, are in view (Mk.10.15; Lk.18.17; 1 Pet.2.2). **6:** *Little ones,* disciples of Jesus, whom he calls "children" (Mk.10.24; compare Mt.11.25).

  18.7–9: Warnings of hell (Mk.9.42–48; Lk.17.1–2). **8–9:** In vivid language Jesus speaks of the terrible danger in yielding to temptation (5.29–30).

  18.10–14: The lost sheep (Lk.15.3–7). **10:** *Little ones,* see v. 6 n. *Angels,* see Acts 12,15 n.

  18.15–20: Discipline among followers (Lk.17.3). 1 Cor.6.1–6; Gal.6.1; Jas.5.19–20; Lev.19.17. **16:** Dt.19.15. **17:** The guilty person excludes himself from the group of followers. **18:** See 16.19 n.; Jn.20.21–23 n.

  18.21–35: Forgiveness. 21–22: Lk.17.4. Forgiveness is beyond calculating. **23:** 25.19. **25:** Lk.7.42. **26:** 8.2; 17.14. **32–33:** Lk.7.41–43.

by the throat he said, 'Pay what you owe,' [29] So his fellow servant fell down and besought him, 'Have patience with me, and I will pay you.' [30] He refused and went and put him in prison till he should pay the debt. [31] When his fellow servants saw what had taken place, they were greatly distressed, and they went and reported to their lord all that had taken place. [32] Then his lord summoned him and said to him, 'You wicked servant! I forgave you all that debt because you besought me; [33] and should not you have had mercy on your fellow servant, as I had mercy on you?' [34] And in anger his lord delivered him to the jailers,[h] till he should pay all his debt. [35] So also my heavenly Father will do to every one of you, if you do not forgive your brother from your heart."

19 Now when Jesus had finished these sayings, he went away from Galilee and entered the region of Judea beyond the Jordan; [2] and large crowds followed him, and he healed them there.

[3] And Pharisees came up to him and tested him by asking, "Is it lawful to divorce one's wife for any cause?" [4] He answered, "Have you not read that he who made them from the beginning made them male and female, [5] and said, 'For this reason a man shall leave his father and mother and be joined to his wife, and the two shall become one flesh'? [6] So they are no longer two but one flesh. What therefore God has joined together, let not man put asunder." [7] They said to him, "Why then did Moses command one to give a certificate of divorce, and to put her away?" [8] He said to them, "For your hardness of heart Moses allowed you to divorce your wives, but from the beginning it was not so. [9] And I say to you: whoever divorces his wife, except for unchastity,[j] and marries another, commits adultery."[k]

[10] The disciples said to him, "If such is the case of a man with his wife, it is not expedient to marry." [11] But he said to them, "Not all men can receive this saying, but only those to whom it is given. [12] For there are eunuchs who have been so from birth, and there are eunuchs who have been made eunuchs by men, and there are eunuchs who have made themselves eunuchs for the sake of the kingdom of heaven. He who is able to receive this, let him receive it."

[13] Then children were brought to him that he might lay his hands on them and pray. The disciples rebuked the people; [14] but Jesus said, "Let the children come to me, and do not hinder them; for to such belongs the kingdom of heaven." [15] And he laid his hands on them and went away.

[16] And behold, one came up to him, saying, "Teacher, what good deed must I do, to have eternal life?" [17] And he said to him, "Why do you ask me about what is good? One there is who is good. If you would enter life, keep the commandments." [18] He said to him, "Which?" And Jesus said, "You shall not kill, You shall not commit adultery, You shall not steal, You shall not bear false witness, [19] Honor your father and mother, and, You shall love your neighbor as yourself." [20] The young man said to him, "All these I have

h Greek *torturers*   j Other ancient authorities, after *unchastity,* read *makes her commit adultery*   k Other ancient authorities insert *and he who marries a divorced woman commits adultery*

19.1–20.34: From Galilee to Jerusalem (Mk.10.1–52; Lk.18.15–19.27).
19.1–12: Marriage and divorce (Mk.10.1–12). **1:** *Finished,* see 7.28 n. **3:** The Mosaic law gives no answer to this question and the rabbis differed in their opinions. **4–6:** Gen.1.27; 2.24. Jesus appeals to God's purpose of unity in marriage as shown in the account of creation. **7:** Dt.24.1–4. **8:** See Mk.10.5 n. **9:** See 5.32 n.; Lk.16.18; 1 Cor.7.10–13. **11–12:** Jesus recognizes a place for voluntary celibacy in the service of God's kingdom (compare 1 Cor.7.1–9).
19.13–15: Blessing the children (Mk.10.13–16; Lk.18.15–17). **14:** See Mk.10:15 n.; compare Mt.18.2–4; 1 Cor.14.20.
19.16–30: The rich young man (Mk.10.17–31; Lk.18.18–30). **16:** Lk.10.25; Lev.18.5. The question concerns the way of life which Jesus will guarantee as satisfying God (see Lk.18.26 n.). **17:** Jesus replies that the good way of life is obedience to God's will (15.2–3,6). **18:** Ex.20.12–16; Dt.5.16–20; Rom.13.9; Jas.2.11. **19:** Lev.19.18; Mt.22.39;

observed; what do I still lack?" [21] Jesus said to him, "If you would be perfect, go, sell what you possess and give to the poor, and you will have treasure in heaven; and come, follow me." [22] When the young man heard this he went away sorrowful; for he had great possessions.

[23] And Jesus said to his disciples, "Truly, I say to you, it will be hard for a rich man to enter the kingdom of heaven. [24] Again I tell you, it is easier for a camel to go through the eye of a needle than for a rich man to enter the kingdom of God." [25] When the disciples heard this they were greatly astonished, saying, "Who then can be saved?" [26] But Jesus looked at them and said to them, "With men this is impossible, but with God all things are possible." [27] Then Peter said in reply, "Lo, we have left everything and followed you. What then shall we have?" [28] Jesus said to them, "Truly, I say to you, in the new world, when the Son of man shall sit on his glorious throne, you who have followed me will also sit on twelve thrones, judging the twelve tribes of Israel. [29] And every one who has left houses or brothers or sisters or father or mother or children or lands, for my name's sake, will receive a hundredfold,[l] and inherit eternal life. [30] But many that are first will be last, and the last first.

20 "For the kingdom of heaven is like a householder who went out early in the morning to hire laborers for his vineyard. [2] After agreeing with the laborers for a denarius[m] a day, he sent them into his vineyard. [3] And going out about the third hour he saw others standing idle in the market place; [4] and to them he said, 'You go into the vineyard too, and whatever is right I will give you.' So they went. [5] Going out again about the sixth hour and the ninth hour, he did the same. [6] And about the eleventh hour he went out and found others standing; and he said to them, 'Why do you stand here idle all day?' [7] They said to him, 'Because no one has hired us.' He said to them, 'You go into the vineyard too.' [8] And when evening came, the owner of the vineyard said to his steward, 'Call the laborers and pay them their wages, beginning with the last, up to the first.' [9] And when those hired about the eleventh hour came, each of them received a denarius. [10] Now when the first came, they thought they would receive more; but each of them also received a denarius. [11] And on receiving it they grumbled at the householder, [12] saying, 'These last worked only one hour, and you have made them equal to us who have borne the burden of the day and the scorching heat.' [13] But he replied to one of them, 'Friend, I am doing you no wrong; did you not agree with me for a denarius? [14] Take what belongs to you, and go; I choose to give to this last as I give to you. [15] Am I not allowed to do what I choose with what belongs to me? Or do you begrudge my generosity?'[n] [16] So the last will be first, and the first last."

[17] And as Jesus was going up to Jerusalem, he took the twelve disciples aside, and

l Other ancient authorities read *manifold*   *m* The denarius was a day's wage for a laborer   *n* Or *is your eye evil because I am good?*

Rom.13.8; Jas.2.8–9. **21:** Jesus consistently turned men's attention from concern over their own religious standing, calling them to involve themselves in the basic, vital interests of others. Neither wealth, poverty, nor formal piety was so important as sharing in the working out of God's life-giving design for all men (5.23–24,43–48; 6.33). Eternal life will be found through utter dependence on God, not through a ritual that wealth makes possible (see Lk.12.33 n.; Acts 2.44–45; 4.34,35). **24:** See Mk.10.25 n. **28:** *The new world* refers to the consummation of God's purpose (compare Rom.8.18–25). **29:** *Inherit eternal life* means *enter the kingdom of God* (vv. 23,24), and *inherit the kingdom* (25.34). **30:** 20.16; Mk.10.31; Lk.13.30.

20.1–16: Laborers in the vineyard. 1: *Early,* approximately 6 a.m. **3:** About nine a.m. **5:** About noon and three p.m. **6:** About five p.m. **8:** Lev.19.13; Dt.24.14–15. **9:** *Denarius,* smaller coins existed (see Lk.12.59 n.); therefore payment could have been made on an hourly basis. **14:** The point of the parable is the willingness of the owner to exceed conventional practices, and his freedom to do so within the limits of agreement. **15:** The first sentence is not a statement of economic theory except as it claims the right to enter into differing contracts. The second sentence expresses the sense of the Greek text, which is literally translated in note *n*. **16:** Compare 19.30.

20.17–19: The Passion foretold a third time (Mk.10.32–34; Lk.18.31–34); compare 16.21; 17.22.

on the way he said to them, [18] "Behold, we are going up to Jerusalem; and the Son of man will be delivered to the chief priests and scribes, and they will condemn him to death, [19] and deliver him to the Gentiles to be mocked and scourged and crucified, and he will be raised on the third day."

20 Then the mother of the sons of Zeb'edee came up to him, with her sons, and kneeling before him she asked him for something. [21] And he said to her, "What do you want?" She said to him, "Command that these two sons of mine may sit, one at your right hand and one at your left, in your kingdom." [22] But Jesus answered, "You do not know what you are asking. Are you able to drink the cup that I am to drink?" They said to him, "We are able." [23] He said to them, "You will drink my cup, but to sit at my right hand and at my left is not mine to grant, but it is for those whom it has been prepared by my Father." [24] And when the ten heard it, they were indignant at the two brothers. [25] But Jesus called them to him and said, "You know that the rulers of the Gentiles lord it over them, and their great men exercise authority over them. [26] It shall not be so among you; but whoever would be great among you must be your servant, [27] and whoever would be first among you must be your slave; [28] even as the Son of man came not to be served but to serve, and to give his life as a ransom for many."

29 And as they went out of Jericho, a great crowd followed him. [30] And behold, two blind men sitting by the roadside, when they heard that Jesus was passing by, cried out,[o] "Have mercy on us, Son of David!" [31] The crowd rebuked them, telling them to be silent; but they cried out the more, "Lord, have mercy on us, Son of David!" [32] And Jesus stopped and called them, saying, "What do you want me to do for you?" [33] They said to him, "Lord, let our eyes be opened." [34] And Jesus in pity touched their eyes, and immediately they received their sight and followed him.

21 And when they drew near to Jerusalem and came to Beth'phage, to the Mount of Olives, then Jesus sent two disciples, [2] saying to them, "Go into the village opposite you, and immediately you will find an ass tied, and a colt with her; untie them and bring them to me. [3] If any one says anything to you, you shall say, 'The Lord has need of them,' and he will send them immediately." [4] This took place to fulfil what was spoken by the prophet, saying,

[5] "Tell the daughter of Zion,
Behold, your king is coming to you,
humble, and mounted on an ass,
and on a colt, the foal of an ass."

[6] The disciples went and did as Jesus had directed them; [7] they brought the ass and the colt, and put their garments on them, and he sat thereon. [8] Most of the crowd spread their garments on the road, and others cut branches from the trees and spread them on the road. [9] And the crowds that went before him and that followed him shouted, "Hosanna to the Son of David! Blessed is he who comes in the name of the Lord! Hosanna in the highest!" [10] And when he entered Jerusalem, all the city was stirred, saying, "Who is this?" [11] And the

o Other ancient authorities insert Lord

20.20–28: James and John seek honor (Mk.10.35–45; Lk.22.24–27). **22:** Cup, see Lk.22.42 n. **23:** Acts 12.2; Rev.1.9; Mt.13.11. **26:** See Mk.9.35. **28:** 26.39; 1 Tim.2.5–6; Jn.13.15–16; Tit.2.14; 1 Pet.1.18. The thought seems to be based on Is. ch. 53.

20.29–34: Two blind men of Jericho (Mk.10.46–52; Lk.18.35–43). Jesus responds not to the Messianic title Son of David (v. 30) but to the cry of need (v. 34; compare 15.22–28).

21.1–27.66: The last week (Mk.11.1–15.47; Lk.19.28–23.56).

21.1–9: Palm Sunday (Mk.11.1–10; Lk.19.28–38; Jn.12.12–18). **1:** See Mk.11.1 n. **5:** Is. 62.11; Zech.9.9. The Hebrew text refers not to two animals but to one. The reference to the two in v. 7 may have arisen through misunderstanding the form of Hebrew poetic expression in Zech.9.9. **8:** Tokens of honor (2 Kg.9.13). **9:** Ps.118.26. Hosanna, originally a Hebrew invocation addressed to God, meaning, "O save!"; later it was used as a cry of joyous acclamation. **11:** The identification reflects an unchanged attitude toward Jesus. His parable (see Mk.11.1 n.) is seen and not understood (Jn.6.14; 7.40; Acts 3.22; Mk.6.15; Lk.13.33).

crowds said, "This is the prophet Jesus from Nazareth of Galilee."

12 And Jesus entered the temple of God[p] and drove out all who sold and bought in the temple, and he overturned the tables of the money-changers and the seats of those who sold pigeons. [13] He said to them, "It is written, 'My house shall be called a house of prayer'; but you make it a den of robbers."

14 And the blind and the lame came to him in the temple, and he healed them. [15] But when the chief priests and the scribes saw the wonderful things that he did, and the children crying out in the temple, "Hosanna to the Son of David!" they were indignant; [16] and they said to him, "Do you hear what these are saying?" And Jesus said to them, "Yes; have you never read,

'Out of the mouth of babes and sucklings
thou hast brought perfect praise'?"

[17] And leaving them, he went out of the city to Bethany and lodged there.

18 In the morning, as he was returning to the city, he was hungry. [19] And seeing a fig tree by the wayside he went to it, and found nothing on it but leaves only. And he said to it, "May no fruit ever come from you again!" And the fig tree withered at once. [20] When the disciples saw it they marveled, saying, "How did the fig tree wither at once?" [21] And Jesus answered them, "Truly, I say to you, if you have faith and never doubt, you will not only do what has been done to the fig tree, but even if you say to this mountain, 'Be taken up and cast into the sea,' it will be done. [22] And whatever you ask in prayer, you will receive, if you have faith."

23 And when he entered the temple, the chief priests and the elders of the people came up to him as he was teaching, and said, "By what authority are you doing these things, and who gave you this authority?" [24] Jesus answered them, "I also will ask you a question; and if you tell me the answer, then I also will tell you by what authority I do these things. [25] The baptism of John, whence was it? From heaven or from men?" And they argued with one another, "If we say, 'From heaven,' he will say to us, 'Why then did you not believe him?' [26] But if we say, 'From men,' we are afraid of the multitude; for all hold that John was a prophet." [27] So they answered Jesus, "We do not know." And he said to them, "Neither will I tell you by what authority I do these things.

28 "What do you think? A man had two sons; and he went to the first and said, 'Son, go and work in the vineyard today.' [29] And he answered, 'I will not'; but afterward he repented and went. [30] And he went to the second and said the same; and he answered, 'I go, sir,' but did not go. [31] Which of the two did the will of his father?" They said, "The first." Jesus said to them, "Truly, I say to you, the tax collectors and the harlots go into the kingdom of God before you. [32] For John came to you in the way of righteousness, and you did not believe him, but the tax collectors and the harlots believed him; and even when you saw it, you did not afterward repent and believe him.

33 "Hear another parable. There was a householder who planted a vineyard, and set a hedge around it, and dug a wine press in it,

p Other ancient authorities omit *of God*

21.12–17: **Cleansing the temple** (Mk.11.11,15–19; Lk.19.45–48; Jn.2.13–17). **12:** The animals for sale were acceptable for sacrifice; the money changers converted Gentile coins into Jewish money that could properly be presented in the temple (Ex.30.13; Lev.1.14). **13:** Is.56.7; Jer.7.11. **15:** Lk.19.39; Mt.21.9. *Hosanna,* see v. 9 n. **16:** Ps.8.2.

21.18–22: **Fig tree cursed** (Mk.11.12–14,20–25). See Mk.11.13 n. **19:** The leaves of the fig tree normally appear after the fruit. **21:** See 17.20 n.

21.23–32: **Jesus' authority** (Mk.11.27–33; Lk.20.1–8). Jn.2.18–22. **26:** 11.9; 14.5; Lk.1.76. **27:** Jesus declined to answer because his listeners declined to heed. **28–32:** 20.1; 21.33; Lk.15.11–32. **32:** Lk.7.29–30. *The way of righteousness* led to reconciliation with God by Faith.

21.33–46: **Parable of the vineyard** (Mk.12.1–12; Lk.20.9–19). **33:** Compare Is.5.1–7, which forms the background of Jesus' parable. **34:** 22.3. **41:** 8.11; Acts 13.46; 18.6; 28.28. **42:** Jesus agrees with his listeners' answer (v. 41) and quotes Ps.118.22–23 to support his teaching (Acts 4.11; 1 Pet.2.7).

and built a tower, and let it out to tenants, and went into another country. [34] When the season of fruit drew near, he sent his servants to the tenants, to get his fruit; [35] and the tenants took his servants and beat one, killed another, and stoned another. [36] Again he sent other servants, more than the first; and they did the same to them. [37] Afterward he sent his son to them, saying, 'They will respect my son.' [38] But when the tenants saw the son, they said to themselves, 'This is the heir; come, let us kill him and have his inheritance.' [39] And they took him and cast him out of the vineyard, and killed him. [40] When therefore the owner of the vineyard comes, what will he do to those tenants?" [41] They said to him, "He will put those wretches to a miserable death, and let out the vineyard to other tenants who will give him the fruits in their seasons."

42 Jesus said to them, "Have you never read in the scriptures:

'The very stone which the builders rejected
has become the head of the corner;
this was the Lord's doing,
and it is marvelous in our eyes'?
[43] Therefore I tell you, the kingdom of God will be taken away from you and given to a nation producing the fruits of it."[q]

45 When the chief priests and the Pharisees heard his parables, they perceived that he was speaking about them. [46] But when they tried to arrest him, they feared the multitudes, because they held him to be a prophet.

22 And again Jesus spoke to them in parables, saying, [2] "The kingdom of heaven may be compared to a king who gave a marriage feast for his son, [3] and sent his servants to call those who were invited to the marriage feast; but they would not come. [4] Again he sent other servants, saying, 'Tell those who are invited, Behold, I have made ready my dinner, my oxen and my fat calves

are killed, and everything is ready; come to the marriage feast.' [5] But they made light of it and went off, one to his farm, another to his business, [6] while the rest seized his servants, treated them shamefully, and killed them. [7] The king was angry, and he sent his troops and destroyed those murderers and burned their city. [8] Then he said to his servants, 'The wedding is ready, but those invited were not worthy. [9] Go therefore to the thoroughfares, and invite to the marriage feast as many as you find.' [10] And those servants went out into the streets and gathered all whom they found, both bad and good; so the wedding hall was filled with guests.

11 "But when the king came in to look at the guests, he saw there a man who had no wedding garment; [12] and he said to him, 'Friend, how did you get in here without a wedding garment?' And he was speechless. [13] Then the king said to the attendants, 'Bind him hand and foot, and cast him into the outer darkness; there men will weep and gnash their teeth.' [14] For many are called, but few are chosen."

15 Then the Pharisees went and took counsel how to entangle him in his talk. [16] And they sent their disciples to him, along with the Hero'dians, saying, "Teacher, we know that you are true, and teach the way of God truthfully, and care for no man; for you do not regard the position of men. [17] Tell us, then, what you think. Is it lawful to pay taxes to Caesar, or not?" [18] But Jesus, aware of their malice, said, "Why put me to the test, you hypocrites? [19] Show me the money for the tax." And they brought him a coin.[r] [20] And Jesus said to them, "Whose likeness and inscription is this?" [21] They said, "Caesar's."

q Other ancient authorities add verse 44, *"And he who falls on this stone will be broken to pieces; but when it falls on any one, it will crush him"*   r Greek *a denarius*

***

22.1–14: **The marriage feast** (Lk.14.16–24). **3:** 21.34. **10:** 13.47. **13:** 8.12.

22.15–22: **Paying taxes to Caesar** (Mk.12.13–17; Lk.20.20–26). **15:** Mk.3.6; 8.15. **16:** *Herodians*, Mk.3.6 n. In asking Jesus for a pronouncement affecting all Jews, his enemies thought to bring him into conflict with sectarian views. **17:** If Jesus approved paying taxes he would offend the nationalistic parties; if he disapproved payment he could be reported as disloyal to the empire. **21:** Rom.13.7; 1 Pet.2.17.

Then he said to them, "Render therefore to Caesar the things that are Caesar's, and to God the things that are God's." 22 When they heard it, they marveled; and they left him and went away.

23 The same day Sad'ducees came to him, who say that there is no resurrection; and they asked him a question, 24 saying, "Teacher, Moses said, 'If a man dies, having no children, his brother must marry the widow, and raise up children for his brother.' 25 Now there were seven brothers among us; the first married, and died, and having no children left his wife to his brother. 26 So too the second and third, down to the seventh. 27 After them all, the woman died. 28 In the resurrection, therefore, to which of the seven will she be wife? For they all had her."

29 But Jesus answered them, "You are wrong, because you know neither the scriptures nor the power of God. 30 For in the resurrection they neither marry nor are given in marriage, but are like angels[s] in heaven. 31 And as for the resurrection of the dead, have you not read what was said to you by God, 32 'I am the God of Abraham, and the God of Isaac, and the God of Jacob'? He is not God of the dead, but of the living." 33 And when the crowd heard it, they were astonished at his teaching.

34 But when the Pharisees heard that he had silenced the Sad'ducees, they came together. 35 And one of them, a lawyer, asked him a question, to test him. 36 "Teacher, which is the great commandment in the law?" 37 And he said to him, "You shall love the Lord your God with all your heart, and with all your soul, and with all your mind. 38 This is the great and first commandment. 39 And a second is like it, You shall love your neighbor as yourself. 40 On these two commandments depend all the law and the prophets."

41 Now while the Pharisees were gathered together, Jesus asked them a question, 42 saying, "What do you think of the Christ? Whose son is he?" They said to him, "The son of David." 43 He said to them, "How is it then that David, inspired by the Spirit,[t] calls him Lord, saying,

44 'The Lord said to my Lord,

Sit at my right hand,

till I put thy enemies under they feet'?

45 If David thus calls him Lord, how is he his son?" 46 And no one was able to answer him a word, nor from that day did any one dare to ask him any more questions.

23 Then said Jesus to the crowds and to his disciples, 2 "The scribes and the Pharisees sit on Moses' seat; 3 so practice and observe whatever they tell you, but not what they do; for they preach, but do not practice. 4 They bind heavy burdens, hard to bear,[u] and lay them on men's shoulders; but they themselves will not move them with their finger. 5 They do all their deeds to be seen by men; for they make their phylacteries broad and their fringes long, 6 and they love the place of honor at feasts and the best seats in the synagogues, 7 and salutations in the market places, and being called rabbi by men. 8 But you are not to be called rabbi, for you have one

s Other ancient authorities add *of God* t Or *David in the Spirit* u Other ancient authorities omit *hard to bear*

22.23–33: Question about the resurrection (Mk.12.18–27; Lk.20.27–40). **23:** Belief in the *resurrection* was held by the Pharisees in Jesus' day, but rejected by the Sadducees (Acts 4.1–2; 23.6–10). **24;** Dt.25.5. **29:** The Sadducees fail to see God's purpose and do not trust his *power.* **31–32:** Ex.3.6. The idea here is that men who are related to God in faith have life even though physically dead. Resurrection is the divine act by which men will achieve the fulness of life intended in creation and lost through sin and death (see Lk.20.34–36 n.).

22.34–40: The great commandment (Mk.12.28–34; Lk.10.25–28). **37:** Dt.6.5. **39:** Lev.19.18; Compare Mt.19.19; Rom.13.9; Gal.5.14; Jas.2.8. **40:** The Law contains many ways of applying to life the principle of love.

22.41–46: David's son (Mk.12.35–37; Lk.20.41–44). **44:** The first *Lord* refers to God, the second *Lord* is taken here to refer to the Messiah (see Ps.110.1; Acts 2.34–35; Heb.1.13; 10.12–13).

23.1–36: Woe to scribes and Pharisees. 4: Lk.11.46; Mt.11.28–30; Acts 15.10. **5:** 6.1; 5.16; Ex.13.9; Dt.6.8. **6–7:** Mk.12.38–39; Lk.11.43; 14.7–11; 20.46. **8:** Jas.3.1. **12:** Lk.14.11; 18.14; Mt.18.4; 1 Pet.5.6. **13:** Lk.11.52. **15:**

teacher, and you are all brethren. [9] And call no man your father on earth, for you have one Father, who is in heaven. [10] Neither be called masters, for you have one master, the Christ. [11] He who is greatest among you shall be your servant; [12] whoever exalts himself will be humbled, and whoever humbles himself will be exalted.

[13] "But woe to you, scribes and Pharisees, hypocrites! because you shut the kingdom of heaven against men; for you neither enter yourselves, nor allow those who would enter to go in.[v] [15] Woe to you, scribes and Pharisees, hypocrites! for you traverse sea and land to make a single proselyte, and when he becomes a proselyte, you make him twice as much a child of hell[w] as yourselves.

[16] "Woe to you, blind guides, who say, 'If any one swears by the temple, it is nothing; but if any one swears by the gold of the temple, he is bound by his oath.' [17] You blind fools! For which is greater, the gold or the temple that has made the gold sacred? [18] And you say, 'If any one swears by the altar, it is nothing; but if any one swears by the gift that is on the altar, he is bound by his oath.' [18] You blind men! For which is greater, the gift or the altar that makes the gift sacred? [20] So he who swears by the altar, swears by it and by everything on it; [21] and he who swears by the temple, swears by it and by him who dwells in it; [22] and he who swears by heaven, swears by the throne of God and by him who sits upon it.

[23] "Woe to you, scribes and Pharisees, hypocrites! for you tithe mint and dill and cummin, and have neglected the weightier matters of the law, justice and mercy and faith; these you ought to have done, without neglecting the others. [24] You blind guides, straining out a gnat and swallowing a camel!

[25] "Woe to you, scribes and Pharisees, hypocrites! for you cleanse the outside of the cup and of the plate, but inside they are full of extortion and rapacity. [26] You blind Pharisee! first cleanse the inside of the cup and of the plate, that the outside also may be clean.

[27] "Woe to you, scribes and Pharisees, hypocrites! for you are like white-washed tombs, which outwardly appear beautiful, but within they are full of dead men's bones and all uncleanness. [28] So you also outwardly appear righteous to men, but within you are full of hypocrisy and iniquity.

[29] "Woe to you, scribes and Pharisees, hypocrites! for you build the tombs of the prophets and adorn the monuments of the righteous, [30] saying, 'If we had lived in the days of our fathers, we would not have taken part with them in shedding the blood of the prophets.' [31] Thus you witness against yourselves, that you are sons of those who murdered the prophets. [32] Fill up, then, the measure of your fathers. [33] You serpents, you brood of vipers, how are you to escape being sentenced to hell?[w] [34] Therefore I send you prophets and wise men and scribes, some of whom you will kill and crucify, and some you will scourge in your synagogues and persecute from town to town, [35] that upon you may come all the righteous blood shed on earth, from the blood of innocent Abel to the blood of Zechari'ah

v Other authorities add here (or after verse 12) verse 14, *Woe to you, scribes and Pharisees, hypocrites! for you devour widows' houses and for a pretense you make long prayers; therefore you will receive the greater condemnation w* Greek *Gehenna*

Acts 2.10; 6.5; 13.43. **16:** 5.33–37; 15.14. **17:** Ex.30.29. **21:** 1 Kg.8.13; Ps.26.8. **23–24:** Lk.11.42; Lev.27.30; Mic.6.8. **25–26:** Lk.11.39–41; Mk.7.4. **27–28:** Lk.11.44; Acts 23.3; Ps.5.9. **28:** See Lk.20.20 n. **29–32:** Lk.11.47–48; Acts 7.51–53. **31:** *Sons of* has two meanings: descendants, or, those of similar character. The scribes and Pharisees would admit to being descendants *of those who murdered the prophets.* Jesus insists that their attitudes are also similar (v. 28). **33:** 3.7; Lk.3.7. **34–36:** Lk.11,49–51. **34:** See Lk.11.49 n.; Mt.10.17,23; 2 Chr.36.15–16. *Prophets and wise men and scribes* are terms of Jewish origin applied here to Christian missionaries. **35:** Gen.4.8; Heb.11.4; 2 Chr.24.20–22; Zech.1.1. The identifying words *son of Barachiah* (not in Lk.11.51) probably were mistakenly added to the text of Matthew at an early date because of confusion over which *Zechariah* was meant. The meaning of the sentence is to indicate the sweep of time from the first to the last victim of murder mentioned in the Old Testament (2 Chronicles stands last in the order of books in the Hebrew Bible).

the son of Barachi'ah, whom you murdered between the sanctuary and the altar. ³⁸ Truly, I say to you, all this will come upon this generation.

37 "O Jerusalem, Jerusalem, killing the prophets and stoning those who are sent to you! How often would I have gathered your children together as a hen gathers her brood under her wings, and you would not! ³⁸ Behold, your house is forsaken and desolate.^x ³⁹ For I tell you, you will not see me again, until you say, 'Blessed is he who comes in the name of the Lord.'"

24 Jesus left the temple and was going away, when his disciples came to point out to him the buildings of the temple. ² But he answered them, "You see all these, do you not? Truly, I say to you, there will not be left here one stone upon another, that will not be thrown down."

3 As he sat on the Mount of Olives, the disciples came to him privately, saying, "Tell us, when will this be, and what will be the sign of your coming and the close of the age?" ⁴ And Jesus answered them, "Take heed that no one leads you astray. ⁵ For many will come in my name, saying, 'I am the Christ,' and they will lead many astray. ⁶ And you will hear of wars and rumors of wars; see that you are not alarmed; for this must take place, but the end is not yet. ⁷ For nation will rise against nation, and kingdom against kingdom, and there will be famines and earthquakes in various places: ⁸ all this is but the beginning of the birthpangs.

9 "Then they will deliver you up to tribulation, and put you to death; and you will be hated by all nations for my name's sake. ¹⁰ And then many will fall away,^y and betray one another, and hate one another. ¹¹ And many false prophets will arise and lead many astray. ¹² And because wickedness is multiplied, most men's love will grow cold. ¹⁸ But he who endures to the end will be saved. ¹⁴ And this gospel of the kingdom will be preached throughout the whole world, as a testimony to all nations; and then the end will come.

15 "So when you see the desolating sacrilege spoken of by the prophet Daniel, standing in the holy place (let the reader understand), ¹⁶ then let those who are in Judea flee to the mountains; ¹⁷ let him who is on the housetop not go down to take what is in his house; ¹⁸ and let him who is in the field not turn back to take his mantle. ¹⁹ And alas for those who are with child and for those who give suck in those days! ²⁰ Pray that your flight may not be in winter or on a sabbath. ²¹ For then there will be great tribulation, such as has not been from the beginning of the world until now, no, and never will be. ²² And if those days had not been shortened, no human being would be saved; but for the sake of the elect those days will be shortened. ²³ Then if any one says to you, 'Lo, here is the Christ!' or 'There he is!' do not believe it. ²⁴ For false Christs and false prophets will arise and show great signs and wonders, so as to lead astray, if possible, even the elect. ²⁵ Lo, I have told you beforehand. ²⁶ So, if they say to you, 'Lo, he is in the wilderness,'

x Other ancient authorities omit *and desolate*
y Or *stumble*

23.37–39: Lament over Jerusalem (Lk.13.34–35). **37:** The words *how often* suggest repeated efforts, made perhaps during an earlier Judean ministry (see Lk.4.44 n.). **38:** 1 Kg.9.7; Jer.12.7; 22.5. **39:** 21.9; Ps.118.26.

24.1–3: Destruction of the temple foretold (Mk.13.1–2; Lk.21.5–7). **1:** These verses, together with the discourse that follows, seem to merge teachings about an immediate destruction of Jerusalem with details associated in Scripture with the end of human history. These teachings were set down by the Evangelist in the light of events between A.D. 30 and 70. It is difficult to be certain what the original form of Jesus' words was. **3:** Lk.17.20–21; Mt.13.39,40,49; 16.27.

24.4–36: On the end of the age (Mk.13.3–37; Lk.21.8–36). **5:** 1 Jn.2.18. **6–7:** Rev.6.3–8; **12–17:** **8:** *The birthpangs* signal the imminence of the new age, which was announced at the beginning of Jesus' public ministry as "at hand" (4.17), but is to be realized only after a period of witness to Jesus' message (v. 14). Verses 5–14 seem to include a larger community of followers than the original disciples. **9:** 10.17–18,22; Jn.15.18; 16.2. **13:** 10.22; Rev.2.7. **14:** 28.19; Rom. 10.18. **15:** Dan.9.27; 11.31; 12.11; see Mk.13.14 n. **17–18:** Lk.17.31. **21:** Dan.12.1; Jl.2.2.

do not go out; if they say, 'Lo, he is in the inner rooms,' do not believe it. [27] For as the lightning comes from the east and shines as far as the west, so will be the coming of the Son of man. [28] Wherever the body is, there the eagles[z] will be gathered together.

[29] "Immediately after the tribulation of those days the sun will be darkened, and the moon will not give its light, and the stars will fall from heaven, and the powers of the heavens will be shaken; [30] then will appear the sign of the Son of man in heaven, and then all the tribes of the earth will mourn, and they will see the Son of man coming on the clouds of heaven with power and great glory; [31] and he will send out his angels with a loud trumpet call, and they will gather his elect from the four winds, from one end of heaven to the other.

[32] "From the fig tree learn its lesson: as soon as its branch becomes tender and puts forth its leaves, you know that summer is near. [33] So also, when you see all these things, you know that he is near, at the very gates. [34] Truly, I say to you, this generation will not pass away till all these things take place. [35] Heaven and earth will pass away, but my words will not pass away.

[36] "But of that day and hour no one knows, not even the angels of heaven, nor the Son,[a] but the Father only. [37] As were the days of Noah, so will be the coming of the Son of man. [38] For as in those days before the flood they were eating and drinking, marrying and giving in marriage, until the day when Noah entered the ark, [39] and they did not know until the flood came and swept them all away, so will be the coming of the Son of man. [40] Then two men will be in the field; one is taken and one is left. [41] Two women will be grinding at the mill; one is taken and one is left. [42] Watch therefore, for you do not know on what day your Lord is coming. [43] But know this, that if the householder had known in what part of the night the thief was coming, he would have watched and would not have let his house be broken into. [44] Therefore you also must be ready; for the Son of man is coming at an hour you do not expect.

[45] "Who then is the faithful and wise servant, whom his master has set over his household, to give them their food at the proper time? [46] Blessed is that servant whom his master when he comes will find so doing. [47] Truly, I say to you, he will set him over all his possessions. [48] But if that wicked servant says to himself, 'My master is delayed,' [49] and begins to beat his fellow servants, and eats and drinks with the drunken, [50] the master of that servant will come on a day when he does not expect him and at an hour he does not know, [51] and will punish[b] him, and put him with the hypocrites; there men will weep and gnash their teeth.

25 "Then the kingdom of heaven shall be compared to ten maidens who took their lamps and went to meet the bridegroom.[c] [2] Five of them were foolish, and five were wise. [3] For when the foolish took their lamps, they took no oil with them; [4] but the wise took flasks of oil with their lamps. [5] As the bridegroom was delayed, they all slumbered and slept. [6] But at midnight there was a cry, 'Behold, the bridegroom! Come out to meet him.' [7] Then all those maidens rose and trimmed their lamps. [8] And the foolish said to

z Or *vultures*   a Other ancient authorities omit *nor the Son*   b Or *cut him in pieces*   c Other ancient authorities add *and the bride*

28: See Lk.17.37 n.; Job 39.30. **29–31:** The language here is drawn from the Old Testament; God's victory over sin is to be established by the Son of man whom he sends (Rev.8.12; Is.13.10; 34.4; Ezek.32.7; Jl.2.10–11; Zeph.1.15). **30:** 16.27; Dan.7.13; Rev.1.7. **31:** 1 Cor.15.52; 1 Th.4.16; Is.27.13; Zech.2.10; 9.14. **34:** 10.23; 16.28. The normal meaning of *this generation* would be "men of our time," and the words would refer to a period of 20–30 years. What Jesus meant, however, is uncertain. **35:** 5.18; Lk.16.17. **36:** Acts 1.6–7. **37–39:** Lk.17.26–27; Gen.6.5–8; 7.6–24. **40–41:** Lk.17.34–35. **42:** Mk.13.35; Lk.12.40; 21.34–46; Mt.25.13. **43–51:** Lk.12.39–46. **43:** 1 Th.5.2; Rev.3.3.
   25.1–46: Teachings on the coming of the kingdom. 1–13: The parable of the wise and foolish maidens is based on the Palestinian custom that *the bridegroom* fetched his bride from her parents' home to his own. **1:** Lk.12.35–38; Mk.13.34. **2:** 7.24–27. **10:** Rev.19.9. **11–12:** Lk.13.25; Mt.7.21–23. **13:** 24.42; Mk.13.35; Lk.12.40.

the wise, 'Give us some of your oil, for our lamps are going out.' [9] But the wise replied, 'Perhaps there will not be enough for us and for you; go rather to the dealers and buy for yourselves.' [10] And while they went to buy, the bridegroom came, and those who were ready went in with him to the marriage feast; and the door was shut. [11] Afterward the other maidens came also, saying, 'Lord, lord, open to us.' [12] But he replied, 'Truly, I say to you, I do not know you.' [13] Watch therefore, for you know neither the day nor the hour.

[14] "For it will be as when a man going on a journey called his servants and entrusted to them his property; [15] to one he gave five talents,[d] to another two, to another one, to each according to his ability. Then he went away. [16] He who had received the five talents went at once and traded with them; and he made five talents more. [17] So also, he who had the two talents made two talents more. [18] But he who had received the one talent went and dug in the ground and hid his master's money. [19] Now after a long time the master of those servants came and settled accounts with them. [20] And he who had received the five talents came forward, bringing five talents more, saying, 'Master, you delivered to me five talents; here I have made five talents more.' [21] His master said to him, 'Well done, good and faithful servant; you have been faithful over a little. I will set you over much; enter into the joy of your master.' [22] And he also who had the two talents came forward, saying, 'Master, you delivered to me two talents; here I have made two talents more.' [23] His master said to him, 'Well done, good and faithful servant; you have been faithful over a little, I will set you over much; enter into the joy of your master.' [24] He also who had received the one talent came forward, saying, 'Master, I knew you to be a hard man, reaping where you did not sow, and gathering where you did not winnow; [25] so I was afraid, and I went and hid your talent in the ground. Here you have what is yours.' [26] But his master answered him, 'You wicked and slothful servant! You knew that I reap where I have not sowed, and gather where I have not winnowed? [27] Then you ought to have invested my money with the bankers, and at my coming I should have received what was my own with interest. [28] So take the talent from him, and give it to him who has the ten talents. [29] For to every one who has will more be given, and he will have abundance; but from him who has not, even what he has will be taken away. [30] And cast the worthless servant into the outer darkness; there men will weep and gnash their teeth.'

[31] "When the Son of man comes in his glory, and all the angels with him, then he will sit on his glorious throne. [32] Before him will be gathered all the nations, and he will separate them one from another as a shepherd separates the sheep from the goats, [33] and he will place the sheep at his right hand, but the goats at the left. [34] Then the King will say to those at his right hand, 'Come, O blessed of my Father, inherit the kingdom prepared for you from the foundation of the world; [35] for I was hungry and you gave me food, I was thirsty and you gave me drink, I was a stranger and you welcomed me, [36] I was naked and you clothed me, I was sick and you visited me, I was in prison and you came to me.' [37] Then the righteous will answer him, 'Lord, when did we see thee hungry and feed thee, or thirsty and give thee drink? [38] And when did we see thee a stranger and welcome thee, or naked and clothe thee? [39] And when did we

d This talent was more than fifteen years' wages of a laborer

---

25.14–30: Parable of the talents. Lk.19.12–27. **15:** On the value of this *talent* see note *d.* **21:** Lk.16.10. **29:** The statement, *From him who has not . . . taken away,* illustrates Jesus' way of speaking in two settings at once: as the master's servant had his original talent, yet had earned nothing by it, so men can have their earthly existence and all that derives from it, yet lack merit in the final judgment (v. 30). **30:** *Worthless,* without value to his master.

25.31–46: The Great Judgment. 31: 16.27; 19.28. **32:** Ezek.34.17. *The nations,* probably those who do not know the God of Israel (compare Rom.2.13–16). **34:** Lk.12.32; Mt.5.3; Rev.13.8; 17.8. **35–36:** Is.58.7; Jas.1.27; 2.15–16;

see thee sick or in prison and visit thee?' [40] And the King will answer them, 'Truly, I say to you, as you did it to one of the least of these my brethren, you did it to me.' [41] Then he will say to those at his left hand, 'Depart from me, you cursed, into the eternal fire prepared for the devil and his angels; [42] for I was hungry and you gave me no food, I was thirsty and you gave me no drink, [43] I was a stranger and you did not welcome me, naked and you did not clothe me, sick and in prison and you did not visit me.' [44] Then they also will answer, 'Lord, when did we see thee hungry or thirsty or a stranger or naked or sick or in prison, and did not minister to thee?' [45] Then he will answer them, 'Truly, I say to you, as you did it not to one of the least of these, you did it not to me.' [46] And they will go away into eternal punishment, but the righteous into eternal life."

26 When Jesus had finished all these sayings, he said to his disciples, [2] "You know that after two days the Passover is coming, and the Son of man will be delivered up to be crucified."

[3] Then the chief priests and the elders of the people gathered in the palace of the high priest, who was called Ca'iaphas, [4] and took counsel together in order to arrest Jesus by stealth and kill him. [5] But they said, "Not during the feast, lest there be a tumult among the people."

[6] Now when Jesus was at Bethany in the house of Simon the leper, [7] a woman came up to him with an alabaster flask of very expensive ointment, and she poured it on his head, as he sat at table. [8] But when the disciples saw it, they were indignant, saying, "Why this waste? [9] For this ointment might have been sold for a large sum, and given to the poor." [10] But Jesus, aware of this, said to them, "Why do you trouble the woman? For she has done a beautiful thing to me. [11] For you always have the poor with you, but you will not always have me. [12] In pouring this ointment on my body she has done it to prepare me for burial. [13] Truly, I say to you, wherever this gospel is preached in the whole world, what she has done will be told in memory of her."

[14] Then one of the twelve, who was called Judas Iscariot, went to the chief priests [15] and said, "What will you give me if I deliver him to you?" And they paid him thirty pieces of silver. [16] And from that moment he sought an opportunity to betray him.

[17] Now on the first day of Unleavened Bread the disciples came to Jesus, saying, "Where will you have us prepare for you to eat the passover?" [18] He said, "Go into the city to a certain one, and say to him, 'The Teacher says, My time is at hand; I will keep the passover at your house with my disciples.'" [19] And the disciples did as Jesus had directed them, and they prepared the passover.

[20] When it was evening, he sat at table with the twelve disciples;[e] [21] and as they were eating, he said, "Truly, I say to you, one of you will betray me." [22] And they were very sorrowful, and began to say to him one after another, "Is it I, Lord?" [23] He answered, "He who has dipped his hand in the dish with me, will betray me. [24] The Son of man goes as it

e Other authorities omit disciples

Heb.13.2; 2 Tim.1.16. **40:** 10.42; Mk.9.41; Heb.6.10; Pr.19.17. **41:** Mk.9.48; Rev.20.10. **46:** Dan.12.2; Jn.5.29. *Go away into eternal life* expresses the same idea as *inherit the kingdom* (v. 34).

26.1–27.66: Jesus' death (Mk.14.1–15.47; Lk.22.1–23.56; Jn.13.1–19.42). **26.1:** *Finished*, see 7.28 n. **2–5:** Mk.14.1–2; Lk.22.1–2; Jn.11.47–53. **2:** *The Passover* commemorated the escape from Egypt under Moses (Ex.12.1–20). **6–13:** Mk.14.3–9; Jn.12.1–8. A similar event is reported in Lk.7.36–50. **6:** The identity of this Simon is unknown. **7:** Jn.12.3; see Lk.7.37 n., 46. **10:** The *beautiful thing* is what is good and fitting under the circumstances of impending death. The same Greek words are translated "good works" in 5.16. **12:** Jn.19.40. **14–16:** Mk.14.10–11; Lk.22.3–6. **14:** See Mk.14.10 n. **15:** Ex.21.32; Zech.11.12. The value of the *thirty pieces of silver* is uncertain. Matthew's quotation refers to silver shekels; at four denarii to the shekel this was one hundred and twenty days' wages (20.2).

26.17–29: The Last Supper. 17–19: Mk.14.12–16; Lk.22.7–13. **17:** See Lk.22.7 n. **18:** Lk.22.10 n., 11 n. Jn.7.6; 12.23; 13.1; 17.1. **19:** 21.6; Dt.16.5–8. **20–25:** Mk.14.17–21; Lk.22.14,21–23; Jn.13.21–30. **24:** Ps.41.9; Lk.24.25; 1

is written of him, but woe to that man by whom the Son of man is betrayed! It would have been better for that man if he had not been born." [25] Judas, who betrayed him, said, "Is it I, Master?"*f* He said to him, "You have said so."

26 Now as they were eating, Jesus took bread, and blessed, and broke it, and gave it to the disciples and said, "Take, eat, this is my body." [27] And he took a cup, and when he had given thanks he gave it to them, saying, "Drink of it, all of you; [28] for this is my blood of the*g* covenant, which is poured out for many for the forgiveness of sins. [29] I tell you I shall not drink again of this fruit of the vine until that day when I drink it new with you in my Father's kingdom."

30 And when they had sung a hymn, they went out to the Mount of Olives. [31] Then Jesus said to them, "You will all fall away because of me this night; for it is written, 'I will strike the shepherd, and the sheep of the flock will be scattered.' [32] But after I am raised up, I will go before you to Galilee." [33] Peter declared to him, "Though they all fall away because of you, I will never fall away." [34] Jesus said to him, "Truly, I say to you, this very night, before the cock crows, you will deny me three times." [35] Peter said to him, "Even if I must die with you, I will not deny you." And so said all the disciples.

36 Then Jesus went with them to a place called Gethsem'ane, and he said to his disciples, "Sit here, while I go yonder and pray." [37] And taking with him Peter and the two sons of Zeb'edee, he began to be sorrowful and troubled. [38] Then he said to them, "My soul is very sorrowful, even to death; remain here, and watch*h* with me." [39] And going a little farther he fell on his face and prayed, "My Father, if it be possible, let this cup pass from me; nevertheless, not as I will, but as thou wilt." [40] And he came to the disciples and found them sleeping; and he said to Peter, "So, could you not watch*h* with me one hour? [41] Watch*h* and pray that you may not enter into temptation; the spirit indeed is willing, but the flesh is weak." [42] Again, for the second time, he went away and prayed, "My Father, if this cannot pass unless I drink it, thy will be done." [43] And again he came and found them sleeping, for their eyes were heavy. [44] So, leaving them again, he went away and prayed for the third time, saying the same words. [45] Then he came to the disciples and said to them, "Are you still sleeping and taking your rest? Behold, the hour is at hand, and the Son of man is betrayed into the hands of sinners. [46] Rise, let us be going; see, my betrayer is at hand."

47 While he was still speaking, Judas came, one of the twelve, and with him a great crowd with swords and clubs, from the chief priests and the elders of the people. [48] Now the betrayer had given them a sign, saying, "The one I shall kiss is the man; seize him." [49] And he came up to Jesus at once and said, "Hail, Master!"*i* And he kissed him. [50] Jesus said to him, "Friend, why are you here?"*j* Then they came up and laid hands on Jesus and seized him. [51] And behold, one of those

f Or *Rabbi*   *g* Other ancient authorities insert *new*
h Or *keep awake*   *i* Or *Rabbi*   *j* Or *do that for which you have come*

Cor.15.3; Acts 17.2–3; Mt.18.7. **25:** Judas' question is phrased to imply that the answer will be in the negative. **26–29:** Mk.14.22–25; Lk.22.15–20; 1 Cor.10.16; 11.23–26; Mt.14.19; 15.36; see Lk.22.17 n. **28:** Heb.9.20; Mt.20.28; Mk.1.4; Ex.24.6–8; see Mk.14.24 n. In the background of Jesus' words are several important ideas of Jewish religion: man's sins lead to death; God has rescued his people, as from Egypt, and may be trusted to deliver from death itself; God forgives men in mercy if they obey him; God will make a new covenant (Jer.31.31–34). **29:** See Lk.14.15; 22.18,30; Rev.19.9.

26.30–56: Gethsemane. 30–35: Mk.14.26–31; Lk.22.31–34,39; Jn.14.31; 18.1; 13.36–38. **30:** Probably the *hymn* was Psalms 115–118. **31:** Zech.13.7; Jn.16.32. **32:** 28.7,10,16. **36–46:** Mk.14.32–42; Lk.22.40–46. **38:** Jn.12.27; Heb.5.7–8; Ps.42.6. *My soul,* i.e. "I." **39:** Ezek. 23.31–34; Jn.18.11; Mt.20.22. Jesus does not desire death but accepts God's will even including death. *Cup,* see Lk.22.42 n. **41:** 6.13; Lk.11.4. *Temptation,* "testing," in which man's best intentions may give way. **42:** Jn.4.34; 5.30; 6.38. **45:** 26.18 n.; Jn.12.23; 13.1; 17.1. **47–56:** Mk.14.43–52; Lk.22.47–53; Jn.18.2–11. **50:** *Friend,* "comrade." The synoptic gospels do not report Judas' movements on this night

who were with Jesus stretched out his hand and drew his sword, and struck the slave of the high priest, and cut off his ear. [52] Then Jesus said to him, "Put your sword back into its place; for all who take the sword will perish by the sword. [53] Do you think that I cannot appeal to my Father, and he will at once send me more than twelve legions of angels? [54] But how then should the scriptures be fulfilled, that it must be so?" [55] At that hour Jesus said to the crowds, "Have you come out as against a robber, with swords and clubs to capture me? Day after day I sat in the temple teaching, and you did not seize me. [56] But all this has taken place, that the scriptures of the prophets might be fulfilled." Then all the disciples forsook him and fled.

[57] Then those who had seized Jesus led him to Ca′iaphas the high priest, where the scribes and the elders had gathered. [58] But Peter followed him at a distance, as far as the courtyard of the high priest, and going inside he sat with the guards to see the end. [59] Now the chief priests and the whole council sought false testimony against Jesus that they might put him to death, [60] but they found none, though many false witnesses came forward. At last two came forward [61] and said, "This fellow said, 'I am able to destroy the temple of God, and to build it in three days.'" [62] And the high priest stood up and said, "Have you no answer to make? What is it that these men testify against you?" [63] But Jesus was silent. And the high priest said to him, "I adjure you by the living God, tell us if you are the Christ, the Son of God." [64] Jesus said to him, "You have said so. But I tell you, hereafter you will see the Son of man seated at the right hand of Power, and coming on the clouds of heaven."

[65] Then the high priest tore his robes, and said, "He has uttered blasphemy. Why do we still need witnesses? You have now heard his blasphemy. [66] What is your judgment?" They answered, "He deserves death." [67] Then they spat in his face, and struck him; and some slapped him, [68] saying, "Prophesy to us, you Christ! Who is it that struck you?

[69] Now Peter was sitting outside in the courtyard. And a maid came up to him, and said, "You also were with Jesus the Galilean." [70] But he denied it before them all, saying, "I do not know what you mean." [71] And when he went out to the porch, another maid saw him, and she said to the bystanders, "This man was with Jesus of Nazareth." [72] And again he denied it with an oath, "I do not know the man." [73] After a little while the bystanders came up and said to Peter, "Certainly you are also one of them, for your accent betrays you." [74] Then he began to invoke a curse on himself and to swear, "I do not know the man." And immediately the cock crowed. [75] And Peter remembered the saying of Jesus, "Before the cock crows, you will deny me three times." And he went out and wept bitterly.

27 When morning came, all the chief priests and the elders of the people took counsel against Jesus to put him to death; [2] and they bound him and led him away and delivered him to Pilate the governor.

[3] When Judas, his betrayer, saw that he was condemned, he repented and brought back the thirty pieces of silver to the chief priest and the elders, [4] saying, "I have sinned in betraying innocent blood." They said, "What is that to us? See to it yourself." [5] And throwing down the pieces of silver in the temple, he departed; and he went and hanged

---

(compare Jn.13.30; 18.3). **51:** Jn.18.10. **52:** Gen.9.6; Rev.13.10. **53:** *Twelve legions,* 72,000. **54:** Faith in God can not claim his promise (4.6) so as to counteract his purpose. **55:** Lk.19.47; Jn.18.19–21.

26.57–75: Jesus before Caiaphas. 57: The reference is to the Jewish supreme court (the Sanhedrin; see Jn.11.47 n.). **59:** See Mk.14.55 n. **61:** 24.2; 27.40; Acts 6.14; Jn.2.19. **63:** 27.11; Jn.18.33. **64:** 16.28; Dan.7.13; Ps.110.1. **65:** Num.14.6; Acts 14.14; Lev.24.16. **66:** Lev.24.16. **73:** Peter spoke with a Galilean accent differing from the Judean. **75:** Compare v. 34.

27.1–26: Jesus before Pilate. 1–2: Mk.15.1; Lk.23.1; Jn.18.28–32. Jewish law required that the Sanhedrin take formal action by daylight. Apparently 26.57–68 describes a pre-dawn hearing. **3–10:** Acts 1.16–20. The details of

himself. [6] But the chief priests, taking the pieces of silver, said, "It is not lawful to put them into the treasury, since they are blood money." [7] So they took counsel, and bought with them the potter's field, to bury strangers in. [8] Therefore that field has been called the Field of Blood to this day. [9] Then was fulfilled what had been spoken by the prophet Jeremiah, saying, "And they took the thirty pieces of silver, the price of him on whom a price had been set by some of the sons of Israel, [10] and they gave them for the potter's field, as the Lord directed me."

11 Now Jesus stood before the governor; and the governor asked him, "Are you the King of the Jews?" Jesus said, "You have said so." [12] But when he was accused by the chief priests and elders, he made no answer. [13] Then Pilate said to him, "Do you not hear how many things they testify against you?" [14] But he gave him no answer, not even to a single charge; so that the governor wondered greatly.

15 Now at the feast the governor was accustomed to release for the crowd any one prisoner whom they wanted. [16] And they had then a notorious prisoner, called Barab'bas.[k] [17] So when they had gathered, Pilate said to them, "Whom do you want me to release for you, Barab'bas[k] or Jesus who is called Christ?" [18] For he knew that it was out of envy that they had delivered him up. [19] Besides, while he was sitting on the judgment seat, his wife sent word to him, "Have nothing to do with that righteous man, for I have suffered much over him today in a dream." [20] Now the chief priests and the elders persuaded the people to ask for Barab'bas and destroy Jesus. [21] The governor again said to them, "Which of the two do you want me to release for you?"

And they said, "Barab'bas." [22] Pilate said to them, "Then what shall I do with Jesus who is called Christ?" They all said, "Let him be crucified." [23] And he said, "Why, what evil has he done?" But they shouted all the more, "Let him be crucified."

24 So when Pilate saw that he was gaining nothing, but rather that a riot was beginning, he took water and washed his hands before the crowd, saying, "I am innocent of this man's blood;[l] see to it yourselves." [25] And all the people answered, "His blood be on us and on our children!" [26] Then he released for them Barab'bas, and having scourged Jesus, delivered him to be crucified.

27 Then the soldiers of the governor took Jesus into the praetorium, and they gathered the whole battalion before him. [28] And they stripped him and put a scarlet robe upon him, [29] and plaiting a crown of thorns they put it on his head, and put a reed in his right hand. And kneeling before him they mocked him, saying, "Hail, King of the Jews!" [30] And they spat upon him, and took the reed and struck him on the head. [31] And when they had mocked him, they stripped him of the robe, and put his own clothes on him, and led him away to crucify him.

32 As they went out, they came upon a man of Cyre'ne, Simon by name; this man they compelled to carry his cross. [33] And when they came to a place called Gol'gotha (which means the place of a skull), [34] they offered him wine to drink, mingled with gall; but when he tasted it, he would not drink it. [35] And when they had crucified him, they divided his garments among them by casting

k Other ancient authorities read *Jesus Barabbas*
l Other authorities read *this righteous blood* or *this righteous man's blood*

Judas' end are obscure. Each account connects him in death with a cemetery for foreigners in Jerusalem. **9–10:** Zech.11.12–13; Jer.18.1–3; 32.6–15. **11–14:** Mk.15.2–5; Lk.23.2–5; Jn.18.29–19.16. **14:** Lk.23.9; Mt.26.62; Mk.14.60; 1 Tim.6.13. **15–26:** Mk.15.6–15; Lk.23.18–25; Jn.18.38–40; 19.4–16. **19:** Lk.23.4. **21:** Acts 3.13–14. **24:** Dt.21.6–9; Ps.26.6. **25:** Acts 5.28; Jos.2.19. **26:** Scourging with a multi-thonged whip ordinarily preceded execution.
27.27–44: The crucifixion. 27–31: Mk.15.16–20; Jn.19.1–3. **27:** The *praetorium* was the governor's residence. *The battalion* at full strength numbered about five hundred men. **32–44:** Mk.15.21–32; Lk.23.26,33–43; Jn.19.17–24. **32:** The procession included Jesus, two other prisoners, a centurion, and a few soldiers. *Simon,* see Mk.15.21 n. **34:** *Gall,* any bitter liquid, possibly the myrrh of Mk.15.23. **35:** Ps.22.18. **37:** Indication of the offense was customary.

lots; [36] then they sat down and kept watch over him there. [37] And over his head they put the charge against him, which read, "This is Jesus the King of the Jews." [38] Then two robbers were crucified with him, one on the right and one on the left. [39] And those who passed by derided him, wagging their heads [40] and saying, "You who would destroy the temple and build it in three days, save yourself! If you are the Son of God, come down from the cross." [41] So also the chief priests, with the scribes and elders, mocked him, saying, [42] "He saved others; he cannot save himself. He is the King of Israel; let him come down now from the cross, and we will believe in him. [43] He trusts in God; let God deliver him now, if he desires him; for he said, 'I am the Son of God.'" [44] And the robbers who were crucified with him also reviled him in the same way.

45 Now from the sixth hour there was darkness over all the land[m] until the ninth hour. [46] And about the ninth hour Jesus cried with a loud voice, "Eli, Eli, la'ma sabach-tha'ni?" that is, "My God, my God, why hast thou forsaken me?" [47] And some of the bystanders hearing it said, "This man is calling Eli'jah." [48] And one of them at once ran and took a sponge, filled it with vinegar, and put it on a reed, and gave it to him to drink. [49] But the others said, "Wait, let us see whether Eli'jah will come to save him."[n] [50] And Jesus cried again with a loud voice and yielded up his spirit.

51 And behold, the curtain of the temple was torn in two, from top to bottom; and the earth shook, and the rocks were split; [52] the tombs also were opened, and many bodies of the saints who had fallen asleep were raised, [53] and coming out of the tombs after his resurrection they went into the holy city and appeared to many. [54] When the centurion and those who were with him, keeping watch over Jesus, saw the earthquake and what took place, they were filled with awe, and said, "Truly this was the Son[x] of God!"

55 There were also many women there, looking on from afar, who had followed Jesus from Galilee, ministering to him; [56] among whom were Mary Mag'dalene, and Mary the mother of James and Joseph, and the mother of the sons of Zeb'edee.

57 When it was evening, there came a rich man from Arimathe'a, named Joseph, who also was a disciple of Jesus. [58] He went to Pilate and asked for the body of Jesus. Then Pilate ordered it to be given to him. [59] And Joseph took the body, and wrapped it in a clean linen shroud, [60] and laid it in his own new tomb, which he had hewn in the rock; and he rolled a great stone to the door of the tomb, and departed. [61] Mary Mag'dalene and the other Mary were there, sitting opposite the sepulchre.

62 Next day, that is, after the day of Preparation, the chief priests and the Pharisees gathered before Pilate [63] and said, "Sir, we remember how that impostor said, while he was still alive, 'After three days I will rise again.' [64] Therefore order the sepulchre to be made secure until the third day, lest his disciples go and steal him away, and tell the

m Or earth   n Other ancient authorities insert And another took a spear and pierced his side, and out came water and blood   x Or a son

---

Since the Romans recognized the ruling Herods, it seems implied that Jesus was alleged to be a pretender and revolutionary. **39:** Ps.22.7–8; 109.25. **40:** 26.61; Acts 6.14; Jn.2.19. **42–43:** The taunts stress religious aspects of Jesus' works and words. *Israel* (rather than *the Jews,* v. 37) refers to the religious community rather than the political state. **43:** Ps.22.8.

27.45–66: The death of Jesus. 45–56: Mk.15.33–41; Lk.23.44–49; Jn.19.28–37. **45:** From about noon to about three p.m. **46:** *Eli . . . sabachthani,* quoted from Ps.22.1. **47:** *Elijah* (similar in sound to *Eli*) was expected to usher in the final period (Mal.4.5–6; Mt.27.49). **48:** Ps.69.21. The *vinegar* was a cheap, sour wine of the poor. The motive in offering it may have been to revive him and hence prolong the ordeal. **51:** Heb.9.8; 10.19; Ex.26.31–35; Mt.28.2; see Mk.15.38 n. **56:** *James,* possibly the James of 10.3; Lk.24.10; Acts 1.13. **57–61:** Mk.15.42–47; Lk.23.50–56; Jn.19.38–42; Acts 13.29. **58:** Bodies of the executed were normally denied burial. **60:** See Mk.16.3–5 n.; Acts 13.29. **61:** 27.56. **62:** *Next day,* the sabbath (Mk.15.42).

people, 'He has risen from the dead,' and the last fraud will be worse than the first." [65] Pilate said to them, "You have a guard[o] of soldiers; go, make it as secure as you can."[p] [66] So they went and made the sepulchre secure by sealing the stone and setting a guard.

28 Now after the sabbath, toward the dawn of the first day of the week, Mary Mag'dalene and the other Mary went to see the sepulchre. [2] And behold, there was a great earthquake; for an angel of the Lord descended from heaven and came and rolled back the stone, and sat upon it. [3] His appearance was like lightning, and his raiment white as snow. [4] And for fear of him the guards trembled and became like dead men. [5] But the angel said to the women, "Do not be afraid; for I know that you seek Jesus who was crucified. [6] He is not here; for he has risen, as he said. Come, see the place where he[q] lay. [7] Then go quickly and tell his disciples that he has risen from the dead, and behold, he is going before you to Galilee; there you will see him. Lo, I have told you." [8] So they departed quickly from the tomb with fear and great joy, and ran to tell his disciples. [9] And behold, Jesus met them and said, "Hail!" And they came up and took hold of his feet and worshiped him. [10] Then Jesus said to them, "Do not be afraid; go and tell my brethren to go to Galilee, and there they will see me."

[11] While they were going, behold, some of the guard went into the city and told the chief priests all that had taken place. [12] And when they had assembled with the elders and taken counsel, they gave a sum of money to the soldiers [13] and said, "Tell people, 'His disciples came by night and stole him away while we were asleep.' [14] And if this comes to the governor's ears, we will satisfy him and keep you out of trouble." [15] So they took the money and did as they were directed; and this story has been spread among the Jews to this day.

[16] Now the eleven disciples went to Galilee, to the mountain to which Jesus had directed them. [17] And when they saw him they worshiped him; but some doubted. [18] And Jesus came and said to them, "All authority in heaven and on earth has been given to me. [19] Go therefore and make disciples of all nations, baptizing them in the name of the Father and of the Son and of the Holy Spirit, [20] teaching them to observe all that I have commanded you; and lo, I am with you always, to the close of the age."

o Or *Take a guard*   *p* Greek *know*
q Other ancient authorities read *the Lord*

28.1–15: The first Easter (Mk.16.1–8; Lk.24.1–11; Jn.20.1–10). **4:** *The guards,* 27.62–66. **7:** 26.32; 28.16; Jn.21.1–23; 1 Cor.15.3–4,12,20. **8:** Compare Lk.24.9,22–23; the sequence of events cannot be worked out. Each account is a separate summary of early Christian testimony to the fact of Jesus' resurrection. **9:** Jn.20.14–18.

28.11–15: Bribing the guard. 11: 27.62–66. **15:** *This day,* i.e. the time when the Gospel according to Matthew was written.

28:16–20: Jesus' commission to his disciples. 17: 1 Cor.15.5–6; Jn.21.1–23; Lk.24.11. **18:** 11.27; Lk.10.22; Phil.2.9; Eph.1.20–22. *All authority,* compare Dan.7.14. **19:** *All nations,* contrast 10.5, and compare Mk.16.15; Lk.24.47; Acts 1.8. According to Hebrew usage *in the name of* means in the possession and protection of (Ps.124.8). **20:** *I am with you,* 18.20; Acts 18.10.

The Gospel According to John

IN THE BEGINNING WAS THE WORD, and the Word was with God, and the Word was God. 2 He was in the beginning with God; 3 all things were made through him, and without him was not anything made that was made. 4 In him was life,*a* and the life was the light of men. 5 The light shines in the darkness, and the darkness has not overcome it.

6 There was a man sent from God, whose name was John. 7 He came for testimony, to bear witness to the light, that all might believe through him. 8 He was not the light, but came to bear witness to the light.

9 The true light that enlightens every man was coming into the world. 10 He was in the world, and the world was made through him, yet the world knew him not. 11 He came to his own home, and his own people received him not. 12 But to all who received him, who believed in his name, he gave power to become children of God; 13 who were born, not of blood nor of the will of the flesh nor of the will of man, but of God.

14 And the Word became flesh and dwelt among us, full of grace and truth; we have beheld his glory, glory as of the only Son from the Father. 15 (John bore witness to him, and cried, "This was he of whom I said, 'He who comes after me ranks before me, for he was before me.'") 16 And from his fulness have we all received, grace upon grace. 17 For the law was given through Moses; grace and truth came through Jesus Christ. 18 No one has ever seen God; the only Son,*b* who is in the bosom of the Father, he has made him known.

19 And this is the testimony of John, when the Jews sent priests and Levites from Jerusalem to ask him, "Who are you?" 20 He confessed, he did not deny, but confessed, "I am not the Christ." 21 And they asked him, "What then? Are you Eli'jah?" He said, "I am not." "Are you the prophet?" And he answered, "No." 22 They said to him then, "Who are you? Let us have an answer for those who sent us. What do you say about yourself?" 23 He said, "I am the voice of one crying in the wilderness, 'Make straight the way of the Lord,' as the prophet Isaiah said."

24 Now they had been sent from the Pharisees. 25 They asked him, "Then why are you baptizing, if you are neither the Christ, nor Eli'jah, nor the prophet?" 26 John answered them, "I baptize with water; but among you stands one whom you do not know, 27 even he who comes after me, the thong of whose sandal I am not worthy to untie." 28 This took place in Bethany beyond the Jordan, where John was baptizing.

29 The next day he saw Jesus coming toward him, and said, "Behold, the Lamb of God, who takes away the sin of the world! 30 This is he of whom I said, 'After me comes a man who ranks before me, for he was before

a Or *was not anything made. That which has been made was life in him* *b* Other ancient authorities read *God*

1.1–18: The Prologue. 1–2: The *Word* (Greek "logos") of God is more than speech; it is God in action, creating (Gen.1.3; Ps.33.6), revealing (Amos 3.7–8), redeeming (Ps.107.19–20). Jesus is this *Word* (v. 14). He was eternal (*in the beginning:* compare Gen.1.1); personal *(with God);* divine *(was God).* Was, not "became" (contrast v. 14). **3:** He was sole agent of creation (Gen. 1.1; Pr.8.27–30; Col.1.16–17; Heb.1.2). **4:** Apart from him both physical (Col.1.17) and spiritual life would recede into nothingness (5.39–40; 8.12). **5:** *Darkness* is total evil in conflict with light; it cannot *overcome.* **6–8:** John, climaxing the Old Testament prophets, was *sent* (commissioned by God, Mal.3.1) to point to Jesus (vv. 19–34). **9:** *True light* is real, underived light, contrasted not with false light, but with such as John, who was but a lamp (5.35). **11:** *His own people,* the Jews. **14–17:** God's *glory* dwelt ("tabernacled") in the *flesh* (human nature) of Jesus, as did his *grace* (redeeming love) and *truth* (faithfulness to his promises). These are available to *all,* exhaustless *(grace upon grace),* a fulfilment of the *law of Moses.* **18:** *The bosom of the Father,* complete communion (vv. 1–2). Men *see* God in Jesus (14.9).

1.19–34: The testimony of John. 19: *Jews,* the religious authorities. **20:** *The Christ,* the Messiah. **21:** *Elijah* (2 Kg.2.11) was expected to return to prepare the Messiah's way (Mal.4.5). John is unconscious of this role, but Jesus later ascribed it to him (see Mt.11.14 n.; Mk.9.13 n.). *The prophet* was likewise an expected Messianic forerunner (6.14; 7.40; see Dt.18.15). **23:** As a *voice* John fulfils a prophetic role announcing the Messiah's coming (Is.40.3). **25:** *Why are you baptizing,* performing an official rite, without official status? **27:** *To untie a sandal thong* was a slave's task. **29:** *Lamb,* Ex. ch. 12; Is.53.7. *Of God,* provided by God. **30:** He outranks me, *for he was* (existed) *before me.*

Bible, THE NEW OXFORD ANNOTATED BIBLE WITH THE APOCRYPHA Revised Standard Edition, Gospel of John, chaps 1–6.

me.' [31] I myself did not know him; but for this I came baptizing with water, that he might be revealed to Israel." [32] And John bore witness, "I saw the Spirit descend as a dove from heaven, and it remained on him. [33] I myself did not know him; but he who sent me to baptize with water said to me, 'He on whom you see the Spirit descend and remain, this is he who baptizes with the Holy Spirit.' [34] And I have seen and have borne witness that this is the Son of God."

35 The next day again John was standing with two of his disciples; [36] and he looked at Jesus as he walked, and said, "Behold, the Lamb of God!" [37] The two disciples heard him say this, and they followed Jesus. [38] Jesus turned, and saw them following, and said to them, "What do you seek?" And they said to him, "Rabbi" (which means Teacher), "where are you staying?" [39] He said to them, "Come and see." They came and saw where he was staying; and they stayed with him that day, for it was about the tenth hour. [40] One of the two who heard John speak, and followed him, was Andrew, Simon Peter's brother. [41] He first found his brother Simon, and said to him, "We have found the Messiah" (which means Christ). [42] He brought him to Jesus. Jesus looked at him, and said, "So you are Simon the son of John? You shall be called Cephas" (which means Peter[c]).

43 The next day Jesus decided to go to Galilee. And he found Philip and said to him, "Follow me." [44] Now Philip was from Bethsa'ida, the city of Andrew and Peter. [45] Philip found Nathan'a-el, and said to him, "We have found him of whom Moses in the law and also the prophets wrote, Jesus of Nazareth, the son of Joseph." [46] Nathan'a-el said to him, "Can anything good come out of Nazareth?" Philip said to him, "Come and see." [47] Jesus saw Nathan'a-el coming to him, and said of him, "Behold, an Israelite indeed, in whom is no guile!" [48] Nathan'a-el said to him, "How do you know me?" Jesus answered him, "Before Philip called you, when you were under the fig tree, I saw you." [49] Nathan'a-el answered him, "Rabbi, you are the Son of God! You are the King of Israel!" [50] Jesus answered him, "Because I said to you, I saw you under the fig tree, do you believe? You shall see greater things than these." [51] And he said to him, "Truly, truly, I say to you, you will see heaven opened, and the angels of God ascending and descending upon the Son of man."

2 On the third day there was a marriage at Cana in Galilee, and the mother of Jesus was there; [2] Jesus also was invited to the marriage, with his disciples. [3] When the wine gave out, the mother of Jesus said to him, "They have no wine." [4] And Jesus said to her, "O woman, what have you to do with me? My hour has not yet come." [5] His mother said to the servants, "Do whatever he tells you." [6] Now six stone jars were standing there, for the Jewish rites of purification, each holding twenty or thirty gallons. [7] Jesus said to them, "Fill the jars with water." And they filled them up to the brim. [8] He said to them, "Now draw some out, and take it to the steward of the feast." So they took it. [9] When the steward of the feast tasted the water now become wine,

c From the word for *rock* in Aramaic and Greek respectively

31–33: John's knowledge of Jesus' significance was given him by God at the baptism. **34:** *Son of God,* the Messiah (v. 49; 11.27).

1.35–51: The testimony of Jesus' first disciples. 39: *Come and see,* a call to personal following (8.12). *The tenth hour,* about 4 p.m. **42:** In Aramaic *Cephas* (Greek *Peter*) means *Rock.* **45:** *Moses . . . prophets,* the Old Testament points to Christ. **46:** *Nathanael,* probably the same person as Bartholomew (Mt.10.3; Mk.3.18; Lk.6.14), lived in Cana, near Nazareth (21.2). **47:** *No guile,* no qualities of Jacob before he became Israel (Gen.27.35; 32.28). **51:** What Jacob saw in vision (Gen.28.12) is now a reality in Jesus. *Son of man,* a messenger from heaven to make God known (3.13), and to be the final judge (5.27; see Mk.2.10 n.).

2.1–12: The wedding at Cana. 4: *Woman,* a term of solemn and respectful address (compare 19.26). The *hour* of Jesus' self-disclosure was determined by God, not by Mary's desires. His final manifestation was at the cross (7.30; 8.20; 12.23,27; 13.1; 17.1). **6:** *Rites of purification* were ceremonial, not hygienic. **8:** *Steward,* head-waiter or toast-

and did not know where it came from (though the servants who had drawn the water knew), the steward of the feast called the bridegroom [10] and said to him, "Every man serves the good wine first; and when men have drunk freely, then the poor wine; but you have kept the good wine until now." [11] This, the first of his signs, Jesus did at Cana in Galilee, and manifested his glory; and his disciples believed in him.

[12] After this he went down to Caper'na-um, with his mother and his brothers and his disciples; and there they stayed for a few days.

[13] The Passover of the Jews was at hand, and Jesus went up to Jerusalem. [14] In the temple he found those who were selling oxen and sheep and pigeons, and the money-changers at their business. [15] And making a whip of cords, he drove them all, with the sheep and oxen, out of the temple; and he poured out the coins of the money-changers and overturned their tables. [16] And he told those who sold the pigeons, "Take these things away; you shall not make my Father's house a house of trade." [17] His disciples remembered that it was written, "Zeal for thy house will consume me." [18] The Jews then said to him, "What sign have you to show us for doing this?" [19] Jesus answered them, "Destroy this temple, and in three days I will raise it up." [20] The Jews then said, "It has taken forty-six years to build this temple, and will you raise it up in three days?" [21] But he spoke of the temple of his body. [22] When therefore he was raised from the dead, his disciples remembered that he had said this; and they believed the scripture and the word which Jesus had spoken.

[23] Now when he was in Jerusalem at the Passover feast, many believed in his name when they saw the signs which he did; [24] but Jesus did not trust himself to them, [25] because he knew all men and needed no one to bear witness of man; for he himself knew what was in man.

3 Now there was a man of the Pharisees, named Nicode'mus, a ruler of the Jews. [2] This man came to Jesus[d] by night and said to him, "Rabbi, we know that you are a teacher come from God; for no one can do these signs that you do, unless God is with him." [3] Jesus answered him, "Truly, truly, I say to you, unless one is born anew,[e] he cannot see the kingdom of God." [4] Nicode'mus said to him, "How can a man be born when he is old? Can he enter a second time into his mother's womb and be born?" [5] Jesus answered, "Truly, truly, I say to you, unless one is born of water and the Spirit, he cannot enter the kingdom of God. [6] That which is born of the flesh is flesh, and that which is born of the Spirit is spirit.[f] [7] Do not marvel that I said to you, 'You must be born anew.'[e] [8] The wind[f] blows where it wills, and you hear the sound of it, but you do not know whence it comes or whither it goes; so it is with every one who is born of the Spirit." [9] Nicode'mus said to him, "How can this be?" [10] Jesus answered him, "Are you a teacher of Israel, and yet you do not understand this? [11] Truly, truly, I say to you, we speak of what we know, and bear witness to what we have seen; but you do not receive our testimony. [12] If I have told you earthly things

d Greek *him* e Or *from above* f The same Greek word means both *wind* and *spirit*

---

master. **11:** Jesus' miracles were not wonders to astound, but *signs* pointing to *his glory* (God's presence in him). *First,* for the second see 4.46–54. **12:** *Brothers,* see Mt.13.55 n.

2.13–25: The cleansing of the temple (compare Mt.21.12–17; Mk.11.15–19; Lk.19.45–48). **14:** Animals were sold for sacrifice; Roman money was changed into Jewish money to pay the temple tax. **15–16:** Not an outburst of temper, but the energy of righteousness against religious leaders to whom religion had become a business. *My Father's house* is a claim to lordship. **17:** Ps.69.9. **23–25:** Faith which rests merely on *signs* and not on him to whom they point is shallow and unstable.

3.1–21: Jesus and official Judaism. 1: *The Pharisees* were the most devout of Jews. *A ruler,* a member of the Sanhedrin (see 11.47 n.). **3:** *The kingdom of God* is entered, not by moral achievement, but by a transformation wrought by God. **5:** Birth into the new order is through *water* (referring to baptism; 1.33; Eph.5.26) and *the Spirit* (Ezek.36.25–27; Tit.3.5). **6:** Like begets like. **8–9:** See note *f* and Ezek.37.5–10. **12:** *Earthly things,* such as the para-

and you do not believe, how can you believe if I tell you heavenly things? [13] No one has ascended into heaven but he who descended from heaven, the Son of man.[g] [14] And as Moses lifted up the serpent in the wilderness, so must the Son of man be lifted up, [15] that whoever believes in him may have eternal life."[h]

16 For God so loved the world that he gave his only Son, that whoever believes in him should not perish but have eternal life. [17] For God sent the Son into the world, not to condemn the world, but that the world might be saved through him. [18] He who believes in him is not condemned; he who does not believe is condemned already, because he has not believed in the name of the only Son of God. [19] And this is the judgment, that the light has come into the world, and men loved darkness rather than light, because their deeds were evil. [20] For every one who does evil hates the light, and does not come to the light, lest his deeds should be exposed. [21] But he who does what is true comes to the light, that it may be clearly seen that his deeds have been wrought in God.

22 After this Jesus and his disciples went into the land of Judea; there he remained with them and baptized. [23] John also was baptizing at Ae′non near Salim, because there was much water there; and people came and were baptized. [24] For John had not yet been put in prison.

25 Now a discussion arose between John's disciples and a Jew over purifying. [26] And they came to John, and said to him, "Rabbi, he who was with you beyond the Jordan, to whom you bore witness, here he is, baptizing,

and all are going to him," [27] John answered, "No one can receive anything except what is given him from heaven. [28] You yourselves bear me witness, that I said, I am not the Christ, but I have been sent before him. [29] He who has the bride is the bridegroom; the friend of the bridegroom, who stands and hears him, rejoices greatly at the bridegroom's voice; therefore this joy of mine is now full. [30] He must increase, but I must decrease."[i]

31 He who comes from above is above all; he who is of the earth belongs to the earth, and of the earth he speaks; he who comes from heaven is above all. [32] He bears witness to what he has seen and heard, yet no one receives his testimony; [33] he who receives his testimony sets his seal to this, that God is true. [34] For he whom God has sent utters the words of God, for it is not by measure that he gives the Spirit; [35] the Father loves the Son, and has given all things into his hand. [36] He who believes in the Son has eternal life; he who does not obey the Son shall not see life, but the wrath of God rests upon him.

4 Now when the Lord knew that the Pharisees had heard that Jesus was making and baptizing more disciples than John [2] (although Jesus himself did not baptize, but only his disciples), [3] he left Judea and departed again to Galilee. [4] He had to pass through Sama′ria. [5] So he came to a city of Sama′ria, called Sy′char, near the field that Jacob gave to his son Joseph. [6] Jacob's well was there, and so Jesus, wearied as he was with his journey,

g Other ancient authorities add *who is in heaven*
h Some interpreters hold that the quotation continues through verse 21   i Some interpreters hold that the quotation continues through verse 36

---

ble of the wind; *heavenly things,* supreme spiritual realities. **13–15:** Jesus *descended from heaven* to bring *eternal life* (participation in God's life), through being *lifted up* on the cross (Num.21.9). **16:** Luther called this verse "the Gospel in miniature." **17–20:** God's purpose is to save; men judge themselves by hiding their *evil deeds* from the *light* of Christ's holiness.

3.22–36: Further testimony of John (compare 1.19–34). **25:** *Purifying,* Jewish religious ceremonies. **27–29:** John was only the *friend of the bridegroom,* leading Israel, the bride, to Jesus, the bridegroom. He *rejoices* in their union (see Mk.2.19–20 n.). **32–35:** *No one,* a generalization about the Jews. The author and others do believe, and attest that Jesus authentically speaks *the words of God.* **36:** Unbelief is disobedience. *Wrath* is the consuming fire of God's holiness.

4.1–42: Jesus and the Samaritans. 1–3: *The Pharisees,* hostile to John, now turn on Jesus. **4:** *Samaria,* between Judea and Galilee, with a mixed people (see Acts 8.5 n.). **5:** Gen.33.19; 48.22; Jos.24.32. **6:** *Wearied,* shows Jesus'

sat down beside the well. It was about the sixth hour.

7 There came a woman of Sama'ria to draw water. Jesus said to her, "Give me a drink." [8] For his disciples had gone away into the city to buy food. [9] The Samaritan woman said to him, "How is it that you, a Jew, ask a drink of me, a woman of Sama'ria?" For Jews have no dealings with Samaritans. [10] Jesus answered her, "If you knew the gift of God, and who it is that is saying to you, 'Give me a drink,' you would have asked him, and he would have given you living water." [11] The woman said to him, "Sir, you have nothing to draw with, and the well is deep; where do you get that living water? [12] Are you greater than our father Jacob, who gave us the well, and drank from it himself, and his sons, and his cattle?" [13] Jesus said to her, "Every one who drinks of this water will thirst again, [14] but whoever drinks of the water that I shall give him will never thirst; the water that I shall give him will become in him a spring of water welling up to eternal life." [15] The woman said to him, "Sir, give me this water, that I may not thirst, nor come here to draw."

16 Jesus said to her, "Go, call your husband, and come here." [17] The woman answered him, "I have no husband." Jesus said to her, "You are right in saying, 'I have no husband'; [18] for you have had five husbands, and he whom you now have is not your husband; this you said truly." [19] The woman said to him, "Sir, I perceive that you are a prophet. [20] Our fathers worshiped on this mountain; and you say that in Jerusalem is the place where men ought to worship." [21] Jesus said to her, "Woman, believe me, the hour is coming when neither on this mountain nor in Jerusalem will you worship the Father. [22] You worship what you do not know; we worship what we know, for salvation is from the Jews. [23] But the hour is coming, and now is, when the true worshipers will worship the Father in spirit and truth, for such the Father seeks to worship him. [24] God is spirit, and those who worship him must worship in spirit and truth." [25] The woman said to him, "I know that Messiah is coming (he who is called Christ); when he comes, he will shows us all things." [26] Jesus said to her, "I who speak to you am he."

27 Just then his disciples came. They marveled that he was talking with a woman, but none said, "What do you wish?" or, "Why are you talking with her?" [28] So the woman left her water jar, and went away into the city, and said to the people, [29] "Come, see a man who told me all that I ever did. Can this be the Christ?" [30] They went out of the city and were coming to him.

31 Meanwhile the disciples besought him, saying, "Rabbi, eat." [32] But he said to them, "I have food to eat of which you do not know." [33] So the disciples said to one another, "Has any one brought him food?" [34] Jesus said to them, "My food is to do the will of him who sent me, and to accomplish his work. [35] Do you not say, 'There are yet four months, then comes the harvest'? I tell you, lift up your eyes, and see how the fields are already white for harvest. [36] He who reaps receives wages, and gathers fruit for eternal life, so that sower and reaper may rejoice together. [37] For here the saying holds true, 'One sows and another reaps.' [38] I sent you to reap that for which you did not labor; others have labored, and you have entered into their labor."

39 Many Samaritans from that city believed in him because of the woman's testi-

---

humanity. *The sixth hour,* about noon. **5:** Gen. 33.19; 48.22; Jos.24.32. **9:** Rabbis avoided speaking to a *woman* in public (v. 27). *Jews* held *Samaritans* in contempt, as religious apostates (2 Kg.17.24–34). **10:** *Living water,* Jer.2.13; 17.13. **14:** Jesus' gift is God's life in man. **19–20:** *A prophet* should be able to settle rival religious claims. **21:** *This mountain,* i.e. Mount Gerizim, where the Samaritans had had a temple. Jesus means that the place of worship is not of primary importance. **24:** Worship *in spirit* is man's response to God's gift of himself (*the Father seeks,* v. 23). *In truth,* in accord with God's nature seen in Christ. **27:** See v. 9 n. **35:** *Already,* see v. 30. **36:** *Wages,* the reward of gathering believers. **37–38:** Jesus *sows* (vv. 7–26), the disciples *reap;* the harvest comes from the *labor* of Jesus' life, death, and resurrection (12.23–24). **39–42:** Faith based on the testimony of another *(the woman)* is vindicated in personal experience.

mony, "He told me all that I ever did." [40] So when the Samaritans came to him, they asked him to stay with them; and he stayed there two days. [41] And many more believed because of his word. [42] They said to the woman, "It is no longer because of your words that we believe, for we have heard for ourselves, and we know that this is indeed the Savior of the world."

43 After the two days he departed to Galilee. [44] For Jesus himself testified that a prophet has no honor in his own country. [45] So when he came to Galilee, the Galileans welcomed him, having seen all that he had done in Jerusalem at the feast, for they too had gone to the feast.

46 So he came again to Cana in Galilee, where he had made the water wine. And at Caper'na-um there was an official whose son was ill. [47] When he heard that Jesus had come from Judea to Galilee, he went and begged him to come down and heal his son, for he was at the point of death. [48] Jesus therefore said to him, "Unless you see signs and wonders you will not believe." [49] The official said to him, "Sir, come down before my child dies." [50] Jesus said to him, "Go; your son will live." The man believed the word that Jesus spoke to him and went his way. [51] As he was going down, his servants met him and told him that his son was living. [52] So he asked them the hour when he began to mend, and they said to him, "Yesterday at the seventh hour the fever left him." [53] The father knew that was the hour when Jesus had said to him, "Your son will live"; and he himself believed, and all his household. [54] This was now the second sign that Jesus did when he had come from Judea to Galilee.

5 After this there was a feast of the Jews, and Jesus went up to Jerusalem.

2 Now there is in Jerusalem by the Sheep Gate a pool, in Hebrew called Beth-za'tha,[j] which has five porticoes. [3] In these lay a multitude of invalids, blind, lame, paralyzed.[k] [5] One man was there, who had been ill for thirty-eight years. [6] When Jesus saw him and knew that he had been lying there a long time, he said to him, "Do you want to be healed?" [7] The sick man answered him, "Sir, I have no man to put me into the pool when the water is troubled, and while I am going another steps down before me." [8] Jesus said to him, "Rise, take up your pallet, and walk." [9] And at once the man was healed, and he took up his pallet and walked.

Now that day was the sabbath. [10] So the Jews said to the man who was cured, "It is the sabbath, it is not lawful for you to carry your pallet." [11] But he answered them, "The man who healed me said to me; 'Take up your pallet, and walk.'" [12] They asked him, "Who is the man who said to you, 'Take up your pallet, and walk'?" [13] Now the man who had been healed did not know who it was, for Jesus had withdrawn, as there was a crowd in the place. [14] Afterward, Jesus found him in the temple, and said to him, "See, you are well! Sin no more, that nothing worse befall you." [15] The man went away and told the Jews that it was Jesus who had healed him. [16] And this was why the Jews persecuted Jesus, because he did

j Other ancient authorities read *Bethesda,* others *Bethsaida*   *k* Other ancient authorities insert, wholly or in part, *waiting for the moving of the water;* [4] *for an angel of the Lord went down at certain seasons into the pool, and troubled the water; whoever stepped in first after the troubling of the water was healed of whatever disease he had*

4.43–54: Jesus and the Gentiles. Illustrates v. 42, Jesus as *Savior of the world* (Jew, Samaritan, Gentile — everyone; compare Is.43.3,11; 45.22). **46:** *An official,* a Gentile military officer. **48:** *You* is plural here, addressed to all who base faith on mere signs (compare v. 45). **49:** He desires life for his child, not a display. **50:** The official *believed* that Jesus' *word* had effected the cure, and he did not return to his home (which was only about eighteen miles away) until the next day (v. 52). **52:** *Seventh hour,* about 1 p.m. **53:** *Believed,* in the deepest sense. **54:** *Second,* for the first see 2.1–11.

5.1–18: Healing the lame man on the sabbath. 3: After the word *paralyzed* later manuscripts add an explanatory statement; see note *k.* **7:** *When the water is troubled* is explained by the addition to v. 3. Movement caused by an intermittent spring was attributed to divine action. **13:** *Jesus had withdrawn* to avoid publicity. **14:** There are *worse things*

this on the sabbath. [17] But Jesus answered them, "My Father is working still, and I am working." [18] This was why the Jews sought all the more to kill him, because he not only broke the sabbath but also called God his own Father, making himself equal with God.

[19] Jesus said to them, "Truly, truly, I say to you, the Son can do nothing of his own accord, but only what he sees the Father doing; for whatever he does, that the Son does likewise. [20] For the Father loves the Son, and shows him all that he himself is doing; and greater works than these will he show him, that you may marvel. [21] For as the Father raises the dead and gives them life, so also the Son gives life to whom he will. [22] The Father judges no one, but has given all judgment to the Son, [23] that all may honor the Son, even as they honor the Father. He who does not honor the Son does not honor the Father who sent him. [24] Truly, truly, I say to you, he who hears my word and believes him who sent me, has eternal life; he does not come into judgment, but has passed from death to life.

[25] "Truly, truly, I say to you, the hour is coming, and now is, when the dead will hear the voice of the Son of God, and those who hear will live. [26] For as the Father has life in himself, so he has granted the Son also to have life in himself, [27] and has given him authority to execute judgment, because he is the Son of man. [28] Do not marvel at this; for the hour is coming when all who are in the tombs will hear his voice [29] and come forth, those who have done good, to the resurrection of life, and those who have done evil, to the resurrection of judgment.

[30] "I can do nothing on my own authority; as I hear, I judge; and my judgment is just, because I seek not my own will but the will of him who sent me. [31] If I bear witness to myself, my testimony is not true; [32] there is another who bears witness to me, and I know that the testimony which he bears to me is true. [33] You sent to John, and he has borne witness to the truth. [34] Not that the testimony which I receive is from man; but I say this that you may be saved. [35] He was a burning and shining lamp, and you were willing to rejoice for a while in his light. [36] But the testimony which I have is greater than that of John; for the works which the Father has granted me to accomplish, these very works which I am doing, bear me witness that the Father has sent me. [37] And the Father who sent me has himself borne witness to me. His voice you have never heard, his form you have never seen; [38] and you do not have his word abiding in you, for you do not believe him whom he has sent. [39] You search the scriptures, because you think that in them you have eternal life; and it is they that bear witness to me; [40] yet you refuse to come to me that you may have life. [41] I do not receive glory from men. [42] But I know that you have not the love of God within you. [43] I have come in my Father's name, and you do not receive me; if another comes in his own name, him you will receive. [44] How can you believe, who receive glory from one another and do not seek the glory that comes from the only God? [45] Do not think that I shall accuse you to the Father; it is Moses who accuses you, on whom you set your hope. [46] If you believed Moses, you would believe me, for he wrote of me. [47] But

---

than illness. **16:** *The Jews,* the religious authorities, opposed Jesus for his break with their legalism. **17:** God continually gives life and judges evil, as does Jesus. **18:** *Equal,* see 10.30–33.

5.19–29: Jesus' relation to God. 19–20: Jesus' sonship involves the identity of his will and actions with the Father's. The *greater works* are giving life (v. 21) and judgment (v. 22). **24:** He who *believes* on the basis of Jesus' word *has passed* into the realm where death does not reign. **25:** The *coming* age is already present in Jesus. To *hear* with the comprehension of faith makes the spiritually *dead* live. **26–29:** They will share in the final *resurrection of life.*

5.30–40: Evidence of Jesus' relation to God. 30: Jesus' judgment is that of God, and therefore *just,* without favoritism or error. **32:** *Another,* the Father. **33–40:** God witnesses to Jesus through the ministry of *John* the Baptist (vv. 33–35), through Jesus' *works* (v. 36), and through *the scriptures* (vv. 37–40).

5.41–47: Jesus condemns the Jews. 41: No human standards apply to him. **42:** No *love of God,* no love of Jesus. **43–44:** Judgment based on human pride. **45:** 9.28; Rom.2.17. **47:** Lk.16.29,31.

if you do not believe his writings, how will you believe my words?"

6 After this Jesus went to the other side of the Sea of Galilee, which is the Sea of Tibe′ri-as. ² And a multitude followed him, because they saw the signs which he did on those who were diseased. ³ Jesus went up on the mountain, and there sat down with his disciples. ⁴ Now the Passover, the feast of the Jews, was at hand. ⁵ Lifting up his eyes, then, and seeing that a multitude was coming to him, Jesus said to Philip, "How are we to buy bread, so that these people may eat?" ⁶ This he said to test him, for he himself knew what he would do. ⁷ Philip answered him, "Two hundred denarii*l* would not buy enough bread for each of them to get a little." ⁸ One of his disciples, Andrew, Simon Peter's brother, said to him, ⁹ "There is a lad here who has five barley loaves and two fish; but what are they among so many?" ¹⁰ Jesus said, "Make the people sit down." Now there was much grass in the place; so the men sat down, in number about five thousand. ¹¹ Jesus then took the loaves, and when he had given thanks, he distributed them to those who were seated; so also the fish, as much as they wanted. ¹² And when they had eaten their fill, he told his disciples, "Gather up the fragments left over, that nothing may be lost." ¹³ So they gathered them up and filled twelve baskets with fragments from the five barley loaves, left by those who had eaten. ¹⁴ When the people saw the sign which he had done, they said, "This is indeed the prophet who is to come into the world!"

15 Perceiving then that they were about to come and take him by force to make him king, Jesus withdrew again to the mountain by himself.

16 When evening came, his disciples went down to the sea, ¹⁷ got into a boat, and started across the sea to Caper′na-um. It was now dark, and Jesus had not yet come to them. ¹⁸ The sea rose because a strong wind was blowing. ¹⁹ When they had rowed about three or four miles,*m* they saw Jesus walking on the sea and drawing near to the boat. They were frightened, ²⁰ but he said to them, "It is I; do not be afraid." ²¹ Then they were glad to take him into the boat, and immediately the boat was at the land to which they were going.

22 On the next day the people who remained on the other side of the sea saw that there had been only one boat there, and that Jesus had not entered the boat with his disciples, but that his disciples had gone away alone. ²³ However, boats from Tibe′ri-as came near the place where they ate the bread after the Lord had given thanks. ²⁴ So when the people saw that Jesus was not there, nor his disciples, they themselves got into the boats and went to Caper′na-um, seeking Jesus.

25 When they found him on the other side of the sea, they said to him, "Rabbi, when did you come here?" ²⁶ Jesus answered them, "Truly, truly, I say to you, you seek me, not because you saw signs, but because you ate your fill of the loaves. ²⁷ Do not labor for the food which perishes, but for the food which endures to eternal life, which the Son of man will give to you; for on him has God the Father set his seal." ²⁸ Then they said to him, "What must we do, to be doing the works of

l The denarius was a day's wage for a laborer
m Greek *twenty-five or thirty stadia*

6.1–15: Feeding the five thousand; the only miracle recorded by all four gospels (Mt.14.13–21; Mk.6.32–44; Lk.9.10–17). **1:** *Tiberias,* named for the Emperor Tiberius. **6:** *To test* Philip's faith. **7:** *Two hundred denarii,* for the value of the denarius, see note *l.* **9:** *Barley loaves,* food of the poor. **12:** *Gather,* an act of reverential economy toward the gift of God. **13:** *Twelve baskets,* one for each disciple. **15:** *To make him king,* as a political Messiah opposing Rome; but Jesus would not accept this (18.36).
    6.16–21: Jesus walks on the sea (Mt.14.22–27; Mk.6.45–51). Jesus is greater than a political ruler (v. 15); he is Lord of the elements (Ps.107.29–30). **17:** *Not yet come,* probably they expected to meet Jesus along the shore. **20–21:** Jesus' presence dispels fear.
    6.22–71: Jesus, the bread of life. 22–25: Note the clamor for more bread. **26:** *Signs,* pointing to Jesus as food for the soul. **27:** *Son of man,* see 1.51 n. *Seal,* God's authentication, perhaps at the baptism (1.32). **28:** *Works,* 3.21;

God?" [29] Jesus answered them, "This is the work of God, that you believe in him whom he has sent." [30] So they said to him, "Then what sign do you do, that we may see, and believe you? What work do you perform? [31] Our fathers ate the manna in the wilderness; as it is written, 'He gave them bread from heaven to eat.'" [32] Jesus then said to them, "Truly, truly, I say to you, it was not Moses who gave you the bread from heaven; my Father gives you the true bread from heaven. [33] For the bread of God is that which comes down from heaven, and gives life to the world." [34] They said to him, "Lord, give us this bread always."

35 Jesus said to them, "I am the bread of life; he who comes to me shall not hunger, and he who believes in me shall never thirst. [36] But I said to you that you have seen me and yet do not believe. [37] All that the Father gives me will come to me; and him who comes to me I will not cast out. [38] For I have come down from heaven, not to do my own will, but the will of him who sent me; [39] and this is the will of him who sent me, that I should lose nothing of all that he has given me, but raise it up at the last day. [40] For this is the will of my Father, that every one who sees the Son and believes in him should have eternal life; and I will raise him up at the last day."

41 The Jews then murmured at him, because he said, "I am the bread which came down from heaven." [42] They said, "Is not this Jesus, the son of Joseph, whose father and mother we know? How does he now say, 'I have come down from heaven'?" [43] Jesus answered them, "Do not murmur among yourselves. [44] No one can come to me unless the Father who sent me draws him; and I will raise him up at the last day. [45] It is written in the prophets, 'And they shall all be taught by God.' Every one who has heard and learned from the Father comes to me. [46] Not that any one has seen the Father except him who is from God; he has seen the Father. [47] Truly, truly, I say to you, he who believes has eternal life. [48] I am the bread of life. [49] Your fathers ate the manna in the wilderness, and they died. [50] This is the bread which comes down from heaven, that a man may eat of it and not die. [51] I am the living bread which came down from heaven; if any one eats of this bread, he will live for ever; and the bread which I shall give for the life of the world is my flesh."

52 The Jews then disputed among themselves, saying, "How can this man give us his flesh to eat?" [53] So Jesus said to them, "Truly, truly, I say to you, unless you eat the flesh of the Son of man and drink his blood, you have no life in you; [54] he who eats my flesh and drinks my blood has eternal life, and I will raise him up at the last day. [55] For my flesh is food indeed, and my blood is drink indeed. [56] He who eats my flesh and drinks my blood abides in me, and I in him. [57] As the living Father sent me, and I live because of the Father, so he who eats me will live because of me. [58] This is the bread which came down from heaven, not such as the fathers ate and died; he who eats this bread will live for ever." [59] This he said in the synagogue, as he taught at Caper'na-um.

60 Many of his disciples, when they heard it, said, "This is a hard saying; who can listen to it?" [61] But Jesus, knowing in himself that

---

Rev.2.26. **29:** *Work,* singular number; not many works (v. 28), but obedient trust *(believe)* is the one thing pleasing to God (1 Jn.3.23). *Him . . . sent,* Jesus who reveals God. **30:** *See,* as a proof; but faith cannot be proved. **31:** The Messiah was expected to reproduce the miracle of the giving of manna (Ex.16.4,15; Num.11.8; Ps.78.24; 105.40). **36–40:** Jesus himself is God's gift of sustenance for time and eternity. Belief, or unbelief involves a mystery known only to God, but no one who *comes* is rejected (v. 37). Faith is God's gift, not a human achievement; it gives *eternal life* now and issues in resurrection *at the last day.* **44–45:** The *drawing* is not coercive or mechanical. *Prophets,* Is.54.13; compare Jl.2.28–29. Had they *heard* and *learned* God's voice in their scriptures, they would have recognized its accents in him who alone has direct communion with God. **51:** *The living bread . . . is my flesh,* the One who became flesh (assumed complete human nature, 1.14) offered himself to God in death, thus releasing his life *for the life of the world.* **53:** The separation of the *blood* from the *flesh* emphasizes the reality of Jesus' death. **54:** To *eat* and *drink* is to believe (v. 47), to appropriate, assimilate, and *abide* in Christ (v. 56). **58:** Since Christ is *bread . . . from heaven* (compare vv. 32–35), to eat him is to *live for ever.* **60:** *Hard saying* means offensive or difficult, but not obscure. **62–63:** The ascen-

his disciples murmured at it, said to them, "Do you take offense at this? [62] Then what if you were to see the Son of man ascending where he was before? [63] It is the spirit that gives life, the flesh is of no avail; the words that I have spoken to you are spirit and life. [64] But there are some of you that do not believe." For Jesus knew from the first who those were that did not believe, and who it was that would betray him. [65] And he said, "This is why I told you that no one can come to me unless it is granted him by the Father."

[66] After this many of his disciples drew back and no longer went about with him. [67] Jesus said to the twelve, "Do you also wish to go away?" [68] Simon Peter answered him, "Lord, to whom shall we go? You have the words of eternal life; [69] and we have believed, and have come to know, that you are the Holy One of God." [70] Jesus answered them, "Did I not choose you, the twelve, and one of you is a devil?" [71] He spoke of Judas the son of Simon Iscariot, for he, one of the twelve, was to betray him.

sion, by which Jesus will be taken away as regards the flesh, will indicate that he has been speaking of spiritual realities and not the actual eating of his flesh. **64–65:** These truths can be discerned only by faith, which is God's gift, not man's achievement (Eph.2.8). **66–71:** To receive God's gift of faith is to *know* God in Christ; to refuse it is to become an ally of the *devil*. Faith and unbelief mark the great divisions among men.

Romans

3 Then what advantage has the Jew? Or what is the value of circumcision? [2] Much in every way. To begin with, the Jews are entrusted with the oracles of God. [3] What if some were unfaithful? Does their faithlessness nullify the faithfulness of God? [4] By no means! Let God be true though every man be false, as it is written,

> "That thou mayest be justified in thy words,
> and prevail when thou art judged."

[5] But if our wickedness serves to show the justice of God, what shall we say? That God is unjust to inflict wrath on us? (I speak in a human way.) [6] By no means! For then how could God judge the world? [7] But if through my falsehood God's truthfulness abounds to his glory, why am I still being condemned as a sinner? [8] And why not do evil that good may come? — as some people slanderously charge us with saying. Their condemnation is just.

9 What then? Are we Jews any better off?[c] No, not at all; for I[d] have already charged that all men, both Jews and Greeks, are under the power of sin, [10] as it is written:

> "None is righteous, no, not one;
> [11] no one understands, no one seeks for God.
> [12] All have turned aside, together they have
>   gone wrong;
> no one does good, not even one."
> [13] "Their throat is an open grave,
> they use their tongues to deceive."
> "The venom of asps is under their lips."
> [14] "Their mouth is full of curses and bitterness."
> [15] "Their feet are swift to shed blood,
> [16] in their paths are ruin and misery,
> [17] and the way of peace they do not know."
> [18] "There is no fear of God before their eyes."

19 Now we know that whatever the law says it speaks to those who are under the law, so that every mouth may be stopped, and the whole world may be held accountable to God. [20] For no human being will be justified in his sight by works of the law, since through the law comes knowledge of sin.

c Or at any disadvantage?   d Greek we

3.1–8: The advantage of the Jews as the covenant people cannot be denied. To them were given the *oracles, i.e.* the Scriptures, and particularly the promises they contain. God's *faithfulness* in making the promises is not invalidated by the failure of the Jews to keep their part of the covenant; nor can that failure be excused on the plea that, because of it, God's truth will shine more brightly when he fulfils his part (Paul will discuss this problem more fully in chs. 9–11). **4:** Ps.51.4.
3.9–20: All are guilty. Jew and Greek, despite the former's advantages, stand on the same ground, *under the power of sin.* **10–18:** Ps.14.1–2; 53.1–2; 5.9; 140.3; 10.7; Is.59.7–8; Ps.36.1. The law succeeds only in making men aware of their condition. That indeed was God's purpose in giving it (7.7; see Gal.3.19–29 n.).

21 But now the righteousness of God has been manifested apart from law, although the law and the prophets bear witness to it, [22] the righteousness of God through faith in Jesus Christ for all who believe. For there is no distinction; [23] since all have sinned and fall short of the glory of God, [24] they are justified by his grace as a gift, through the redemption which is in Christ Jesus, [25] whom God put forward as an expiation by his blood, to be received by faith. This was to show God's righteousness, because in his divine forbearance he had passed over former sins; [26] it was to prove at the present time that he himself is righteous and that he justifies him who has faith in Jesus.

27 Then what becomes of our boasting? It is excluded. On what principle? On the principle of works? No, but on the principle of faith. [28] For we hold that a man is justified by faith apart from works of law. [29] Or is God the God of Jews only? Is he not the God of Gentiles also? Yes, of Gentiles also, [30] since God is one; and he will justify the circumcised on the ground of their faith and the uncircumcised through their faith. [31] Do we then overthrow the law by this faith? By no means! On the contrary, we uphold the law.

4 What then shall we say about[e] Abraham, our forefather according to the flesh? [2] For if Abraham was justified by works, he has something to boast about, but not before God. [3] For what does the scripture say? "Abraham believed God, and it was reckoned to him as righteousness." [4] Now to one who works, his wages are not reckoned as a gift but as his due. [5] And to one who does not work but trusts him who justifies the ungodly, his faith is reckoned as righteousness. [6] So also David pronounces a blessing upon the man to whom God reckons righteousness apart from works:

[7] "Blessed are those whose iniquities are
        forgiven, and whose sins are covered;
[8] blessed is the man against whom the Lord
        will not reckon his sin."

9 Is this blessing pronounced only upon the circumcised, or also upon the uncircumcised? We say that faith was reckoned to Abraham as righteousness. [10] How then was it reckoned to him? Was it before or after he had been circumcised? It was not after, but before he was circumcised. [11] He received circumcision as a sign or seal of the righteousness which he had by faith while he was still uncircumcised. The purpose was to make him the father of all who believe without being circumcised and who thus have righteousness reckoned to them, [12] and likewise the father of the circumcised who are not merely circumcised but also follow the example of the faith which our father Abraham had before he was circumcised.

13 The promise to Abraham and his descendants, that they should inherit the world, did not come through the law but through the righteousness of faith. [14] If it is the adherents of the law who are to be the heirs, faith is null

e Other ancient authorities read *was gained by*

3.21–26: The true righteousness, now revealed in Christ, rests not upon obedience to law, but on faith in God's act of *redemption . . . in Christ Jesus.* **21:** *The law and the prophets,* the Hebrew scriptures. **24:** *Redemption* means a ransoming or "buying back" (as of a slave or captive), and therefore emancipation or deliverance. Slaves of sin are set free through God's act in Christ (Eph.1.7; Col.1.14; Heb.9.15). **25:** *Expiation by his blood,* a reference to the death of Christ as a sacrifice for sin (1 Jn.2.2), demonstrating the seriousness with which God regards sin (despite his *forbearance*); it also reveals the measure of his love (Jn.3.16). **3.27–31: Boasting is excluded.** *On the principle of works* there might be ground for boasting, but if salvation is by faith, pride *is excluded.* **30:** Since *God is one,* he will deal with Jews and Gentiles on the same basis. **4.1–8: Abraham justified by faith,** not by works. **2:** *But not before God;* the full statement would be: "But actually if he had anything to boast about, it was not before God." **3:** According to Paul's understanding of Gen.15.6, Abraham's faith in God was credited to him as righteousness. **6–8:** God's blessing belongs not to those who perfectly obey the law (as though that were possible), but to those who in faith accept God's free gift of forgiveness (Ps.32.1–2). **9–12:** This justification of Abraham occurred *before he was circumcised,* and therefore cannot have been dependent upon circumcision; it depended only upon faith. **11:** Gen.17.10. **12:** *Follow the example,* i.e. rely only on faith, as Abraham did.

and the promise is void. [15] For the law brings wrath, but where there is no law there is no transgression.

16 That is why it depends on faith, in order that the promise may rest on grace and be guaranteed to all his descendants — not only to the adherents of the law but also to those who share the faith of Abraham, for he is the father of us all, [17] as it is written, "I have made you the father of many nations"— in the presence of the God in whom he believed, who gives life to the dead and calls into existence the things that do not exist. [18] In hope he believed against hope, that he should become the father of many nations; as he had been told, "So shall your descendants be." [19] He did not weaken in faith when he considered his own body, which was as good as dead because he was about a hundred years old, or when he considered the barrenness of Sarah's womb. [20] No distrust made him waver concerning the promise of God, but he grew strong in his faith as he gave glory to God, [21] fully convinced that God was able to do what he had promised. [22] That is why his faith was "reckoned to him as righteousness." [23] But the words, "it was reckoned to him," were written not for his sake alone, [24] but for ours also. It will be reckoned to us who believe in him that raised from the dead Jesus our Lord, [25] who was put to death for our trespasses and raised for our justification.

5 Therefore, since we are justified by faith, we[f] have peace with God through our Lord Jesus Christ. [2] Through him we have obtained access[g] to this grace in which we stand, and we[h] rejoice in our hope of sharing the glory of God. [3] More than that, we[h] rejoice in our sufferings, knowing that suffering produces endurance, [4] and endurance produces character, and character produces hope, [5] and hope does not disappoint us, because God's love has been poured into our hearts through the Holy Spirit which has been given to us.

6 While we were still weak, at the right time Christ died for the ungodly. [7] Why, one will hardly die for a righteous man — though perhaps for a good man one will dare even to die. [8] But God shows his love for us in that while we were yet sinners Christ died for us. [9] Since, therefore, we are now justified by his blood, much more shall we be saved by him from the wrath of God. [10] For if while we were enemies we were reconciled to God by the death of his Son, much more, now that we are reconciled, shall we be saved by his life. [11] Not only so, but we also rejoice in God through our Lord Jesus Christ, through whom we have now received our reconciliation.

12 Therefore as sin came into the world through one man and death through sin, and so death spread to all men because all men sinned — [13] sin indeed was in the world before the law was given, but sin is not counted where there is no law. [14] Yet death reigned from Adam to Moses, even over those whose sins were not like the transgression of Adam, who was a type of the one who was to come.

15 But the free gift is not like the trespass. For if many died through one man's trespass, much more have the grace of God and the free

f Other ancient authorities read *let us*   g Other ancient authorities add *by faith*   h Or *let us*

4.13–25: The true descendants of Abraham are those who have faith in Christ, whether Jews or Gentiles. To them the benefits promised to Abraham belong (Gen.17.4–6; 22.17–18; Gal.3.29). **17:** Gen.17.5. **18:** Gen.15.5. **19:** Gen.17.17; 18.11; Heb.11.12. **22–23:** See v. 3.

5.1–11: Consequences of justification. 1–5: When we rely utterly upon God's grace and not at all upon ourselves, *we have peace,* i.e. reconciliation, or a state of harmony *with God. Hope of . . . the glory of God,* though we had fallen short of the glorious destiny God intended for us (3.23), we now find ourselves confidently expecting it. **6–11:** Christ in his death has borne the consequences of our sin and thus has reconciled us to God. Note that Paul never speaks of a reconciliation of God to us; it is we who were estranged. **9–10:** Being *now justified* (and reconciled) *by Christ's death,* we *shall . . . be saved* in the final Judgment *by his life,* i.e. through our participation in his present *life* as the risen Lord. **11:** *Now,* under the gospel.

5.12–21: Adam and Christ; analogy and contrast. Sin and death for all men followed upon Adam's disobedi-

gift in the grace of that one man Jesus Christ abounded for many. [16] And the free gift is not like the effect of that one man's sin. For the judgment following one trespass brought condemnation, but the free gift following many trespasses brings justification. [17] If, because of one man's trespass, death reigned through that one man, much more will those who receive the abundance of grace and the free gift of righteousness reign in life through the one man Jesus Christ.

18 Then as one man's trespass led to condemnation for all men, so one man's act of righteousness leads to acquittal and life for all men. [19] For as by one man's disobedience many were made sinners, so by one man's obedience many will be made righteous. [20] Law came in, to increase the trespass; but where sin increased, grace abounded all the more, [21] so that, as sin reigned in death, grace also might reign through righteousness to eternal life through Jesus Christ our Lord.

6 What shall we say then? Are we to continue in sin that grace may abound? [2] By no means! How can we who died to sin still live in it? [3] Do you not know that all of us who have been baptized into Christ Jesus were baptized into his death? [4] We were buried therefore with him by baptism into death, so that as Christ was raised from the dead by the glory of the Father, we too might walk in newness of life.

5 For if we have been united with him in a death like his, we shall certainly be united with him in a resurrection like his. [6] We know that our old self was crucified with him so that the sinful body might be destroyed, and we might no longer be enslaved to sin. [7] For he

who has died is freed from sin. [8] But if we have died with Christ, we believe that we shall also live with him. [9] For we know that Christ being raised from the dead will never die again; death no longer has dominion over him. [10] The death he died he died to sin, once for all, but the life he lives he lives to God. [11] So you also must consider yourselves dead to sin and alive to God in Christ Jesus.

12 Let not sin therefore reign in your mortal bodies, to make you obey their passions. [13] Do not yield your members to sin as instruments of wickedness, but yield yourselves to God as men who have been brought from death to life, and your members to God as instruments of righteousness. [14] For sin will have no dominion over you, since you are not under law but under grace.

15 What then? Are we to sin because we are not under law but under grace? By no means! [16] Do you not know that if you yield yourselves to any one as obedient slaves, you are slaves of the one whom you obey, either of sin, which leads to death, or of obedience, which leads to righteousness? [17] But thanks be to God, that you who were once slaves of sin have become obedient from the heart to the standard of teaching to which you were committed, [18] and, having been set free from sin, have become slaves of righteousness. [19] I am speaking in human terms, because of your natural limitations. For just as you once yielded your members to impurity and to greater and greater iniquity, so now yield your members to righteousness for sanctification.

20 When you were slaves of sin, you were free in regard to righteousness. [21] But then

---

ence (Gen.2.17; 3.17–19). **13–16:** 1 Cor.15.21–23,45–49. **18:** *Acquittal and life for all* followed upon Christ's perfect obedience. **20:** *Law . . . to increase the trespass,* this is explained in 7.7–13.

6.1–14: Dying and rising with Christ. Paul's insistence that salvation is entirely a gracious and undeserved gift of God may seem to have laid him open to the charge of encouraging sin. This charge Paul vigorously rejects. When the Christian is *baptized,* he is united with Christ. We share in his death and in the *newness of life* (v. 4), which his resurrection has made possible for us. But this death is a *death . . . to sin,* and the new life is *life . . . to God* (v. 10). *How then can we who died to sin still live in it?* (v. 2). **6:** *The sinful body,* not the physical body as such, but the sinful self. **13:** *Your members,* all the organs and functions of the person.

6.15–23: The two slaveries. In rejecting again the same charge (see v. 1 n.), Paul draws an analogy from slavery. The sinner is sin's slave; but if he becomes God's slave, how can he longer obey his old master? **19:** *Sanctification,* the process and result of being entirely devoted, consecrated, to God (v. 22).

what return did you get from the things of which you are now ashamed? The end of those things is death. [22] But now that you have been set free from sin and have become slaves of God, the return you get is sanctification and its end, eternal life. [23] For the wages of sin is death, but the free gift of God is eternal life in Christ Jesus our Lord.

7 Do you not know, brethren — for I am speaking to those who know the law — that the law is binding on a person only during his life? [2] Thus a married woman is bound by law to her husband as long as he lives; but if her husband dies she is discharged from the law concerning the husband. [3] Accordingly, she will be called an adulteress if she lives with another man while her husband is alive. But if her husband dies she is free from that law, and if she marries another man she is not an adulteress.

4 Likewise, my brethren, you have died to the law through the body of Christ, so that you may belong to another, to him who has been raised from the dead in order that we may bear fruit for God. [5] While we were living in the flesh, our sinful passions, aroused by the law, were at work in our members to bear fruit for death. [6] But now we are discharged from the law, dead to that which held us captive, so that we serve not under the old written code but in the new life of the Spirit.

7 What then shall we say? That the law is sin? By no means! Yet, if it had not been for the law, I should not have known sin. I should not have known what it is to covet if the law had not said, "You shall not covet." [8] But sin, finding opportunity in the commandment, wrought in me all kinds of covetousness. Apart from the law sin lies dead. [9] I was once alive apart from the law, but when the commandment came, sin revived and I died; [10] the very commandment which promised life proved to be death to me. [11] For sin, finding opportunity in the commandment, deceived me and by it killed me. [12] So the law is holy, and the commandment is holy and just and good.

13 Did that which is good, then, bring death to me? By no means! It was sin, working death in me through what is good, in order that sin might be shown to be sin, and through the commandment might become sinful beyond measure. [14] We know that the law is spiritual; but I am carnal, sold under sin. [15] I do not understand my own actions. For I do not do what I want, but I do the very thing I hate. [16] Now if I do what I do not want, I agree that the law is good. [17] So then it is no longer I that do it, but sin which dwells within me. [18] For I know that nothing good dwells within me, that is, in my flesh. I can will what is right, but I cannot do it. [19] For I do not do the good I want, but the evil I do not want is what I do. [20] Now if I do what I do not want, it is no longer I that do it, but sin which dwells within me.

21 So I find it to be a law that when I want to do right, evil lies close at hand. [22] For I delight in the law of God, in my inmost self, [23] but I see in my members another law at war

---

7.1–6: An analogy from marriage. One who has died to sin is no more bound to it than is a woman to her deceased husband. **1–2:** *The law* here probably means Roman law. **4–6:** *The law* here refers to God's commandments, as in chs. 2–4.

7.7–13: The law and sin. 7: Though the law is *holy . . . and good* (v. 12), it not only makes man conscious of sin (see Gal.3.19 n.), but also incites to sin (e.g. covetousness; compare Ex.20.17; Dt.5.21). **9:** Probably a reminiscence of a thoughtless, carefree boyhood brought to an end *(death)* by the dawning sense of moral obligation and guilt. **10:** Lev.18.5. **13:** The real enemy is sin, which uses even *what is good* (the law) to make a man more sinful than he would otherwise be.

7.14–23: The inner conflict. Sin is personified as an evil power that enters a man's life and brings his true self into slavery to its rule or *law* (still another use of this term). **14:** *The law is spiritual,* divine in origin and nature, and holy (v. 12). *I am carnal,* Greek "fleshly," referring not merely to man's physical nature, but to his whole nature in so far as he is ruled by selfish interests (compare v. 18 and v. 25). **17:** In emphasizing the reality of sin's power over a man's *inmost self* (v. 22), Paul seems almost to deny one's responsibility for sin (compare v. 20). Other passages in his letters, however, prevent our inferring that he means this (e.g. Rom.1.31–2.5).

with the law of my mind and making me captive to the law of sin which dwells in my members. ²⁴ Wretched man that I am! Who will deliver me from this body of death? ²⁵ Thanks be to God through Jesus Christ our Lord! So then, I of myself serve the law of God with my mind, but with my flesh I serve the law of sin.

8 There is therefore now no condemnation for those who are in Christ Jesus. ² For the law of the Spirit of life in Christ Jesus has set me free from the law of sin and death. ³ For God has done what the law, weakened by the flesh, could not do: sending his own Son in the likeness of sinful flesh and for sin,ⁱ he condemned sin in the flesh, ⁴ in order that the just requirement of the law might be fulfilled in us, who walk not according to the flesh but according to the Spirit. ⁵ For those who live according to the flesh set their minds on the things of the flesh, but those who live according to the Spirit set their minds on the things of the Spirit. ⁶ To set the mind on the flesh is death, but to set the mind on the Spirit is life and peace. ⁷ For the mind that is set on the flesh is hostile to God; it does not submit to God's law, indeed it cannot; ⁸ and those who are in the flesh cannot please God.

9 But you are not in the flesh, you are in the Spirit, if in fact the Spirit of God dwells in you. Any one who does not have the Spirit of Christ does not belong to him. ¹⁰ But if Christ is in you, although your bodies are dead because of sin, your spirits are alive because of righteousness. ¹¹ If the Spirit of him who raised Jesus from the dead dwells in you, he who raised Christ Jesus from the dead will give life to your mortal bodies also through his Spirit which dwells in you.

12 So then, brethren, we are debtors, not to the flesh, to live according to the flesh — ¹³ for if you live according to the flesh you will die, but if by the Spirit you put to death the deeds of the body you will live. ¹⁴ For all who are led by the Spirit of God are sons of God. ¹⁵ For you did not receive the spirit of slavery to fall back into fear, but you have received the spirit of sonship. When we cry. "Abba! Father!" ¹⁶ it is the Spirit himself bearing witness with our spirit that we are children of God, ¹⁷ and if children, then heirs, heirs of God and fellow heirs with Christ, provided we suffer with him in order that we may also be glorified with him.

18 I consider that the sufferings of this present time are not worth comparing with the glory that is to be revealed to us. ¹⁹ For the creation waits with eager longing for the revealing of the sons of God; ²⁰ for the creation was subjected to futility, not of its own will but by the will of him who subjected it in hope; ²¹ because the creation itself will be set free from its bondage to decay and obtain the

i Or *and as a sin offering*

7.24–25: Despair and release. Threatened by utter defeat in the struggle with our enemy entrenched in our own souls, we cast ourselves upon God's mercy in Christ; only then do we find freedom from both the guilt and the power of sin. **24:** *This body of death,* i.e. the body, which is the instrument of sin, is under the dominion of death. **25:** *Flesh,* compare "carnal," v. 14 n.

8.1–4: God's saving act. 1: *Condemnation* means more than judgment; it means doom. There is to be no doom or death *for us,* because God has sentenced sin to death (*condemned sin,* v. 3). **2:** *The Spirit* is the divine principle (*law*) of life in the new order which God has created through Christ. To be *in Christ* is to belong to this new order and thus to know the Spirit, who is the actual presence of God in our midst and in our hearts. **4:** Only through the power of *the Spirit* can we hope for the righteousness which *the law* requires but cannot enable us in our weakness to attain.

8.5–11: Life in the flesh and in the Spirit. 5: To live *according to the flesh* (see 7.14 n.) is to be dominated by selfish passions; to *live according to* (or *in,* v. 9) *the Spirit* is to belong to the new community of faith where God dwells as the Spirit. **9–10:** Note the similar, almost interchangeable, use of "the Spirit of God," "the Spirit of Christ," and "Christ." **10:** Gal.2.20; Eph.3.17. **11:** Jn.5.21.

8.12–17: The Spirit and sonship. The Spirit does not make slaves of us, but sons. **15:** *Abba,* the Aramaic word meaning "Father," which Jesus used in his own prayers (Mk.14.36) and which passed into the liturgy of the early church. **16:** The fact that *the Spirit* prompts this ecstatic prayer proves our sonship (Gal.4.6).

8.18–25: The hope of fulfillment. 18: The Christian life involves *sufferings* (this was more obviously true then than now), but Paul rejoices in the sure hope of *glory* (5.2). **20:** *Of him,* God (Gen.3.17). **21:** When man (in Christ) is

glorious liberty of the children of God. ²² We know that the whole creation has been groaning in travail together until now; ²³ and not only the creation, but we ourselves, who have the first fruits of the Spirit, groan inwardly as we wait for adoption as sons, the redemption of our bodies. ²⁴ For in this hope we were saved. Now hope that is seen is not hope. For who hopes for what he sees? ²⁵ But if we hope for what we do not see, we wait for it with patience.

26 Likewise the Spirit helps us in our weakness; for we do not know how to pray as we ought, but the Spirit himself intercedes for us with sighs too deep for words. ²⁷ And he who searches the hearts of men knows what is the mind of the Spirit, because*ʲ* the Spirit intercedes for the saints according to the will of God.

28 We know that in everything God works for good*ᵏ* with those who love him,*ˡ* who are called according to his purpose. ²⁹ For those whom he foreknew he also predestined to be conformed to the image of his Son, in order that he might be the first-born among many brethren. ³⁰ And those whom he predestined he also called; and those whom he called he also justified; and those whom he justified he also glorified.

31 What then shall we say to this? If God is for us, who is against us? ³² He who did not spare his own Son but gave him up for us all, will he not also give us all things with him? ³³ Who shall bring any charge against God's

elect? It is God who justifies; ³⁴ who is to condemn? Is it Christ Jesus, who died, yes, who was raised from the dead, who is at the right hand of God, who indeed intercedes for us?*ᵐ* ³⁵ Who shall separate us from the love of Christ? Shall tribulation, or distress, or persecution, or famine, or nakedness, or peril, or sword? ³⁶ As it is written,

"For thy sake we are being killed all the
    day long;
we are regarded as sheep to be slaugh-
    tered."

³⁷ No, in all these things we are more than conquerors through him who loved us. ³⁸ For I am sure that neither death, nor life, nor angels, nor principalities, nor things present, nor things to come, nor powers, ³⁹ nor height, nor depth, nor anything else in all creation, will be able to separate us from the love of God in Christ Jesus our Lord.

9 I am speaking the truth in Christ, I am not lying; my conscience bears me witness in the Holy Spirit ² that I have great sorrow and unceasing anguish in my heart. ³ For I could wish that I myself were accursed and cut off from Christ for the sake of my brethren, my kinsmen by race. ⁴ They are Israelites, and to them belong the sonship, the glory, the covenants, the giving of the law, the worship, and the promises; ⁵ to them belong the patriarchs, and of their race, according to the flesh, is the

j Or *that*   *k* Other ancient authorities read *in everything he works for good,* or *everything works for good*   *l* Greek *God*   *m* Or *It is Christ Jesus . . . for us*

finally restored to his true nature and destiny, nature will also share in the freedom from *bondage to decay* and in the *glorious liberty.* **22–23:** Nature is thought of as sharing in the stress, anxiety, and pain which we ourselves feel as we wait for the promised *redemption. The first fruits of the Spirit,* the Spirit, already received, is an advanced installment of the full sonship we are yet to receive. *Our bodies,* as usually in Paul, our "selves," our "personalities." **24–25:** 1 Cor.2.9; 2 Cor.5.7; Heb.11.1.

8.26–30: Human weakness is sustained by the Spirit's intercession and by the knowledge of God's loving purpose. **28:** *His purpose,* or plan, is set forth in vv. 29–30. **29:** *To be conformed to . . . his Son* is to share the resurrection life of Christ, to be a "fellow heir" (compare v. 17), to be *glorified.*

8.31–39: Our confidence in God. 31: Ps.118.6. **32:** 4.25; 5.8; Jn.3.16. **35:** To be a Christian in the first century was both difficult and dangerous. **36:** Ps.44.22. **38:** *Neither death, nor life,* i.e. whether we live or die we shall not be separated. *Angels . . . principalities . . . powers* are supernatural beings, whether evil or good, and of various ranks (see Eph.6.12.n.). **39:** *Height* and *depth,* the highest point to which the stars rise and the abyss out of which they were thought to ascend; i.e. no supposed astrological power can separate us from Christ or defeat God's purpose for us.

9.1–5: The problem of Israel's unbelief. 3: Ex.32.32. **4:** *Sonship,* Ex.4.22; Jer.31.9. *Glory,* God's presence (Ex.16.10; 24.16). *Covenants,* plural because the covenant with Israel was often renewed (Gen.6.18; 9.9; 15.8; 17.2,7,9; Ex.2.24). *Giving the law,* Ex.20.1–17; Dt.5.1–21. *Worship,* in tabernacle and temple.

Christ. God who is over all be blessed for ever.[n] Amen.

6 But it is not as though the word of God had failed. For not all who are descended from Israel belong to Israel, [7] and not all are children of Abraham because they are his descendants; but "Through Isaac shall your descendants be named." [8] This means that it is not the children of the flesh who are the children of God, but the children of the promise are reckoned as descendants. [9] For this is what the promise said, "About this time I will return and Sarah shall have a son." [10] And not only so, but also when Rebecca had conceived children by one man, our forefather Isaac, [11] though they were not yet born and had done nothing either good or bad, in order that God's purpose of election might continue, not because of works but because of his call, [12] she was told, "The elder will serve the younger." [13] As it is written, "Jacob I loved, but Esau I hated."

14 What shall we say then? Is there injustice on God's part? By no means! [15] For he says to Moses, "I will have mercy on whom I have mercy, and I will have compassion on whom I have compassion." [16] So it depends not upon man's will or exertion, but upon God's mercy. [17] For the scripture says to Pharaoh, "I have raised you up for the very purpose of showing my power in you, so that my name may be proclaimed in all the earth." [18] So then he has mercy upon whomever he wills, and he hardens the heart of whomever he wills.

19 You will say to me then, "Why does he still find fault? For who can resist his will?" [20] But who are you, a man, to answer back to God? Will what is molded say to its molder, "Why have you made me thus?" [21] Has the potter no right over the clay, to make out of the same lump one vessel for beauty and another for menial use? [22] What if God, desiring to show his wrath and to make known his power, has endured with much patience the vessels of wrath made for destruction, [23] in order to make known the riches of his glory for the vessels of mercy, which he has prepared beforehand for glory, [24] even us whom he has called, not from the Jews only but also from the Gentiles? [25] As indeed he says in Hose'a,

"Those who were not my people
I will call 'my people,'
and her who was not beloved
I will call 'my beloved.'"
[26] "And in the very place where it was said to
them, 'You are not my people,'
they will be called 'sons of the living
God.'"

27 And Isaiah cries out concerning Israel: "Though the number of the sons of Israel be as the sand of the sea, only a remnant of them will be saved; [28] for the Lord will execute his sentence upon the earth with rigor and dispatch." [29] And as Isaiah predicted,

"If the Lord of hosts had not left us children,
we would have fared like Sodom and been
made like Gomor'rah."

30 What shall we say, then? That Gentiles who did not pursue righteousness have attained it, that is, righteousness through faith; [31] but that Israel who pursued the righteousness which is based on law did not succeed in fulfilling that law. [32] Why? Because they did not pursue it through faith, but as if it were based on works. They have stumbled over the stumbling stone, [33] as it is written,

n Or *Christ, who is God over all, blessed for ever*

9.6–13: **God's promise to Israel has not failed,** because the promise was not made to Abraham's physical descendants merely as such, but to those whom God chose. 7: Gen.21.12. 9: Gen.18.10. 10–12: Gen.25.21,23. 13: Mal.1.2–3.

9.14–29: **God's right to choose.** 15: Ex.33.19. 17: Ex.9.16. 19–21: Is.29,16; 45.9; 64.8; Jer.18.6. 24: God's choice or election is not limited to *the Jews* (compare 3.29). 25–26: The passage *in Hosea* (Hos.2.23; 1.10) refers to God's reclaiming of Israel after she had forsaken God and lost her covenant status; Paul (as also 1 Pet.2.10) applies the promise to the Gentiles. 27–29: God's promise never included all Israelites (Is.10.22; 1.9). *Sodom* and *Gomorrah*, Gen.19.24–25.

9.30–10.13: **True righteousness is by faith. 9.30:** 3.22; 10.6,20; Gal.2.16; 3.24; Phil.3.9; Heb.11.7. **33:** Is.28.16

"Behold, I am laying in Zion a stone that
   will make men stumble,
a rock that will make them fall;
and he who believes in him will not be put
   to shame."

10 Brethren, my heart's desire and prayer to God for them is that they may be saved. [2] I bear them witness that they have a zeal for God, but it is not enlightened. [3] For, being ignorant of the righteousness that comes from God, and seeking to establish their own, they did not submit to God's righteousness. [4] For Christ is the end of the law, that every one who has faith may be justified.

5 Moses writes that the man who practices the righteousness which is based on the law shall live by it. [6] But the righteousness based on faith says, Do not say in your heart, "Who will ascend into heaven?" (that is, to bring Christ down) [7] or "Who will descend into the abyss?" (that is, to bring Christ up from the dead). [8] But what does it say? The word is near you, on your lips and in your heart (that is, the word of faith which we preach); [9] because, if you confess with your lips that Jesus is Lord and believe in your heart that God raised him from the dead, you will be saved. [10] For man believes with his heart and so is justified, and he confesses with his lips and so is saved. [11] The scripture says, "No one who believes in him will be put to shame." [12] For there is no distinction between Jew and Greek; the same Lord is Lord of all and bestows his riches upon all who call upon him. [13] For, "every one who calls upon the name of the Lord will be saved."

14 But how are men to call upon him in whom they have not believed? And how are they to believe in him of whom they have never heard? And how are they to hear without a preacher? [15] And how can men preach unless they are sent? As it is written, "How beautiful are the feet of those who preach good news!" [16] But they have not all obeyed the gospel; for Isaiah says, "Lord, who has believed what he has heard from us?" [17] So faith comes from what is heard, and what is heard comes by the preaching of Christ.

18 But I ask, have they not heard? Indeed they have; for
"Their voice has gone out to all the earth,
   and their words to the ends of the world."
[19] Again I ask, did Israel not understand?
   First Moses says,
"I will make you jealous of those who are
   not a nation;
with a foolish nation I will make you
   angry."
[20] Then Isaiah is so bold as to say,
"I have been found by those who did not
   seek me;
I have shown myself to those who did not
   ask for me."
[21] But of Israel he says, "All day long I have held out my hands to a disobedient and contrary people."

11 I ask, then, has God rejected his people? By no means! I myself am an Israelite, a descendant of Abraham, a member of the tribe of Benjamin. [2] God has not rejected his people whom he foreknew. Do you not know what the scripture says of Eli'jah, how he pleads with God against Israel? [3] "Lord, they have killed thy prophets, they have demolished thy altars, and I alone am left, and they seek my life." [4] But what is God's reply to

and 8.14–15. The "stone" is a symbol of God's help, but if neglected it becomes an instrument of judgment. Christ is this *stone.* **10.4:** Gal.3.23–26. **5:** Lev.18.5; Gal.3.12. One must actually *practice* the law if one is to find life through it; this Paul has already shown to be impossible (3.9–20). But one has only to *accept* the free gift of the salvation in Christ (vv. 6–9; compare Dt.30.11–14). **10:** Both faith and confession are essential for justification and salvation. **11:** Is.28.16. **13:** Jl.2.32. The early Christians often applied to Jesus Old Testament references to the *Lord,* which in their original context refer to God.

10.14–21: Israel responsible for its failure. 14–18: The nation cannot claim that it has not had the opportunity of hearing the gospel. **15:** Is.52.7. **16:** Is.53.1. **18:** Ps.19.4. **19–21:** Nor can Israel claim that it has not understood the gospel; even Gentiles have been able to understand it. **19:** Dt.32.21. **20–21:** Is.65.1–2.

11.1–16: Israel's rejection not final. 1–6: As in Elijah's time (1 Kg.19.10,18), there is a *remnant* of the faithful.

him? "I have kept for myself seven thousand men who have not bowed the knee to Ba'al." ⁵ So too at the present time there is a remnant, chose by grace. ⁶ But if it is by grace, it is no longer on the basis of works; otherwise grace would no longer be grace.

7 What then? Israel failed to obtain what it sought. The elect obtained it, but the rest were hardened, ⁸ as it is written,

"God gave them a spirit of stupor,
eyes that should not see and ears that
      should not hear,
down to this very day."
⁹ And David says,
"Let their table become a snare and a trap,
a pitfall and a retribution for them;
¹⁰ let their eyes be darkened so that they can-
      not see,
and bend their backs for ever."

11 So I ask, have they stumbled so as to fall? By no means! But through their trespass salvation has come to the Gentiles, so as to make Israel jealous. ¹² Now if their trespass means riches for the world, and if their failure means riches for the Gentiles, how much more will their full inclusion mean!

13 Now I am speaking to you Gentiles. Inasmuch then as I am an apostle to the Gentiles, I magnify my ministry ¹⁴ in order to make my fellow Jews jealous, and thus save some of them. ¹⁵ For if their rejection means the reconciliation of the world, what will their acceptance mean but life from the dead? ¹⁶ If the dough offered as first fruits is holy, so is the whole lump; and if the root is holy, so are the branches.

17 But if some of the branches were broken off, and you, a wild olive shoot, were grafted in their place to share the richness⁰ of the olive tree, ¹⁸ do not boast over the branches. If you do boast, remember it is not you that support the root, but the root that supports you. ¹⁹ You will say, "Branches were broken off so that I might be grafted in." ²⁰ That is true. They were broken off because of their unbelief, but you stand fast only through faith. So do not become proud, but stand in awe. ²¹ For if God did not spare the natural branches, neither will he spare you. ²² Note then the kindness and the severity of God: severity toward those who have fallen, but God's kindness to you, provided you continue in his kindness; otherwise you too will be cut off. ²³ And even the others, if they do not persist in their unbelief, will be grafted in, for God has the power to graft them in again. ²⁴ For if you have been cut from what is by nature a wild olive tree, and grafted, contrary to nature, into a cultivated olive tree, how much more will these natural branches be grafted back into their own olive tree.

25 Lest you be wise in your own conceits, I want you to understand this mystery, brethren: a hardening has come upon part of Israel, until the full number of the Gentiles come in; ²⁶ and so all Israel will be saved; as it is written,

"The Deliverer will come from Zion,
he will banish ungodliness from Jacob";
²⁷ "and this will be my covenant with them
when I take away their sins."

o Other ancient authorities read *rich root*

Paul as a Jew is no more alone than Elijah was. **7–12:** The resistance to the gospel on the part of the masses of Jews is providential; God has *hardened* their *hearts* for a loving purpose, namely, that the Gentiles might have an opportunity to hear and receive the gospel. **8:** Is.29.10. **9:** Ps.69.22–23. **13–16:** The *reconciliation* of Gentiles will have the effect of making Israelites *jealous* and thus of drawing *some of them* to Christ. **16:** *The dough* and *the root* (Num.15.19–20 Septuagint; Jer.11.16–17) stand for the patriarchs, through whom all Israel has been consecrated.

11.17–24: The metaphor of the olive tree. The tree, including root and branches, is Israel. The branches broken off are the unbelieving Jews; the branches grafted in are Gentiles who believe in Christ. **20–22:** Having been made a part of the tree only because of faith (not merit or works), Gentile believers have no reason for pride, else God who has grafted them into the tree may later cut them off. **24:** The restoration of Israel will be easier than the call of the Gentiles.

11.25–36: All Israel will be saved. 25–26: A *mystery,* a truth once hidden, but now revealed by God. The *full number of the Gentiles* may mean the elect from among the Gentiles; and *all Israel* may mean Israel as a whole, not every

[28] As regards the gospel they are enemies of God, for your sake; but as regards election they are beloved for the sake of their forefathers. [29] For the gifts and the call of God are irrevocable. [30] Just as you were once disobedient to God but now have received mercy because of their disobedience, [31] so they have now been disobedient in order that by the mercy shown to you they also may[p] receive mercy. [32] For God has consigned all men to disobedience, that he may have mercy upon all.

[33] O the depth of the riches and wisdom and knowledge of God! How unsearchable are his judgments and how inscrutable his ways!
[34] "For who has known the mind of the Lord,
or who has been his counselor?"
[35] "Or who has given a gift to him
that he might be repaid?"
[36] For from him and through him and to him are all things. To him be glory for ever. Amen.

12 [1] I appeal to you therefore, brethren, by the mercies of God, to present your bodies as a living sacrifice, holy and acceptable to God, which is your spiritual worship. [2] Do not be conformed to this world[q] but be transformed by the renewal of your mind, that you may prove what is the will of God, what is good and acceptable and perfect.[r]

[3] For by the grace given to me I bid every one among you not to think of himself more highly than he ought to think, but to think with sober judgment, each according to the measure of faith which God has assigned him. [4] For as in one body we have many members, and all the members do not have the same function, [5] so we, though many, are one body in Christ, and individually members one of another. [6] Having gifts that differ according to the grace given to us, let us use them: if prophecy, in proportion to our faith; [7] if service, in our serving; he who teaches, in his teaching; [8] he who exhorts, in his exhortation; he who contributes, in liberality; he who gives aid, with zeal; he who does acts of mercy, with cheerfulness.

[9] Let love be genuine; hate what is evil, hold fast to what is good; [10] love one another with brotherly affection; outdo one another in showing honor. [11] Never flag in zeal, be aglow with the Spirit, serve the Lord. [12] Rejoice in your hope, be patient in tribulation, be constant in prayer. [13] Contribute to the needs of the saints, practice hospitality.

[14] Bless those who persecute you; bless and do not curse them. [15] Rejoice with those who rejoice, weep with those who weep. [16] Live in harmony with one another; do not be haughty, but associate with the lowly;[s] never be conceited. [17] Repay no one evil for evil, but take thought for what is noble in the sight of all. [18] If possible, so far as it depends upon you, live peaceably with all. [19] Beloved, never avenge yourselves, but leave it[t] to the wrath of God; for it is written, "Vengeance is mine, I will repay, says the Lord." [20] No, "if your enemy is hungry, feed him; if he is thirsty, give him drink; for by so doing you will heap burning coals upon his head." [21] Do not be overcome by evil, but overcome evil with good.

p Other ancient authorities add *now*   q Greek *age*
r Or *what is the good and acceptable and perfect will of God*   s Or *give yourselves to humble tasks*
t Greek *give place*

---

particular Israelite. **26–27:** Is.59.20–21; 27.9. **28–32:** Although temporarily *enemies* of the *gospel*, the *election* of the Jews is *irrevocable*. **33:** The wonder of God's providence. **34:** Is.40.13. **35:** Job 35.7; 41.11. **36:** 1 Cor.8.6; 11.12; Col.1.16; Heb.2.10.

12.1–8: The consecrated life. 1: *Bodies,* as usually in Paul, means "selves." *Living sacrifice,* as contrasted to the sacrifice of a slain beast. **2:** Christians are to live as belonging to the coming age, not this present age (Eph.4.23; 1 Jn.2.15). *Prove* means "have sure knowledge of." **3:** *Measure of faith,* measure of the Spirit which one has received by faith (1 Cor.4.7). **4–8:** 1 Cor.12.4–31. **8:** *He who gives aid,* or "he who rules."

12.9–21: The Christian's duty. 9–18: The law of love (compare 1 Cor.13). **13:** *Hospitality,* see 16.1–2 n.; Heb.13.2 n.; 3 Jn.5–8 n. **14:** Mt.5.44. **19:** The vindication of justice is God's prerogative, not ours (Dt.32.35). We are neither wise enough nor good enough to punish our enemies justly. **20:** To *heap burning coals. . . ,* is to make the enemy feel ashamed by meeting his *evil* with *good* (Pr.25.21–22).

13 Let every person be subject to the governing authorities. For there is no authority except from God, and those that exist have been instituted by God. ² Therefore he who resists the authorities resists what God has appointed, and those who resist will incur judgment. ³ For rulers are not a terror to good conduct, but to bad. Would you have no fear of him who is in authority? Then do what is good, and you will receive his approval, ⁴ for he is God's servant for your good. But if you do wrong, be afraid, for he does not bear the sword in vain; he is the servant of God to execute his wrath on the wrongdoer. ⁵ Therefore one must be subject, not only to avoid God's wrath but also for the sake of conscience. ⁶ For the same reason you also pay taxes, for the authorities are ministers of God, attending to this very thing. ⁷ Pay all of them their dues, taxes to whom taxes are due, revenue to whom revenue is due, respect to whom respect is due, honor to whom honor is due.

8 Owe no one anything, except to love one another; for he who loves his neighbor has fulfilled the law. ⁹ The commandments, "You shall not commit adultery, You shall not kill, You shall not steal, You shall not covet," and any other commandment, are summed up in this sentence, "You shall love your neighbor as yourself." ¹⁰ Love does no wrong to a neighbor; therefore love is the fulfilling of the law.

11 Besides this you know what hour it is, how it is full time now for you to wake from sleep. For salvation is nearer to us now than when we first believed; ¹² the night is far gone, the day is at hand. Let us then cast off the works of darkness and put on the armor of light; ¹³ let us conduct ourselves becomingly as in the day, not in reveling and drunkenness, not in debauchery and licentiousness, not in quarreling and jealousy. ¹⁴ But put on the Lord Jesus Christ, and make no provision for the flesh, to gratify its desires.

13.1–7: The Christian and the state. Though the Christian has no right to punish (12.19–21), the state does have that right and the Christian must respect it. Paul's confidence that the Roman state is, on the whole, just and beneficent is matched in 1 Pet.2.13–17; 3.13.

13.8–10: Love fulfils the law. 8a: Pay every debt; do not stand under any obligation except the obligation to love. **8b–10:** Mk.12.31; Jas.2.8.

13.11–14: The imminence of Christ's second coming makes it the more urgent that Christians *conduct* themselves *becomingly*. **14:** To *put on the Lord Jesus Christ* is to enter fully into the new order of existence which God has created through Christ (see 6.1–14 n.).

Augustine

CONFESSIONS

Introduction by Michael Graham

Augustine, second only to St. Paul in his influence on Christian theology, was born in 354 in a town which is today in Algeria. In his late teens, he went off to study at Carthage, a major city in north Africa. After a short stint teaching in his native town, he returned to Carthage for several years, before departing for Italy in 383. The following year he became a professor of rhetoric in Milan, the northern Italian city which had become home to the Roman emperor, and came under the influence of Ambrose, bishop of Milan. In 386, at the age of 32, he converted to Christianity, the religion of his mother Monica as well as his friend Ambrose. In 388 he returned to north Africa, and in 391, at the age of 37, became a priest there, in the port city of Hippo. In 396 he became bishop of Hippo, a post he held for the rest of his life. Augustine died in 430 while Hippo was under siege by the Vandals, invaders from Germany.

Augustine was charismatic, intelligent and curious. These qualities made him popular with friends, and helped him rise to prominence once he embarked on a career in the Church. His best-known theological work was *City of God,* a book he was moved to write after the Visigoths, another Germanic tribe, sacked Rome in 410. Many Romans blamed this historic defeat on the suppression of Roman pagan cults by Christian rulers, and suggested that if Christianity had been the right choice for Rome, the city would not have fallen. In *City of God,* Augustine, who was a great admirer of many aspects of Roman civilization, responded that empires would rise and fall but only God's kingdom was eternal. No earthly empire could remain impregnable, Augustine argued, because life on earth was a passing thing. God's kingdom, ultimately far more important, would last. Augustine was also an active controversialist, defending (and in the process helping to define) Church doctrines against various heresies, including the Pelagians, who rejected the idea of Original Sin and claimed that people could earn eternal salvation through their own good behavior.

But most interestingly for our purposes, Augustine was a seeker. In his youth he experimented with many lifestyles and philosophies, before deciding that Christianity offered the answers for which he had been searching. He became well-acquainted with Roman culture and Greek philosophy, as well as the ideas of the Manicheans, who saw the world as sharply divided between the forces of good and evil. Also, as a teenager he became involved with a girl by whom he had a child, and with whom he lived for many years, although they never married.

Years later, he recorded his spiritual and philosophical journey in his *Confessions,* a landmark in autobiographical literature, which covers Augustine's life up to age 35. It is important to remember that the *Confessions,* only a part of which you are about to read, is an autobiography, not a diary. Rather than copying down a daily or weekly record of events, Augustine was, as a mature adult, recalling his early years. He was thus telling a story for which he already knew the outcome—that he would convert to Christianity. How might this have affected the way he told the story? Not surprisingly, Augustine's father and mother loomed large in his recollection of his early life. What roles did they, particularly his mother, play in his upbringing? What particular sins and temptations did Augustine seem most troubled by? Many of us go through long periods of personal development, often labeled "growing up," before choosing a course to follow in life. Some never find that course. Do you see something of yourself in Augustine? Also of interest in this work is the extent to which Greek and Roman culture dominated the Mediterranean world, including Augustine's corner of north Africa. What were some of his major intellectual influences? Do you think this work is timeless, or does it no longer carry a message for us?

Confessions

BOOK I

14

If this was so, why did I dislike Greek literature, which tells these tales, as much as the Greek language itself? Homer, as well as Virgil, was a skilful spinner of yarns and he is most delightfully imaginative. Nevertheless, as a boy, I found him little to my taste. I suppose that Greek boys think the same about Virgil when they are forced to study him as I was forced to study Homer. There was of course the difficulty which is found in learning any foreign language, and this soured the sweetness of the Greek romances. For I understood not a single word and I was constantly subjected to violent threats and cruel punishments to make me learn. As a baby, of course, I knew no Latin either, but I learned it without fear and fret, simply by keeping my ears open while my nurses fondled me and everyone laughed and played happily with me. I learned it without being forced by threats of punishment, because it was my own wish to be able to give expression to my thoughts. I could never have done this if I had not learnt a few words, not from schoolmasters, but from people who spoke to me and listened when I delivered to their ears whatever thoughts I had conceived. This clearly shows that we learn better in a free spirit of curiosity than under fear and compulsion. But your law, O God, permits the free flow of curiosity to be stemmed by force. From the schoolmaster's cane to the ordeals of martyrdom, your law prescribes bitter medicine to retrieve us from the noxious pleasures which cause us to desert you.

15

Grant my prayer, O Lord, and do not allow my soul to wilt under the discipline which you prescribe. Let me not tire of thanking you for your mercy in rescuing me from all my wicked ways, so that you may be sweeter to me than all the joys which used to tempt me; so that I may love you most intensely and clasp your hand with all the power of my devotion; so that you may save me from all temptation until the end of my days.

You, O Lord, are my King and my God, and in your service I want to use whatever good I learned as a boy. I can speak and write, read and count, and I want these things to be used to serve you, because when I studied other subjects you checked me and forgave me the sins I committed by taking pleasure in such worthless things. It is true that these studies taught me many useful words, but the same words can be learnt by studying something that matters, and this is the safe course for a boy to follow.

Augustine, *Confessions* (R.S. Pine-Coffin, trans.), Penguin, 1961, original pp. 35–70 (Book I, chap. 14–end of Book III).

16

But we are carried away by custom to our own undoing and it is hard to struggle against the stream. Will this torrent never dry up? How much longer will it sweep the sons of Adam down to that vast and terrible sea which cannot easily be passed, even by those who climb upon the ark of the Cross?

This traditional education taught me that Jupiter punishes the wicked with his thunderbolts and yet commits adultery himself. The two roles are quite incompatible. All the same he is represented in this way, and the result is that those who follow his example in adultery can put a bold face on it by making false pretences of thunder. But can any schoolmaster in his gown listen unperturbed to a man who challenges him on his own ground and says 'Homer invented these stories and attributed human sins to the gods. He would have done better to provide men with examples of divine goodness'?[1] It would be nearer the truth to say that Homer certainly invented the tales but peopled them with wicked human characters in the guise of gods. In this way their wickedness would not be reckoned a crime, and all who did as they did could be shown to follow the example of the heavenly gods, not that of sinful mortals.

And yet human children are pitched into this hellish torrent, together with the fees which are paid to have them taught lessons like these. Much business is at stake, too, when these matters are publicly debated, because the law decrees that teachers would be paid a salary in addition to the fees paid by their pupils. And the roar of the torrent beating upon its boulders seems to say 'This is the school where men are made masters of words. This is where they learn the art of persuasion, so necessary in business and debate'—as much as to say that, but for a certain passage in Terence, we should never have heard of words like 'shower', 'golden', 'lap', 'deception', 'sky', and the other words which occur in the same scene. Terence brings on to the stage a dissolute youth who excuses his own fornication by pointing to the example of Jupiter. He looks at a picture painted on the wall, which 'shows how Jupiter is said to have deceived the girl Danae by raining a golden shower into her lap.'[2] These are the words with which he incites himself to lechery, as though he had heavenly authority for it: 'What a god he is! His mighty thunder rocks the sky from end to end. You may say that I am only a man, and thundering is beyond my power. But I played the rest of the part well enough, and willingly too'![2]

The words are certainly not learnt any the more easily by reason of the filthy mortal, but filth is committed with greater confidence as a result of learning the words. I have nothing against the words themselves. They are like choice and costly glasses, but they contain the wine of error which had already gone to the heads of the teachers who poured it out for us to drink. If we refused to drink, we were beaten for it, without the right to appeal to a sober judge. With your eyes upon me, my God, my memory can safely recall those days. But it is true that I learned all these things gladly and took a sinful pleasure in them. And for this very reason I was called a promising boy.

17

Let me tell you, my God, how I squandered the brains you gave me on foolish delusions. I was set a task which troubled me greatly, for if I were successful, I might win some praise: if not, I was afraid of disgrace or a beating. I had to recite the speech of Juno,[3] who was pained and angry because she could not prevent Aeneas from sailing to Italy. I had been told that Juno had never really spoken the words, but we were compelled to make believe and follow the flight of the poet's fancy by repeating in prose what he had said in verse. The contest was to be won by the boy who found the best words to suit the meaning and best expressed feelings of sorrow and anger appropriate to the majesty of the character he impersonated.

What did all this matter to me, my God, my true Life? Why did my recitation win more praise than those of the many other boys in my class? Surely it was all so much smoke without fire? Was there no other subject on which I might have sharpened my wits and my tongue? I might have used them, O Lord, to praise you in the words of your Scriptures, which could have been a prop to support my heart, as if it were a young vine, so that it would not have produced this crop of worthless fruit, fit only for the birds to peck at. For offerings can be made to those birds of prey, the fallen angels, in more ways than one.

18

But was it surprising that I was lured into these fruitless pastimes and wandered away from you, my God? I was expected to model myself upon men who were disconcerted by the rebukes they received if they used outlandish words or strange idioms to tell of some quite harmless thing they might have done, but revelled in the applause they earned for the fine flow of well-ordered and nicely balanced phrases with which they described their own acts of indecency. You see all these things, Lord, and yet you keep silence, because you are patient and full of compassion and can tell no lie.[4] Will you be silent for ever? This very day you are ready to rescue from this fearsome abyss any soul that searches for you, any man who says from the depths of his heart, *I have eyes only for you; I long, Lord, for your presence;*[5] for the soul that is blinded by wicked passions is far from you and cannot see your face. The path that leads us away from you and brings us back again is not measured by footsteps or milestones. The prodigal son of the Scriptures went to live in a distant land to waste in dissipation all the wealth which his father had given him when he set out. But, to reach that land, he did not hire horses, carriages, or ships; he did not take to the air on real wings to set one foot before the other. For you were the Father who gave him riches. You loved him when he set out and you loved him still more when he came home without a penny. But he set his heart on pleasure and his soul was blinded, and this blindness was the measure of the distance he travelled away from you, so that he could not see your face.

O Lord my God, be patient, as you always are, with the men of this world as you watch them and see how strictly they obey the rules of grammar which have been handed down to them, and yet ignore the eternal rules of everlasting salvation which they have received from you. A man who has learnt the traditional rules of pronunciation, or teaches them to others, gives greater scandal if he breaks them by dropping the aitch from 'human being' than if he breaks your rules and hates another human, his fellow man. This is just as perverse as to imagine that our enemies can do us more harm than we do to ourselves by hating them, or that by persecuting another man we can damage him more fatally than we damage our own hearts in the process. O God, alone in majesty, high in the silence of heaven, unseen by man! we can see how your unremitting justice punishes unlawful ambition with blindness, for a man who longs for fame as a fine speaker will stand up before a human judge, surrounded by a human audience, and lash his opponent with malicious invective, taking the greatest care not to say ''uman' instead of 'human' by a slip of the tongue, and yet the thought that the frenzy in his own mind may condemn a human being to death disturbs him not at all.

19

It was at the threshold of a world such as this that I stood in peril as a boy. I was already being prepared for its tournaments by a training which taught me to have a horror of faculty grammar instead of teaching me, when I committed these faults, not to envy others who avoided them. All this, my God, I admit and confess to you. By these means I won praise from the people whose favour I sought, for I thought that the right way to live was to do as they wished. I was blind to the whirlpool of debasement in which I had been plunged away from the sight of your eyes. For in your eyes nothing could be more debased than I was then, since I was even trouble-some to the people whom I set out to please. Many and many a time I lied to my tutor, my masters, and my parents, and deceived them because I wanted to play games or watch some futile show or was impatient to imitate what I saw on the stage. I even stole from my parents' larder and from their table, either from greed or to get something to give to other boys in exchange for their favourite toys, which they were willing to barter with me. And in the games I played with them I often cheated in order to come off the better, simply because a vain desire to win had got the better of me. And yet there was nothing I could less easily endure, nothing that made me quarrel more bitterly, than to find others cheating me as I cheated them. All the same, if they found me out and blamed me for it, I would lose my temper rather than give in.

Can this be the innocence of childhood? Far from it, O Lord! But I beg you to forgive it. For commanders and kings may take the place of tutors and schoolmasters, nuts and balls and pet birds may give way to money and estates and servants, but these same passions remain with us while one stage of life follows upon another, just as more severe punishments follow upon the schoolmaster's cane. It was, then, simply because they are small that you used children to symbolize humility when, as our King, you commended it by saying that *the kingdom of heaven belongs to such as these.*[6]

20

And yet, Lord, even if you had willed that I should not survive my childhood, I should have owed you gratitude, because you are our God, the supreme God, the Creator and Ruler of the universe. For even as a child I existed, I was alive, I had the power of feeling; I had an instinct to keep myself safe and sound, to preserve my own being, which was a trace of the single unseen Being from whom it was derived; I had an inner sense which watched over my bodily senses and kept them in full vigour; and even in the small things which occupied my thoughts I found pleasure in the truth. I disliked finding myself in the wrong; my memory was good; I was acquiring the command of words; I enjoyed the company of friends; and I shrank from pain, ignorance, and sorrow. Should I not be grateful that so small a creature possessed such wonderful qualities? But they were all gifts from God, for I did not give them to myself. His gifts are good and the sum of them all is my own self. Therefore, the God who made me must be good and all the good in me is his. I thank him and praise him for all the good in my life, even my life as a boy. But my sin was this, that I looked for pleasure, beauty, and truth not in him but in myself and his other creatures, and the search led me instead to pain, confusion, and error. My God, in whom is my delight, my glory, and my trust, I thank you for your gifts and beg you to preserve and keep them for me. Keep me, too, and so your gifts will grow and reach perfection and I shall be with you myself, for I should not even exist if it were not by your gift.

BOOK II

1

I must now carry my thoughts back to the abominable things I did in those days, the sins of the flesh which defiled my soul. I do this, my God, not because I love those sins, but so that I may love you. For love of your love I shall retrace my wicked ways. The memory is bitter, but it will help me to savour your sweetness, the sweetness that does not deceive but brings real joy and never fails. For love of your love I shall retrieve myself from the havoc of disruption which tore me to pieces when I turned away from you, whom alone I should have sought, and lost myself instead on many a different quest. For as I grew to manhood I was inflamed with desire for a surfeit of hell's pleasures. Foolhardy as I was, I ran wild with lust that was manifold and rank. In your eyes my beauty vanished and I was foul to the core, yet I was pleased with my own condition and anxious to be pleasing in the eyes of men.

2

I cared for nothing but to love and be loved. But my love went beyond the affection of one mind for another, beyond the arc of the bright beam of friendship. Bodily desire, like a morass, and adolescent sex welling up within me exuded mists which clouded over and obscured my heart, so that I could not distinguish the clear light of true love from the murk of lust. Love and lust together seethed within me. In my tender youth they swept me away over the precipice of my body's appetites and plunged me in the whirlpool of sin. More and more I angered you, unawares. For I had been deafened by the clank of my chains, the fetters of the death which was my due to punish the pride in my soul. I strayed still farther from you and you did not restrain me. I was tossed and spilled, floundering in the broiling sea of my fornication, and you said no word. How long it was before I learned that you were my true joy! You were silent then, and I went on my way, farther and farther from you, proud in my distress and restless in fatigue, sowing more and more seeds whose only crop was grief.

Was there no one to lull my distress, to turn the fleeting beauty of these new-found attractions to good purpose and set up a goal for their charms, so that the high tide of my youth might have rolled in upon the shore of marriage? The surge might have been calmed and contented by the procreation of children, which is the purpose of marriage, as your law prescribes, O Lord. By this means you form the offspring of our fallen nature, and with a gentle hand you prune back the thorns that have no place in your paradise. For your almighty power is not far from us, even when we are far from you. Or, again, I might have listened more attentively to your voice from the clouds, saying of those who marry that they will *meet with outward distress, but I leave you your freedom;*[7] that *a man does well to abstain from all commerce with women,*[8] and that *he who is unmarried is concerned with God's claim, asking how he is to please God; whereas the married man is concerned with the world's claim, asking how he is to please his wife.*[9] These were the words to which I should have listened with more care, and if I had made myself a *eunuch for love of the kingdom of heaven,*[10] I should have awaited your embrace with all the greater joy.

But instead, I was in a ferment of wickedness. I deserted you and allowed myself to be carried away by the sweep of the tide. I broke all your lawful bounds and did not escape your lash. For what man can escape it? You were always present, angry and merciful at once, strewing the pangs of bitterness over all my lawless pleasures to lead me on to look for others unallied with pain. You meant me to find them nowhere but in yourself, O Lord, for you teach us by inflicting pain,[11] you smite so that you may heal,[12] and you kill us so that we may not die away from you. Where was I then and how far was I banished from the bliss of your house in that sixteenth year of my life? This was the age at which the frenzy gripped me and I surrendered myself entirely to lust, which your law forbids but human hearts are not ashamed to sanction. My family made no effort to save me from my fall by marriage. Their only concern was that I should learn how to make a good speech and how to persuade others by my words.

3

In the same year my studies were interrupted. I had already begun to go to the near-by town of Madaura to study literature and the art of public speaking, but I was brought back home while my father, a modest citizen of Thagaste whose determination was greater than his means, saved up the money to send me farther afield to Carthage. I need not tell all this to you, my God, but in your presence I tell it to my own kind, to those other men, however few, who may perhaps pick up this book. And I tell it so that I and all who read my words may realize the depths from which we are to cry to you. Your ears will surely listen to the cry of a penitent heart which lives the life of faith.

No one had anything but praise for my father who, despite his slender resources, was ready to provide his son with all that was needed to enable him to travel so far for the purpose of study. Many of our townsmen, far richer than my father, went to no such trouble for their children's sake. Yet this same father of mine took no trouble at all to see how I was growing in your sight or whether I was chaste or not. He cared only that I should have a fertile tongue, leaving my heart to bear none of your fruits, my God, though you are the only Master, true and good, of its husbandry.

In the meanwhile, during my sixteenth year, the narrow means of my family obliged me to leave school and live idly at home with my parents. The brambles of lust grew high above my head and there was no one to root them out, certainly not my father. One day at the public baths he saw the signs of active virility coming to life in me and this was enough to make him relish the thought of having grandchildren. He was happy to tell my mother about it, for his happiness was due to the intoxication which causes the world to forget you, its Creator, and to love the things you have created instead of loving you, because the world is drunk with the invisible wine of its own perverted, earthbound will. But in my mother's heart you had already begun to build your temple and laid the foundations of your holy dwelling, while my father was still a catechumen and a new one at that. So in her piety, she became alarmed and apprehensive, and although I had not yet been baptized, she began to dread that I might follow in the crooked path of those who do not keep their eyes on you but turn their backs instead.

How presumptuous it was of me to say that you were silent, my God, when I drifted farther and farther away from you! Can it be true that you said nothing to me at that time? Surely the words which rang in my ears, spoken by your faithful servant, my mother, could have come from none but you? Yet none of them sank into my heart to make me do as you said. I well remember what her wishes were and how she most earnestly warned me not to commit fornication and above all not to seduce any man's wife. It all seemed womanish advice to me and I should have blushed to accept it. Yet the words were yours, though I did not know it. I thought that you were silent and that she was speaking, but all the while you were speaking to me through her, and when I disregarded her, your handmaid, I was disregarding you, though I was both her son and your servant. But I did this unawares and continued headlong on my way. I was so blind to the truth that among my companions I was ashamed to be less dissolute than they were. For I heard them bragging of their depravity, and the greater the sin the more they gloried in it, so that I took pleasure in the same vices not only for the enjoyment of what I did, but also for the applause I won.

Nothing deserves to be despised more than vice; yet I gave in more and more to vice simply in order not to be despised. If I had not sinned enough to rival other sinners, I used to pretend that I had done things I had not done at all, because I was afraid that innocence would be taken for cowardice and chastity for weakness. These were the companions with whom I walked the streets of Babylon. I wallowed in its mire as if it were made of spices and precious ointments, and to fix me all the faster in the very depths of sin the unseen enemy trod me underfoot and enticed me to himself, because I was an easy prey for his seductions. For even my mother, who by now had escaped from the centre of Babylon, though she still loitered in its outskirts, did not act upon what she had heard about me from her husband with the same earnestness as she had advised me about chastity. She saw that I was already infected with a disease that would become dangerous later on, but if the growth of my passions could not be cut back to the quick, she did not think it right to restrict them to the bounds of married love. This was because she was afraid that the bonds of marriage might be a hindrance to my hopes for the future—not of course the hope of the life to come, which she reposed in you, but my hopes of success at my studies. Both my parents were unduly eager for me to learn, my father because he gave next to no thought to you and only shallow thought to me, and my mother because she thought the usual course of study would certainly not hinder me, but would even help me, in my approach to you. To the best of my memory this is how I construe the characters of my parents. Furthermore, I was given a free rein to amuse myself beyond the strict limits of discipline, so that I lost myself in many kinds of evil ways, in all of which a pall of darkness hung between me and the bright light of your truth, my God. What malice proceeded from my pampered heart![13]

4

It is certain, O Lord, that theft is punished by your law, the law that is written in men's hearts and cannot be erased however sinful they are. For no thief can bear that another thief should steal from him, even if he is rich and the other is driven to it by want. Yet I was willing to steal, and steal I did, although I was not compelled by any lack, unless it were the lack of a sense of justice or a distaste for what was right and a greedy love of doing wrong. For what I stole I already had plenty, and much better at that, and I had no wish to enjoy the things I coveted by stealing, but only to enjoy the theft itself and the sin. There was a pear-tree near our vineyard, loaded with fruit that was attractive neither to look at nor to taste. Late one night a band of ruffians, myself included, went off to shake down the fruit and carry it away, for we had continued our games out of doors until well after dark, as was our pernicious habit. We took away an enormous quantity of pears, not to eat them ourselves, but simply to throw them to the pigs. Perhaps we ate some of them, but our real pleasure consisted in doing something that was forbidden.

Look into my heart, O God, the same heart on which you took pity when it was in the depths of the abyss. Let my heart now tell you what prompted me to do wrong for no purpose, and why it was only my own love of mischief that made me do it. The evil in me was foul, but I loved it. I loved my own perdition and my own faults, not the things for which I committed wrong, but the wrong itself. My soul was vicious and broke away from your safe keeping to seek its own destruction, looking for no profit in disgrace but only for disgrace itself.

5

The eye is attracted by beautiful objects, by gold and silver and all such things. There is great pleasure, too, in feeling something agreeable to the touch, and material things have various qualities to please each of the other senses. Again, it is gratifying to be held in esteem by other men and to have the power of giving them orders and gaining the mastery over them. This is also the reason why revenge is sweet. But our ambition to obtain all these things must not lead us astray from you, O Lord, nor must we depart from what your law allows. The life we live on earth has its own attractions as well, because it has a certain beauty of its own in harmony with all the rest of this world's beauty. Friendship among men, too, is a delightful bond, uniting many souls in one. All these things and their like can be occasions of sin because, good though they are, they are of the lowest order of good, and if we are too much tempted by them we abandon those higher and better things, your truth, your law, and you yourself, O Lord our God. For these earthly things, too, can give joy, though not such joy as my God, who made them all, can give, because *honest men will rejoice in the Lord; upright hearts will not boast in vain.*[14]

When there is an inquiry to discover why a crime has been committed, normally no one is satisfied until it has been shown that the motive might have been either the desire of gaining, or the fear of losing, one of those good things which I said were of the lowest order. For such things are attractive and have beauty, although they are paltry trifles in comparison with the worth of God's blessed treasures. A man commits murder and we ask the reason. He did it because he wanted his victim's wife or estates for himself, or so that he might live on the proceeds of robbery, or because he was afraid that the other might defraud him of something, or because he had been wronged and was burning for revenge. Surely no one would believe that he would commit murder for no reason but the sheer delight of killing? Sallust tells us that Catiline was a man of insane ferocity, 'who chose to be cruel and vicious without apparent reason';[15] but we are also told that his purpose was 'not to allow his men to lose heart or waste their skill through lack of practice'.[16] If we ask the reason for this, it is obvious that he meant that once he had made himself master of the government by means of this continual violence, he would obtain honour, power, and wealth and would no longer go in fear of the law because of his crimes or have to face difficulties through lack of funds. So even Catiline did not love crime for crime's sake. He loved something quite different, for the sake of which he committed his crimes.

6

If the crime of theft which I committed that night as a boy of sixteen were a living thing, I could speak to it and ask what it was that, to my shame, I loved in it. I had no beauty because it was a robbery. It is true that the pears which we stole had beauty, because they were created by you, the good God, who are the most beautiful of all beings and the Creator of all things, the supreme Good and my own true Good. But it was not the pears that my unhappy soul desired. I had plenty of my own, better than those, and I only picked them so that I might steal. For no sooner had I picked them than I threw them away, and tasted nothing in them but my own sin, which I relished and enjoyed. If any part of one of those pears passed my lips, it was the sin that gave it flavour.

And now, O Lord my God, now that I ask what pleasure I had in that theft, I find that it had no beauty to attract me. I do not mean beauty of the sort that justice and prudence possess, nor the beauty that is in man's mind and in his memory and in the life that animates him, nor the beauty of the stars in their allotted places or of the earth and sea, teeming with new life born to replace the old as it passes away. It did not even have the shadowy, deceptive beauty which makes vice attractive—pride, for instance, which is a pretence of superiority, imitating yours, for you alone are God, supreme over all; or ambition, which is only a craving for honour and glory, when you alone are to be honoured before all and you alone are glorious for ever. Cruelty is the weapon of the powerful, used to make others fear them: yet no one is to be feared but God alone, from whose power nothing can be snatched away or stolen by any man at any time or place or by any means. The lustful use caresses to win the love they crave for, yet no one caress is sweeter than your charity and no love is more rewarding than the love of your truth, which shines in beauty above all else. Inquisitiveness has all the appearance of a thirst for knowledge, yet you have supreme knowledge of all things. Ignorance, too, and stupidity choose to go under the mask of simplicity and innocence, because you are simplicity itself and no innocence is greater than yours. You are innocent even of the harm which overtakes the wicked, for it is the result of their own actions. Sloth poses as the love of peace: yet what certain peace is there besides the Lord? Extravagance masquerades as fullness and abundance: but you are the full, unfailing store of never-dying sweetness. The spendthrift makes a pretence of liberality: but you are the most generous dispenser of all good. The covetous want many possessions for themselves: you possess all. The envious struggle for preferment: but what is to be preferred before you? Anger demands revenge: but what vengeance is as just as yours? Fear shrinks from any sudden, unwonted danger which threatens the things that it loves, for its only care is safety: but to you nothing is strange, nothing unforeseen. No one can part you from the things that you love, and safety is assured nowhere but in you. Grief eats away its heart for the loss of things which it took pleasure in desiring, because it wants to be like you, from whom nothing can be taken away.

So the soul defiles itself with unchaste love when it turns away from you and looks elsewhere for things which it cannot find pure and unsullied except by returning to you. All who desert you and set themselves up against you merely copy you in a perverse way; but by this very act of imitation they only show that you are the Creator of all nature and, consequently, that there is no place whatever where man may hide away from you.

What was it, then, that pleased me in the act of theft? Which of my Lord's powers did I imitate in a perverse and wicked way? Since I had no real power to break his law, was it that I enjoyed at least the pretence of doing so, like a prisoner who creates for himself the illusion of liberty by doing something wrong, when he has no fear of punishment, under a feeble hallucination of power? Here was the slave who ran away from his master and chased a shadow instead! What an abomination! What a parody of life! What abysmal death! Could I enjoy doing wrong for no other reason than that it was wrong?

7

What return shall I make to the Lord[17] for my ability to recall these things with no fear in my soul? I will love you, Lord, and thank you, and praise your name, because you have forgiven me such great sins and such wicked deeds. I acknowledge that it was by your grace and mercy that you melted away my sins like ice. I acknowledge, too, that by your grace I was preserved from whatever sins I did not commit, for there was no knowing what I might have done, since I loved evil even if it served no purpose. I avow that you have forgiven me all, both the sins which I committed of my own accord and those which by your guidance I was spared from committing.

What man who reflects upon his own weakness can dare to claim that his own efforts have made him chaste and free from sin, as though this entitled him to love you the less, on the ground that he had less need of the mercy by which you forgive the sins of the penitent? There are some who have been called by you and because they have listened to your voice they have avoided the sins which I here record and confess for them to read. But let them not deride me for having been cured by the same Doctor who preserved them from sickness, or at least from such grave sickness as mine. Let them love you just as much, or even more, than I do, for they can see that the same healing hand which rid me of the great fever of my sins protects them from falling sick of the same disease.

8

It brought me no happiness, for *what harvest did I reap from acts which now make me blush,*[18] particularly from the act of theft? I loved nothing in it except the thieving, though I cannot truly speak of that as a 'thing' that I could love, and I was only the more miserable because of it. And yet, as I recall my feelings at the time, I am quite sure that I would not have done it on my own. Was it then that I also enjoyed the company of those with whom I committed the crime? If this is so, there was something else I loved besides the act of theft; but I cannot call it 'something else', because companionship, like theft, is not a thing at all.

No one can tell me the truth of it except my God, who enlightens my mind and dispels its shadows. What conclusion am I trying to reach from these questions and this discussion? It is true that if the pears which I stole had been to my taste, and if I had wanted to get them for myself, I might have committed the crime on my own if I had needed to do no more than that to win myself the pleasure. I should have had no need to kindle my glowing desire by rubbing shoulders with a gang of accomplices. But as it was not the fruit that gave me pleasure, I must have got it from the crime itself, from the thrill of having partners in sin.

9

How can I explain my mood? It was certainly a very vile frame of mind and one for which I suffered; but how can I account for it? *Who knows his own frailties?*[19]

We were tickled to laughter by the prank we had played, because no one suspected us of it although the owners were furious. Why was it, then, that I thought it fun not to have been the only culprit? Perhaps it was because we do not easily laugh when we are alone. True enough: but even when a man is all by himself and quite alone, sometimes he cannot help laughing if he thinks or hears or sees something especially funny. All the same, I am quite sure that I would never have done this thing on my own.

My God, I lay all this before you, for it is still alive in my memory. By myself I would not have committed that robbery. It was not the takings that attracted me but the raid itself, and yet to do it by myself would have been no fun and I should not have done it. This was friendship of a most unfriendly sort, bewitching my mind in an inexplicable way. For the sake of a laugh, a little sport, I was glad to do harm and anxious to damage another; and that without thought of profit for myself or retaliation for injuries received! And all because we are ashamed to hold back when others say 'Come on! Let's do it!'

10

Can anyone unravel this twisted tangle of knots? I shudder to look at it or think of such abomination. I long instead for innocence and justice, graceful and splendid in eyes whose sight is undefiled. My longing fills me and yet it cannot cloy. With them is certain peace and life that cannot be disturbed. The man who enters their domain goes to *share the joy of his Lord.*[20] He shall know no fear and shall lack no good. In him that is goodness itself he shall find his own best way of life. But I deserted you, my God. In my youth I wandered away, too far from your sustaining hand, and created of myself a barren waste.

BOOK III

1

I went to Carthage, where I found myself in the midst of a hissing cauldron of lust. I had not yet fallen in love, but I was in love with the idea of it, and this feeling that something was missing made me despise myself for not being more anxious to satisfy the need. I began to look around for some object for my love, since I badly wanted to love something. I had no liking for the safe path without pitfalls, for although my real need was for you, my God, who are the food of the soul, I was not aware of this hunger. I felt no need for the food that does not perish, not because I had had my fill of it, but because the more I was starved of it the less palatable it seemed. Because of this my soul fell sick. It broke out in ulcers and looked about desperately for some material, worldly means of relieving the itch which they caused. But material things, which have no soul, could not be true objects for my love. To love and to have my love returned was my heart's desire, and it would be all the sweeter if I could also enjoy the body of the one who loved me.

So I muddied the stream of friendship with the filth of lewdness and clouded its clear waters with hell's black river of lust. And yet, in spite of this rank depravity, I was vain enough to have ambitions of cutting a fine figure in the world. I also fell in love, which was a snare of my own choosing. My God, my God of mercy, how good you were to me, for you mixed much bitterness in that cup of pleasure! My love was returned and finally shackled me in the bonds of its consummation. In the midst of my joy I was caught up in the coils of trouble, for I was lashed with the cruel, fiery rods of jealousy and suspicion, fear, anger, and quarrels.

2

I was much attracted by the theatre, because the plays reflected my own unhappy plight and were tinder to my fire. Why is it that men enjoy feeling sad at the sight of tragedy and suffering on the stage, although they would be most unhappy if they had to endure the same fate themselves? Yet they watch the plays because they hope to be made to feel sad, and the feeling of sorrow is what they enjoy. What miserable delirium this is! The more a man is subject to such suffering himself, the more easily he is moved by it in the theatre. Yet when he suffers himself, we call it misery: when he suffers out of sympathy with others, we call it pity. But what sort of pity can we really feel for an imaginary scene on the stage? The audience is not called upon to offer help but only to feel sorrow, and the more they are pained the more they applaud the author. Whether this human agony is based on fact or is simply imaginary, if it is acted so badly that the audience is not moved to sorrow, they leave the theatre in a disgruntled and critical mood; whereas, if they are made to feel pain, they stay to the end watching happily.

This shows that sorrow and tears can be enjoyable. Of course, everyone wants to be happy; but even if no one likes being sad, is there just the one exception that, because we enjoy pitying others, we welcome their misfortunes, without which we could not pity them? If so, it is because friendly feelings well up in us like the waters of a spring. But what course do these waters follow? Where do they flow? Why do they trickle away to join that stream of boiling pitch, the hideous flood of lust? For by their own choice they lose themselves and become absorbed in it. They are diverted from their true course and deprived of their original heavenly calm.

Of course this does not mean that we must arm ourselves against compassion. There are times when we must welcome sorrow on behalf of others. But for the sake of our souls we must beware of uncleanness. My God must be the Keeper of my soul, the God of our fathers, who is to be exalted and extolled for ever more. My soul must guard against uncleanness.

I am not nowadays insensible to pity. But in those days I used to share the joy of stage lovers and their sinful pleasure in each other even though it was all done in make-believe for the sake of entertainment; and when they were parted, pity of a sort led me to share their grief. I enjoyed both these emotions equally. But now I feel more pity for a man who is happy in his sins than for one who has to endure the ordeal of forgoing some harmful pleasure or being deprived of some enjoyment which was really an affliction. Of the two, this sort of pity is certainly the more genuine, but the sorrow which it causes is not a source of pleasure. For although a man who is sorry for the sufferings of others deserves praise for his charity, nevertheless, if his pity is genuine, he would prefer that there should be no cause for his sorrow. If the impossible could happen and kindness were unkind, a man whose sense of pity was true and sincere might want others to suffer so that he could pity them. Sorrow may therefore be commendable but never desirable. For it is powerless to stab you, Lord God, and this is why the love you bear for our souls and the compassion you show for them are pure and unalloyed, far purer than the love and pity which we feel ourselves. But *who can prove himself worthy of such a calling?*[21]

However, in those unhappy days I enjoyed the pangs of sorrow. I always looked for things to wring my heart and the more tears an actor caused me to shed by his performance on the stage, even though he was portraying the imaginary distress of others, the more delightful and attractive I found it. Was it any wonder that I, the unhappy sheep who strayed from your flock, impatient of your shepherding, became infected with a loathsome mange? Hence my love of things which made me sad. I did not seek the kind of sorrow which would wound me deeply, for I had no wish to endure the sufferings which I saw on the stage; but I enjoyed fables and fictions, which could only graze the skin. But where the fingers scratch, the skin becomes inflamed. It swells and festers with hideous pus. And the same happened to me. Could the life I led be called true life, my God?

3

Yet all the while, far above, your mercy hovered faithfully about me. I exhausted myself in depravity, in the pursuit of an unholy curiosity. I deserted you and sank to the bottom-most depths of scepticism and the mockery of devil-worship. My sins were a sacrifice to the devil, and for all of them you chastised me. I defied you even so far as to relish the thought of lust, and gratify it too, within the walls of your church during the celebration of your mysteries. For such a deed I deserved to pluck the fruit of death, and you punished me for it with a heavy lash. But, compared with my guilt, the penalty was nothing. How infinite is your mercy, my God! You are my Refuge from the terrible dangers amongst which I wandered, head on high, intent upon withdrawing still further from you. I loved my own way, not yours, but it was a truant's freedom that I loved.

Besides these pursuits I was also studying for the law. Such ambition was held to be honourable and I determined to succeed in it. The more unscrupulous I was, the greater my reputation was likely to be, for men are so blind that they even take pride in their blindness. By now I was at the top of the school of rhetoric. I was pleased with my superior status and swollen with conceit. All the same, as you well know, Lord, I behaved far more quietly than the 'Wreckers', a title of ferocious devilry which the fashionable set chose for themselves. I had nothing whatever to do with their outbursts of violence, but I lived amongst them, feeling a perverse sense of shame because I was not like them. I kept company with them and there were times when I found their friendship a pleasure, but I always had a horror of what they did when they lived up to their name. Without provocation they would set upon some timid newcomer, gratuitously affronting his sense of decency for their own amusement and using it as fodder for their spiteful jests. This was the devil's own behaviour or not far different. 'Wreckers' was a fit name for them, for they were already adrift and total wrecks themselves. The mockery and trickery which they loved to practise on others was a secret snare of the devil, by which they were mocked and tricked themselves.

4

These were the companions with whom I studied the art of eloquence at that impressionable age. It was my ambition to be a good speaker, for the unhallowed and inane purpose of gratifying human vanity. The prescribed course of study brought me to a work by an author named Cicero, whose writing nearly everyone admires, if not the spirit of it. The title of the book is *Hortensius* and it recommends the reader to study philosophy. It altered my outlook on life. It changed my prayers to you, O Lord, and provided me with new hopes and aspirations. All my empty dreams suddenly lost their charm and my heart began to throb with a bewildering passion for the wisdom of eternal truth. I began to climb out of the depths to which I had sunk, in order to return to you. For I did not use the book as a whetstone to sharpen my tongue. It was not the style of it but the contents which won me over, and yet the allowance which my mother paid me was supposed to be spent on putting an edge on my tongue. I was now in my nineteenth year and she supported me, because my father had died two years before.

My God, how I burned with longing to have wings to carry me back to you, away from all earthly things, although I had no idea what you would do with me! For *yours is the wisdom.*[22] In Greek the word 'philosophy' means 'love of wisdom', and it was with this love that the *Hortensius* inflamed me. There are people for whom philosophy is a means of misleading others, for they misuse its great name, its attractions, and its integrity to give colour and gloss to their own errors. Most of these so-called philosophers who lived in Cicero's time and before are noted in the book. He shows them up in their true colours and makes quite clear how wholesome is the admonition which the Holy Spirit gives in the words of your good and true servant, Paul: *Take care not to let anyone cheat you with his philosophizings, with empty fantasies drawn from human tradition, from worldly principles; they were never Christ's teaching. In Christ the whole plenitude of Deity is embodied and dwells in him.*[23]

But, O Light of my heart, you know that at that time, although Paul's words were not known to me, the only thing that pleased me in Cicero's book was his advice not simply to admire one or another of the schools of philosophy, but to love wisdom itself, whatever it might be, and to search for it, pursue it, hold it, and embrace it firmly. These were the words which excited me and set me burning with fire, and the only check to this blaze of enthusiasm was that they made no mention of the name of Christ. For by your mercy, Lord, from the time when my mother fed me at the breast my infant heart had been suckled dutifully on his name, the name of your Son, my Saviour. Deep inside my heart his name remained, and nothing could entirely captivate me, however learned, however neatly expressed, however true it might be, unless his name were in it.

5

So I made up my mind to examine the holy Scriptures and see what kind of books they were. I discovered something that was at once beyond the understanding of the proud and hidden from the eyes of children. Its gait was humble, but the heights it reached were sublime. It was enfolded in mysteries, and I was not the kind of man to enter into it or bow my head to follow where it led. But these were not the feelings I had when I first read the Scriptures. To me they seemed quite unworthy of comparison with the stately prose of Cicero, because I had too much conceit to accept their simplicity and not enough insight to penetrate their depths. It is surely true that as the child grows these books grow with him. But I was too proud to call myself a child. I was inflated with self-esteem, which made me think myself a great man.

6

I fell in with a set of sensualists, men with glib tongues who ranted and raved and had the snares of the devil in their mouths. They baited the traps by confusing the syllables of the names of God the Father, God the Son Our Lord Jesus Christ, and God the Holy Ghost, the Paraclete, who comforts us. These names were always on the tips of their tongues, but only as sounds which they mouthed aloud, for in their hearts they had no inkling of the truth. Yet 'Truth and truth alone' was the motto which they repeated to me again and again, although the truth was nowhere to be found in them. All that they said was false, both what they said about you, who truly are the Truth, and what they said about this world and its first principles, which were your creation. But I ought not to have been content with what the philosophers said about such things, even when they spoke the truth. I should have passed beyond them for love of you, my supreme Father, my good Father, in whom all beauty has its source.

Truth! Truth! How the very marrow of my soul within me yearned for it as they dinned it in my ears over and over again! To them it was no more than a name to be voiced or a word to be read in their libraries of huge books. But while my hunger was for you, for Truth itself, these were the dishes on which they served me up the sun and the moon, beautiful works of yours but still only your works, not you yourself nor even the greatest of your created things.[24] For your spiritual works are greater than these material things, however brightly they may shine in the sky.

But my hunger and thirst were not even for the greatest of your works, but for you, my God, because you are Truth itself *with whom there can be no change, no swerving from your course.*[25] Yet the dishes they set before me were still loaded with dazzling fantasies, illusions with which the eye deceives the mind. It would have been better to love the sun itself, which at least is real as far as we can see. But I gulped down this food, because I thought that it was you. I had no relish for it, because the taste it left in my mouth was not the taste of truth—it could not be, for it was not you but an empty sham. And it did not nourish me, but starved me all the more. The food we dream of is very like the food we eat when we are awake, but it does not nourish because it is only a dream. Yet the things they gave me to eat were not in the least like you, as now I know since you have spoken to me. They were dream-substances, mock realities, far less true than the real things which we see with the sight of our eyes in the sky or on the earth. These things are seen by bird and beast as well as by ourselves, and they are far more certain than any image we conceive of them. And in turn we can picture them to ourselves with greater certainty than the vaster, infinite things which we surmise from them. Such things have no existence at all, but they were the visionary foods on which I was then fed but not sustained.

But you, O God whom I love and on whom I lean in weakness so that I may be strong, you are not the sun and the moon and the stars, even though we see these bodies in the heavens; nor are you those other bodies which we do not see in the sky, for you created them and, in your reckoning, they are not even among the greatest of your works. How far, then, must you really be from those fantasies of mine, those imaginary material things which do not exist at all! The images we form in our mind's eyes, when we picture things that really do exist, are far better founded than these inventions; and the things themselves are still more certain than the images we form of them. But you are not these things. Neither are you the soul, which is the life of bodies and, since it gives them life, must be better and more certain than they are themselves. But you are the life of souls, the life of lives. You live, O Life of my soul, because you are life itself, immutable.

Where were you in those days? How far away from me? I was wandering far from you and I was not even allowed to eat the husks on which I fed the swine. For surely the fables of the poets and the penmen are better than the traps which those impostors set! There is certainly

more to be gained from verses and poems and tales like the flight of Medea than from their stories of the five elements disguised in various ways because of the five dens of darkness. These
things simply do not exist and they are death to those who believe in them. Verses and poems
can provide real food for thought, but although I used to recite verses about Medea's flight
through the air, I never maintained that they were true; and I never believed the poems which I
heard others recite. But I did believe the tales which these men told.

These were the stages of my pitiful fall into the depths of hell, as I struggled and strained
for lack of the truth. My God, you had mercy on me even before I had confessed to you; but I
now confess that all this was because I tried to find you, not through the understanding of the
mind, by which you meant us to be superior to the beasts, but through the senses of the flesh. Yet
you were deeper than my inmost understanding and higher than the topmost height that I could
reach. I had blundered upon that woman in Solomon's parable who, ignorant and unabashed,
sat at her door and said *Stolen waters are sweetest, and bread is better eating when there is none
to see.*[26] She inveigled me because she found me living in the outer world that lay before my
eyes, the eyes of the flesh, and dwelling upon the food which they provided for my mind.

7

There is another reality besides this, though I knew nothing of it. My own specious reasoning
induced me to give in to the sly arguments of fools who asked me what was the origin of evil,
whether God was confined to the limits of a bodily shape, whether he had hair and nails, and
whether men could be called just if they had more than one wife at the same time, or killed other
men, or sacrificed living animals. My ignorance was so great that these questions troubled me,
and while I thought I was approaching the truth, I was only departing the further from it. I did
not know that evil is nothing but the removal of good until finally no good remains. How could
I see this when with the sight of my eyes I saw no more than material things and with the sight
of my mind no more than their images? I did not know that God is a spirit, a being without bulk
and without limbs defined in length and breadth. For bulk is less in the part than in the whole,
and if it is infinite, it is less in any part of it which can be defined within fixed limits than it is in
its infinity. It cannot, therefore, be everywhere entirely whole, as a spirit is and as God is. Nor
had I the least notion what it is in us that gives us our being, or what the Scriptures mean when
they say that we are made in God's image.

I knew nothing of the true underlying justice which judges, not according to convention,
but according to the truly equitable law of Almighty God. This is the law by which each age and
place forms rules of conduct best suited to itself, although the law itself is always and everywhere the same and does not differ from place to place or from age to age. I did not see that by
the sanction of this law Abraham and Isaac, Jacob, Moses, David, and the others whom God
praised were just men, although they have been reckoned sinners by men who are not qualified
to judge, for they try them by human standards and assess all the rights and wrongs of the
human race by the measure of their own customs. Anyone who does this behaves like a man
who knows nothing about armour and cannot tell which piece is meant for which part of the
body, so that he tries to cover his head with a shin-piece and fix a helmet on his foot, and then
complains because they will not fit; or like a shopkeeper who is allowed to sell his wares in the
morning, but grumbles because the afternoon is a public holiday and he is not allowed to trade;
or like a man who sees one of the servants in a house handling things which the cellar-man is
not allowed to touch, or finds something being done in the stableyard which is not allowed in
the dining-room, and is then indignant because the members of the household, living together in
one house, are not all given the same privileges in all parts of the house.

The people of whom I am speaking have the same sort of grievance when they hear that things which good men could do without sin in days gone by are not permitted in ours, and that God gave them one commandment and has given us another. He has done this because the times have demanded it, although men were subject to the same justice in those days as we are in these. Yet those who complain about this understand that when we are dealing with a single man, a single day, or a single house, each part of the whole has a different function suited to it. What may be done at one time of day is not allowed at the next, and what may be done, or must be done, in one room is forbidden and punished in another. This does not mean that justice is erratic or variable, but that the times over which it presides are not always the same, for it is the nature of time to change. Man's life on earth is short and he cannot, by his own perception, see the connexion between the conditions of earlier times and of other nations, which he has not experienced himself, and those of his own times, which are familiar to him. But when only one individual, one day, or one house is concerned, he can easily see what is suitable for each part of the whole and for each member of the household, and what must be done at which times and places. These things he accepts: but with the habits of other ages he finds fault.

I knew nothing of this at that time. I was quite unconscious of it, quite blind to it, although it stared me in the face. When I composed verses, I could not fit any foot in any position that I pleased. Each metre was differently scanned and I could not put the same foot in every position in the same line. And yet the art of poetry, by which I composed, does not vary from one line to another: it is the same for all alike. But I did not discern that justice, which those good and holy men obeyed, in a far more perfect and sublime way than poetry contains in itself at one and the same time all the principles which it prescribes, without discrepancy; although, as times change, it prescribes and apportions them, not all at once, but according to the needs of the times. Blind to this, I found fault with the holy patriarchs not only because, in their own day, they acted as God commanded and inspired them, but also because they predicted the future as he revealed it to them.

8

Surely it is never wrong at any time or in any place for a man to *love God with his whole heart and his whole soul and his whole mind* and to *love his neighbour as himself*?[27] Sins against nature, therefore, like the sin of Sodom, are abominable and deserve punishment wherever and whenever they are committed. If all nations committed them, all alike would be held guilty of the same charge in God's law, for our Maker did not prescribe that we should use each other in this way. In fact the relationship which we ought to have with God is itself violated when our nature, of which he is the Author, is desecrated by perverted lust.

On the other hand, offences against human codes of conduct vary according to differences of custom, so that no one, whether he is a native or a foreigner, may, to suit his own pleasure, violate the conventions established by the customary usage or the law of the community or the state. For any part that is out of keeping with the whole is at fault. But if God commands a nation to do something contrary to its customs or constitutions, it must be done even if it has never been done in that country before. If it is a practice which has been discontinued, it must be resumed, and if it was not a law before, it must be enacted. In his own kingdom a king has the right to make orders which neither he nor any other has ever made before. Obedience to his orders is not against the common interest of the community; in fact, if they were disobeyed, the common interest would suffer, because it is the general agreement in human communities that the ruler is obeyed. How much more right, then, has God to give commands, since he is the Ruler of all creation and all his creatures must obey his commandments without demur! For all must yield to God just as, in the government of human society, the lesser authority must yield to the greater.

With sins of violence the case is the same as with sins against nature. Here the impulse is to injure others, either by word or by deed, but by whichever means it is done, there are various reasons for doing it. A man may injure his enemy for the sake of revenge; a robber may assault a traveller to secure for himself something that is not his own; or a man may attack someone whom he fears in order to avoid danger to himself. Or the injury may be done from envy, which will cause an unhappy man to harm another more fortunate than himself or a rich man to harm someone whose rivalry he fears for the future or already resents. Again, it may be done for the sheer joy of seeing others suffer, as is the case with those who watch gladiators or make fun of other people and jeer at them.

These are the main categories of sin. They are hatched from the lust for power, from gratification of the eye, and from gratification of corrupt nature—from one or two of these or from all three together. Because of them, O God most high, most sweet, our lives offend against your *ten-stringed harp,*[28] your commandments, the three which proclaim our duty to you and the seven which proclaim our duty to men.

But how can sins of vice be against you, since you cannot be marred by perversion? How can sins of violence be against you, since nothing can injure you? Your punishments are for the sins which men commit against themselves, because although they sin against you, they do wrong to their own souls and their malice is self-betrayed.[29] They corrupt and pervert their own nature, which you made and for which you shaped the rules, either by making wrong use of the things which you allow, or by becoming inflamed with passion to make unnatural use of things which you do not allow. Or else their guilt consists in raving against you in their hearts and with their tongues and *kicking against the goad,*[30] or in playing havoc with the restrictions of human society and brazenly exulting in private feuds and factions, each according to his fancies or his fads.

This is what happens, O Fountain of life, when we abandon you, who are the one true Creator of all that ever was or is, and each of us proudly sets his heart on some one part of your creation instead of on the whole. So it is by the path of meekness and devotion that we must return to you. You rid us of our evil habits and forgive our sins when we confess to you. You *listen to the groans of the prisoners*[31] and free us from the chains which we have forged for ourselves. This you do for us unless we toss our heads against you in the illusion of liberty and in our greed for gain, at the risk of losing all, love our own good better than you yourself, who are the common good of all.

9

Among these vices and crimes and all the endless ways in which men do wrong there are also the sins of those who follow the right path but go astray. By the rule of perfection these lapses are condemned, if we judge them aright, but the sinners may yet be praised, for they give promise of better fruit to come, like the young shoots which later bear the ears of corn. Sometimes we also do things which have every appearance of being sins against nature or against our fellow men, but are not sins because they offend neither you, the Lord our God, nor the community in which we live. For example, a man may amass a store of goods to meet the needs of life or some contingency, but it does not necessarily follow that he is a miser. Or he may be punished by those whose duty it is to correct misdemeanours, but it is by no means certain that they do it out of wanton cruelty. Many of the things we do may therefore seem wrong to men but are approved in the light of your knowledge, and many which men applaud are condemned in your eyes. This is because the appearance of what we do is often different from the intention with which we do it, and the circumstances at the time may not be clear.

But when you suddenly command us to do something strange and unforeseen, even if you had previously forbidden it, none can doubt that the command must be obeyed, even though, for the time being, you may conceal the reason for it and it may conflict with the established rule of custom in some forms of society; for no society is right and good unless it obeys you. But happy are they who know that the commandment was yours. For all that your servants do is done as an example of what is needed for the present or as a sign of what is yet to come.

10

I was ignorant of this and derided those holy servants and prophets of yours. But all that I achieved by deriding them was to earn your derision for myself, for I was gradually led to believe such nonsense as that a fig wept when it was plucked, and that the tree which bore it shed tears of mother's milk. But if some sanctified member of the sect were to eat the fig— someone else, of course, would have committed the sin of plucking it—he would digest it and breathe it out again in the form of angels or even as particles of God, retching them up as he groaned in prayer. These particles of the true and supreme God were supposed to be imprisoned in the fruit and could only be released by means of the stomach and teeth of one of the elect. I was foolish enough to believe that we should show more kindness to the fruits of the earth than to mankind, for whose use they were intended. If a starving man, not a Manichee, were to beg for a mouthful, they thought it a crime worthy of mortal punishment to give him one.

11

But *you sent down your help from above*[32] and rescued my soul from the depths of this darkness because my mother, your faithful servant, wept to you for me, shedding more tears for my spiritual death than other mothers shed for the bodily death of a son. For in her faith and in the spirit which she had from you she looked on me as dead. You heard her and did not despise the tears which streamed down and watered the earth in every place where she bowed her head in prayer. You heard her, for how else can I explain the dream with which you consoled her, so that she agreed to live with me and eat at the same table in our home? Lately she had refused to do this, because she loathed and shunned the blasphemy of my false beliefs.

She dreamed that she was standing on a wooden rule, and coming towards her in a halo of splendour she saw a young man who smiled at her in joy, although she herself was sad and quite consumed with grief. He asked her the reason for her sorrow and her daily tears, not because he did not know, but because he had something to tell her, for this is what happens in visions. When she replied that her tears were for the soul I had lost, he told her to take heart for, if she looked carefully, she would see that where she was, there also was I. And when she looked, she saw me standing beside her on the same rule.

Where could this dream have come from, unless it was that you listened to the prayer of her heart? For your goodness is almighty; you take good care of each of us as if you had no others in your care, and you look after all as you look after each. And surely it was for the same reason that, when she told me of the dream and I tried to interpret it as a message that she need not despair of being one day such as I was then, she said at once and without hesitation 'No! He did not say "Where he is, you are", but "Where you are, he is".'

I have often said before and, to the best of my memory, I now declare to you, Lord, that I was much moved by this answer, which you gave me through my mother. She was not disturbed by my interpretation of her dream, plausible though it was, but quickly saw the true meaning, which I had not seen until she spoke. I was more deeply moved by this than by the dream itself, in which the joy for which this devout woman had still so long to wait was foretold so long before to comfort her in the time of her distress. For nearly nine years were yet to come during which I wallowed deep in the mire and the darkness of delusion. Often I tried to lift myself, only to plunge the deeper. Yet all the time this chaste, devout, and prudent woman, a widow such as is close to your heart, never ceased to pray at all hours and to offer you the tears she shed for me. The dream had given new spirit to her hope, but she gave no rest to her sighs and her tears. *Her prayers reached your presence*[33] and yet you still left me to twist and turn in the dark.

12

I remember that in the meantime you gave her another answer to her prayers, though there is much besides this that escapes my memory and much too that I must omit, because I am in haste to pass on to other things, which I am more anxious to confess to you.

This other answer you gave her through the mouth of one of your priests, a bishop who had lived his life in the Church and was well versed in the Scriptures. My mother asked him, as a favour, to have a talk with me, so that he might refute my errors, drive the evil out of my mind, and replace it with good. He often did this when he found suitable pupils, but he refused to do it for me—a wise decision, as I afterwards realized. He told her that I was still unripe for instruction because, as she had told him, I was brimming over with the novelty of the heresy and had already upset a great many simple people with my casuistry. 'Leave him alone', he said. 'Just pray to God for him. From his own reading he will discover his mistakes and the depth of his profanity.'

At the same time he told her that when he was a child his misguided mother had handed him over to the Manichees. He had not only read almost all their books, but had also made copies of them, and even though no one argued the case with him or put him right, he had seen for himself that he ought to have nothing to do with the sect; and accordingly he had left it. Even after she had heard this my mother still would not be pacified, but persisted all the more with her tears and her entreaties that he should see me and discuss the matter. At last he grew impatient and said 'Leave me and go in peace. It cannot be that the son of these tears should be lost.'

In later years, as we walked together, she used to say that she accepted these words as a message from heaven.

Notes

1. Cicero, *Tusculanae disputationes* I, 26.
2. Terence, *Eunuchus* III, 5.
3. Virgil, *Aeneid* I, 37–49.
4. See Ps. 85: 15 (86: 15).
5. Ps. 26: 8 (27: 8).
6. Matt. 19: 14.
7. I Cor. 7: 28.
8. I Cor. 7: 1.
9. I Cor. 7:32, 33.
10. Matt. 19: 12.
11. See Ps. 93: 20 (94: 20).
12. See Deut. 32: 39.

13. See Ps. 72: 7 (73: 7).
14. Ps. 63: 11 (64: 10).
15. Sallust, *Catilina* XVI.
16. Sallust, *Catilina* XVI.
17. Ps. 115: 12 (116: 12).
18. Rom. 6: 21.
19. Ps. 18: 13 (19: 12).
20. Matt. 25: 21.
21. II Cor. 2: 16.
22. Job 12: 13.
23. Col. 2: 8, 9.
24. Saint Augustine is here speaking of the Manichees, for whom astronomy was a part of theology.
25. James I: 17.
26. Prov. 9: 17.
27. Matt. 22: 37, 39.
28. Ps. 143: 9 (144: 9)
29. See Ps. 26: 12 (27: 12).
30. Acts, 9:5.
31. Ps. 101: 21 (102: 20).
32. Ps. 143: 7 (144: 7).
33. Ps. 87: 3 (88: 2).

THE KORAN

Introduction by Michael Levin

In the year 610 A.D., a man named Muhammed was praying alone in a cave just outside the city of Mecca, in what is now Saudi Arabia. Suddenly he heard a great voice command him to "read!" Mystified Muhammed asked "what should I read?" The voice answered, "read that which man knew not." Then Muhammed turned and saw who was speaking to him—the angel Gabriel (or, in Arabic, Jibrail), who told Muhammed that God had chosen him to receive the last and greatest of divine revelations. When Muhammed emerged from the cave, he had the words of the Koran (which means "reading" or "recitation") inscribed in his heart. Muhammed began to preach the message of God (Allah) in Mecca, and quickly won many converts. Thus was born the religion of Islam.

The Koran is the scared text for Moslems, as the Bible is for Jews and Christians. Like the Bible, the Koran is a source of moral instruction and practical laws for society, as well as a guide for getting into Heaven. And also like the Bible, the Koran contains beautiful poetry. In fact, the poetic nature of the Koran may be its most confusing aspect for those reading it for the first time. The Koran has little narrative structure; stories and poetic images appear side-by-side with discussions of legal problems. This may seem strange, but new readers may also be surprised by how many similarities there are between the Koran and the Bible. The values and ideals of Islam derive from the Judeo-Christian tradition, a fact which should become clear upon reading the Koran.

The Koran is divided into chapters, called "suras," each with its own title. We have chosen the first two suras, "The Opening" and "The Cow." The first is only a few lines long, but it is important because it encapsulates many of the basics of Islam. We are told here about Allah—who He is, and what His relationship with humanity is like. Compare this vision of God with the God of the Old Testament, or with Jesus as he is described in the Gospel of Matthew. Does it seem familiar?

The second sura is much longer, and contains a great deal of information. One of the key themes of this section is the relationship between Islam and the two older religions, Judaism and Christianity. Jews and Christians are often addressed directly—what are they told? Also, note how many references to the Hebrew Scriptures there are in this sura. What purpose do they serve in the text? Incidentally, the title of this sura is a reference to the Golden Calf which the Israelites worshipped at the foot of Mount Sinai, when they lost faith in God (Exodus 32). In this sura there is a different account of this event. What point is being made about the Israelites?

Another important theme in the second sura is the question of social laws and how to be a righteous person. When reading this section, keep in mind the laws described in the Book of Exodus, as well as Jesus' explication of the Mosaic laws in the Sermon on the Mount in the Gospel of Matthew. What is similar, and what is different? Again, those encountering Islam for the first time may be surprised at how familiar much of it seems. In the modern Western world, Islam has received a great deal of bad press. Hopefully, the more we read about Islam, the less alien it will seem. Today Islam is one of the fastest growing religions in the world. As you read in the Koran, ask yourself what makes this religion so appealing to so many people?

The Koran Interpreted

I

The Opening

In the Name of God, the Merciful, the Compassionate

Praise belongs to God, the Lord of all Being,
the All-merciful, the All-compassionate,
the master of the Day of Doom.

Thee only we serve; to Thee alone we pray for succour.   5
Guide us in the straight path,
the path of those whom Thou hast blessed,
not of those against whom Thou art wrathful,
nor of those who are astray.

II

The Cow

In the Name of God, the Merciful, the Compassionate

Alif Lam Mim

That is the Book, wherein is no doubt,
a guidance to the godfearing
who believe in the Unseen, and perform the prayer,
and expend of that We have provided them;
who believe in what has been sent down to thee
and what has been sent down before thee,
and have faith in the Hereafter;
those are upon guidance from their Lord,
those are the ones who prosper.

The Koran, Oxford University Press, 1964 (ISBN 0192505963), original pp. 1–44 (Suras 1 and 2).

As for the unbelievers, alike it is to them   5
whether thou hast warned them or hast not warned them,
they do not believe.
God has set a seal on their hearts and on their hearing,
and on their eyes is a covering,
and there awaits them a mighty chastisement.

And some men there are who say,
'We believe in God and the Last Day';
but they are not believers.
They would trick God and the believers,
and only themselves they deceive,
and they are not aware.
In their hearts is a sickness,
and God has increased their sickness,
and there awaits them a painful chastisement
for that they have cried lies.
When it is said to them, 'Do not corruption in the land',   10
they say, 'We are only ones that put things right.'
Truly, they are the workers of corruption
but they are not aware.
When it is said to them, 'Believe as the people believe',
they say, 'Shall we believe, as fools believe?'
Truly, they are the foolish ones,
but they do not know.
When they meet those who believe, they say, 'We believe';
but when they go privily to their Satans, they say,
'We are with you; we were only mocking.'
God shall mock them, and shall lead them on
blindly wandering in their insolence.
Those are they that have bought error   15
at the price of guidance,
and their commerce has not profited them,
and they are not right-guided.
The likeness of them is as the likeness of a man
who kindled a fire, and when it lit all about him
God took away their light, and left them in darkness
unseeing,
deaf, dumb, blind—
so they shall not return;
or as a cloudburst out of heaven
in which is darkness, and thunder, and lightning—
they put their fingers in their ears
against the thunderclaps, fearful of death;
and God encompasses the unbelievers;
the lightning wellnigh snatches away their sight;

whensoever it gives them light, they walk in it,
and when the darkness is over them, they halt;
had God willed, He would have taken away
their hearing and their sight.
Truly, God is powerful over everything.

O you men, serve your Lord Who created you,
and those that were before you; haply so
you will be godfearing;
who assigned to you the earth for a couch,   20
and heaven for an edifice, and sent down
out of heaven water, wherewith He brought forth
fruits for your provision; so set not up
compeers to God wittingly.
And if you are in doubt concerning that We have
sent down on Our servant, then bring a sura
like it, and call your witnesses, apart from
God, if you are truthful.
And if you do not—and you will not—then
fear the Fire, whose fuel is men and stones,
prepared for unbelievers.

Give thou good tidings to those who believe
and do deeds of righteousness, that for them
await gardens underneath which rivers flow;
whensoever they are provided with fruits therefrom
they shall say, 'This is what wherewithal
we were provided before'; that they shall be
given in perfect semblance; and there
for them shall be spouses purified; therein
they shall dwell forever.

God is not ashamed to strike a similitude
even of a gnat, or aught above it.
As for the believers, they know it is the truth
from their Lord; but as for unbelievers,
they say, 'What did God desire by this
for a similitude?' Thereby He leads
many astray, and thereby He guides
many; and thereby He leads none astray
save the ungodly
such as break the covenant of God   25
after its solemn binding, and such as cut
what God has commanded should be joined,
and such as do corruption in the land—
they shall be the losers.

How do you disbelieve in God, seeing you were dead
and He gave you life, then He shall make you dead,
then He shall give you life, then unto Him
you shall be returned?
It is He who created for you all that is
in the earth, then He lifted Himself to heaven
and levelled them seven heavens; and He has
knowledge of everything.

And when thy Lord said to the angels,
'I am setting the earth a viceroy.'
They said, 'What, wilt Thou set therein one
who will do corruption there, and shed blood,
while We proclaim Thy praise and call Thee Holy?'
He said, 'Assuredly I know
that you know not.'
And He taught Adam the names, all of them;
then He presented them unto the angels
and said, 'Now tell Me the names of these,
if you speak truly.'
They said, "Glory be to Thee! We know not   30
save what Thou hast taught us. Surely Thou art
the All-knowing, the All-wise.'
He said, 'Adam, tell them their names.'
And when he had told them their names
He said, 'Did I not tell you I know
the unseen things of the heavens and earth?
And I know what things you reveal, and
what you were hiding.'
And when We said to the angels, 'Bow
yourselves to Adam'; so they bowed
themselves, save Iblis; he refused,
and waxed proud, and so he became
one of the unbelievers.
And We said, 'Adam, dwell thou, and thy wife,
in the Garden, and eat thereof easefully
where you desire; but draw not nigh this tree,
lest you be evildoers.'
Then Satan caused them to slip therefrom
and brought them out of that they were in;
and We said, 'Get you all down, each
of you an enemy of each; and in
the earth a sojourn shall be yours, and
enjoyment for a time.'
Thereafter Adam received certain words   35
from his Lord, and He turned towards him;
truly He turns, and is All-compassionate.

We said, 'Get you down out of it, all together;
yet there shall come to you guidance from Me,
and whosoever follows My guidance,
no fear shall be on them, neither shall they sorrow.
As for the unbelievers who cry lies to Our signs,
those shall be the inhabitants of the Fire,
therein dwelling forever.'

Children of Israel, remember My blessing
wherewith I blessed you, and fulfil My covenant
and I shall fulfil your covenant; and have awe of Me.
And believe in that I have sent down, confirming
that which is with you, and be not the first
to disbelieve in it. And sell not My signs
for a little price; and fear you Me.
And do not confound the truth with vanity,
and do not conceal the truth wittingly.
And perform the prayer, and pay the alms,   40
and how with those that bow. Will you bid
others to piety, and forget yourselves
while you recite the Book? Do you not understand?
Seek you help in patience and prayer,
for grievous it is, save to the humble
who reckon that they shall meet their Lord
and that unto Him they are returning.

Children of Israel, remember My blessing
wherewith I blessed you, and that I
have preferred you above all beings;
and beware of a day when no soul for another
shall give satisfaction, and no intercession   45
shall be accepted from it, nor any counterpoise
be taken, neither shall they be helped.

And when We delivered you from the folk of Pharaoh
who were visiting you with evil chastisement,
slaughtering your sons, and sparing your women;
and in that was a grievous trial from your Lord.
And when We divided for you the sea
and delivered you, and drowned Pharaoh's folk
while you were beholding.
And when We appointed with Moses forty nights
then you took to yourselves the Calf after him
and you were evildoers;
then We pardoned you after that, that haply
you should be thankful.

And when We gave to Moses the Book   50
and the Salvation, that haply
you should be guided.
And when Moses said to his people,
'My people, you have done wrong against yourselves
by your taking the Calf; now turn to your Creator
and slay one another. That will be better for you
in your Creator's sight, and He will turn to you;
truly He turns, and is All-compassionate.'
And when you said, 'Moses, we will not believe thee
till we see God openly'; and the thunderbolt took you
while you were beholding.
Then We raised you up after you were dead, that haply
you should be thankful.
And We outspread the cloud to overshadow you,
and We sent down manna and quails upon you:
'Eat of the good things wherewith We have provided you.
And they worked no wrong upon Us, but
themselves they wronged.
And when We said, 'Enter this township,   55
and eat easefully of it wherever you will,
and enter in at the gate, prostrating,
and say, Unburdening; We will forgive you
your transgressions, and increase the good-doers.'
Then the evildoers substituted a saying
other than that which had been said to them;
so We sent down upon the evildoers
wrath out of heaven for their ungodliness.
And when Moses sought water for his people,
so We said, 'Strike with thy staff the rock';
and there gushed forth from it twelve fountains;
all the people knew now their drinking-place.
'Eat and drink of God's providing, and
mischief not in the earth, doing corruption.'
And when you said, 'Moses, we will not endure
one sort of food; pray to thy Lord for us, that He
may bring forth for us of that the earth produces—
green herbs, cucumbers, corn, lentils, onions.'
He said, 'Would you have in exchange what is meaner
for what is better? Get you down to Egypt;
you shall have there that you demanded.'
And abasement and poverty were pitched upon them,
and they were laden with the burden of God's anger;
that, because they had disbelieved the signs of God
and slain the Prophets unrightfully; that,
because they disobeyed, and were transgressors.
Surely they that believe, and those of Jewry,

and the Christians, and those Sabaeans,
whoso believes in God and the Last Day, and works
righteousness—their wage awaits them with their Lord,
and no fear shall be on them, neither shall they sorrow.

And when We took compact with you, and raised above you   60
the Mount: 'Take forcefully what We have given you, and
remember what is in it; haply you shall be godfearing.'
Then you turned away thereafter, and but for the bounty
and mercy of God towards you, you had been of the losers.
And well you know there were those among you
that transgressed the Sabbath, and We said to them,
'Be you apes, miserably slinking!'
And We made it a punishment exemplary
for all the former times and for the latter,
and an admonition to such as are godfearing.
And when Moses said to his people,
'God commands you to sacrifice a cow.' They said,
'Dost thou take us in mockery?' He said,
'I take refuge with God, lest I should be
one of the ignorant.' They said, 'Pray to thy Lord
for us, that He may make clear to us what she may be.'
He said, 'He says she is a cow neither old, nor virgin,
middling between the two; so do that you are bidden.'
They said, 'Pray to thy Lord for us, that He make clear   65
to us what her colour may be.' He said, 'He says
she shall be a golden cow, bright her colour,
gladdening the beholders.' They said, 'Pray
to thy Lord for us, that He make clear to us
what she may be; cows are much alike to us;
and, if God will, we shall then be guided.'
He said, 'He says she shall be a cow not broken
to plough the earth or to water the tillage,
one kept secure, with no blemish on her.' They said,
'Now thou hast brought the truth'; and therefore they
sacrificed her, a thing they had scarcely done.
And when you killed a living soul, and disputed
thereon—and God disclosed what you were hiding—
so We said, 'Smite him with part of it'; even so
God brings to life the dead, and He shows you
His signs, that haply you may have understanding.
Then your hearts became hardened thereafter
and are like stones, or even yet harder;
for there are stones from which rivers come gushing,
and others split, so that water issues from them,
and others crash down in the fear of God.
And God is not heedless of the things you do.

Are you then so eager that they should believe you,   70
seeing there is a party of them that heard
God's word, and then tampered with it, and that
after they had comprehended it, wittingly?
And when they meet those who believe, they say
'We believe'; and when they go privily
one to another, they say, 'Do you speak to them
of what God has revealed to you, that they may
thereby dispute with you before your Lord?
Have you no understanding?'
Know they not that God knows what they keep secret
and what they publish?
And some there are of them that are common folk
not knowing the Book, but only fancies
and mere conjectures. So woe to those
who write the Book with their hands, then say,
'This is from God,' that they may sell it
for a little price; so woe to them
for what their hands have written, and woe
to them for their earnings.
And they say, 'The Fire shall not touch us
save a number of days.' Say: 'Have you taken
with God a covenant? God will not fail in His
covenant; or say you things against God
of which you know nothing?
Not so; whoso earns evil, and is encompassed by   75
his transgression—those are the inhabitants of the Fire;
there they shall dwell forever.
And those that believe, and do deeds of
righteousness—those are the inhabitants of Paradise;
there they shall dwell forever.'

And when We took compact with the Children of Israel:
'You shall not serve any save God;
and to be good to parents, and the near kinsman,
and to orphans, and to the needy;
and speak good to men, and perform the prayer,
and pay the alms.' Then you turned away,
all but a few of you, swerving aside.
And when We took compact with you: 'You shall not
shed your own blood, neither expel your own
from your habitations'; then you confirmed it
and yourselves bore witness. Then there you are
killing one another, and expelling a party of you
from their habitations, conspiring against them
in sin and enmity; and if they come to you
as captives, you ransom them; yet their expulsion

was forbidden you. What, do you believe
in part of the Book, and disbelieve in part?
What shall be the recompense of those of you who
do that, but degradation in the present life,
and on the Day of Resurrection to be returned
unto the most terrible of chastisement?
And God is not heedless of the things you do.
Those who have purchased the present life at the price   80
of the world to come—for them the chastisement
shall not be lightened, neither shall they be helped.

And We gave to Moses the Book, and after him
sent succeeding Messengers; and We gave Jesus
son of Mary the clear signs, and confirmed him
with the Holy Spirit; and whensoever
there came to you a Messenger with that your souls
had not desire for, did you become arrogant,
and some cry lies to, and some slay?

And they say, 'Our hearts are uncircumcised.'
Nay, but God has cursed them for their unbelief;
little will they believe. When there came to them
a Book from God, confirming what was with them—
and they aforetimes prayed for victory
over the unbelievers—when there came to them
that they recognized, they disbelieved in it;
and the curse of God is on the unbelievers.
Evil is the thing they have sold themselves for,
disbelieving in that which God sent down,
grudging that God should send down of His bounty
on whomsoever He will of His servants,
and they were laden with anger upon anger;
and for unbelievers awaits a humbling chastisement.
And when they were told, 'Believe in that   85
God has sent down,' they said, 'We believe
in what was sent down on us'; and they disbelieve
in what is beyond that, yet it is the truth
confirming what is with them. Say: 'Why then
were you slaying the Prophets of God
in former time, if you were believers?'

And Moses came to you with the clear signs,
then you took to yourselves the Calf after him
and you were evildoers.
And when We took compact with you, and raised over you
the Mount: 'Take forcefully what We have given you
and give ear.' They said, 'We hear, and rebel';

and they were made to drink the Calf in their hearts
for their unbelief. Say: 'Evil is the thing
your faith bids you to, if you are believers.
Say: 'If the Last Abode with God is yours
exclusively, and not for other people,
then long for death—if you speak truly.'
But they will never long for it, because of that
their hands have forwarded; God knows the evildoers;
and thou shalt find them the eagerest of men   90
for life. And of the idolaters; there is one of them
wishes if he might be spared a thousand years,
yet his being spared alive shall not remove him
from the chastisement. God sees the things they do.
Say: 'Whosoever is an enemy to Gabriel—
he it was that brought it down upon thy heart
by the leave of God, confirming what was before it,
and for a guidance and good tidings to the believers.
Whosoever is an enemy to God and His angels
and His Messengers, and Gabriel, and Michael—
surely God is an enemy to the unbelievers.'
And We have sent down unto thee signs, clear signs,
and none disbelieves in them except the ungodly.

Why, whensoever they have made a covenant,
does a party of them reject it?
Nay, but the most of them are unbelievers.
When there has come to them a Messenger from God   95
confirming what was with them, a party of them
that were given the Book reject the Book of God
behind their backs, as though they knew not,
and they follow what the Satans recited
over Solomon's kingdom. Solomon disbelieved not,
but the Satans disbelieved, teaching
the people sorcery, and that which was sent down
upon Babylon's two angels, Harut and Marut;
they taught not any man, without they said,
'We are but a temptation; do not disbelieve.'
From them they learned how they might divide
a man and his wife, yet they did not hurt
any man thereby, save by the leave of God,
and they learned what hurt them, and did not
profit them, knowing well that whoso buys it
shall have no share in the world to come;
evil then was that they sold themselves for,
if they had but known.
Yet had they believed, and been godfearing,

a recompense from God had been better,
if they had but known.

O believers; do not say, 'Observe us,'
but say, 'Regard us'; and give ear;
for unbelievers awaits a painful chastisement.

Those unbelievers of the People of the Book
and the idolaters wish not that any good
should be sent down upon you from your Lord;
but God singles out for His mercy whom He will;
God is of bounty abounding.

And for whatever verse We abrogate   100
or cast into oblivion, We bring a better
or the like of it; knowst thou not that God
is powerful over everything?
Knowest thou not that to God belongs
the kingdom of the heavens and the earth,
and that you have none, apart from God,
neither protector nor helper?
Or do you desire to question your Messenger
as Moses was questioned in former time?
Whoso exchanges belief for unbelief has surely
strayed from the right way.

Many of the People of the Book wish they might
restore you as unbelievers, after you have believed,
in the jealousy of their souls, after the truth
has become clear to them; yet do you pardon
and be forgiving, till God brings His command;
truly God is powerful over everything.
And perform the prayer, and pay the alms; whatever
good you shall forward to your souls' account,
you shall find it with God; assuredly God
sees the things you do.
And they say, 'None shall enter Paradise   105
except that they be Jews or Christians.'
Such are their fancies. Say: 'Produce your proof,
if you speak truly.'
Nay, but whosoever submits his will to God,
being a good-doer, his wage is with his Lord,
and no fear shall be on them, neither shall they sorrow.

The Jews say, 'The Christians stand not on anything';
the Christians say, 'The Jews stand not on anything';

yet they recite the Book. So too the ignorant
say the like of them. God shall decide between them
on the Day of Resurrection touching their differences.
And who does greater evil than he who bars
God's places of worship, so that His Name
be not rehearsed in them, and strives to destroy them?
Such men might never enter them, save in fear;
for them is degradation in the present world,
and in the world to come a mighty chastisement.

To God belong the East and West;
whithersoever you turn, there is the Face of God;
God is All-embracing, All-knowing.

And they say, 'God has taken to Him a son.'   110
Glory be to Him! Nay, to Him belongs
all that is in the heavens and the earth;
all obey His will—
the Creator of the heavens and the earth;
and when He decrees a thing, He but says to it
'Be,' and it is.
And they that know not say, 'Why does God not
speak to us? Why does a sign not come to us?'
So spoke those before them as these men say;
their hearts are much alike. Yet We have made
clear the signs unto a people who are sure.
We have sent thee with the truth, good tidings
to bear, and warning. Thou shalt not be questioned
touching the inhabitants of Hell.
Never will the Jews be satisfied with thee,
neither the Christians, not till thou followest
their religion. Say: 'God's guidance
is the true guidance.' If thou followest
their caprices, after the knowledge that
has come to thee, thou shalt have against God
neither protector nor helper.
Those to whom We have given the Book   115
and who recite it with true recitation,
they believe in it; and whoso disbelieves in it,
they shall be the losers

Children of Israel, remember My blessing
wherewith I blessed you, and that I
have preferred you above all beings;
and beware a day when no soul for another
shall give satisfaction, and no counterpoise
shall be accepted from it, nor any

intercession shall be profitable to it,
neither shall they be helped.

And when his Lord tested Abraham
with certain words, and he fulfilled them.
He said, 'Behold, I make you a leader
for the people.' Said he, 'And of my seed?'
He said 'My covenant shall not reach
the evildoers.'
And when We appointed the House to be
a place of visitation for the people,
and a sanctuary,
and: 'Take to yourselves Abraham's station
for a place of prayer.' And We made covenant
with Abraham and Ishmael: 'Purify
My House for those that shall go about it
and those that cleave to it, to those who bow
and prostrate themselves.'
And when Abraham said, 'My Lord, make this   120
a land secure, and provide its people
with fruits, such of them as believe in
God and the Last Day.'
He said, 'And whoso disbelieves, to him
I shall give enjoyment a little, then I
shall compel him to the chastisement of the Fire—
how evil a homecoming!'
And when Abraham, and Ishmael with him,
raised up the foundations of the House:
'Our Lord, receive this from us; Thou art
the All-hearing, the All-knowing;
and, our Lord, make us submissive to Thee,
and of our seed a nation submissive
to Thee; and show us our holy rites, and
turn towards us; surely Thou turnest, and art
All-compassionate;
and, our Lord, do Thou send among them
a Messenger, one of them, who shall recite
to them Thy signs, and teach them the Book
and the Wisdom, and purify them; Thou art
the All-mighty, the All-wise.'
Who therefore shrinks from the religion
of Abraham, except he be foolish-minded?
Indeed, We chose him in the present world,
and in the world to come he shall be
among the righteous.
When his Lord said to him, 'Surrender,'   125
he said, 'I have surrendered me to

the Lord of all Being.'
And Abraham charged his sons with this
and Jacob likewise: 'My sons, God has chosen
for you the religion; see that you die not
save in surrender.'
Why, were you witnesses, when death came
to Jacob? When he said to his sons,
'What will you serve after me?' They said,
'We will serve thy God and the God of thy fathers
Abraham, Ishmael and Isaac, One God;
to Him we surrender.'
That is a nation that has passed away;
there awaits them that they have earned,
and there awaits you that you have earned;
you shall not be questioned concerning
the things they did.

And they say, 'Be Jews or Christians and
you shall be guided.' Say thou: 'Nay, rather
the creed of Abraham, a man of pure faith;
he was no idolater.'
Say you: 'We believe in God, and   130
in that which has been sent down on us
and sent down on Abraham, Ishmael,
Isaac and Jacob, and the Tribes,
and that which was given to Moses and Jesus
and the Prophets, of their Lord; we
make no division between any of them, and
to Him we surrender.
And if they believe in the like of that you
believe in, then they are truly guided; but if
they turn away, then they are clearly in schism;
God will suffice you for them; He is
the All-hearing, the All-knowing;
the baptism of God; and who is there
that baptizes fairer than God?
Him we are serving.
Say: 'Would you then dispute with us
concerning God, who is our Lord
and your Lord? Our deeds belong to us,
and to you belong your deeds; Him
we serve sincerely.
Or do you say, "Abraham, Ishamel,
Isaac and Jacob, and the Tribes—
they were Jews, or they were Christians"?'
Say: 'Have you then greater knowledge,

or God? And who does greater evil than
he who conceals a testimony received
from God? And God is not heedless of
the things you do.'
That is a nation that has passed away;   135
there awaits them that they have earned,
and there awaits you that you have earned;
you shall not be questioned concerning
the things they did.

The fools among the people will say,
'What has turned them from the direction
they were facing in their prayers aforetime?'
Say:
'To God belong the East and the West;
He guides whomsoever He will
to a straight path.'

Thus We appointed you a midmost nation
that you might be witnesses to the people,
and that the Messenger might be a witness
to you; and We did not appoint the direction
thou wast facing, except that We might know
who followed the Messenger from him who turned
on his heels—though it were a grave thing
save for those whom God has guided; but
God would never leave your faith to waste—
truly, God is All-gentle with the people,
All-compassionate.
We have seen thee turning thy face about
in the heaven; now We will surely turn thee
to a direction that shall satisfy thee.
Turn thy face towards the Holy Mosque; and
wherever you are, turn your faces towards it.
Those who have been given the Book know it is
the truth from their Lord; God is not heedless of
the things they do.
Yet if thou shouldst bring to those that have been   140
given the Book every sign, they will not follow
thy direction; thou art not a follower
of their direction, neither are they followers
of one another's direction. If thou followest
their caprices, after the knowledge
that has come to three, then thou wilt surely be
among the evildoers
whom We have given the Book, and they recognize

as they recognize their sons, even though
there is a party of them conceal the truth
and that wittingly.
The truth comes from thy Lord; then be not
among the doubters.
Every man has his direction to which he turns;
so be you forward in good works. Wherever
you may be, God will bring you all together;
surely God is powerful over everything.
From whatsoever place thou issuest, turn
thy face towards the Holy Mosque; it is
the truth from thy Lord. God is not heedless of
the things you do.
From whatsoever place thou issuest, turn   145
thy face towards the Holy Mosque; and
wherever you may be, turn your faces
towards it, that the people may not have
any argument against you, excepting
the evildoers of them; and fear you them not,
but fear you Me; and that I may perfect
My blessing upon you, and that haply so
you may be guided;
as also We have sent among you, of yourselves,
a Messenger, to recite Our signs to you
and to purify you, and to teach you
the Book and the Wisdom, and to teach you
that you knew not.
So remember Me, and I will remember
you; and be thankful to Me; and be you not
ungrateful towards Me.
O all you who believe, seek you help
in patience and prayer; surely God is
with the patient.
And say not of those slain in God's way,
'They are dead'; rather they are living,
but you are not aware.
Surely We will try you with something of fear   150
and hunger, and diminution of goods
and lives and fruits; yet give thou good tidings
unto the patient
who, when they are visited by an affliction,
say, 'Surely we belong to God, and
to Him we return';
upon those rest blessings and mercy
from their Lord, and those—they are
the truly guided.

Safa and Marwa are among the waymarks
of God; so whosoever makes the Pilgrimage
to the House, or the Visitation,
it is no fault in him to circumambulate
them; and whoso volunteers good, God is
All-grateful, All-knowing.

Those who conceal the clear signs and the guidance
that We have sent down, after We have shown them
clearly in the Book—they shall be cursed by
God and the cursers,
save such as repent and make amends, and show   155
clearly—towards them I shall turn; I turn,
All-compassionate.
But those who disbelieve, and die disbelieving—
upon them shall rest the curse of God
and the angels, and of men altogether,
therein dwelling forever; the chastisement
shall not be lightened for them; no respite
shall be given them.

Your God is One God;
there is no god but He,
the All-merciful, the All-compassionate.

Surely in the creation of the heavens and the earth
and the alternation of night and day
and the ship that runs in the sea with profit
to men, and the water God sends down from heaven
therewith reviving the earth after it is dead
and His scattering abroad in it all manner of
crawling thing, and the turning about of the winds
and the clouds compelled between heaven and earth—
surely there are signs for a people having understanding.

Yet there be men who take to themselves compeers   160
apart from God, loving them as God is loved;
but those that believe love God more ardently.
O if the evildoers might see, when they see
the chastisement, that the power altogether
belongs to God, and that God is terrible
in chastisement,
when those that were followed disown their followers,
and they see the chastisement, and their cords
are cut asunder,
and those that followed say, 'O if only we might

return again and disown them, as they have disowned
us!' Even so God shall show them their works.
O bitter regrets for them! Never shall they
issue from the Fire.

O men, eat of what is in the earth
lawful and good; and follow not the steps
of Satan; he is a manifest foe to you.
he only commands you to evil and indecency,
and that you should speak against God such things
as you know not.

And when it is said to them, 'Follow what God   165
has sent down,' they say, 'No; but we will follow
such things as we found our fathers doing.'
What? And if their fathers had no understanding
of anything, and if they were not guided?
The likeness of those who disbelieve is as
the likeness of one who shouts to that
which hears nothing, save a call and a cry;
deaf, dumb, blind—they do not understand.

O believers, eat of the good things
wherewith We have provided you, and give thanks
to God, if it be Him that you serve.
These things only has He forbidden you:
carrion, blood, the flesh of swine,
what has been hallowed to other than God.
Yet whoso is constrained, not desiring
nor transgressing, no sin shall be on him;
God is All-forgiving, All-compassionate.

Those who conceal what of the Book God has sent down
on them, and sell it for a little price—they shall eat
naught but the Fire in their bellies; God shall not
speak to them on the Day of Resurrection
neither purify them; there awaits them
a painful chastisement.
Those are they that have bought error at   170
the price of guidance, and chastisement at
the price of pardon; how patiently they
shall endure the Fire!
That, because God has sent down the Book
with the truth; and those that are
at variance regarding the Book
are in wide schism.

It is not piety, that you turn your faces
to the East and to the West.
True piety is this:
to believe in God, and the Last Day,
the angels, the Book, and the Prophets,
to give of one's substance, however cherished,
to kinsmen, and orphans,
the needy, the traveller, beggars,
and to ransom the slave,
to perform the prayer, to pay the alms.
And they who fulfil their covenant
when they have engaged in a covenant,
and endure with fortitude
misfortune, hardship and peril,
these are they who are true in their faith,
these are the truly godfearing.

O believers, prescribed for you is
retaliation, touching the slain;
freeman for freeman, slave for slave,
female for female. But if aught is pardoned
a man by his bother, let the pursuing
be honourable, and let the payment be
with kindliness. That is a lightening
granted you by your Lord, and a mercy;
and for him who commits aggression
after that—for him there awaits
a painful chastisement.
In retaliation there is life for you,   175
men possessed of minds; haply you
will be godfearing.

Prescribed for you, when any of you
is visited by death, and he leaves behind
some goods, is to make testament
in favour of his parents and kinsmen
honourably—an obligation
on the godfearing.
Then if any man changes it after
hearing it, the sin shall rest upon
those who change it; surely God is
All-hearing, All-knowing.
But if any man fears injustice or
sin from one making testament, and so
makes things right between them, then
sin shall not rest upon him; surely God is
All-forgiving, All-compassionate.

O believers, prescribed for you is
the Fast, even as it was prescribed for
those that were before you—haply you
will be godfearing—
for days numbered; and if any of you
be sick, or if he be on a journey,   180
then a number of other days; and for those
who are able to fast, a redemption
by feeding a poor man. Yet better
it is for him who volunteers good,
and that you should fast is better for you,
if you but know;
the month of Ramadan, wherein the Koran
was sent down to be a guidance
to the people, and as clear signs
of the Guidance and the Salvation
So let those of you, who are present
at the month, fast it; and if any of you be sick, or if he be on a journey,
then a number of other days; God desires
ease for you, and desires not hardship
for you; and that you fulfil the number, and
magnify God that He has guided you, and haply
you will be thankful.

And when My servants question thee
concerning Me—I am near to answer
the call of the caller, when he calls
to Me; so let them respond to Me,
and let them believe in Me; haply so
they will go aright.

Permitted to you, upon the night of
the Fast, is to go to your wives;
they are a vestment for you, and you are
a vestment for them. God knows that you have been
betraying yourselves, and has turned to you
and pardoned you. So now lie with them,
and seek what God has prescribed for you.
And eat and drink, until the white thread
shows clearly to you from the black thread
at the dawn; then complete the Fast
unto the night, and do not lie with them
while you cleave to the mosques. Those are
God's bounds; keep well within them. So God
makes clear His signs to men; haply they
will be godfearing.

Consume not your goods between you
in vanity; neither proffer it
to the judges, that you may sinfully
consume a portion of other men's goods,
and that wittingly.

They will question thee concerning
the new moons. Say: 'They are appointed
times for the people, and the Pilgrimage.'

185

It is not piety to come to the houses
from the backs of them; but piety is
to be godfearing; so come to the houses
by the doors, and fear God; haply so
you will prosper.

And fight in the way of God with those
who fight with you, but aggress not: God loves
not the aggressors.
And slay them wherever you come upon them,
and expel them from where they expelled you;
persecution is more grievous than slaying.
But fight them not by the Holy Mosque
until they should fight you there;
then, if they fight you, slay them—
such is the recompense of unbelievers—
but if they give over, surely God is
All-forgiving, All-compassionate.
Fight them, till there is no persecution
and the religion is God's; then if they
give over, there shall be no enmity
save for evildoers.
The holy month for the holy month;
holy things demand retaliation.
Whoso commits aggression against you,
do you commit aggression against him
like as he has committed against you;
and fear you God, and know that God is
with the godfearing.

190

And expend in the way of God;
and cast not yourselves by your own hands
into destruction, but be good-doers; God
loves the good-doers.

Fulfil the Pilgrimage and the Visitation
unto God; but if you are prevented,

then such offering as may be feasible.
And shave not your heads, till the offering
reaches its place of sacrifice. If any
of you is sick, or injured in his head,
then redemption by fast, or freewill offering,
or ritual sacrifice. When you are secure,
then whosoever enjoys the Visitation
until the Pilgrimage, let his offering
be such as may be feasible; or if he
finds none, then a fast of three days
in the Pilgrimage, and of seven when
you return, that is ten completely;
that is for him whose family are not
present at the Holy Mosque. And fear
God, and know that God is terrible
in retribution.

The Pilgrimage is in months well-known;
whoso undertakes the duty of Pilgrimage
in them shall not go in to his womenfolk
nor indulge in ungodliness and disputing
in the Pilgrimage.Whatever good you do,
God knows it. And take provision;
but the best provision is godfearing,
so fear you Me, men possessed of minds!
It is no fault in you, that you should seek
bounty from your Lord; but when you press on
from Arafat, then remember God
at the Holy Waymark, and remember Him
as He has guided you, though formerly you
were gone astray.
Then press on from where the people   195
press on, and pray for God's forgiveness;
God is All-forgiving, All-compassionate.
And when you have performed your holy rites
remember God, as you remember your fathers
or yet more devoutly. Now some men
there are who say, 'Our Lord, give to us
in this world'; such men shall have no part
in the world to come.
And others there are who say, 'Our Lord,
give to us in this world good, and good
in the world to come, and guard us against the
chastisement of the Fire';
those—they shall have a portion from
what they have earned; and God is swift

at the reckoning.
And remember God during certain days
numbered. If any man hastens on
in two days, that is no sin in him;
and if any delays, it is not a sin
in him, if he be godfearing. And
fear you God, and know that unto Him
you shall be mustered.

And some men there are whose saying   200
upon the present world pleases thee,
and such a one calls on God to witness
what is in his heart, yet he is most stubborn
in altercation,
and when he turns his back, he hastens about
the earth, to do corruption there and to
destroy the tillage and the stock; and God
loves not corruption;
and when it is said to him, 'Fear God',
vainglory seizes him in his sin.
So Gehenna shall be enough for him—how
evil a cradling!
But other men there are that sell themselves
desiring God's good pleasure; and God is gentle
with His servants.
O believers, enter the peace, all of you,
and follow not the steps of Satan;
he is a manifest foe to you. But   205
if you slip, after the clear signs
have come to you, know then that God is
All-mighty, All-wise.

What do they look for, but that God
shall come to them in the cloud-shadows,
and the angels? The matter is determined,
and unto God all matters are returned.
Ask the Children of Israel how many a clear sign
We gave them. Whoso changes God's blessing
after it has come to him, God is terrible
in retribution.
Decked out fair to the unbelievers
is the present life, and they deride
the believers; but those who were godfearing
shall be above them on the Resurrection Day;
and God provides whomsoever He will
without reckoning.

The people were one nation; then God sent forth
the Prophets, good tidings to bear
and warning, and He sent down with them
the Book with the truth, that He might
decide between the people touching their differences;
and only those who had been given it
were at variance upon it, after the
clear signs had come to them, being insolent
one to another; then God guided those
who believed to the truth, touching which
they were at variance, by His leave;
and God guides whomsoever He will
to a straight path.
Or did you suppose you should enter Paradise   210
without there had come upon you the like
of those who passed away before you?
They were afflicted by misery and hardship
and where so convulsed, that the Messenger
and those who believed with him said,
'When comes God's help?' Ah, but surely
God's help is nigh.

They will question thee concerning
what they should expend. Say: 'Whatsoever good
you expend is for parents and kinsmen,
orphans, the needy, and the traveller;
and whatever good you may do, God has
knowledge of it.'

Prescribed for you is fighting, though it be
hateful to you.
Yet it may happen that you will hate a thing
which is better for you;
and it may happen that you
will love a thing which is worse for you; God knows,
and you know not.

They will question thee concerning
the holy month, and fighting in it.
Say: 'Fighting in it is a henious thing,
but to bar from God's way, and disbelief in Him,
and the Holy Mosque, and to expel its people
from it—that is more heinous in God's sight;
and persecution is more heinous than slaying.'
They will not cease to fight with you,
till they turn you from your religion,
if they are able; and whosoever of you

turns from his religion, and dies disbelieving—
their works have failed in this world and the next;
those are the inhabitants of the Fire; therein
they shall dwell forever.
But the believers, and those who emigrate
and struggle in God's way—those have hope of
God's compassion; and God is All-forgiving,
All-compassionate.   215

They will question thee concerning
wine, and arrow-shuffling. Say: 'In both
is heinous sin, and uses for men,
but the sin in them is more heinous
than the usefulness.'

They will question thee concerning
what they should expend. Say: 'The abundance.'
So god makes clear His signs to you; haply
you will reflect;
in this world, and the world to come.

They will question thee concerning
the orphans. Say: 'To set their affairs
aright is good.
And if you intermix with them, they are
your brothers. God knows well
him who works corruption from him
who sets aright; and had He willed
He would have harassed you. Surely God is
All-mighty, All-wise.'

Do not marry idolatresses, until   220
they believe; a believing slavegirl
is better than an idolatress, though
you may admire her. And do not marry
idolaters, until they believe. A believing
slave is better than an idolater, though
you may admire him.
Those call unto the Fire; and God calls unto
Paradise, and pardon, by His leave, and He
makes clear His signs to the people; haply
they will remember.

They will question thee concerning
the monthly course. Say: 'It is hurt;
so go apart from women during
the monthly course, and do not approach them

till they are clean. When they have cleansed
themselves, then come unto them as God
has commanded you.' Truly, God loves
those who repent, and He loves those
who cleanse themselves.
Your women are a tillage for you; so come
unto your tillage as you wish, and forward
for your souls; and fear God, and know that
you shall meet Him. Give thou good tidings
to the believers.

Do not make God a hindrance, through your oath
to being pious and godfearing, and putting
things right between men. Surely God is
All-hearing, All-knowing.
God will not take you to task for a slip   225
in your oaths; but He will take you to task
for what your hearts have earned; and God is
All-forgiving, All-clement.

For those who foreswear their women
a wait of four months; if they revert,
God is All-forgiving, All-compassionate;
but if they resolve on divorce, surely God is
All-hearing, All-knowing.
Divorced women shall wait by themselves
for three periods; and it is not lawful
for them to hide what God has created
in their wombs; if they believe in God
and the Last Day. In such time their mates
have better right to restore them, if they
desire to set things right. Women have
such honourable rights as obligations, but
their men have a degree above them; God is
All-mighty, All-wise.
Divorce is twice; then honourable retention
or setting free kindly. It is not lawful
for you to take of what you have given them
unless the couple fear they may not maintain
Gods' bounds; if you fear they may not maintain
God's bounds, it is no fault in them for her
to redeem herself. Those are God's bounds;
do not transgress them. Whosoever
transgresses the bounds of God—those
are the evildoers.
If he divorces her finally, she shall not   230

be lawful to him after that, until she
marries another husband. If he divorces her,
then it is no fault in them to return
to each other, if they suppose that they will
maintain God's bounds. Those are God's bounds;
He makes them clear unto a people
that have knowledge.
When you divorce women, and they have reached
their term, then retain them honourably
or set them free honourably; do not retain them
by force, to transgress; whoever does that
has wronged himself. Take not God's signs
in mockery, and remember God's blessing
upon you, and the Book and the Wisdom He
has sent down on you, to admonish you.
And fear God, and know that God has knowledge
of everything.
When you divorce women, and they have reached
their term, do not debar them from marrying
their husbands, when they have agreed together
honourably. That is an admonition for
whoso of you believes in God and the Last Day;
that is cleaner and purer for you; God knows,
and you know not.

Mothers shall suckle their children two years
completely, for such as desire to fulfil
the suckling. It is for the father to provide them
and clothe them honourably. No soul is charged
save to its capacity; a mother shall not be pressed
for her child, neither a father for his child.
The heir has a like duty. But if the couple
desire by mutual consent and consultation
to wean, then it is no fault in them.
And if you desire to seek nursing
for your children, it is no fault in you
provide you hand over what you have given
honourably; and fear God, and know that God sees
the things you do.

And those of you who die, leaving wives,
they shall wait by themselves for four months
and ten nights; when they have reached their term
then it is no fault in you what they may do
with themselves honourably. God is aware of
the things you do.

There is no fault in you touching the proposal   235
to women you offer, or hide in your hearts;
God knows that you will be mindful of them;
but do not make troth with them secretly
without you speak honourable words.
And do not resolve on the knot of marriage
until the book has reached its term; and know
that God knows what is in your hearts,
so be fearful of Him; and know that God is
All-forgiving, All-clement.

There is no fault in you, if you divorce
women while as yet you have not touched them
nor appointed any marriage-portion for them;
yet make provision for them, the affluent man
according to his means, and according to his means
the needy man, honourably—an obligation
on the good-doers.
And if you divorce them before you have
touched them, and you have already appointed
for them a marriage-portion, then one-half
of what you have appointed, unless it be
they make remission, or he makes remission
in whose hand is the knot of marriage;
yet that you should remit is nearer
to godfearing. Forget not to be bountiful
one towards another. Surely God sees
the things you do.

Be you watchful over the prayers,
and the middle prayer; and do you stand
obedient to God.
And if you are in fear, then afoot   240
or mounted; but when you are secure, then
remember God, as He taught you the things
that you knew not.

And those of you who die, leaving wives,
let them make testament for their wives,
provision for a year without expulsion; but if
they go forth, there is no fault in you what
they may do with themselves honourably; God is
All-mighty, All-wise.
There shall be for divorced women
provision honourable—an obligation
on the godfearing.

So God makes clear His signs for you; haply
you will understand.

Hast thou not regarded those who went forth
from their habitations in their thousands
fearful of death? God said to them, 'Die!'
Then He gave them life. Truly God is bounteous
to the people, but most of the people
are not thankful.
So fight in God's way, and know that God is   245
All-hearing, All-knowing.
Who is he that will lend God a good loan,
and He will multiply it for him manifold?
God grasps, and outspreads; and unto Him
you shall be returned.

Hast thou not regarded the Council
of the Children of Israel, after Moses,
when they said to a Prophet of theirs,
'Raise up for us a king, and we will fight
in God's way.' He said, 'Might it be
that, if fighting is prescribed for you,
you will not fight?' They said, 'Why should we
not fight in God's way, who have been
expelled from our habitations
and our children?' Yet when fighting was
prescribed for them, they turned their backs
except a few of them; and God has knowledge
of the evildoers.
Then their Prophet said to them, 'Verily
God has raised up Saul for you as king.'
They said, 'How should he be king over us
who have better right than he to kingship,
seeing he has not been given amplitude
of wealth?' He said, 'God has chosen him
over you, and has increased him
broadly in knowledge and body. God gives
the kingship to whom He will; and God is
All-embracing, All-knowing.'
And their Prophet said to them, 'The sign
of his kingship is that the Ark will come to you,
in it a Shechina from your Lord, and a remnant
of what the folk of Moses and Aaron's folk
left behind, the angels bearing it.
Surely in that shall be a sign for you if
you are believers.'

And when Saul went forth with the hosts   250
he said, 'God will try you with a river;
whosoever drinks of it is not of me,
and whoso tastes it not, he is of me,
saving him who scoops up with his hand.'
But they drank of it, except a few
of them; and when he crossed it, and those
who believed with him, they said, 'We have no
power today against Goliath and his hosts.'
Said those who reckoned they should meet God,
'How often a little company has overcome
a numerous company, by God's leave! And God
is with the patient.'
So, when they went forth against Goliath
and his hosts, they said, 'Our Lord, pour out
upon us patience, and make firm our feet,
and give us aid against the people of
the unbelievers!'
And they routed them, by the leave of God,
and David slew Goliath; and God gave him
the kingship, Wisdom, and He taught him
such as He willed. Had God not driven back
the people, some by the means of others,
the earth had surely corrupted; but God is bounteous
unto all beings.

These are the signs of God We recite to thee
in truth,
and assuredly thou art of the number
of the Envoys.
And those Messengers, some We have preferred
above others;
some there are to whom god spoke, and some He
raised in rank.

And We gave Jesus son of Mary the clear signs
and confirmed him with the Holy Spirit.
And had God willed, those who came after him
would not have fought one against the other
after the clear signs had come to them;
but they fell into variance, and some of them
believed, and some disbelieved; and had God willed
they would not have fought one against the other;
but God does whatsoever He desires.

O believers, expend of that wherewith
We have provided you, before there comes a day

wherein shall be neither traffick, nor friendship,
nor intercession; and the unbelievers—they
are the evildoers.

God
there is no god but He, the
Living, the Everlasting.
Slumber seizes Him not, neither sleep;
to Him belongs
all that is in the heavens and the earth.
Who is there that shall intercede with Him
save by His leave?
He knows what lies before them
and what is after them,
and they comprehend not anything of His knowledge
save such as He wills.
His Throne comprises the heavens and earth;
the preserving of them oppresses Him not;
He is the All-high, the All-glorious.

No compulsion is there in religion.
Rectitude has become clear from error.
So whosoever disbelieves in idols
and believes in God, has laid hold of
the most firm handle, unbreaking; God is
All-hearing, All-knowing.

God is the Protector of the believers;
He brings them forth from the shadows
into the light.
And the unbelievers—their protectors are
idols, that bring them forth from the light
into the shadows;
those are the inhabitants of the Fire,
therein dwelling forever.

Hast thou not regarded him who disputed   260
with Abraham, concerning his Lord,
that God had given him the kingship? When
Abraham said, 'My Lord is He who gives
life, and makes to die,' he said, 'I give
life, and make to die.' Said Abraham, 'God
brings the sun from the east; so bring thou
it from the west.' Then the unbeliever
was confounded. God guides not the people
of the evildoers.
Or such as he who passed by a city

that was fallen down upon its turrets;
he said, 'How shall God give life to this
now it is dead?' So God made him die
a hundred years, then He raised him up,
saying, 'How long hast thou tarried?' He said,
'I have tarried a day, or part of a day.'
Said He, 'Nay; thou hast tarried a hundred years.
Look at thy food and drink—it has not spoiled;
and look at thy ass. So We would make thee
a sign for the people. And look at the bones,
how We shall set them up, and then clothe them
with flesh.' So, when it was made clear
to him, he said, 'I know that God is powerful
over everything.'
And when Abraham said, 'My Lord, show me
how Thou wilt give life to the dead,' He said,
'Why, dost thou not believe?' 'Yes,' he said,
'but that my heart may be at rest.' Said He,
'Take four birds, and twist them to thee,
then set a part of them on every hill,
then summon them, and they will come to thee
running. And do thou know that God is
All-mighty, All-wise.'

The likeness of those who expend their wealth
in the way of God is as the likeness
of a grain of corn that sprouts seven ears,
in every ear a hundred grains. So God
multiplies unto whom He will; God is
All-embracing, All-knowing.
Those who expend their wealth in the way of God
then follow not up what they have expended with
reproach and injury, their wage is with their Lord,
and no fear shall be on them, neither shall they sorrow.
Honourable words, and forgiveness, are better than
a freewill offering followed by injury; and God is
All-sufficient, All-clement.
O believers, void not your freewill offerings
with reproach and injury, as one who expends
of his substance to show off to men
and believes not in God and the Last Day.
The likeness of him is as the likeness
of a smooth rock on which is soil,
and a torrent smites it, and leaves it barren.
They have no power over anything that they
have earned. God guides not the people
of the unbelievers.

But the likeness of those who expend their
wealth, seeking God's good pleasure, and to
confirm themselves, is as the likeness
of a garden upon a hill; a torrent smites it
and it yields its produce twofold; if no
torrent smites it, yet dew; and God sees
the things you do.
Would any of you wish to have a garden
of palms and vines, with rivers flowing
beneath it, and all manner of fruit there
for him, then old age smites him, and he has
seed, but weaklings, then a whirlwind with
fire smites it, and it is consumed?
So God makes clear the signs to you; haply
you will reflect.
O believers, expend of the good things
you have earned, and of that We
have produced for you from the earth,
and intend not the corrupt of it for
your expending;
for you would never take it yourselves, except
you closed an eye on it; and know that God is
All-sufficient, All-laudable.
Satan promises you poverty, and bids you
unto indecency; but God promises you
His pardon and His bounty; and God is
All-embracing, All-knowing.
He gives the Wisdom to whomsoever He will,
and whoso is given the Wisdom, has been
given much good; yet none remembers but men
possessed of minds.
And whatever expenditure you expend,
and whatever vow you vow, surely God
knows it. No helpers have the evildoers.
If you publish your freewill offerings, it is
excellent; but if you conceal them, and give them
to the poor, that is better for you, and will
acquit you of your evil deeds; God is aware of
the things you do.

Thou art not responsible for guiding them;
but God guides whomsoever He will.

And whatever good you expend is for yourselves,
for then you are expending, being desirous
only of God's Face; and whatever good
you expend shall be repaid to you

270

in full, and you will not be wronged,
it being for the poor who are restrained
in the way of God, and are unable
to journey in the land; the ignorant man
supposes them rich because of their abstinence,
but thou shalt know them by their mark—
they do not beg of men importunately.
And whatever good you expend, surely God has
knowledge of it.
Those expend their wealth night and day, secretly   275
and in public, their wage awaits them with their Lord,
and no fear shall be on them, neither shall they sorrow.

Those who devour usury shall not rise again
except as he rises, whom Satan of the touch
prostrates; that is because they say,
'Trafficking is like usury.' God has
permitted trafficking, and forbidden usury.
Whosoever receives an admonition
from his Lord and gives over, he shall have
his past gains, and his affair is
committed to God; but whosoever reverts—
those are the inhabitants of the Fire,
therein dwelling forever.
God blots out usury, but freewill offerings
He augments with interest. God loves not
any guilty ingrate.

Those who believe and do deeds of righteousness,
and perform the prayer, and pay the alms—
their wage awaits them with their Lord,
and no fear shall be on them, neither shall they sorrow.

O believers, fear you God; and
give up the usury that is outstanding, if
you are believers.
But if you do not, then take notice that
God shall war with you, and His Messenger; yet
if you repent, you shall have your principal,
unwronging and unwronged.
And if any man should be in difficulties,   280
let him have respite till things are easier; but
that you should give freewill offerings is better for you,
did you but know.
And fear a day wherein you shall be
returned to God, and every soul shall be

paid in full what it has earned; and they
shall not be wronged.

O believers, when you contract a debt
one upon another for a stated term,
write it down, and let a writer
write it down between you justly,
and let not any writer refuse
to write it down, as God has taught him;
so let him write, and let the debtor
dictate, and let him fear God his Lord
and not diminish aught of it. And if
the debtor be a fool, or weak, or unable
to dictate himself, then let his guardian
dictate justly. And call in to witness
two witnesses, men; or if the two
 be not men, then one man and two women,
such witnesses as you approve of,
that if one of the two women errs
the other will remind her; and let the witnesses
not refuse, whenever they are summoned.
And be not loath to write it down,
whether it be small or great, with its term;
that is more equitable in God's sight,
more upright for testimony, and likelier
that you will not be in doubt. Unless it be
merchandise present that you give and take
between you; then it shall be no fault in you
if you do not write it down. And take witnesses
when you are trafficking one with another.
And let not either writer or witness be
pressed; or if you do, that is ungodliness in you.
And fear God; God teaches you, and God has
knowledge of everything.
And if you are upon a journey, and
you do not find a writer, then a pledge
in hand. but If one of you trusts another,
let him who is trusted deliver his trust,
and let him fear God his Lord. And do not
conceal the testimony; whoso conceals it,
his heart is sinful; and God has knowledge of
the things you do.
To God belongs all that is in the heavens and
earth. Whether you publish what is in your hearts
or hide it, God shall make reckoning with you
for it. He will forgive whom He will,

and chastise whom He will; God is powerful
over everything.

The Messenger believes in what was sent down to   285
him from his Lord,
and the believers; each one believes in God
and His angels,
and in His Books and His Messengers; we
make no division
between any one of His Messengers. They say,
'We hear, and obey.
Our Lord, grant us Thy forgiveness; unto Thee
is the homecoming.'

God charges no soul save to its capacity;
standing to its account is what it has earned,
and against its account what it has merited.

Our Lord,
take us not to task
if we forget, or make mistake.
Our Lord,
charge us not with a load such
as Thou didst lay upon those before us.
Our Lord,
do Thou not burden us
beyond what we have the strength to bear.
And pardon us,
and forgive us,
and have mercy on us;
Thou art our Protector.
And help us against the people
of the unbelievers.

Saint Benedict of Nursia

THE BENEDICTINE RULE

The monastic way of life soon spread from Egypt to Palestine and Syria and eventually throughout the Christian Roman Empire. In Italy, Benedict of Nursia (c. 480–547), scion of a wealthy Roman family, founded twelve monasteries, the best known being at Monte Cassino in the mountains of southern Italy. Benedict wrote a set of rules for the governance of his monks; the Benedictine Rule became the model for many monasteries throughout Latin Christendom. In the following extract, Benedict summarizes the purpose and principles of monastic life.

. . . Therefore we are constrained to found a school for the service of the Lord. In its organization we hope we shall ordain nothing severe, nothing burdensome; but if there should result anything a little irksome by the demands of justice for the correction of vices and the persevering of charity, do not therefore, through fear, avoid the way of salvation, which cannot be entered upon save through a narrow entrance, but in which, as life progresses and the heart becomes filled with faith, one walks in the unspeakable sweetness of love; but never departing from His control, and persevering in His doctrine in the monastery until death, let us with patience share in the sufferings of Christ, that we may be worthy to be partakers in His kingdom. . . .

What the Abbot Should Be Like

The abbot who is worthy to rule a monastery ought to remember by what name they are called, and to justify by their deeds the name of a superior. For he is believed to take the place of Christ in the monastery, since he is called by his name, as the apostle says: "Ye have received the spirit of adoption of sons, whereby we call, Abba, Father."

And so the abbot ought not (God forbid) to teach or decree or order anything apart from the precept of the Lord; but his rules and his teaching ought always to be leavened with the leaven of divine justice in the minds of his disciples; and let the abbot be always mindful that in the great judgment of God, both his teaching and the obedience of his disciples will be weighed in the balance. And let the abbot know that whatever the master finds lacking in the sheep will be

Perry, Peden, Von Laue, eds., *Sources of the Western Tradition,* Volume 1, Houghton Mifflin, (ISBN: 0–395–89201–5), original pp. 181–4, (Benedictine Rule).

charged to the fault of the shepherd. Only in case the pastor has shown the greatest diligence in his management of an unruly and disobedient flock, and has given his whole care to the correction of their evil doings, will that pastor be cleared at the judgment of God and be able to say with the prophet, "I have not hid thy righteousness within my heart, I have declared thy faithfulness and thy salvation, but they despising have scorned me"; then let the punishment of eternal death itself fall upon the disobedient sheep of his care.

Therefore when anyone takes on himself the name of abbot, he should govern his disciples by a twofold teaching, that is, let him show forth all the good and holy things by his deeds rather than by his words; to ready disciples he ought to set forth the commands of God in words, but to the hard of heart, and to the simple-minded he ought to illustrate the divine precepts in his deeds. And all things which he has taught his disciples to be wrong, let him demonstrate in his action that they should not be done, lest sometime God should say to him, a sinner: "Why dost thou declare my statutes or take my testimony in thy mouth? Thou hast hated instruction and cast My word behind thee"; and again: "Thou who hast seen the mote in thy brother's eyes, hast not seen the beam in thine own eye."

Let him not be a respecter of persons in the monastery. Let not one be loved more than another, unless he shall have found someone to be better than another in good deeds and in obedience; let not a freeman be preferred to one coming from servitude, unless there be some good and reasonable cause; but if according to the dictates of justice it shall have seemed best to the abbot, let him do this with anyone of any rank whatsoever; otherwise let each keep his own place, since, whether bond or free, we are all one in Christ, and under one God we bear the same burden of service, for there is no respect of persons with God; only in this regard are we distinguished with him if we are found better and more humble than others in our good deeds. Therefore let his love for all be the same, and let one discipline be put upon all according to merit. . . .

About Calling the Brothers to Council

Whenever anything especial is to be done in the monastery, the abbot shall convoke the whole body and himself set forth the matter at issue. And after listening to the advice of the brothers, he shall consider it by himself, and shall do what he shall have judged most useful. Now we say all should be called to the council, because the Lord often reveals to the younger brother what is best to be done.

But let the brothers give advice with all subjection of humility and not presume to defend boldly what seemed good to them, but rather rely on the judgment of the abbot, and all obey him in what he has judged to be for their welfare. But just as it is fitting that the disciples obey the master, so is it incumbent on him to dispose everything wisely and justly.

Therefore, let all follow the rule of the master in all things, and let no one depart from it rashly; let no one in the monastery follow the desire of his own heart. And let no one strive with his abbot shamelessly either within or without the monastery; and if he shall have presumed to do so, let him be subjected to the regular discipline. And let the abbot himself do all things in the fear of God and in the observance of the rule, knowing that he must without doubt render account unto God, the most just judge, for all his judgments.

If there are any matters of minor importance to be done for the welfare of the monastery, let the abbot take the advice only of the elders, as it is written: "Do all things with counsel, and after it is done thou wilt not repent."

Concerning Those Who, Being Often Rebuked, Do Not Amend

If any brother, having frequently been rebuked for any fault, do not amend even after he has been excommunicated, a more severe rebuke shall fall upon him;—that is, the punishment of the lash shall be inflicted upon him. But if he do not even then amend; or, if perchance—which God forbid,—swelled with pride he try even to defend his works: then the abbot shall act as a wise physician. If he have applied . . . the ointments of exhortation, the medicaments [medicines] of the Divine Scriptures; if he have proceeded to the last blasting of excommunication, or to blows with rods, and if he sees that his efforts avail nothing: let him also—what is greater— call in the prayer of himself and all the brothers for him: that God who can do all things may work a cure upon an infirm brother. But if he be not healed even in this way, then at last the abbot may use the pruning knife, as the apostle says: "Remove evil from you," etc.: lest one diseased sheep contaminate the whole flock.

Whether Brothers Who Leave the Monastery Ought Again To Be Received

A brother who goes out, or is cast out, of the monastery for his own fault, if he wish to return, shall first promise every amends for the fault on account of which he departed; and thus he shall be received into the lowest degree—so that thereby his humility may be proved. But if he again depart, up to the third time he shall be received. Knowing that after this every opportunity of return is denied to him.

Concerning Boys Under Age, How They Shall Be Corrected

Every age or intelligence ought to have its proper bounds. Therefore as often as boys or youths, or those who are less able to understand how great is the punishment of excommunication: as often as such persons offend, they shall either be afflicted with excessive fasts, or coerced with severe blows, that they may be healed.

Concerning the Reception of Guests

All guests who come shall be received as though they were Christ; for He Himself said: "I was a stranger and ye took Me in." And to all, fitting honour shall be shown; but, most of all, to servants of the faith and to pilgrims. When, therefore, a guest is announced, the prior or the brothers shall run to meet him, with every office of love. And first they shall pray together; and thus they shall be joined together in peace. Which kiss of peace shall not first be offered, unless a prayer have preceded; on account of the wiles of the devil. In the salutation itself, moreover, all humility shall be exhibited. In the case of all guests arriving or departing: with inclined head, or with prostrating of the whole body upon the ground, Christ, who is also received in them, shall be adored.

> The monks gathered together for prayer seven times in the course of the day. Prayers were chanted from set texts.

Concerning the Art of Singing

Whereas we believe that there is a divine presence, and that the eyes of the Lord look down everywhere upon the good and the evil: chiefly then, without any doubt, we may believe that this is the case when we are assisting at divine service. Therefore let us always be mindful of what the prophets say: "Serve the Lord in all fear"; and before the face of the Divinity and His angels; and let us so stand and again, "Sing wisely"; and "in the sight of the angels I will sing unto thee." Therefore let us consider how we ought to conduct ourselves and sing that our voice may accord with our intention.

Concerning Reverence for Prayer

If when to powerful men we wish to suggest anything, we do not presume to do it unless with reverence and humility: how much more should we supplicate with all humility, and devotion of purity, God who is the Lord of all. And let us know that we are heard, not for much speaking, but for purity of heart and compunction of tears. And, therefore, prayer ought to be brief and pure; unless perchance it be prolonged by the influence of the inspiration of the divine grace. When assembled together, then, let the prayer be altogether brief; and, the sign being given by the prior, let us rise together.

Concerning the Daily Manual Labor

Idleness is the enemy of the soul. And therefore, at fixed times, the brothers ought to be occupied in manual labour; and again, at fixed times, in sacred reading.

Concerning Humility

. . . If we wish to attain to the height of the greatest humility, and to that divine exaltation which is attained by the humility of this present life, we must mount by our own acts that ladder which appeared in a dream to Jacob,[1] upon which angels appeared unto him ascending and descend-

---

[1]Jacob, a patriarch of ancient Israel, had a dream about angels ascending and descending a ladder between heaven and earth; the dream is recounted in the Old Testament.

ing. For that ascent and descent can only be understood by us to be this: to ascend by humility, to descend through pride. . . .

Now the first grade of humility is this: keeping the fear of God before his eyes, let him avoid forgetfulness and ever remember all the precepts of the Lord; and continually consider in his heart that eternal life which is prepared for those who fear God, just as the mockers of God fall into hell. . . .

The fifth grade of humility is this, if one reveals to the abbot in humble confession all the vain imaginings that come into his heart, and all the evil he has done in secret. . . .

This is the eighth grade of humility; if a monk do nothing except what the common rule of the monastery or the examples of his superior urges him to do.

The ninth grade of humility is this: if a monk keep his tongue from speaking and keeping silence speaks only in answer to questions, since the Scripture says that "sin is not escaped by much speaking," and "a talkative man is not established in the earth."

The tenth grade of humility is this, that he be not easily moved nor prompt to laughter, since it is written: "The fool raiseth his voice in laughter."

The eleventh grade of humility is this: if, when the monk speaks, he says few words and those to the point, slowly and without laughter, humbly and gravely; and be not loud of voice, as it is written: "A wise man is known by his few words."

The twelfth grade of humility is this: that a monk conduct himself with humility not only in his heart but also in his bearing, in the sight of all; that is, in the service of God, in the oratory [chapel], in the monastery, in the garden, on the road, in the field; and everywhere, sitting or walking or standing, let him always have his head bowed, and his eyes fixed on the ground. Always mindful of his sins, let him think of himself as being already tried in the great judgment, saying in his heart what that publican, spoken of in the gospel, said with his eyes fixed on the earth: "Lord, I a sinner am not worthy to lift mine eyes to the heavens;" and again with the prophet: "I am bowed down and humbled wheresoever I go." . . .

Saint Thomas Aquinas

SUMMA THEOLOGICA
AND SUMMA CONTRA GENTILES

For most of the middle ages, religious thought was dominated by the influence of Saint Augustine (d. 430), the greatest of the Latin church fathers (see page 185). Augustine placed little value on the study of nature; for him, the City of Man (the world) was a sinful place from which people tried to escape in order to enter the City of God (heaven). Regarding God as the source of knowing, he held that reason by itself was an inadequate guide to knowledge: without faith in revealed truth, there could be no understanding. An alternative approach to that of Augustine was provided by Thomas Aquinas (1225–1274), a friar of the Order of Preachers (Dominicans), who taught theology at Paris and later in Italy. Both Augustine and Aquinas believed that God was the source of all truth, that human nature was corrupted by the imprint of the original sin of Adam and Eve, and that God revealed himself through the Bible and in the person of Jesus Christ. But, in contrast to Augustine, Aquinas expressed great confidence in the power of reason and favored applying it to investigate the natural world.

Aquinas held that as both faith and reason came from God, they were not in opposition to each other; properly understood, they supported each other. Because reason was no enemy of faith, it should not be feared. In addition to showing renewed respect for reason, Aquinas—influenced by Aristotelian empiricism (the acquisition of knowledge of nature through experience)—valued knowledge of the natural world. He saw the natural and supernatural worlds not as irreconcilable and hostile to each other, but as a continuous ascending hierarchy of divinely created orders of being moving progressively toward the Supreme Being. In constructing a synthesis of Christianity and Aristotelianism, Aquinas gave renewed importance to the natural world, human reason, and the creative human spirit. Nevertheless, by holding that reason was subordinate to faith, he remained a typically medieval thinker.

In the opening reading from his most ambitious work, the *Summa Theologica,* Thomas Aquinas asserts that reason by itself is insufficient to lead human beings to salvation. Also included in this grouping is a selection from another work, *Summa Contra Gentiles,* a theological defense of Christian doctrines that relies extensively on natural reason.

Summa Theologica

Whether, Besides the Philosophical Sciences, Any Further Doctrine Is Required?

It was necessary for man's salvation that there should be a knowledge revealed by God, besides the philosophical sciences investigated by human reason. First, because man is directed to God as to an end that surpasses the grasp of his reason. . . . But the end must first be known by men who are to direct their thoughts and actions to the end. Hence it was necessary for the salvation of man that certain truths which exceed human reason should be made known to him by divine revelation. Even as regards those truths about God which human reason can investigate, it was necessary that man be taught by a divine revelation. For the truth about God, such as reason can know it, would only be known by a few, and that after a long time, and with the admixture of many errors: whereas man's whole salvation, which is in God, depends upon the knowledge of this truth. Therefore, in order that the salvation of men might be brought about more fitly and more surely, it was necessary that they be taught divine truths by divine revelation. It was therefore necessary that, besides the philosophical sciences investigated by reason, there should be a sacred science by way of revelation.

> In the next selection, Aquinas uses the categories of Aristotelian philosophy to demonstrate through natural reason God's existence.

Whether God Exists?

The existence of God can be proved in five ways.

The first and more manifest way is the argument from motion. It is certain, and evident to our senses, that in the world some things are in motion. Now whatever is moved is moved by another, for nothing can be moved except it is in potentiality to that towards which it is moved; whereas a thing moves inasmuch as it is in act. For motion is nothing else than the reduction of something from potentiality to actuality. But nothing can be reduced from potentiality to actuality, except by something in a state of actuality. Thus that which is actually hot, as fire, makes wood, which is potentially hot, to be actually hot, and thereby moves and changes it. Now it is not possible that the same thing should be at once in actuality and potentiality in the same respect, but only in different respects. For what is actually hot cannot simultaneously be potentially hot; but it is simultaneously potentially cold. It is therefore impossible that in the same

Perry, Peden, Von Laue, eds., *Sources of the Western Tradition,* Volume 1, Houghton Mifflin, (ISBN 0-395-89201-5), original pp. 236–240 (selections from Thomas Aquinas).

respect and in the same way a thing should be both mover and moved, *i.e.,* that it should move itself. Therefore, whatever is moved must be moved by another. If that by which it is moved be itself moved, then this also must needs be moved by another, and that by another again. But this cannot go on to infinity, because then there would be no first mover, and, consequently, no other mover, seeing that subsequent movers move only inasmuch as they are moved by the first mover; as the staff moves only because it is moved by the hand. Therefore it is necessary to arrive at a first mover, moved by no other; and this everyone understands to be God.

The second way if from the nature of efficient cause. In the world of sensible things we find there is an order of efficient causes. There is no case known (neither is it, indeed, possible) in which a thing is found to be the efficient cause of itself; for so it would be prior to itself, which is impossible. Now in efficient causes it is not possible to go on to infinity, because in all efficient causes following in order, the first is the cause of the intermediate cause, and the intermediate is the cause of the ultimate cause, whether the intermediate cause be several, or one only. Now to take away the cause is to take away the effect. Therefore, if there be no first cause among efficient causes, there will be no ultimate, nor any intermediate, cause. But if in efficient causes it is possible to go on to infinity, there will be no first efficient cause, neither will there be an ultimate effect, nor any intermediate efficient causes; all of which is plainly false. Therefore, it is necessary to admit a first efficient cause, to which everyone gives the name of God.

The third way is taken from possibility and necessity, and runs thus. We find in nature things that are possible to be and not to be, since they are found to be generated, and to be corrupted, and consequently, it is possible for them to be and not to be. But it is impossible for these always to exist, for that which can not-be at some time is not. Therefore, if everything can not-be, then at one time there was nothing in existence. Now if this were true, even now there would be nothing in existence, because that which does not exist begins to exist only through something already existing. Therefore, if at one time nothing was in existence, it would have been impossible for anything to have begun to exist; and thus even now nothing would be in existence—which is absurd. Therefore, not all beings are merely possible, but there must exist something the existence of which is necessary. But every necessary thing either has its necessity caused by another, nor not. Now it is impossible to go on to infinity in necessary things which have their necessity caused by another, as has been already proved in regard to efficient causes. Therefore we cannot but admit the existence of some being having of itself its own necessity, and not receiving it from another, but rather causing in others their necessity. This all men speak of as God.

The fourth way is taken from the graduation to be found in things. Among beings there are some more and some less good, true, noble, and the like. But *more* and *less* are predicated of different things according as they resemble in their different ways something which is the maximum, as a thing is said to be hottest according as it more nearly resembles that which is hottest; so that there is something which is truest, something best, something noblest, and, consequently, something which is most being, for those things that are greatest in truth are greatest in being. . . . Now the maximum in any genus is the cause of all in that genus, as fire, which is the maximum of heat, is the cause of all hot things. . . . Therefore there must also be something which is to all beings the cause of their being, goodness, and every other perfection; and this we call God.

The fifth way is taken from the governance of the world. We see that things which lack knowledge, such as natural bodies, act for an end, and this is evident from their acting always, or nearly always, in the same way, so as to obtain the best result. Hence it is plain that they achieve their end, not fortuitously, but designedly. Now whatever lacks knowledge cannot move towards an end, unless it be directed by some being endowed with knowledge and intelligence; as the arrow is directed by the archer. Therefore some intelligent being exists by whom all natural things are directed to their end; and this being we call God.

> The next reading shows Aquinas' great respect for reason. He defines a human being by the capacity to regulate actions through reason and will.

Does Man Choose with Necessity or Freely?

Man does not choose of necessity. . . . For man can will and not will, act and not act . . . can will this or that, and do this or that. The reason for this is to be found in the very power of the reason. For the will can tend to whatever the reason can apprehend as good. Now the reason can apprehend as good not only this, viz., *to will* or *to act,* but also this, viz., *not to will* and *not to act.* Again, in all particular goods, the reason can consider the nature of some good, and the lack of some good, which has the nature of an evil; and in this way, it can apprehend any single one of such goods as to be chosen or to be avoided. . . . Therefore, man chooses, not of necessity, but freely.

> In the following selection Aquinas stresses the necessity of assenting to the truths of faith even if they are beyond the grasp of reason.

Summa Contra Gentiles

Another benefit that comes from the revelation to men of truths that exceed the reason is the curbing of presumption, which is the mother of error. For there are some who have such a presumptuous opinion of their own ability that they deem themselves able to measure the nature of everything: I mean to say that, in their estimation, everything is true that seems to them so, and everything is false that does not. So that the human mind, therefore, might be freed from this presumption and come to a humble inquiry after truth, it was necessary that some things should be proposed to man by God that would completely surpass his intellect.

A still further benefit may also be seen in what Aristotle says in the *Ethics.* There was a certain Simonides who exhorted people to put aside the knowledge of divine things and to apply their talents to human occupations. He said that "he who is a man should know human things, and he who is mortal, things that are mortal." Against Simonides Aristotle says that "man should draw himself towards what is immortal and divine as much as he can." And so he says in the *De animalibus* that, although what we know of the higher substances is very little, yet that little is loved and desired more than all the knowledge that we have about less noble substances. He also says in the *De caelo et mundo* that when questions about the heavenly bodies can be given a modest and merely plausible solution, he who hears this experiences intense joy. From all these considerations it is clear that even the most imperfect knowledge about the most noble realities brings the greatest perfection to the soul. Therefore, although the human reason cannot grasp fully the truths that are above it, yet, if it somehow holds these truths at least by faith, it acquires great perfection for itself.

Therefore it is written: "For many things are shown to thee above the understanding of men" (Ecclus. 3:25). . . .

Those who place their faith in this truth, however, "for which the human reason offers no experimental evidence," do not believe foolishly, as though "following artificial fables" (II Peter 1:16). For these "secrets of divine Wisdom" (Job 11:6) the divine Wisdom itself, which knows all things to the full, has deigned to reveal to men. It reveals its own presence, as well as the truth of its teaching and inspiration, by fitting arguments; and in order to confirm those truths that exceed natural knowledge, it gives visible manifestation to works that surpass the ability of all nature. Thus, there are the wonderful cures of illnesses, there is the raising of the dead. . . . [A]nd what is more wonderful, there is the inspiration given to human minds, so that simple and untutored persons, filled with the gift of the Holy Spirit, come to possess instantaneously the highest wisdom and the readiest eloquence. When these arguments were examined [in Roman times], . . . in the midst of the tyranny of the persecutors, an innumerable throng of people, both simple and most learned, flocked to the Christian faith. In this faith there are truths preached that surpass every human intellect, the pleasures of the flesh are curbed; it is taught that the things of the world should be spurned. Now, for the minds of mortal men to assent to these things is the greatest of miracles, just as it is a manifest work of divine inspiration that, spurning visible things, men should seek only what is invisible. Now, that this has happened . . . as a result of the disposition of God, is clear from the fact that through many pronouncements of the ancient prophets God had foretold that He would do this. The books of these prophets are held in veneration among us Christians, since they give witness to our faith.

Guillaume d' Orange

THE CONQUEST OF ORANGE

Introduction by Constance Bouchard

During the twelfth century "vernacular" literature emerged for the first time, that is, litera-ture written not in the Latin of the church or the schoolroom, but in the everyday spoken language (early forms of French, German, Italian, and so on). Some of the most popular stories were those now called epics, tales of adventure, war, conquest, and often death. Most of these epics had as their heroes semi-legendary, semi-historical figures, usually noble lords and often kings. By creating these larger-than-life characters and placing them in an imaginary past, the authors were able to make comments on their own society.

These marvelous, vaguely-historical figures included King Arthur, Charlemagne, and William of Orange, the hero of the following selection. William was based ultimately on a real person, a great lord who had served Charlemagne for many years and finally retired to a monastery, some three centuries before epics were created about him. There were more than half a dozen different William of Orange epics written in the twelfth century, roughly linked into a "cycle" of stories. This selection tells how William captured the castle of Orange, a real city in southern France, located on the Rhone river, which, according to legend, became his capital.

This particular story is set in the context of conflict between Christians and Muslims. The southern part of France had been dominated by Muslims during the time of the real William, in the eighth and ninth centuries, and in the twelfth century the French knights and nobles who would have enjoyed this story most were also very interested in the conflict between those who followed the two different religions. The twelfth century was the period of the Crusades, when many French knights went to the Holy Land to try to conquer the Muslims who controlled the region, and when many more French knights fought against Muslims in Spain. The person who wrote this story had no trouble making the Muslims into the villains; clearly he saw little use for religious tolerance.

As well as highlighting the differences between Christians and Muslims, as perceived by Christians who actually knew very little about Islam, this story's plot turns on the power of love. Romantic love, in which people alter their whole life-span after falling for someone, act more nobly and more bravely because of the beloved's inspiration, and get happily married at the end, may seem normal in America in the twenty-first century, but it was a real novelty in the twelfth century. At the time the William of Orange stories were being written, the knights and nobles who made up their audience mostly took spouses in marriages arranged for them by their relatives. The presence and power of love in these stories, with its ability to bring together even a Christian and a Muslim, and to inspire both male and female into fearless action, thus had a distinctly subversive quality.

Although most of the stories in the William of Orange cycle were very serious, this one was intended to be funny. Certainly it has moments of tension and danger, but the basic plot of William creeping into a castle in disguise, and his nephew repeatedly blaming him for being about to get them all killed, would certainly have been humorous to those who read this tale or heard it being read. Its humor would not have undercut, and indeed would have strengthened, the author's ideas about courage, religion, and the roles and relations of men and women.

The Conquest of Orange

Translated by Joan M. Ferrante

i

Listen my lords, and may God give you grace,
the glorious son of Holy Mary,
to a good song that I would offer you.
It is not a tale of pride or folly,
or deception plotted and carried out
but of brave men who conquered in Spain.
They know it well, who have been to St. Gilles,
who have seen the relics kept at Brioude,
the shield of William and the white buckler,
and Bertrand's too, his noble nephew.   10
I think that no clerk will belie me,
nor any writing that's found in a book.
They have all sung of the city of Nîmes,
which William holds among his possessions,
the great high walls and the rooms built of stone,
and the palace and the many castles
and by God, he had not yet won Orange!
There are few men who have told it truly,
but I shall tell what I learned long ago,
how Orange was destroyed and undone.   20
This William did, of the bold countenance.
He expelled the pagans from Almeria,
and the Saracens of Eusce and Pincernie,
those of Baudas and of Tabarie.
He took as his wife Orable the queen—
she had been born of a pagan race—
the wife of Tiebaut, king of Africa.

Guillaume d'Orange: *Four Twelfth-Century Epics* (Joan Ferrante, trans.), Columbia UP, 1991 (ISBN 0231-09634-8),
original pp. 141–195 ("Conquest of Orange" epic).

Then she turned to God, blessed Mary's son,
and founded churches and monasteries.
There are not many who could tell you of them.   30

ii

Hear me, my lords, noble knights and worthy,
if it please you to hear a good deed sung,
how Count William took and destroyed Orange
and took to wife the wise Lady Orable,
who had been Tiebaut of Persia's queen.
Before he was able to win her love,
he had, in truth, to suffer great pains,
many days he fasted, and waked many nights.

iii

It was in May, in the early summer,
the woods blossoming, and the meadows green,   40
the sweet waters withdrawing into streams
and the birds singing sweetly and soft.
One morning Count William arises,
and goes to the church to hear the service.
He comes out when the service is over
and mounts the palace of the heathen Otran,
whom he had conquered by his fierce courage.
He goes to look from the great windows
and gazes far out across the kingdom.
He sees the fresh grass and the rose gardens,   50
he hears the song-thrush and the blackbird sing,
then he remembers the joy and pleasure
that he used to feel when he was in France.
He calls Bertrand: "Sir nephew, come here.
We came out of France in great poverty,
we brought with us no harpers or minstrels,
or young ladies to delight our bodies.
We have our share of fine well-groomed horses,
and strong chain-mail and gilded helmets,
sharp, cutting swords and fine buckled shields,   60
and splendid spears fashioned of heavy iron,
and bread and wine and salted meat and grain;
but God confound the Saracens and Slavs
who leave us to sleep and rest here so long
for they have not yet crossed the sea in force,
to give us the chance to prove ourselves.
It tires me to stay so quiet here,
shut up so tight inside these walls,
as if we were all held as prisoners."
His mind is led astray in this folly,   70

but before the sun is hid or vespers sung,
he will be brought news of such a nature
that he'll be filled with anger and fury.

iv
William stands at the windows in the wind,
sixty of his Franks in attendance,
not one of them without new white ermine,
stockings of silk and cordovan sandals.
Most of them loose their falcons in the wind.
Count William, feeling great joy in his heart,
looks into the valley through the steep mountains;　　　　　　　80
he sees the green grass, the roses in bloom,
and the oriole and the blackbird in song.
He calls Guielin and Bertrand to his side,
his two nephews, whom he loves so well:
"Listen to me, worthy and valiant knights,
we came from France not very long ago;
if only we now had a thousand girls,
maidens from France, with graceful charming forms,
so that our barons might be entertained,
and I too might delight in making love;　　　　　　　　　90
that would be greatly to my liking.
We have enough fine chargers, swift and strong,
sturdy chain-mail and good shining helmets,
sharp, cutting spears and splendid heavy shields,
good swords whose hilts are fashioned of silver,
and bread and wine, cheeses and salted meat.
God confound the Saracens and Persians
who do not cross the sea to do battle.
Our stay inside here starts to weary me,
for I have no chance to test my courage."　　　　　　　100
He wanders distracted in his folly,
but the sun won't set nor will evening come,
before he is brought such a piece of news,
that it will make him both angry and sad.

v
William is at the windows on the wall,
with him there are a hundred Franks and more;
there is not one who is not clothed in ermine.
He looks below where the Rhone river roars
and to the East, where the roadway runs;
he sees some wretch emerge from the water;　　　　　　110
it is Gilbert, from the city, Lenu.
He was captured on a bridge of the Rhone,
the Turks, shouting, brought him back to Orange.

Three years they held him in prison there,
until one morning as the day appeared,
when it was God's will that he should escape,
a Saracen untied him by the gate
and then began to beat and insult him.
When the knight had as much as he could bear,
he seized him by the hair and pulled him down;   120
with his huge fist, he struck him such a blow,
that it shattered both his chest and his spine.
Dead at his feet, he has thrown down his foe.
Down from the window, now, he throws himself,
he can no longer be restrained or held.
From there to Nîmes he comes without a stop,
he will report such tidings here today
to our barons, who talk now of trifles,
that will relieve William of his boredom
and bring delight with ladies in the nude.   130

vi
William the noble is at the window.
The fleeing captive has crossed the Rhone,
climbed the hills and gone down the valleys,
from there to Nîmes, he has not made a stop.
He enters the gates of the good city
and finds William beneath the full pine,
and, in his train, many excellent knights.
Beneath the pine, a minstrel is singing
an ancient song, of venerable age.
It is quite good and it pleases the count.   140
And now Gilbert begins to climb the steps;
William sees him and looks at him closely,
he is black and dirty and yet he's pale,
sickly and pallid, tired and thin.
He thinks he must be Saracen or Slav
who has been sent from across the sea
to bring him a message and take one back.
But then the poor wretch begins to greet him:
"May the Lord God who made both wine and grain,
and gives us light and brightness from heaven,   150
who made man and woman to walk and speak,
preserve William, the marquis of the short nose,
the flower of France and his noble knights,
the fighters whom I see assembled here!"
"My good friend and brother, may God bless you!
But tell us now, do not keep it hidden,
who taught you to call this William by name?"
"Sire," he answers, "you will hear the truth now;

inside Orange I have been a long time,
and could not find any way to escape,
until one morning as day was breaking,
it was Jesus' will that I be set free."
And William says: "God be praised for that!
But tell me now, do not hide it from me,
what is your name, in what land were you born?"
"Sire," he says, "you will soon hear the truth,
but I have suffered so much torment and pain,
I have waked through the nights and fasted all day,
it is four days since I have eaten at all."
And William says: "You will have all you wish."
The count then summons his chamberlains:
"Bring this man plenty of food to eat,
with bread and wine, mixed with spices and honey,
cranes and geese, and peacocks with pepper."
And this was done, as he had commanded.
When he has been richly entertained,
he sits willingly at the feet of the count
and begins to relate the news he brought.

vii

Count William has seen the strange messenger,
he summons him and then asks this question:
"Where were you born, friend, and in what country?
What is your name, where in France have you been?"
Gilbert replies, a most valiant knight:
"I am Guion's son, the Duke of Ardennes,
and of Vermendois, which he also holds.
Through Burgundy I came from Alemaigne,
I set sail on the waters of Lausanne,
but a wind caught me and a great tempest
and carried me to the port of Geneva.
Pagans captured me at Lyons on the Rhone
and led me off to the port at Orange.
There's no fortress like it from here to the Jordan;
the walls are high, the tower large and wide,
the courtyards, too, and the whole enclosure.
Twenty thousand pagans armed with lances,
seven score Turks, bearing standards—
the city of Orange is guarded well,
for they're afraid that Louis will take it,
and you, sweet lord, and the barons of France.
There's Aragon, a rich Saracen king,
the son of Tiebaut, of the land of Spain,
and lady Orable, a noble queen;
there is none so lovely from here to the East,

160

170

180

190

200

a beautiful body, slender and fine;
her skin is white, like a flower on the stem.
God, what good is her body or her youth,
she doesn't know God, our father almighty!"
"It's true," says William, "their power is great,
but by Him, in whom I have placed my faith,
I shall not bear shield or lance any more   210
if I do not manage to meet them soon."

viii
Count William has listened to the baron
who is sitting beside him on the step;
he addresses him and speaks with affection:
"Fair brother, friend, you have told quite a tale.
Did the Saracens keep you long in prison?"
"Yes, they did, sire, three years and fifteen days,
and there was no way for me to escape
until one morning when God gave us day,
a Saracen, evil and arrogant,   220
wanted to beat me, as he had each day.
I seized him by the hair on his forehead,
struck him so hard on the neck with my fist,
that I shattered all the bones of his throat.
Then I escaped through the window, alone,
so that not one of the enemy saw.
To Beaucaire, the port at Oriflor, came
Turks and Persians, the king of Aragon,
the elder son of King Tiebaut the Slav;
he is large and heavy and strong and tall,   230
his head is broad and his brow bound with iron,
his nails are long and pointed and sharp,
there is no tyrant like him under the world's cloak.
He murders our Christians and destroys them.
Whoever could win that city and tower
and put to death the treacherous villain,
he would have spent his labor very well."

ix
"Good brother, friend," says Count William the brave,
"Is Orange really as you have described?"
Gilbert answers: "It is even better.   240
If you could see the principal palace,
how high it is and enclosed all around,
as you look at it from any view;
if you were there the first day of summer,
you would hear the birds as they sing there then,

the falcons' cry and the moulting goshawks,
the horses' whinny and the braying mules
that entertain and delight the Saracens.
The sweet herbs smell most fragrant there,
spices and cinammon which he had planted.   250
There you might see the fair Lady Orable
who is the wife of Sir Tiebaut the Slav;
there is no one so fair in all Christendom,
nor in pagan lands wherever you seek.
Her body is lovely, slender and soft,
and her eyes change color like a moulting falcon,
but of what use is all her beauty
when she does not know God and his goodness?
A noble man could be well pleased with her,
she could be saved if she wished to believe."   260
Then William says: "By the faith of St. Omer,
good brother, friend, you sing her praises well.
But by Him who has all mankind to save,
I will not carry lance or shield again
if I don't win the lady and the city."

x

"Good brother, friend, is Orange then so rich?"
The fugitive answers: "God help me, my lord,
if you could see the palace of the city
with its many vaults and its palisades,
as it was built by Grifon of Almeria,   270
a Saracen of most marvelous vice.
No flower grows from here to Pavia
that is not painted there in gold artfully.
Within is Lady Orable, the queen,
the wife of King Tiebaut of Africa.
There is none so lovely in all pagandom,
her body is beautiful, slender and fine,
her skin is as white as the flower of the thorn,
her eyes bright and hazel and always laughing;
But what good is her gay spirit to her   280
when she doesn't know God, blessed Mary's son."
"You have set," William says, "great worth on her,
and by the faith that I owe to my love,
I shall eat no more bread made from flour,
no salted meat, I shall drink no more wine,
until I have seen how Orange is set.
And I must see that tower of marble,
and Lady Orable, the gracious queen.
Love of her has me so in its power,

that I could not describe or conceive it.   290
If I can't have her soon, I shall lose my life."
The fugitive says: "This idea is insane,
if you were now inside that palace
and could see the vast Saracen array,
God confound me, if I thought I should live
long enough to see such a thing achieved.
Best let it be, the whole idea is mad."

xi
Count William listens to the troubled words
that the fugitive has spoken to him.
He summons the people of his country: 300
"Give me advice, noble men of honor.
This poor wretch has praised a city to me,
I was never there, I don't know the land.
But the Rhone runs here, a swift, moving stream,
except for it I should have gone by now."
The fugitive says: "This whole plan is mad.
If you had a hundred thousand with swords,
with beautiful weapons and golden shields,
and you wished to engage the enemy,
if there'd been no water or obstacle   310
before you could even enter the gates,
a thousand blows of the sword would be struck
and belts would be torn and many shields pierced
and many fine men struck down in the streets.
Let it all be, it is madness to try."

xii
"Look here," William says, "You have disturbed me,
you have just told me about this city
that no count or king possesses its like
and you would prevent me from going there.
By St. Maurice, who is sought at Amiens,   320
I tell you, you shall accompany me,
and we shall not take horses or palfreys
or white chain-mail or helmets from Amiens,
no shield or lance or Poitevin spears—
but javelins, like greedy fugitives.
You have spoken enough Turkish in that land
and African, Basque and Bedouin tongues."
The wretch hears him, imagine how he feels—
he wishes he were at Chartres or Blois
or at Paris in the land of the king,   330
for he does not know how to get out of this.

xiii
Now William is angry and filled with wrath,
his nephew Bertrand undertakes to speak:
"Uncle," he says, "give up this madness,
if you were now in that city's palace
and you could look at those Saracen hordes,
you would be known by your bump and your laugh,
they would quickly suspect that you were a spy.
Then, I'm afraid, you'd be brought to Persia,   340
they would not feed you on bread or flour,
nor would they wait long before they killed you;
they would throw you into a stone prison,
and you wouldn't come out again in your lives
until King Tiebaut of Africa came
and Desramé and Golias of Bile,
they would sentence you however they wished.
If, because of love, you come to judgment,
the people of your kingdom will say
that you were cursed for the sight of Orable the queen."   350
"Look," says William, "I have no fear of that
for, by the apostle sought in Galicia,
I would far rather die and lose my life
than go on eating bread made from flour
or salted flesh and fermented wine.
Instead I shall see how Orange is set
and Gloriete with its marble tower
and lady Orable, the gracious queen.
The love of her torments and governs me—
a man in love is reckless and a fool."

xiv
Now William is troubled about Orange,   360
his nephew Bertrand begins to chide him:
"Uncle," he says, "you'll bring shame on yourself
and dishonor, and have your limbs torn off."
"Look," says the count, "that is not what I fear,
a man who's in love is completely mad.
I would not give up, though I lose my limbs,
not for any man who might beg me to,
going to see how Orange is set,
and Lady Orable, so worthy of praise.
Love for her has so taken hold of me   370
I can't sleep in the night or take any rest,
I am unable to drink or to eat
or carry arms or to mount on my horse
or go to mass, or to enter a church."

He orders ink ground up in a mortar
and other herbs that the baron knew of;
he and Gilbert, who does not dare leave him,
paint their bodies in front and behind,
their faces and their chests, even their feet,
so they resemble devils and demons.   380
Guielin says: "By St. Riquier's body,
you have both been transformed by a miracle,
now you could wander throughout the world,
you wouldn't be recognized anywhere.
But, by the apostle who's sought in Rome,
I would not give up, though I lose my limbs,
going with you to see how it will be."
With the ointment he too is painted and swabbed;
there are the three all prepared to set forth,
they take their leave and depart the city.   390
"God," says Bertrand, "good and righteous father,
how we have been deceived and betrayed!
In what madness was this affair begun
which will bring us all dishonor and shame,
if God does not help, who must judge us all."

xv
William goes forth, the marquis of the fierce look,
with brave Gilbert and the proud Guielin.
Count Bertrand has already turned back
but these go on without further delay.
Below Beaucaire they have found the Rhone   400
and at Dourance they've crossed over it.
Thereabouts they begin to swim quietly,
they cross the Sorgues without barge or ship.
By Aragon, they have gotten across;
straight towards the walls and moats of Orange
the high halls and the fortified palace
adorned with golden pommels and eagles.
Inside they can hear the little birds sing,
the falcons cry and the moulting goshawks,
the horses whinny and the braying mules,   410
and the Saracens entertained in the tower,
the soft fragrance of spices and cinammon,
all the sweet herbs they have in plenty.
"God," says William, "who gave me life and breath,
what wealth there is in this wondrous city!"
How rich he must be who possesses it."
They do not stop until they reach the gate
and then Gilbert addresses the porter

in his own tongue, he speaks courteously:
"Open these gates, porter, let us come in,
we are interpreters from Africa
and men of King Tiebaut the Slav."
The porter says: "I have not heard of you.
What people are you who call me out there?
King Aragon is not yet awake,
and I do not dare to open the gate,
so much do we fear William of the short nose,
who captured Nîmes with such violent force.
You remain here, I shall go to the king;
if he commands, then I'll let you enter."
"Go right away," says the baron William,
"quickly so that we lose no more time."
The porter leaves without any delay,
he climbs the marble steps of the palace.
He finds Aragon seated by a pillar,
surrounded by his Saracens and Slavs.
Courteously he begins to address him:
"Sire," he says, "listen to this report:
at the gate there are three honorable Turks
who claim to be from Africa beyond the seas."
"Then go, good brother, and let them come in;
there are many things I should like to ask
about my lord who has waited so long."
And so he runs back to open the gate.
Now William has gotten inside Orange,
with him Gilbert and the worthy Guielin.
They will not get out once the gates are shut
before they have suffered distress and pain.

xvi

Now William has gotten inside Orange
with Guielin and the noble Gilbert.
They are disguised by alum and black dye,
so that they look like Saracen tyrants.
In the palace they find two Saracens,
they call to them and speak their idiom,
one tells the other: "They're from Africa,
today we shall hear some good news from there."
But Count William keeps walking straight ahead,
towards the palace of the Persian Tiebaut.
The columns and the walls are built of marble
and the windows sculpted of fine silver;
a gold eagle sparkles and shines.
The sun doesn't enter, nor a breath of wind.

420

430

440

450

460

"God," says William, "redeemer and father—
who ever saw such a splendid palace!
How rich he must be, the lord of this hall,
would it were God's will, who formed all mankind,
that I had with me my palatine Bertrand,
and all the ten thousand Frank warriors!
We would bury the unlucky Saracens.
I would kill a good hundred before noon."   470
He finds Aragon beside a column
and around him fifteen thousand Persians.
William is dead, if he can't deceive them.
Now you shall hear how he speaks to them:
"Emir and lord, noble and valiant knight,
Mohammed greets you and the God Tervagant."
Says the emir: "Baron, you may approach.
Where are you from?" "The African kingdom
of your father, the mighty king Tiebaut.
Yesterday morning as nones was sounded,   480
we got to Nîmes, the strong and rich city,
where we expected to find King Otran
and Sinagon and the tyrant Harpin.
But William had killed him, with his Frank troops;
our men were murdered, bleeding and torn.
He put the three of us in his prison, too,
but he is so rich in family and friends
that somehow we were allowed to escape.
We don't know how—may the devil take him!"
Aragon says: "How sad this makes me.   490
By Mohammed, in whom I believe,
if I had William in my power now,
he would be dead and suffering torment,
his bones and ashes scattered to the winds."
William hears him and he lowers his head.
He wishes that he were at Paris or Sens;
he calls on God, his merciful father:
"Glorious sire, who has formed all mankind,
who was born of the Virgin in Bethlehem,
if the three kings came in search of you   500
and if you were hung on the cross by tyrants,
and by the lance, you were pierced in the side—
Longinus did it, who could not see—
and blood and water ran down from the point;
he rubbed his eyes and the light was restored.
If this is true, just as I have told it,
guard our bodies against death and torment.
Don't let Saracens or Persians kill us!"

xvii

William is in the palace at the tower.
He calls his other companions to him   510
quietly, so the pagans cannot hear:
"My lords," he says, "we shall be in prison
if God does not help by His most holy name."
"Uncle William," Guielin answers him,
"Noble lord, sire, you came here seeking love,
you see Gloriete, the palace and tower,
why don't you ask where the ladies are kept.
You might well find a way to deceive them."
And the count says: "You are right, my young squire."
Now King Aragon begins to question him: 520
"Baron, when were you in Africa?"
"My dear lord, no more than two months ago."
"Did you see King Tiebaut of Aragon?"
"Yes, my good lord, when he was at Vaudon.
He embraced us and sent you this message,
that you maintain his honor and city.
Where is his wife? Will you show her to us?"
"Of course, my lords," says the king Aragon.
"There is none lovelier up to the clouds.
But barons," he adds, "I have need of my father;   530
the Franks are taking our castles and towers.
William is the one, with his two nephews.
But, by Mohammed's and Tervagant's faith,
if I now held William in my prison,
he would soon be burned in fire and coals,
his bones and ashes scattered through the air."
William hears him, he holds his head down
and wishes he could be at Reims or Laon.
He calls on God and His glorious name:
"Glorious father, who made Lazarus,   540
and became incarnate in the Virgin,
preserve my body from death and prison.
Don't let these evil Saracens kill us!"

xviii

Now William is in the noble palace;
pagans and Saracens call for water,
the tables are placed, they sit down to eat.
William sits too and his nephew Guielin;
they speak softly and hold their heads down,
they're in great fear that they will be captured.
King Aragon has them served splendidly.   550
They have plenty of bread and wine at the meal,

cranes and geese and well-roasted peacocks,
and other foods I cannot describe.
There is as much as anyone could wish.
When they have eaten and drunk to their pleasure,
the cup-bearers come to take up the cloths.
Pagan and Saracens start to play chess.
William hears all the palace resound,
which is sculpted of green marble and dark,
he sees the birds and lions depicted: 560
"God," says the count, "who was hung on the cross,
who ever saw so splendid a palace!
If it pleased God, who never deceives us,
that we had the palatine Bertrand here,
and the twenty thousand Franks with their arms,
the pagans would meet a bad end today.
By my head, I would kill eighty myself."

xix
King Aragon has summoned Count William
to sit beside him beneath a pillar
and in his ear he questions him softly: 570
"Noble Turk," he asks, "now tell me the truth,
what sort of man is William of the short nose,
who captured Nîmes with his powerful force
and murdered King Harpin and his brother?
He had you thrown into his prison, too."
And William answers: "You will hear the truth now.
He is so rich, in pride of possessions,
that he has no care for gold or silver;
instead he let us escape for nothing
except that he made us swear by our laws.   580
He sent you a message we cannot hide,
that you flee over seas to Africa,
you will not see the month of May go by
before he attacks with twenty thousand men;
your towers and columns will not save you,
your magnificent halls, nor your deep moats.
With iron clubs they will all be destroyed.
If he captures you, you will suffer torture.
You will hang from the gallows in the wind."
Aragon says: "What madness is this—   590
I shall send overseas to Africa,
my father will come with his mighty nobles,
with Golias and the king Desramé,
Corsolt of Mables, his brother Aceré,
and Clariau and the king Atriblez
and Quinzepaumes and the king Sorgalez,

the king of Egypt and King Codroez,
and King Moranz and the king Anublez,
and the prince of Sorgremont on the sea,
my uncle Borreaus and all his sons,   600
and the thirty kings who were born in Spain.
Each one will bring twenty thousand armed men
and we will fight at the walls and the moats;
William will be dead and go to his end
and his nephews will be hung from the gallows."
William hears him and almost loses his mind;
between his teeth, he answers him softly:
"By God," he says, "you pig, you are lying,
instead three thousand Turks will be killed,
before you conquer or hold Nîmes in fief."   610
If he had arms to equip himself now,
he would hold all the palace in terror
for he can no longer control his rage.

xx

Now William is in the great stone hall:
"King Aragon," he begins his address,
"Sire," he says, "will you show me the queen
whom Africa's emperor seems to love so?"
Aragon says: "It is madness in him,
for he is old and his beard is snow-white,
and she is a young and beautiful girl,   620
there is none so fair in all pagandom.
In Gloriete he enjoys his loves—
better if he loved Soribant of Venice,
a young bachelor who still has his first beard,
who knows how to live with arms and pleasure
better than Tiebaut of Slavonia.
An old man is mad to love a young girl,
he is soon cuckolded and driven mad."
When William hears him he begins to laugh.
"Tell me," asks William, "you don't love her at all?"   630
"Not I, certainly, God curse the woman!
I only wish she were in Africa
or at Baudas, in Almeria."

xxi

In the palace is William the noble,
and Gilbert too and the mighty Guielin;
they go out through the center of the hall,
led by an unsuspecting pagan,
to the queen who is so loved by the king.
Better for them if they would return

beyond the Rhone and go back to Nîmes;   640
before evening comes or the sun can set,
unless God acts with his noble power,
they will suffer what will cause them sorrow.
At Gloriete, they have now arrived,
of marble are its pillars and walls,
and the windows sculpted in fine silver,
the golden eagle, resplendent and bright,
the sun cannot enter, nor does the wind blow;
it is beautifully done, pleasant and charming.
In one part of the chamber, inside,   650
there is a pine grown in such a way,
as you shall hear, if that is your wish:
the branches are long and the leaves are large,
the flower it bears wond'rously fair;
it is white and blue, and even red.
There's an abundance of carob-trees there,
spices, cinnamon, galingale, and incense,
sweet fragrances, of hyssop and allspice.
There sits Orable, the African lady,
dressed in a gown of marvelous stuff,   660
tightly laced on her noble body,
and sewn along the sides with rich silks,
and Rosiane, the niece of Rubiant,
makes a gentle breeze with a silver fan.
She is more white than snow in the sunlight,
she is more red than the most fragrant rose.
William sees her and his blood turns cold,
he greets her nobly and courteously.
"May that God save you, in whom we believe!"
The queen answers: "Baron, please approach me.   670
Mohammed save you, on whom the world depends."
Beside her, she has them sit on a bench,
that is sculpted in silver and gold.
Now they can speak somewhat of their wishes.
"God," says William, "this is paradise here!"
Says Guielin: "I've seen nothing finer,
I would like to spend all my life here.
There would never be a reason to leave."

xxii
Now William is seated in Gloriete,
and Gilbert and the worthy Guielin,   680
near the ladies in the shade of the pine.
There sits Orable, of the bright face,
wearing a piece of ermine fur
and underneath a samite tunic,

tightened with laces on her lovely body.
William sees her, all his body trembles.
"God," says William, "it is Paradise here!"
"If God would help me," Guielin responds,
"I would remain here most willingly.
I would not seek either food or sleep." 690
Then the noble lady begins to ask:
"Where are you from, noble and gentle knight?"
"Lady we are from the Persian kingdom,
from the land of your husband, Tiebaut.
Yesterday morning, when day was breaking,
we were at Nîmes, that marvelous city,
we expected to find people of our race,
King Sinagon and Otran and Harpin,
but Fierebrace had killed all three of them.
The Franks captured us at the gates of the city 700
and led us before the palatine,
but he is so rich and supported by friends
that he does not care for silver or gold.
Instead he let us escape in this way:
first we had to swear an oath by our laws
and carry This message which I bring to you,
that you must flee to the Persian kingdom,
for you will not see the month of April pass
before he comes with twenty thousand men.
The palace and the walls will not save you, 710
nor the broad halls, not the strong palisades,
with iron clubs they will all be destroyed.
If he captures Aragon the Arab,
your stepson, the prince that you love so much,
he will make him die an unpleasant death,
by hanging or burning in fire and flame."
The lady hears him and sighs tenderly.

xxiii

The lady listens to the strange message,
then she asks them, she is anxious to know:
"My lord barons, I am versed in your tongue. 720
What sort of a man is William Fierebrace,
who captured Nîmes, the palace and the halls
and killed my men, and is still threatening me?"
"Indeed," says the count, "he has a fierce heart,
his fists are huge and his arm is mighty.
There is no man from here to Arabia
who, if William strikes him with his sharp sword,
would not be hacked apart, body and arms,
straight to the ground drives that sword as it cuts."

"Indeed," says the lady, "this is distressing.   730
By Mohammed, he will hold great domains.
Happy the lady who possesses his heart."
Then the villainous pagans come in a crowd;
today William will find more trouble
than he has encountered in all his life.
May God protect him against loss and harm!

xxiv
Now William has climbed inside the tower,
and Gilbert and the worthy Guielin;
beside the ladies under the pine,
he sits chatting softly with the queen.   740
The treacherous pagans are massed outside
to watch the barons and look at them.
Unless God helps, who was hung on the cross,
today William will be badly abused,
for there is a pagan, Salatré—
may He confound him who must save us all—
one whom the count had captured at Nîmes,
but one evening the scoundrel had escaped
and had fled through the moats and found his way,
so that he could not be recaptured or found.   750
He causes terrible trouble for William,
as you are about to hear recounted.
To Aragon, the scoundrel now comes,
into his ear he pours out a whole tale:
"By Mohammed, sire, arouse your barons.
We can avenge now the fierce cruelty
that would have struck me at the city of Nîmes.
You see that strong figure in the tower?
That is William, the marquis of the short nose,
and his nephew is the other young knight,   760
the third one, who carries the heavy club,
is the marquis who escaped from here.
To deceive you, they have donned this disguise,
for they hope to capture this good city."
Aragon asks: "Do you tell me the truth?"
"Sire," he answers, "you'll be sorry if you doubt me.
That is William who had me imprisoned,
he would have had me hanging in the wind
if Mohammed had not protected me.
This is the day that he'll be rewarded."   770
Now hear me tell, noble barons and good,
for the love of God who hung on the cross,
of that villain, what evil he worked.
He takes a tunic, made of pure gold,

and hurls it straight into William's face,
it strikes William just above the nose,
he is discovered, his color comes off;
his skin is white like a summer flower.
When William sees this, he almost goes mad,   780
throughout his body the blood runs cold.
He calls on God, the king in majesty:
"Glorious father, who must save us all,
who deigned to become flesh in the Virgin,
all for the people whom You wished to save,
You gave up Your body to pain and torment,
to be wounded and injured upon the cross,
as this is all true, lord, in Your goodness,
guard my body from death and destruction.
Don't let the Slavs and Saracens kill us!"

xxv

When Aragon hears what the Slav tells him,   790
that he recognizes the three companions,
he rises to his feet and begins to speak:
"Sir William, your name is well known here,
you'll be sorry you crossed the Rhone, by Mohammed!
You will all be put to dreadful death,
your bones and ashes scattered in the wind.
I would not, for a dungeon filled with gold,
rescue you from death and burning to coals."
William hears him, his color like ashes;
he wishes he were at Reims or Laon;   800
Guielin sees that they can't hide any longer,
he wrings his hands and tears at his hair.
"God," says William, "by Your most holy name,
glorious Father who made Lazarus
and in the Virgin took on human form,
who saved Jonah in the belly of the whale
and Daniel the prophet in the lion's den,
who granted pardon to Mary Magdalene,
brought the body of St. Peter to Rome,
and converted his companion, St. Paul,   810
who was, at that time, a very cruel man,
but then became one of the believers,
together with them he walked in processions,
as this is true, sire, and we believe it,
protect us against death and foul prison.
Don't let treacherous Saracens kill us!"
He has a stick, large and sturdy and long;
with his two hands, he raises it high
and brings it down on the false Salatré,

who had denounced him to King Aragon.   820
Right through his head comes the blow of the club,
so that his brains pour out on the ground.
"Montjoy!" he cries, "strike ahead, barons!"

xxvi
William has all the palace in terror.
Before the king he has killed a pagan.
Count William has found himself a club
that had been brought there to make a fire.
He runs over to it, swiftly and sweating,
grabs it in his fists and lifts it high.
He strikes Baitaime, the reckless pagan,   830
a vigorous blow of the club on his skull,
which causes his brains to fly from his head.
Before the king he has struck him dead.
And Gilbert, too, goes to strike Quarré,
he shoves his club into his stomach
and forces a good part of it out the side.
He throws him down before the pillar, dead.
"Montjoy!" he cries, "barons, come, strike ahead!
Since we are certainly destined to die,
let's sell ourselves high as long as we last!"   840
Aragon hears; he thinks he will go mad.
Aloud he cries: "Barons, capture these men!
By Mohammed, they will be killed straightway
and tossed and thrown into the Rhone,
or burned in fire and scattered to the wind."
Guielin shouts at them "Barons stand aside,
for by the apostle we seek at Rome,
you won't take me without paying for it."
In fierce anger, he brandishes his stick.
Count William begins to strike with his club   850
and Gilbert with his iron-bound cudgel,
mighty blows the noble barons strike;
fourteen Turks they have thrown to their deaths
and so terrified all the others
that, striking, they chase them out through the gates.
Then the towers are bolted and shut,
and by the great chains, the bridge is hauled up.
May God now help, who was hung on the cross!
For William is in a dangerous spot,
and Gilbert and the worthy Guielin,   860
In Gloriete where they have been trapped,
and the Saracens, the raging cowards,
attack them from outside with no respite.

xxvii

The Saracens are fierce and arrogant,
they attack them by hundreds and thousands,
throwing their lances and piercing steel darts.
The Franks defend themselves like noble knights,
casting those pigs into moats and channels,
more than fourteen have already fallen.
The most fortunate has his neck splintered.   870
Aragon sees it and begins to rage,
from sorrow and anger he is nearly mad.
With a loud, clear voice, he begins to shout:
"Are you up there, William of the fierce look?"
The count answers: "Certainly I am here.
By my prowess I have found good lodging,
may God help me, who was raised on the cross!"

xxviii

Now William has entered Gloriete
and begun to speak to the Saracens:
"Damned be he who thinks he can hide!   880
I entered this city in order to spy
and I have deceived and tricked you so well
that I have chased you out of Gloriete.
Henceforth you will be guardians of this tower,
protect it well, your reward will be high!"
Aragon hears him and begins to rage.
He summons the Saracens and pagans:
"Quickly to arms, now, my noble knights.
The assault must now be begun in force.
Whoever captures this William for me   890
will bear the standard for all my kingdom;
all my treasures will be open to him."
When his men hear this they are pleased and encouraged,
the craven flatterers run for their arms
and attack William in front and behind.
The count sees them and nearly goes mad.
He invokes God, the true and righteous judge.

xxix

Now William is angered and sorrowful,
and brave Guielin and the noble Gilbert.
At Gloriete, where they are trapped inside,   900
they are sought by all of that pagan race,
they throw their lances and piercing steel darts.
William sees them and nearly loses his mind.
"Nephew Guielin, what is holding us back?

Never can we hope to return to France,
if God does not help us, with his power,
we shall not see cousins or family."
But Guielin of the graceful body:
"Uncle William, you're speaking to no end.
Because of your love you made your way here;   910
there is Orable, the African lady,
and none so fair alive in this world.
Go now and sit beside her on the bench,
put both your arms around her lovely form
and don't be slow to embrace and kiss her,
for by the apostle penitents seek,
we shall not have the value of that kiss
unless it costs twenty thousand silver marks
and great suffering to all our people."
"God," says William, "your words so incite me   920
that I can barely keep my reason."

xxx
Count William is now angry and enraged,
and Gilbert and the worthy Guielin;
inside Gloriete where they have been trapped
with the Saracen pagans pressing hard;
they defend themselves like skillful knights,
throwing down clubs and huge heavy cudgels.
Now the queen begins to counsel them:
"Barons," she says, "Franks, give yourselves up.
The villainous pagans hate you fiercely,   930
you will soon see them climbing the steps,
you'll all be dead, murdered, and dismembered."
William hears her, his mind is distraught.
He runs to the chamber beneath the pine
and wildly begins to beg the queen:
"My lady," he says, "please give me armor,
for the love of God who was hung on the cross!
For, by St. Peter, if I live through this,
you will be richly rewarded for it."
The lady hears him and weeps with pity.   940
She runs to the chamber without delay,
to a coffer, which she quickly opens.
She takes from it a good golden shirt of mail
and a bright golden helmet, set with jewels;
William runs to take the things from her,
and to receive what he has so desired.
He dons the hauberk and laces the helm,
and Lady Orable girds on the sword
which belonged to her lord, Tiebaut the Slav.

She had not wished any man to have it,   950
not even Aragon, who wanted it so,
and was the son of her wedded husband.
At his neck she hangs a strong polished shield,
on it a lion wearing a gold crown.
In his fist he holds a good, heavy lance,
its standard held by five golden nails.
"God," says William, "how well armed I am now.
For God, I beg you to think of the others!"

xxxi

When Guielin sees that his uncle is armed,
he too runs into the lady's chamber   960
and calls to her, sweetly begging her aid:
"Lady," he asks, "by St. Peter of Rome,
please give me arms, we have such great need."
"My child," she says, "you are so very young,
if you live long you will be a brave man.
But the Vavars and Hongars hate you to death."
In her chamber she takes out a mail-shirt
which Isaac of Barcelone had forged—
there was no sword that could pierce that mail.
He puts it on and his uncle is glad;   970
he laces the Alfar of Babylon's helm,
the first king who had held that city.
There is no sword that can destroy it
or knock off a stone or ruby flower.
She girds the sword of Tornemont of Valsone
which was stolen from him by thieves at Valdonne,
and then sold to Tiebaut at Voirconbe;
he gave a thousand besants for it
for he hoped to pass it on to his son.
She girds it at his side, the straps are long,   980
at his neck she hangs a large, round shield,
and hands him a lance, my lady of Valronne,
the handle is large and the blade is long.
He is well armed and Gilbert as well.
Today Gloriete will be contested.

xxxii

William and his nephew are now well armed,
and Gilbert, too, and they all rejoice.
On his back a strong, double shirt of mail,
on his head they lace a green barred helmet,
then they gird a sword of steel at his side,   990
and they hang a quartered shield from his neck.
But before he takes the good sharp spear,

the evil pagans have advanced so far
that they are beginning to mount the steps.
Count William goes to strike down Haucebier
and Gilbert, the gate-keeper, Maretant,
and Guielin goes to attack Turfier.
These three pagans do not escape death;
they smash the tips of the pointed spears
so that the splinters shoot up toward the sky.   1000
They are now forced to rely on their swords
which they are anxious to try out and prove.
Count William has drawn his sword of steel,
he strikes a pagan across the back
and cuts him down like an olive branch.
Down into the palace the two halves fall.
And Gilbert goes to strike Gaifier
and sends his head flying into the palace.
Guielin too is not at all frightened.
He holds his sword and grasps his good shield;   1010
whoever he meets is destined to die.
Pagans see him and begin to retreat,
the craven flatterers take to flight.
The Franks chase them, the noble warriors,
more than fourteen they've already destroyed,
and terrified all the others so
that they drive them back out through the gates.
The Franks run to shut them and bolt them;
by the great chains they have pulled up the bridge
and attached it fast against the tower.   1020
Now let God think of them who judges all!
Aragon sees it and his mind rages.

xxxiii
Now William is sorrowful and angry
and Gilbert and the worthy Guielin;
they are pressed hard by the pagan masses
who throw their lances and well-turned darts
and beat down the walls with clubs of iron.
William sees it, he is consumed by rage.
"Nephew Guielin," he asks "what shall we do?
Never, it seems, will we return to France.   1030
Nor will we kiss nephews and relatives again."
"Uncle William, this is useless talk,
for by the apostle who's sought at Rome,
I'll sell myself high before we give up."
They climb down the steps of the tower
and strike the pagans on their rounded helmets;
they cut straight through their chests and their chins

until seventeen lie dead in the sand.
The most fortunate has his lungs cut out.
When the pagans see this, their hearts tremble,   1040
they cry aloud to mighty Aragon:
"Make a truce with them, we'll never get in."
Aragon hears them, nearly dissolved in rage,
he swears by Mohammed he will make them pay.

xxxiv
Aragon sees the pagans hesitate,
he calls them graciously and then he says:
"Sons of bitches, pigs, you'll be sorry you came.
You'll never hold fiefs or marches from me,
you can look for them in fiercer fighting."
And so they do, the miscreant swine,   1050
they throw their darts and miserable lances,
with iron clubs they beat down the walls.
William sees it, nearly mad with fury:
"Nephew Guielin, now what can we do?
We are all dead, and doomed to destruction."
"Uncle William, you're talking like a fool,
for by the apostle we seek in the ark,
I'll make them pay before pagans get me."
The points of their spears have all been shattered,
but each of the three picks up an axe   1060
which the noble Lady Orable gave them.
They go out again, bearing new weapons
and strike the pagans on their red targes,
cutting straight through to their faces and chests.
More than fourteen now lie on the marble,
some of them dead, the others unconscious.
Never did three men do so much damage.
Aragon sees it and nearly goes mad.

xxxv
When Aragon sees his people so pressed,
then he grieves and almost bursts with anger.   1070
In a clear voice, he cries out to the Franks:
"Are you up there, William of the fine body,
the son of Aimeri of Narbonne the great?
Do something for me that I greatly desire,
leave Gloriete, the palace, right now
and go away healthy, safe and alive,
before you lose all your limbs and your blood.
If you refuse, you will suffer for it.
By Mohammed, in whom I believe,
here in this place, a great pyre will be built,   1080

you will all be burned and roasted in there."
William answers: "Your talk is for nothing.
We have plenty of bread and wine and cheese
and salted meat and wines, honeyed and spiced,
and white hauberks and green shining helmets,
excellent swords with hilts of silver,
sharp piercing spears and good heavy shields
and lovely ladies to entertain us.
I shall not leave while I am yet alive,
and soon the noble king Louis will know,   1090
my brother Bernard, who is hoary and white,
and the warrior, Garin of Anseune,
and the mighty duke Bueves of Commarch,
my nephew Bertrand, who is brave and valiant,
whom we just left behind us at Nîmes.
Each one of them, whenever he wishes,
can well send twenty thousand warriors.
When they find out what is happening here,
how we are established here within,
they will come to our aid most graciously   1100
with as many men as they can gather.
I tell you, these walls will be no defense,
nor this palace, where gold shines in splendor;
you will see it shattered in a thousand parts.
If they capture you, it will not go easy,
you will be hooked and hung in the wind."
Aragon says: "We shall grieve all the more."
Pharaon speaks, the king of Bonivent,
"Emir, sire, you are not worth a glove.
By Mohammed, you have very little sense.   1110
Your father was worthy and valiant,
and he left this city to you to defend,
and the palace, Gloriete, as well.
These three scoundrels who are challenging you
have been killing your men and your people;
by Mohammed, you are not worth much
if you can't burn them in stinking Greek fire."

xxxvi
"Pharaon, sir," says the king Aragon,
give me better counsel, for Mohammed's sake,
you see Gloriete, the palace and tower,   1120
whose foundation is set so deep and strong.
All the people from here to Moncontor
could not make any opening in it.
Where the devil would we get the coals?

We have no wooden branches or sticks.
Those three pigs got in there by their arrogance,
but they won't get out in seven years."

xxxvii
"Pharaon, sir," says the king Aragon,
"for Mohammed, whose laws we uphold,
you must advise me immediately.   1130
Behold Gloriete, the splendid palace
the foundation is laid in solid rock.
All the men from here to the port of Vauquois
could not make a hole in its walls in a month.
From what devils could we get the coals
when we haven't a twig of wood or laurel?
In their arrogance those three got inside,
but in seven years, they will not get out."
Now a pagan, Orquenois steps forward,
his beard is black, but his hair white with age,   1140
his eyebrows white, if I judge them rightly.
In a loud voice, he cries out three times:
"Emir, sire, will you listen to me,
and tell me if it would be worth my while
to deliver William the Frank to you
so that you might hold him in your prison?"
Aragon answers: "Yes, by my faith.
Ten mules laden with the best Spanish gold
I would give to one who could tell me that."
Orquenois says: "Then listen to me.   1150
If you will give me your promise straightway,
I shall do it, whatever may happen."
Aragon says: "I swear this to you,
and I pledge faithfully here and now
that when you wish you shall have those riches."
The pagan replies: "I give you my word."

xxxviii
Orquenois says: "By Mohammed, sweet lord,
I shall tell you how to take him with guile:
there is Gloriete, the marble tower,
it foundation set well in the stone.   1160
It was built by Grifaigne of Almeria,
a Saracen of great cleverness.
You never knew what tricks they had designed:
Beneath the earth, a solitary vault,
a portcullis into your palace.
Take a thousand Turks and go there yourself

to lay a siege at the front of the tower
and attack at the same time from behind.
William will soon be dead and in torment."
Aragon says: "By Mohammed, that's true.   1170
You'll be rich for this, by my lord Apollo!"

xxxix
When Aragon has learned of this secret,
that there is a cave in the earth beneath him,
his joy is such that it makes his heart leap.
He takes a thousand Turks, their helmets laced,
and another thousand he leaves in front
to keep up the siege of Guielin and William;
the others turn round and go quickly
not stopping until they reach the entrance,
carrying candles and lanterns along.   1180
They enter the cave, that foul hostile race.
The honorable knights know nothing of them
until they're already inside the palace.
William is the first to find out they are there.
"God," says the count, "glorious in heaven,
we are all dead and delivered to pain."
Guielin says: "By St. Hilaire's body,
as God helps me, Orable has betrayed us.
May God confound the whole Saracen race!"

xl
Count William sees the palace being filled   1190
with Saracens who come there in anger;
he sees the hauberks and the helmets shine.
"God," says the count, "who never deceives us,
we are all dead and doomed to destruction."
"In faith, my good lord," answers Guielin,
"we were betrayed by Orable the fair.
May God confound pagans and Saracens!
This is the day that we must meet our end.
Let us help ourselves, as long as we can,
for we have no friends or relatives here."   1200
Count William brandishes the sword of steel,
in fury he moves to strike a pagan
back-handed and cuts him straight through the middle.
The pagans are terrified by this blow.
They rush at him enraged and distressed.
They defend themselves like emboldened knights;
he strikes great blows, the count palatine.
The assault is fierce and the slaughter great,
but it won't end until they're defeated.

No battle was ever fought so well.   1210
In their defense they have killed thirty Turks.
Who cares, if they can never finish them!
The pagans and Saracens lay hold of him,
Turks and Persians and the Almoravi,
Acoperts, Esclamors and Bedouins;
by Mohammed they swear vengeance will be had.
They will avenge the death of their friends.

xli
William is captured by deadly treason
and with him Gilbert and the brave Guielin.
The Saracen villains have them in their hands   1220
and swear by Mohammed to take revenge.
They send twenty boys into the city
to dig a ditch that will be wide and deep,
and to fill it with kindling wood and twigs
for they intend to grill our barons.
Orable comes, she is fair of visage,
and addresses her stepson Aragon:
"My friend," she says, "give these prisoners to me,
I shall place them in my deepest dungeon,
where toads and adders will feed on them   1230
and small serpents will devour them."
"My lady, queen," says the king Aragon,
"you were the cause of this trouble
when you armed these treacherous swine up there.
Damned be the man who would give them to you!"
The lady hears him and trembles with rage.
"You'll be sorry for that, you bastard pig!
By Mohammed, whom I praise and adore,
if it were not for these other barons,
I would strike you on the nose with my fist.   1240
Get yourself out of my tower quickly,
if you stay longer you will regret it."
She addresses the treacherous villains:
"Vile thieves," she says, "put them in your prison
until Tiebaut returns from Valdon,
and Desramé and Golias the blond.
They will take the vengeance they desire."
"I swear it, lady," says King Aragon,
William is cast into the deep dungeon,
and Guielin and the valiant Gilbert.   1250
For a while we must let our barons be;
when it is time we will come back to them.
Now we must sing of the pagan people.

xlii

King Aragon does not rest with his deed,
he sends his messengers over the seas
and they depart, without pause or halt,
from here to the Rhone they don't rest or stop,
and there they embark on a galley,
on the ship of Maudoine of Nubie.
It is artfully covered with silk,   1260
and does not fear a storm or temptest.
They lift their anchor and hoist their sails,
they take to sea, leave the city behind,
they glide and skim and they steer and they sail,
they have a good wind to carry them straight.
When they reach the port beneath Almeria,
they drop anchor and lower their sails.
Mounting their horses, they still do not stop.
They do not pause or rest from their ride
until they reach the African city.   1270
They dismount in the shade of an olive
and begin to climb to the great stone hall.
They find Tiebaut and his pagan nation
and greet him as Saracen custom bids:
"That Mohammed, who holds all in his power,
preserve King Tiebaut of Esclavonie!
Your son, of the bold look, sends you this plea,
that you come to his aid with all your knights.
He has captured William, I'll hide nothing,
the son of Aimeri, from Narbonne the rich,   1280
inside Orange, the well-protected city;
in disguise he had entered the town,
intending to take it as he had Nîmes
and make love to Lady Orable.
But their devilish scheme did not succeed.
They gave us a hard time from Gloriete
which he managed to hold for seven days;
if it hadn't been for the underground cave
whose stones are set beneath the palace,
you would no longer possess Orable,   1290
your wife, who is such a noble lady.
But Mohammed sent you aid in your need,
we have him now in a lonely prison
from which he will never escape alive.
Vengeance will be taken as you will it."
When Tiebaut hears this he begins to laugh,
he summons the people of his empire.
"Now quickly to arms, noble knights and free!"
and they obey without any delay,

mounting horses from Russia and Puglia.   1300
When Tiebaut leaves the African city,
he takes with him pagans of Almeria
and others from Suite and Esclavonie.
At the head, before him, are sixty thousand.
They don't pause or rest till they reach the sea.
In little time the ships are prepared
with wine and meat and biscuits and grain.
They embark quickly, that Saracen race,
raise their anchors and hoist their sails.
The wind blows hard and drives them straight on,   1310
they reach the sea; they are on their way.
Then might you hear such horns and trumpets,
horses neighing and greyhounds barking,
braying of mules and whinnying chargers,
sparrow-hawks crying out on their perches.
You might hear those sounds from a great distance.
Eight days they sail, on the ninth they arrive,
but before they reach Orange the rich,
Tiebaut will know such sorrow and anger,
as he has not felt in his life before.   1320
For he will lose his fortified city
and his wife, the elegant Orable.

xliii

William is deep inside the prison,
Gilbert too and the noble Guielin.
"God," says the count, "Father and redeemer,
we are dead and abandoned to torment!
God, if only King Louis knew of it,
and my brother Bernard, hoary and white,
and Garin the mighty, of Anseune,
and Bueves the great warrior of Commarch,   1330
and my nephew, Bertrand, valiant and brave,
whom we left behind at the city of Nîmes,
and all twenty thousand fighting Franks.
We could derive great comfort from their aid."
Guielin says, the knight of gracious bearing:
"Uncle William, there's no point to such words.
Send for Orable, the African's lady,
to help, for the love she bears her lover!"
"God," says William "you have taunted me so,
it will not take much for my heart to burst."   1340

xliv

Now William is angry and depressed
and Gilbert too, and the worthy Guielin,

inside the prison where they await death.
But while they are lamenting their lot,
Orable suddenly appears at their cell.
When she sees the counts, she begins to speak:
"Listen to me, noble, valiant knights,
pagans and Saracens hate you unto death.
They intend to hang you tonight or tomorrow."
"We can do nothing, lady," says Guielin,   1350
"but consider, noble, gentle lady,
if we could be let out of this dungeon,
I would become your man by oath and vow
and happily I would render service
whenever you, noble lady, might wish."
"But," says William, "it is she who betrayed us,
because of her we are in this dungeon."
The lady hears him and breathes a sigh.

xlv
"My lord baron," says the gracious Orable,
"by Mohammed, you accuse me wrongly.   1360
It was I who armed you in that tower;
if you could keep fighting in the palace
until word reaches Louis, the son of King Charles,
and Sir Bernard of Brabant and the others,
and Aimeri and all your magnificent line,
the treacherous swine would not know of it
until they had reached the marvelous tower,
and then they'd be able to free this land,
its narrow passes, its fords and gorges."
Guielin replies: "Lady, you've spoken well.   1370
If we were now let out of this prison,
I should be your man the rest of my life."
"By my faith," Orable the queen answers,
"if I thought that my pains would thus be repaid,
if William Fierebrace promised to take me,
I would set all three of you free
and would swiftly become a Christian."
William hears her, his spirit's restored.
"Lady," he says, "I shall give you my gage,
I swear this to you by God and St. James,   1380
and by the apostle we seek in the ark."
"Then," says the lady, "I require no more."
She unlocks all the doors of the prison
and they leave it, valiant men;
each of them rejoices in his heart.

xlvi

Now the lady has received the counts' oaths,
and set them free from their prison;
she leads and guides them into Gloriete.
Up in the palace, they sit down to dine.
When they have all been richly feasted,   1390
the noble lady addresses them thus:
"My lords, barons, listen to me now.
I have taken you out of your prison,
I have led you into my palace,
but I do not know how you will escape.
What I have in mind, I had best tell you:
beneath us here, there is a secret cave
which no man yet born of woman knows,
except my ancestor who had it dug;
from here to the Rhone a tunnel was carved.   1400
If you manage to send a messenger
to Count Bertrand and the other barons,
they might come to speak to you underground,
and the infidel pagans would not know
until they had entered the tiled palace
and begun to strike with their broad swords.
In this way they could set the city free
and all its passes, its gorges and moats."
And William says: "My lady, that is so.
But where can we find a messenger."   1410

xlvii

"Nephew Guielin," Count William then says,
from here to Nîmes do not stop or pause,
you must tell your brother Bertrand of us
and bring him to our aid with all his men."
"Uncle William," says Guielin, "what the devil—
may God help me, this must be a joke.
For by the faith I owe to St. Stephen,
I would rather die in this lovely tower
than in sweet France or at Aix-la-chapelle."

xlviii

"Nephew Guielin," says the noble William,   1420
"you must find your way through the cave below,
not stop for a moment from here to Nîmes,
and tell the palatine Bertrand for me
to bring me help immediately."
"Uncle William, there is no point to all this;
I would not desert you, to save my limbs.
I would rather die inside this tower

than in sweet France among my relatives.
Send Gilbert of Flanders instead."
"Will you go, brother?" asks the good William.   1430
And the baron replies: "I shall go, indeed,
and carry your message faithfully."
"Go, then, good brother, I commend you to Jesus,
and tell the palatine Bertrand for me,
that he must help without any delay.
If he does not, by God the redeemer,
he will never see his uncle again."

xlix
When the messenger hears that he must go,
then he begins to rage and wonder
how he can ever escape from there.   1440
"I've never been there, I don't know where to go."
But the lady says: "I shall guide you there.
You need not fear any man born of woman,
except Jesus Christ, the almighty lord."
Next to a pillar she has a stone moved,
which measures a fathom in length and width.
"My brother," she says, "you can enter here.
At its head, you will find three pillars,
formed and designed with vaulted archways."
He leaves them and begins to wander,   1450
not knowing where, underneath the city.
Count William accompanies him quite far
with lady Orable and baron Guielin.
They do not stop until the three pillars;
through their midst, he reaches the outside
and comes to the Rhone where he finds a boat;
then he moves softly across the water.
Count William has already turned back
with Guielin and Orable of the bright face;
All three of them have entered Gloriete.   1460
It would have been better if they had gone on
and descended to the dungeon below,
for not a thing have they done and plotted
that was not overheard by a pagan
who goes to tell it to King Aragon.

l
This Saracen is evil and deceitful,
he goes to denounce them to King Aragon;
as soon as he sees him, he starts to speak:
"Emir and lord, grant me peace and listen
to what your stepmother has been plotting   1470

with the captives whom you held in your prison.
She has taken them all out of the dungeon
and conducted them up to the palace;
in Gloriete they sat down to a meal."
Aragon asks: "Is this true, messenger?"
"Sire," he answers, "I am not a liar,
I have seen them taking secret counsel
and kissing and embracing one another.
She loves them more, and William in bed,
than your father or the king Haucebier."   1480
Aragon hears and almost loses his mind;
he summons his Saracens and Slavs.
"Barons," he says, "give me counsel on this,
tell me in what way I ought to proceed
against my stepmother who has shamed me,
disgraced me and dishonored my father."

li

Aragon says: "Good and powerful knights,
by Mohammed, gather up all your arms.
Whoever now takes armor and weapons
will pay for it before we capture them."   1490
His men answer: "Just as you command."
Fifteen thousand men rush to arm.
God, what trouble when William finds out,
and Lady Orable and brave Guielin.
In Gloriete where they are hidden,
they play at chess, in all confidence;
they suspect nothing, the noble counts,
when the Slavs and Saracens fall on them.

lii

Aragon finds William beneath the pine,
and Lady Orable and bold Guielin;   1500
the palatine counts know nothing of it
until they are taken by Saracens,
Turks and Persians and evil Bedouins.
By Mohammed they swear they'll have revenge;
Pharaon says, he lays claim to finesse,
"Emir and lord, listen to what I say.
Tiebaut your father is brave and noble,
who left this city to you to protect,
and Gloriete the royal palace.
These swine have dared to challenge you for it,   1510
they have murdered your men, hacked and killed them.
By Mohammed, I am not worth a cent,
if I do not have all their limbs torn off;

and your stepmother, who has shamed you so,
I shall see burn and roast in a fire."
But Escanors, who is white-haired and old:
"King Pharaon, you have not spoken well."

liii

Says Escanors, who is hoary and old:
"King Pharaon, you have not judged this well.
You ought never engage in such folly.   1520
If it once starts, you cannot control it.
Emir, my lord, grant me peace and hear me:
Tiebaut your father is a noble man,
he left this city to you to protect,
and Gloriete, the palace and the fief.
If you were really to burn his lady,
he would only be furious with you.
But have these counts thrown back into prison
and put lady Orable in with them.
Then send a messenger over the seas;   1530
your father will come, with King Haucebier,
and let them decide how they'll be avenged."
Aragon says: "You have spoken well.
You'll be rewarded, you will lack nothing.
But I have already sent a messenger
to my father, the king who rules Africa.
Within eight days he should have returned."
They throw William into prison again
with Guielin, who is bold and skillful.
and Lady Orable is cast in with them.   1540
God save them now, who is judge of us all!

liv

Now William has been cast into prison
with Guielin and the gracious Orable;
the unhappy lady cries in despair.
"God," she says, "our good, heavenly father,
this poor creature has not been baptized yet.
I hoped to become one of God's faithful.
Sir William, your valor has brought me harm,
your noble body and knightly honor,
for you I've been thrown into this dungeon,   1550
in anguish as if I had been a whore."
Guielin says: "What nonsense is this,
you and my uncle are not badly off;
through your great love, you should bear this trouble."
William hears him and rages with anger,
in his fury, he swears by St. James:

"If it were not to my shame and disgrace,
I would give you a good blow on the neck."
Guielin says: "That would only be madness.
From now on I shall say, no matter who hears,   1560
you used to be called William the strong-armed,
but now you will be William the lover.
It was for love that you entered this town."
The count hears him, he looks down at the ground.

lv

Now William is furious and distressed,
and lady Orable and Guielin his nephew,
inside the dungeon where they have been thrown.
"God," says the count, "glorious king of heaven.
We are all dead, betrayed and deceived!"
"What folly it was to start this affair,   1570
by which we are all dishonored and shamed,
unless He, who judges all, rescues us.
Alas, if King Louis the fierce only knew,
my brother Bernard, the white-haired and old,
and valiant Sir Garin of Anseune,
and within Nîmes, the powerful Bertrand.
We certainly have great need of their aid."
"Uncle William," says the fierce Guielin,
"let that be, we have no need of them here.
Here is Orable, the gracious lady,   1580
for you to kiss and embrace as you wish,
I can think of no lovelier lady."
"God," says the count, "now I shall go mad."
The pagans hear them quarrel in the prison,
more than forty, they rush in and seize them
and throw the two men out of their dungeon.
They leave Orable, the gracious lady,
but lead uncle and nephew to the palace.
Pharaon speaks, who is fiercest of all:
"Emir, sire, grant me peace and hear me.   1590
Your father, Tiebaut, must be respected.
He left this city to you to protect
and Gloriete, the palace and the fief.
You see this pig, this young bachelor,
nothing you say does he hold worth a cent.
By Mohammed, you're no more than a clown
if you do not have him torn limb from limb,
him and his uncle, William, the warrior."
Guielin hears him, his sense begins to stray,
he grinds his teeth, his eyes roll in his head;   1600
he steps forward, he has pulled his sleeves back;

with his left fist, he grabs him by the hair,
raises the right and plants it on his neck.
The bone in his throat is almost shattered.
He lets the pagan fall, dead, at his feet.
William watches and rejoices in it.
"God," says the count, "who are judge of us all,
now we are dead and abandoned in pain!"

lvi
William sees Pharaon who has fallen:
"God," says the count, "good king of paradise,   1610
now we are dead, and given up to pain."
"Do not despair, uncle," says Guielin,
"in this palace you are not without friends."
"Indeed," says William, "there are few of those."
Then the young Guielin looks around.
He notices a huge axe near a pillar,
moves forward and seizes it with both hands,
and goes to strike a barbarous pagan.
He cuts through him all the way to the chest.
Aragon looks, almost loses his mind,   1620
he cries aloud: "Seize him, Saracens!
By Mohammed, they shall be abused,
they will be swung and dropped into the Rhone."
Guielin says: "You swine, get away from here.
You have had us led out of your prison
and conducted up here to the palace,
but by the apostle who is blessed at Rome,
you have thus acquired such companions,
they'll make you angry and very sad."
At these words two Saracens appear,   1630
bearing in their hands a serving of wine,
which they intend to serve in the palace,
but when they see such mighty blows struck,
they run away and let everything fall.
Count William runs to seize the huge tray.
Swiftly, he takes it in both his hands
and strikes great blows at pagan Saracens.
Anyone he reaches does not rejoice.

lvii
Now William is inside the tiled palace,
and Guielin his renowned nephew.   1640
One has an axe, the other the tray;
the noble vassals strike great blows with them.
Fourteen Turks have already been killed,
and the others are so terrified,

that they chase them out through the doors,
which they run to bolt and lock after them.
By its great chains, they have pulled up the bridge.
Aragon sees it and his mind rages.
He calls on all his Saracens and Slavs:
"Give me counsel, by Mohammed, my God.   1650
This William has badly abused me,
he has seized my principal palace,
I don't see how we can enter again."
Let us leave the Saracens here for a while,
for we must sing once more of Gilbert,
the messenger who has crossed the Rhone.
He mounts the peaks and descends the valleys,
from here to Nîmes, he has never paused.
It is morning, Count Bertrand has arisen,
he climbs the palace of the heathen Otran   1660
whom he had conquered by his fierce courage.
The count stands at the great windows
and looks down across the kingdom.
He sees the green grass and the rose gardens
and hears the oriole and blackbird sing.
He remembers William of the short nose
and his brother, the highly praised Guielin,
and tenderly then he begins to weep,
grieving for them as you will now hear:
"Uncle William, what madness it was   1670
to go to Orange just to look at it,
disguised in rags like some poor beggar.
Brother Guielin, how worthy you were!
Now you've been killed by Saracens and Slavs,
and I am left all alone in this land.
I see no man here of all my great race
to whom I can go for good counsel.
The Slavs will soon return to this place,
Golias and the king Desramé,
Clareaus and his brother Aceré,   1680
Aguisant and the king Giboé,
and the royal prince of Reaumont by the sea,
the kings Eubron, Borreaus and Lorré,
and Quinzepaumes and his brother Gondrez,
the thirty kings who were born here in Spain.
Each one will have thirty thousand armed men
and they will attack the city of Nîmes;
they will capture me by powerful force,
I shall be dead, murdered or killed.
But there is one thing I have determined: 1690
I would not fail, for the gold of ten cities,

to return to the land where I was born,
and bring back with me all my barons,
whom William of the short nose once led here.
And when I come to the city, Paris,
I will descend on the enameled stones;
sergeants and squires will come to greet me
and they will certainly ask for William,
and for Guielin my worthy brother.
Alas, I will not know what to tell them,   1700
except that the pagans killed them at Orange!"
Twice he falls in a faint on the marble step,
and his barons run to lift him up.

lviii
Count Bertrand is saddened and desolate,
for Guielin and the noble William.
He grieves with fine and courteous words:
"Uncle William, how madly you acted
when you decided to go to Orange
as a poor beggar, disguised in rags.
Brother Guielin, what a good man you were!   1710
Now Persians have killed you and Saracens
and I am alone in this pagan land,
I have no cousin or brother with me.
Now King Tiebaut will return from Africa
and Desramé and the huge Golias,
the thirty kings with their vast forces,
and they will lay siege to me here at Nîmes.
I shall be dead and doomed to torments,
but by the apostle penitents seek,
I shall not, even if I lose my limbs,   1720
give up until I reach Orange the great
to avenge the sorrow and the torment
that Saracens made our people suffer.
Alas, poor wretch, why do I hesitate
to go and present myself before them!"

lix
Count Bertrand is sad and filled with anger,
but just when he is weeping and sighing,
Gilbert arrives and enters the city.
He climbs the steps of the great stone chamber.
Bertrand sees him and he begins to laugh,   1730
in a loud, clear voice he cries out to him:
"You are most welcome, here, good, noble knight!
Where is my uncle of the bold countenance,
and Guielin? Don't hide it from me!"

And Gilbert answers as a noble knight:
"Within Orange, the fortified city,
in Gloriete, the tower of marble;
evil pagans hold them in their power.
It won't be long before they are both killed.
William sent me, I hide nothing from you,   1740
to ask you to help with all of your knights,
immediately, without any delay."
Bertrand hears him, then he begins to laugh.
He calls on everyone who can hear him:
"To arms, now, quickly, my good, noble knights!"
And they obey, without any delay,
mounting their Spanish and Sulian horses.
When Bertrand leaves the city of Nîmes,
he brings every man in his command,
at the head are more than fifteen thousand.   1750
From here to the Rhone they don't pause or stop,
they all embark on ships and galleys.
The Franks put to sea, they sail and steer.
Beneath Orange, there is the vast plains,
the proud companies disembark,
they pitch their tents and raise their pavilions.
Count Bertrand has allowed no delay,
he looks at the messenger and says:
"Now, Sir Gilbert, do not lie to me.
Should we attack this city of Orange,   1760
can we break down the walls and the stone halls?"
Gilbert answers: "Your idea is mad.
She does not fear the whole kingdom of France—
you couldn't take her any day of your life."
Bertrand hears him and nearly goes mad.

lx

"Gilbert, brother," Count Bertrand demands,
"shall we attack the mighty Orange,
could we break down these walls, these high buildings?"
Gilbert answers: "There is no sense in this.
You could not take her in all your lifetime."   1770
Bertrand is enraged by that answer
and the messenger tries to comfort him:
"Sire," he says, "listen to my plan:
I shall get you into the city
without the Persians or Saracens' knowledge."
"Go ahead, good brother, with Jesus' aid!"
He goes, because he knows what is needed,
with thirteen thousand Frankish fighting men,
leaving the others behind at the tents.

They do not stop before they reach the cave,   1780
through the pillars they make their way in—
they are without candles or burning lights—
one after the other in deep darkness.
Bertrand begins to lose heart at this,
he calls the messenger and asks aloud:
"Gilbert, my brother, don't conceal the truth,
my uncle is dead, I'm beginning to see,
and you've sold us to the infidel race."
Gilbert answers: "You're talking nonsense—
I could not do that to save my own limbs.   1790
You will arrive soon inside Gloriete,
by God, I beg you, do it quietly."
"Go on, good brother, with God's protection."
And as they move along, speaking thus,
they suddenly find themselves in Gloriete.
Count William has seen them as they arrive:
"God," says the count, "good father, redeemer,
now I see what I have needed so long."
The valiant fighters unlace their helmets,
they embrace and kiss, weeping in their joy.   1800
Count Bertrand is the first to address him:
"How are you, uncle? Hide nothing from me."
"I'm fine, good nephew, by the grace of God,
though I have suffered great pain and distress.
I didn't expect to see you while I lived,
for the torments of Saracens and Persians."
"Uncle William, you will soon be avenged."
Up in the palace an olifant sounds,
outside in tents and pavilions, men arm.
Count William is bold and valiant.   1810
They approach the gates of the fine city,
the bridge is lowered, they quickly descend
to open the gates as fast as they can,
and the men outside begin to pour in,
shouting "Montjoy!" in the front and the rear.
At their joy, the pagans are terrified,
they run to arm, the treacherous cowards;
from their lodgings they begin to come forth,
running to equip themselves for defense.
But all their armor is not worth a glove,   1820
for there are too many Franks by then;
Bertrand has taken over the city.
To win that strong and valiant fortress,
you might have seen such a furious combat,
so many lances broken and shields crashing,
so many hauberks of Moorish chain pierced,

so many Saracens bleeding and dead.
When Aragon sees his people killed,
his grief is such, he almost goes mad.
He leaps in the saddle of a spirited horse,   1830
grabbing a shield he had taken from a Frank,
he looks on the ground and sees a sharp spear,
he leans down to take it with both his hands
and urges the horse with his sharpened spurs.
He thrusts himself in the thick of the fight.
First he kills our Folquer of Meliant
and then another and a third after him.
Bertrand sees him and almost goes mad,
he draws his sword, whose blade cuts so well,
and strikes Aragon, he does not spare him.   1840
The blow he strikes with such vicious intent,
he cuts through him all the way to his chest.
He knocks him dead from his spirited horse.
Pagans begin to lose force and courage.
But why should I extend this tale further?
Cursed be he who would have escaped it!
Over the earth flows a river of blood.
Count William does not wait any longer,
he runs immediately to the dungeon
and frees Orable of the graceful form.   1850
He calls Bertrand and says this before all:
"Good nephew," he says, "hear what I intend:
this lady of the noble, charming form,
who rescued me, certainly, from death,
I made her a most faithful promise
that I would indeed take her as my wife."
And Bertrand says: "Then why do you delay?
Keep the covenant you have made with her,
and marry her in happiness and joy."
"Nephew," says William, "just as you command."   1860

lxi

Count William is most noble and worthy.
When he has conquered the city by force,
he has a great vessel prepared
and clear water is poured into it.
Then comes the bishop of the city, Nîmes;
they have Orable take off her robes,
and baptize her to the honor of God,
divesting her of her pagan name.
The barons, Bertrand and Guielin, sponsor her
and Gilbert, the worthy and wise.   1870
By Christian law, they call her Guiborc.

To a church consecrated by them,
where Mohammed had once been invoked,
Count William goes to make her his wife.
The mass is sung by the bishop Guimer.
After the mass they return from the church
and the lady is led into Gloriete,
in the paved halls the wedding is splendid.
Count Bertrand serves them as is fitting,
and Gilbert and the worthy Guielin.   1880
Eight days they feast in joy together;
there are harpers and minstrels in plenty,
and robes of silk and delicate ermine,
and mules of Spain and well-groomed horses.

lxii
Count William has married his lady;
now he remains thirty years in Orange,
and no day goes by without a challenge.

Dante

THE DIVINE COMEDY

Introduction by Constance Bouchard

Dante Alighieri (1265–1321), usually known by his first name, is generally considered the greatest vernacular writer of the late Middle Ages. He was from the city of Florence, and his influence was such that the Florentine version of Italian in which he wrote became, and still is, the standard for written Italian. He was born into a noble family of Florence and became involved in the politics and internal quarrels of his hometown. The two major political parties there were the Guelfs and the Ghibellines, the former party further divided among subgroups that called themselves the White and the Black Guelfs. Dante was a prominent figure in the former, and when the Black Guelfs came to power in 1302, he was exiled from his beloved city.

It was during his exile from Florence that he began writing his masterpiece, the *Divine Comedy*. It is not a comedy in the sense of something knee-slappingly hilarious, but rather in the sense of a story in which good triumphs in the end. It was written as a very long poem, divided into short sections of a few pages each, called Cantos. Each Canto in turn is a series of three-line verses, which rhymed in the original Italian, although modern English translators prefer to avoid forcing the lines to rhyme, which can be much more awkward in English than in Italian. The "Comedy" overall is the story of a Pilgrim on a long journey which leads him, over the course of three books, first through Hell, then through Purgatory, and finally to Paradise. The following selection is from the beginning of the first volume, the "Inferno."

The *Divine Comedy* is much more than the story of the human journey toward salvation. Rather, Dante used it as a vehicle to discuss philosophy, theology, politics—especially the relative authority of pope and emperor within the Holy Roman Empire—and history. Most of the people the narrator meets on the course of the journey are historical figures, who would have been well-known to the educated Italian audience for whom Dante was writing. Some were figures out of classical mythology, such as Odysseus (Ulysses). Others were people that Dante had known personally. Virtually all of them are given the opportunity in the poem to speak with the Pilgrim and explain how they ended up in their present position in the afterlife. Dante wrote in a very long tradition of visions of heaven and hell, even though his Divine Comedy is far longer and more complex than any of the earlier accounts of a visit to the afterlife.

A motif that he developed from these previous accounts was that the Pilgrim would need a guide to help direct him and explain what he was seeing. In the "Inferno," the guide is Virgil, the classical Roman poet. Virgil, according to the poem, was chosen to be the Pilgrim's guide by Beatrice, a long-dead lady whom Dante had admired from afar in his youth, and who herself became the Pilgrim's guide when he reached Heaven in the third book (the name means "she who blesses"). Although Virgil, not having been a Christian, would have to remain in Hell according to Christian doctrine (or at least in Limbo, its outermost circle), Dante clearly admired him. It was also appropriate that as Dante set out to write his monumental poem he should have chosen for his first guide Virgil, best known for the *Aeneid,* a monumental poem on the founders of Rome.

The Hell that the Pilgrim and Virgil explore is divided into circles, where people are placed depending on the severity of their sin. The following selection involves only the outer circles, but as they descend into the center of hell, they see Lucifer, frozen on his throne, chewing on the three worst sinners of all, those who had betrayed those who trusted them most: Judas, who betrayed Christ, and Brutus and Cassius, who betrayed Caesar. The inclusion of Caesar's betrayers both indicates the continued relevance of Roman history in Dante's time and, especially, reflects his belief that Roman emperors, of which Caesar was regarded as the first, should have a crucial role in the governance of human society. Among the other people found in Hell were well-known sinners from throughout literature and history, as well as several of Dante's own enemies, and even some popes. Although the *Divine Comedy* is thus a deeply religious work, it thus did not hesitate to criticize where Dante felt criticism was needed, including the organized church.

The Divine Comedy

CANTO I

Halfway through his life, Dante the Pilgrim wakes to find himself lost in a dark wood. Terrified at being alone in so dismal a valley, he wanders until he comes to a hill bathed in sunlight, and his fear begins to leave him. But when he starts to climb the hill his path is blocked by three fierce beasts: first a Leopard, then a Lion, and finally a She-Wolf. They fill him with fear and drive him back down to the sunless wood. At that moment the figure of a man appears before him; it is the shade of Virgil, and the Pilgrim begs for help. Virgil tells him that he cannot overcome the beasts which obstruct his path; they must remain until a "Greyhound" comes who will drive them back to Hell. Rather by another path will the Pilgrim reach the sunlight, and Virgil promises to guide him on the path through Hell and Purgatory, after which another spirit, more fit than Virgil, will lead him to Paradise. The Pilgrim begs Virgil to lead on, and the Guide starts ahead. The Pilgrim follows.

Midway along the journey of our life
   I woke to find myself in a dark wood,
   for I had wandered off from the straight path.   3

How hard it is to tell what it was like,
   this wood of wilderness, savage and stubborn
   (the thought of it brings back all my old fears),   6

a bitter place! Death could scarce be bitterer.
   But if I would show the good that came of it
   I must talk about things other than the good.   9

---

1. The imaginary date of the poem's beginning is the night before Good Friday in 1300, the year of the papal jubilee proclaimed by Boniface VIII. Born in 1265, Dante would be thirty-five years old, which is half the seventy years allotted to man in the Bible.

The Portable Dante (ed. Mark Musa), Viking/Penguin, 1995 (ISBN 0253209307), original pp. 1–31 (first six cantos of Divine Comedy).

How I entered there I cannot truly say,
    I had become so sleepy at the moment
    when I first strayed, leaving the path of truth;   12

but when I found myself at the foot of a hill,
    at the edge of the wood's beginning, down in the valley,
    where I first felt my heart plunged deep in fear,   15

I raised my head and saw the hilltop shawled
    in morning rays of light sent from the planet
    that leads men straight ahead on every road.   18

And then only did terror start subsiding
    in my heart's lake, which rose to heights of fear
    that night I spent in deepest desperation.   21

Just as a swimmer, still with panting breath,
    now safe upon the shore, out of the deep,
    might turn for one last look at the dangerous waters,   24

so I, although my mind was turned to flee,
    turned round to gaze once more upon the pass
    that never let a living soul escape.   27

I rested my tired body there awhile
    and then began to climb the barren slope
    (I dragged my stronger foot and limped along).   30

Beyond the point the slope begins to rise
    sprang up a leopard, trim and very swift!
    It was covered by a pelt of many spots.   33

And, everywhere I looked, the beast was there
    blocking my way, so time and time again
    I was about to turn and go back down.   36

The hour was early in the morning then,
    the sun was climbing up with those same stars
    that had accompanied it on the world's first day,   39

31–51. The three beasts that block the Pilgrim's path could symbolize the three major divisions of Hell. The spotted Leopard (32) represents Fraud (cf. Canto XVI, 106–108) and reigns over the Eighth and Ninth Circles where the Fraudulent are punished (Cantos XVIII-XXXIV). The Lion (45) symbolizes all forms of Violence that are punished in the Seventh Circle (XII-XVII). The She-Wolf (49) represents the different types of Concupisence or Incontinence that are punished in Circles Two to Five (V–VIII).

the day Divine Love set their beauty turning;
   so the hour and sweet season of creation
   encouraged me to think I could get past   42

that gaudy beast, wild in its spotted pelt,
   but then good hope gave way and fear returned
   when the figure of a lion loomed up before me,   45

and he was coming straight toward me, it seemed,
   with head raised high, and furious with hunger—
   the air around him seemed to fear his presence.   48

And now a she-wolf came, that in her leanness
   seemed racked with every kind of greediness
   (how many people she has brought to grief!).   51

This last beast brought my spirit down so low
   with fear that seized me at the sight of her,
   I lost all hope of going up the hill.   54

As a man who, rejoicing in his gains,
   suddenly seeing his gain turn into loss,
   will grieve as he compares his then and now,   57

so she made me do, that relentless beast;
   coming toward me, slowly, step by step,
   she forced me back to where the sun is mute.   60

While I was rushing down to that low place,
   my eyes made out a figure coming toward me
   of one grown faint, perhaps from too much silence. 63

And when I saw him standing in this wasteland,
   "Have pity on my soul," I cried to him,
   "whichever you are, shade or living man!"   66

"No longer living man, though once I was,"
   he said, "and my parents were from Lombardy,
   both of them were Mantuans by birth.   69

---

62. The approaching figure represents (though not exclusively, for he has other meanings) Reason or Natural Philosophy. The Pilgrim cannot proceed to the light of Divine Love (the mountaintop) until he has overcome the three beasts of his sin; and because it is impossible for man to cope with the beasts unaided, Virgil has been summoned to guide the Pilgrim.
63. The voice of Reason has been silent in the Pilgrim's ear for a long time.

I was born, though somewhat late, *sub Julio,*
　and lived in Rome when good Augustus reigned,
　when still the false and lying gods were worshipped.　　72

I was a poet and sang of that just man,
　son of Anchises, who sailed off from Troy
　after the burning of proud Ilium.　　75

But why retreat to so much misery?
　Why not climb up this blissful mountain here,
　the beginning and the source of all man's joy?"　　78

"Are you then Virgil, are you then that fount
　from which pours forth so rich a stream of words?"
　I said to him, bowing my head modestly.　　81

"O light and honor of the other poets,
　may my long years of study, and that deep love
　that made me search your verses, help me now!　　84

You are my teacher, the first of all my authors,
　and you alone the one from whom I took
　the noble style that was to bring me honor.　　87

You see the beast that forced me to retreat;
　save me from her, I beg you, famous sage,
　she makes me tremble, the blood throbs in my veins."　　90

"But you must journey down another road,"
　he answered, when he saw me lost in tears,
　"if ever you hope to leave this wilderness;　　93

this beast, the one you cry about in fear,
　allows no soul to succeed along her path,
　she blocks his way and puts an end to him.　　96

She is by nature so perverse and vicious,
　her craving belly is never satisfied,
　still hungering for food the more she eats.　　99

She mates with many creatures, and will go on
　mating with more until the greyhound comes
　and tracks her down to make her die in anguish.　　102

---

91. Dante must choose another road because, in order to arrive at the Divine Light, it is necessary first to recognize the true nature of sin, renounce it, and pay penance for it.

He will not feed on either land or money:
    his wisdom, love, and virtue shall sustain him;
    he will be born between Feltro and Feltro.   105

He comes to save that fallen Italy
    for which the maid Camilla gave her life
    and Turnus, Nisus, Euryalus died of wounds.   108

And he will hunt for her through every city
    until he drives her back to Hell once more,
    whence Envy first unleashed her on mankind.   111

And so, I think it best you follow me
    for your own good, and I shall be your guide
    and lead you out through an eternal place   114

where you will hear desperate cries, and see
    tormented shades, some old as Hell itself,
    and know what second death is, from their screams.   117

And later you will see those who rejoice
    while they are burning, for they have hope of coming,
    whenever it may be, to join the blessèd—   120

to whom, if you too wish to make the climb,
    a spirit, worthier than I, must take you;
    I shall go back, leaving you in her care,   123

because that Emperor dwelling on high
    will not let me lead any to His city,
    since I in life rebelled against His law.   126

101–111. The Greyhound has been identified with Henry VII, Charles Martel, and even Dante himself. It seems more plausible that the Greyhound represents Can Grande della Scala, the ruler of Verona from 1308 to 1329, whose "wisdom, love, and virtue" (104) were certainly well-known to Dante. Whoever the Greyhound may be, the prophecy would seem to indicate in a larger sense the establishment of a spiritual kingdom on earth in which "wisdom, love, and virtue" will replace the bestial sins of the world. Perhaps Dante had no specific person in mind.

107. Camilla was the valiant daughter of King Metabus, who was slain while fighting against the Trojans (*Aeneid* XI).

108. Turnus was the king of the Rutulians. Nisus and Euryalus were young Trojan warriors slain during a nocturnal raid on the camp of the Rutulians.

117. The "second" death is that of the soul, which occurs when the soul is damned.

122. Just as Virgil, the pagan Roman poet, cannot enter the Christian Paradise because he lived before the birth of Christ and lacks knowledge of Christian salvation, so Reason can only guide the Pilgrim to a certain point: In order to enter Paradise, the Pilgrim's guide must be Christian Grace or Revelation (Theology) in the figure of Beatrice.

124. Note the pagan terminology of Virgil's reference to God: It expresses, as best it can, his unenlightened conception of the Supreme Authority.

Everywhere He reigns, and there He rules;
    there is His city, there is His high throne.
    Oh, happy the one He makes His citizen!"   129

And I to him: "Poet, I beg of you,
    in the name of God, that God you never knew,
    save me from this evil place and worse,   132

lead me there to the place you spoke about
    that I may see the gate Saint Peter guards
    and those whose anguish you have told me of."   135

Then he moved on, and I moved close behind him.

CANTO II

*But the Pilgrim begins to waver; he expresses to Virgil his misgivings about his ability to under-
take the journey proposed by Virgil. His predecessors have been Aeneas and Saint Paul, and he
feels unworthy to take his place in their company. But Virgil rebukes his cowardice, and relates
the chain of events that led him to come to Dante. The Virgin Mary took pity on the Pilgrim in
his despair and instructed Saint Lucia to aid him. The Saint turned to Beatrice because of
Dante's great love for her, and Beatrice in turn went down to Hell, into Limbo, and asked Virgil
to guide her friend until that time when she herself would become his guide. The Pilgrim takes
heart at Virgil's explanation and agrees to follow him.*

The day was fading and the darkening air
    was releasing all the creatures on our earth
    from their daily tasks, and I, one man alone,   3

was making ready to endure the battle
    of the journey, and of the pity it involved,
    which my memory, unerring, shall now retrace.   6

O Muses! O high genius! Help me now!
    O memory that wrote down what I saw,
    here your true excellence shall be revealed!   9

Then I began: "O poet come to guide me,
    tell me if you think my worth sufficient
    before you trust me to this arduous road.   12

You wrote about young Sylvius's father,
    who went beyond, with flesh corruptible,
    with all his senses, to the immortal realm;   15

but if the Adversary of all evil
    was kind to him, considering who he was,
      and the consequence that was to come from him,   18

this cannot seem, to thoughtful men, unfitting,
    for in the highest heaven he was chosen
      father of glorious Rome and of her empire,   21

and both the city and her lands, in truth,
    were established as the place of holiness
      where the successors of great Peter sit.   24

And from this journey you celebrate in verse,
    Aeneas learned those things that were to bring
      victory for him, and for Rome, the Papal seat;   27

then later the Chosen Vessel, Paul, ascended
    to ring back confirmation of that faith
      which is the first step on salvation's road.   30

But why am I to go? Who allows me to?
    I am not Aeneas, I am not Paul,
      neither I nor any man would think me worthy;   33

and so, if I should undertake the journey,
    I fear it might turn out an act of folly—
      you are wise, you see more than my words express."   36

As one who unwills what he willed, will change
    his purpose with some new second thought,
      completely quitting what he first had started,   39

so I did, standing there on that dark slope,
    thinking, ending the beginning of that venture
      I was so quick to take up at the start.   42

"If I have truly understood your words,"
    that shade of magnanimity replied,
      "your soul is burdened with that cowardice   45

which often weighs so heavily on man,
    it turns him from a noble enterprise
      like a frightened beast that shies at its own shadow.   48

28–30. In his Second Epistle to the Corinthians (12:2–4), the apostle Paul alludes to his mystical elevation to the third heaven and to the arcane messages pronounced there.

To free you from this fear, let me explain
    the reason I came here, the words I heard
    that first time I felt pity for your soul: 51

I was among those dead who are suspended,
    when a lady summoned me. She was so blessed
    and beautiful, I implored her to command me.   54

With eyes of light more bright than any star,
    in low, soft tones she started to address me
    in her own language, with an angel's voice: 57

'O noble soul, courteous Mantuan,
    whose fame the world continues to preserve
    and will preserve as long as world there is,   60

my friend, who is no friend of Fortune's, strays
    on a desert slope; so many obstacles
    have crossed his path, his fright has turned him back   63

I fear he may have gone so far astray,
    from what report has come to me in Heaven,
    that I may have started to his aid too late.   66

Now go, and with your elegance of speech,
    with whatever may be needed for his freedom,
    give him your help, and thereby bring me solace.   69

I am Beatrice, who urges you to go;
    I come from the place I am longing to return to;
    love moved me, as it moves me now to speak.   72

When I return to stand before my Lord,
    often I shall sing your praises to Him.'
    And then she spoke no more. And I began,   75

'O Lady of Grace, through whom alone mankind
    may go beyond all worldly things contained
    within the sphere that makes the smallest round,   78

your plea fills me with happy eagerness—
    to have obeyed already would still seem late!
    You needed only to express your wish.   81

But tell me how you dared to make this journey
    all the way down to this point of spacelessness,
    away from your spacious home that calls you back.'   84

'Because your question searches for deep meaning,
    I shall explain in simple words,' she said,
    'just why I have no fear of coming here.   87

A man must stand in fear of just those things
    that truly have the power to do us harm,
    of nothing else, for nothing else is fearsome.   90

God gave me such a nature through His Grace,
    the torments you must bear cannot affect me,
    nor are the fires of Hell a threat to me.   93

A gracious lady sits in Heaven grieving
    for what happened to the one I send you to,
    and her compassion breaks Heaven's stern decree.   96

She called Lucia and making her request,
    she said, "Your faithful one is now in need
    of you, and to you I now commend his soul."   99

Lucia, the enemy of cruelty,
    hastened to make her way to where I was,
    sitting by the side of ancient Rachel,   102

and said to me: "Beatrice, God's true praise,
    will you not help the one whose love was such
    it made him leave the vulgar crowd for you?   105

Do you not hear the pity of his weeping,
    do you not see what death it is that threatens him
    along that river the sea shall never conquer?"   108

There never was a wordly person living
    more anxious to promote his selfish gains
    than I was at the sound of words like these—   111

to leave my holy seat and come down here
    and place my trust in you, in your noble speech
    that honors you and all those who have heard it!'   114

When she had finished reasoning, she turned
    her shining eyes away, and there were tears.
    How eager then I was to come to you!   117

---

94. The lady is the Virgin Mary.
102. In the Dantean Paradise Rachel is seated by Beatrice.

And I have come to you just as she wished,
    and I have freed you from the beast that stood
    blocking the quick way up the mount of bliss.   120

So what is wrong? Why, why do you delay?
    Why are you such a coward in your heart,
    why aren't you bold and free of all your fear,   123

when three such gracious ladies, who are blessed,
    watch out for you up there in Heaven's court,
    and my words, too, bring promise of such good?"   126

As little flowers from the frosty night
    are closed and limp, and when the sun shines down
    on them, they rise to open on their stem,   129

my wilted strength began to bloom within me,
    and such warm courage flowed into my heart
    that I spoke like a man set free of fear.   132

"O she, compassionate, who moved to help me!
    And you, all kindness, in obeying quick
    those words of truth she brought with her for you—   135

you and the words you spoke have moved my heart
    with such desire to continue onward
    that now I have returned to my first purpose.   138

Let us start, for both our wills, joined now, are one.
    You are my guide, you are my lord and teacher."
    These were my words to him and, when he moved,   141

I entered on that deep and rugged road.

CANTO III

As the two poets enter the vestibule that leads to Hell itself, Dante sees the inscription above the gate, and he hears the screams of anguish from the damned souls. Rejected by God and not accepted by the powers of Hell, the first group of souls are "nowhere," because of their cowardly refusal to make a choice in life. Their punishment is to follow a banner at a furious pace forever, and to be tormented by flies and hornets. The Pilgrim recognizes several of these shades but mentions none by name. Next they come to the River Acheron, where they are greeted by the infernal boatman, Charon. Among those doomed souls who are to be ferried across the river, Charon sees the living man and challenges him, but Virgil lets it be known that his companion must pass. Then across the landscape rushes a howling wind, which blasts the Pilgrim out of his senses, and he falls to the ground.

I AM THE WAY INTO THE DOLEFUL CITY,
   I AM THE WAY INTO ETERNAL GRIEF,
   I AM THE WAY TO A FORSAKEN RACE.   3

JUSTICE IT WAS THAT MOVED MY GREAT CREATOR;
   DIVINE OMNIPOTENCE CREATED ME,
   AND HIGHEST WISDOM JOINED WITH PRIMAL LOVE.   6

BEFORE ME NOTHING BUT ETERNAL THINGS
   WERE MADE, AND I SHALL LAST ETERNALLY.
   ABANDON EVERY HOPE, ALL YOU WHO ENTER.   9

I saw these words spelled out in somber colors
   inscribed along the ledge above a gate;
   "Master," I said, "these words I see are cruel."   12

He answered me, speaking with experience:
   "Now here you must leave all distrust behind;
   let all your cowardice die on this spot.   15

We are at the place where earlier I said
   you could expect to see the suffering race
   of souls who lost the good of intellect."   18

Placing his hand on mine, smiling at me
   in such a way that I was reassured,
   he led me in, into those mysteries.   21

Here sighs and cries and shrieks of lamentation
   echoed throughout the starless air of Hell;
   at first these sounds resounding made me weep: 24

tongues confused, a language strained in anguish
   with cadences of anger, shrill outcries
   and raucous groans that joined with sounds of hands,   27

raising a whirling storm that turns itself
   forever through that air of endless black,
   like grains of sand swirling when a whirlwind blows.   30

And I, in the midst of all this circling horror,
   began, "Teacher, what are these sounds I hear?
   What souls are these so overwhelmed by grief?"   33

5–6. Divine Omnipotence, Highest Wisdom, and Primal Love are, respectively, the Father, the Son, and the Holy Ghost. Thus, the gate of Hell was created by the Trinity moved by Justice.
18. Souls who have lost sight of God.

And he to me: "This wretched state of being
   is the fate of those sad souls who lived a life
   but lived it with no blame and with no praise.   36

They are mixed with that repulsive choir of angels
   neither faithful nor unfaithful to their God,
   who undecided stood but for themselves.   39

Heaven, to keep its beauty, cast them out,
   but even Hell itself would not receive them,
   for fear the damned might glory over them."   42

And I. "Master, what torments do they suffer
   that force them to lament so bitterly?"
   He answered: "I will tell you in few words: 45

these wretches have no hope of truly dying,
   and this blind life they lead is so abject
   it makes them envy every other fate.   48

The world will not record their having been there;
   Heaven's mercy and its justice turn from them.
   Let's not discuss them; look and pass them by."   51

And so I looked and saw a kind of banner
   rushing ahead, whirling with aimless speed
   as though it would not ever take a stand;   54

behind it an interminable train
   of souls pressed on, so many that I wondered
   how death could have undone so great a number.   57

When I had recognized a few of them,
   I saw the shade of the one who must have been
   the coward who had made the great refusal.   60

At once I understood, and I was sure
   this was the sect of evil souls who were
   hateful to God and His enemies.   63

52–69. In the *Inferno* divine retribution assumes the form of the *contrapasso*, i.e., the just punishment of
sin, effected by a process either resembling or contrasting to the sin itself. In this canto the *contrapasso*
opposes the sin of neutrality, or inactivity: The souls who in their early lives had no banner, no leader to
follow, now run forever after one.
60. The coward could be Pontius Pilate, who refused to pass sentence on Christ.

These wretches, who had never truly lived,
　　went naked, and were stung and stung again
　　by the hornets and the wasps that circled them　　　　66

and made their faces run with blood in streaks;
　　their blood, mixed with their tears, dripped to their feet,
　　and disgusting maggots collected in the pus.　　　　69

And when I looked beyond this crowd I saw
　　a throng upon the shore of a wide river,
　　which made me ask, "Master, I would like to know:　　　　72

who are these people, and what law is this
　　that makes those souls so eager for the crossing—
　　as I can see, even in this dim light?"　　　　75

And he: "All this will be made plain to you
　　as soon as we shall come to stop awhile
　　upon the sorrowful shore of Acheron."　　　　78

And I, with eyes cast down in shame, for fear
　　that I perhaps had spoken out of turn,
　　said nothing more until we reached the river.　　　　81

And suddenly, coming toward us in a boat,
　　a man of years whose ancient hair was white
　　shouted at us, "Woe to you, perverted souls!　　　　84

Give up all hope of ever seeing Heaven:
　　I come to lead you to the other shore,
　　into eternal darkness, ice, and fire.　　　　87

And you, the living soul, you over there,
　　get away from all these people who are dead."
　　But when he saw I did not move aside,　　　　90

he said, "Another way, by other ports,
　　not here, shall you pass to reach the other shore;
　　a lighter skiff than this must carry you."　　　　93

And my guide, "Charon, this is no time for anger!
　　It is so willed, there where the power is
　　for what is willed; that's all you need to know."　　　　96

These words brought silence to the woolly cheeks
　　of the ancient steersman of the livid marsh,
　　whose eyes were set in glowing wheels of fire.　　　　99

But all those souls there, naked, in despair,
  changed color and their teeth began to chatter
  at the sound of his announcement of their doom.   102

They were cursing God, cursing their own parents,
  the human race, the time, the place, the seed
  of their beginning, and their day of birth.   105

Then all together, weeping bitterly,
  they packed themselves along the wicked shore
  that waits for every man who fears not God.   108

The devil, Charon, with eyes of glowing coals,
  summons them all together with a signal,
  and with an oar he strikes the laggard sinner.   111

As in autumn when the leaves begin to fall,
  one after the other (until the branch
  is witness to the spoils spread on the ground),   114

so did the evil seed of Adam's Fall
  drop from that shore to the boat, one at a time,
  at the signal, like the falcon to its lure.   117

Away they go across the darkened waters,
  and before they reach the other side to land,
  a new throng starts collecting on this side.   120

"My son," the gentle master said to me,
  "all those who perish in the wrath of God
  assemble here from all parts of the earth;   123

they want to cross the river, they are eager;
  it is Divine Justice that spurs them on,
  turning the fear they have into desire.   126

A good soul never comes to make this crossing,
  so, if Charon grumbles at the sight of you,
  you see now what his words are really saying."   129

He finished speaking, and the grim terrain
  shook violently; and the fright it gave me
  even now in recollection makes me sweat.   132

124–126. It is perhaps a part of the punishment that the souls of all the damned are eager for their punishment to begin; those who were so willing to sin on earth, are in hell damned with a willingness to receive their just retribution.

Out of the tear-drench land a wind arose
  which blasted forth into a reddish light,
    knocking my senses out of me completely,   135

and I fell as one falls tired into sleep.

CANTO IV

Waking from his swoon, the Pilgrim is led by Virgil to the First Circle of Hell, known as Limbo, where the sad shades of the virtuous non-Christians dwell. The souls here, including Virgil, suffer no physical torment, but they must live, in desire, without hope of seeing God. Virgil tells about Christ's descent into Hell and His salvation of several Old Testament figures. The poets see a light glowing in the darkness, and as they proceed toward it, they are met by the four greatest (other than Virgil) pagan poets: Homer, Horace, Ovid, and Lucan, who take the Pilgrim into their group. As they come closer to the light, the Pilgrim perceives a splendid castle, where the greatest non-Christian thinkers dwell together with other famous historical figures. Once within the castle, the Pilgrim sees, among others, Electra, Aeneas, Caesar, Saladin, Aristotle, Plato, Orpheus, Cicero, Avicenna, and Averroës. But soon they must leave; and the poets move from the radiance of the castle toward the fearful encompassing darkness.

A heavy clap of thunder! I awoke
  from the deep sleep that drugged my mind—startled,
    the way one is when shaken out of sleep.   3

I turned my rested eyes from side to side,
  already on my feet and, staring hard,
    I tried my best to find out where I was,   6

and this is what I saw: I found myself
  upon the brink of grief's abysmal valley
    that collects the thunderings of endless cries.   9

So dark and deep and nebulous it was,
  try as I might to force my sight below,
    I could not see the shape of anything.   12

"Let us descend into the sightless world,"
  began the poet (his face was deathly pale):
    "I will go first, and you will follow me."   15

And I, aware of his changed color, said:
  "But how can I go on if you are frightened?
    You are my constant strength when I lose heart."   18

And he to me: "The anguish of the souls
  that are down here paints my face with pity—
    which you have wrongly taken to be fear.   21

Let us go, the long road urges us."
   He entered then, leading the way for me
   down to the first circle of the abyss.   24

Down there, to judge only by what I heard,
   there were no wails but just the sounds of sighs
   rising and trembling through the timeless air,   27

the sounds of sighs of untormented grief
   burdening these groups, diverse and teeming,
   made up of men and women and of infants.   30

Then the good master said, "You do not ask
   what sort of souls are these you see around you.
   Now you should know before we go on farther,   33

they have not sinned. But their great worth alone
   was not enough, for they did not know Baptism,
   which is the gateway to the faith you follow,   36

and if they came before the birth of Christ,
   they did not worship God the way one should;
   I myself am a member of this group.   39

For this defect, and for no other guilt,
   we here are lost. In this alone we suffer:
   cut off from hope, we live on in desire."   42

The words I heard weighed heavy on my heart;
   to think that souls as virtuous as these
   were suspended in that limbo, and forever!   45

"Tell me, my teacher, tell me, O my master,"
   I began (wishing to have confirmed by him
   the teachings of unerring Christian doctrine),   48

"did any leave here, through his merit
   or with another's help, and go to bliss?"
   And he, who understood my hidden question,   51

answered: "I was a novice in this place
   when I saw a mighty lord descend to us
   who wore the sign of victory as his crown.   54

He took from us the shade of our first parent,
   of Abel, his good son, of Noah, too,
   and of obedient Moses, who made the laws;   57

Abram, the Patriarch, David the King,
    Israel with his father and his children,
    with Rachel, whom he worked so hard to win;   60

and many more he chose for blessedness;
    and you should know, before these souls were taken,
    no human soul had ever reached salvation."   63

We did not stop our journey while he spoke,
    but continued on our way along the woods—
    I say the woods, for souls were thick as trees.   66

We had not gone too far from where I woke
    when I made out a fire up ahead,
    a hemisphere of light that lit the dark.   69

We were still at some distance from that place,
    but close enough for me vaguely to see
    that honorable souls possessed that spot.   72

"O glory of the sciences and arts,
    who are these souls enjoying special honor,
    dwelling apart from all the others here?"   75

And he to me: "The honored name they bear
    that still resounds above in your own world
    wins Heaven's favor for them in this place."   78

And as he spoke I heard a voice announce:
    "Now let us honor our illustrious poet,
    his shade that left is now returned to us."   81

And when the voice was silent and all was quiet
    I saw four mighty shades approaching us,
    their faces showing neither joy or sorrow.   84

Then my good master started to explain:
    "Observe the one who comes with sword in hand,
    leading the three as if he were their master.   87

It is the shade of Homer, sovereign poet,
    and coming second, Horace, the satirist;
    Ovid is the third, and last comes Lucan.   90

---

69. The "hemisphere of light" emanates from a "splendid castle" (106), the dwelling place of the virtuous men of wisdom in Limbo. The light is the illumination of human intellect, which those who dwell in the castle had in such high measure on earth.

86–88. Because his name was inseparably linked with the Trojan War, Homer is portrayed by Dante as a sword-bearing poet, one who sang of arms and martial heroes.

Since they all share one name with me, the name
    you heard resounding in that single voice,
    they honor me and do well doing so."   93

So I saw gathered there the noble school
    of the master singer of sublimest verse,
    who soars above all others like the eagle.   96

And after they had talked awhile together,
    they turned and with a gesture welcomed me,
    and at that sign I saw my master smile.   99

Greater honor still they deigned to grant me:
    they welcomed me as one of their own group,
    so that I numbered sixth among such minds.   102

We walked together toward the shining light,
    discussing things that here are best kept silent,
    as there they were most fitting for discussion.   105

We reached the boundaries of a splendid castle
    that seven times was circled by high walls
    defended by a sweetly flowing stream.   108

We walked right over it as on hard ground;
    through seven gates I passed with those wise spirits,
    and then we reached a meadow fresh in bloom.   111

There people were whose eyes were calm and grave,
    whose bearing told of great authority;
    seldom they spoke and always quietly.   114

Then moving to one side we reached a place
    spread out and luminous, higher than before,
    allowing us to view all who were there.   117

106–111. The allegorical construction of the castle is open to question. It may represent natural philosophy unilluminated by divine wisdom, in which case the seven walls serving to protect the castle would be
the seven moral and speculative virtues (prudence, justice, fortitude, temperance, intellect, science, and
knowledge); and the seven gates that provide access to the castle would be the seven liberal arts that
formed the medieval school curriculum (music, arithmetic, geometry, astronomy—the *quadrivium;* and
grammar, logic, and rhetoric—the *trivium*). The symbolic value of the stream also remains uncertain; it
could signify eloquence, a "stream" that the eloquent Virgil and Dante should have no trouble crossing—
and indeed, they "walked right over it as on hard ground" (109).

112–144. The inhabitants of the great castle are important pagan philosophers and poets as well as
famous writers. Three of the shades named (Saladin, Avicenna, Averroës) lived only one hundred or two
hundred years before Dante. Modern readers might wonder at the inclusion of medieval non-Christians
among the virtuous pagans of antiquity, but the three just mentioned were among the non-Christians
respected, particularly during the Middle Ages.

And right before us on the lustrous green
　　the mighty shades were pointed out to me
　　(my heart felt glory when I looked at them).　　　　　120

There was Electra standing with a group,
　　among whom I saw Hector and Aeneas,
　　and Caesar, falcon-eyed and fully armed.　　　　　123

I saw Camilla and Penthesilea;
　　across the way I saw the Latian King,
　　with Lavinia, his daughter, by his side.　　　　　126

I saw the Brutus who drove out the Tarquin;
　　Lucretia, Julia, Marcia, and Cornelia;
　　off, by himself, I noticed Saladin,　　　　　129

and when I raised my eyes a little higher
　　I saw the master sage of those who know,
　　sitting with his philosophic family.　　　　　132

All gaze at him, all pay their homage to him;
　　and there I saw both Socrates and Plato,
　　each closer to his side than any other;　　　　　135

Democritus, who said the world was chance,
　　Diogenes, Thales, Anaxagoras,
　　Empedocles, Zeno, and Heraclitus;　　　　　138

---

121. Electra was the daughter of Atlas, the mother of Dardanus, and the founder of Troy; thus, her followers include all members of the Trojan race. She should not be confused with Electra, daughter of Agamemnon, the character in plays by Aeschylus, Sophocles, and Euripides.
122. Among Electra's descendants are Hector, the eldest son of Priam, king of Troy, and Aeneas (cf. Canto I, 73–75; and Canto II, 13–24).
123. Julius Caesar proclaimed himself the first emperor of Rome after defeating numerous opponents in civil conflicts.
124–126. For Camilla see Canto I, note on line 107. Penthesilea was the glamorous queen of the Amazons who aided the Trojans against the Greeks and was slain by Achilles during the conflict. King Latinus commanded the central region of the Italian peninsula, the site where Aeneas founded Rome. He gave Lavinia to the Trojan conqueror in marriage.
127–129. Outraged by the murder of his brother and the rape (and subsequent suicide) of his sister (Lucretia), Lucius Brutus incited the Roman populace to expel the Tarquins, the perpetrators of the offenses. This accomplished, he was elected first consul and consequently became the founder of the Roman Republic. The four women were famous Roman wives and mothers. Lucretia was the wife of Collatinus; Julia the daughter of Julius Caesar and wife of Pompey; Marcia the second wife of Cato of Utica (in the *Convivio* Dante makes her the symbol of the noble soul); and Cornelia the daughter of Scipio Africanus Major and mother of the Gracchi, the tribunes Tiberius and Caius. A distinguished soldier, Saladin became sultan of Egypt in 1174. Medieval opinion of Saladin was favorable; he was lauded for his generosity and his magnanimity.
131. To Dante, Aristotle represented the summit of human reason, that point which man could reach on his own without the benefit of Christian revelation.

I saw the one who classified our herbs:
    Dioscorides I mean. And I saw Orpheus,
    Tully, Linus, Seneca the moralist,   141

Euclid the geometer, and Ptolemy,
    Hippocrates, Galen, Avicenna,
    and Averroës, who made the Commentary.   144

I cannot tell about them all in full;
    my theme is long and urges me ahead,
    often I must omit things I have seen.   147

The company of six becomes just two;
    my wise guide leads me by another way
    out of the quiet into tempestuous air.   150

I come into a place where no light is.

CANTO V

From Limbo Virgil leads his ward down to the threshold of the Second Circle of Hell, where for the first time he will see the damned in Hell being punished for their sins. There, barring their way, is the hideous figure of Minòs, the bestial judge of Dante's underworld; but after strong words from Virgil, the poets are allowed to pass into the dark space of this circle, where can be heard the wailing voices of the Lustful, whose punishment consists in being forever whirled

---

137. Diogenes was the Cynic philosopher who believed that the only good lies in virtue secured through self-control and abstinence. Anaxagoras was a Greek philosopher of the Ionian school (500–428 B.C.). Among his famous students were Pericles and Euripides. Thales (ca. 635–ca. 545 B.C.), an early Greek philosopher born at Miletus, founded the Ionian school of philosophy and in his main doctrine maintained that water is the elemental principle of all things.
140. Dioscorides was a Greek natural scientist and physician of the first century A.D. Orpheus was a mythical Greek poet and musician whose lyrical talent was such that it moved rocks and trees and tamed wild beasts.
141. Tully was Marcus Tullius Cicero, celebrated Roman orator, writer, and philosopher (106–43 B.C.). Linus was a mythical Greek poet and musician who is credited with inventing the dirge. Lucius Annaeus Seneca (4 B.C.–A.D. 65) followed the philosophy of the Stoics in his oral treatises. Dante calls him "the moralist" to distinguish him from Seneca the tragedian, who was thought (erroneously) during the Middle Ages to be another person.
142. Euclid was a Greek mathematician (ca. 300 B.C.) who wrote a treatise on geometry that was the first codification and exposition of mathematical principles. Ptolemy was a Greek mathematician, astronomer, and geographer. The universe, according to the Ptolemaic system (which was accepted by the Middle Ages), so named although he did not invent it, had the earth as its fixed center encircled by nine spheres.
143. Hippocrates was a Greek physician (ca. 460–377 B.C.) who founded the medical profession and introduced the scientific art of healing. Galen was a celebrated physician (ca. A.D. 130–ca. 200) who practiced his art in Greece, Egypt, and Rome. Avicenna (or Ibn-Sina) was an Arabian philosopher and physician (A.D. 980–1037) who was a prolific writer.
144. Ibn-Rushd, called Averroës (ca. A.D. 1126–ca. 1198), was a celebrated Arabian scholar born in Spain. He was widely known in the Middle Ages for his commentary on Aristotle, which served as the basis for the work of St. Thomas Aquinas.

about in a dark, stormy wind. After seeing a thousand or more famous lovers—including Semi-ramis, Dido, Helen, Achilles, and Paris—the Pilgrim asks to speak to two figures he sees together. They are Francesca da Rimini and her lover, Paolo, and the scene in which they appear is probably the most famous episode of the Inferno. *At the end of the scene, the Pilgrim, who has been overcome by pity for the lovers, faints to the ground.*

This way I went, descending from the first
    into the second round, that holds less space
    but much more pain—stinging the soul to wailing.   3

There stands Minòs grotesquely, and he snarls,
    examining the guilty at the entrance;
    he judges and dispatches, tail in coils.   6

By this I mean that when the evil soul
    appears before him, it confesses all,
    and he, who is the expert judge of sins,   9

knows to what place in Hell the soul belongs;
    the times he wraps his tail around himself
    tell just how far the sinner must go down.   12

The damned keep crowding up in front of him:
    they pass along to judgment one by one;
    they speak, they hear, and then are hurled below.   15

"O you who come to the place where pain is host,"
    Minòs spoke out when he caught sight of me,
    putting aside the duties of his office,   18

"be careful how you enter and whom you trust
    it's easy to get in, but don't be fooled!"
    And my guide said to him: "Why keep on shouting?   21

Do not attempt to stop his fated journey;
    it is so willed there where the power is
    for what is willed; that's all you need to know."   24

And now the notes of anguish start to play
    upon my ears; and now I find myself
    where sounds on sounds of weeping pound at me.   27

4. Minòs was the son of Zeus and Europa. As king of Crete he was revered for his wisdom and judicial gifts. For these qualities he became chief magistrate of the underworld in classical literature. (See Virgil, *Aeneid* VI, 432–433.) Although Dante did not alter Minòs' official function, he transformed him into a demonic figure, both in his physical characteristics and in his bestial activity.

I came to a place where no light shone at all,
    bellowing like the sea racked by a tempest,
    when warring winds attack it from both sides.   30

The infernal storm, eternal in its rage,
    sweeps and drives the spirits with its blast:
    it whirls them, lashing them with punishment.   33

When they are swept back past their place of judgment,
    then come the shrieks, laments, and anguished cries;
    there they blaspheme God's almighty power.   36

I learned that to this place of punishment
    all those who sin in lust have been condemned,
    those who make reason slave to appetite;   39

and as the wings of starlings in the winter
    bear them along in wide-spread, crowded flocks,
    so does that wind propel the evil spirits: 42

now here, then there, and up and down, it drives them
    with never any hope to comfort them—
    hope not of rest but even of suffering less.   45

And just like cranes in flight, chanting their lays,
    stretching an endless line in their formation,
    I saw approaching, crying their laments,   48

spirits carried along by the battling winds.
    And so I asked, "Teacher, tell me, what souls
    are these punished in the sweep of the black wind?"   51

"The first of those whose story you should know,"
    my master wasted no time answering,
    "was empress over lands of many tongues;   54

her vicious tastes had so corrupted her
    she licensed every form of lust with laws
    to cleanse the stain of scandal she had spread;   57

she is Semiramis, who, legend says,
    was Ninus' wife as well as his successor;
    she governed all the land the Sultan rules.   60

31–32. The *contrapasso* or punishment suggests that lust (the "infernal storm") is pursued without the light of reason (in the darkness).

The next is she who killed herself for love
    and broke faith with the ashes of Sichaeus;
    and there is Cleopatra, who loved men's lusting.   63

See Helen there, the root of evil woe
    lasting long years, and see the great Achilles,
    who lost his life to love, in final combat;   66

see Paris, Tristan"—then, more than a thousand
    he pointed out to me, and named them all,
    those shades whom love cut off from life on earth.   69

After I heard my teacher call the names
    of all these knights and ladies of ancient times,
    pity confused my senses, and I was dazed.   72

I began: "Poet, I would like, with all my heart,
    to speak to those two there who move together
    and seem to be so light upon the winds."   75

And he: "You'll see when they are closer to us;
    if you entreat them by that love of theirs
    that carries them along, they'll come to you."   78

When the winds bent their course in our direction
    I raised my voice to them, "O wearied souls,
    come speak with us if it be not forbidden."   81

As doves, called by desire to return
    to their sweet nest, with wings raised high and poised,
    float downward through the air, guided by will,   84

---

64. Helen of Troy.

65–66. Enticed by the beauty of Polyxena, a daughter of the Trojan king, Achilles desired her to be his wife, but Hecuba, Polyxena's mother, arranged a counterplot with Paris so that when Achilles entered the temple for his presumed marriage, he was treacherously slain by Paris.

67. Paris was the son of Priam, king of Troy, whose abduction of Helen ignited the Trojan War. Tristan was the central figure of numerous medieval French, German, and Italian romances. Sent as a messenger by his uncle, King Mark of Cornwall, to obtain Isolt for him in marriage, Tristan became enamored of her, and she of him. After Isolt's marriage to Mark, the lovers continued their love affair, and in order to maintain its secrecy they necessarily employed many deceits and ruses. According to one version, Mark, increasingly suspicious of their attachment, finally discovered them together and ended the incestuous relationship by mortally wounding Tristan with a lance.

74. The two are Francesca, daughter of Guido Vecchio da Polenta, lord of Ravenna; and Paolo Malatesta, third son of Malatesta da Verrucchio, lord of Rimini. Around 1275 the aristocratic Francesca was married for political reasons to Gianciotto, the physically deformed second son of Malatesta da Verrucchio. In time a love affair developed between Francesca and Gianciotto's youngest brother, Paolo. One day the betrayed husband discovered them in an amorous embrace and slew them both.

so these two left the flock where Dido is
   and came toward us through the malignant air,
   such was the tender power of my call.   87

"O living creature, gracious and so kind,
   who makes your way here through this dingy air
   to visit us who stained the world with blood,   90

if we could claim as friend the King of Kings,
   we would beseech him that he grant you peace,
   you who show pity for our atrocious plight.   93

Whatever pleases you to hear or speak
   we will hear and we will speak about with you
   as long as the wind, here where we are, is silent.   96

The place where I was born lies on the shore
   where the river Po with its attendant streams
   descends to seek its final resting place.   99

Love, quick to kindle in the gentle heart,
   seized this one for the beauty of my body,
   torn from me. (How it happened still offends me!)   102

Love, that excuses no one loved from loving,
   seized me so strongly with delight in him
   that, as you see, he never leaves my side.   105

Love led us straight to sudden death together.
   Caïna awaits the one who quenched our lives."
   These were the words that came from them to us.   108

When those offended souls had told their story,
   I bowed my head and kept it bowed until
   the poet said, "What are you thinking of?"   111

When finally I spoke, I sighed, "Alas,
   all those sweet thoughts, and oh, how much desiring
   brought these two down into this agony."   114

And then I turned to them and tried to speak;
   I said, "Francesca, the torment that you suffer
   brings painful tears of pity to my eyes.   117

---

107. Caïna was one of the four divisions of Cocytus, the lower part of Hell, wherein those souls who treacherously betrayed their kin are tormented.

But tell me, in that time of your sweet sighing
   how, and by what signs, did love allow you
   to recognize your dubious desires?"

       120

And she to me: "There is no greater pain
   than to remember, in our present grief,
   past happiness (as well your teacher knows)!

       123

But if your great desire is to learn
   the very root of such a love as ours,
   I shall tell you, but in words of flowing tears.

       126

One day we read, to pass the time away,
   of Lancelot, of how he fell in love;
   we were alone, innocent of suspicion.

       129

Time and again our eyes were brought together
   by the book we read; our faces flushed and paled.
   To the moment of one line alone we yielded:

       132

it was when we read about those longed-for lips
   now being kissed by such a famous lover,
   that this one (who shall never leave my side)

       135

then kissed my mouth, and trembled as he did.
   Our Galehot was that book and he who wrote it.
   That day we read no further." And all the while

       138

the one of the two spirits spoke these words,
   the other wept, in such a way that pity
   blurred my senses; I swooned as though to die,

       141

and fell to Hell's floor as a body, dead, falls.

Petrarch

LETTER TO POSTERITY

Introduction by Michael Levin

Francesco Petrarch (1304–74) is often referred to as "the father of the Italian Renaissance." Born into an exiled Florentine family, Petrarch spent most of his life wandering about Italy, much like Dante. As a young man he attended law school, but he hated it. At one point he took holy orders, but that did not take either—much to his own disgust, Petrarch could never completely renounce the pleasures of the world. His only true loves were classical literature and a woman named Laura, and both would contribute to his profound effect on the Italian Renaissance.

Petrarch felt much more at ease with the history and literature of classical Rome than with the events and people of his own time. He often bemoaned the ignorance and vulgarity of his contemporaries, and longed for a return to the spirit of the classical age. This desire to revive classical ideas and ideals is of course at the heart of the Renaissance (which means "rebirth"), and Petrarch was the first of the Renaissance humanists who sought to rejuvenate their society. It was Petrarch who first coined the term "Dark Ages," referring to the centuries separating classical Rome from himself, and we still owe the idea of the "Middle Ages" to Petrarch and the Renaissance writers who followed his example. In order to return to the virtues of classical Rome, Petrarch advocated the use of the Latin language as the Romans knew it, particularly the great orator and writer Cicero. Petrarch spent his whole life trying to perfect a "Ciceronian" Latin prose style, which subsequently became the model of eloquence for generations of scholars.

But Petrarch isn't important only for his Latin works; his poetry in vernacular Italian was equally influential. Like Dante, Petrarch wrote a great deal of love poetry dedicated to a perfect, unattainable woman. Petrarch's love object was a blonde beauty named Laura, who may or may not have been aware of Petrarch's existence. He wrote a collection of 366 poems about Laura, called the *Canzoniere* ("Songbook"). These poems served as models for love poetry for at least three centuries—Shakespeare's sonnets often echo Petrarch. To the end of his life Petrarch wrestled with his conflicted emotions about earthly love. On the other hand, Laura served as Petrarch's muse, inspiring him to write great poetry. On the other hand Petrarch genuinely yearned to live a pure Christian life, and reject the ephemeral glories of this world. Petrarch expressed this conflict in a work called *Secretum,* in which he imagined a dialogue between himself and St. Augustine, one of the biggest influences on Petrarch's intellectual life. The character of St. Augustine berates Petrarch for caring too much about earthly love and fame, but Petrarch never really changes his mind.

For Petrarch did care about being famous. He promoted the idea of reviving the ancient Roman tradition of granting the title of poet laureate, so that he could win it. And he also wrote the letter we present here, the "Letter to Posterity." Petrarch wrote many letters, to contemporaries and to his long-dead heroes like Cicero. But this letter is written to us, his future readers. Petrarch is often called a "modern" author because of his self-awareness, his individualism, and his desire for immortality through his art. All of these things are evident in this letter. Read this letter and you will hear the voice of a man who has been dead for over six centuries. Petrarch would no doubt be pleased to know his work does indeed live on.

Letter to Posterity

It is possible that some word of me may have come to you, though even this is doubtful, since an insignificant and obscure name will scarcely penetrate far in either time or space. If, however, you should have heard of me, you may desire to know what manner of man I was, or what was the outcome of my labors, especially those of which some description or, at any rate, the bare titles may have reached you.

To begin with myself, then, the utterances of men concerning me will differ widely, since in passing judgment almost every one is influenced not so much by truth as by preference, and good and evil report alike know no bounds. I was, in truth, a poor mortal like yourself, neither very exalted in my origin, nor, on the other hand, of the most humble birth, but belonging, as Augustus Caesar says of himself, to an ancient family. As to my disposition, I was not naturally perverse or wanting in modesty, however the contagion of evil associations may have corrupted me. My youth was gone before I realized it; I was carried away by the strength of manhood; but a riper age brought me to my senses and taught me by experience the truth I had long before read in books, that youth and pleasure are vanity—nay, that the Author of all ages and times permits us miserable mortals, puffed up with emptiness, thus to wander about, until finally, coming to a tardy consciousness of our sins, we shall learn to know ourselves. In my prime I was blessed with a quick and active body, although not exceptionally strong; and while I do not lay claim to remarkable personal beauty, I was comely enough in my best days. I was possessed of a clear complexion, between light and dark, lively eyes, and for long years a keen vision, which however deserted me, contrary to my hopes, after I reached my sixtieth birthday, and forced me, to my great annoyance, to resort to glasses. Although I had previously enjoyed perfect health, old age brought with it the usual array of discomforts.

I have always possessed an extreme contempt for wealth; not that riches are not desirable in themselves, but because I hate the anxiety and care which are invariably associated with them. I certainly do not long to be able to give gorgeous banquets. I have, on the contrary, led a happier existence with plain living and ordinary fare than all the followers of Apicius,[1] with their elaborate dainties. So-called *convivia,* which are but vulgar bouts, sinning against sobriety and good manners, have always been repugnant to me. I have ever felt that it was irksome and profitless to invite others to such affairs, and not less so to be bidden to them myself. On the other hand, the pleasure of dining with one's friends is so great that nothing has ever given me more delight

Kenneth R. Bartlett, ed., *The Civilization of the Italian Renaissance*, Heath, 1992 (ISBN 0669-20900-7), original pp. 17–25 (Petrarch, "Letter to Posterity").

than their unexpected arrival, nor have I ever willingly sat down to table without a companion. Nothing displeases me more than display, for not only is it bad in itself, and opposed to humility, but it is troublesome and distracting.

I struggled in my younger days with a keen but constant and pure attachment, and would have struggled with it longer had not the sinking flame been extinguished by death—premature and bitter, but salutary.[2] I should be glad to be able to say that I had always been entirely free from irregular desires, but I should lie if I did so. I can, however, conscientiously claim that, although I may have been carried away by the fire of youth or by my ardent temperament, I have always abhorred such sins from the depths of my soul. As I approached the age of forty, while my powers were unimpaired and my passions were still strong, I not only abruptly threw off my bad habits, but even the very recollection of them, as if I had never looked upon a woman. This I mention as among the greatest of my blessings, and I render thanks to God, who freed me, while still sound and vigorous, from a disgusting slavery which had always been hateful to me.[3] But let us turn to other matters.

I have perceived pride in others, never in myself, and however insignificant I may have been, I have always been still less important in my own judgment. My anger has very often injured myself, but never others. I make this boast without fear, since I am confident that I speak truly: While I am very prone to take offense, I am equally quick to forget injuries, and have a memory tenacious of benefits. I have always been most desirous of honorable friendships, and have faithfully cherished them. But it is the cruel fate of those who are growing old that they can commonly only weep for friends who have passed away. In my familiar associations with kings and princes, and in my friendship with noble personages, my good fortune has been such as to excite envy. I fled, however, from many of those to whom I was greatly attached; and such was my innate longing for liberty, that I studiously avoided those whose very name seemed incompatible with the freedom that I loved. The greatest kings of this age have loved and courted me. They may know why; I certainly do not. With some of them I was on such terms that they seemed in a certain sense my guests rather than I theirs; their lofty position in no way embarrassing me, but, on the contrary, bringing with it many advantages.

I possessed a well-balanced rather than a keen intellect, one prone to all kinds of good and wholesome study, but especially inclined to moral philosophy and the art of poetry. The latter, indeed, I neglected as time went on, and took delight in sacred literature. Finding in that a hidden sweetness which I had once esteemed but lightly, I came to regard the works of the poets as only amenities. Among the many subjects which interested me, I dwelt especially upon antiquity, for our own age has always repelled me, so that, had it not been for the love of those dear to me, I should have preferred to have been born in any other period than our own. In order to forget my own time, I have constantly striven to place myself in spirit in other ages, and consequently I delighted in history; not that the conflicting statements did not offend me, but when in doubt I accepted what appeared to me most probable, or yielded to the authority of the writer.

My style, as many claimed, was clear and forcible; but to me it seemed weak and obscure. In ordinary conversation with friends, or with those about me, I never gave thought to my language, and I have always wondered that Augustus Caesar should have taken such pains in this respect.[4] When, however, the subject itself, or the place or listener, seemed to demand it, I gave some attention to style, with what success I cannot pretend to say; let them judge in whose presence I spoke. If only I have lived well, it matters little to me how I talked. Mere elegance of language can produce at best but an empty renown.

My parents were honorable folk, Florentine in their origin, of medium fortune, or, I may as well admit it, in a condition verging on poverty. They had been expelled from their native city,[5] and consequently I was born in exile, at Arezzo, in the year 1304 of this latter age which begins with Christ's birth, July the twentieth, on a Monday, at dawn. My life up to the present has, either through fate or my own choice, fallen into the following divisions. A part only of my first year was spent at Arezzo, where I first saw the light. The six following years were, owing to the recall of my mother from exile, spent upon my father's estate at Incisa, about fourteen miles above Florence. I passed my eighth year at Pisa, the ninth and following years in Farther Gaul, at Avignon, on the left bank of the Rhone, where the Roman Pontiff holds and has long held the Church of Christ in shameful exile.[6] It seemed a few years ago as if Urban V was on the point of restoring the Church to its ancient seat, but it is clear that nothing is coming of this effort, and, what is to me the worst of all, the Pope seems to have repented him of his good work, for failure came while he was still living.[7] Had he lived but a little longer, he would certainly have learned how I regarded his retreat. My pen was in my hand when he abruptly surrendered at once his exalted office and his life. Unhappy man, who might have died before the altar of Saint Peter and in his own habitation! Had his successors remained in their capital he would have been looked upon as the cause of this benign change, while, had they left Rome, his virtue would have been all the more conspicuous in contrast with their fault.[8]

But such laments are somewhat remote from my subject. On the windy banks of the river Rhone I spent my boyhood, guided by my parents, and then, guided by my own fancies, the whole of my youth. Yet there were long intervals spent elsewhere, for I first passed four years at the little town of Carpentras, somewhat to the east of Avignon: in these two places I learned as much of grammar, logic, and rhetoric as my age permitted, or rather, as much as it is customary to teach in school: you know how little that is, dear reader. I then set out for Montpellier to study law, and spent four years there, then three at Bologna. I heard the whole body of the civil law, and would, as many thought, have distinguished myself later, had I but continued my studies. I gave up the subject altogether, however, so soon as it was no longer necessary to consult the wishes of my parents.[9] My reason was that, although the dignity of the law, which is doubtless very great, and especially the numerous references it contains to Roman antiquity, did not fail to delight me, I felt it to be habitually degraded by those who practice it. It went against me painfully to acquire an art which I would not practice dishonestly, and could hardly hope to exercise otherwise. Had I made the latter attempt, my scrupulousness would doubtless have been ascribed to simplicity.

So at the age of two and twenty I returned home. I call my place of exile home, Avignon, where I had been since childhood; for habit has almost the potency of nature itself. I had already begun to be known there, and my friendship was sought by prominent men; wherefore I cannot say. I confess this is now a source of surprise to me, although it seemed natural enough at an age when we are used to regard ourselves as worthy of the highest respect. I was courted first and foremost by that very distinguished and noble family, the Colonnesi, who, at that period, adorned the Roman Curia with their presence. However it might be now, I was at that time certainly quite unworthy of the esteem in which I was held by them. I was especially honored by the incomparable Giacomo Colonna, then Bishop of Lombez,[10] whose peer I know not whether I have ever seen or ever shall see, and was taken by him to Gascony; there I spent such a divine summer among the foot-hills of the Pyrenees, in happy intercourse with my master and the members of our company, that I can never recall the experience without a sigh of regret.[11]

Returning thence, I passed many years in the house of Giacomo's brother, Cardinal Giovanni Colonna, not as if he were my lord and master, but rather my father, or better, a most affectionate brother—nay, it was as if I were in my own home.[12] About this time, a youthful desire impelled me to visit France and Germany. While I invented certain reasons to satisfy my elders of the propriety of the journey, the real explanation was a great inclination and longing to see new sights. I first visited Paris, as I was anxious to discover what was true and what fabulous in the accounts I had heard of that city. On my return from this journey I went to Rome, which I had since my infancy ardently desired to visit. There I soon came to venerate Stephano, the noble head of the family of the Colonnesi, like some ancient hero, and was in turn treated by him in every respect like a son. The love and good-will of this excellent man toward me remained constant to the end of his life, and lives in me still, nor will it cease until I myself pass away.

On my return, since I experienced a deep-seated and innate repugnance to town life, especially in that disgusting city of Avignon, which I heartily abhorred, I sought some means of escape. I fortunately discovered, about fifteen miles from Avignon, a delightful valley, narrow and secluded, called Vaucluse, where the Sorgue, the prince of streams, takes its rise. Captivated by the charms of the place, I transferred thither myself and my books. Were I to describe what I did there during many years, it would prove a long story. Indeed, almost every bit of writing which I have put forth was either accomplished or begun, or at least conceived, there, and my undertakings have been so numerous that they still continue to vex and weary me. My mind, like my body, is characterized by a certain versatility and readiness, rather than by strength, so that many tasks that were easy of conception have been given up by reason of the difficulty of their execution. The character of my surroundings suggested the composition of a sylvan or bucolic song.[13] I also dedicated a work in two books upon *The Life of Solitude,* to Philip, now exalted to the Cardinal-bishopric of Sabina. Although always a great man, he was, at the time of which I speak, only the humble Bishop of Cavaillon.[14] He is the only one of my old friends who is still left to me, and he has always loved and treated me not as a bishop (as Ambrose did Augustine), but as a brother.

While I was wandering in those mountains upon Friday in Holy Week, the strong desire seized me to write an epic in an heroic strain, taking as my theme Scipio Africanus the Great, who had, strange to say, been dear to me from my childhood. But although I began the execution of this project with enthusiasm, I straightway abandoned it, owing to a variety of distractions. The poem was, however, christened *Africa,* from the name of its hero, and, whether from his fortunes or mine, it did not fail to arouse the interest of many before they had seen it.[15]

While leading a leisurely existence in this region, I received, remarkable as it may seem, upon one and the same day,[16] letters both from the Senate at Rome and the Chancellor of the University of Paris, pressing me to appear in Rome and Paris, respectively, to receive the poet's crown of laurel.[17] In my youthful elation I convinced myself that I was quite worthy of this honor; the recognition came from eminent judges, and I accepted their verdict rather than that of my own better judgment. I hesitated for a time which I should give ear to, and sent a letter to Cardinal Giovanni Colonna, of whom I have already spoken, asking his opinion. He was so near that, although I wrote late in the day, I received his reply before the third hour on the morrow. I followed his advice, and recognized the claims of Rome as superior to all others. My acceptance of his counsel is shown by my twofold letter to him on that occasion, which I still keep. I set off accordingly; but although, after the fashion of youth, I was a most indulgent judge of my own work, I still blushed to accept in my own case the verdict even of such men as those who summoned me, despite the fact that they would certainly not have honored me in this way, had they not believed me worthy.

Notes

1. Proverbial gourmet from the age of Tiberius.
   SOURCE: Excerpts from D. Thompson (ed. and trans.), *Petrarch: A Humanist Among Princes.* (New York: Harper and Row, 1971), pp. 1–13. Reprinted by permission of HarperCollins Publishers.

2. While it is tempting to see here a reference to Laura, there are chronological difficulties. The period of life described *(adolescentia)* extended from age 15 to 28, but Petrarch's attachment to Laura lasted until her death many years later. Perhaps we must simply accept this as one of those not infrequent instances where Petrarch has altered the account of his life.

3. Though a cleric, Petrarch was the father of two illegitimate children: Giovanni, born in 1337; and Francesca, born six years later.

4. Suetonius, *Life of Augustus,* p. 87.

5. Petrarch's father, a "White" Guelph, was banished by the victorious "Black" Guelphs on October 20, 1302 (nine months after the expulsion of Dante, whom he had known).

6. The French pope, Clement V (1305–14), had moved the papal court to Avignon in 1309.

7. Urban V (1362–70) left Avignon in April, 1367; returned there from Rome in September, 1370; and died on December 19 of the same year.

8. Petrarch had sent metrical epistles to Urban's predecessors, Benedict XII (1334–42) and Clement VI (1342–52), urging them to restore the papacy to Rome.

9. Petrarch left Bologna in April 1326, probably on receiving news of his father's death. His mother had died some years earlier.

10. Some thirty miles southwest of Toulouse. Giacomo had been elected bishop in 1328. He died in 1341.

11. It was during this summer of 1330 that Petrarch formed his lifelong friendship with "Socrates" (the Flemish Ludwig van Kempen, chanter in the chapel of Cardinal Giovanni Colonna), who resided at Avignon; and with "Laelius" (a Roman, Lello di Pietro Stefano dei Tosetti), who also resided at Avignon until the cardinal's death in 1348. Many of Petrarch's letters are addressed to these two friends.

12. As a household chaplain Petrarch was an active member of the cardinal's staff from 1330 to 1337, and an occasionally active member for another ten years. This was his first ecclesiastical appointment. On his ecclesiastical career, see E. H. Wilkins, *Studies in the Life and Works of Petrarch* (Cambridge, Mass., 1955), pp. 3–32.

13. Petrarch conflates his first stay in Vaucluse (1337–41) with his third (1345–47); for the *Bucolicum Carman* and the *De Vita Solitaria* were both begun during the latter period. Petrarch began one or more major works during each of his four periods of residence at Vaucluse.

14. Philippe de Cabassoles, whose diocese included Vaucluse, was about Petrarch's age, and they shared similar tastes for books and country life. Philippe became cardinal in 1368, cardinal-bishop in 1370, and died in 1372.

15. Begun in 1338 or 1339, the *Africa* was never finished; and aside from a fragment that circulated during Petrarch's lifetime, it was not published until after his death. It proved something of a disappointment to Coluccio Salutati and others after they had seen it.

16. September 1, 1340.

17. Albertino Mussato had been crowned with laurel in Padua in 1315; and Dante had been offered a crown by Bologna but had declined (see *Paradiso* XXV, 1–9 on his desire to receive the crown in Florence). For the whole complicated question see E. H. Wilkins, "The Coronation of Petrarch" (*The Making of the "Cansoniere" and Other Petrarchan Studies* [Rome, 1951], pp. 9–69), who concludes: "the sum of the matter would seem to be that Petrarch succeeded, after persistent and varied efforts, in getting two invitations to receive the laurel crown; that the specific basis for the invitations was a rather limited amount of published Latin verse, together with the knowledge that he was engaged in the writing of a grandiose epic; that he had convinced the Colonna family and Roberto de' Bardi [Chancellor at the University of Paris, and a Florentine] that he was in truth a great poet; that their sense of his poetic worth was presumably enhanced by their knowledge that he was engaged in the writing of historical works and by the obvious range of his classical scholarship; and—just possibly—that the beauty of some of his belittled Italian lyrics was in their minds" (p. 35).

Pico della Mirandola

ORATION ON THE DIGNITY OF MAN

In the opening section of the *Oration,* Pico declares that unlike other creatures, human beings have not been assigned a fixed place in the universe. Our destiny is not determined by anything outside us. Rather, God has bestowed upon us a unique distinction: the liberty to determine the form and value our lives shall acquire. The notion that people have the power to shape their own lives is a key element in the emergence of the modern outlook.

I have read in the records of the Arabians, reverend Fathers, that Abdala the Saracen,[1] when questioned as to what on this stage of the world, as it were, could be seen most worthy of wonder, replied: "There is nothing to be seen more wonderful than man." In agreement with this opinion is the saying of Hermes Trismegistus: "A great miracle, Asclepius, is man."[2] But when I weighed the reason for these maxims, the many grounds for the excellence of human nature reported by many men failed to satisfy me—that man is the intermediary between creatures, the intimate of the gods, the kings of the lower beings, by the acuteness of his senses, by the discernment of his reason, and by the light of his intelligence the interpreter of nature, the interval between fixed eternity and fleeting time, and (as the Persians say) the bond, nay, rather, the marriage song of the world, on David's [biblical king] testimony but little lower than the angels. Admittedly great though these reasons be, they are not the principal grounds, that is, those which may rightfully claim for themselves the privilege of the highest admiration. For why should we not admire more the angels themselves and the blessed choirs of heaven? At last it seems to me I have come to understand why man is the most fortunate of creatures and consequently worthy of all admiration and what precisely is that rank which is his lot in the universal chain of Being—a rank to be envied not only by brutes but even by the stars and by minds beyond this world. It is a matter past faith and a wondrous one. Why should it not be? For it is on this very account that man is rightly called and judged a great miracle and a wonderful creature indeed. . . .

. . . God the Father, the supreme Architect, had already built this cosmic home we behold, the most sacred temple of His godhead, by the laws of His mysterious wisdom. The region above the heavens He had adorned with Intelligences, the heavenly spheres He had quickened with eternal souls, and the excrementary and filthy parts of the lower world He had filled with a multitude of animals of every kind. But, when the work was finished, the Craftsman kept wishing

Perry, Peden, Von Laue, eds., *Sources of the Western Tradition,* Volume 1, Houghton Mifflin (ISBN: 0-395-89201-5), original pp. 286–7 (Pico della Mirandola, "Oration on the Dignity of Man").

that there was someone to ponder the plan of so great a work, to love its beauty, and to wonder at its vastness. Therefore, when everything was done (as Moses and Timaeus[3] bear witness), He finally took thought concerning the creation of man. But there was not among His archetypes that from which He could fashion a new offspring, nor was there in His treasurehouses anything which He might bestow on His new son as an inheritance, nor was there in the seats of all the world a place where the latter might sit to contemplate the universe. All was now complete; all things had been assigned to the highest, the middle, and the lowest orders. But in its final creation it was not the part of the Father's power to fail as though exhausted. It was not the part of His wisdom to waver in a needful matter through poverty of counsel. It was not the part of His kindly love that he who was to praise God's divine generosity in regard to others should be compelled to condemn it in regard to himself.

At last the best of artisans [God] ordained that that creature to whom He had been able to give nothing proper to himself should have joint possession of whatever had been peculiar to each of the different kinds of being. He therefore took man as a creature of indeterminate nature and, assigning him a place in the middle of the world, addressed him thus: "Neither a fixed abode nor a form that is thine alone nor any function peculiar to thyself have we given thee, Adam, to the end that according to thy longing and according to thy judgment thou mayest have and possess what abode, what form, and what functions thou thyself shalt desire. The nature of all other beings is limited and constrained within the bounds of laws prescribed by Us. Thou, constrained by no limits, in accordance with thine own free will, in whose hand We have placed thee, shalt ordain for thyself the limits of thy nature. We have set thee at the world's center that thou mayest from thence more easily observe whatever is in the world. We have made thee neither of heaven nor of earth, neither mortal nor immortal, so that with freedom of choice and with honor, as though the maker and molder of thyself, thou mayest fashion thyself in whatever shape thou shalt prefer. Thou shalt have the power to degenerate into the lower forms of life, which are brutish. Thou shalt have the power, out of thy soul's judgment, to be reborn into the higher forms, which are divine."

O supreme generosity of God the Father, O highest and most marvelous felicity of man! To him it is granted to have whatever he chooses, to be whatever he wills. Beasts as soon as they are born (so says Lucilius)[4] bring with them from their mother's womb all they will ever possess. Spiritual beings [angels], either from the beginning or soon thereafter, become what they are to be for ever and ever. On man when he came into life the Father conferred the seeds of all kinds and the germs of every way of life. Whatever seeds each man cultivates will grow to maturity and bear in him their own fruit. If they be vegetative, he will be like a plant. If sensitive, he will become brutish. If rational, he will grow into a heavenly being. If intellectual, he will be an angel and the son of God. And if, happy in the lot of no created thing, he withdraws into the center of his own unity, his spirit, made one with God, in the solitary darkness of God, who is set above all things, shall surpass them all.

Notes

1. Abdala the Saracen possibly refers to the eighth-century A.D. writer Abd-Allah Ibn al-Muqaffa.
2. Ancient writings dealing with magic, alchemy, astrology, and occult philosophy were erroneously attributed to an assumed Egyptian priest, Hermes Trismegistus. Asclepius was a Greek god of healing.
3. Timaeus, a Greek Pythagorean philosopher, was a central character in Plato's famous dialogue *Timaeus*.
4. Lucilius, a first-century A.D. Roman poet and Stoic philosopher, was a close friend of Seneca, the philosopher-dramatist.

John Calvin

GENEVAN ECCLESIASTICAL ORDINANCES

Introduction by Michael Graham

Martin Luther published a lot and retracted a lot; John Calvin didn't publish nearly as much, but he never took back a word. Whatever one may think of his ideas, they were consistent and systematic. For Luther, the Reformation was an effort to bring the individual believer closer to Christ and His sacrifice on the cross; for Calvin it became an effort to reshape society, and it is in this area that Calvinism had its most dramatic impact, both in Europe and North America.

Calvin was a second-generation reformer. Born in northern France in 1509, he was only eight years old when Luther began his public criticism of the Catholic Church with the publication of his "Ninety-five Theses." He attended the College de Montaigu in Paris, where Erasmus had studied (and been bored) in the 1490s, and which Ignatius Loyola would attend as well. In 1528, having finished his master's degree at age 18, he left Paris to study law at the University of Orleans. But in 1531 his father (who may have been pushing him toward a legal career) died, and Calvin returned to Paris, associating with a group of evangelical academics who were critical of some aspects of Catholic worship. His first publication was a 1532 commentary on Seneca's *De Clementia*. This was not an explicitly religious work, but an exposition of the musings of an important Stoic philosopher who had tutored the Roman Emperor Nero, and later been persecuted by his former pupil. Soon Calvin would find himself in hot water with his own ruler, Francis I, king of France. On 1 November 1533, Calvin's friend Nicholas Cop gave his inaugural address as rector of the University of Paris and criticized the persecution in France of those who "strive purely and sincerely to penetrate the minds of believers with the Gospel." Calvin probably had a hand in writing this address, and when it drew the king's wrath, he and Cop fled Paris. The king ordered the *parlement* of Paris (France's highest court) to root out "heretics,"and Calvin fled the kingdom entirely the following autumn after anonymous placards criticizing the "Roman Mass" as an "act of idolatry" were posted throughout Paris and its suburbs (one even turned up on the door of the king's bedchamber!).

Calvin spent the next two years wandering from place to place, and at Basel in 1536 he published the first edition of his *Institutes of the Christian Religion,* a systematic work expounding his view of the nature of God, the nature of humanity, the proper relationship between God and humanity (including preaching, the practice of prayer and the sacraments of Baptism and Communion), and how the Christian Church ought to be organized. It was a work he would expand many times between that initial publication and his death in 1564. Later in 1536 he stopped overnight in the independent city-state of Geneva (now part of Switzerland), which had recently declared its protestantism in rebellion against its prince-bishop.

This chance stopover would prove fateful. The fiery preacher Guillaume Farel, who provided early leadership for Geneva's reform movement met Calvin and decided he was the sort of preacher-administrator Geneva needed. He asked Calvin to stay, and when the latter resisted, Farel tried to make him feel guilty, suggesting that God had sent him to Geneva for a reason. So Calvin stayed. But his and Farel's efforts to discourage traditional social behaviors such as dancing, gambling and heavy drinking by excluding from Communion those who engaged in such activities drew the wrath of many of Geneva's leading citizens, and Calvin and Farel were kicked out of the city in 1538. Calvin headed for Strasbourg, which he had visited before, and there witnessed the reform efforts being pushed by Martin Bucer. But conflicts in the turbulent internal politics of Geneva led to Calvin being invited back to become that city's leading pastor. He held out, insisting to Genevan officials that he could only take up the post if he was given a free hand to reform the Church in Geneva. The authorities agreed to this demand, and the Genevan *Ecclesiastical Ordinances* of 1541 were the result. Calvin would remain Geneva's leading pastor until his death. Meanwhile, Geneva would become both a haven for French-speaking protestants and the nerve center of "Calvinism," the international religious movement which by 1550 would replace Lutheranism as the leading challenge to the Catholic Church in Europe.

As you read these ordinances, what elements strike you as most important? If you were living in Geneva under these ordinances, how would your life most obviously be affected? Who are the elders, and what are their primary responsibilities? (Note: the Little Council and the Council of Two Hundred were parts of Geneva's city government.) What about the deacons? Is there some historical model that Calvin seems to be employing? What does Calvin see as the proper relationship between church authorities and civic authorities? Can you see any influence of Calvinism in contemporary American society?

16. *Ecclesiastical Ordinances*. Geneva (1541)*

Of the Frequency, Place and Time of Preaching

Each Sunday, at daybreak, there shall be a sermon in St. Peter's and St. Gervaise's, also at the customary hour at St. Peter, Magdalene and St. Gervaise. At three o'clock, as well, in all three parishes, the second sermon.

For purposes of catechetical instruction and the administration of the sacraments, the boundaries of the parishes are to be observed as possible. St. Gervaise is to be used by those who have done so in the past; likewise with Magdalene. Those who formerly attended St. Germain, Holy Cross, the new church of Our lady and St. Legier are to attend St. Peter's.

On work days, besides the two sermons mentioned, there shall be preaching three times each week, on Monday, Wednesday, and Friday. These sermons shall be announced for an early hour so that they may be finished before the day's work begins. On special days of prayer the Sunday order is to be observed.

To carry out these provisions and the other responsibilities pertaining to the ministry, five ministers and three coadjutors will be needed. The latter will also be ministers and help and reinforce the others as the occasion arises.

Concerning the Second Order, Called Teachers

The proper duty of teachers is to instruct the faithful in sound doctrine so that the purity of the gospel is not corrupted by ignorance or evil opinions. We include here the aids and instructions necessary to preserve the doctrines and to keep the church from becoming desolate for lack of pastors and ministers. To use a more familiar expression, we shall call it the order of the schools.

The order nearest to the ministry and most closely associated with the government of the church is that of lecturer in theology who teaches the Old and the New Testament.

Since it is impossible to profit by such instruction without first knowing languages and the humanities, and also since it is necessary to prepare for the future in order that the church may not be neglected by the young, it will be necessary to establish a school to instruct the youth, to prepare them not only for the ministry but for government.

First of all, a proper place for teaching purposes must be designated, fit to accommodate children and others who wish to profit by such instruction; to secure someone who is both learned in subject matter and capable of looking after the building, who can also read. This per-

1. Hans Hillerbrand, ed., *The Protestant Reformation*, (New York: Harper and Row, 1968), ISBN 0061313424, pp. 172–178 ("Genevan Ecclesiastical Ordinances")

*Reprinted with the help of Corpus Reformatorum 38, 21 ff. from Hans J. Hillerbrand, *The Reformation. A Narrative History* (New York, 1965), pp. 191–94.

son is to be employed and placed under contract on condition that he provide under his charge readers in the languages and in dialectics, if it be possible. Also to secure men with bachelor degrees to teach the children. This we hope to do to further the work of God.

These teachers shall be subject to the same ecclesiastical discipline as the ministers. There shall be no other school in the city for small children; the girls shall have their school apart, as before.

No one shall be appointed unless he is approved by the ministers, who will make their selection known to the authorities, after which he shall be presented to the council with their recommendation. In any case, when he is examined, two members of the Little Council shall be present.

The Third Order Is That of Elders, Those Commissioned or Appointed to the Consistory by the Authorities

Their office is to keep watch over the lives of everyone, to admonish in love those whom they see in error and leading disorderly lives. Whenever necessary they shall make a report concerning these to the ministers who will be designated to make brotherly corrections and join, with the others in making such corrections.

If the church deems it wise, it will be well to choose two from the Little Council, four from the Council of Two Hundred, honest men of good demeanor, without reproach and free from all suspicion, above all fearing God and possessed of good and spiritual judgment. It will be well to elect them from every part of the city so as to be able to maintain supervision over all. This we desire to be instituted.

This shall be the manner of their selection, inasmuch as the Little Council advises that the best men be nominated, and to call the minister so as to confer with them, after which those whom they suggest may be presented to the Council of Two Hundred for their approval. If they are found worthy, after being approved, they shall take an oath similar to that required of the ministers. At the end of the year, after the election of the council, they shall present themselves to the authorities in order that it may be decided if they are to remain in office or be replaced. It will not be expedient to replace them often without cause, or so long as they faithfully perform their duties.

The Fourth Order or the Deacons

There were two orders of deacons in the ancient church, the one concerned with receiving, distributing and guarding the goods of the poor, their possessions, income and pensions as well as the quarterly offerings; the other, to take heed to and care for the sick and administer the pittance for the poor. This custom we have preserved to the present. In order to avoid confusion, for we have both stewards and managers, one of the four stewards of the hospital is to act as receiver of all its goods and is to receive adequate remuneration in order that he may better exercise his office.

The number of four stewards shall remain as it is, of which number one shall be charged with the common funds, as directed, not only that there may be greater efficiency, but also that those who wish to make special gifts may be better assured that these will be distributed only as they desire. If the income which the officials assign is not sufficient, or if some emergency should arise, the authorities shall instruct him to make adjustments according to the need.

The election of the managers, as well as of the stewards, is to be conducted as that of the elders; in their election the rule is to be followed which was delivered by St. Paul respecting deacons.

Concerning the office and authority of stewards, we confirm the articles which have already been proposed, on condition that, in urgent matters, especially when the issue is no great matter and the expenditure involved is small, they not be required to assemble for every action taken, but that one or two of them may be permitted to act in the absence of the others, in a reasonable way.

It will be his task to take diligent care that the public hospital is well administered and that it is open not only to the sick but also to aged persons who are unable to work, to widows, orphans and other needy persons. Those who are sick are to be kept in a separate lodging, away from those who cannot work, old persons, widows, orphans and other needy persons.

Also the care of the poor who are scattered throughout the city is to be conducted as the stewards may order.

Also, that another hospital is established for the transients who should be helped. Separate provision is to be made for any who are worthy of special charity. To accomplish this, a room is to be set aside for those who shall be recommended by the stewards, and it is to be used for no other purpose.

Above all, the families of the managers are to be well managed in an efficient and godly fashion, since they are to manage the houses dedicated to God.

The ministers and the commissioners or elders, with one of the syndics, for their part, are carefully to watch for any fault or negligence of any sort, in order to beg and admonish the authorities to set it in order. Every three months they are to cause certain of their company, with the stewards, to visit the hospital to ascertain if everything is in order.

It will be necessary, also, for the benefit of the poor in the hospital and for the poor of the city who cannot help themselves, that a doctor and a competent surgeon be secured from among those who practice in the city to have the care of the hospital and to visit the poor.

The hospital, for the pestilence in any case, is to be set apart; especially should it happen that the city is visited by this rod from God.

Moreover, to prevent begging, which is contrary to good order, it will be necessary that the authorities delegate certain officers. They are to be stationed at the doors of the churches to drive away any who try to resist and, if they act impudently or answer insolently, to take them to one of the syndics. In like manner, the heads of the precincts should always watch that the law against begging is well observed.

The Persons Whom the Elders Should Admonish, and Proper Procedure in This Regard

If there shall be anyone who lays down opinions contrary to received doctrine, he is to be summoned. If he recants, he is to be dismissed without prejudice. If he is stubborn, he is to be admonished from time to time until it shall be evident that he deserves greater severity. Then, he is to be excommunicated and this action reported to the magistrate.

If anyone is negligent in attending worship so that a noticeable offense is evident for the communion of the faithful, or if anyone shows himself contemptuous of ecclesiastical discipline, he is to be admonished. If he becomes obedient, he is to be dismissed in love. If he persists, passing from bad to worse, after having been admonished three times, he is to be excommunicated and the matter reported to the authorities.

For the correction of faults, it is necessary to proceed after the ordinance of our Lord. That is, vices are to be dealt with secretly and no one is to be brought before the church for accusation if the fault is neither public nor scandalous, unless he has been found rebellious in the matter.

For the rest, those who scorn private admonitions are to be admonished again by the church. If they will not come to reason nor recognize their error, they are to be ordered to abstain from communion until they improve.

As for obvious and public evil, which the church cannot overlook: if the faults merit nothing more than admonition, the duty of the elders shall be to summon those concerned, deal with them in love in order that they may be reformed and, if they correct the fault, to dismiss the matter. If they persevere, they are to be admonished again. If, in the end, such procedure proves unsuccessful, they are to be denounced as contemptuous of God, and ordered to abstain from communion until it is evident that they have changed their way of life.

As for crimes that merit not only admonition but punitive correction: if any fall into such error, according to the requirements of the case, it will be necessary to command them to abstain from communion so that they humble themselves before God and repent of their error.

If anyone by being contumacious or rebellious attempts that which is forbidden, the duty of the ministers shall be to reject him, since it is not proper that he receive the sacrament.

Nevertheless, let all these measures be moderate; let there not be such a degree of rigor that anyone should be cast down, for all corrections are but medicinal, to bring back sinners to the Lord.

And let all be done in such a manner as to keep from the ministers any civil jurisdiction whatever, so that they use only the spiritual sword of the word of God as St. Paul ordered them. Thus the consistory may in no wise take from the authority of the officers or of civil justice. On the contrary, the civil power is to be kept intact. Likewise, when it shall be necessary to exercise punishment or restraint against any party, the ministers and the consistory are to hear the party concerned, deal with them and admonish them as it may seem good, reporting all to the council which, for its part, shall deliberate and then pass judgment according to the merits of the case.

Ignatius of Loyola

SPIRITUAL EXERCISES

Introduction by Michael Levin

St. Ignatius of Loyola was born in 1491 on the northern coast of Spain. As he wrote in his autobiography, as a young man "he was given over to the vanities of the world." He desired fame and fortune, especially as a great soldier. In 1521 he led a heroic defense of a fortress against a French army, during which one of his legs was shattered by gunfire. He spent several years recovering; when the leg healed crooked, he volunteered to have the leg rebroken and reset (long before the invention of anaesthetic). During his second recovery he began reading religious literature, especially the lives of famous saints, and he experienced a spiritual conversion. Ignatius dedicated the rest of his life to the greater glory of God, and to the service of the Catholic Church. By the time of his death in 1556, he had become a leader of the Catholic cause, and in 1622 the Church declared him to be a saint.

Ignatius is most famous for founding the Society of Jesus, a new religious order, better known as the Jesuits. A teaching order, the Jesuits established many schools which combined traditional education with religious instruction. They were also great missionaries; by 1600 Jesuit priests had traveled to India, China and Japan, as well as to the Americas. All the members of this order swore a special oath of allegiance to the Pope, which was important in this age of Reformation and Counter-Reformation. Ignatius, the ex-soldier, envisioned his order as a military company fighting for God and the Pope against paganism and the heresies of the protestants. Every one of his followers had to be mentally prepared to do battle with evil, which is where the *Spiritual Exercises* come in.

The *Spiritual Exercises,* which Ignatius began writing in 1522 and first published in 1548, is a manual for how to get closer to God. Ignatius set up a system for people who truly wanted to know how best to serve God: they could retreat from the world for a month, and under the guidance of a Jesuit spiritual director, use these mental exercises to clear their minds of worldly concerns. The book begins with an explanation of the purpose of the exercises, and then describes a logical sequence of "weeks," or periods of contemplation. In each of these weeks the subject is told to concentrate on a concrete image, such as Jesus suffering on the cross. The person performing the exercises is supposed to submerge himself completely into these images, and totally give himself up to the experience. The subject is thus encouraged to use his imagination, willpower, and emotions in the quest for inner peace and the knowledge of God's love.

If this sounds strange, compare it to modern self-help books or the power of positive thinking. Ask yourself, could this work? What was Ignatius trying to do? Also, think about this work in the context of the "quest for order" in the sixteenth and seventeenth centuries. Compare the *Spiritual Exercises* to the Genevan *Ecclesiastical Ordinances* of John Calvin. Are Calvin and Ignatius trying to accomplish similar things?

The Spiritual Exercises of St. Ignatius Loyola have been reprinted and republished many times in the last four centuries, and have lately been more popular than ever. Why do you think this might be?

The Spiritual Exercises

[1]   **IHS**

Introductory Explanations, to Gain Some Understanding of the Spiritual Exercises Which Follow, and to Aid Both the One Who Gives Them and the One Who Receives Them.

The First Explanation. By the term Spiritual Exercises we mean every method of examination of conscience, meditation, contemplation, vocal or mental prayer, and other spiritual activities, such as will be mentioned later. For, just as taking a walk, traveling on foot, and running are physical exercises, so is the name of spiritual exercises given to any means of preparing and disposing our soul to rid itself of all its disordered affections and then, after their removal, of seeking and finding God's will in the ordering of our life for the salvation of our soul.

[2]   *The Second.* The person who gives to another the method and procedure for meditating or contemplating should accurately narrate the history contained in the contemplation or meditation, going over the points with only a brief or summary explanation. For in this way the person who is contemplating, by taking this history as the authentic foundation, and by going over it and reasoning about it for oneself, can thus discover something that will bring better understanding or a more personalized concept of the history — either through one's own reasoning or to the extent that the understanding is enlightened by God's grace. This brings more spiritual relish and spiritual fruit than if the one giving the Exercises had lengthily explained and amplified the meaning of the history. For, what fills and satisfies the soul consists, not in knowing much, but in our understanding the realities profoundly and in savoring them interiorly.

[3]   *The Third.* In all the following Spiritual Exercises we use the acts of the intellect in reasoning and of the will in eliciting acts of the affections. In regard to the affective acts which spring from the will we should note that when we are conversing with God our Lord or his saints vocally or mentally, greater reverence is demanded of us than when we are using the intellect to understand.

[4]   *The Fourth.* Four Weeks are taken for the following Exercises, corresponding to the four parts into which they are divided. That is, the First Week is devoted to the consideration and contemplation of sins; the Second, to the life of Christ our Lord up to and including Palm Sunday; the Third, to the Passion of Christ our Lord; and the Fourth, to the Resurrection and Ascension. To this week are appended the Three Methods of Praying. However, this does not mean that each week must necessarily consist of seven or eight days. For during the First Week some

Ignatius of Loyola: *The Spiritual Exercises and Selected Works* ed. George E. Ganss (Paulist Press, 1991) ISBN 0809132168, pp. 121–45.

persons happen to be slower in finding what they are seeking, that is, contrition, sorrow, and tears for their sins. Similarly, some persons work more diligently than others, and are more pushed back and forth and probed by different spirits. In some cases, therefore, the week needs to be shortened, and in others lengthened. This holds as well for all the following weeks, while the retreatant is seeking for what corresponds to their subject matter. But the Exercises ought to be completed in thirty days, more or less.

[5]   *The Fifth.* The persons who receive the Exercises will benefit greatly by entering upon them with great spirit and generosity toward their Creator and Lord, and by offering all their desires and freedom to him so that his Divine Majesty can make use of their persons and of all they possess in whatsoever way is according to his most holy will.

[6]   *The Sixth.* When the one giving the Exercises notices that the person making them is not experiencing any spiritual motions in his or her soul, such as consolations or desolations, or is not being moved one way or another by different spirits, the director should question the exercitant much about the Exercises: Whether the exercitant is making them at the appointed times, how they are being made, and whether the Additional Directives are being diligently observed. The director should ask about each of these items in particular. Consolation and desolation are treated in [316–324], the Additional Directives in [73–90].

[7]   *The Seventh.* When the giver of the Exercises sees that the recipient is experiencing desolation and temptation, he or she should not treat the retreatant severely or harshly, but gently and kindly. The director should encourage and strengthen the exercitant for the future, unmask the deceptive tactics of the enemy of our human nature, and help the retreatant to prepare and dispose himself or herself for the consolation which will come.

[8]   *The Eighth.* According to the need perceived in the recipient with respect to the desolations and deceptive tactics of the enemy, and also the consolations, the giver of the Exercises may explain to the retreatant the rules of the First and Second Weeks for recognizing the different kinds of spirits, in [313–327 and 328–336].

[9]   *The Ninth.* This point should be noticed. When an exercitant spiritually inexperienced is going through the First Week of the Exercises he or she may be tempted grossly and openly, for example, by being shown obstacles to going forward in the service of God our Lord, in the form of hardships, shame, fear about worldly honor, and the like. In such a case the one giving the Exercises should not explain to this retreatant the rules on different kinds of spirits for the Second Week. For to the same extent that the rules of the First Week will help him or her, those of the Second Week will be harmful. They are too subtle and advanced for such a one to understand.

[10]   *The Tenth.* When the one giving the Exercises perceives that the recipient is being assailed and tempted under the appearance of good, the proper time has come to explain to the retreatant the rules of the Second Week mentioned just above. For ordinarily the enemy of human nature tempts under the appearance of good more often when a person is performing the Exercises in the illuminative life, which corresponds to the Exercises of the Second Week, than in the purgative life, which corresponds to those of the First Week.

[11]   *The Eleventh.* It is helpful for a person receiving the Exercises of the First Week to know nothing about what is to be done in the Second, but to work diligently during the First Week at obtaining what he or she is seeking, just as if there were no anticipation of finding anything good in the Second.

[12]   *The Twelfth.* The one giving the Exercises should insist strongly with the person receiving them that he or she should remain for a full hour in each of the five Exercises or contemplations which will be made each day; and further, that the recipient should make sure always to have the satisfaction of knowing that a full hour was spent on the exercise — indeed, more rather than less. For the enemy usually exerts special efforts to get a person to shorten the hour of contemplation, meditation, or prayer.

[13]   *The Thirteenth.* This too should be noted. In time of consolation it is easy and scarcely taxing to remain in contemplation for a full hour, but during desolation it is very hard to fill out the time. Hence, to act against the desolation and overcome the temptations, the exercitant ought to remain always a little longer than the full hour, and in this way become accustomed not merely to resist the enemy but even to defeat him.

[14]   *The Fourteenth.* If the one giving the Exercises sees that the exercitant is proceeding with consolation and great fervor, he or she should warn the person not to make some promise or vow which is unconsidered or hasty. The more unstable the director sees the exercitant to be, the more earnest should be the forewarning and caution. For although it is altogether right for someone to advise another to enter religious life, which entails the taking of vows of obedience, poverty, and chastity; and although a good work done under a vow is more meritorious than one done without it; still one ought to bestow much thought on the circumstances and character of each person, and on the helps or hindrances one is likely to meet with in carrying out what one wishes to promise.

[15]   *The Fifteenth.* The one giving the Exercises should not urge the one receiving them toward poverty or any other promise more than toward their opposites, or to one state or way of life more than to another. Outside the Exercises it is lawful and meritorious for us to counsel those who are probably suitable for it to choose continence, virginity, religious life, and all forms of evangelical perfection. But during these Spiritual Exercises when a person is seeking God's will, it is more appropriate and far better that the Creator and Lord himself should communicate himself to the devout soul, embracing it with love, inciting it to praise of himself, and disposing it for the way which will most enable the soul to serve him in the future. Accordingly, the one giving the Exercises ought not to lean or incline in either direction but rather, while standing by like the pointer of a scale in equilibrium, to allow the Creator to deal immediately with the creature and the creature with its Creator and Lord.

[16]   *The Sixteenth.* For this purpose — namely, that the Creator and Lord may with greater certainty be the one working in his creature — if by chance the exercitant feels an affection or inclination to something in a disordered way, it is profitable for that person to strive with all possible effort to come over to the opposite of that to which he or she is wrongly attached. Thus, if someone is inclined to pursue and hold on to an office or benefice, not for the honor and glory of God our Lord or for the spiritual welfare of souls, but rather for one's own temporal

advantages and interests, one should try to bring oneself to desire the opposite. One should make earnest prayers and other spiritual exercises and ask God our Lord for the contrary; that is, to have no desire for this office or benefice or anything else unless his Divine Majesty has put proper order into those desires, and has by this means so changed one's earlier attachment that one's motive in desiring or holding on to one thing rather than another will now be only the service, honor, and glory of his Divine Majesty.

[17]   *The Seventeenth.* Although the one giving the Exercises should not endeavor to ask about or know the personal thoughts or sins of the exercitant, it is very advantageous for the director to be faithfully informed about the various agitations and thoughts which the different spirits stir up in the retreatant. For then, in accordance with the person's greater or lesser progress, the director will be able to communicate spiritual exercises adapted to the needs of the person who is agitated in this way.

[18]   *The Eighteenth.* The Spiritual Exercises should be adapted to the disposition of the persons who desire to make them, that is, to their age, education, and ability. In this way someone who is uneducated or has a weak constitution will not be given things he or she cannot well bear or profit from without fatigue.

Similarly exercitants should be given, each one, as much as they are willing to dispose themselves to receive, for their greater help and progress.

Consequently, a person who wants help to get some instruction and reach a certain level of peace of soul can be given the Particular Examen ([24–31]), and then the General Examen ([32–43]), and farther, the Method of Praying for a half hour in the morning on the Commandments ([238–243]), the Capital Sins ([244–245]), and other such procedures ([238; 246–260]). Such a person can also be encouraged to weekly confession of sins and, if possible, to reception of the Eucharist every two weeks or, if better disposed, weekly. This procedure is more appropriate for persons who are rather simple or illiterate. They should be given an explanation of each of the commandments, the seven capital sins, the precepts of the Church, the five senses, and the works of mercy.

Likewise, if the one giving the Exercises sees that the recipient is a person poorly qualified or of little natural capacity from whom much fruit is not to be expected, it is preferable to give to such a one some of these light Exercises until he or she has confessed, and then to give ways of examining one's conscience and a program for confession more frequent than before, that the person may preserve what has been acquired. But this should be done without going on to matters pertaining to the Election or to other Exercises beyond the First Week. This is especially the case when there are others with whom greater results can be achieved and time is insufficient to do everything.

[19]   *The Nineteenth.* A person who is involved in public affairs or pressing occupations but educated or intelligent may take an hour and a half each day to perform the Exercises. To such a one the director can explain the end for which human beings are created. Then he or she can explain for half an hour the particular examen, then the general examen, and the method of confessing and receiving the Eucharist. For three days this exercitant should make a meditation for an hour each morning on the first, second, and third sins ([45–53]); then for another three days at the same hour the meditation on the court-record of one's own sins ([55–56]); then for a further three days at the same hour the meditation on the punishment corresponding to sins ([65–72]). During these three meditations the ten Additional Directives ([73–90]) should be

given the exercitant. For the mysteries of Christ our Lord this exercitant should follow the same procedure as is explained below and at length throughout the Exercises themselves.

[20]　　*The Twentieth.* A person who is more disengaged, and who desires to make all the progress possible, should be given all the Spiritual Exercises in the same sequence in which they proceed below. Ordinarily, in making them an exercitant will achieve more progress the more he or she withdraws from all friends and acquaintances, and from all earthly concerns; for example, by moving out of one's place of residence and taking a different house or room where one can live in the greatest possible solitude, and thus be free to attend Mass and Vespers daily without fear of hindrance from acquaintances. Three principal advantages flow from this seclusion, among many others.

First, by withdrawing from friends and acquaintances and likewise from various activities that are not well ordered, in order to serve and praise God our Lord, we gain much merit in the eyes of his Divine Majesty.

Second, by being secluded in this way and not having our mind divided among many matters, but by concentrating instead all our attention on one alone, namely, the service of our Creator and our own spiritual progress, we enjoy a freer use of our natural faculties for seeking diligently what we so ardently desire.

Third, the more we keep ourselves alone and secluded, the more fit do we make ourselves to approach and attain to our Creator and Lord; and the nearer we come to him in this way, the more do we dispose ourselves to receive graces and gifts from his divine and supreme goodness.

[21]

Spiritual Exercises

To Overcome Oneself, and To Order One's Life, Without Reaching a Decision Through Some Disordered Affection.

[22]
Presupposition

That both the giver and the receiver of the Spiritual Exercises may be of greater help and benefit to each other, it should be presupposed that every good Christian ought to be more eager to put a good interpretation on a neighbor's statement than to condemn it. Further, if one cannot interpret it favorably, one should ask how the other means it. If that meaning is wrong, one should correct the person with love; and if this is not enough, one should search out every appropriate means through which, by understanding the statement in a good way, it may be saved.

The First Week

[23]
Principle and Foundation

Human beings are created to praise, reverence, and serve God our Lord, and by means of this to save their souls.

The other things on the face of the earth are created for the human beings, to help them in working toward the end for which they are created.

From this it follows that I should use these things to the extent that they help me toward my end, and rid myself of them to the extent that they hinder me.

To do this, I must make myself indifferent to all created things, in regard to everything which is left to my freedom of will and is not forbidden. Consequently, on my own part I ought not to seek health rather than sickness, wealth rather than poverty, honor rather than dishonor, a long life rather than a short one, and so on in all other matters.

I ought to desire and elect only the thing which is more conducive to the end for which I am created.

[24]
Daily Particular Examination of Conscience.

It comprises three times in the day and two examinations of conscience.

The First Time is in the morning. Upon arising the person should resolve to guard carefully against the particular sin or fault he or she wants to correct or amend.

[25]   *The Second Time* is after the noon meal. One should ask God our Lord for what one desires, namely, grace to recall how often one has fallen into the particular sin or fault, in order to correct it in the future. Then one should make the first examination, exacting an account of oneself with regard to the particular matter one has decided to take for correction and improve-

ment. One should run through the time, hour by hour or period by period, from the moment of rising until the present examination. On the upper line of the G═══ one should enter a dot for each time one fell into the particular sin or fault. Then one should renew one's resolution to do better during the time until the second examination which will be made later.

[26]   *The Third Time* is after supper. The person should make the second examination, likewise hour by hour starting from the previous examination down to the present one. For each time he or she fell into the particular sin or fault, a dot should be entered on the lower line of the g═══ .

[27]   Four Additional Directives to help toward quicker riddance of the particular sin or fault.

The First Directive. Each time one falls into the particular sin or fault, one should touch one's hand to one's breast in sorrow for having fallen. This can be done even in public without its being noticed by others.

[28]   *The Second.* Since the upper line of the G═══ represents the first examination and the lower line the second, the person should look at night to see if there was any improvement from the first line to the second, that is, from the first examination to the second.

[29]   *The Third.* The person should compare the second day with the first, that is, the two examinations of each day with those of the previous day, to see whether any improvement has been made from one day to the next.

[30]   *The Fourth.* The person should compare this week with the previous one, to see if any improvement has been made during the present week in comparison with the one before.

[31]   It should be noted that the first large G═══ on the top line indicates Sunday, the second and smaller g═══ Monday, the third Tuesday, and so on.

[32]   General Examination of Conscience to purify oneself, and to make a better confession.

I assume that there are three kinds of thoughts in myself, That is, one kind is my own, which arises strictly from my own freedom and desire; and the other two come from outside myself, the one from the good spirit and the other from the evil.

[33]   *Thoughts*

There are two ways in which I can merit from an evil thought that comes from outside myself.

The first occurs when a thought of committing a mortal sin comes to me, and I resist it immediately, and it remains banished.

[34]   The second way to merit occurs when this same bad thought comes to me, and I resist it, but it keeps coming back and I resist it continually, until it is overcome and goes away. This second way gains more merit than the first.

[35]   I sin venially when this same thought of committing a mortal sin comes to me and I give some heed to it — dwelling on it somewhat or experiencing some pleasure in the senses; or when there is some slackness in repulsing the thought.

[36]   There are two ways of sinning mortally. The first occurs when I consent to the bad thought, intending at that time to carry out what I have assented to, or to do so if it becomes possible.

[37]   The second way of sinning mortally occurs when one actually carries out the sin. This is graver, for three reasons: the longer time involved, the greater intensity, and the worse harm to the two persons.

[38]   **Words**

It is not permissible to swear, either by God or by a creature, unless it is done with truth, necessity, and reverence. With necessity, that is, to affirm with an oath, not just any truth at all, but only one of some importance for the good of the soul, or the body, or temporal interests. With reverence, that is, when in pronouncing the name of our Creator and Lord one acts with consideration and manifests that honor and reverence which are due to him.

[39]   In an unnecessary oath, it is a more serious sin to swear by the Creator than by a creature. However, we should note, it is harder to swear by a creature with the proper truth, necessity, and reverence than to swear by the Creator, for the following reasons.

The First. When we desire to swear by a creature, our very desire to name a creature makes us less careful and cautious about speaking the truth or affirming it with necessity than is the case when our urge is to name the Lord and Creator of all things.

The Second. When we swear by a creature, it is not as easy to maintain reverence and respect for the Creator as it is when we swear by the name of the Creator and Lord himself. For our very desire to name God our Lord carries with it greater respect and reverence than desire to name a creature. Consequently, to swear by a creature is more permissible for persons spiritually far advanced than for those less advanced. The perfect, through constant contemplation and enlightenment of their understanding, more readily consider, meditate, and contemplate God our Lord as being present in every creature by his essence, presence, and power. Thus when they swear by a creature, they are more able and better disposed than the imperfect to render respect and reverence to their Creator and Lord.

The Third. To swear continually by a creature brings a risk of idolatry that is greater in the imperfect than in the perfect.

[40]   It is not permissible to speak idle words. I take this to mean words that are of no benefit to myself or anyone else, and are not ordered toward such benefit. Consequently, words that benefit or are intended to benefit my own or another's soul, body, or temporal goods are never idle. Nor are they idle merely because they are about matters outside one's state of life; for example, if a religious talks about wars or commerce. However, in all that has been mentioned, there is merit if the words are ordered to a good end, and sin if they are directed to a bad end, or by one's talking uselessly.

[41]   We may not say anything to harm the reputation of others or to disparage them. If I reveal another person's mortal sin that is not publicly known, I sin mortally; if a venial sin, venially; if a defect, I expose my own defect.

When one has a right intention, there are two cases where it is permissible to speak about someone else's sin or fault.

The first. When the sin is public, for example, in the case of a known prostitute, a judicial sentence, or a public error infecting the minds of those with whom we live.

The second. When a hidden sin is revealed to another person so that he or she can help the sinner arise from this state. But in that case there must be conjectures or probable reasons to think that this person will be able to help the sinner.

[42]

Deeds

Here the subject matter takes in the ten commandments, the precepts of the Church, and the official recommendations of our superiors. Any action performed against these three headings is a sin, more serious or less in accordance with its nature. By official recommendations of our superiors I mean, for example, the bulls about crusades and other indulgences, such as those for peaceful reconciliations on condition of confession and reception of the Eucharist. For it is no small sin to act or cause others to act against these pious exhortations and recommendations of our superiors.

[43]

A Method for Making the General Examination of Conscience.

It contains five points.

The First Point is to give thanks to God our Lord for the benefits I have received from him.

The Second is to ask grace to know my sins and rid myself of them.

The Third is to ask an account of my soul from the hour of rising to the present examen, hour by hour or period by period; first as to thoughts, then words, then deeds, in the same order as was given for the particular examination [in 25].

The Fourth is to ask pardon of God our Lord for my faults.

The Fifth is to resolve, with his grace, to amend them. Close with an Our Father.

[44]

General Confession, with Holy Communion

For a person who voluntarily desires to make a general confession, to make it here in the time of retreat will bring three benefits, among others.

The First. It is granted that a person who confesses annually is not obliged to make a general confession. Nevertheless, to make it brings greater profit and merit, because of the greater sorrow experienced at present for all the sins and evil deeds of one's entire life.

The Second. During these Spiritual Exercises one reaches a deeper interior understanding of the reality and malice of one's sins than when one is not so concentrated on interior concerns. In this way, by coming to know and grieve for the sins more deeply during this time, one will profit and merit more than was the case on earlier occasions.

The Third. As a result of having made a better confession and come to a better disposition, one is worthier and better prepared to receive the Holy Sacrament. Furthermore, the reception of it helps, not only to avoid failing into sin, but also to preserve the increase of grace.

The general confession is best made immediately after the Exercises of the First Week.

[45]
The First Exercise
Is a Meditation By Using the Three Powers of the Soul About the First, Second, and Third Sins.

*It contains, after a preparatory prayer and two preludes,
three main points and a colloquy.*

[46]   *The Preparatory Prayer* is to ask God our Lord for the grace that all my intentions, actions, and operations may be ordered purely to the service and praise of his Divine Majesty.

[47]   *The First Prelude* is a composition made by imagining the place. Here we should take notice of the following. When a contemplation or meditation is about something that can be gazed on, for example, a contemplation of Christ our Lord, who is visible, the composition consists of seeing in imagination the physical place where that which I want to contemplate is taking place. By physical place I mean, for instance, a temple or a mountain where Jesus Christ or Our Lady happens to be, in accordance with the topic I desire to contemplate.

When a contemplation or meditation is about something abstract and invisible, as in the present case about the sins, the composition will be to see in imagination and to consider my soul as imprisoned in this corruptible body, and my whole compound self as an exile in this valley [of tears] among brute animals. I mean, my whole self as composed of soul and body.

[48]   *The Second Prelude* is to ask God our Lord for what I want and desire. What I ask for should be in accordance with the subject matter. For example, in a contemplation on the Resurrection, I will ask for joy with Christ in joy; in a contemplation on the Passion, I will ask for pain, tears, and suffering with Christ suffering.

In the present meditation it will be to ask for shame and confusion about myself, when I see how many people have been damned for committing a single mortal sin, and how many times I have deserved eternal damnation for my many sins.

[49]   *Note.* All the contemplations or meditations ought to be preceded by this same preparatory prayer, which is never changed, and also by the two preludes, which are sometimes changed in accordance with the subject matter.

[50]   *The First Point* will be to use my memory, by going over the first sin, that of the angels; next, to use my understanding, by reasoning about it; and then my will. My aim in remembering and reasoning about all these matters is to bring myself to greater shame and confusion, by comparing the one sin of the angels with all my own many sins. For one sin they went to hell; then how often have I deserved hell for my many sins!

In other words, I will call to memory the sin of the angels: How they were created in grace and then, not wanting to better themselves by using their freedom to reverence and obey their Creator and Lord, they fell into pride, were changed from grace to malice, and were hurled from heaven into hell. Next I will use my intellect to ruminate about this in greater detail, and then move myself to deeper affections by means of my will.

[51]   *The Second Point* will be meditated in the same way. That is, I will apply the three faculties to the sin of Adam and Eve. I will recall to memory how they did long penance for their sin, and the enormous corruption it brought to the human race, with so many people going to hell.

Again in other words, I will call to memory the second sin, that of our first parents: How Adam was created in the plain of Damascus and placed in the earthly paradise; and how Eve was created from his rib; how they were forbidden to eat of the tree of knowledge, but did eat, and thus sinned; and then, clothed in garments of skin and expelled from paradise, they lived out their whole lives in great hardship and penance, deprived of the original justice which they had lost. Next I will use my intellect to reason about this in greater detail, and then use the will, as is described just above.

[52]   *The Third Point* will likewise be to use the same method on the third sin, the particular sin of anyone who has gone to hell because of one mortal sin; and further, of innumerable other persons who went there for fewer sins than I have committed.

That is, about this third particular sin too I will follow the same procedure as above. I will call to memory the gravity and malice of the sin against my Creator and Lord; then I will use my intellect to reason about it — how by sinning and acting against the Infinite Goodness the person has been justly condemned forever. Then I will finish by using the will, as was described above.

[53]   *Colloquy.* Imagine Christ our Lord suspended on the cross before you, and converse with him in a colloquy: How is it that he, although he is the Creator, has come to make himself a human being? How is it that he has passed from eternal life to death here in time, and to die in this way for my sins?

In a similar way, reflect on yourself and ask: What have I done for Christ? What am I doing for Christ? What ought I to do for Christ?

In this way, too, gazing on him in so pitiful a state as he hangs on the cross, speak out whatever comes to your mind.

[54]   A colloquy is made, properly speaking, in the way one friend speaks to another, or a servant to one in authority — now begging a favor, now accusing oneself of some misdeed, now telling one's concerns and asking counsel about them. Close with an Our Father.

[55]   ## The Second Exercise Is a Meditation On Our Own Sins.

*It comprises, after the preparatory prayer and preludes,
five points and a colloquy.*

The Preparatory Prayer will be the same.

The First Prelude will be the same composition of place.

The Second Prelude will be to ask for what I desire. Here it will be to ask for growing and intense sorrow and tears for my sins.

[56]   *The First Point* is the court-record of my sins. I will call to memory all the sins of my life, looking at them year by year or period by period. For this three things will he helpful: first, the locality or house where I lived; second, the associations which I had with others; third, the occupation I was pursuing.

[57]   *The Second Point* is to ponder these sins, looking at the foulness and evil which every mortal sin would contain in itself, even if it were not forbidden.

[58]   *The Third Point.* I will reflect upon myself, by using examples which humble me:

First, what am I when compared with all other human beings?

Second, what are they when compared with all the angels and saints in paradise?

Third, what is all of creation when compared with God? and then, I alone — what can I be?

Fourth, I will look at all the corruption and foulness of my body.

Fifth, I will look upon myself as a sore or abscess from which have issued such great sins and iniquities and such foul poison.

[59]   *The Fourth Point.* I will consider who God is against whom I have sinned, by going through his attributes and comparing them with their opposites in myself: his wisdom with my

ignorance, his omnipotence with my weakness, his justice with my iniquity, his goodness with my malice.

[60]   *The Fifth Point.* This is an exclamation of wonder and surging emotion, uttered as I reflect on all creatures and wonder how they have allowed me to live and have preserved me in life. The angels: How is it that, although they are the swords of God's justice, they have borne with me, protected me, and prayed for me? The saints: How is it that they have interceded and prayed for me? Likewise, the heavens, the sun, the moon, the stars, and the elements; the fruits, birds, fishes, and animals. And the earth: How is it that it has not opened up and swallowed me, creating new hells for me to suffer in forever?

[61]   *I will conclude with a colloquy* of mercy — speaking and giving thanks to God our Lord for giving me life until now, and proposing, with his grace, amendment for the future. Our Father.

The Third Exercise Is a Repetition of the First and Second Exercises, By Making Three Colloquies.

[62]

After the preparatory prayer and two preludes, this exercise will be a repetition of the first and the second exercises. I should notice and dwell on those points where I felt greater consolation or desolation, or had a greater spiritual experience. Then I will make three colloquies in the manner which follows.

[63]   *The First Colloquy* will be with Our Lady, that she may obtain for me from her Son and Lord grace for three things:

First, that I may feel an interior knowledge of my sins and also an abhorrence of them;

Second, that I may perceive the disorder in my actions, in order to detest them, amend myself, and put myself in order;

Third, that I may have a knowledge of the world, in order to detest it and rid myself of all that is worldly and vain. Then I will say a Hail Mary.

The Second Colloquy. I will make the same requests to the Son, asking him to obtain these graces for me from the Father. Then I will say the prayer Soul of Christ.

The Third Colloquy. I will address these same requests to the Father, asking that he himself, the eternal Lord, may grant me these graces. Then I will say an Our Father.

The Fourth Exercise Is to Make a Résumé of the Third.

[64]

I have used the word résumé because the intellect, without rambling, should strive assiduously to recall the matters contemplated in the previous exercises. It concludes with the same three colloquies.

The Fifth Exercise Is a Meditation on Hell.

[65]

It contains, after the preparatory prayer and two preludes,
five points and a colloquy.

The Preparatory Prayer will be the same as usual.

The First Prelude, the composition of place. Here it will be to see in imagination the length, breadth, and depth of hell.

The Second Prelude, to ask for what I desire. Here it will be to ask for an interior sense of the pain suffered by the damned, so that if through my faults I should forget the love of the Eternal Lord, at least the fear of those pains will serve to keep me from falling into sin.

[66]   *The First Point* will be to see with the eyes of the imagination the huge fires and, so to speak, the souls within the bodies full of fire.

[67]   *The Second Point.* In my imagination I will hear the wailing, the shrieking, the cries, and the blasphemies against our Lord and all his saints.

[68]   *The Third Point.* By my sense of smell I will perceive the smoke, the sulphur, the filth, and the rotting things.

[69]   *The Fourth Point.* By my sense of taste I will experience the bitter flavors of hell: tears, sadness, and the worm of conscience.

[70]   *The Fifth Point.* By my sense of touch, I will feel how the flames touch the souls and burn them.

[71]   *The Colloquy.* I will carry on a colloquy with Christ our Lord. I will call to mind the souls who are in hell: Some are there because they did not believe in Christ's coming; and others who, although they believed, did not act according to his commandments. I will group these persons into three classes.

First, those lost before Christ came.

Second, those condemned during his lifetime.

Third, those lost after his life in this world.

Thereupon I will thank Christ because he has not, by ending my life, let me fall into any of these classes. I will also thank him because he has shown me, all through my life up to the present moment, so much pity and mercy. I will close with an Our Father.

[72]   *Note.* The first exercise will be made at midnight; the second, soon after arising in the morning; the third, before or after Mass, but always before the noon meal; the fourth, at the time of Vespers; and the fifth, an hour before the evening meal. This distribution of the hours is intended to be followed, more or less, throughout the four Weeks. The norm is the help found by the exercitant in making the five exercises or fewer, in accordance with his or her age, disposition, and health.

[73]   ## Additional Directives for Making the Exercises Better and Finding More Readily What One Desires.

The First Directive. Upon going to bed at night, just before I fall asleep, I will think for the length of a Hail Mary about the hour when I should arise, and for what purpose; and I will briefly sum up the exercise I am to make.

[74]   *The Second.* Upon awakening, while keeping out any other thoughts, I will immediately turn my attention to what I will contemplate in the first exercise, at midnight. I will strive to feel shame for my many sins, by using examples, such as that of a knight who stands before his king and his whole court, shamed and humiliated because he has grievously offended him, from whom he had received numerous gifts and favors.

Similarly, in the second exercise I will imagine myself as a great sinner in chains; that is, as if I were being brought in chains to appear before the supreme and eternal Judge; taking as an example how chained prisoners, already deserving death, appear before their earthly judge. As I dress I will keep thoughts like these in mind, or others proper to the subject matter.

[75]   *The Third.* A step or two away from the place where I will make my contemplation or meditation, I will stand for the length of an Our Father. I will raise my mind and think how God our Lord is looking at me, and other such thoughts. Then I will make an act of reverence or humility.

[76]   *The Fourth.* I will enter upon the contemplation, now kneeling, now prostrate on the floor, or lying face upward, or seated, or standing — but always intent on seeking what I desire. Two things should be noted. First, if I find what I desire while kneeling, I will not change to another posture; so too, if I find it while prostrate, and so on.

Second, if in any point I find what I am seeking, there I will repose until I am fully satisfied, without any anxiety to go on.

[77]   *The Fifth.* After finishing the exercise, for a quarter of an hour, either seated or walking about, I will examine how well I did in the contemplation or meditation. If poorly, I will seek the reasons; and if I find them, I will express sorrow in order to do better in the future. If I did well, I will thank God our Lord and use the same procedure next time.

[78]   *The Sixth.* I should not think about pleasant or joyful things, such as heavenly glory, the Resurrection, and so forth. For if we desire to experience pain, sorrow, and tears for our sins, any thought of happiness or joy will be an impediment. Instead, I should keep myself intent on experiencing sorrow and pain; and for this it is better to think about death and judgment.

[79]   *The Seventh.* For the same purpose I will deprive myself of all light, by closing the shutters and doors while I am in my room, except for times when I want to read the office or other matters, or eat.

[80]   *The Eighth.* I should not laugh, or say anything that would arouse laughter.

[81]   *The Ninth.* I should restrain my sight, except to receive or say goodbye to someone with whom I speak.

[82]   *The Tenth.* This pertains to penance, which is divided into interior and exterior. Interior penance is grieving for one's sins with a firm intention not to commit those or any other sins again. Exterior penance, a fruit of the former, is self-punishment for the sins one has committed. This is done in three principal ways.

[83]   The first way pertains to eating. That is, when we abstain from what is superfluous we are practicing, not penance, but temperance. We practice penance when we abstain from what is ordinarily suitable. And the more we subtract the better is the penance, provided that we do not weaken our constitution or bring on noteworthy illness.

[84]   The second way pertains to our manner of sleeping. Again, when we abstain from the superfluous in things delicate and soft, this is not penance. But we do practice penance when we deprive ourselves of what is ordinarily suitable; and the more we so deprive ourselves, the better is the penance, provided we do not harm ourselves or weaken our constitution. However, we should not deprive ourselves of the amount of sleep ordinarily good for us, except perhaps in an effort to find the right mean when one has a bad habit of sleeping too much.

[85]   The third way is to chastise the body, that is, to inflict pain on it, by wearing hairshirts, cords, or iron chains; by scourging or wounding oneself; and by similar austerities.

[86]   *Note.* The best and safest form of penance seems to be that which produces physical pain but does not penetrate to the bones, so that it brings pain but not illness. Therefore the most suitable form of penance is to hurt oneself with light cords that inflict the pain on the surface, rather than some other manner which might cause noteworthy illness inside.

[87]   *A First Observation.* Exterior penances are performed chiefly for three purposes.

First, to satisfy for one's past sins.

Second, to overcome ourselves; that is, to keep our bodily nature obedient to reason and all our bodily faculties subject to the higher.

Third, to seek and obtain some grace or gift which one wishes and desires, such as interior contrition for one's sins, abundant tears because of them or of the pains and sufferings which Christ our Lord underwent in his Passion; or to obtain a solution to some doubt in which one finds oneself.

[88]   *A Second Observation.* The first and second additional directives should be used for the exercises at midnight and early morning, but not for those which will be made at other times. The fourth additional directive will never be practiced in church in the presence of others, but only privately, for example, in one's house, and so forth.

[89]   *A Third Observation.* When someone making the Exercises fails to find what he or she desires, such as tears, consolation, and the like, it is often useful to make some change in eating, sleeping, and other forms of penance, so that we do penance for two or three days, and then omit it for two or three days. Furthermore, for some persons more penance is suitable, and for others less. Further still, on many occasions we give up penance because of love of our bodies and judge erroneously that a human being cannot endure such penance without notable illness. On the other hand, we sometimes do excessive penance, thinking that the body can bear it. Now since God our Lord knows our nature infinitely better than we do, through changes of this sort he often enables each of us to know what is right for her or him.

[90]   *A Fourth Observation.* The particular examination should be made to get rid of faults and negligences pertaining to the exercises and Additional Directives. This holds true also during the Second, Third, and Fourth Weeks.

Michel de Montaigne

"ON THE CANNIBALS"

Introduction by Michael Levin

When Christopher Columbus discovered the "New World," it of course caused a sensation all over Europe. Descriptions of these previously unknown continents and civilizations quickly became best sellers. People were especially fascinated with stories of Native Americans, who seemed "primitive" compared to Western Civilization. Early accounts of European explorers in the Americas often describe the natives as child-like or innocent, like Adam and Eve before the Fall. Other natives, however, were called "savages." They practiced human sacrifice, and some of them were reported to be cannibals. In the sixteenth century Europeans brought back a number of these "Indians" to their homelands, to be gawked at by everyone. One person who saw three such natives was the French writer Michel de Montaigne (1533–1592).

Montaigne was one of the greatest thinkers and writers of the French Renaissance. Extremely well educated in the Renaissance humanist tradition, he was fluent in Latin by the age of six. We see evidence of his classical education in the numerous quotations from Greek and Roman authors which pepper his work. Montaigne also exemplifies the same humanist fondness for self-examination, which Petrarch had displayed two centuries earlier. As he says on the opening page of his most famous work, *Essays,* "I am myself the matter of my book." In these essays (including the one we include here) Montaigne presents us with a self-portrait, and gives us a detailed account of what he felt and thought, as well as what he observed about his fellow men. But what he had to say about other people was often not very complimentary, for Montaigne lived in a confused and violent world.

In the sixteenth century, France was torn apart by religious and civil war. Many French subjects, drawn to the ideas of Martin Luther and John Calvin, became protestants (in France called Huguenots), while others remained loyal to the Catholic Church. Both sides committed atrocities, the most famous being the St. Bartholomew's Day Massacre of 1572, when royal troops slaughtered thousands of protestants in the streets of Paris. Throughout his life Montaigne tried to remain neutral, but he witnessed the horrors of war and religious conflict. In this essay, "On the Cannibals," written around 1580, Montaigne compares the behavior and values of Native Americans with those of his countrymen. He asks a simple yet profound question: who is more savage?

One of the themes of this course is the nature of civilization. What does it mean to be civilized? Is Western civilization superior to others? Montaigne was interested in these same questions, and wanted his readers to question their assumptions about themselves. During Montaigne's lifetime, European soldiers and colonists conquered the Americas, and they often used the Native Americans' lack of civilization as justification for their conquest. Were the Europeans justified?

Pay particular attention to the last line of this essay. What point is Montaigne trying to make?

31. On the Cannibals

A] When King Pyrrhus crossed into Italy, after noting the excellent formation of the army which the Romans had sent ahead towards him he said, 'I do not know what kind of Barbarians these are' (for the Greeks called all foreigners Barbarians) 'but there is nothing barbarous about the ordering of the army which I can see!' The Greeks said the same about the army which Flaminius brought over to their country, [C] as did Philip when he saw from a hill-top in his kingdom the order and plan of the Roman encampment under Publius Sulpicius Galba.[1] [A] We should be similarly wary of accepting common opinions; we should judge them by the ways of reason not by popular vote.

I have long had a man with me who stayed some ten or twelve years in that other world which was discovered in our century when Villegaignon made his landfall and named it *La France Antartique*.[2] This discovery of a boundless territory seems to me worthy of reflection. I am by no means sure that some other land may not be discovered in the future, since so many persons, [C] greater than we are, [A] were wrong about this one! I fear that our eyes are bigger than our bellies, our curiosity more[3] than we can stomach. We grasp at everything but clasp nothing but wind.

Plato brings in Solon to relate that he had learned from the priests of the town of Saïs in Egypt how, long ago before the Flood, there was a vast island called Atlantis right at the mouth of the Straits of Gibraltar, occupying an area greater than Asia and Africa combined; the kings of that country, who not only possessed that island but had spread on to the mainland across the breadth of Africa as far as Egypt and the length of Europe as far as Tuscany, planned to stride

---

Montaigne's Essays trans. M. A. Screech (New York: Penguin, 1993) ISBN 0140446028, pp. 79–95, "Of Cannibals."

1. Plutarch, *Life of Pyrrhus* and *Life of Flaminius.*

2. Durand de Villegagnon struck land, in Brazil, in 1557. Cf. *Lettres sur la navigation du chevalier de Villegaignon es terres de l'Amérique*, Paris, 1557, by an author who calls himself simply N.B.

3. '80: our bellies, *as they say, applying it to those whose appetite and hunger make them desire more meat than they can manage: I fear that we too have* curiosity *far* more . . .

over into Asia and subdue all the peoples bordering on the Mediterranean as far as the Black Sea. To this end they had traversed Spain, Gaul and Italy and had reached as far as Greece when the Athenians withstood them; but soon afterwards those Athenians, as well as the people of Atlantis and their island, were engulfed in that Flood.[4]

It is most likely that that vast inundation should have produced strange changes to the inhabitable areas of the world; it is maintained that it was then that the sea cut off Sicily from Italy —

[B] *Hæc loca, vi quondam et vasta convulsa ruina,*
Dissiluisse ferunt, cum protinus utraque tellus
Una foret.

[Those places, they say, were once wrenched apart by a violent convulsion, whereas they had formerly been one single land.][5]

— [A] as well as Cyprus from Syria, and the island of Negropontus from the Boeotian mainland, while elsewhere lands once separated were joined together by filling in the trenches between them with mud and sand:

sterilisque diu palus aptaque remis
Vicinas urbes alit, et grave sentit aratrum.

[Barren swamps which you could row a boat through now feed neighbouring cities and bear the heavy plough.][6]

Yet there is little likelihood of that island's being the New World which we have recently discovered, for it was virtually touching Spain; it would be unbelievable for a flood to force it back more than twelve hundred leagues to where it is now; besides our modern seamen have already all but discovered that it is not an island at all but a mainland, contiguous on one side with the East Indies and on others with lands lying beneath both the Poles — or that if it is separated from them, it is by straits so narrow that it does not deserve the name of 'island' on that account.

[B] It seems that large bodies such as these are subject, as are our own, to changes, [C] some natural, some [B] feverish.[7] When I consider how my local river the Dordogne has, during my own lifetime, been encroaching on the right-hand bank going downstream and has taken over so much land that it has robbed many buildings of their foundation, I realize that it has been suffering from some unusual upset: for if it had always gone on like this or were to do so in the future, the whole face of the world would be distorted. But their moods change: sometimes they incline one way, then another: and sometimes they restrain themselves. I am not discussing those sudden floodings whose causes we know. By the coast-line in Médoc, my brother the Sieur d'Arsac can see lands of his lying buried under sand spewed up by the sea: the tops of some of the buildings are still visible: his rents and arable fields have been changed into very sparse grazing. The locals say that the sea has been thrusting so hard against them for some time

---

4. Plato, *Timaeus,* 24E etc., and Girolamo Benzoni, *Historia del mondo novo,* Venice 1565. Cf. also Plato, *Critias,* 113 A ff.

5. Virgil, *Aeneid,* *I*II, 414–17.

6. Horace, *Ars poetica,* 65–6.

7. '88: changes *sickly* and feverish. When . . .

now that they have lost four leagues of land. These sands are the sea's pioneer-corps: [C] and we can see those huge shifting sand-dunes marching a half-league ahead in the vanguard, capturing territory.

[A] The other testimony from Antiquity which some would make relevant to this discovery is in Aristotle — if that little book about unheard wonders is really his.[8] He tells how some Carthaginians struck out across the Atlantic beyond the Straits of Gibraltar, sailed for a long time and finally discovered a large fertile island entirely clothed in woodlands and watered by great deep rivers but very far from any mainland; they and others after them, attracted by the richness and fertility of the soil, emigrated with their wives and children and started living there. The Carthaginian lords, seeing that their country was being gradually depopulated, expressly forbade any more to go there on pain of death and drove out those new settlers, fearing it is said that they would in time increase so greatly that they would supplant them and bring down their State.

But that account in Aristotle cannot apply to these new lands either.

That man of mine was a simple, rough fellow — qualities which make for a good witness: those clever chaps notice more things more carefully but are always adding glosses; they cannot help changing their story a little in order to make their views triumph and be more persuasive; they never show you anything purely as it is: they bend it and disguise it to fit in with their own views. To make their judgement more credible and to win you over they emphasize their own side, amplify it and extend it. So you need either a very trustworthy man or else a man so simple that he has nothing in him on which to build such false discoveries or make them plausible; and he must be wedded to no cause. Such was my man; moreover on various occasions he showed me several seamen and merchants whom he knew on that voyage. So I am content with what he told me, without inquiring what the cosmographers have to say about it.

What we need is topographers who would make detailed accounts of the places which they had actually been to. But because they have the advantage of visiting Palestine, they want to enjoy the right of telling us tales about all the rest of the world! I wish everyone would write only about what he knows — not in this matter only but in all others. A man may well have detailed knowledge or experience of the nature of one particular river or stream, yet about all the others he knows only what everyone else does; but in order to trot out his little scrap of knowledge he will write a book on the whole of physics! From this vice many great inconveniences arise.

Now to get back to the subject, I find (from what has been told me) that there is nothing savage or barbarous about those peoples, but that every man calls barbarous anything he is not accustomed to; it is indeed the case that we have no other criterion of truth or right-reason than the example and form of the opinions and customs of our own country. There we always find the perfect religion, the perfect polity, the most developed and perfect way of doing anything! Those 'savages' are only wild in the sense that we call fruits wild when they are produced by Nature in her ordinary course: whereas it is fruit which we have artificially perverted and misled from the common order which we ought to call savage. It is in the first kind that we find their true, vigorous, living, most natural and most useful properties and virtues, which we have bastardized in the other kind by merely adapting them to our corrupt tastes. [C] Moreover, there is a delicious savour which even our taste finds excellent in a variety of fruits produced in those countries, without cultivation: they rival our own. [A] It is not sensible that artifice should be reverenced more than Nature, our great and powerful Mother. We have so overloaded the richness and

---

8. The *Secreta secretorum* is supposititious. Montaigne is following Girolamo Benzoni.

beauty of her products by our own ingenuity that we have smothered her entirely. Yet wherever her pure light does shine, she wondrously shames our vain and frivolous enterprises:

> [B] *Et veniunt ederæ sponte sua melius,*
> *Surgit et in solis formosior arbutus antris,*
> *Et volucres nulla dulcius arte canunt.*

[Ivy grows best when left untended; the strawberry tree flourishes more beautifully in lonely grottoes, and birds sing the sweeter for their artlessness.][9]

[A] All our strivings cannot even manage to produce the nest of the smallest little bird, with its beauty and appropriateness to its purpose; we cannot even reproduce the web of the wretched spider. [C] Plato says that all things are produced by nature, fortune or art, the greatest and fairest by the first two, the lesser and least perfect by the last.[10]

[A] Those peoples, then, seem to me to be barbarous only in that they have been hardly fashioned by the mind of man, still remaining close neighbours to their original state of nature. They are still governed by the laws of Nature and are only very slightly bastardized by ours; but their purity is such that I am sometimes seized with irritation at their not having been discovered earlier, in times when there were men who could have appreciated them better than we do. It irritates me that neither Lycurgus nor Plato had any knowledge of them, for it seems to me that what experience has taught us about those peoples surpasses, not only all the descriptions with which poetry has beautifully painted the Age of Gold[11] and all its ingenious fictions about Man's blessed early state, but also the very conceptions and yearnings of philosophy. They could not even imagine a state of nature so simple and so pure as the one we have learned about from experience; they could not even believe that societies of men could be maintained with so little artifice, so little in the way of human solder. I would tell Plato that those people have no trade of any kind, no acquaintance with writing, no knowledge of numbers, no terms for governor or political superior, no practice of subordination or of riches or poverty, no contracts, no inheritances, no divided estates, no occupation but leisure, no concern for kinship — except such as is common to them all — no clothing, no agriculture, no metals, no use of wine or corn. Among them you hear no words for treachery, lying, cheating, avarice, envy, backbiting or forgiveness. How remote from such perfection would Plato find that Republic which he thought up — [C] *'viri a diis recentes'* [men fresh from the gods].[12]

> [B] *Hos natura modos primum dedit.*

[These are the ways which Nature first ordained.][13]

[A] In addition they inhabit a land with a most delightful countryside and a temperate climate, so that, from what I have been told by my sources, it is rare to find anyone ill there;[14] I

---

9. Propertius, I, ii, 10–12.

10. Plato, *Laws*, X, 888A–B.

11. Cf. Elizabeth Armstrong, *Ronsard and the Age of Gold*, Cambridge, 1968.

12. Seneca, *Epist. moral.*, XC, 44. (This epistle is a major defence of the innocence of natural man before he was corrupted by philosophy and progress.)

13. Virgil, *Georgics,* II, 208.

14. One of Montaigne's sources was Simon Goulart's *Histoire du Portugal, Pa*ris, 1587, based on a work by Bishop Jeronimo Osorio (da Fonseca) and others.

have been assured that they never saw a single man bent with age, toothless, blear-eyed or tottering. They dwell along the sea-shore, shut in to landwards by great lofty mountains, on a stretch of land some hundred leagues in width. They have fish and flesh in abundance which bear no resemblance to ours; these they eat simply cooked. They were so horror-struck by the first man who brought a horse there and rode it that they killed him with their arrows before they could recognize him, even though he had had dealings with them on several previous voyages. Their dwellings are immensely long, big enough to hold two or three hundred souls; they are covered with the bark of tall trees which are fixed into the earth, leaning against each other in support at the top, like some of our barns where the cladding reaches down to the ground and acts as a side. They have a kind of wood so hard that they use it to cut with, making their swords from it as well as grills to cook their meat. Their beds are woven from cotton and slung from the roof like hammocks on our ships; each has his own, since wives sleep apart from their husbands. They get up at sunrise and have their meal for the day as soon as they do so; they have no other meal but that one. They drink nothing with it, [B] like those Eastern peoples who, according to Suidas,[15] only drink apart from meals. [A] They drink together several times a day, and plenty of it. This drink is made from a certain root and has the colour of our claret. They always drink it lukewarm; it only keeps for two or three days; it tastes a bit sharp, is in no ways heady and is good for the stomach; for those who are not used to it it is laxative but for those who are, it is a very pleasant drink. Instead of bread they use a certain white product resembling coriander-cakes. I have tried some: it tastes, sweet and somewhat insipid.

They spend the whole day dancing; the younger men go off hunting with bow and arrow. Meanwhile some of the women-folk are occupied in warming up their drink: that is their main task. In the morning, before their meal, one of their elders walks from one end of the building to the other, addressing the whole barnful of them by repeating one single phrase over and over again until he has made the rounds, their building being a good hundred yards long. He preaches two things only: bravery before their enemies and love for their wives. They never fail to stress this second duty, repeating that it is their wives who season their drink and keep it warm. In my own house, as in many other places, you can see the style of their beds and rope-work as well as their wooden swords and the wooden bracelets with which they arm their wrists in battle, and the big open-ended canes to the sound of which they maintain the rhythm of their dances. They shave off all their hair, cutting it more cleanly than we do, yet with razors made of only wood or stone. They believe in the immortality of the soul: souls which deserve well of the gods dwell in the sky where the sun rises; souls which are accursed dwell where it sets. They have some priests and prophets or other, but they rarely appear among the people since they live in the mountains. When they do appear they hold a great festival and a solemn meeting of several villages — each of the barns which I have described constituting a village situated about one French league distant from the next. The prophet then addresses them in public, exhorting them to be virtuous and dutiful, but their entire system of ethics contains only the same two articles: resoluteness in battle and love for their wives. He foretells what is to happen and the results they must expect from what they undertake; he either incites them to war or deflects them from it, but only on condition that if he fails to divine correctly and if things turn out other than he foretold, then — if they can catch him — he is condemned as a false prophet and hacked to pieces. So the prophet who gets it wrong once is seen no more.

---

15. Suidas, *Historica, caeteraque omnia quae ad cognitionem rerum spectant,* Basle, 1564.

[C] Prophecy is a gift of God.[16] That is why abusing it should be treated as a punishable deceit. Among the Scythians, whenever their soothsayers got it wrong they were shackled hand and foot and laid in ox-carts full of bracken where they were burned.[17] Those who treat subjects under the guidance of human limitations can be excused if they have done their best; but those who come and cheat us with assurances of powers beyond the natural order and then fail to do what they promise, should they not be punished for it and for the foolhardiness of their deceit?

[A] These peoples have their wars against others further inland beyond their mountains; they go forth naked, with no other arms but their bows and their wooden swords sharpened to a point like the blades of our pig-stickers. Their steadfastness in battle is astonishing and always ends in killing and bloodshed: they do not even know the meaning of fear or flight. Each man brings back the head of the enemy he has slain and sets it as a trophy over the door of his dwelling. For a long period they treat captives well and provide them with all the comforts which they can devise; afterwards the master of each captive summons a great assembly of his acquaintances; he ties a rope to one of the arms of his prisoner [C] and holds him by it, standing a few feet away for fear of being caught in the blows, [A] and allows his dearest friend to hold the prisoner the same way by the other arm: then, before the whole assembly, they both hack at him with their swords and kill him. This done, they roast him and make a common meal of him, sending chunks of his flesh to absent friends. This is not as some think done for food — as the Scythians used to do in antiquity — but to symbolize ultimate revenge. As a proof of this, when they noted that the Portuguese who were allied to their enemies practised a different kind of execution on them when taken prisoner — which was to bury them up to the waist, to shoot showers of arrows at their exposed parts and then to hang them — they thought that these men from the Other World, who had scattered a knowledge of many a vice throughout their neighbourhood and who were greater masters than they were of every kind of revenge, which must be more severe than their own; so they began to abandon their ancient method and adopted that one. It does not sadden me that we should note the horrible barbarity in a practice such as theirs: what does sadden me is that, while judging correctly of their wrong-doings we should be so blind to our own. I think there is more barbarity in eating a man alive than in eating him dead; more barbarity in lacerating by rack and torture a body still fully able to feel things, in roasting him little by little and having him bruised and bitten by pigs and dogs (as we have not only read about but seen in recent memory, not among enemies in antiquity but among our fellow-citizens and neighbours and, what is worse, in the name of duty and religion) than in roasting him and eating him after his death.

Chrysippus and Zeno, the leaders of the Stoic school, certainly thought that there was nothing wrong in using our carcasses for whatever purpose we needed, even for food — as our own forebears did when, beleaguered by Caesar in the town of Alesia, they decided to relieve the hunger of the besieged with the flesh of old men, women and others who were no use in battle:

[B] *Vascones, fama est, alimentis talibus usi*
Produxere animas.

[By the eating of such food it is notorious that the Gascons prolonged their lives.][18]

---

16. Cf. Cicero, *De divinatione,* I, i.1; I Peter 1:2; I Corinthians 12:20; 13:2.

17. Herodotus, *History,* IV, lxix.

18. Sextus Empiricus, *Hypotyposes, III,* xxiv; Caesar, *Gallic Wars,* VII, lvii–lviii; Juvenal, *Satires,* XV, 93–4.

[A] And our medical men do not flinch from using corpses in many ways, both internally and externally, to cure us.[19] Yet no opinion has ever been so unruly as to justify treachery, disloyalty, tyranny and cruelty, which are everyday vices in us. So we can indeed call those folk barbarians by the rules of reason but not in, comparison with ourselves, who surpass them in every kind of barbarism. Their warfare is entirely noble and magnanimous; it has as much justification and beauty as that human malady allows: among them it has no other foundation than a zealous concern for courage. They are not striving to conquer new lands, since without toil or travail they still enjoy that bounteous Nature who furnishes them abundantly with all they need, so that they have no concern to push back their frontiers. They are still in that blessed state of desiring nothing beyond what is ordained by their natural necessities: for them anything further is merely superfluous. The generic term which they use for men of the same age is 'brother'; younger men they call 'sons'. As for the old men, they are the 'fathers' of everyone else; they bequeath all their goods, indivisibly, to all these heirs in common, there being no other entitlement than that with which Nature purely and simply endows all her creatures by bringing them into this world. If the neighbouring peoples come over the mountains to attack them and happen to defeat them, the victors' booty consists in fame and in the privilege of mastery in virtue and valour: they have no other interest in the goods of the vanquished and so return home to their own land, which lacks no necessity; nor do they lack that great accomplishment of knowing how to enjoy their mode-of-being in happiness and to be content with it. These people do the same in their turn: they require no other ransom from their prisoners-of-war than that they should admit and acknowledge their defeat — yet there is not one prisoner in a hundred years who does not prefer to die rather than to derogate from the greatness of an invincible mind by look or by word; you cannot find one who does not prefer to be killed and eaten than merely to ask to be spared. In order to make their prisoners love life more they treat them generously in every way,[20] but occupy their thoughts with the menaces of the death awaiting all of them, of the tortures they will have to undergo and of the preparations being made for it, of limbs to be lopped off and of the feast they will provide. All that has only one purpose: to wrench some weak or unworthy word from their lips or to make them wish to escape, so as to enjoy the privilege of having frightened them and forced their constancy.[21]

Indeed, if you take it the right way, true victory[22] consists in that alone:

> [C] *victoria nulla est*
> *Quam quæ confessos animo quoque subjugat hostes.*

[There is no victory unless you subjugate the minds of the enemy and make them admit defeat.][23]

In former times those warlike fighters the Hungarians never pressed their advantage beyond making their enemy throw himself on their mercy. Once having wrenched this admission from him, they let him go without injury or ransom, except at most for an undertaking never again to bear arms against them.[24]

---

19. Mummies were imported for use in medicines. (Othello's handkerchief was steeped in 'juice of mummy'.)

20. '80: generously in every way, *and furnish them with all the comforts they can devise* but . . .

21. '80: their *virtue and their* constancy . . .

22. '80: true *and solid* victory . . .

23. Claudian, *De sexto consulatu Honorii,* 248–9.

24. Nicolas Chalcocondylas (tr. Blaise de Vigenère), *De la décadence de l'empire grec,* V, ix.

[A] Quite enough of the advantages we do gain over our enemies are mainly borrowed ones not truly our own. To have stronger arms and legs is the property of a porter not of Valour; agility is a dead and physical quality, for it is chance which causes your opponent to stumble and which makes the sun dazzle him; to be good at fencing is a matter of skill and knowledge which may light on a coward or a worthless individual. A man's worth and reputation lie in the mind and in the will: his true honour is found there. Bravery does not consist in firm arms and legs but in firm minds and souls: it is not a matter of what our horse or our weapons are worth but of what we are. The man who is struck down but whose mind remains steadfast, [C] *'si succiderit, de genu pugnat'* [if his legs give way, then on his knees doth he fight];[25] [B] the man who relaxes none of his mental assurance when threatened with imminent death and who faces his enemy with inflexible scorn as he gives up the ghost is beaten by Fortune not by us: [C] he is slain but not vanquished.[26] [B] Sometimes it is the bravest who may prove most unlucky. [C] So there are triumphant defeats rivalling victories; Salamis, Plataea, Mycale and Sicily are the fairest sister-victories which the Sun has ever seen, yet they would never dare to compare their combined glory with the glorious defeat of King Leonidas and his men at the defile of Thermopylae.[27] Who has ever run into battle with a greater desire and ambition for victory than did Captain Ischolas when he was defeated? Has any man ever assured his safety more cleverly or carefully than he assured his destruction?[28] His task was to defend against the Arcadians a certain pass in the Peleponnesus. He realized that he could not achieve this because of the nature of the site and of the odds against him, concluding that every man who faced the enemy must of necessity die in the battlefield; on the other hand he judged it unworthy of his own courage, of his greatness of soul and of the name of Sparta to fail in his duty; so he chose the middle path between these two extremes and acted thus: he saved the youngest and fittest soldiers of his unit to serve for the defence of their country and sent them back there. He then determined to defend that pass with men whose loss would matter less and who would, by their death, make the enemy purchase their breakthrough as dearly as possible. And so it turned out. After butchering the Arcadians who beset them on every side, they were all put to the sword. Was ever a trophy raised to a victor which was not better due to those who were vanquished? True victory lies in your role in the conflict, not in coming through safely: it consists in the honour of battling bravely not battling through.

[A] To return to my tale, those prisoners, far from yielding despite all that was done to them during the two or three months of their captivity, maintain on the contrary a joyful countenance: they urge their captors to hurry up and put them to the test; they defy them, insult them and reproach them for cowardice and for all the battles they have lost against their country. I have a song made by one such prisoner which contains the following: Let them all dare to come and gather to feast on him, for with him they will feast on their own fathers and ancestors who have served as food and sustenance for his body. 'These sinews,' he said, 'this flesh and these veins — poor fools that you are — are your very own; you do not realize that they still contain the very substance of the limbs of your forebears: savour them well, for you will find that they taste of your very own flesh!' There is nothing 'barbarous' in the contriving of that topic. Those who tell how they die and who describe the act of execution show the prisoners spitting at their

---

25. Seneca, *De constantia,* II.

26. '80: by us: *he is vanquished in practice but not by reason; it is his bad luck which we may indict not his cowardice.* Sometimes . . .

27. Cf. Cicero, *Tusc. disput.,* I, xli, 100 for the glory of Leonidas' death in the defile of Thermopylae.

28. Diodorus Siculus, XV, xii.

killers and pulling faces at them. Indeed, until their latest breath, they never stop braving them and defying them with word and look. It is no lie to say that these men are indeed savages — by our standards; for either they must be or we must be: there is an amazing gulf between their [C] souls [A] and ours.[29]

The husbands have several wives: the higher their reputation for valour the more of them they have. One beautiful characteristic of their marriages is worth noting: just as our wives are zealous in thwarting our love and tenderness for other women, theirs are equally zealous in obtaining them for them. Being more concerned for their husband's reputation than for anything else, they take care and trouble to have as many fellow-wives as possible, since that is a testimony to their husband's valour.

— [C] Our wives will scream that that is a marvel, but it is not: it is a virtue proper to matrimony, but at an earlier stage. In the Bible Leah, Rachel, Sarah and the wives of Jacob all made their fair handmaiden available to their husbands; Livia, to her own detriment, connived at the lusts of Augustus, and Stratonice the consort of King Deiotarus not only provided her husband with a very beautiful chambermaid who served her but carefully brought up their children and lent a hand in enabling them to succeed to her husband's rank.[30]

— [A] Lest anyone should think that they do all this out of a simple slavish subjection to convention or because of the impact of the authority of their ancient customs without any reasoning or judgement on their part, having minds so dulled that they could never decide to do anything else, I should cite a few examples of what they are capable of.

Apart from that war-song which I have just given an account of, I have another of their songs, a love-song, which begins like this:

> O Adder, stay: stay O Adder! From your colours
>   let my sister take the pattern for a girdle
>   she will make for me to offer to my love;
> So may your beauty and your speckled hues be for
>   ever honoured above all other snakes.

This opening couplet serves as the song's refrain. Now, I know enough about poetry to make the following judgement: not only is there nothing 'barbarous' in this conceit but it is thoroughly anacreontic.[31] Their language incidentally is [C] a pleasant one with an agreeable sound [A] and has terminations[32] rather like Greek.

Three such natives, unaware of what price in peace and happiness they would have to pay to buy a knowledge of our corruptions, and unaware that such commerce would lead to their downfall — which I suspect to be already far advanced — pitifully allowing themselves to be cheated by their desire for novelty and leaving the gentleness of their regions to come and see ours, were at Rouen at the same time as King Charles IX.[33] The King had a long interview with them: they were shown our manners, our ceremonial and the layout of a fair city. Then someone asked them what they thought of all this and wanted to know what they had been most amazed

---

29. '80: their *constancy* and ours . . .

30. Standard examples: cf. Tiraquellus, *De legibus connubialibus,* XIII, 35, for all these un-jealous wives. (But Leah and Sarah were in fact Jacob's wives.)

31. Anacreon was the great love-poet of Teos (*fl.* 540 B.C.).

32. '80: their language *is the pleasantest language in the world; its* sound *is agreeable to the ear* and has terminations . . .

33. In 1562, when Rouen was retaken by Royalist forces.

by. They made three points; I am very annoyed with myself for forgetting the third, but I still remember two of them. In the first place they said (probably referring to the Swiss Guard) that they found it very odd that all those full-grown bearded men, strong and bearing arms in the King's entourage, should consent to obey a boy rather than choosing one of themselves as a Commander; secondly — since they have an idiom in their language which calls all men 'halves' of one another — that they had noticed that there were among us men fully bloated with all sorts of comforts while their halves were begging at their doors, emaciated with poverty and hunger: they found it odd that those destitute halves should put up with such injustice and did not take the others by the throat or set fire to their houses.

I had a very long talk with one of them (but I used a stupid interpreter who was so bad at grasping my meaning and at understanding my ideas that I got little joy from it). When I asked the man (who was a commander among them, our sailors calling him a king) what advantage he got from his high rank, he told me that it was to lead his troops into battle; asked how many men followed him, he pointed to an open space to signify as many as it would hold — about four or five thousand men; questioned whether his authority lapsed when the war was over, he replied that he retained the privilege of having paths cut for him through the thickets in their forests so that he could easily walk through them when he visited villages under his sway.

Not at all bad, that. — Ah! But they wear no breeches . . .

Thomas Hobbes

LEVIATHAN

Introduction by Michael Graham

The Englishman Thomas Hobbes was born in 1588, the year England's navy, aided by what was called "the Protestant Wind" defeated the Spanish Armada, an attempted invasion by sixteenth century Europe's leading superpower. To patriotic English people, it seemed that God had taken their side (and that of their popular queen, Elizabeth) against Catholic Spain; they were David, and Spain was Goliath.

Thus Hobbes was born into a kingdom and a European continent in which religious views dominated political outlooks. This was the "era of religious warfare" when protestants (viewed by Catholics as schismatic heretics) and Catholics (viewed by protestants as minions of Antichrist) squared off across Europe. Hobbes' own family had a professional as well as a confessional interest in protestantism; his father was an Anglican (i.e. Church of England) priest, although allegedly abusive and prone to drinking too much. However this may have affected Hobbes' outlook later in life, he must have inherited some longevity genes as well as good luck; he died in 1679, having attained what to contemporaries was the truly remarkable age of 91. Indeed, he was still translating Homer's poetry at 86!

He studied at the University of Oxford, earning a bachelor's degree in 1608. After this, he spent twenty years as tutor and then private secretary to William Cavendish (later earl of Devonshire) and his son. Hobbes published a translation of the ancient Greek historian Thucydides in 1629. Over the next several years he spent quite a bit of time in Paris, and visited Italy, where he met the natural philosopher Galileo. He also became friendly with the English royal physician William Harvey, who discovered how blood circulates through the body. This contact with (and interest in the work of) leading figures in what has been called the "Scientific Revolution" influenced Hobbes' assessments of how humans interact in society.

By 1641, the threat of domestic strife, based partly on religious differences, was looming over England. Relations between King Charles I, with whom Hobbes' patrons the Cavendishes were closely allied, and the English Parliament, many of whose "puritan" members favored neither the "high church" policies pursued by the king nor the fact that the queen (a French princess) practiced Catholicism, had reached an impasse. Hobbes headed for Paris again, spending the next eleven years there while England descended into civil war and eventually (in 1649) the execution of the twice-defeated king and the proclamation of an English Republic (i.e. a state ruled without a king). Meanwhile, Hobbes tutored Charles I's exiled eldest son (the future Charles II) in mathematics, and ruminated on the disorders rocking his homeland. *Leviathan,* published in 1651, was the product of these meditations.

In this work, Hobbes sought to explain the reasons why people form governments in the first place. To do so, he first theorized on human nature. What were people like before they created governments? What are their primary instincts? This led him to explain why he thought some form of government was needed. Compare Hobbes' view of the purpose of government with your own. Would you be happy with the kind of government he suggests? Do you agree with his assessment of what we, as humans, are naturally like? Under what circumstances did he think it was permissible to rebel against government? Do you agree?

While *Leviathan* (the title comes from a sea monster mentioned in the Old Testament) may not shock its readers today, it was quite controversial at the time of its publication. Not surprisingly, supporters of Parliament disagreed with it. But Hobbes' royalist friends, many of whom had supported Charles I on the grounds that he was "God's anointed," were equally troubled, even shocked. Hobbes was accused of "atheism" for having written what appears to be a thoroughly rational defense of strong monarchy. What is it about this tract that would have bothered them so much? How does it seem to differ with traditional thinking? Can you see the influence of "scientific" thought in it?

In 1660 military and parliamentary leaders in England, weary of eleven years without a monarchy, offered Hobbes' former pupil Charles II the throne from which his father had been removed. Hobbes himself received a pension from the new king, but few were willing to embrace his political philosophy, and it was only the protection of the king which kept officials of the Church of England from troubling him. Nevertheless, his ideas grew in influence after his death, and the adjective "Hobbesian" is often employed today. After reading these selections from *Leviathan,* you should have some idea of what a "Hobbesian" world would be. Do we live in one?

Leviathan

On the Difference of Manners

In the first place, I put as a general inclination of all mankind a perpetual and restless desire of power after power that ceases only in death. And the cause of this is not always that a man hopes for a more intensive delight than he has already attained to, or that he cannot be content with a moderate power, but because he cannot assure the power and means to live well which he already has without the acquisition of more. And from hence it is that kings, whose power is greatest, turn their endeavors to the assuring it at home by laws or abroad by wars; and when that is done, there succeeds a new desire — in some, of fame from new conquest; in others, of case and sensual pleasure; in others, of admiration or being flattered for excellence in some art or other ability of the mind.

On the Natural Condition of Mankind as Concerning Their Happiness and Misery

Nature has made men so equal in the faculties of the body and mind that, though there be found one man sometimes stronger in body or of quicker mind than another, yet, when all is reckoned together, the difference between man and man is not so considerable that one man can claim for himself any benefit to which another may not put forward a claim as well as he. For as to the strength of body, the weakest has strength enough to kill the strongest, either by secret plotting or in alliance with others that are in the same danger. . . .

From this equality of ability arises equality of hope in the attaining of our ends. And therefore if any two men desire the same thing, which nevertheless they cannot both enjoy, they become enemies; and to achieve their end, which is principally their own preservation, and sometimes their pleasure only, endeavor to destroy or subdue one another. And from hence it comes to pass that where an invader has no more to fear than another man's single power, if one plant, sow, build, or possess an estate, others may be expected to come prepared with forces united to dispossess and deprive him, not only of the fruit of his labor, but also of his life or liberty. And the invader again is in the like danger of another. . . .

In the nature of man, we find three principal causes for quarrel: first, competition; secondly, distrust; thirdly, glory.

The first makes men invade for gain; the second, for safety; and the third for reputation. The first use violence to make themselves masters of other men's persons, wives, children, and

Edgar E. Knoebel, ed., *Classics of Western Thought Volume III: The Modern World* (Fourth Edition), (New York: Harcourt Brace Jovanovich, 1988), ISBN 0155076841, pp. 31–42 (Selection from Hobbes, "Leviathan.")

LEVIATHAN Adapted by editor, from Thomas Hobbes, *Leviathan*, in *The Ethics of Hobbes*, ed. by E. Hershey Sneath (Boston: Ginn and Company, 1898), 119, 139–46, 177–82, 319–20, 330–32, 336.

cattle; the second, to defend them; the third, for trifles, as a word, a smile, a different opinion, and any other sign of insult, either direct to their persons or by reflection in their kindred, their friends, their nation, their profession, or their name.

It is certain, that during the time men live without a common power to keep them all in awe, they are in that condition which is called war; and such a war is of every man against every man. For war, consists not in battle only, or the act of fighting, but in a time span, where the will to fight is sufficiently known; and therefore the notion of time is to be considered in the nature of war as it is in the nature of weather. For as the nature of foul weather lies not in a shower or two of rain but in an inclination thereto over many days, so the nature of war consists not in actual fighting but in the known disposition thereto during all the time there is no assurance to the contrary. All other time is peace.

Whatsoever, therefore, follows in a time of war where every man is enemy to every man; the same follows in a time, when men live without other security than what their own strength and their own invention shall furnish them. In such condition there is no place for industry, because the fruit thereof is uncertain, and consequently no culture of the earth; no navigation nor use of the commodities that may be imported by sea; no spacious building; no instruments of moving and removing such things as require much force; no knowledge of the face of the earth; no account of time; no arts; no letters; no society; and, which is worst of all, continual fear and danger of violent death; and the life of man solitary, poor, nasty, brutish, and short.

It may seem strange to somebody who has not considered these things that nature should thus dissociate and render men apt to invade, and destroy one another; . . . But let us observe that when a man takes a journey he arms himself, and seeks to go well accompanied; when going to sleep he locks his doors; when even in his house he locks his chests, and this when he knows there are laws and public officers, armed, to revenge all injuries done to him. What opinion has he of his fellow man when he rides armed, of his fellow citizens when he locks his doors; and of his children, and servants, when he locks his chests? Does he not thereby as much accuse mankind by his actions as I do by my words? But neither of us accuse man's nature in it. The desires and other passions of man are in themselves no sin. No more are the actions that proceed from those passions till they know a law that forbids them, which, till laws are made, they cannot know, nor can any law be made till they have agreed upon the person that shall make it. . . .

To this war of every man against every man, this also follows: that nothing can be unjust. The notions of right and wrong, justice and injustice, have there no place. Where there is no common power, there is no law; where no law, no injustice. Force and fraud are in war the two cardinal virtues. Justice and injustice are none of the faculties of the body or mind. If they were, they might be in a man who was alone in the world, including his senses and passions. They are qualities that relate to men in society, not in solitude. It follows also from the same condition that there be no property, no dominion, no *mine* and *thine;* but only that is every man's what he can get, and for so long as he can keep it. And so much for the ill condition which man by mere nature is actually placed in, though with a possibility to come out of it, consisting partly in the passions, partly in his reason.

The passions that incline men to peace are fear of death, desire for such things as are necessary for comfortable living; and a hope by their labor to obtain them. And reason suggests convenient terms of peace, upon which men may be drawn to agreement. These terms are those which otherwise are called the laws of nature, whereof I shall speak more particularly. . . .

Of the First and Second Natural Laws

The right of nature, . . . is the liberty each man has to use his own power, as he himself desires, for the preservation of his own nature — that is to say, of his own life and consequently, of doing anything, which in his own judgment and reason, he shall believe to be the best means thereunto.

By liberty is understood, according to the proper meaning of the word, the absence of external obstructions which may take away part of a man's power to do what he desires; but cannot hinder him from using the power left him, according as his judgment, and as reason shall dictate to him.

A law of nature is a general rule, found out by reason, by which a man is forbidden to do that which is destructive of his life or takes away the means of preserving it. . . .

And because the condition of man, as has been declared before, is a state of war of every one against every one — in which every one is governed by his own reason and there is nothing he can make use of that may not be a help unto him in preserving his life against his enemies — it follows that in such a condition every man has a right to everything, even to one another's body. And therefore, as long as this natural right of every man to everything endures, there can be no security to any man, how strong or wise he may be, during the time which nature ordinarily allows men to live. And consequently it is a general rule of reason that every man ought to seek peace, as far as he has hope of obtaining it; and when he cannot obtain it, that he may seek and use all help and advantages of war. The first branch of that rule contains the first and fundamental law of nature, which is *to seek peace and follow it.* The second, the sum of the right of nature, which is, *by all means we can to defend ourselves.*

From this fundamental law of nature, by which men are commanded to seek peace, is derived this second law: that a man be willing, when others are so too, as far as for peace and defense of himself he shall judge it necessary, to lay down his right to all things; and be contented with so much liberty against other men as he would allow other men against himself. For as long as every man holds the right of doing anything he likes, so long are all men in a state of war. But if other men will not lay down their right as well as he, then there is no reason for anyone, to divest himself of his, because that would expose himself to prey, which no man is bound to, rather than to incline himself to peace. This is that law of the Gospel: *whatsoever you wish that others should do to you, that do unto them.* And that law of all men: *what you would not have done to you, do not unto them.*

Of the Causes, Development, and Definition of a Commonwealth

The final cause, end, or design of men, who naturally love liberty and authority over others, in the introduction of that restraint upon themselves in which we see them live in commonwealths, is the desire for their own preservation. and of a more contented life thereby; that is to say, of getting themselves out from that miserable condition of war which necessarily follows . . . from the natural passions of men when there is no visible power to keep them in awe and tie them by fear of punishment to the performance of their agreements and observation of the laws of nature. . . .

For the laws of nature, as "justice," "equity," "modesty," "mercy," and, in sum, "doing to others as we would be done to," of themselves, without the terror of some power to cause them to be observed, are contrary to our natural passions, that carry us to partiality, pride, revenge, and the like. And agreements without the sword are but words, and of no strength to secure a man at all. . . . And in all places where men have lived in small families, to rob and spoil one another has been the custom. . . . And as small families did then, so now do cities and kingdoms, which are but greater families, for their own security enlarge their dominions . . . and endeavor as much as possible to subdue or weaken their neighbors by open force and secret arts, for lack of other protection, justly; and are remembered for it in later ages with honor.

Nor is it the joining together of a small number of men that gives them this security, because in small numbers small additions on the one side or the other make the advantage of strength so great as is sufficient to carry the victory; and therefore gives encouragement to an invasion. The multitude sufficient to confide in for our security is not determined by any certain number but by comparison with the enemy we fear; and is then sufficient when the advantage of the enemy is not so visible and conspicuous to determine the event of war as to move him to attempt it.

And should there not be so great a multitude, even if their actions be directed according to their particular judgments and particular appetites, they can expect thereby no defense nor protection, neither against a common enemy nor against the injuries of one another. For being divided in opinions concerning the best use and application of their strength, they do not help but hinder one another, and reduce their strength by mutual opposition to nothing; whereby they are easily not only subdued by a very few that agree together, but also, when there is no common enemy, they make war upon each other for their particular interests. For if we could suppose a great multitude of men to consent in the observation of justice and other laws of nature without a common power to keep them all in awe, we might as well suppose all mankind to do the same; and then there neither would be, nor need to be, any civil government or commonwealth at all, because there would be peace without subjection.

Nor is it enough for the security which men want to last all the time of their life that they be governed and directed by one judgment for a limited time, as in one battle or one war. For though they obtain a victory by their unanimous endeavor against a foreign enemy, yet afterwards, when either they have no common enemy or he that by one group is held for an enemy is by another group held for a friend, they must, by the difference of their interests, dissolve, and fall again into a war among themselves.

It is true that certain living creatures, as bees and ants, live harmoniously with each other. They are therefore called by Aristotle[1] political creatures and have no other direction, than their particular judgments and appetites; nor speech whereby one of them can signify to another what he thinks expedient for the common benefit; and therefore some man may perhaps desire to know why mankind cannot do the same. To which I answer:

First, that men are continually in competition for honor and dignity, which these creatures are not; and consequently among men there arises envy and hatred and finally war, but among these creatures not so.

Secondly, that among these creatures the common good differ not from the private; and being by nature inclined to their private, they procure thereby the common benefit. But man, whose joy consists in comparing himself with other men, can savor nothing but his own superiority.

---

1. Greek philosopher (384–322 B.C.)

Thirdly, that these creatures, having not, as man, the use of reason, do not see nor think they see any fault, in the administration of their common business; whereas among men, there are very many that think themselves wiser and abler to govern the public better than the rest; and these strive to reform and innovate, one this way, another that way, and thereby bring it into division and civil war.

Fourthly, that these creatures, though they have some use of voice in making known to one another their desires and other affections, yet they lack that art of words by which some men can represent to others that which is good in the likeness of evil; and evil in the likeness of good; and increase or diminish the apparent greatness of good and evil, making men discontented and troubling their peace at their pleasure.

Fifthly, irrational creatures cannot distinguish between "injury" and "damage"; and, therefore, as long as they be at ease they are not offended with their fellows; whereas man is then most troublesome when he is most at ease; for then it is that he loves to show his wisdom and control the actions of them that govern the commonwealth.

Lastly, the harmony of these creatures is natural, that of men is by agreement only, which is artificial; and therefore, it is no wonder if there be something else required besides agreement to make it constant and lasting; that is, a common power to keep them in awe and to direct their actions to the common benefit.

The only way to erect such a common power which may defend them from the invasion of foreigners and the injuries of one another, and thereby to secure them so that by their own labors and by the fruits of the earth they may nourish themselves and live contentedly, is to confer all their power and strength upon one man, or upon one assembly of men that may reduce all their wills, by majority of voices, unto one will; which is as much as to say, to appoint one man or assembly of men to speak for them; and every one to accept and acknowledge himself to be author of whatsoever he that speaks for him shall act or cause to be acted in those things which concern the common peace and safety, and therein to submit their wills to his will, and their judgments to his judgment. This is more than consent or concord; it is a real unity of them all in one and the same person, made by agreement of every man with every man, in such manner as if every man should say to every man, "I authorize and give up my right of governing myself to this man, or to this assembly of men, on this condition, that you give up your right to him and authorize all his actions in like manner." This done, the multitude so united in one person is called a "commonwealth," in Latin *civitas*. This is the origin of that great "leviathan," or rather, to speak more reverently, of that "mortal god," to which we owe, under the "immortal God," our peace and defense. For by this authority, given him by every particular man in the commonwealth, he has the use of so much power and strength conferred on him that, by terror thereof, he is enabled to form the wills of them all to peace at home and mutual aid against their enemies abroad. And in him consists the essence of the commonwealth, which, to define it, is "one person, of whose acts a great multitude, by mutual covenants one with another, have made themselves the author, to the end he may use the strength and means of them all as he shall think wise for their peace and common defense."

And he that carries this person is called "sovereign" and said to have "sovereign power"; and every one besides, his "subject."

The attaining to this sovereign power is by two ways. One, by natural force, as when a man makes his children to submit themselves and their children to his rule, as being able to destroy them if they refuse; or by war subdues his enemies to his will, giving them their lives on that condition. The other is when men agree among themselves to submit to some man or assembly of men voluntarily, on confidence that they will be protected by him against all others. This latter, may be called a political commonwealth, or commonwealth by "institution," and the former, a commonwealth by "acquisition."

Of the Function of the Sovereign Representative

The function of the sovereign, be it a monarch or an assembly, consists in the purpose for which he was trusted with the sovereign power, namely, the securing of "the safety of the people"; to which he is obliged by the law of nature, and to render an account thereof to God, the author of that law, and to none but him. But by safety here is not meant a bare preservation but also all other contentments of life which every man by lawful labor, without danger or hurt to the commonwealth, shall acquire for himself.

And this is to be done, not by care applied to individuals further than their protection from injuries when they shall complain, but by a general provision contained in public instruction, both of doctrine and example, and in the making and executing of good laws to which individual persons may apply their own cases.

And because, if the essential rights of sovereignty . . . be taken away, the commonwealth is thereby dissolved and every man returns into the condition and calamity of a war with every other man, which is the greatest evil that can happen in this life; it is the duty of the sovereign, to maintain those rights entire, and consequently against his duty, first, to transfer to another or to remove from himself any of them. For he that deserts the means deserts the ends; and he deserts the means when, being the sovereign, he acknowledges himself subject to the civil laws and renounces supreme judicial authority or the making of war or peace by his own authority; or of judging of the necessities of the commonwealth; or of levying money and soldiers when and as much he shall judge necessary; or of making officers and ministers both of war and peace; or of appointing teachers and examining what doctrines are conformable or contrary to the defense, peace, and good of the people. Secondly, it is against his duty to let the people be ignorant or misinformed of the reasons for his essential rights, because thereby men are easy to be seduced and drawn to resist him when the commonwealth shall require their use and exercise. . . .

To the care of the sovereign belongs the making of good laws. But what is a good law? By a good law I mean not a just law; for no law can be unjust. The law is made by the sovereign power, and all that is done by such power is warranted and owned by every one of the people; and that which every man will have so, no man can say is unjust. It is in the laws of a commonwealth as in the laws of games whatsoever the players all agree on is injustice to none of them. A good law is that which is "needed" for the "good of the people" and "clearly understood."

For the use of laws, which are but rules authorized, is not to bind the people from all voluntary actions but to direct and keep them from hurting themselves by their own impulsive desires, rashness, or indiscretion; as hedges are set not to stop travelers, but to keep them in their way. And, therefore, a law that is not needed, having not the true purpose of a law, is not good. A law may be thought to be good when it is for the benefit of the sovereign, though it be not necessary for the people, but it is not so. For the good of the sovereign and people cannot be separated. It is a weak sovereign, that has weak subjects; and a weak people, whose sovereign lacks power to rule them at his will. . . .

It belongs also to the function of the sovereign to make a right application of punishments and rewards. And seeing the end of punishing is not revenge and discharge of anger, but correction, either of the offender, or of others by his example; the severest punishments are to be inflicted for those crimes that are of most danger to the public; such as are those which proceed from malice to the government established; those that spring from contempt of justice; those that provoke indignation in the multitude; and those which, unpunished, seem authorized, as when they are committed by sons, servants, or favorites of men in authority. For indignation carries men not only against the actors and authors of injustice, but against all power that is likely to protect them; as in the case of Tarquin,[2] when for the insolent act of one of his sons he was driven out of Rome and the monarchy itself dissolved.[3] But crimes which proceed from great provocation, from great fear, great need, or from ignorance, whether the fact be a great crime or not, there is often a place for leniency without prejudice to the commonwealth; and leniency, when there is such place for it, is required by the law of nature. The punishment of the leaders and teachers in a rebellion, not the poor seduced people, when they are punished, can profit the commonwealth by their example. To be severe to the people is to punish that ignorance which may in great part be blamed on the sovereign, whose fault it was that they were not better instructed.

In like manner it belongs to the duty of the sovereign, to apply his rewards so that there may arise from them benefit to the commonwealth, wherein consists their use, and purpose; and is then done when they that have well served the commonwealth are, with as little expense of the common treasure as is possible, so well recompensed as others thereby may be encouraged both to serve the same as faithfully as they can and to study the arts by which they may be enabled to do it better. . . .

Concerning the relationships of one sovereign to another, which are included in that law commonly called the "law of nations,"[4] I need not say anything in this place because the law of nations and the law of nature is the same thing. And every sovereign has the same right, in securing the safety of his people that any particular man can have in securing the safety of his own body. And the same law that dictates to men that have no civil government what they ought to do and what to avoid in regard of one another dictates the same to commonwealths, that is, to the consciences of sovereign princes and sovereign assemblies. For there is no court of natural justice except the conscience only; where not man but God reigns whose laws, . . . since God is the author of nature, are "natural," and as God is King of kings, are "laws."

---

2. Lucius Tarquinius Superbus (that is, the "Proud," 534–510 B.C.), last of the Roman kings; said to have been a cruel despot, though a capable ruler.

3. The offending son was Tarquinius Sextus (died ca. 496 b.c.). According to legend, the Romans drove his father from the throne because Sextus had raped Lucretia, the virtuous wife of his cousin, Lucius Tarquinius Collatinus. Following the successful rebellion, the Romans transformed their state into a republic (509 b.c.), with Lucius Tarquinius Collatinus, the wronged husband, serving as one of the first two consuls (chief executives).

4. International law.

John Locke

SECOND TREATISE ON GOVERNMENT

Introduction by Michael Graham

John Locke had a lot in common with Thomas Hobbes. Both were English, both questioned traditional religious dogma, both lived through (and wrote about) the constitutional conflicts that shook seventeenth-century England, both had friends in high places, and both spent time in exile on the continent. But these common experiences left them with markedly different outlooks.

Locke was born in 1632, meaning he was only ten years old when Charles I and Parliament went to war in 1642. He attended Westminster School and then Oxford University, where he completed a master's degree in 1658. After that, he became a lecturer in Greek language (1660) and rhetoric (1662). In the 1660s, with a king (Charles II) once again ruling in England, Locke earned the patronage of Anthony Ashley Cooper, later earl of Shaftesbury, who was for a while a leading figure in Charles II's government. But Locke's patron fell out of favor with the king in the 1670s, as some of the issues left unsettled by the 1660 restoration of the monarchy arose again. Two major political groupings, the ancestors of modern political parties, were emerging in England's Parliament. One group, the Tories, favored royal power, the legitimate succession to the throne, and a strong Church of England. On the other side, the Whigs felt that kings had to rule with the advice and consent of Parliament, that Parliament could alter the succession (i.e. choose a king) if it had good reasons for doing so, and that protestant dissenters (those who were not members of the Church of England) ought to have full political rights. Locke and his patron favored the Whigs.

The question of who should succeed Charles II, who had no legitimate children, would prove to be the most vexing issue. According to the traditional succession, Charles' heir was his younger brother James, duke of York. But James was a practicing Catholic, making him an unpopular choice in protestant England. In addition, both Charles and his brother seemed to hold to the Tory view that kings did not need to consult Parliament if they did not wish to. In 1679 Shaftesbury and the Whigs sought to have James excluded from the succession, supporting instead Charles' illegitimate (and protestant) son the Duke of Monmouth. The king refused to go along with this, but the issue of "Exclusion" did not go away, particularly in light of (probably fictional) allegations that Catholics were plotting to assassinate the king.

In 1684 Shaftesbury was forced into exile in the Dutch Republic, and Locke went with him. Both men became close to William of Orange, Stadholder (i.e. governor-general) of the Dutch Republic, who was married to Mary, the protestant daughter of James, duke of York. The next

year, Charles II died (proclaiming his own Catholicism on his deathbed), and his brother succeeded him as James II. Needless to say, this made Locke and Shaftesbury's return to England
even less likely. But within three years, the new king had so alienated England's political leadership (particularly with his suspension of laws against Catholicism) that Tories as well as Whigs
invited William of Orange to invade England and restore their "liberties." The declaration he
issued upon his landing in England was written by none other than John Locke. James II made
things easy by fleeing to France, and William and Mary were proclaimed jointly as king and
queen. England had experienced a bloodless revolution, labeled "glorious" by its supporters.

In retrospect, Locke's *Second Treatise on Government* seems almost a commentary on the
Glorious Revolution. It was published in 1690, just after the events described above. But in
fact, it had been written in the early 1680s. Like Hobbes before him, Locke imagined what
human life was like before the existence of government. How does his view of this situation differ with that of Hobbes? Then, also like Hobbes, Locke suggested why government was found
to be necessary, and what purpose it ought to serve. Compare his positions with those espoused
by Hobbes. What attitude did Locke take to rebellion? It is worth noting that his ideas proved
popular in some of Britain's North American colonies in the 1770s. Finally, whose view of
humanity do you prefer — Hobbes' or Locke's?

Of Civil Government

Of the State of Nature

To understand political power correctly, and derive it from its origins, we must consider what state all men are naturally in: a state of perfect freedom to order their actions and dispose of their possessions and persons as they think fit, within the bounds of the law of nature, without asking permission or depending upon the will of any other man.

A state also of equality, wherein all the power and jurisdiction is mutual, no one having more than another; there being nothing more evident than that creatures of the same species, born to all the same advantages of nature and the use of the same faculties, should also be equal one among another without subordination or subjection; unless the Lord and Master of them all should, by an open declaration of his will, set one above another, and confer on him by an evident and clear appointment an undoubted right to rule over others.

But though this be a state of liberty, yet it is not a state of license;[1] though man in that state has an unrestricted liberty to dispose of his person or possessions, yet he has not liberty to destroy himself, or any creature under his control. . . . The state of nature has a law of nature to govern it which obliges every one; and *reason,* which is that law, teaches all mankind who will but consult it that, being all equal and independent, no one ought to harm another in his life, health, liberty, or possessions. Since all men are the creation of one omnipotent and infinitely wise Maker, all are the servants of one sovereign Master, sent into the world by his order, and doing his work; they are his property, made to live for his, not one another's, pleasure; and being furnished with like faculties, sharing all in one community of nature, there cannot be supposed any such subordination among us that may authorize us to destroy another — as if we were made for one another's uses as the inferior ranks of creatures are for ours. Every one, as he is bound to preserve himself, . . . so by the like reason, when his own preservation is not in jeopardy, ought, as much as he can, to preserve the rest of mankind. He may not, unless it be to do justice to an offender, take away or impair the life, or what tends to the preservation of life: the liberty, health, limb, or goods of another.

And that all men may be restrained from invading others' rights and from doing hurt to one another, and the law of nature be observed which wills the peace and preservation of all mankind, the execution of the law of nature is, in that state, put into every man's hands, whereby every one has a right to punish the breakers of that law to such a degree as may hinder its violation. For the law of nature would, as all other laws that concern men in this world, be in vain, if there were nobody that in the state of nature had a power to execute that law and thereby

Of Civil Government, Adapted by editor, from John Locke, *Two Treatises of Government,* in *The Works of John Locke* (London: Thomas Tegg, 1823), V, 339–42, 353–54, 357, 387–89, 394–96, 411–13, 416–17, 423–24, 457, 459, 469–72, 483–85.

Edgar E. Knoebel, ed., *Classics of Western Thought Volume III: The Modern World* (Fourth Edition), (New York: Harcourt Brace Jovanovich, 1988), ISBN 0155076841, pp. 68–82 (Selection from John Locke, "Of Civil Government.")

1. Abuse of liberty.

preserve the innocent and restrain offenders. And if any one in the state of nature may punish another for any evil he has done, every one may do so; for in that state of perfect equality, where naturally there is no superiority or jurisdiction of one over another, what any may do in prosecution of that law, every one must have a right to do.

And thus in the state of nature one man takes power over another; but yet no absolute or arbitrary power to abuse a criminal, when he has got him in his hands, according to the intensity of anger or whims of his own will; but only to punish him, so far as calm reason and conscience dictate, according to his crime. . . . In breaking the law of nature, the offender declares himself to live by another rule than that of reason and justice, which is that measure God has set to the actions of men for their mutual security; and so he becomes dangerous to mankind, the tie which is to secure them from injury and violence being slighted and broken by him. Which being a trespass against the whole species and the peace and safety of it provided for by the law of nature, every man upon this reason, by the right he has to preserve mankind in general, may restrain, or, where it is necessary, destroy things harmful to them. He thus may bring such evil on any one who has broken that law, in order to make him repent the doing of it and thereby deter him, and by his example others, from doing the like harm. And in this case, and upon this ground, every man has a right to punish the offender and be executioner of the law of nature. . . .

Of Property

God, who has given the world to men in common, has also given them reason to make use of it to the best advantage of life and convenience. The earth and all that is therein, is given to men for the support and comfort of their being. And though all the fruits it naturally produces and beasts it feeds belong to mankind in common, as they are produced by the spontaneous hand of nature; and nobody has *originally* a private estate exclusive of the rest of mankind, in any of them, since they are in their natural state; yet, being given for the use of men, there must be a means to take them some way or other before they can be of any use or at all beneficial to any particular man. The fruit or venison which nourishes the wild Indian, who knows no enclosure[2] and is still a tenant in common,[3] must be his, and so his, that is, a part of him, that another can no longer have any right to it before it can do him any good for the support of his life.

Though the earth and all inferior creatures be common to all men, yet every man has a property in his own person; this nobody has any right to but himself. The labor of his body and the work of his hands, we may say, are properly his. Whatsoever then he removes out of the state that nature has provided and left it in, he has mixed his labor with, and joined to it something that is his own, and thereby makes it his *property*. It being by him removed from the common state nature has placed it in, it has by this labor something added to it that excludes the common right of other men. For this labor being the unquestionable property of the laborer, no man but he can have a right to what that is once joined to, at least where there is enough and as good left in common for others. . . .

God gave the world to men in common; but since he gave it them for their benefit and the greatest conveniences of life they were capable to draw from it, it cannot be supposed he meant it should always remain common and uncultivated. He gave it to the use of the industrious and rational — and labor was to be his title to it — not to the whim or greed of the quarrelsome. . . .

---

2. Boundary enclosing private property.
3. Sharing ownership with others.

Of Political or Civil Society

Man, being born, as has been proved, with a title to perfect freedom and an unrestricted enjoyment of all the rights and privileges of the law of nature equally with any other man or number of men in the world, has by nature a power not only to preserve his property[4] — that is, his life, liberty, and estate[5] — against the injuries and attempts of other men, but also to judge and punish the violations of that law by others as he is persuaded the offense deserves — even with death itself in those crimes where the heinousness in his opinion requires it. But because no political society can exist without having the power to preserve the property and also to punish the offenses of all those of that society, there and there only is political society where every one of the members has given up his natural power, surrendered it into the hands of the community. . . . And thus, all private judgment of every particular member being excluded, the community comes to be umpire by settled standing rules, impartial and the same to all parties, and by men having authority from the community for the execution of those rules. The community decides all the differences that may happen between any members of that society concerning any matter of right, and punishes those offenses which any member has committed against the society with such penalties as the law has established; whereby it is easy to see who are, and who are not, in political society together. Those who are united into one body and have a common established law and courts to appeal to, with authority to decide controversies between them and punish offenders, are in civil society one with another; but those who have no such common appeal are still in the state of nature, each being, where there is no other, judge for himself and executioner, which is, as I have before shown it, the perfect state of nature.

And thus the commonwealth[6] receives power to set down what punishment shall fit the various crimes committed by the members of that society — which is the power of making laws — as well as it has the power to punish any injury done unto any of its members by any one that is not of it — which is the power of war and peace — and all this for the preservation of the property of all the members of that society as far as is possible. But though every man who has entered into civil society and has become a member of any commonwealth has thereby surrendered his power to punish offenses against the law of nature in prosecution of his own private judgment, yet, with the judgment of offenses which he has given up to the legislative . . . he has given a right to the commonwealth to employ his force for the execution of judgments of the commonwealth, whenever he shall be called to it. These are, indeed, his own judgments, they being made by himself or his representative. And herein we have the origin of the legislative and executive power of civil society which is to judge by standing laws how far offenses are to be punished when committed within the commonwealth, and also to determine, by occasional judgments founded on the present circumstances of the fact, how far injuries from without are to be punished, and in both these to employ all the force of all the members when there shall be need.

Whenever, therefore, any number of men are so united into one society, and when every one gives up his executive power of the law of nature and surrenders it to the public, there and there only is a political or civil society. And this is done wherever any number of men, in the state of nature, enter into society to make one people, one body politic, under one supreme government, or else when any one joins himself to any government already made; for hereby he authorizes the society or, which is the same, the legislative thereof, to make laws for him as the

---

4. Whatever belongs to an individual.

5. Material possessions.

6. Political community (state).

public good of the society shall require. . . . And this puts men out of a state of nature into that of a commonwealth by setting up a judge on earth, with authority to determine all the controversies and redress the injuries that may happen to any member of the commonwealth; which judge is the legislative, or magistrates appointed by it. And wherever there are any number of men, however associated, that have no such decisive power to appeal to, there they are still in the state of nature. . . .

Of the Beginning of Political Societies

Men being, as has been said, by nature all free, equal, and independent, no one can be put out of this condition and subjected to the political power of another without his own consent. The only way whereby any one divests himself of his natural liberty, and puts on the bonds of civil society, is by agreeing with other men to join and unite into a community for their comfortable, safe, and peaceable living one among another, in a secure enjoyment of their properties and a greater security against any that are not of it. This any number of men may do, because it injures not the freedom of the rest; they are left as they were in the liberty of the state of nature. When any number of men have so consented to make one community or government, they are thereby incorporated and make one body politic wherein the majority have a right to act and govern the rest.

For when any number of men have, by the consent of every individual, made a community, they have thereby made that community one body, with a power to act as one body, which is only by the will and determination of the *majority*. For that which moves any community, which is the consent of the individuals of it, and it being necessary to that which is one body to move one way, it is necessary the body should move that way where the greater force carries it, which is the consent of the majority; or else it is impossible it should act or continue one body, one community, which the consent of every individual that united into it agreed that it should. Therefore, every one is bound by that consent to be governed by the majority. And therefore we see that in assemblies empowered to act by positive laws, where no other number is set by that positive law which empowers them, the act of the majority passes for the act of the whole. . . .

And thus every man, by consenting with others to make one body politic under one government, puts himself under an obligation to every one of that society to submit to the determination of the majority, and to be governed by it; or else this original compact, whereby he with others incorporates into one society, would signify nothing, and be no compact, if he be left free and under no other ties than he was in before in the state of nature. For what appearance would there be of any compact? What new engagement if he were no further tied by any decrees of the society than he himself thought fit and did actually consent to? This would be still as great a liberty as he himself had before his compact, or any one else in the state of nature has who may submit himself and consent to any acts of it if he thinks fit.

For if the consent of the majority shall not for good reason be accepted as the will of the whole and govern every individual, nothing but the consent of every individual can make any thing to be the act of the whole; but such a consent is next to impossible ever to be had if we consider the infirmities of health and duties of business which in a number, though much less than that of a commonwealth, will necessarily keep many away from the public assembly. To which, if we add the variety of opinions and diversities of interests which unavoidably happen

in all groups of men, the entering into society upon such terms would be only like Cato's[7] entering into the theater, only to go out again. Such a constitution as this would make the mighty
leviathan[8] of a shorter duration than the feeblest creatures, and not let it outlast the day it was
born in; which cannot be supposed that rational creatures should desire and constitute societies
only to be dissolved; for where the majority cannot govern the rest, there they cannot act as one
body, and consequently will be immediately dissolved again.

Whosoever, therefore, out of a state of nature unite into a community must be understood
to give up all the power necessary for the purposes for which they unite into society to the
majority of the community, unless they expressly agreed in any number greater than the majority. And this is done by simply agreeing to unite into one political society, which is all the compact that is, or needs be, between the individuals that enter into or make up a commonwealth.
And thus that which begins and actually constitutes any political society is nothing but the consent of any number of freemen capable of a majority to unite and incorporate into such a society. And this is that, and that only, which did or could give beginning to any lawful government
in the world. . . .

Of the Ends of Political Society and Government

If man in the state of nature be so free, as has been said, if he be absolute lord of his own person
and possessions, equal to the greatest, and subject to nobody, why will he part with his freedom,
why will he give up his independence and subject himself to the rule and control of any other
power? To which it is obvious to answer that though in the state of nature he has such a right,
yet the enjoyment of it is very uncertain and constantly exposed to the attacks of others; for all
being kings as much as he, every man his equal, and the greater part no strict observers of
equity and justice, the enjoyment of the property he has in this state is very unsafe, very inse-
cure. This makes him willing to give up a condition which, however free, is full of fears and
continual dangers; and it is not without reason that he seeks out and is willing to join in society
with others, who are already united, or have a mind to unite, for the mutual preservation of their
lives, liberties, and estates, which I call by the general name "property."

The great and chief end, therefore, of men's uniting into commonwealths and putting themselves under government, is the preservation of their property. To which in the state of nature
there are many things lacking:

First, there lacks an established, settled, known law, received and allowed by common consent to be the standard of right and wrong and the common measure to decide all controversies
between them; for though the law of nature be plain and intelligible to all rational creatures, yet
men, being biased by their interest as well as ignorant for lack of studying it, are not apt to allow
it as a law binding to them in the application of it to their particular cases.

Secondly, in the state of nature there lacks a known and impartial judge with authority to
determine all differences according to the established law; for every one in that state being both
judge and executioner of the law of nature, men being partial to themselves, passion and

---

7. Marcus Porcius Cato (234–149 B.C.), also known as "Cato the Elder," was a Roman statesman and orator. He
endeavored to keep alive the ancient Roman virtues such as austerity, simplicity, discipline, and obedience to authority. He loathed Greek philosophy and demonstrated his contempt for the theater by walking ostentatiously through it
without sitting down for a moment.

8. A legendary monster; the term used by Hobbes and others to symbolize the awesome power of the state.

revenge is very apt to carry them too far and with too much intensity of feeling in their own cases, as well as negligence and unconcernedness to make them too remiss in other men's.

Thirdly, in the state of nature, there often lacks power to back and support the sentence when right, and to give it due execution. And they who by any injustice offend will seldom fail, where they are able, by force, to make good their injustice; such resistance many times makes their punishment dangerous and frequently destructive to those who attempt it.

Thus mankind, notwithstanding all the privileges of the state of nature, being but in an ill condition while they remain in it, are quickly driven into society. Hence it comes to pass that we seldom find any number of men to live any time together in this state. The inconveniences that they are therein exposed to by the irregular and uncertain exercise of the power every man has of punishing the transgressions of others make them take protection under the established laws of government and therein seek the preservation of their property. It is this that makes every one of them so willing to give up his single power of punishing, to be exercised by such alone as shall be appointed; and by such rules as the community, or those authorized by them for that purpose, shall agree on. And in this we have the origin of the right of both the legislative and executive power, as well as of the governments and societies themselves. . . .

Of the Extent of the Legislative Power

The great purposes of men's entering into society being the enjoyment of their properties in peace and safety, and the great instrument and means of that being the laws established in that society, the first and fundamental positive law of all commonwealths is the establishment of the legislative power. The first and fundamental natural law which is to govern even the legislative itself, is the preservation of the society and, as far as will agree with the public good, of every person in it. This legislative is not only the supreme power of the commonwealth, but sacred and unalterable in the hands where the community has once placed it; nor can any edict of anybody else, in whatever form conceived or by whatever power backed, have the force and obligation of a law which has not its approval from that legislative which the public has chosen and appointed. Nor without this the law could not have that which is absolutely necessary to its being a law: the consent of the society over whom nobody can have a power to make laws, but by their own consent and by authority received from them. And therefore all the obedience, which by the most solemn ties any one can be obliged to pay, ultimately ends in this supreme power and is directed by those laws which it enacts. Nor can any oaths to any foreign power, or any domestic lesser power, free any member of the society from his obedience to the legislative acting pursuant to their trust, nor oblige him to any obedience contrary to the laws so enacted. . . .

These are the bounds which the trust that is put in them by the society and the law of God and nature have set to the legislative power of every commonwealth, in all forms of government:

First, they are to govern by published established laws, not to be varied in particular cases, but to have one rule for rich and poor, for the favorite at court and the farmer at his plow.

Secondly, these laws also ought to be designed for no other purpose than the good of the people.

Thirdly, they must not raise taxes on the property of the people without the consent of the people, given by themselves or their representatives. . . .

Fourthly, the legislative cannot transfer the power of making laws to anybody else, or place it anywhere but where the people have placed it.

Of Tyranny

As *usurpation* is the exercise of power which another has a right to, so *tyranny* is the exercise of power beyond right, which nobody can have a right to. And this is making use of the power any one has in his hands, not for the good of those who are under it, but for his own private advantage — when the executive officer makes not the law, but [copy out] the rule, and his commands and actions are not directed to the [copy out] of the properties of his people, but the satisfaction of [copy out] ambition, revenge, greed, or any other unlawful passion. . . .

Wherever law ends tyranny begins, if the law be violated to another's harm. And whosoever in authority exceeds the power given him by the law, and makes use of the force he has under his command to enforce that upon the subject which the law does not allow, ceases in that to be a legitimate official and, acting without authority, may be opposed as any other man who by force invades the right of another. This is acknowledged in minor officials. He who has authority to seize my person in the street may be opposed as a thief and a robber if he endeavors to break into my house to serve a warrant, notwithstanding that I know he has such a warrant and such a legal authority as will impower him to arrest me in the street. And why should this not [copy out] the highest as well as in the lowest official? I would gladly be informed. Is it reasonable that the eldest brother, because he has the greatest part of his father's estate, should thereby have a right to take away any of his younger brother's portions? Or that a rich man who possessed a whole country should have a right to seize, when he pleased, the cottage and garden of his poor neighbor? Having great power and riches . . . can be no excuse or reason for plunder and oppression. . . . Exceeding the bounds of authority is no more a right in a great than in a petty officer, no more justifiable in a king than a constable;[9] and is so much the worse in him because he has more trust put in him, has already a much greater share than his fellow citizens, and is supposed, from the advantage of his education, work, and advisers, to be more knowing in matters of right and wrong. . . .

Of the Dissolution of Government

The reason why men enter into society is the preservation of their property; and the aim of their choosing and authorizing a legislature that there may be laws made and rules set as guards and fences for for the properties of all the members of the society in order to limit and moderate the power of every part and member of the society. For it can never be supposed to be the will of the society that the legislative should have a power to destroy that which every one aims to secure by entering into society, and for which the people submitted themselves to legislators of their own making. Whenever the legislators endeavor to take away and destroy the property of the people, or to reduce them to slavery under arbitrary power, they put themselves into a state of war with the people who are thereupon freed from any further obedience, and are left to the common shelter which God has provided for all men against force and violence. Whenever, therefore, the legislative shall break this fundamental rule of society, and either by ambition,

---

9. A minor official, empowered to make arrests.

fear, folly, or corruption, endeavor to grasp for themselves, or put into the hands of any other, an absolute power over the lives, liberties, and estates of the people, by this breach of trust they forfeit the power the people had put into their hands for quite contrary ends. It reverts then to the people, who have a right to resume their original liberty, and, by the establishment of a new legislative, such as they shall think fit, provide for their own safety and security, which is the purpose for which they are in society. What I have said here concerning the legislative in general holds true also concerning the supreme executive, who having a double trust in him — both to have a part in the legislative and the supreme execution of the law — acts against both when he goes about to set up his own arbitrary will as the law of the society. He acts also contrary to his trust when he either employs the force, money, and offices of the society to corrupt the representatives and win them to his purposes, or openly manipulates the electors and prescribes to their choice such whom he has by bribes, threats, promises, or otherwise won to his schemes and employs them to bring in those who have promised beforehand how to vote and what to enact. Thus to regulate candidates and electors, and alter the ways of elections, what is it but to destroy the government by the roots, and poison the very fountain of public security? For the people, having reserved to themselves the choice of their representatives, for the protection of their properties, could do it for no other end but that they might always be freely chosen, and, so chosen, freely act and advise as the necessity of the commonwealth and the public good should upon examination and mature debate be judged to require. This, those who give their votes before they hear the debate and have weighed the reasons on all sides, are not capable of doing. To prepare such an assembly as this, and endeavor to set up appointed supporters of his own choosing for the true representatives of the people and lawmakers of society, is certainly as great a breach of trust and a perfect declaration of a scheme to subvert the government. . . .

To this perhaps it will be said that, the people being ignorant and always discontented, to lay the foundation of government in the unsteady opinion and uncertain temperament of the people is to expose it to certain ruin; and no government will be able to endure long if the people may set up a new legislative whenever they take offense at the old one. To this I answer: Quite the contrary. People are not so easily got out of their old forms as some are apt to suggest. They are hardly to be moved to change the acknowledged faults in the circumstances they have been accustomed to. And if there be any original defects, or accidental ones introduced by time or corruption, it is not an easy thing to get them changed, even when all the world sees there is an opportunity for it. This slowness and aversion in the people to abandon their old constitutions has in the many revolutions which have been seen in this kingdom, in this and former ages, . . . still brought us back to our old legislative of king, lords, and commons;[10] and whatever provocations caused the crown to be taken from some of our princes' heads, they never carried the people so far as to place it on another dynasty.

But it will be said this theory lays the foundation for frequent rebellion. To which I answer:

First, no more than any other theory; for when the people are made miserable, and find themselves exposed to the abuses of arbitrary power, revere their governors as sons of Jupiter,[11] let them be sacred or divine, descended, or authorized from heaven, give them out for whom or what you please, the same will happen. The people generally ill-treated, and contrary to right, will be ready upon any occasion to ease themselves of a burden that sits heavy upon them. They

10. Representatives of the non-noble classes of England (House of Commons).
11. The principal Roman god.

will wish and seek for the opportunity, which in the change, weakness, and accidents of human affairs seldom delays long to offer itself. He must have lived but a little while in the world who has not seen examples of this in his time, and he must have read very little who cannot produce examples of it in all sorts of governments in the world.

Secondly, I answer, such revolutions happen not upon every little mismanagement in public affairs. Great mistakes of the ruling party, many wrong and inconvenient laws, and all the slips of human frailty will be borne by the people without mutiny or murmur. But if a long train of abuses, lies, and tricks, all tending the same way, make the scheme visible to the people, and they cannot but feel what they are subjected to and see where they are going, it is not to be wondered that they should then rouse themselves and endeavor to put the rule into such hands which may secure to them the ends for which government was at first formed. . . .

Thirdly, I answer that this doctrine of a power in the people of providing for their safety anew by a new legislative, when their legislators have acted contrary to their trust by invading their property, is the best defense against rebellion, and the most likely means to hinder it. For rebellion is an opposition, not to persons, but authority which is founded only on the constitutions and laws of the government; those, whoever they may be, who by force break through, and by force justify their violation of them, are truly and properly the *rebels*. . . .

Here, probably, the common question will be asked: Who shall be judge whether the prince or legislative act contrary to their trust? This, perhaps, ill-affected and devisive men may spread among the people, when the prince only makes use of his due prerogative. To this I reply: The people shall be judge; for who shall be judge whether his trustee or deputy acts well and according to the trust placed in him but he who hired him and must, by having hired him, have still the power to discard him when he fails in his trust? If this be reasonable in particular cases of private men, why should it be otherwise in that of the greatest moment where the welfare of millions is concerned, and also where the evil, if not prevented, is greater and the redress very difficult, costly, and dangerous? . . .

If a controversy should arise between a prince and some of the people in a matter where the law is silent or doubtful, and the matter is of great consequence, I should think the proper umpire in such a case should be the body of the people. For in cases where the prince has a trust placed in him and is exempted from the common ordinary rules of the law, there, if any men find themselves aggrieved and think the prince acts contrary to or beyond that trust, who is so proper to judge as the body of the people (who, at first, placed that trust in him) as to how far they meant it should extend? But if the prince, or whoever they may be in the administration, decline that way of decision, the appeal then lies nowhere but with heaven. Force between persons, who have no known superior on earth or which permits no appeal to a judge on earth, is properly a state of war wherein the appeal lies only to heaven; and in that state the injured party must judge for himself when he will think fit to make use of that appeal and put himself to it.

To conclude, the power that every individual gave the society when he entered into it can never revert to the individuals again as long as the society lasts, but will always remain in the *community*, because without this there can be no community, no commonwealth, which is contrary to the original agreement. So also when the society has placed the legislative in any assembly of men, to continue in them and their successors with direction and authority for providing such successors, the legislative can never revert to the people while that government lasts, because having provided a legislative with power to continue forever, they have given up their political power to the legislative and cannot reclaim it. But if they have set limits to the duration of their legislative and made this supreme power in any person or assembly only temporary, or else when by the miscarriages of those in authority it is forfeited, upon the forfeiture, or at the determination of the time set, it reverts to the society. The people then have a right to act as supreme and continue the legislative in themselves, or erect a new form, or under the old form place it in new hands, as they think good.

Galileo Galilei

THE STARRY MESSENGER

Introduction by Michael Levin

In the summer of 1609, an Italian professor of mathematics named Galileo Galilei (1564–1642) learned of a new invention called a spyglass (later renamed "telescope"). When two glass lenses, one convex and the other concave, were placed a certain distance from each other and then looked through simultaneously, they appeared to magnify the image of an object many times. Intrigued, Galileo constructed a spyglass for himself. As its name suggests, this invention was originally prized for its military applications, but Galileo did something no one else had: he pointed the spyglass up, into the heavens. What he saw there would forever change our understanding of the universe and our place in it.

For several thousand years before Galileo, the accepted view of the cosmos was that Earth is at the center of everything, and that all the heavenly bodies revolve around us. Aristotle, the greatest secular authority of classical civilization expressed this opinion, and the Bible apparently confirmed him. Since God made man in His image, it made sense that we are the center of the universe. Aristotle also claimed that the heavenly spheres are perfect and eternal, while the earthly sphere is imperfect and subject to changes which again fits very well with the Christian worldview. Nonetheless, in 1543, the Polish astronomer Nicholas Copernicus published *On the Revolution of the Spheres,* arguing that in fact the Earth orbits around the Sun. Few people read this work, and fewer believed it. After all, if the Earth is moving, shouldn't we be able to feel it move? And how could Aristotle and the Bible be wrong? It is in this context that we must read Galileo's work, *The Starry Messenger,* published in 1610. For Galileo claimed to have proof that the "Copernican system," with the Sun at the center, was correct.

When reading this work, remember that Galileo is describing things that *no one* in history had ever before seen. How does he try to convince us that what he says is true? Pay particular attention to the drawings that he includes — what purpose do they serve? One of the hallmarks of the modern idea of "science" (which dates from the time of Galileo) is that an experiment can be performed more than once and produce the same results, thus providing the hypothesis on which the experiment is based. This applies to Galileo's results as well: if you take a telescope and look through it, you will see exactly the same thing he saw.

Perhaps the most exciting section of this work is Galileo's discussion of his discovery of moons orbiting the planet Jupiter. Recall that the Aristotelian system insists that everything revolve around the Earth — so how then could there be something orbiting a different planet? Likewise, when Galileo describes looking at the Moon, he says it is covered with craters and mountains, "much like the Earth" — so what happens to Aristotle's perfect heavenly spheres? Finally, think about the philosophical implications of Galileo's discovery of thousands of new stars. If the universe is much bigger than we previously thought, what does that do to our sense of self-importance? And if the Earth is a planet like other planets, what happens to our belief in our own unique nature?

In 1633, the Pope and the Roman Inquisition put Galileo on trial. They accused him of being a heretic, and of promoting dangerous ideas, which went counter to Scripture and Church doctrine. In order to avoid punishment, Galileo publicly declared that he had been in error, but he still spent the rest of his life under house arrest. This is but one incident in the long conflict between "scientific truth" and "religious faith." Can you think of more recent examples of this same problem?

THE STARRY MESSENGER

Revealing great, unusual, and remarkable

spectacles, opening these

to the consideration of every man,

and especially of philosophers and

astronomers;

AS OBSERVED BY GALILEO GALILEI

Gentleman of Florence

Professor of Mathematics in the

University of Padua,

WITH THE AID OF A SPYGLASS

lately invented by him,

In the surface of the Moon, in innumerable

Fixed Stars, in Nebulae, and above all

in FOUR PLANETS

swiftly revolving about Jupiter at

differing distances and periods,

and known to no one before the

Author recently perceived them

and decided that they should

be named

THE MEDICEAN STARS

Venice

1610

Discoveries and Opinions of Galileo, trans. Stillman Drake (New York: Anchor Books, 1957) ISBN 0385092393, pp. 21–58, "Starry Messenger."

To the Most Serene
Cosimo II de' Medici
Fourth Grand Duke of Tuscany

Surely a distinguished public service has been rendered by those who have protected from envy the noble achievements of men who have excelled in virtue, and have thus preserved from oblivion and neglect those names which deserve immortality. In this way images sculptured in marble or cast in bronze have been handed down to posterity; to this we owe our statues, both pedestrian and equestrian; thus have we those columns and pyramids whose expense (as the poet says)[1] reaches to the stars; finally, thus cities have been built to bear the names of men deemed worthy by posterity of commendation to all the ages. For the nature of the human mind is such that unless it is stimulated by images of things acting upon it from without, all remembrance of them passes easily away.

Looking to things even more stable and enduring, others have entrusted the immortal fame of illustrious men not to marble and metal but to the custody of the Muses and to imperishable literary monuments. But why dwell upon these things as though human wit were satisfied with earthly regions and had not dared advance beyond? For, seeking further, and well understanding that all human monuments ultimately perish through the violence of the elements or by old age, ingenuity has in fact found still more incorruptible monuments over which voracious time and envious age have been unable to assert any rights. Thus turning to the sky, man's wit has inscribed on the familiar and everlasting orbs of most bright stars the names of those whose eminent and godlike deeds have caused them to be accounted worthy of eternity in the company of the stars. And so the fame of Jupiter, of Mars, of Mercury, Hercules, and other heroes by whose names the stars are called, will not fade before the extinction of the stars themselves.

Yet this invention of human ingenuity, noble and admirable as it is, has for many centuries been out of style. Primeval heroes are in possession of those bright abodes, and hold them in their own right. In vain did the piety of Augustus attempt to elect Julius Caesar into their number, for when he tried to give the name of "Julian" to a star which appeared in his time (one of those bodies which the Greeks call "comets" and which the Romans likewise named for their hairy appearance), it vanished in a brief time and mocked his too ambitious wish. But we are able, most serene Prince, to read Your Highness in the heavens far more accurately and auspiciously. For scarce have the immortal graces of your spirit begun to shine on earth when in the heavens bright stars appear as tongues to tell and celebrate your exceeding virtues to all time. Behold, then, four stars reserved to bear your famous name; bodies which belong not to the inconspicuous multitude of fixed stars, but to the bright ranks of the planets. Variously moving about most noble Jupiter as children of his own, they complete their orbits with marvelous velocity — at the same time executing with one harmonious accord mighty revolutions every dozen years about the center of the universe; that is, the sun.[2]

Indeed, the Maker of the stars himself has seemed by clear indications to direct that I assign to these new planets Your Highness's famous name in preference to all others. For just as these stars, like children worthy of their sire, never leave the side of Jupiter by any appreciable distance, so (as indeed who does not know?) clemency, kindness of heart, gentleness of manner,

---

1. Propertius iii, 2, 17.

2. This is the first published intimation by Galileo that he accepted the Copernican system. Tycho had made Jupiter revolve about the sun, but considered the earth to be the center of the universe. It was not until 1613, however, that Galileo unequivocally supported Copernicus in print.

splendor of royal blood, nobility in public affairs, and excellency of authority and rule have all fixed their abode and habitation in Your Highness. And who, I ask once more, does not know that all these virtues emanate from the benign star of Jupiter, next after God as the source of all things good? Jupiter; Jupiter, I say, at the instant of Your Highness's birth, having already emerged from the turbid mists of the horizon and occupied the midst of the heavens, illuminating the eastern sky from his own royal house, looked out from that exalted throne upon your auspicious birth and poured forth all his splendor and majesty in order that your tender body and your mind (already adorned by God with the most noble ornaments) might imbibe with their first breath that universal influence and power.

But why should I employ mere plausible arguments, when I may prove my conclusion absolutely? It pleased Almighty God that I should instruct Your Highness in mathematics, which I did four years ago at that time of year when it is customary to rest from the most exacting studies. And since clearly it was mine by divine will to serve Your Highness and thus to receive from near at hand the rays of your surpassing clemency and beneficence, what wonder is it that my heart is so inflamed as to think both day and night of little else than how I, who am indeed your subject not only by choice but by birth and lineage, may become known to you as most grateful and most anxious for your glory? And so, most serene Cosimo, having discovered under your patronage these stars unknown to every astronomer before me, I have with good right decided to designate them by the august name of your family. And if I am first to have investigated them, who can justly blame me if I likewise name them, calling them the Medicean Stars, in the hope that this name will bring an much honor to them as the names of other heroes have bestowed on other stars? For, to say nothing of Your Highness's most serene ancestors, whose everlasting glory is testified by the monuments of all history, your virtue alone, most worthy Sire, can confer upon these stars an immortal name. No one can doubt that you will fulfill those expectations, high though they are, which you have aroused by the auspicious beginning of your reign, and will not only meet but far surpass them. Thus when you have conquered your equals you may still vie with yourself, and you and your greatness will become greater every day.

Accept then, most clement Prince, this gentle glory reserved by the stars for you. May you long enjoy those blessings which are sent to you not so much from the stars as from God, their Maker and their Governor.

Your Highness's most devoted servant,

GALILEO GALILEI

PADUA, March 12, 1610

Astronomical Message

**Which contains and explains recent observations
made with the aid of a new spyglass[3]
concerning the surface of the moon,
the Milky Way, nebulous stars, and
innumerable fixed stars,
as well as four planets never before seen,
and now named
THE MEDICEAN STARS**

Great indeed are the things which in this brief treatise I propose for observation and consideration by all students of nature. I say great, because of the excellence of the subject itself, the
entirely unexpected and novel character of these things, and finally because of the instrument
by means of which they have been revealed to our senses.

Surely it is a great thing to increase the numerous host of fixed stars previously visible to
the unaided vision, adding countless more which have never before been seen, exposing these
plainly to the eye in numbers ten times exceeding the old and familiar stars.

It is a very beautiful thing, and most gratifying to the sight, to behold the body of the moon,
distant from us almost sixty earthly radii,[4] as if it were no farther away than two such
measures — so that its diameter appears almost thirty times larger, its surface nearly nine hundred times, and its volume twenty-seven thousand times as large as when viewed with the
naked eye. In this way one may learn with all the certainty of sense evidence that the moon is
not robed in a smooth and polished surface but is in fact rough and uneven, covered everywhere, just like the earth's surface, with huge prominences, deep valleys, and chasms.

Again, it seems to me a matter of no small importance to have ended the dispute about the
Milky Way by making its nature manifest to the very senses as well as to the intellect. Similarly
it will be a pleasant and elegant thing to demonstrate that the nature of those stars which
astronomers have previously called "nebulous" is far different from what has been believed
hitherto. But what surpasses all wonders by far, and what particularly moves us to seek the
attention of all astronomers and philosophers, is the discovery of four wandering stars not
known or observed by any man before us. Like Venus and Mercury, which have their own periods about the sun, these have theirs about a certain star that is conspicuous among those already
known, which they sometimes precede and sometimes follow, without ever departing from it
beyond certain limits. All these facts were discovered and observed by me not many days ago
with the aid of a spyglass which I devised, after first being illuminated by divine grace. Perhaps

---

3. The word "telescope" was not coined until 1611. A detailed account of its origin is given by Edward Rosen in *The
Naming of the Telescope* (New York, 1947). In the present translation the modern term has been introduced for the
sake of dignity and ease of reading, but only after the passage in which Galileo describes the circumstances which led
him to construct the instrument (pp. 28–29).

4. The original text reads "diameters" here and in another place. That this error was Galileo's and not the printer's has
been convincingly shown by Edward Rosen (*Isis,* 1952, pp. 344 ff.). The slip was a curious one, as astronomers of all
schools had long agreed that the maximum distance of the moon was approximately sixty terrestrial radii. Still more
curious is the fact that neither Kepler nor any other correspondent appears to have called Galileo's attention to this
error; not even a friend who ventured to criticize the calculations in this very passage.

other things, still more remarkable, will in time be discovered by me or by other observers with the aid of such an instrument, the form and construction of which I shall first briefly explain, as well as the occasion of its having been devised. Afterwards I shall relate the story of the observations I have made.

About ten months ago a report reached my ears that a certain Fleming[5] had constructed a spyglass by means of which visible objects, though very distant from the eye of the observer, were distinctly seen as if nearby. Of this truly remarkable effect several experiences were related, to which some persons gave credence while others decried them. A few days later the report was confirmed to me in a letter from a noble Frenchman at Paris, Jacques Badovere,[6] which caused me to apply myself wholeheartedly to inquire into the means by which I might arrive at the invention of a similar instrument. This I did shortly afterwards, my basis being the theory of refraction. First I prepared a tube of lead, at the ends of which I fitted two glass lenses, both plane on one side while on the other side one was spherically convex and the other concave. Then placing my eye near the concave lens I perceived objects satisfactorily large and near, for they appeared three times closer and nine times larger than when seen with the naked eye alone. Next I constructed another one, more accurate, which represented objects as enlarged more than sixty times. Finally, sparing neither labor nor expense, I succeeded in constructing for myself so excellent an instrument that objects seen by means of it appeared nearly one thousand times larger and over thirty times closer than when regarded with our natural vision.

It would be superfluous to enumerate the number and importance of the advantages of such an instrument at sea as well as on land. But forsaking terrestrial observations, I turned to celestial ones, and first I saw the moon from as near at hand as if it were scarcely two terrestrial radii away. After that I observed often with wondering delight both the planets and the fixed stars, and since I saw these latter to be very crowded, I began to seek (and eventually found) a method by which I might measure their distance apart.

Here it is appropriate to convey certain cautions to all who intend to undertake observations of this sort, for in the first place it is necessary to prepare quite a perfect telescope, which will show all objects bright, distinct, and free from any haziness, while magnifying them at least four hundred times and thus showing them twenty times closer. Unless the instrument is of this kind it will be vain to attempt to observe all the things which I have seen in the heavens, and which will presently be set forth. Now in order to determine without much trouble the magnifying power of an instrument, trace on paper the contour of two circles or two squares of which one is four hundred times as large as the other, as it will be when the diameter of one is twenty times that of the other. Then, with both these figures attached to the same wall, observe them simultaneously from a distance, looking at the smaller one through the telescope and at the larger one with the other eye unaided. This may be done without inconvenience while holding both eyes open at the same time; the two figures will appear to be of the same size if the instrument magnifies objects in the desired proportion.

Such an instrument having been prepared, we seek a method of measuring distances apart. This we shall accomplish by the following contrivance.

---

5. Credit for the original invention is generally assigned to Hans Lipperhey, a lens grinder in Holland who chanced upon this property of combined lenses and applied for a patent on it in 1608.

6. Badovere studied in Italy toward the close of the sixteenth century and is said to have been a pupil of Galileo's about 1598. When he wrote concerning the new instrument in 1609 he was in the French diplomatic service at Paris, where he died in 1620.

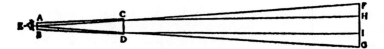

Let ABCD be the tube and E be the eye of the observer. Then if there were no lenses in the tube, the rays would reach the object FG along the straight lines ECF and EDG. But when the lenses have been inserted, the rays go along the refracted lines ECH and EDI; thus they are brought closer together, and those which were previously directed freely to the object FG now include only the portion of it HI. The ratio of the distance EH to the line HI then being found, one may by means of a table of sines determine the size of the angle formed at the eye by the object HI, which we shall find to be but a few minutes of arc. Now, if to the lens CD we fit thin plates, some pierced with larger and some with smaller apertures, putting now one plate and now another over the lens as required, we may form at pleasure different angles subtending more or fewer minutes of arc, and by this means we may easily measure the intervals between stars which are but a few minutes apart, with no greater error than one or two minutes. And for the present let it suffice that we have touched lightly on these matters and scarcely more than mentioned them, as on some other occasion we shall explain the entire theory of this instrument.

Now let us review the observations made during the past two months, once more inviting the attention of all who are eager for true philosophy to the first steps of such important contemplations. Let us speak first of that surface of the moon which faces us. For greater clarity I distinguish two parts of this surface, a lighter and a darker; the lighter part seems to surround and to pervade the whole hemisphere, while the darker part discolors the moon's surface like a kind of cloud, and makes it appear covered with spots. Now those spots which are fairly dark and rather large are plain to everyone and have been seen throughout the ages; these I shall call the "large" or "ancient" spots, distinguishing them from others that are smaller in size but so numerous as to occur all over the lunar surface, and especially the lighter part. The latter spots had never been seen by anyone before me. From observations of these spots repeated many times I have been led to the opinion and conviction that the surface of the moon is not smooth, uniform, and precisely spherical as a great number of philosophers believe it (and the other heavenly bodies) to be, but is uneven, rough, and full of cavities and prominences, being not unlike the face of the earth, relieved by chains of mountains and deep valleys. The things I have seen by which I was enabled to draw this conclusion are as follows.

On the fourth or fifth day after new moon, when the moon is seen with brilliant horns, the boundary which divides the dark part from the light does not extend uniformly in an oval line as would happen on a perfectly spherical solid, but traces out an uneven, rough, and very wavy line as shown in the figure below. Indeed, many luminous excrescences extend beyond the boundary into the darker portion, while on the other hand some dark patches invade the illuminated part. Moreover a great quantity of small blackish spots, entirely separated from the dark region, are scattered almost all over the area illuminated by sun with the exception only of that part which is occupied by the large and ancient spots. Let us note, however, that the said small spots always agree in having their blackened parts directed toward the sun, while on the side opposite the sun they are crowned with bright contours, like shining summits. There is a similar sight on earth about sunrise, when we behold the valleys not yet flooded with light though the mountains surrounding them are already ablaze with glowing splendor on the side opposite the

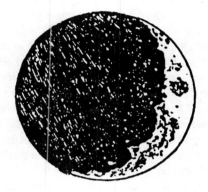

as the shadows in the hollows on earth diminish in size as the sun rises higher, so these spots on the moon lose their blackness as the illuminated region grows larger and larger.

Again, not only are the boundaries of shadow and light in the moon seen to be uneven and wavy, but still more astonishingly many bright points appear within the darkened portion of the moon, completely divided and separated from the illuminated part and at a considerable distance from it. After a time these gradually increase in size and brightness, and an hour or two later they become joined with the rest of the lighted part which has now increased in size. Meanwhile more and more peaks shoot up as if sprouting now here, now there, lighting up within the shadowed portion; these become larger, and finally they too are united with that same luminous surface which extends ever further. An illustration of this is to be seen in the figure above. And on the earth, before the rising of the sun, are not the highest peaks of the mountains illuminated by the sun's rays while the plains remain in shadow? Does not the light go on spreading while the larger central parts of those mountains are becoming illuminated? And when the sun has finally risen, does not the illumination of plains and hills finally become one? But on the moon the variety of elevations and depressions appears to surpass in every way the roughness of the terrestrial surface, as we shall demonstrate further on.

At present I cannot pass over in silence something worthy of consideration which I observed when the moon was approaching first quarter, as shown in the previous figure. Into the luminous part there extended a great dark gulf in the neighborhood of the lower cusp. When I had observed it for a long time and had seen it completely dark, a bright peak began to emerge, a little below its center, after about two hours. Gradually growing, this presented itself in a triangular shape, remaining completely detached and separated from the lighted surface. Around it three other small points soon began to shine, and finally, when the moon was about to set, this triangular shape (which had meanwhile become more widely extended) joined with the rest of the illuminated region and suddenly burst into the gulf of shadow like a vast promontory of light, surrounded still by the three bright peaks already mentioned. Beyond the ends of the cusps, both above and below, certain bright points emerged which were quite detached from the remaining lighted part, as may be seen depicted in the same figure. There were also a great number of dark spots in both the horns, especially in the lower one; those nearest the boundary of light and shadow appeared larger and darker, while those more distant from the boundary were not so dark and distinct. But in all cases, as we have mentioned earlier, the blackish portion of each spot is turned toward the source of the sun's radiance, while a bright rim surrounds the spot on the side away from the sun in the direction of the shadowy region of the moon. This part of the moon's surface, where it is spotted as the tail of a peacock is sprinkled with azure eyes, resembles those glass vases which have been plunged while still hot into cold water and have thus acquired a crackled and wavy surface, from which they receive their common name of "ice-cups."

As to the large lunar spots, these are not seen to be broken in the above manner and full of cavities and prominences; rather, they are even and uniform, and brighter patches crop up only here and there. Hence if anyone wished to revive the old Pythagorean[7] opinion that the moon is like another earth, its brighter part might very fitly represent the surface of the land and its darker region that of the water. I have never doubted that if our globe were seen from afar when flooded with sunlight, the land regions would appear brighter and the watery regions darker.[8] The large spots in the moon are also seen to be less elevated than the brighter tracts, for whether the moon is waxing or waning there are always seen, here and there along its boundary of light and shadow, certain ridges of brighter hue around the large spots (and we have attended to this in preparing the diagrams); the edges of these spots are not only lower, but also more uniform, being uninterrupted by peaks or ruggedness.

Near the large spots the brighter part stands out particularly in such a way that before first quarter and toward last quarter, in the vicinity of a certain spot in the upper (or northern) region of the moon, some vast prominences arise both above and below as shown in the figures reproduced below. Before last quarter this same spot is seen to be walled about with certain blacker contours which, like the loftiest mountaintops, appear darker on the side away from the sun and brighter on that which faces the sun. (This is the opposite of what happens in the cavities, for there the part away from the sun appears brilliant, while that which is turned toward the sun is dark and in shadow.) After a time, when the lighted portion of the moon's surface has diminished in size and when all (or nearly all) the said spot is covered with shadow, the brighter ridges of the mountains gradually emerge from the shade. This double aspect of the spot is illustrated in the ensuing figures.

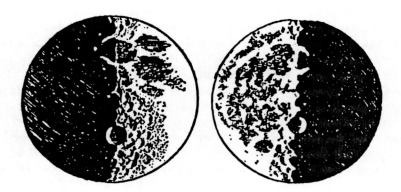

7. Pythagoras was a mathematician and philosopher of the sixth century B.C., a semilegendary figure whose followers were credited at Galileo's time with having anticipated the Copernican system. This tradition was based upon a misunderstanding. The Pythagoreans made the earth revolve about a "central fire" whose light and heat were reflected to the earth by the sun.

8. Leonardo da Vinci had previously suggested that the dark and light regions of the moon were bodies of land and water, though Galileo probably did not know this. Da Vinci, however, had mistakenly supposed that the water would appear brighter than the land.

There is another thing which I must not omit, for I beheld it not without a certain wonder; this is that almost in the center of the moon there is a cavity larger than all the rest, and perfectly round in shape. I have observed it near both first and last quarters, and have tried to represent it as correctly as possible in the second of the above figures. As to light and shade, it offers the same appearance as would a region like Bohemia[9] if that were enclosed on all sides by very lofty mountains arranged exactly in a circle. Indeed, this area on the moon is surrounded by such enormous peaks that the bounding edge adjacent to the dark portion of the moon is seen to be bathed in sunlight before the boundary of light and shadow reaches halfway across the same space. As in other spots, its shaded portion faces the sun while its lighted part is toward the dark side of the moon; and for a third time I draw attention to this as a very cogent proof of the ruggedness and unevenness that pervades all the bright region of the moon. Of these spots, moreover, those are always darkest which touch the boundary line between light and shadow, while those farther off appear both smaller and less dark, so that when the moon ultimately becomes full (at opposition[10] to the sun), the shade of the cavities is distinguished from the light of the places in relief by a subdued and very tenuous separation.

The things we have reviewed are to be seen in the brighter region of the moon. In the large spots, no such contrast of depressions and prominences is perceived as that which we are compelled to recognize in the brighter parts by the changes of aspect that occur under varying illumination by the sun's rays throughout the multiplicity of positions from which the latter reach the moon. In the large spots there exist some holes rather darker than the rest, as we have shown in the illustrations. Yet these present always the same appearance, and their darkness is neither intensified nor diminished, although with some minute difference they appear sometimes a little more shaded and sometimes a little lighter according as the rays of the sun fall on them more or less obliquely. Moreover, they join with the neighboring regions of the spots in a gentle linkage, the boundaries mixing and mingling. It is quite different with the spots which occupy the brighter surface of the moon; these, like precipitous crags having rough and jagged peaks, stand

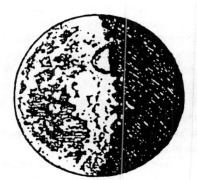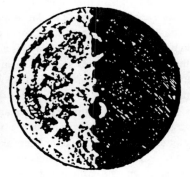

9. This casual comparison between a part of the moon and a specific region on earth was later the basis of much trouble for Galileo; see the letter of Piero Dini, p. 158. Even in antiquity the idea that the moon (or any other heavenly body) was of the same nature as the earth had been dangerous to hold. The Athenians banished the philosopher Anaxagoras for teaching such notions, and charged Socrates with blasphemy for repeating them.

10. Opposition of the sun and moon occurs when they are in line with the earth between them (full moon, or lunar eclipse); conjunction, when they are in line on the same side of the earth (new moon, or eclipse of the sun).

out starkly in sharp contrasts of light and shade. And inside the large spots there are observed certain other zones that are brighter, some of them very bright indeed. Still, both these and the darker parts present always the same appearance; there is no change either of shape or of light and shadow; hence one may affirm beyond any doubt that they owe their appearance to some real dissimilarity of parts. They cannot be attributed merely to irregularity of shape, wherein shadows move in consequence of varied illuminations from the sun, as indeed is the case with the other, smaller, spots which occupy the brighter part of the moon and which change, grow, shrink, or disappear from one day to the next, as owing their origin only to shadows of prominences.

But here I foresee that many persons will be assailed by uncertainty and drawn into a grave difficulty, feeling constrained to doubt a conclusion already explained and confirmed by many phenomena. If that part of the lunar surface which reflects sunlight more brightly is full of chasms (that is, of countless prominences and hollows), why is it that the western edge of the waxing moon, the eastern edge of the waning moon, and the entire periphery of the full moon are not seen to be uneven, rough, and wavy? On the contrary they look as precisely round as if they were drawn with a compass; and yet the whole periphery consists of that brighter lunar substance which we have declared to be filled with heights and chasms. In fact not a single one of the great spots extends to the extreme periphery of the moon, but all are grouped together at a distance from the edge.

Now let me explain the twofold reason for this troublesome fact, and in turn give a double solution to the difficulty. In the first place, if the protuberances and cavities in the lunar body existed only along the extreme edge of the circular periphery bounding the visible hemisphere, the moon might (indeed, would necessarily) look to us almost like a toothed wheel, terminated by a warty or wavy edge. Imagine, however, that there is not a single series of prominences arranged only along the very circumference, but a great many ranges of mountains together with their valleys and canyons disposed in ranks near the edge of the moon, and not only in the hemisphere visible to us but everywhere near the boundary line of the two hemispheres. Then an eye viewing them from afar will not be able to detect the separation of prominences by cavities, because the intervals between the mountains located in a given circle or a given chain will be hidden by the interposition of other heights situated in yet other ranges. This will be especially true if the eye of the observer is placed in the same straight line with the summits of these elevations. Thus on earth the summits of several mountains close together appear to be situated in one plane if the spectator is a long way off and is placed at an equal elevation. Similarly in a rough sea the tops of the waves seem to lie in one plane, though between one high crest and another there are many gulfs and chasms of such depth as not only to hide the hulls but even the bulwarks, masts, and rigging of stately ships. Now since there are many chains of mountains and chasms on the moon in addition to those around its periphery, and since the eye, regarding these from a great distance, lies nearly in the plane of their summits, no one need wonder that they appear as arranged in a regular and unbroken line.

To the above explanation another may be added; namely, that there exists around the body of the moon, just as around the earth, a globe of some substance denser than the rest of the aether.[11] This may serve to receive and reflect the sun's radiations without being sufficiently opaque to prevent our seeing through it, especially when it is not illuminated. Such a globe, lighted by the sun's rays, makes the body of the moon appear larger than it really is, and if it were thicker it would be able to prevent our seeing the actual body of the moon. And it actually is thicker near the circum-

---

11. The aether, or "ever-moving," was the special substance of which the sky and all the heavenly bodies were supposed to be made, a substance essentially different from all the earthly "elements." In later years Galileo abandoned his suggestion here that the moon has a vaporous atmosphere

ference of the moon; I do not mean in an absolute sense, but relatively to the rays of our vision, which cut it obliquely there. Thus it may obstruct our vision, especially when it is lighted, and cloak the lunar periphery that is exposed to the sun. This may be more clearly understood from the figure below, in which the body of the moon, ABC, is surrounded by the vaporous globe DEG. The eyesight from F reaches the moon in the central region, at A for example, through a lesser thickness of the vapors DA, while toward the extreme edges a deeper stratum of vapors, EB, limits and shuts out our sight. One indication of this is that the illuminated portion of the moon appears to be larger in circumference than the rest of the orb, which lies in shadow. And perhaps this same cause will appeal to some as reasonably explaining why the larger spots on the moon are nowhere seen to reach the very edge, probable though it is that some should occur there. Possibly they are invisible by being hidden under a thicker and more luminous mass of vapors.

That the lighter surface of the moon is everywhere dotted with protuberances and gaps has, I think, been made sufficiently clear from the appearances already explained. It remains for me to speak of their dimensions, and to show that the earth's irregularities are far less than those of the moon. I mean that they are absolutely less, and not merely in relation to the sizes of the respective globes. This is plainly demonstrated as follows.

I had often observed, in various situations of the moon with respect to the sun, that some summits within the shadowy portion appeared lighted, though lying some distance from the boundary of the light. By comparing this separation to the whole diameter of the moon, I found that it sometimes exceeded one-twentieth of the diameter. Accordingly, let CAF be a great circle of the lunar body, E its center, and CF a diameter, which is to the diameter of the earth as two is to seven.

Since according to very precise observations the diameter of the earth is seven thousand miles, CF will be two thousand, CE one thousand, and one-twentieth of CF will be one hundred miles. Now let CF be the diameter of the great circle which divides the light part of the moon from the dark part (for because of the very great distance of the sun from the moon, this does not differ appreciably from a great circle), and let A be distant from C by one-twentieth of this. Draw the radius EA, which, when produced, cuts the tangent line GCD (representing the illuminating ray) in the point D. Then the arc CA, or rather the straight line CD, will consist of one hundred units whereof CE contains one thousand, and the sum of the squares of DC and CE will be 1,010,000. This is equal to the square of DE; hence ED will exceed 1,004, and AD will be more than four of those units of which CE contains one thousand. Therefore the altitude AD on the moon, which represents a summit reaching up to the solar ray GCD and standing at the distance CD from C, exceeds four miles. But on the earth we have no mountains which reach to a perpendicular height of even one mile.[12] Hence it is quite clear that the prominences on the moon are loftier than those on the earth.

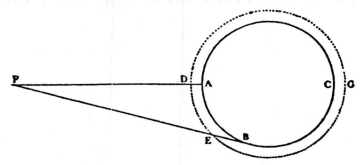

12. Galileo's estimate of four miles for the height of some lunar mountains was a very good one. His remark about the maximum height of mountains on the earth was, however, quite mistaken. An English propagandist for his views, John Wilkins, took pains to correct this error in his anonymous *Discovery of a New World . . . in the Moon* (London, 1638), Prop. ix.

Here I wish to assign the cause of another lunar phenomenon well worthy of notice. I observed this not just recently, but many years ago, and pointed it out to some of my friends and pupils, explaining it to them and giving its true cause. Yet since it is rendered more evident and easier to observe with the aid of the telescope, I think it not unsuitable for introduction in this place, especially as it shows more clearly the connection between the moon and the earth.

When the moon is not far from the sun, just before or after new moon, its globe offers itself to view not only on the side where it is adorned with shining horns, but a certain faint light is also seen to mark out the periphery of the dark part which faces away from the sun, separating this from the darker background of the aether. Now if we examine the matter more closely, we shall see that not only does the extreme limb of the shaded side glow with this uncertain light, but the entire face of the moon (including the side which does not receive the glare of the sun) is whitened by a not inconsiderable gleam. At first glance only a thin luminous circumference appears, contrasting with the darker sky coterminous with it; the rest of the surface appears darker from its contact with the shining horns which distract our vision. But if we place ourselves so as to interpose a roof or chimney or some other object at a considerable distance from the eye, the shining horns may be hidden while the rest of the lunar globe remains exposed to view. It is then found that this region of the moon, though deprived of sunlight, also shines not a little. The effect is heightened if the gloom of night has already deepened through departure of the sun, for in a darker field a given light appears brighter.

Moreover, it is found that this secondary light of the moon (so to speak) is greater according as the moon is closer to the sun. It diminishes more and more as the moon recedes from that body until, after the first quarter and before the last, it is seen very weakly and uncertainly even when observed in the darkest sky. But when the moon is within sixty degrees of the sun it shines remarkably, even in twilight; so brightly indeed that with the aid of a good telescope one may distinguish the large spots. This remarkable gleam has afforded no small perplexity to philosophers, and in order to assign a cause for it some have offered one idea and some another. Some would say it is an inherent and natural light of the moon's own; others, that it is imparted by Venus; others yet, by all the stars together; and still others derive it from the sun, whose rays they would have permeate the thick solidity of the moon. But statements of this sort are refuted and their falsity evinced with little difficulty. For if this kind of light were the moon's own, or were contributed by the stars, the moon would retain it and would display it particularly during eclipses, when it is left in an unusually dark sky. This is contradicted by experience, for the brightness which is seen on the moon during eclipses is much fainter and is ruddy, almost copper-colored, while this is brighter and whitish. Moreover the other light is variable and movable, for it covers the face of the moon in

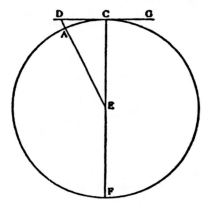

such a way that the place near the edge of the earth's shadow is always seen to be brighter than the rest of the moon; this undoubtedly results from contact of the tangent solar rays with some denser zone which girds the moon about.[13] By this contact a sort of twilight is diffused over the neighboring regions of the moon, just as on earth a sort of crepuscular light is spread both morning and evening; but with this I shall deal more fully in my book on the system of the world.[14]

To assert that the moods secondary light is imparted by Venus is so childish as to deserve no reply. Who is so ignorant as not to understand that from new moon to a separation of sixty degrees between moon and sun, no part of the moon which is averted from the sun can possibly be seen from Venus? And it is likewise unthinkable that this light should depend upon the sun's rays penetrating the thick solid mass of the moon, for then this light would never dwindle, inasmuch as one hemisphere of the moon is always illuminated except during lunar eclipses. And the light does diminish as the moon approaches first quarter, becoming completely obscured after that is passed.

Now since the secondary light does not inherently belong to the moon, and is not received from any star or from the sun, and since in the whole universe there is no other body left but the earth, what must we conclude? What is to be proposed? Surely we must assert that the lunar body (or any other dark and sunless orb) is illuminated by the earth. Yet what is there so remarkable about this? The earth, in fair and grateful exchange, pays back to the moon an illumination similar to that which it receives from her throughout nearly all the darkest gloom of night

Let us explain this matter more fully. At conjunction the moon occupies a position between the sun and the earth; it is then illuminated by the sun's rays on the side which is turned away from the earth. The other hemisphere, which faces the earth, is covered with darkness; hence the moon does not illuminate the surface of the earth at all. Next, departing gradually from the sun, the moon comes to be lighted partly upon the side it turns toward us, and its whitish horns, still very thin, illuminate the earth with a faint light. The sun's illumination of the moon increasing now as the moon approaches first quarter, a reflection of that light to the earth also increases. Soon the splendor on the moon extends into a semicircle, and our nights grow brighter; at length the entire visible face of the moon is irradiated by the sun's resplendent rays, and at full moon the whole surface of the earth shines in a flood of moonlight. Now the moon, waning, sends us her beams more weakly, and the earth is less strongly lighted; at length the moon returns to conjunction with the sun, and black night covers the earth.

In this monthly period, then, the moonlight gives us alternations of brighter and fainter illumination; and the benefit is repaid by the earth in equal measure. For while the moon is between us and the sun (at new moon), there lies before it the entire surface of that hemisphere of the earth which is exposed to the sun and illuminated by vivid rays. The moon receives the light which this reflects, and thus the nearer hemisphere of the moon — that is, the one deprived of sunlight — appears by virtue of this illumination to be not a little luminous. When the moon is ninety degrees away from the sun it sees but half the earth illuminated (the western half), for the other (the eastern half) is enveloped in night. Hence the moon itself is illuminated less brightly from the earth, and as a result its secondary light appears fainter to us. When the moon is in opposition to the sun, it faces a hemisphere of the earth that is steeped in the gloom of night, and if this position occurs in the plane of the ecliptic the moon will receive no light at all,

---

13. Kepler had correctly accounted for the existence of this light and its ruddy color. It is caused by refraction of sunlight in the earth's atmosphere, and does not require a lunar atmosphere as supposed by Galileo.

14. The book thus promised was destined not to appear for more than two decades. Events which will presently be recounted prevented its publication for many years, and then it had to be modified to present the arguments for both the Ptolemaic and Copernican systems instead of just the latter as Galileo here planned. Even then it was suppressed, and the author was condemned to life imprisonment.

being deprived of both the solar and the terrestrial rays. In its various other positions with respect to the earth and sun, the moon receives more or less light according as it faces a greater or smaller portion of the illuminated hemisphere of the earth. And between these two globes a relation is maintained such that whenever the earth is most brightly lighted by the moon, the moon is least lighted by the earth, and vice versa.

Let these few remarks suffice us here concerning this matter, which will be more fully treated in our *System of the world*. In that book, by a multitude of arguments and experiences, the solar reflection from the earth will be shown to be quite real — against those who argue that the earth must be excluded from the dancing whirl of stars for the specific reason that it is devoid of motion and of light. We shall prove the earth to be a wandering body surpassing the moon in splendor, and not the sink of all dull refuse of the universe; this we shall support by an infinitude of arguments drawn from nature.

Thus far we have spoken of our observations concerning the body of the moon. Let us now set forth briefly what has thus far been observed regarding the fixed stars. And first of all, the following fact deserves consideration: The stars, whether fixed or wandering,[15] appear not to be enlarged by the telescope in the same proportion as that in which it magnifies other objects, and even the moon itself. In the stars this enlargement seems to be so much less that a telescope which is sufficiently powerful to magnify other objects a hundredfold is scarcely able to enlarge the stars four or five times. The reason for this is as follows.

When stars are viewed by means of unaided natural vision, they present themselves to us not as of their simple (and, so to speak, their physical) size, but as irradiated by a certain fulgor and as fringed with sparkling rays, especially when the night is far advanced. From this they appear larger than they would if stripped of those adventitious hairs of light, for the angle at the eye is determined not by the primary body of the star but by the brightness which extends so widely about it. This appears quite clearly from the fact that when stars first emerge from twilight at sunset they look very small, even if they are of the first magnitude; Venus itself, when visible in broad daylight, is so small as scarcely to appear equal to a star of the sixth magnitude. Things fall out differently with other objects, and even with the moon itself; these, whether seen in daylight or the deepest night, appear always of the same bulk. Therefore the stars are seen crowned among shadows, while daylight is able to remove their headgear; and not daylight alone, but any thin cloud that interposes itself between a star and the eye of the observer. The same effect is produced by black veils or colored glasses, through the interposition of which obstacles the stars are abandoned by their surrounding brilliance. A telescope similarly accomplishes the same result. It removes from the stars their adventitious and accidental rays, and then it enlarges their simple globes (if indeed the stars are naturally globular) so that they seem to be magnified in a lesser ratio than other objects. In fact a star of the fifth or sixth magnitude when seen through a telescope presents itself as one of the first magnitude.

Deserving of notice also is the difference between the appearances of the planets and of the fixed stars.[16] The planets show their globes perfectly round and definitely bounded, looking like little moons, spherical and flooded all over with light; the fixed stars are never seen to be bounded by a circular periphery, but have rather the aspect of blazes whose rays vibrate about them and

---

15. That is, planets. Among these bodies Galileo counted his newly discovered satellites of Jupiter. The term "satellites" was introduced somewhat later by Kepler.

16. Fixed stars are so distant that their light reaches the earth as from dimensionless points. Hence their images are not enlarged by even the best telescopes, which serve only to gather more of their light and in that way increase their visibility. Galileo was never entirely clear about this distinction. Nevertheless, by applying his knowledge of the effects described here, he greatly reduced the prevailing overestimation of visual dimensions of stars and planets.

The Belt and Sword of Orion

scintillate a great deal. Viewed with a telescope they appear of a shape similar to that which they present to the naked eye, but sufficiently enlarged so that a star of the fifth or sixth magnitude seems to equal the Dog Star, largest of all the fixed stars. Now, in addition to stars of the sixth magnitude, a host of other stars are perceived through the telescope which escape the naked eye; these are so numerous as almost to surpass belief. One may, in fact, see more of them than all the stars included among the first six magnitudes. The largest of these, which we may call stars of the seventh magnitude, or the first magnitude of invisible stars, appear through the telescope as larger and brighter than stars of the second magnitude when the latter are viewed with the naked eye. In order to give one or two proofs of their almost inconceivable number, I have adjoined pictures of two constellations. With these as samples, you may judge of all the others.

In the first I had intended to depict the entire constellation of Orion, but I was overwhelmed by the vast quantity of stars and by limitations of time, so I have deferred this to another occasion. There are more than five hundred new stars distributed among the old ones within limits of one or two degrees of arc. Hence to the three stars in the Belt of Orion and the six in the Sword which were previously known, I have added eighty adjacent stars discovered recently, preserving the intervals between them as exactly as I could. To distinguish the known or ancient stars, I have depleted them larger and have outlined them doubly; the other (invisible) stars I have drawn smaller and without the extra line. I have also preserved differences of magnitude as well as possible.

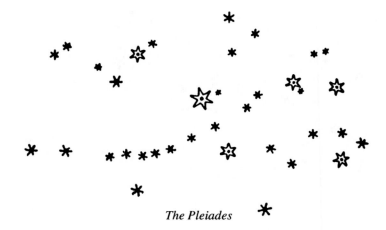

The Pleiades

In the second example I have depleted the six stars of Taurus known as the Pleiades (I say six, inasmuch as the seventh is hardly ever visible) which lie within very narrow limits in the sky. Near them are more than forty others, invisible, no one of which is much more than half a degree away from the original six. I have shown thirty-six of these in the diagram; as in the case of Orion I have preserved their intervals and magnitudes, as well as the distinction between old stars and new.

Third, I have observed the nature and the material of the Milky Way. With the aid of the telescope this has been scrutinized so directly and with such ocular certainty that all the disputes which have vexed philosophers through so many ages have been resolved, and we are at last freed from wordy debates about it. The galaxy is, in fact, nothing but a congeries of innumerable stars grouped together in clusters. Upon whatever part of it the telescope is directed, a vast crowd of stars is immediately presented to view. Many of them are rather large and quite bright, while the number of smaller ones is quite beyond calculation.

But it is not only in the Milky Way that whitish clouds are seen; several patches of similar aspect shine with faint light here and there throughout the aether, and if the telescope is turned upon any of these it confronts us with a tight mass of stars. And what is even more remarkable, the stars which have been called "nebulous" by every astronomer up to this time turn out to be groups of very small stars arranged in a wonderful manner. Although each star separately escapes our sight on account of its smallness or the immense distance from us, the mingling of their rays gives rise to that gleam which was formerly believed to be some denser part of the aether that was capable of reflecting rays from stars or from the sun. I have observed some of these constellations and have decided to depict two of them.

In the first you have the nebula called the Head of Orion, in which I have counted twenty-one stars. The second contains the nebula called Praesepe,[17] which is not a single star but a mass of more than forty starlets. Of these I have shown thirty-six, in addition to the Aselli, arranged in the order shown.

We have now briefly recounted the observations made thus far with regard to the moon, the fixed stars, and the Milky Way. There remains the matter which in my opinion deserves to be considered the most important of all — the disclosure of four PLANETS never seen from the

---

17. Praesepe, "the Manger," is a small whitish cluster of stars lying between the two Aselli (ass-colts) which are imagined as feeding from it. It lies in the constellation Cancer.

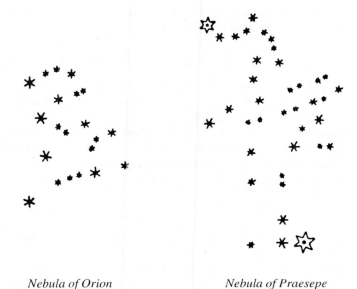

Nebula of Orion   *Nebula of Praesepe*

creation of the world up to our own time, together with the occasion of my having discovered and studied them, their arrangements, and the observations made of their movements and alterations during the past two months. I invite all astronomers to apply themselves to examine them and determine their periodic times, something which has so far been quite impossible to complete, owing to the shortness of the time. Once more, however, warning is given that it will be necessary to have a very accurate telescope such as we have described at the beginning of this discourse.

On the seventh day of January in this present year 1610, at the first hour of night, when I was viewing the heavenly bodies with a telescope, Jupiter presented itself to me; and because I had prepared a very excellent instrument for myself, I perceived (as I had not before, on account of the weakness of my previous instrument) that beside the planet there were three starlets, small indeed, but very bright. Though I believed them to be among the host of fixed stars, they aroused my curiosity somewhat by appearing to lie in an exact straight line parallel to the ecliptic, and by their being more splendid than others of their size. Their arrangement with respect to Jupiter and each other was the following:

East   *   *   O   *   *West*

that is, there were two stars on the eastern side and one to the west. The most easterly star and the western one appeared larger than the other. I paid no attention to the distances between them and Jupiter, for at the outset I thought them to be fixed stars, as I have said.[18] But returning to the same investigation on January eighth — led by what, I do not know — I found a very different

18. The reader should remember that the telescope was nightly revealing to Galileo hundreds of fixed stars never previously observed. His unusual gifts for astronomical observation are illustrated by his having noticed and remembered these three merely by reason of their alignment, and recalling them so well that when by chance he happened to see them the following night he was certain that they had changed their positions. No such plausible and candid account of the discovery was given by the rival astronomer Simon Mayr, who four years later claimed priority.

arrangement. The three starlets were now all to the west of Jupiter, closer together, and at equal intervals from one another as shown in the following sketch.

East   ○ ✳ ✳ ✳   *West*

At this time, though I did not yet turn my attention to the way the stars had come together, I began to concern myself with the question how Jupiter could be east of all these stars when on the previous day it had been west of two of them. I commenced to wonder whether Jupiter was not moving eastward at that time, contrary to the computations of the astronomers, and had got in front of them by that motion.[19] Hence it was with great interest that I awaited the next night. But I was disappointed in my hopes, for the sky was then covered with clouds everywhere.

On the tenth of January, however, the stars appeared in this position with respect to Jupiter:

East   ✳   ✳   ○   *West*

that is, there were but two of them, both easterly, the third (as I supposed) being hidden behind Jupiter. As at first, they were in the same straight line with Jupiter and were arranged precisely in the line of the zodiac. Noticing this, and knowing that there was no way in which such alterations could be attributed to Jupiter's motion, yet being certain that these were still the same stars I had observed (in fact no other was to be found along the line of the zodiac for a long way on either side of Jupiter), my perplexity was now transformed into amazement. I was sure that the apparent changes belonged not to Jupiter but to the observed stars, and I resolved to pursue this investigation with greater care and attention.

And thus, on the eleventh of January, I saw the following disposition:

East   ✳ ✳   ○   *West*

There were two stars, both to the east, the central one being three times as far from Jupiter as from the one farther east. The latter star was nearly double the size of the former, whereas on the night before they had appeared approximately equal.

I had now decided beyond all question that there existed in the heavens three stars wandering about Jupiter as do Venus and Mercury about the sun, and this became plainer than daylight from observations on similar occasions which followed. Nor were there just three such stars; four wanderers complete their revolutions about Jupiter, and of their alterations as observed more precisely later on we shall give a description here. Also I measured the distances between them by means of the telescope, using the method explained before. Moreover I recorded the times of the observations, especially when more than one was made during the same night — for the revolutions of these planets are so speedily completed that it is usually possible to take even their hourly variations.

Thus on the twelfth of January at the first hour of night I saw the stars arranged in this way:

East   ✳ ●○ ✳   *West*

---

19. See note 4, p. 12. Jupiter was at this time in "retrograde" motion; that is, the earth's motion made the planet appear to be moving westward among the fixed stars.

The most easterly star was larger than the western one, though both were easily visible and quite bright. Each was about two minutes of arc distant from Jupiter. The third star was invisible at first, but commenced to appear after two hours; it almost touched Jupiter on the east, and was quite small. All were on the same straight line directed along the ecliptic.

On the thirteenth of January four stars were seen by me for the first time, in this situation relative to Jupiter:

East   ✳ ⭕ ✳✳✳   *West*

Three were westerly and one was to the east; they formed a straight line except that the middle western star departed slightly toward the north. The eastern star was two minutes of arc away from Jupiter, and the intervals of the rest from one another and from Jupiter were about one minute. All the stars appeared to be of the same magnitude, and though small were very bright, much brighter than fixed stars of the same size.[20]

· · · · ·

On the twenty-sixth of February, midway in the first hour of night, there were only two stars:

East   ✳   ⭕   ✳   *West*

One was to the east, ten minutes from Jupiter; the other to the west, six minutes away. The eastern one was somewhat smaller than the western. But at the fifth hour three stars were seen:

East   ✳   ⭕ ✳   ✳   *West*

In addition to the two already noticed, a third was discovered to the west near Jupiter; it had at first been hidden behind Jupiter and was now one minute away. The eastern one appeared farther away than before, being eleven minutes from Jupiter.

This night for the first time I wanted to observe the progress of Jupiter and its accompanying planets along the line of the zodiac in relation to some fixed star, and such a star was seen to the east, eleven minutes distant from the easterly starlet and a little removed toward the south, in the following manner:

East   ✳   ⭕✳   ✳   *West*

         ★

On the twenty-seventh of February, four minutes after the first hour, the stars appeared in this configuration:

East   ✳   ✳⭕   ✳ ✳   *West*

         ★

---

20. Galileo's day-by-day journal of observations continued in unbroken sequence until ten days before publication of the book, which he remained in Venice to supervise. The observations omitted here contained nothing of a novel character.

The most easterly was ten minutes from Jupiter; the next, thirty seconds; the next to the west was two minutes thirty seconds from Jupiter, and the most westerly was one minute from that. Those nearest Jupiter appeared very small, while the end ones were plainly visible, especially the westernmost. They marked out an exactly straight line along the course of the ecliptic. The progress of these planets toward the east is seen quite clearly by reference to the fixed star mentioned, since Jupiter and its accompanying planets were closer to it, as may be seen in the figure above. At the fifth hour, the eastern star closer to Jupiter was one minute away.

At the first hour on February twenty-eighth, two stars only were seen; one easterly, distant nine minutes from Jupiter, and one to the west, two minutes away. They were easily visible and on the same straight line. The fixed star, perpendicular to this line, now fell under the eastern planet as in this figure:

At the fifth hour a third star, two minutes east of Jupiter, was seen in this position:

On the first of March, forty minutes after sunset, four stars all to the east were seen, of which the nearest to Jupiter was two minutes away, the next was one minute from this, the third two seconds from that and brighter than any of the others; from this in turn the most easterly was four minutes distant, and it was smaller than the rest. They marked out almost a straight line, but the third one counting from Jupiter was a little to the north. The fixed star formed an equilateral triangle with Jupiter and the most easterly star, as in this figure:

On March second, half an hour after sunset, there were three planets, two to the east and one to the west, in this configuration:

East   ✳•   ◯   ✳   West

★

The most easterly was seven minutes from Jupiter and thirty seconds from its neighbor; the western one way two minutes away from Jupiter. The end stars were very bright and were larger than that in the middle, which appeared very small. The most easterly star appeared a little elevated toward the north from the straight line through the other planets and Jupiter. The fixed star previously mentioned was eight minutes from the western planet along the line drawn from it perpendicularly to the straight line through all the planets, as shown above.

I have reported these relations of Jupiter and its companions with the fixed star so that anyone may comprehend that the progress of those planets, both in longitude and latitude, agrees exactly with the movements derived from planetary tables.

Such are the observations concerning the four Medicean planets recently first discovered by me, and although from these data their periods have not yet been reconstructed in numerical form, it is legitimate at least to put in evidence some facts worthy of note. Above all, since they sometimes follow and sometimes precede Jupiter by the same intervals, and they remain within very limited distances either to east or west of Jupiter, accompanying that planet in both its retrograde and direct movements in a constant manner, no one can doubt that they complete their revolutions about Jupiter and at the same time effect all together a twelve-year period about the center of the universe. That they also revolve in unequal circles is manifestly deduced from the fact that at the greatest elongation[21] from Jupiter it is never possible to see two of these planets in conjunction, whereas in the vicinity of Jupiter they are found united two, three, and sometimes all four together. It is also observed that the revolutions are swifter in those planets which describe smaller circles about Jupiter, since the stars closest to Jupiter are usually seen to the east when on the previous day they appeared to the west, and vice versa, while the planet which traces the largest orbit appears upon accurate observation of its returns to have a semimonthly period.

Here we have a fine and elegant argument for quieting the doubts of those who, while accepting with tranquil mind the revolutions of the planets about the sun in the Copernican system, are mightily disturbed to have the moon alone revolve about the earth and accompany it in an annual rotation about the sun. Some have believed that this structure of the universe should be rejected as impossible. But now we have not just one planet rotating about another while both run through a great orbit around the sun; our own eyes show us four stars which wander around Jupiter as does the moon around the earth, while all together trace out a grand revolution about the sun in the space of twelve years.

And finally we should not omit the reason for which the Medicean stars appear sometimes to be twice as large as at other times, though their orbits about Jupiter are very restricted. We certainly cannot seek the cause in terrestrial vapors, as Jupiter and its neighboring fixed stars are not seen to change size in the least while this increase and diminution are taking place. It is quite unthinkable that the cause of variation should be their change of distance from the earth at perigee and apogee, since a small circular rotation could by no means produce this effect, and an oval motion (which in this case would have to be nearly straight) seems unthinkable and quite inconsistent with the appearances.[22] But I shall gladly explain what occurs to me on this matter, offering it freely to the judgment and criticism of thoughtful men. It is known that the interposition of territorial vapors makes the sun and moon appear large, while the fixed stars and planets are made to appear smaller. Thus the two great luminaries are seen larger when close to the horizon, while the stars appear smaller and for the most part hardly visible. Hence

---

21. By this is meant the greatest angular separation from Jupiter attained by any of the satellites.

22. The marked variation in brightness of the satellites which Galileo observed may be attributed mainly to markings upon their surfaces, though this was not determined until two centuries later. The mention here of a possible oval shape of the orbits is the closest Galileo ever came to accepting Kepler's great discovery of the previous year. Even here, however, he was probably not thinking of Kepler's work but of an idea proposed by earlier astronomers for the moon and the planet Venus.

the stars appear very feeble by day and in twilight, though the moon does not, as we have said. Now from what has been said above, and even more from what we shall say at greater length in our *System*, it follows that not only the earth but also the moon is surrounded by an envelope of vapors, and we may apply precisely the same judgment to the rest of the planets. Hence it does not appear entirely impossible to assume that around Jupiter also there exists an envelope denser than the rest of the aether, about which the Medicean planets revolve as does the moon about the elemental sphere. Through the interposition of this envelope they appear larger when they are in perigee by the removal, or at least the attenuation, of this envelope.

Time prevents my proceeding further, but the gentle reader may expect more soon.

Cesare Beccaria

ON CRIMES AND PUNISHMENTS

Introduction by Michael Graham

For as long as humans have misbehaved in various ways ("misbehavior" being in the eyes of those who lead a society) law and cultural practices have sought to discourage and punish their actions. Crime is as old as the law itself (indeed, it only finds definition in the law) and seems every bit as serious a concern today as it was in 1764, when Cesare Beccaria published the work from which this selection is taken.

Beccaria was born in 1738 in Milan (today in Italy, then under the control of Austria); his family was noble, and he was sent to a Jesuit school before studying law at the University of Bologna. In his twenties he became interested in the works of leading *philosophes,* and he discussed their ideas with friends, two of whom were involved in Milan's penal administration. Their discussions turned to the criminal justice system and how it might be reformed, and his friends urged Beccaria to publish his own views on the issue. Timid and introverted, he did not put his name on the book, but it soon became known that he was its author.

Contrary to Beccaria's expectations, the book was a huge success. It was translated into several languages and won the praise of several monarchs, although not the Pope — it was placed on the *Index of Forbidden Books* by the Vatican two years after its publication. Beccaria's sudden celebrity status brought him an invitation to Paris, the leading city of the Enlightenment movement. Beccaria made the trip, but his shyness left him unequipped for the trendy world of the Parisian salons. Having bombed out on that social stage, he returned to Milan and never published again. Rumors spread that he had been silenced by the Milanese authorities, but this was not true. In fact, local officials were receptive to his ideas, and he held a succession of jobs in the government of Milan. He just never felt the urge to publish again. Beccaria died in 1794, having lived long enough to see some of his ideas put in practice.

The justice systems of medieval and early modern Europe were so far removed from those of today that it might be worth highlighting some of the differences. Early medieval law codes were usually restitutive, meaning that they established scales of compensation to which a crime victim (or, in the case of homicide, the victim's family) would be entitled should the perpetrator be found guilty. Such compensation scales were rarely egalitarian — the injury or death of a nobleman would be much costlier than that of a peasant, for example. The settlement of a crime was often a private transaction.

But as governments became more interested in the administration of justice in the high and late middle ages, there was a shift toward retributive justice. In addition to compensating victims, the guilty (often convicted by juries or judges representing the state) would also have to pay a debt to society, usually extracted by some physical (and very public) punishment such as whipping, mutilation or even death. Indeed, death was often the punishment mandated for a broad range of crimes. There were no prison systems; local jails could only accommodate those awaiting trial (usually at their own expense!), so long-term imprisonment was rarely an option. Relatively few crimes were resolved with convictions (police forces did not exist, so local magistrates had to rely on the help of the community), so those that were resolved brought dramatic punishments designed to warn off others who might be contemplating similar offenses.

The prison as a place of long-term incarceration was a new idea in Beccaria's time. Prisons were still rare, and authorities were reluctant to pay much to keep them up. In London, for example, the rotting hulls of old ships were used for this purpose. Torture was still employed in most European states as a means of gathering evidence. It was thought that those in pain were more likely to tell the truth. You should keep this background in mind when reading Beccaria's work. What did he see as the purpose of punishment? Did he favor restitution, retribution or something else entirely? How would you compare his views of human nature with those of Locke, Hobbes or (going back to the first half of this course) St. Augustine? What were his major criticisms of the justice systems of his own time? Finally, how do you think he would feel about our justice system today?

On Crimes and Punishments

Introduction

If we open our histories, we shall see that laws which are, or should be, pacts between free men, have for the most part been only the instrument of the passions of the few, or the product of an accidental and temporary need. They have never been dictated by a cool scrutineer of human nature, able to condense to one particular the activities of a multitude of men, and consider them from this point of view: *the greatest happiness of the greatest number.*[1] Happy those rare nations who, instead of waiting for human changes . . . to proceed at their sluggish pace from the extremities of evil to the first steps in goodness, have hastened the stages in between with good laws. Worthy, too, of men's gratitude that philosopher who, from the despised obscurity of his study, had the courage to sow widely the first seeds of useful truths, fruitless for so long.

We are now aware of the right relationship between sovereign and subject, between nation and nation; trade has been quickened in the light of philosophic truths disseminated by the printing press; and there has been kindled between the nations a tacit war[2] of industry, altogether more humane, and more worthy of rational beings. Such are the fruits we owe to this enlightened [eighteenth] century. But how very few men have examined and set themselves against the cruelty of punishments and the irregularity of criminal procedure, a part of legislation so fundamental and so neglected through most of Europe. How few have blotted out, by a return to commonly-accepted principles, those errors which have accumulated through the

Edgar E. Knoebel, ed., *Classics of Western Thought Volume III: The Modern World* (Fourth Edition), (New York: Harcourt Brace Jovanovich, 1988), ISBN 0155076841, pp. 154–165 (Selection from Cesare Beccaria, "Of Crimes and Punishments.")

On Crimes and Punishments Reprinted from *Of Crimes and Punishments* by Cesare Beccaria, trans. Jane Grigson (1964), copyright © 1964 Oxford University Press, 11–13, 42–47, 49–51, 55–56, 91–93, 95–96. Reprinted by permission of Oxford University Press.

1. A principle built upon by the English philosopher and lawyer Jeremy Bentham (1748–1833).

2. Silent war (as opposed to military conflict).

centuries — or have attempted at least to curb, with the force of accepted truth, the unbridled advance of ill-directed power, which until our day has exhibited nothing but one long example of cold, legalized barbarity. Yet the groans of the weak, sacrificed to cruel ignorance and wealthy indifference; the barbarous tortures, multiplied with prodigal and useless severity for crimes either illusory or unproved; the filth and horrors of a prison, augmented by that most cruel tormenter of the wretched, uncertainty, ought surely to have struck home to those magisterial persons[3] who guide the opinions of mankind.

The immortal President de Montesquieu[4] has touched briefly on this matter; truth, which is indivisible, has compelled me to follow in the shining path of this great man. But thoughtful men, for whom I write, will know how to distinguish his steps from mine. I shall be happy if, like him, I also can earn, in secret, the thanks of reason's obscure and pacific followers, if I too can inspire that sweet tremor with which feeling spirits respond to those who uphold the cause of humanity.

At this point order should lead us to examine, and distinguish between, the different kinds of crime, and the ways in which they are punished. Crimes and punishments, however, vary so much in their nature according to the differing circumstances of the age and the country, that this would involve us in too great an immensity of tiresome detail. Enough if I indicate the most general principles, and the commonest and most ruinous errors, disabusing in that way no less those who would introduce anarchy, out of a wrong conception of the love of freedom, than those others who would so willingly reduce mankind to the regularity of the cloister.

What punishment is best suited to a given crime? Is death a punishment which is really *useful,* and *necessary* for the security and good order of society? Are torture and instruments of torture *just,* and do they attain the ends propounded by law? What is the best way of preventing crimes? Are the same penalties always equally useful? What influence have they on social custom? These are the problems which ought to be solved with a precision so geometric that it cannot be overcome by mists of sophistry,[5] seductive eloquence, or timidity and doubt.

If it were my sole merit to be the first to make much clearer to Italy those things which other nations have dared to put into writing and now into practice, I should consider myself happy. But if, by upholding the rights of man and the rights of invincible truth, I should help also to rescue from the pains and anguish of death some hapless victim of tyranny and ignorance, which are equally fateful, then the thanks and the tears of that one innocent man, in the transports of his joy, would console me for the contempt of all men.

Mildness of Punishment

. . . It is evident that the purpose of punishments is neither to torture and afflict a sentient[6] creature nor to undo a crime already done. . . . Can one suppose that the shrieks of some poor wretch will call back out of ever-advancing time actions already consummated?

---

3. Important officials and writers.

4. Charles Louis de Secondat Montesquieu (1689–1755), French writer on politics and law.

5. Deceptive, false arguments.

6. Capable of feeling and perception.

The aim, then, of punishment can only be to prevent the criminal from committing new crimes against his countrymen, and to keep others from doing likewise. Punishments, therefore, and the method of inflicting them, should be chosen in due proportion to the crime, so as to make the most efficacious[7] and most lasting impression on the minds of men, and the least painful of impressions on the body of the criminal. Can one read history without horror and disgust at the useless barbarity of the tortures so coldly invented and inflicted by men who were reckoned wise? Must one not shudder at the sight of thousands of unhappy men reduced by misery, either willed or tolerated by the law (which has always favored the few and outraged the many), to a desperate state of nature? The sight of thousands accused of impossible crimes, fabricated by fearfulness and ignorance, or guilty of nothing except loyalty to their own principles, whom men endowed with the same senses, and so with the same passions, have lacerated with the premeditated, protracted formalities of torture, making them a blithe show for a fanatical populace?

For a punishment to be efficacious, it is enough that the disadvantage of the punishment should exceed the advantage anticipated from the crime; in which excess should be calculated the certainty of punishment and the loss of the expected benefit. Everything beyond this, accordingly, is superfluous, and therefore tyrannical. Men regulate the conduct in response to the repeated action of the disadvantages they know, not of the disadvantages they do not know. If we take two nations, in which the scale of crime and the scale of punishment are in due proportion to each other, and if in one the heaviest punishment is perpetual servitude and in the other the wheel,[8] I say that the one will have as much fear of its maximum penalty as the other. . . .

As punishments become more cruel, men's minds, adjusting themselves like fluids to the level of surrounding objects, become increasingly hardened; and human emotion has such an always lively force that after a hundred years of cruel punishment of that kind the wheel would seem only as terrifying as the prison had been earlier on.

The worse the ill that confronts them, the more men are driven to evade it. The very savagery of a punishment has this effect, and to avoid the penalty for the one crime they have already committed, men commit other crimes. Countries and times in which punishments have been most savage have always been those of the bloodiest and most inhuman acts, inasmuch as the spirit of ferocity which guided the hand of the lawgiver also guided the hand of the parricide[9] and the cutthroat. . . .

Two other grievous consequences derive from cruelty of punishment, contrary to that very purpose of preventing crime. One is that cruelty makes it difficult to maintain the necessary proportion between the crime and the punishment, for however much an ingenious cruelty may have multiplied and diversified the modes of punishment, still these cannot exceed that ultimate of force which human physique and sensibility are capable of enduring. When this extreme has been reached it is impossible to find, for more damaging and more atrocious crimes, penalties correspondingly greater such as are required to prevent those crimes. The other consequence is that atrocity in punishment breeds impunity.[10] Men are hedged within certain bounds, whether

---

7. Effective.

8. Torture by stretching a prisoner's body on a wheel as a prelude to death.

9. One who kills a parent.

10. Disdain of, and scoffing at punishment.

of good and evil. A spectacle too atrocious for mankind can result only from a passing frenzy and can never partake of a settled system, proper to law. If the laws are indeed cruel, either they are altered or they occasion a fatal tendency not to punish.

I end with this reflection, that the weight of punishment should be relative to the condition of the nation itself. Stronger and more palpable[11] impress must be made upon the hardened minds of a people who have barely emerged from a state of savagery. A thunderbolt is required to subdue a ferocious lion which walks off at the touch of a bullet. But as men's minds become gentler from living in a state of society, so their sensibility increases; and with that increase there must be diminution in the severity of punishment, if a constant relation is to be maintained between object and feeling.

Of Capital Punishment

This useless prodigality[12] of punishment, which has never made men better, drives me to ask whether death can be inflicted either usefully or justly in a well-organized state. By what right do men take it upon themselves to slaughter other men? Certainly it cannot be that right which gives birth to sovereignty and law — which are nothing but the sum of the smallest portions of each man's personal liberty, representing the public will (which is the aggregate of individual wills). But who has ever been willing to give other men authority to kill him? How can the least possible sacrifice of each individual's liberty ever be equated with the greatest of all good things, that is with human life itself? And were it possible, how would it accord with that other principle, that a man is not master of his own life and death? Which he must be, if he has been able to give that right to others, or to the whole of society.

The penalty of death is not therefore a *right* — I have shown that it cannot be — but a war of the nation against a citizen; because it has been judged necessary or useful to destroy him. But if I shall demonstrate that his death is neither useful nor necessary, I shall have won the cause of humanity.

The death of a citizen can only be thought necessary for two reasons. First, that although he has been deprived of liberty, he still has such connections and such power that the safety of the nation is endangered — and that he can provoke by his existence a revolution dangerous to the settled form of government. The death of such a citizen, then, becomes necessary when a nation is regaining or losing its freedom, or in a period of anarchy, when disorder takes the place of law. But under the calm rule of law, under a form of government which unites the suffrages of the nation, which is secured within and without both by its strength and (perhaps more efficacious than strength itself) by public opinion, . . . I see no need to destroy a citizen, unless his death be the only true way of keeping other men from crime (which is the second reason for believing that the penalty of death can be just or necessary). . . .

It is not intensity of pain which most greatly affects the mind, but its continuance — since human sensibility is more easily and permanently influenced by very small but repeated impressions than by a strong yet transient impact. The power of habit is universal in every living creature; and just as habit helps man to walk and talk and satisfy his needs, so it takes a steady repetition of blows to impress moral ideas upon his mind. It is not the terrible but tran-

---

11. Easily perceptible.
12. Excess.

sient spectacle of a criminal's execution, but the long sustained example of a man's loss of liberty, of a man paying for his offense to society by labors resembling those of a beast of burden, which is the most powerful brake upon crime. 'If we do such misdeeds,' we say to ourselves, 'we shall be reduced to the same endless state of wretchedness.' This is efficacious, because the thought occurs to us over and over again; and it is much more powerful than the notion of death, which is always obscurely in sight on man's horizon. . . .

To be just, a punishment must not exceed that degree of intensity which will deter other men from crime. Now there is no one who, on reflection, would choose the total, permanent loss of his individual liberty, no matter what advantages a crime might bring him. It follows that the severity of a sentence of imprisonment for life, substituted for the penalty of death, would be as likely to deflect the most determined spirit — indeed I should think it more likely to do so. A great many men contemplate death with a steady, tranquil gaze; some out of fanaticism, some out of vanity, . . . some out of a last desperate effort to free themselves from life and misery. But neither fanaticism nor vanity can subsist among the fetters and the chains, under the rod, or under the yoke, or in the iron cage, where the desperate man rather begins than ends his misery. . . .

The penalty of death is ineffectual because of the barbarity of the example it gives to men. If the passions, or the necessity of war, have taught the spilling of human blood, the law, which is the moderator of the conduct of men, ought not to augment[13] so cruel an example — made all the more grievous, the more legalized death is inflicted with deliberation and formality. To me it appears absurd that the laws, which are the expression of the public will, which detest and punish murder, should themselves commit murder; and, to deter citizens from killing, should ordain a killing in public. . . . What are men to think when they look on the wise magistrates and the solemn priests of justice, who with tranquil indifference have a criminal dragged with slow ceremony to his death; or when they see a judge, with unfeeling coldness and perhaps a secret self-satisfaction in his own power, walk past a poor creature who writhes in his last anguish and awaits the fatal blow, on his way to enjoy the comforts and the pleasures of life? 'Ah,' they say, 'these laws are nothing but the pretexts of force; and the cruel, premeditated formalities of justice are no more than a conventional language for . . . [killing]. . . . Murder, which they preach to us as so terrible a misdeed, we see them employing coolly and without aversion. . . .'

If it is objected that in almost all ages and almost all nations some crimes have been punished by death, I shall reply that the objection vanishes in the face of truth, which triumphs over all prescription: that the history of mankind appears a vast sea of errors, among which there float a few confused truths, each one far from the next. Human sacrifices were common to almost every nation; and who would dare to excuse them? That very few societies, and only for a very brief time, have forborne to inflict death, is more favorable than contrary to my case; since it accords with the fate of all great truths, which endure for no longer than a flash, compared with that long dark night in which mankind is enveloped. . . .

The voice of a single philosopher is too weak to overcome the tumult and the cries of so great a multitude whose guide is the blindness of habit. But the few wise men scattered across the face of the earth will echo my words in their innermost hearts. . . .

---

13. Strengthen.

Promptness of Punishment

The more prompt the punishment and the sooner it follows the crime, the more just it will be and the more effective. I say the more just, because the guilty man will thereby be spared the useless and harrowing torments of uncertainty, which grow with the vigor of the imagination and the feeling of his own weakness; the more just, because deprivation of liberty, in itself a punishment, should not precede sentence beyond the requirements of necessity.

Custody, then, is simply the holding of a citizen until he can be judged; and this custody, which is essentially unpleasant, should last as short a time as possible, and should be as little harsh as possible. This short period should be measured both by the length of time necessary for preparing the case, and by the prior rights of those who are already awaiting trial. Confinement should be strict enough only to prevent flight or concealment of the proofs of crime. The trial itself should be over in the shortest possible time. What contrast more cruel than the indolence of a judge and the anguish of the accused? Or the convenience and pleasures of an unfeeling magistrate set against the tears and wretchedness of a prisoner? In general the weight of punishment and the consequences of a crime should have the greatest possible effect on others and an effect as little harsh as possible on the sufferer, since the only just society is one based upon the infallible principle that men's purpose in coming together was to subject themselves to as few evils as possible.

I have said that promptness of punishment is more effective, because the shorter the time between punishment and misdeed, the stronger and more durable in the human spirit is the association of these two ideas of *crime* and *punishment;* so that they come . . . to be considered, one as cause, the other as necessary and unfailing consequence. It has been shown that the association of ideas is the cement of the whole structure of the human intellect, without which pleasure and pain would be isolated sensations devoid of effect. . . .

The proximity of crime and punishment is therefore of the greatest importance, if we desire that in clumsy, commonplace minds, the seductive picture of the rewards of crime be followed at once by the associated idea of punishment. Long delay can only have the effect of separating these two ideas more and more; and any impression made by the chastisement of crime will be made less as chastisement than as spectacle — and only after the horror of a particular crime, which would have served to reinforce the idea of punishment, has weakened in the minds of the spectators. . . .

How Crimes May Be Prevented

It is better to prevent crimes than to punish them. That is the chief purpose of all good legislation, which is the art of leading men — if one may apply the language of mathematics to the blessings and evils of life — toward the maximum of possible happiness and the minimum of possible misery.

But the means hitherto employed are for the most part mistaken, and contrary to the end proposed. It is impossible to reduce the turbulent activities of mankind to a geometrical order devoid of irregularity and confusion. Just as nature's immutable[14] and very simple laws do not prevent disturbance in the movement of the planets, so human laws cannot prevent disturbances

---

14. Unchangeable.

and disorders in the infinite and utterly opposed attractions of pleasure and pain. Yet such is the chimera[15] entertained by men of narrow mind, who have authority in their hands. To prohibit a multitude of trivial acts is not to prevent the crimes which they may occasion, but to create new ones, and to define at pleasure virtues and vices, which we are exhorted to regard as eternal and immutable. What a situation it would reduce us to, if everything which might tempt us to crime were forbidden! Man would have to be deprived of the use of his sense. For every single thing that drives men to commit a single real crime, there are a thousand things which drive them to some trivial act that a bad law insists on calling a crime; and if the likelihood of crimes is proportionate to the number of motives, then to extend the sphere of crime is to increase the likelihood that they will be committed. The majority of laws are nothing but privileges, a tribute, that is to say, by all to the comfort of the few.

We want crime to be prevented? Then we must see to it that laws are clear and simple, and that the whole strength of the nation is concentrated upon their defense, and that no part of its strength is used to destroy them. We must see that the law favors individual men more than classes of men, that men fear the law and nothing but the law. Fear of the laws is salutary,[16] but fear between man and man is dangerous and productive of crime. Men in a state of slavery are more sensual, more debauched,[17] more cruel, than men who are free. Those who are free study the sciences, study the interests of the nation, look upon great things and imitate them; slaves, content with the day, seek in the clamor of debauchery a distraction from the emptiness of their lives. . . .

We want crime to be prevented? Then see to it we must that light and freedom go hand in hand. The evils born of knowledge are in inverse[18] ratio to its diffusion; the benefits in direct ratio. A daring impostor, always a man above the ordinary, wins the adulation of an ignorant people and the hisses of an enlightened one. By making comparisons easier and by multiplying points of view, knowledge opposes sentiment to sentiment and makes them modify each other, a process which becomes all the easier when different people may be expected to hold the same views or advance the same objections. When light fails profusely over a nation, slanderous ignorance is reduced to silence, authority is disarmed of its reasons and starts to tremble, and nothing can shift the forceful vigor of the law; because there exists no enlightened man who does not approve the compacts, public, open, and effective, which uphold the security of the people. . . .

Another way of preventing crime is that of rewarding virtue. On this proposition I observe a total silence in the laws of every nation at the present time. If prizes awarded by academies for the discovery of useful truths have multiplied both knowledge and good books, why should prizes distributed by the sovereign's beneficent hand not increase virtuous actions? The coin of honor is always inexhaustible and fruitful in the hands of one who distributes it wisely.

Finally, the surest but most difficult way of preventing crime is to improve education; this is too vast a subject, and one which exceeds the limits I have set myself. . . . One great man,[19] who gives light to the humanity which persecutes him, has explained in detail the principles of an education truly useful to mankind; which should comprise, not a sterile multitude of sub-

---

15. Fantasy.

16. Healthy, beneficial.

17. Self-indulgent.

18. Opposite.

19. Meant here is the French writer and philosopher Jean Jacques Rousseau (1712–1778) and his educational novel, *Émile.* (See selection 11.)

jects, but subjects chosen with precision and care; which should substitute, both in the moral and the physical phenomena . . . [presented] to the fresh minds of the young, originals for copies; which should lead to virtue along the easy path of feeling, and divert from evil along the never-failing path of necessity and trouble, instead of using the uncertain method of command which produces no more than a momentary and counterfeit obedience.

Conclusion

From all I have written a very useful theorem may be deduced, little though it conforms to custom, that common lawgiver of the nations. It is this: *In order that punishment should never be an act of violence committed by one or many against a private citizen, it is essential that it be public, speedy, and necessary, as little as the circumstances will allow, proportionate to the crime, and established by law.*

The Declaration of Independence

THE DECLARATION OF THE RIGHTS OF MAN AND THE CITIZEN

Introduction by Stephen Harp

In the late eighteenth century, revolutionaries in both the United States and France justified their actions with written documents. Much like earlier *philosophes,* revolutionaries either took for granted or spelled out the "natural laws" they believed inherent in humankind, but unlike most *philosophes* they did so within political assemblies that generated declarations and constitutions. In the course of the American and French Revolutions, revolutionaries attempted to define the rights and responsibilities of "citizens" (a word implying equal political participation in a constitutional state rather than the implied monarchy of the term "subjects"). Although the American *Declaration of Independence* and the French *Declaration of the Rights of Man and the Citizen* reflect the different social and political contexts in which they were written, we have grouped them together here in order to point out the international character of the growing political impact of the notion of human rights at the end of the eighteenth century.

As you know, Thomas Jefferson wrote the *Declaration of Independence* in 1776, and it was revised, then accepted by the revolutionary Congress on July 4th. Crafted early in the former colonies' struggles with Great Britain, the Declaration lays out the transgressions of King George III. Signers of the Declaration, who largely saw themselves as British people wronged by their government, did not want to alienate the British parliament or other sympathizers within Britain any more than necessary, so the king became a focal point of their criticisms. As a declaration of independence, rather than a bill of rights (various states, including Virginia, passed bills of citizens' rights as early as 1776, well before the more familiar first ten amendments to the U.S. Constitution), the *Declaration of Independence* does not generally lay out the rights and responsibilities of citizens. Instead, you'll need to read through the critiques of George III in order to infer what rights the kind had denied the colonists. What are the various rights that revolutionaries are implicitly claiming? Where do they come from — God or nature? What is the vision of kingship? In what ways do the criticisms of the king hint at the later U.S. Constitution's Bill of Rights? What is the influence of Locke and the *philosophes* on the

Declaration? Your version of the Declaration includes both Jefferson's original text and the changes made by the revolutionary Congress. As you read, note the differences because they reveal contentious issues among the new states, notably slavery.

Whereas the Americans were fighting for independence from the British king, French revolutionaries in 1789 attempted to transform France's absolute monarchy into a constitutional monarchy. In June 1789, the Estates General had been transformed into a National Assembly dominated by members of the former Third Estate. The members of the National Assembly claimed to represent the nation, or people of France as a whole, not merely their own estate. By August, both the streets of Paris (you no doubt know of the storming of the Bastille on July 14, 1789) and the French countryside had experienced widespread rioting of crowds demanding change. In August 1879, the Assembly forged the *Declaration of Rights of Man and the Citizen,* which was meant to be a preamble to an eventual constitution establishing a constitutional monarchy in France.

The *Declaration of Rights of Man and the Citizen* focuses quite specifically on the rights and responsibilities of citizens. Although not really implemented during the French Revolution, the Declaration lays out ideas that would define the meaning of political liberalism. (By defining "liberty") for much of Europe in the nineteenth century. What are the rights of man and where do they originate? How does the Declaration define liberty? What are the protections that a citizen has from the state? What responsibilities does the citizen have to the state? In what ways does the French Declaration differ from the American *Declaration of Independence?* The French Declaration was essentially a contemporary of the U.S. Bill of Rights, and you'll notice many parallels. What are they? What are the differences? Why do you suppose there is no equivalent of the states' rights so important in the American Bill of Rights?

Both the Declarations proclaim the natural rights of man. While the American Declaration focuses very obviously on the thirteen states, the French Declaration has an even more universal quality. All men in the world presumably share these rights. Yet, by refusing to define who specifically was included, much as the American Declaration avoids mentioning slavery, the French Declaration did not guarantee equal rights to all of the humankind. Do the poor have political rights (voting and holding office) as well as civil rights (freedom of expression, presumption of innocence and so on)? And what about women? When Olympe de Gouges wrote a Declaration of Rights for women during a more radical phase of the French Revolution, she found little support even among more radical revolutionaries. Yet declarations such as these can be used by the oppressed, even though framers did not intend to give rights to women and people of color. In what ways might you use the arguments of either declaration to prove that all people, despite their differences of race and gender, might be included as full-fledged citizens? Do you believe the documents to be a sham for white men to get and maintain power?

The Declaration of Independence

[*July 4, 1776*]

WHEN, IN THE COURSE OF HUMAN EVENTS, it becomes necessary for one people to dissolve the political bands which have connected them with another, and to assume among the powers of the earth the separate and equal station to which the laws of nature and of nature's God entitle them, a decent respect to the opinions of mankind requires that they should declare the causes which impel them to the separation.

We hold these truths to be self evident; that all men are created equal; that they are endowed by their Creator with CERTAIN [*inherent and*] inalienable rights; that among these are life, liberty, and the pursuit of happiness; that to secure these rights, governments are instituted among men, deriving their just powers from the consent of the governed; that whenever any form of government becomes destructive of these ends, it is the right of the people to alter or to abolish it, and to institute new government, laying its foundation on such principles, and organizing its powers in such form, as to them shall seem most likely to effect their safety and happiness. Prudence, indeed, will dictate that governments long established should not be changed for light and transient causes; and accordingly all experience hath shown that mankind are more disposed to suffer while evils are sufferable, than to right themselves by abolishing the forms to which they are accustomed. But when a long train of abuses and usurpations, [*begun at a distinguished period and*] pursuing invariably the same object, evinces a design to reduce them under absolute despotism, it is their right, it is their duty to throw off such government, and to provide new guards for their future security. Such has been the patient sufferance of these colonies; and such is now the necessity which constrains them to ALTER [*expunge*] their former systems of government. The history of the present king of Great Britain is a history of REPEATED [*unremitting*] injuries and usurpations, ALL HAVING [*among which appears no solitary fact to contradict the uniform tenor of the rest, but all have*] in direct object the establishment of an absolute tyranny over these states. To prove this, let facts be submitted to a candid world [*for the truth of which we pledge a faith yet unsullied by falsehood*].

He has refused his assent to laws the most wholesome and necessary for the public good.

He has forbidden his governors to pass laws of immediate and pressing importance, unless suspended in their operation till his assent should be obtained; and, when so suspended, he has utterly neglected to attend to them.

He has refused to pass other laws for the accommodation of large districts of people, unless those people would relinquish the right of representation in the legislature, a right inestimable to them, and formidable to tyrants only.

Merrill Peterson, ed., *The Portable Thomas Jefferson* (New York: Viking/Penguin, 1975) ISBN 0140150803, pp. 235–241 ("Declaration of Independence").

The text is taken from Jefferson's Autobiography. The form of the Declaration as reported is printed in roman type, the parts stricken by Congress are bracketed in italics, while the parts substituted are in small capitals. [Ed.]

He has called together legislative bodies at places unusual, uncomfortable, and distant from the depository of their public records, for the sole purpose of fatiguing them into compliance with his measures.

He has dissolved representative houses repeatedly [*and continually*] for opposing with manly firmness his invasions on the rights of the people.

He has refused for a long time after such dissolutions to cause others to be elected, whereby the legislative powers, incapable of annihilation, have returned to the people at large for their exercise, the state remaining, in the meantime, exposed to all the dangers of invasion from without and convulsions within.

He has endeavored to prevent the population, of these states; for that purpose obstructing the laws for naturalization of foreigners, refusing to pass others to encourage their migrations hither, and raising the conditions of new appropriations of lands.

He has OBSTRUCTED [*suffered*] the administration of justice BY [*totally to cease in some of these states*] refusing his assent to laws for establishing judiciary powers.

He has made [*our*] judges dependent on his will alone for the tenure of their offices, and the amount and payment of their salaries.

He has erected a multitude of new offices, [*by a self-assumed power*] and sent hither swarms of new officers to harass our people and eat out their substance.

He has kept among us in times of peace standing armies [*and ships of war*] without the consent of our legislatures.

He has affected to render the military independent of, and superior to, the civil power.

He has combined with others to subject us to a jurisdiction foreign to our constitutions and unacknowledged by our laws, giving his assent to their acts of pretended legislation for quartering large bodies of armed troops among us; for protecting them by a mock trial from punishment for any murders which they should commit on the inhabitants of these states; for cutting off our trade with all parts of the world; for imposing taxes on us without our consent; for depriving us IN MANY CASES of the benefits of trial by jury; for transporting us beyond seas to be tried for pretended offences; for abolishing the free system of English laws in a neighboring province, establishing therein an arbitrary government, and enlarging its boundaries, so as to render it at once an example and fit instrument for introducing the same absolute rule into these COLONIES [*states*]; for taking away our charters, abolishing our most valuable laws, and altering fundamentally the forms of our governments; for suspending our own legislatures, and declaring themselves invested with power to legislate for us in all cases whatsoever.

He has abdicated government here BY DECLARING US OUT OF HIS PROTECTION, AND WAGING WAR AGAINST US [*withdrawing his governors, and declaring us out of his allegiance and protection*].

He has plundered our seas, ravaged our coasts, burnt our towns, and destroyed the lives of our people.

He is at this time transporting large armies of foreign mercenaries to complete the works of death, desolation and tyranny already begun with circumstances of cruelty and perfidy SCARCELY PARALLELED IN THE MOST BARBAROUS AGES, AND TOTALLY unworthy the head of a civilized nation.

He has constrained our fellow citizens taken captive on the high seas, to bear arms against their country, to become the executioners of their friends and brethren, or to fall themselves by their hands.

He has EXCITED DOMESTIC INSURRECTION AMONG US, AND HAS endeavored to bring on the inhabitants of our frontiers, the merciless Indian savages, whose known rule of warfare is an undistinguished destruction of all ages, sexes and conditions [*of existence*].

He has waged cruel war against human nature itself, violating its most sacred rights of life and liberty in the persons of a distant people who never offended him, captivating and carrying them into slavery in another hemisphere, or to incur miserable death in their transportation hither. This piratical warfare, the opprobrium of INFIDEL powers, is the warfare of the CHRISTIAN king of Great Britain. Determined to keep open a market where MEN should be bought and sold, he has prostituted his negative for suppressing every legislative attempt to prohibit or to restrain this execrable commerce. And that this assemblage of horrors might want no fact of distinguished die, he is now exciting those very people to rise in arms among us, and to purchase that liberty of which he has deprived them, by murdering the people on whom he also obtruded them: thus paying off former crimes committed against the LIBERTIES of one people, with crimes which he urges them to commit against the LIVES of another.]

In every stage of these oppressions we have petitioned for redress in the most humble terms: our repeated petitions have been answered only by repeated injuries.

A prince whose character is thus marked by every act which may define a tyrant is unfit to be the ruler of a FREE people [*who mean to be free. Future ages will scarcely believe that the hardiness of one man adventured, within the short compass of twelve years only, to lay a foundation so broad and so undisguised for tyranny over a people fostered and fixed in principles of freedom.*]

Nor have we been wanting in attentions to our British brethren. We have warned them from time to time of attempts by their legislature to extend AN UNWARRANTABLE [*a*] jurisdiction over US [*these our states*]. We have reminded them of the circumstances of our emigration and settlement here, [*no one of which could warrant so strange a pretension: that these were effected at the expense of our own blood and treasure, unassisted by the wealth or the strength of Great Britain: that in constituting indeed our several forms of government, we had adopted one common king, thereby laying a foundation for perpetual league and amity with them: but that submission to their parliament was no part of our constitution, nor even in idea, if history may be credited: and,*] we have, appealed to their native justice and magnanimity AND WE HAVE CONJURED THEM BY [*as well as to*] the ties of our common kindred to disavow these usurpations which WOULD INEVITABLY [*were likely to*] interrupt our connection and correspondence. They too have been deaf to the voice of justice and of consanguinity. WE MUST THEREFORE [*and when occasions have been given them, by the regular course of their laws, of removing from their councils the disturbers of our harmony, they have, by their free election, re-established them in power. At this very time too, they are permitting their chief magistrate to send over not only soldiers of our common blood, but Scotch and foreign mercenaries to invade and destroy us. These facts have given the last stab to agonizing affection, and manly spirit bids us to renounce forever these unfeeling brethren. We must endeavor to forget our former love for them, and hold them as we hold the rest of mankind, enemies in war, in peace friends. We might have a free and a great people together; but a communication of grandeur and of freedom, it seems, is below their dignity. Be it so, since they will have it. The road to happiness and to glory is open to us, too. We will tread it apart from them, and*] acquiesce in the necessity which denounces our [*eternal*] separation AND HOLD THEM AS WE HOLD THE REST OF MANKIND, ENEMIES IN WAR, IN PEACE FRIENDS!

We, therefore, the representatives of the United States of America in General Congress assembled, appealing to the supreme judge of the world for the rectitude of our intentions, do in the name, and by the authority of the good people of these COLONIES, SOLEMNLY PUBLISH AND DECLARE, THAT THESE UNITED COLONIES ARE, AND OF RIGHT OUGHT TO BE FREE AND INDEPENDENT STATES; THAT THEY ARE ABSOLVED FROM ALL ALLEGIANCE TO THE BRITISH CROWN AND THAT ALL POLITICAL CONNECTION BETWEEN THEM AND THE STATE OF GREAT BRITAIN IS, AND OUGHT TO BE, TOTALLY DISSOLVED; [*states reject and renounce all allegiance and subjection to the kings of Great Britain and all others who may hereafter claim by, through or under them; we utterly dissolve all political connection which may heretofore have subsisted between us and the people or parliament of Great Britain: and finally we do assert and declare these colonies to be free and independent states,*] and that as free and independent states, they have full power to levy war, conclude peace, contract alliances, establish commerce, and to do all other acts and things which independent states may of right do.

And for the support of this declaration, with a firm reliance on the protection of divine providence, we mutually pledge to each other our lives, our fortunes, and our sacred honor.

22. Declaration of the Rights of Man and of the Citizen

After the dramatic assertion of revolutionary principles on the Night of the Fourth of August, the National Assembly moved quite quickly to the formulation of a declaration of rights that was to serve as a preamble to the new national constitution. The final articles of the declaration were adopted on 26 August 1789.

The representatives of the French people, constituted as the National Assembly, considering that ignorance, disregard, or contempt for the rights of man are the sole causes of public misfortunes and the corruption of governments, have resolved to set forth, in a solemn declaration, the natural, inalienable, and sacred rights of man, so that the constant presence of this declaration may ceaselessly remind all members of the social body of their rights and duties; so that the acts of the legislative power and those of the executive power may be the more respected, since it will be possible at each moment to compare them against the goal of every political institution; and so that the demands of the citizens, grounded henceforth on simple and incontestable principles, may always be directed to the maintenance of the constitution and to the welfare of all.

Consequently, the National Assembly recognizes and declares, in the presence and under the auspices of the Supreme Being, the following rights of man and the citizen:

Article 1. Men are born and remain free and equal in rights. Social distinctions can be based only on public utility.

Article 2. The aim of every political association is the preservation of the natural and imprescriptible rights of man. These rights are liberty, property, security, and resistance to oppression.

Article 3. The source of all sovereignty resides essentially in the nation. No body, no individual can exercise authority that does not explicitly proceed from it.

Article 4. Liberty consists in being able to do anything that does not injure another; thus the only limits upon each man's exercise of his natural rights are those that guarantee enjoyment of these same rights to the other members of society. These limits can be determined only by law.

Article 5. The law has the right to forbid only actions harmful to society. No action may be prevented that is not forbidden by law, and no one may be constrained to do what the law does not order.

Article 6. The law is the expression of the general will. All citizens have the right to participate personally, or through their representatives, in its formation. It must be the same for all,

Keith Baker, ed., *Readings in Western Civilization Vol. 7: The Old Regime and the French Revolution* (Chicago: University of Chicago Press, 1987) ISBN 0226069508, pp. 237–9 ("Declaration of the Rights of Man and the Citizen").

From *Archives parlementaires de 1787 à 1860, première série (1787 à 1799)*, edited by M. J. Mavidal and M. E. Laurent, 2d ed., 82 vols. (Paris: Dupont, 1879–1913), vol. 9, pp. 236–37. Translated for this volume by the editor, Keith Michael Baker.

whether it protects or punishes. All citizens, being equal in its eyes, are equally admissible to all public dignities, positions, and employments, according to their ability, and on the basis of no other distinction than that of their virtues and talents.

Article 7. No man may be accused, arrested, or detained except in cases determined by the law and according to the forms it has prescribed. Those who solicit, expedite, execute, or effect the execution of arbitrary orders must be punished; but every citizen summoned or seized by virtue of the law must obey at once; he makes himself guilty by resistance.

Article 8. The law must lay down only those penalties that are strictly and evidently necessary, and no one may be punished except by virtue of a law established and promulgated prior to the offense, and legally applied.

Article 9. Every man is presumed innocent until he has been found guilty; if it is considered indispensable to arrest him, any severity not necessary to secure his person must be strictly repressed by law.

Article 10. No one must be disturbed because of his opinions, even in religious matters, provided their expression does not trouble the public order established by law.

Article 11. The free expression of thought and opinions is one of the most precious rights of man: thus every citizen may freely speak, write, and print, subject to accountability for abuse of this freedom in the cases determined by law.

Article 12. To guarantee the rights of man and the citizen requires a public force; this force is therefore instituted for the benefit of all, and not for the personal advantage of those to whom it is entrusted.

Article 13. A common tax is indispensable to maintain the public force and support the expenses of administration. It must be shared equally among all the citizens in proportion to their means.

Article 14. All citizens have the right to ascertain, personally or through their representatives, the necessity of the public tax, to consent to it freely, to know how it is spent, and to determine its amount, basis, mode of collection, and duration.

Article 15. Society has the right to demand that every public agent give an account of his administration.

Article 16. A society in which the guarantee of rights is not secured, or the separation of powers not clearly established, has no constitution.

Article 17. Property being an inviolable and sacred right, no one can be deprived of it, unless legally established public necessity obviously demands it, and upon condition of a just and prior indemnity.

William Wordsworth

"TABLES TURNED" AND "TINTERN ABBEY"

Introduction by Stephen Harp

In the late eighteenth and early nineteenth centuries, an artistic and literary movement known as Romanticism had an important philosophical role in questioning the fundamental ideas of the Enlightenment. The Enlightenment stood above all for reason, embodied in our intellects, as a means to understanding the truth of the universe. In contrast, Romantics instead maintained that the influence of nature on our imaginative and emotionally creativity was crucial; Romantics wanted to give free rein to our emotions as the best means for attaining truth.

Romantic artists (including writers and musicians as well as painters) criticized not only the mechanistic rationality of the Enlightenment but also its means for discovering truth. For Romantics who prized the individual artist's genius above all, prose writing so important during the eighteenth century was like a straightjacket, constraining the creative impulses of the artist's exploration of the truth. Among writers, poetry was often preferred over prose as giving freer rein to the writer's imagination. The ambiguities and multiple meanings of individual words allowed poets to evoke a complex reality not unlike nature's own, whereas good prose writing — like your essays — was supposed to be clear so that readers could grasp the meaning.

The British poet William Wordsworth (1770–1850) was a leading Romantic writer. In the preface to *Lyrical Ballads*, Wordsworth laid out a virtual manifesto of Romanticism. Wordsworth maintained the importance of feelings and imagination in the discovery of truth. He argued that both could be better expressed in the form of poetry. The role of the natural world was also critical for Wordsworth; truth could be found in nature and expressed in poetry. The role of the natural world was also critical for Wordsworth; truth could be found in nature and expressed in poetry. Wordsworth was a very popular poet in nineteenth-century Britain. Early tourists to natural sights, such as the Lake District in Northern England, schlepped their volume of Wordsworth to the places he had visited and described, read him along the way, and attempted to appreciate Wordsworth's aesthetically-defined truth.

The first poem you will read is "Tables Turned." According to Wordsworth, where might true knowledge be found? As you read, assess the contention that poetry might be a more adequate means for relaying truth. Do you agree that "we murder to dissect" or that books are mere "barren leaves"? How does Wordsworth's suggestion of color and sound — thus our senses — help to make his point that one might gain a richer understanding of the world from nature than from books?

Our second poem, "Tintern Abbey," is the last in *Lyrical Ballads*. It is more complex poem, illustrating the fusion of self-reflection and nature that Wordsworth calls for in "Tables Turned." As you read "Tintern Abbey," how does Wordsworth describe his own coming of age with constant reference to his experience and his memory of his natural surroundings? How does he use natural changes (such as the five summers and five winters at the beginning) to enrich a sense of time having passed?

Romantics are often described not as having interest in nature for nature's sake so much as an interest in nature for its use in self-discovery and reflection. Nature is thus an inspiration, and it is closely tied to the poet's own genius. The Romantics have had an incredible influence on later understandings of landscapes and the value of nature for human beings. Do you sense any parallels between the nature of "Tintern Abbey" and that of modern environmentalism?

Despite all of the differences between the *philosophes* and the Romantics, there is at least one important similarity. Whereas the *philosophes* focused on an individual's self-discovery by throwing off the chains of superstition and ignorance, Romantics argued for individual artistic discovery inspired by nature. Both thus give the individual a pride of place. Do you get a sense of the primacy of the individual in Wordsworth's poetry?

It is very normal, even desirable, to read a poem several times so that you can appreciate the richness of the language.

The Tables Turned

AN EVENING SCENE ON THE SAME SUBJECT

Up! up! my friend, and quit your books,
Or surely you'll grow double;
Up! up! my friend, and clear your looks;
Why all this toil and trouble?

The sun, above the mountain's head,   5
A freshening luster mellow
Through all the long green fields has spread,
His first sweet evening yellow.

Books! 'tis a dull and endless strife:
Come, hear the woodland linnet,[1]   10
How sweet his music! on my life,
There's more of wisdom in it.

And hark! how blithe the throstle[2] sings!
He, too, is no mean preacher;
Come forth into the light of things,   15
Let Nature be your teacher.

She has a world of ready wealth,
Our minds and hearts to bless —
Spontaneous wisdom breathed by health,
Truth breathed by cheerfulness.   20

M. H. Abrams, General Editor, *The Norton Anthology of English Literature* Vol. 2 (Fourth Edition), (New York: W. W. Norton, 1979) ISBN 0393950514, pp. 154–8 (William Wordsworth, "Tables Turned" and "Tintern Abbey")

1. A small finch, common in Europe.
2. The song thrush.

One impulse from a vernal wood
May teach you more of man,
Of moral evil and of good,
Than all the sages can.

Sweet is the lore which Nature brings;   25
Our meddling intellect
Misshapes the beauteous forms of things —
We murder to dissect.

Enough of Science and of Art;
Close up those barren leaves;
Come forth, and bring with you a heart   30
That watches and receives.

1798

Lines[1]

COMPOSED A FEW MILES ABOVE TINTERN ABBEY
ON REVISITING THE BANKS OF THE WYE
DURING A TOUR. JULY 13, 1798

Five years have passed; five summers, with the length
Of five long winters! and again I hear
These waters, rolling from their mountain-springs
With a soft inland murmur. Once again
Do I behold these steep and lofty cliffs,   5
That on a wild secluded scene impress
Thoughts of more deep seclusion; and connect
The landscape with the quiet of the sky.
The day is come when I again repose
Here, under this dark sycamore, and view   10
These plots of cottage ground, these orchard tufts,
Which at this season, with their unripe fruits,
Are clad in one green hue, and lose themselves
'Mid groves and copses. Once again I see
These hedgerows, hardly hedgerows, little lines   15
Of sportive wood run wild; these pastoral farms,
Green to the very door; and wreaths of smoke
Sent up, in silence, from among the trees!
With some uncertain notice, as might seem
Of vagrant dwellers in the houseless woods,   20
Or of some Hermit's cave, where by his fire
The Hermit sits alone.

                These beauteous forms,
Through a long absence, have not been to me
As is a landscape to a blind man's eye;

---

1. "No poem of mine was composed under circumstances more pleasant for me to remember than this. I began it upon leaving Tintern, after crossing the Wye, and concluded it just as I was entering Bristol in the evening after a ramble of 4 or 5 days, with my sister. Not a line of it was altered, and not any part of it written down till I reached Bristol" (Wordsworth). The poem was printed as the last item in *Lyrical Ballads*.

    Wordsworth had first visited the Wye valley and the ruins of Tintern Abbey, in Monmouthshire, while on a solitary walking tour in August of 1793, when he was 23 years old. The puzzling difference between the present landscape and the remembered "picture of the mind" (line 61) gives rise to an intricately organized meditation, in which the poet reviews his past, evaluates the present, and (through his sister as intermediary) anticipates the future, until he ends by rounding back quietly upon the scene which had been his point of departure.

But oft, in lonely rooms, and 'mid the din   25
Of towns and cities, I have owed to them,
In hours of weariness, sensations sweet,
Felt in the blood, and felt along the heart;
And passing even into my purer mind,
With tranquil restoration — feelings too   30
Of unremembered pleasure; such, perhaps,
As have no slight or trivial influence
On that best portion of a good man's life,
His little, nameless, unremembered, acts
Of kindness and of love. Nor less, I trust,   35
To them I may have owed another gift,
Of aspect more sublime; that blessed mood,
In which the burthen of the mystery,
In which the heavy and the weary weight
Of all this unintelligible world,   40
Is lightened — that serene and blessed mood,
In which the affections gently lead us on —
Until, the breath of this corporeal frame
And even the motion of our human blood
Almost suspended, we are laid asleep   45
In body, and become a living soul;
While with an eye made quiet by the power
Of harmony, and the deep power of joy,
We see into the life of things.

           If this
Be but a vain belief, yet, oh! how oft —   50
In darkness and amid the many shapes
Of joyless daylight; when the fretful stir
Unprofitable, and the fever of the world,
Have hung upon the beatings of my heart —
How oft, in spirit, have I turned to thee,   55
O sylvan Wye! thou wanderer through the woods,
How often has my spirit turned to thee!

    And now, with gleams of half-extinguished thought
With many recognitions dim and faint,
And somewhat of a sad perplexity,   60
The picture of the mind revives again;
While here I stand, not only with the sense
Of present pleasure, but with pleasing thoughts
That in this moment there is life and food
For future years. And so I dare to hope,   65
Though changed, no doubt, from what I was when first
I came among these hills; when like a roe
I bounded o'er the mountains, by the sides

Of the deep rivers, and the lonely streams,
Wherever nature led — more like a man   70
Flying from something that he dreads than one
Who sought the thing he loved. For nature then
(The coarser pleasures of my boyish days,
And their glad animal movements all gone by)
To me was all in all. — I cannot paint   75
What then I was. The sounding cataract
Haunted me like a passion; the tall rock,
The mountain, and the deep and gloomy wood,
Their colors and their forms, were then to me
An appetite; a feeling and a love,   80
That had no need of a remoter charm,
By thought supplied, nor any interest
Unborrowed from the eye. –– That time is past,
And all its aching joys are now no more,
And all its dizzy raptures.[2] Not for this   85
Faint[3] I, nor mourn nor murmur; other gifts
Have followed; for such loss, I would believe,
Abundant recompense. For I have learned
To look on nature, not as in the hour
Of thoughtless youth; but hearing oftentimes   90
The still, sad music of humanity,
Nor harsh nor grating, though of ample power
To chasten and subdue. And I have felt
A presence that disturbs me with the joy
Of elevated thoughts; a sense sublime   95
Of something far more deeply interfused,
Whose dwelling is the light of setting suns,
And the round ocean and the living air,
And the blue sky, and in the mind of man:
A motion and a spirit, that impels   100
All thinking things, all objects of all thought,
And rolls through all things. Therefore am I still
A lover of the meadows and the woods,
And mountains; and of all that we behold
From this green earth; of all the mighty world   105

---

2. Lines 66 ff. contain Wordsworth's famous description of the three stages of his growing up, defined in terms of his evolving relations to the natural scene: the young boy's purely physical responsiveness (lines 73–74); the post-adolescent's aching, dizzy, and equivocal passions — a love which is more like dread (lines 67–72, 75–85: this was his state of mind on the occasion of his first visit); his present state (lines 85 ff.), in which for the first time he adds thought to sense. All his knowledge of human suffering, so painfully acquired in the interim, chastens him while it enriches the visible scene like a chord of music, and he has gained also awareness of an immanent "presence" which links his mind and all the elements of the external world.

3. Lose heart.

Of eye, and ear — both what they half create,[4]
And what perceive; well pleased to recognize
In nature and the language of the sense
The anchor of my purest thoughts, the nurse,
The guide, the guardian of my heart, and soul   110
Of all my moral being.

                    Nor perchance,
If I were not thus taught, should I the more
Suffer my genial spirits[5] to decay:
For thou art with me here upon the banks
Of this fair river; thou my dearest Friend,[6]   115
My dear, dear Friend; and in thy voice I catch
The language of my former heart, and read
My former pleasures in the shooting lights
Of thy wild eyes. Oh! yet a little while
May I behold in thee what I was once,   120
My dear, dear Sister! and this prayer I make,
Knowing that Nature never did betray
The heart that loved her; 'tis her privilege,
Through all the years of this our life, to lead
From joy to joy: for she can so inform   125
The mind that is within us, so impress
With quietness and beauty, and so feed
With lofty thoughts, that neither evil tongues,
Rash judgments, nor the sneers of selfish men,
Nor greetings where no kindness is, nor all   130
The dreary intercourse of daily life,
Shall e'er prevail against us, or disturb
Our cheerful faith, that all which we behold
Is full of blessings. Therefore let the moon
Shine on thee in thy solitary walk;   135
And let the misty mountain winds be free
To blow against thee: and, in after years,
When these wild ecstasies shall be matured
Into a sober pleasure; when thy mind
Shall be a mansion for all lovely forms,   140
Thy memory be as a dwelling place

---

4. The fact that apparent changes in the sensible world have turned out to be projected by the changing mind of the observer gives evidence that the faculties "half create" the world; the part that is "perceived" (line 107) is what has remained unchanged between the two visits. This view that the "creative sensibility" contributes to its own perceptions is often reiterated in the early books of *The Prelude*.

5. "Genial" is here the adjectival form of the noun "genius" ("native powers"). The sense of lines 111–13 is: "Perhaps, even if I had not learned to look at nature in the way I have just described, I would not have suffered a decay in my creative powers."

6. His sister Dorothy.

For all sweet sounds and harmonies; oh! then,
If solitude, or fear, or pain, or grief
Should be thy portion, with what healing thoughts
Of tender joy wilt thou remember me,   145
And these my exhortations! Nor, perchance —
If I should be where I no more can hear
Thy voice, nor catch from thy wild eyes these gleams
Of past existence[7] — wilt thou then forget
That on the banks of this delightful stream   150
We stood together; and that I, so long
A worshiper of Nature, hither came
Unwearied in that service; rather say
With warmer love — oh! with far deeper zeal
Of holier love. Nor wilt thou then forget,   155
That after many wanderings, many years
Of absence, these steep woods and lofty cliffs,
And this green pastoral landscape, were to me
More dear, both for themselves and for thy sake!

1798

---

7. I.e., his own "past experience" five years before; see lines 116–19.

Charles Darwin

THE ORIGIN OF SPECIES

THE DESCENT OF MAN

Introduction by Shelley Baranowski

The British naturalist Charles Darwin (1809–1882) considered two careers, one as a physician, the other as an Anglican clergyman, before embarking on a five-year scientific expedition that laid the foundations of modern evolutionary theory. After receiving his bachelor's degree from the University of Cambridge in 1831, Darwin sailed around the world on the HMS Beagle to observe different geological formations, fossils, and living organisms.

Already influenced by the geologist Sir Charles Lyell, whose work challenged the prevailing scientific view that species remained essentially unchanged after their origination, Darwin grew increasingly convinced that present species evolved from earlier life forms, which he observed had been preserved as fossils, rather than emerging as unique and discrete acts of creation. Further swayed by the work on population by the classical liberal economist Thomas Malthus, Darwin argued that the evolution of species came from "natural selection" arising from the competition for limited food supplies. The "survival of the fittest" among the offspring of species resulted in the transmission of favorable variations to future generations; variations that would bring further adaptability and improvement in that species. Darwin spent over two decades after returning from his voyage in 1836 compiling additional data to support his hypothesis, finally publishing *The Origin of Species* in 1859. Although in ill health, he produced other works, among them *The Descent of Man* (1871), which postulated that human beings had evolved from lower primates.

On the surface, Darwin's theory of evolution seemed consistent with notions of progress stemming from the Enlightenment that reigned during the nineteenth century. Yet it depicted a slow but ceaseless process of change and adaptation that appeared to serve no grand underlying purpose. Darwin insisted that his work affirmed God's ultimate role in creation, yet his work infuriated his religious opponents because it challenged the Biblical view of creation and the place of humankind in it. The on-going controversy over the teaching of "creationism" indicates that the debate over Darwin's implications for religion continues to this day. Yet the acceptance that Darwin's theories achieved during the second half of the nineteenth century went well beyond scientific circles. Although Darwin did not intend it, "social Darwinists" appropriated Darwin's ideas, especially the "survival of the fittest," to justify European imperialism and the construction of racial hierarchies to support it, the intensifying arms race among the European great powers before World War I, and even middle and upper class attacks on socialism and the working class.

As you read the selections from Darwin below, ask yourself how Darwin's work, so dependent on observation and the meticulous collection of data, might have challenged the assumptions of science in place since the seventeenth century. Despite Darwin's insistence to the contrary, why would clergymen, theologians, and many religious believers have objected to evolution, especially the evolution of human beings? Why might Darwin's ideas have seemed appropriate to social Darwinists as explanations for the evolution, prosperity, or decline of human societies, even if Darwin objected to that sort of appropriation of his theories?

The Origin of Species

As this whole volume is one long argument, it may be convenient to the reader to have the leading facts and inferences briefly recapitulated.

That many and serious objections may be advanced against the theory of descent with modification through variation and natural selection, I do not deny. I have endeavored to give to them their full force. Nothing at first can appear more difficult to believe than that the more complex organs and instincts have been perfected, not by means superior to, though analogous with, human reason, but by the accumulation of innumerable slight variations, each good for the individual possessor. Nevertheless, this difficulty, though appearing to our imagination insuperably great, cannot be considered real if we admit the following propositions, namely, that all parts of the organization and instincts offer, at least, individual differences — that there is a struggle for existence leading to the preservation of profitable deviations[1] of structure or instinct — and, lastly, that gradations in the state of perfection of each organ may have existed, each good of its kind. The truth of these propositions cannot, I think, be disputed.

It is, no doubt, extremely difficult even to conjecture by what gradations many structures have been perfected, more especially among broken and failing groups of organic beings, which have suffered much extinction; but we see so many strange gradations in nature, that we ought to be extremely cautious in saying that any organ or instinct, or any whole structure, could not have arrived at its present state by many graduated steps. There are, it must be admitted, cases of special difficulty opposed to the theory of natural selection; and one of the most curious of these is the existence in the same community of two or three defined casts of workers or sterile female ants; but I have attempted to show how these difficulties can be mastered. . . .

As according to the theory of natural selection, an interminable[2] number of intermediate forms must have existed, linking together all the species in each group by gradations as fine as are our existing varieties, it may be asked, Why do we not see these linking forms all around us? Why are not all organic beings blended together in an inextricable chaos? With respect to existing forms, we should remember that we have no right to expect (excepting in rare cases) to discover *directly* connecting links between them, but only between each and some extinct and supplanted form. Even on a wide area, which has during a long period remained continuous,

Edgar E. Knoebel, ed., *Classics of Western Thought Volume III: The Modern World* (Fourth Edition), (New York: Harcourt Brace Jovanovich, 1988), ISBN 0155076841, pp. 350–366 (Charles Darwin, "The Origin of Species" and "The Descent of Man")

THE ORIGIN OF SPECIES Adapted by editor from *The Origin of Species by Means of Natural Selection, or the Preservation of the Favored Races in the Struggle for Life*, 6th ed., by Charles Darwin (New York: Appleton, 1892), II, 267–68, 271–82, 290–95, 298–301, 304–306.

1. Variations.

2. Endless.

and of which the climatic and other conditions of life change insensibly in proceeding from a closely allied species, we have no just right to expect often to find intermediate varieties in the intermediate zones. For we have reason to believe that only a few species of a genus[3] ever undergo change; the other species becoming utterly extinct and leaving no modified progeny.[4] Of the species which do change, only a few within the same country change at the same time; and all modifications are slowly effected. I have also shown that the intermediate varieties which probably at first existed in the intermediate zones, would be liable to be supplanted by the allied forms on either hand; for the latter, from existing in greater numbers, would generally be modified and improved at a quicker rate than the intermediate varieties, which existed in lesser numbers; so that the intermediate varieties would, in the long run, be supplanted and exterminated.

On this doctrine of the extermination of an infinity of connecting links, between the living and extinct inhabitants of the world, and at each successive period between the extinct and still older species, why is not every geological formation charged with such links? Why does not every collection of fossil remains afford plain evidence of the gradation and mutation of the forms of life? Although geological research has undoubtedly revealed the former existence of many links, bringing numerous forms of life much closer together, it does not yield the infinitely many fine gradations between past and present species required on the theory; and this is the most obvious of the many objections which may be urged against it. Why, again, do whole groups of allied species appear, though this appearance is often false, to have come in suddenly on the successive geological stages? Although we now know that organic beings appeared on this globe, at a period incalculably remote, long before the lowest bed of the Cambrian system[5] was deposited, why do we not find beneath this system great piles of strata stored with the remains of the progenitors[6] of the Cambrian fossils?[7] For on the theory, such strata must somewhere have been deposited at these ancient and utterly unknown epochs of the world's history.

I can answer these questions and objections only on the supposition that the geological record is far more imperfect than most geologists believe. The number of specimens in all our museums is absolutely as nothing compared with the countless generations of countless species which have certainly existed. The parent-form of any two or more species would not be in all its characters directly intermediate between its modified offspring, any more than the rock-pigeon is directly intermediate in crop and tail between its descendants, the pouter and fantail pigeons. We should not be able to recognize a species as the parent of another and modified species, if we were to examine the two ever so closely, unless we possessed most of the intermediate links; and owing to the imperfection of the geological record, we have no just right to expect to find so many links. If two or three, or even more linking forms were discovered, they would simply be ranked by many naturalists as so many new species, more especially if found in different geological sub-stages, let their differences be ever so slight. Numerous existing doubtful forms could be named which are probably varieties;[8] but who will pretend that in future ages so many fossil links will be discovered, that naturalists will be able to decide whether or not these doubtful forms ought to be called varieties? Only a small portion of the world has been geologically explored. Only organic beings

---

3. A biological classification including a number of related *species*.
4. Offspring.
5. An early geological formation (earth stratum).
6. Ancestors.
7. Remains of creatures.
8. Variations *within* a species.

of certain classes can be preserved in a fossil condition, at least in any great number. Many species when once formed never undergo any further change but become extinct without leaving modified descendants; and the periods, during which species have undergone modification, though long as measured by years, have probably been short in comparison with the periods during which they retained the same form. It is the dominant and widely ranging species which vary most frequently and vary most, and varieties are often at first local — both causes rendering the discovery of intermediate links in any one formation less likely. Local varieties will not spread into other and distant regions until they are considerably modified and improved; and when they have spread, and are discovered in a geological formation, they appear as if suddenly created there, and will be simply classed as new species. Most formations have been intermittent in their accumulation; and their duration has probably been shorter than the average duration of specific forms. Successive formations are in most cases separated from each other by blank intervals of time of great length; for fossiliferous formations thick enough to resist future degradation can as a general rule be accumulated only where much sediment is deposited on the subsiding bed of the sea. During the alternate periods of elevation and of stationary level the record will generally be blank. During these latter periods there will probably be more variability in the forms of life; during periods of subsidence, more extinction. . . .

That the geological record is imperfect all will admit; but that it is imperfect to the degree required by our theory, few will be inclined to admit. If we look at long enough intervals of time, geology plainly declares that species have all changed; and they have changed in the manner required by the theory, for they have changed slowly and in a graduated manner. We clearly see this in the fossil remains from consecutive formations invariably being much more closely related to each other, than are the fossils from widely separated formations. . . .

Under domestication[9] we see much variability, caused, or at least excited, by changed conditions of life; but often in so obscure a manner, that we are tempted to consider the variations as spontaneous. Variability is governed by many complex laws, — by correlated growth, compensation, the increased use and disuse of parts, and the definite action of the surrounding conditions. There is much difficulty in ascertaining how largely our domestic productions have been modified; but we may safely infer that the amount has been large, and that modifications can be inherited for long periods. As long as the conditions of life remain the same, we have reason to believe that a modification, which has already been inherited for many generations, may continue to be inherited for an almost infinite number of generations. On the other hand, we have evidence that variability when it has once come into play, does not cease under domestication for a very long period; nor do we know that it ever ceases, for new varieties are still occasionally produced by our oldest domesticated productions.

Variability is not actually caused by man; he only unintentionally exposes organic beings to new conditions of life, and then nature acts on the organization and causes it to vary. But man can and does select the variations given to him by nature, and thus accumulates them in any desired manner. He thus adapts animals and plants for his own benefit or pleasure. He may do this methodically, or he may do it unconsciously by preserving the individuals most useful or pleasing to him without any intention of altering the breed. It is certain that he can largely influence the character of a breed by selecting, in each successive generation, individual differences so slight as to be inappreciable except by an educated eye. This unconscious process of selection has been the great agency[10] in the formation of the most distinct and useful domestic

---

9. Taming and using animals to serve human purposes.

10. Factor.

breeds. That many breeds produced by man have to a large extent the character of natural species, is shown by the inextricable doubts whether many of them are varieties or aboriginally[11] distinct species.

There is no reason why the principles which have acted so efficiently under domestication should not have acted under nature. In the survival of favored individuals and races, during the constantly recurrent Struggle for Existence, we see a powerful and everacting form of Selection. The struggle for existence inevitably follows from the high geometrical ratio of increase which is common to all organic beings. This high rate of increase is proved by calculation, — by the rapid increase of many animals and plants during a succession of peculiar seasons, and when naturalized in new countries. More individuals are born than can possibly survive. A grain in the balance may determine which individuals shall live and which shall die, — which variety or species shall increase in number, and which shall decrease, or finally become extinct. As the individuals of the same species come in all respects into the closest competition with each other, the struggle will generally be most severe between them; it will be almost equally severe between the varieties of the same species, and next in severity between the species of the same genus. On the other hand the struggle will often be severe between beings remote in the scale of nature. The slightest advantage in certain individuals, at any age or during any season, over those with which they come into competition, or better adaptation in however slight a degree to the surrounding physical conditions, will, in the long run, turn the balance.

With animals having separated sexes, there will be in most cases a struggle between the males for the possession of the females. The most vigorous males, or those which have most successfully struggled with their conditions of life, will generally leave most progeny. But success will often depend on the males having special weapons, or means of defense, or charms; and a slight advantage will lead to victory.

As geology plainly proclaims that each land has undergone great physical changes, we might have expected to find that organic beings have varied under nature, in the same way as they have varied under domestication. And if there has been any variability under nature, it would be an unaccountable fact if natural selection had not come into play. It has often been asserted, but the assertion is incapable of proof, that the amount of variation under nature is a strictly limited quantity. Man, though acting on external characters alone and often capriciously, can produce within a short period a great result by adding up mere individual differences in his domestic productions; and every one admits that species present individual differences. But, besides such differences, all naturalists admit that natural varieties exist which are considered sufficiently distinct to be worthy of record in systematic works. No one has drawn any clear distinction between individual differences and slight varieties; or between more plainly marked varieties and sub-species, and species. On separate continents, and on different parts of the same continent when divided by barriers of any kind, and on outlying islands, what a multitude of forms exist, which some experienced naturalists rank as varieties, others as geographical races or sub-species, and others as distinct, though closely allied species!

If, then, animals and plants do vary, let it be ever so slightly or slowly, why should not variations or individual differences, which are in any way beneficial, be preserved and accumulated through natural selection, or the survival of the fittest? If man can by patience select variations useful to him, why, under changing and complex conditions of life, should not variations useful to nature's living products often arise, and be preserved or selected? What limit can be put to

---

11. From the beginning.

this power, acting during long ages and rigidly scrutinizing the whole constitution, structure, and habits of each creature, — favoring the good and rejecting the bad? I can see no limit to this power, in slowly and beautifully adapting each form to the most complex relations of life. The theory of natural selection, even if we look no farther than this, seems to be in the highest degree probable. I have already recapitulated, as fairly as I could, the opposed difficulties and objections: now let us turn to the special facts and arguments in favor of the theory.

On the view that species are only strongly marked and permanent varieties, and that each species first existed as a variety, we can see why it is that no line of demarcation can be drawn between species, commonly supposed to have been produced by special acts of creation, and varieties which are acknowledged to have been produced by secondary laws. On this same view we can understand how it is that in a region where many species of a genus have been produced, and where they now flourish, these same species should present many varieties; for where the production of species has been active, we might expect, as a general rule, to find it still in action; and this is the case if varieties be incipient[12] species. Moreover, the species of the larger genera,[13] which afford the greater number of varieties or incipient species, retain to a certain degree the character of varieties; for they differ from each other by a less amount of difference than do the species of smaller genera. The closely allied species also of the larger genera apparently have restricted ranges, and in their affinities[14] they are clustered in little groups round other species — in both respects resembling varieties. These are strange relations on the view that each species was independently created, but are intelligible if each existed first as a variety. . . .

As natural selection acts solely by accumulating slight, successive, favorable variations, it can produce no great or sudden modifications; it can act only by short and slow steps. Hence, the canon[15] of "Natura non facit saltum,"[16] which every fresh addition to our knowledge tends to confirm, is on this theory intelligible. We can see why throughout nature the same general end is gained by an almost infinite diversity of means, for every peculiarity when once acquired is long inherited, and structures already modified in many different ways have to be adapted for the same general purpose. We can, in short, see why nature is prodigal[17] in variety, though stingy in innovation. But why this should be a law of nature if each species has been independently created, no man can explain. . . .

The fact, as we have seen, that all past and present organic beings can be arranged within a few great classes, in groups subordinate to groups, and with the extinct groups often falling in between the recent groups, is intelligible on the theory of natural selection with its contingencies of extinction and divergence of character. On these same principles we see how it is, that the mutual affinities of the forms within each class are so complex. We see why certain characters are far more serviceable than others for classification; — why adaptive characters, though of paramount importance to the beings, are often of high classificatory value; and why embryological characters are often the most valuable of all. The real affinities of all organic beings, in contradistinction to their adaptive resemblances, are due to inheritance or community of descent. The Natural System is a genealogical arrangement, with the acquired grades of difference, marked by the terms, varieties, species, genera, families, and so forth; and we have to

---

12. At the beginning stage.

13. Plural of genus (see footnote 3).

14. Similarities.

15. Rule.

16. Latin: nature makes no leap — that is, there are no large gaps, or jumps, in natural development.

17. Extravagant.

discover the lines of descent by the most permanent characters whatever they may be and of however slight vital importance.

The similar framework of bones in the hand of a man, wing of a bat, fin of the porpoise, and leg of the horse, — the same number of vertebrae forming the neck of the giraffe and of the elephant, — and innumerable other such facts, at once explain themselves on the theory of descent with slow and slight successive modifications. The similarity of pattern in the wing and in the leg of a bat, though used for such different purpose, — in the jaws and legs of a crab, — in the petals, stamens,[18] and pistils[19] of a flower, is likewise, to a large extent, intelligible on the view of the gradual modification of parts or organs which were aboriginally alike in an early progenitor in each of these classes. On the principle of successive variations not always appearing at an early age, and being inherited at a corresponding not early period of life, we clearly see why the embryos of mammals, birds, reptiles, and fishes should be so closely similar, and so unlike the adult forms. We may cease marvelling at the embryo of an air-breathing mammal or bird having branchial[20] slits and arteries running in loops, like those of a fish which has to breathe the air dissolved in water by the aid of well-developed branchiae.

Disuse, aided sometimes by natural selection, will often have reduced organs when rendered useless under changed habits or conditions of life; and we can understand on this view the meaning of rudimentary organs.[21] But disuse and selection will generally act on each creature, when it has come to maturity and has to play its full part in the struggle for existence, and will thus have little power on an organ during early life; hence the organ will not be reduced or rendered rudimentary at this early age. The calf, for instance, has inherited teeth, which never cut through the gums of the upper jaw, from an early progenitor having well-developed teeth; and we may believe that the teeth in the mature animal were formerly reduced by disuse, owing to the tongue and palate, or lips, having become excellently fitted through natural selection to browse without their aid; whereas in the calf, the teeth have been left unaffected, and on the principle of inheritance at corresponding ages have been inherited from a remote period to the present day. On the view of each organism with all its separate parts having been specially created, how utterly inexplicable is it that organs bearing the plain stamp of inutility, such as the teeth in the embryonic calf or the shrivelled wings under the soldered wing-covers of many beetles, should so frequently occur. Nature may be said to have taken pains to reveal her scheme of modification, by means of rudimentary organs, of embryological and homologous[22] structures, but we are too blind to understand her meaning.

I have now recapitulated the facts and considerations which have thoroughly convinced me that species have been modified, during a long course of descent. This has been effected chiefly through the natural selection of numerous successive, slight, favorable variations aided in an important manner by the inherited effects of the use and disuse of parts; and in an unimportant manner, that is in relation to adaptive structures, whether past or present, by the direct action of external conditions, and by variations which seem to us in our ignorance to arise spontaneously. It appears that I formerly underrated the frequency and value of these latter forms of variation, as leading to permanent modifications of structure independently of natural selection. But as my conclusions have lately been much misrepresented, and it has been stated that I attribute the

---

18. The pollen-bearing organs.
19. The seed-bearing organs.
20. Gill-like.
21. Remnants of organs no longer used.
22. Organs of different species that have the same or similar embryological origin.

modification of species exclusively to natural selection, I may be permitted to remark that in the first edition of this work, and subsequently, I placed in a most conspicuous position — namely, at the close of the Introduction — the following words: "I am convinced that natural selection has been the main but not the exclusive means of modification." This has been of no avail. Great is the power of steady misrepresentation; but the history of science shows that fortunately this power does not long endure. . . .

I see no good reason why the views given in this volume should shock the religious feelings of any one. It is satisfactory, as showing how transient such impressions are, to remember that the greatest discovery ever made by man, namely the law of the attraction of gravity, was also attacked by Leibnitz,[23] "as subversive of natural, and inferentially of revealed, religion." A celebrated author and divine[24] has written to me that "he has gradually learned to see that it is just as noble a conception of the Deity to believe that He created a few original forms capable of self-development into other and needful forms, as to believe that He required a fresh act of creation to supply the voids caused by the action of His laws."

Why, it may be asked, until recently did nearly all the most eminent living naturalists and geologists disbelieve in the mutability[25] of species. It cannot be asserted that organic beings in a state of nature are subject to no variation; it cannot be proved that the amount of variation in the course of long ages is a limited quantity; no clear distinction has been, or can be, drawn between species and well-marked varieties. It cannot be maintained that species when intercrossed are invariably sterile, and varieties invariably fertile; or that sterility is a special endowment and sign of creation. The belief that species were immutable productions was almost unavoidable as long as the history of the world was thought to be of short duration; and now that we have acquired some idea of the lapse of time, we are too apt to assume, without proof, that the geological record is so perfect that it would have afforded us plain evidence of the mutation of species, if they had undergone mutation.

But the chief cause of our natural unwillingness to admit that one species has given birth to other and distinct species, is that we are always slow in admitting great changes of which we do not see the steps. The difficulty is the same as that felt by so many geologists, when Lyell[26] first insisted that long lines of inland cliffs had been formed, and great valleys excavated, by the force which we see still at work. The mind cannot possibly grasp the full meaning of the term of even a million years; it cannot add up and perceive the full effects of many slight variations, accumulated during an almost infinite number of generations. . . .

It may be asked how far I extend the doctrine of the modification of species. The question is difficult to answer, because the more distinct the forms are which we consider, by so much the arguments in favor of community of descent become fewer in number and less in force. But some arguments of the greatest weight extend very far. All the members of whole classes are connected together by a chain of affinities, and all can be classed on the same principle, in groups subordinate to groups. Fossil remains sometimes tend to fill up very wide intervals between existing orders.

Organs in a rudimentary condition plainly show that an early progenitor had the organ in a fully developed condition; and this in some cases implies an enormous amount of modification

---

23. Gottfried Wilhelm von Leibnitz (1646–1716), German philosopher and mathematician.

24. Clergyman.

25. Changeability.

26. Charles Lyell (1797–1875), British geologist.

in the descendants. Throughout whole classes various structures are formed on the same pattern, and at a very early age the embryos closely resemble each other. Therefore I cannot doubt that the theory of descent with modification embraces all the members of the same great class or kingdom. I believe that animals are descended from at most only four or five progenitors, and plants from an equal or lesser number.

Analogy would lead me one step farther, namely, to the belief that all animals and plants are descended from some one prototype. But analogy may be a deceitful guide. Nevertheless all living things have much in common, in their chemical composition, their cellular structure, their laws of growth, and their liability to injurious influences. We see this even in so trifling a fact as that the same poison often similarly affects plants and animals; or that the poison secreted by the gall-fly produces monstrous growths on the wild rose or oak-tree. With all organic beings, excepting perhaps some of the very lowest, sexual reproduction seems to be essentially similar. With all, as far as is at present known, the germinal vesicle[27] is the same; so that all organisms start from a common origin. If we look even to the two main divisions — namely, to the animal and vegetable kingdoms — certain low forms are so far intermediate in character that naturalists have disputed to which kingdom they should be referred. As Professor Asa Gray[28] has remarked, "the spores and other reproductive bodies of many of the lower algae may claim to have first a characteristically animal, and then an unequivocally vegetable existence." Therefore, on the principle of natural selection with divergence of character, it does not seem incredible that, from some such low and intermediate form, both animals and plants may have been developed; and, if we admit this, we must likewise admit that all the organic beings which have ever lived on this earth may be descended from some one primordial form. But this inference is chiefly grounded on analogy, and it is immaterial whether or not it be accepted. No doubt it is possible, as Mr. G. H. Lewes[29] has urged, that at the first commencement of life many different forms were evolved; but if so, we may conclude that only a very few have left modified descendants. For, as I have recently remarked in regard to the members of each great kingdom, such as the Vertebrata, Articulata,[30] and so forth, we have distinct evidence in their embryological, homologous, and rudimentary structures, that within each kingdom all the members are descended from a single progenitor.

When the views advanced by me in this volume, and by Mr. Wallace,[31] or when analogous views on the origin of species are generally admitted, we can dimly foresee that there will be a considerable revolution in natural history. Systematists will be able to pursue their labors as at present; but they will not be incessantly haunted by the shadowy doubt whether this or that form be a true species. This, I feel sure and I speak after experience, will be no slight relief. The endless disputes whether or not some fifty species of British brambles are good species will cease. Systematists will have only to decide (not that this will be easy) whether any form be sufficiently constant and distinct from other forms, to be capable of definition; and if definable, whether the differences be sufficiently important to deserve a specific name. This latter point will become a far more essential consideration than it is at present; for differences, however

---

27. A small cavity or sac.

28. Asa Gray (1810–1888), American botanist.

29. George Henry Lewes (1817–1878), English philosopher and literary critic.

30. Invertebrates which have jointed bodies like worms, insects, spiders, and crustaceans.

31. Alfred Russel Wallace (1823–1913), an English biologist who advanced, independently, an evolutionary view similar to that of Darwin.

slight, between any two forms, if not blended by intermediate gradations, are looked at by most naturalists as sufficient to raise both forms to the rank of species.

Hereafter we shall be compelled to acknowledge that the only distinction between species and well-marked varieties is, that the latter are known, or believed, to be connected at the present day by intermediate gradations, whereas species were formerly thus connected. Hence, without rejecting the consideration of the present existence of intermediate gradations between any two forms, we shall be led to weigh more carefully and to value higher the actual amount of difference between them. It is quite possible that forms now generally acknowledged to be merely varieties may hereafter be thought worthy of specific names; and in this case scientific and common language will come into accordance. In short, we shall have to treat species in the same manner as those naturalists treat genera, who admit that genera are merely artificial combinations made for convenience. This may not be a cheering prospect; but we shall at least be freed from the vain search for the undiscovered and undiscoverable essence of the term species. . . .

Authors of the highest eminence seem to be fully satisfied with the view that each species has been independently created. To my mind it accords better with what we know of the laws impressed on matter by the Creator, that the production and extinction of the past and present inhabitants of the world should have been due to secondary causes, like those determining the birth and death of the individual. When I view all beings not as special creations, but as the lineal descendants of some few beings which lived long before the first bed of the Cambrian system was deposited, they seem to me to become ennobled. Judging from the past, we may safely infer that not one living species will transmit its unaltered likeness to a distant future. And of the species now living very few will transmit progeny of any kind to a far distant future; for the manner in which all organic beings are grouped, shows that the greater number of species in each genus, and all the species in many genera, have left no descendants, but have become utterly extinct. We can so far take a prophetic glance into the future as to fortell that it will be the common and widely-spread species, belonging to the larger and dominant groups within each class, which will ultimately prevail and procreate new and dominant species. As all the living forms of life are the lineal descendants of those which lived long before the Cambrian epoch, we may feel certain that the ordinary succession by generation has never once been broken, and that no cataclysm has desolated the whole world. Hence we may look with some confidence to a secure future of great length. And as natural selection works solely by and for the good of each being, all corporeal and mental endowments will tend to progress toward perfection.

It is interesting to contemplate a tangled bank, clothed with many plants of many kinds, with birds singing in the bushes, with various insects flitting about, and with worms crawling through the damp earth, and to reflect that these elaborately constructed forms, so different from each other, and dependent upon each other in so complex a manner, have all been produced by laws acting around us. These laws, taken in the largest sense, being Growth with Reproduction; Inheritance which is almost implied by reproduction; Variability from the indirect and direct action of the conditions of life, and from use and disuse: a Ratio of Increase so high as to lead to a Struggle for Life, and as a consequence to Natural Selection, entailing Divergence of Character and the Extinction of less-improved forms. Thus, from the war of nature, from famine and death, the most exalted object which we are capable of conceiving, namely, the production of the higher animals, directly follows. There is grandeur in this view of life, with its several powers, having been originally breathed by the Creator into a few forms or into one; and that, while this planet has gone cycling on according to the fixed law of gravity, from so simple a beginning endless forms most beautiful and most wonderful have been, and are being evolved.

The Descent of Man

Man, like every other animal, has no doubt advanced to his present high condition through a struggle for existence resulting from his rapid multiplication; and if he is to advance still higher, it is to be feared that he must remain subject to a severe struggle. Otherwise he would sink into indolence,[32] and the more gifted men would not be more successful in the battle of life than the less gifted. Hence our natural rate of increase, though leading to many and obvious evils, must not be greatly diminished by any means. There should be open competition for all men; and the most able should not be prevented by laws or customs from succeeding best and rearing the largest number of offspring. Important as the struggle for existence has been and even still is, yet as far as the highest part of man's nature is concerned there are other factors more important. For the moral qualities are advanced, either directly or indirectly, much more through the effects of habit, the reasoning powers, instruction, religion, and so forth, than through natural selection. . . .

The main conclusion arrived at in this work, namely that man is descended from some lowly organized form, will, I regret to think, be highly distasteful to many. But there can hardly be a doubt that we are descended from barbarians. The astonishment which I felt on first seeing a group of Fuegians[33] on a wild and broken shore will never be forgotten by me, for the thought at once rushed into my mind — such were our ancestors. These men were absolutely naked and smeared with paint, their long hair was tangled, their mouths frothed with excitement, and their expression was wild, startled, and distrustful. They possessed hardly any skills, and like wild animals lived on what they could catch; they had no government, and were merciless to everyone not of their own small tribe. He who has seen a savage . . . will not feel much shame, if forced to acknowledge that the blood of some more humble creature flows in his veins. For my own part I would as soon be descended from that heroic little monkey, who braved his dreaded enemy in order to save the life of his keeper, or from that old baboon, who descending from the mountains, carried away in triumph his young comrade from a crowd of astonished dogs — as from a savage who delights to torture his enemies, offers up bloody sacrifices, practices infanticide[34] without remorse, treats his wives like slaves, knows no decency, and is haunted by the grossest superstitions.

Man may be excused for feeling some pride at having risen, though not through his own exertions, to the very summit of the organic scale; and the fact of his having thus risen, instead of having been simply placed there, may give him hope for a still higher destiny in the distant future. But we are not here concerned with hopes or fears, only with the truth as far as our reason permits us to discover it; and I have given the evidence to the best of my ability. We must, however, acknowledge, as it seems to me, that man with all his noble qualities, with sympathy which feels for the most debased, with benevolence which extends not only to other men but to the humblest living creature, with his god-like intellect which has penetrated into the movements and make-up of the solar system — with all these exalted powers — Man still bears in his bodily frame the indelible stamp of his lowly origin.

THE DESCENT OF MAN Adapted by editor from *The Descent of Man and Selection in Relation to Sex,* 2nd ed., revised, by Charles Darwin (New York: D. Appleton and Company, 1898), 633–34.

32. Laziness.

33. Native Indians of the Land of Fire, the southernmost tip of South America.

34. The killing of an infant.

Friedrich Nietzsche

THE GAY SCIENCE
(PARABLE OF THE MADMAN)

BEYOND GOOD AND EVIL

Introduction by Shelley Baranowski

Friedrich Nietzsche (1844–1901) is arguably the most influential philosopher since the Enlightenment because many of the philosophical movements that have arisen since, among them existentialism and postmodernism, have derived many of their ideas from his work. Irascible and provocative, Nietzsche radically questioned the principal values and institutions of Western civilization. Born in Prussia, the son of a Lutheran pastor, Nietzsche studied classical philology at the Universities of Bonn and Leipzig, becoming a professor in that field in Basel by the age of 24. Dogged by ill health for most of his life, he completed most of his major works, including *The Gay Science* (of which the story of the madman is a part) and *Beyond Good and Evil* before suffering a nervous breakdown twelve years before his death.

Nietzsche argued that not only God, but also Jewish and Christian morality that composed the ethical underpinnings of the West, no longer held sway in contemporary life. That the "herd," or masses, remained unaware of the extent to which conditions had swept away traditional values was because the comforting nostrums of Christian "slave morality" encouraged them to cling to the past. According to Nietzsche, the solution lay in the emergence of new values. But how? To answer that question, he conceived of an overman *(Übermensch)* or overmen, unique individuals who would be original, creative, and independent enough to affirm the essence of life that the "slave morality" had undermined, the will to power. When the "herd" feared change and adhered to the precept of turning the other cheek, the overman would bravely assert his individualism, vitality, and leadership. Nietzsche conceived of several models for the overman, Socrates, Julius Caesar, Shakespeare, and Napoleon among them. The qualities of such models drawn from the past, appearing in individuals who had not yet arrived on the scene, would bring the indictment and destruction of democracy and socialism, the nineteenth-century heirs to Christian values. Nietzsche did not become a German nationalist after Germany was unified in 1871. In fact, he considered nationalism yet another symptom of the herd mentality, which complicated his friendship with the ultra nationalist composer Richard Wagner. Yet as some scholars have pointed out recently, Nietzsche was an imperialist. He believed that European overmen could assert European domination over the globe. They would accomplish this on their own initiative, bypassing the instruments of mass democracy, political parties and parliaments.

Below are excerpts from two of Nietzsche's works, the parable of the madman from *The Gay Science*, and a chapter from *Beyond Good and Evil*. Why does the madman's audience not hear his message about the "death of God?" Why does it seem fitting that a madman should proclaim this message? Might there be a relationship between the silence that greets the madman and Nietzsche's comments in *Beyond Good and Evil* on "slave morality," democracy and socialism? Some scholars have argued for similarities between Nietzsche's ideas and those of Adolf Hitler and the Nazi party. Do you think there are grounds for such claims?

The Gay Science

125

The madman. — Have you not heard of that madman who lit a lantern in the bright morning hours, ran to the market place, and cried incessantly: "I seek God! I seek God!" — As many of those who did not believe in God were standing around just then, he provoked much laughter. Has he got lost? asked one. Did he lose his way like a child? asked another. Or is he hiding? Is he afraid of us? Has he gone on a voyage? emigrated? — Thus they yelled and laughed.

The madman jumped into their midst and pierced them with his eyes. "Whither is God?" he cried; "I will tell you. *We have killed him* — you and I. All of us are his murderers. But how did we do this? How could we drink up the sea? Who gave us the sponge to wipe away the entire horizon? What were we doing when we unchained this earth from its sun? Whither is it moving now? Whither are we moving? Away from all suns? Are we not plunging continually? Backward, sideward, forward, in all directions? Is there still any up or down? Are we not straying as through an infinite nothing? Do we not feel the breath of empty space? Has it not become colder? Is not night continually closing in on us? Do we not need to light lanterns in the morning? Do we hear nothing as yet of the noise of the gravediggers who are burying God? Do we smell nothing as yet of the divine decomposition? Gods, too, decompose. God is dead. God remains dead. And we have killed him.

"How shall we comfort ourselves, the murderers of all murderers? What was holiest and mightiest of all that the world has yet owned has bled to death under our knives: who will wipe this blood off us? What water is there for us to clean ourselves? What festivals of atonement, what sacred games shall we have to invent? Is not the greatness of this deed too great for us? Must we ourselves not become gods simply to appear worthy of it? There has never been a greater deed; and whoever is born after us — for the sake of this deed he will belong to a higher history than all history hitherto."

Here the madman fell silent and looked again at his listeners; and they, too, were silent and stared at him in astonishment. At last he threw his lantern on the ground, and it broke into pieces and went out. "I have come too early," he said then; "my time is not yet. This tremendous event is still on its way, still wandering; it has not yet reached the ears of men. Lightning and thunder require time; the light of the stars requires time; deeds, though done, still require time to be seen and heard. This deed is still more distant from them than the most distant stars — *and yet they have done it themselves.*"

It has been related further that on the same day the madman forced his way into several churches and there struck up his *requiem aeternam deo*. Led out and called to account, he is said always to have replied nothing but: "What after all are these churches now if they are not the tombs and sepulchers of God?"[1]

Friedrich Nietzsche, *The Gay Science* trans. Walter Kaufmann (New York: Vintage Books, 1974), pp. 181–2.

1. This is one of the most famous sections in this book. See the first note on section 108 above, which calls attention to other passages in Nietzsche that use the same, or similar, imagery. Above all, however, it should be noted how this section fits into its immediate context, and how the de-deification in section 109 and all of the intermediate sections build up to the parable of the madman. It has often been asked what Nietzsche means by saying that "God is dead." One might fairly answer: what he means is what he says in sections 108 through 125 — and in the sections after that. The problem is created in large measure by tearing a section out of its context, on the *false* assumption that what we are offered is merely a random collection of "aphorisms" that are intended for browsing.

126

Mystical explanations. — Mystical explanations are considered deep. The truth is that they are not even superficial.[2]

---

2. Cf. Twilight of the Idols, Chapter I, section 27 (VPN, 470) — which is an aphorism, and a poor one at that. But although the wording is almost the same, section 126 has its place between 125 and 127 as a meaningful transition, and it makes a point: Mystical explanations are not even superficial explanations — because they are not explanations at all. They only seem to explain something.

Beyond Good and Evil

186

The moral sentiment in Europe today is as refined, old, diverse, irritable, and subtle, as the "science of morals" that accompanies it is still young, raw, clumsy, and butterfingered — an attractive contrast that occasionally even becomes visible and incarnate in the person of a moralist. Even the term "science of morals" is much too arrogant considering what it designates, and offends *good* taste — which always prefers more modest terms.

One should own up in all strictness to what is still necessary here for a long time to come, to what alone is justified so far: to collect material, to conceptualize and arrange a vast realm of subtle feelings of value and differences of value which are alive, grow, beget, and perish — and perhaps attempts to present vividly some of the more frequent and recurring forms of such living crystallizations — all to prepare a *typology* of morals.

To be sure, so far one has not been so modest. With a stiff seriousness that inspires laughter, all our philosophers demanded something far more exalted, presumptuous, and solemn from themselves as soon as they approached the study of morality: they wanted to supply a *rational foundation* for morality — and every philosopher so far has believed that he has provided such a foundation. Morality itself, however, was accepted as "given." How remote from their clumsy pride was that task which they considered insignificant and left in dust and must — the task of description — although the subtlest fingers and senses can scarcely be subtle enough for it.

Just because our moral philosophers knew the facts of morality only very approximately in arbitrary extracts or in accidental epitomes — for example, as the morality of their environment, their class, their church, the spirit of their time, their climate and part of the world — just because they were poorly informed and not even very curious about different peoples, times, and past ages — they never laid eyes on the real problems of morality; for these emerge only when we compare *many* moralities. In all "science of morals" so far one thing was *lacking,* strange as it may sound: the problem of morality itself; what was lacking was any suspicion that there was something problematic here. What the philosophers called "a rational foundation for morality" and tried to supply was, seen in the right light, merely a scholarly variation of the common *faith* in the prevalent morality; a new means of *expression* for this faith; and thus just another fact within a particular morality; indeed, in the last analysis a kind of denial that this morality might ever be considered problematic — certainly the very opposite of an examination, analysis, questioning, and vivisection of this very faith.

Friedrich Nietzsche, *Beyond Good and Evil* trans. Walter Kaufmann (New York: Vintage Books, 1996), pp. 99–118.

Listen, for example, with what almost venerable innocence Schopenhauer still described his task, and then draw your conclusions about the scientific standing of a "science" whose ultimate masters still talk like children and little old women: "The principle," he says (p. 136 of *Grundprobleme der Moral*),[1] "the fundamental proposition on whose contents all moral philosophers are *really*[2] agreed — *neminem laede, immo omnes, quantum potes, juva*[3] — that is *really* the proposition for which all moralists endeavor to find the rational foundation . . . the *real* basis of ethics for which one has been looking for thousands of years as for the philosopher's stone."

The difficulty of providing a rational foundation for the principle cited may indeed be great — as is well known, Schopenhauer did not succeed either — and whoever has once felt deeply how insipidly false and sentimental this principle is in a world whose essence is will to power, may allow himself to be reminded that Schopenhauer, though a pessimist, *really* — played the flute. Every day, after dinner: one should read his biography on that. And incidentally: a pessimist, one who denies God and the world but *comes to a stop* before morality — who affirms morality and plays the flute — the *laede neminem* morality — what? is that really — a pessimist?

187

Even apart from the value of such claims as "there is a categorical imperative in us," one can still always ask: what does such a claim tell us about the man who makes it? There are moralities which are meant to justify their creator before others. Other moralities are meant to calm him and lead him to be satisfied with himself. With yet others he wants to crucify himself and humiliate himself. With others he wants to wreak revenge, with others conceal himself, with others transfigure himself and place himself way up, at a distance. This morality is used by its creator to forget, that one to have others forget him or something about him. Some moralists want to vent their power and creative whims on humanity; some others, perhaps including Kant, suggest with their morality: "What deserves respect in me is that I can obey — and you *ought* not to be different from me." — In short, moralities are also merely a *sign language of the affects.*

---

1. First edition of 1886 and second edition of 1891: "das Princip, sagt er (p. 136 der Grundprobleme der Moral), der Grundsatz . . ."

   Musarion edition of the *Werke:* "das Princip, sagt er (p. 137 der Grundprobleme der Ethik), der Grundsatz . . ."

   Schlechta's edition, which purports to follow the original edition, actually departs even a little further from it than the Musarionausgabe: "das Princip" sagt er (S. 137 der Grundprobleme der Ethik), "der Grundsatz . . ."

   The correct title of Schopenhauer's book is *Die beiden Grundprobleme der Ethik* (the two fundamental problems of ethics), and in the original edition of 1841 the quoted passage is found on p. 138. Nietzsche neither placed the title in quotes nor italicized it, and his slight variation of the title is less odd than the fact that on Schopenhauer's own title page of 1841 the title of the second essay, which Nietzsche cites, is given as *"Ueber das Fundament der Moral, nicht gekrönt von der K. Dänischen Societät der Wissenschaften, zu Kopenhagen, den 30. Januar 1840"* ("On the Foundation of Morals, not awarded a prize by the Danish Royal Society . . ."). Turning the page, one finds the table of contents, in which the title of the second essay is given as follows: *"Preisschrift über die Grundlage der Moral"* (Prize essay on the basis of morals). (The heading on p. 101 agrees with the table of contents, not with Schopenhauer's title page.) If Schopenhauer could say in one instance *Fundament* and in the other *Grundlage,* Nietzsche might as well say *Moral* instead of *Ethik;* moreover, the word in the title that concerned Nietzsche was *Moral,* not *Ethik.*

   The editors who changed the title and page reference given by Nietzsche failed to insert three dots in the quotation itself, to indicate a minor omission of two and a half lines between "agreed" and the Latin quotation. This omission does not change the sense and is in no way unfair to Schopenhauer.

2. "Really" and "real": *eigentlich.* The emphasis is Nietzsche's, not Schopenhauer's.

3. "Hurt no one; rather, help all as much as you can."

188

Every morality is, as opposed to *laisser aller*,[4] a bit of tyranny against "nature"; also against "reason"; but this in itself is no objection, as long as we do not have some other morality which permits us to decree that every kind of tyranny and unreason is impermissible. What is essential and inestimable in every morality is that it constitutes a long compulsion: to understand Stoicism or Port-Royal or Puritanism, one should recall the compulsion under which every language so far has achieved strength and freedom — the metrical compulsion of rhyme and rhythm.

How much trouble the poets and orators of all peoples have taken — not excepting a few prose writers today in whose ear there dwells an inexorable conscience — "For the sake of some foolishness," as utilitarian dolts say, feeling smart — "submitting abjectly to capricious laws," as anarchists say, feeling "free," even "free-spirited." But the curious fact is that all there is or has been on earth of freedom, subtlety, boldness, dance, and masterly sureness, whether in thought itself or in government, or in rhetoric and persuasion, in the arts just as in ethics, has developed only owing to the "tyranny of such capricious laws"; and in all seriousness, the probability is by no means small that precisely this is "nature" and "natural" — and *not* that *laisser aller*.

Every artist knows how far from any feeling of letting himself go his "most natural" state is — the free ordering, placing, disposing, giving form in the moment of "inspiration" — and how strictly and subtly he obeys thousandfold laws precisely then, laws that precisely on account of their hardness and determination defy all formulation through concepts (even the firmest concept is, compared with them, not free of fluctuation, multiplicity, and ambiguity).

What is essential "in heaven and on earth" seems to be, to say it once more, that there should be *obedience* over a long period of time and in a *single* direction: given that, something always develops, and has developed, for whose sake it is worth while to live on earth; for example, virtue, art, music, dance, reason, spirituality — something transfiguring, subtle, mad, and divine. The long unfreedom of the spirit, the mistrustful constraint in the communicability of thoughts, the discipline thinkers imposed on themselves to think within the directions laid down by a church or court, or under Aristotelian presuppositions, the long spiritual will to interpret all events under a Christian schema and to rediscover and justify the Christian god in every accident — all this, however forced, capricious, hard, gruesome, and anti-rational, has shown itself to be the means through which the European spirit has been trained to strength, ruthless curiosity, and subtle mobility, though admittedly in the process an irreplaceable amount of strength and spirit had to be crushed, stifled, and ruined (for here, as everywhere, "nature" manifests herself as she is, in all her prodigal and indifferent magnificence which is outrageous but noble).

That for thousands of years European thinkers thought merely in order to prove something — today, conversely, we suspect every thinker who "wants to prove something" — that the conclusions that *ought* to be the result of their most rigorous reflection were always settled from the start, just as it used to be with Asiatic astrology, and still is today with the innocuous Christian-moral interpretation of our most intimate personal experiences "for the glory of God" and "for the salvation of the soul" — this tyranny, this caprice, this rigorous and grandiose stupidity has *educated* the spirit. Slavery is, as it seems, both in the cruder and in the more subtle sense, the indispensable means of spiritual discipline and cultivation,[5] too. Consider

---

4. Letting go.
5. *Zucht und Züchtung.*

any morality with this in mind: what there is in it of "nature" teaches hatred of the *laisser aller,* of any all-too-great freedom, and implants the need for limited horizons and the nearest tasks — teaching the *narrowing of our perspective,* and thus in a certain sense stupidity, as a condition of life and growth.

"You shall obey — someone and for a long time: *else* you will perish and lose the last respect for yourself " — this appears to me to be the moral imperative of nature which, to be sure, is neither "categorical" as the old Kant would have it (hence the "else") nor addressed to the individual (what do individuals matter to her?), but to peoples, races, ages, classes — but above all to the whole human animal, to *man.*

189

Industrious races find it very troublesome to endure leisure: it was a masterpiece of *English* instinct to make the Sabbath so holy and so boring that the English begin unconsciously to lust again for their work- and week-day. It is a kind of cleverly invented, cleverly inserted *fast,* the like of which is also encountered frequently in the ancient world (although, in fairness to southern peoples, not exactly in regard to work). There have to be fasts of many kinds; and wherever powerful drives and habits prevail, legislators have to see to it that intercalary days are inserted on which such a drive is chained and learns again to hunger. Viewed from a higher vantage point, whole generations and ages that make their appearance, infected with some moral fanaticism, seem to be such times of constraint and fasting during which a drive learns to stoop and submit, but also to *purify* and *sharpen* itself. A few philosophical sects, too, permit such an interpretation (for example, the Stoa in the midst of Hellenistic culture with its lascivious atmosphere, overcharged with aphrodisiac odors).

This is also a hint for an explanation of the paradox: why it was precisely during the most Christian period of Europe and altogether only under the pressure of Christian value judgments that the sex drive sublimated[6] itself into love *(amour-passion).*

190

There is something in the morality of Plato that does not really belong to Plato but is merely encountered in his philosophy — one might say, in spite of Plato: namely, the Socratism for which he was really too noble. "Nobody wants to do harm to himself, therefore all that is bad is done involuntarily. For the bad do harm to themselves: this they would not do if they knew that the bad is bad. Hence the bad are bad only because of an error; if one removes the error, one necessarily makes them — good."

This type of inference smells of the *rabble* that sees nothing in bad actions but the unpleasant consequences and really judges, "it is *stupid* to do what is bad," while "good" is taken without further ado to be identical with "useful and agreeable." In the case of every moral utilitarianism one may immediately infer the same origin and follow one's nose: one will rarely go astray.

Plato did everything he could in order to read something refined and noble into the proposition of his teacher — above all, himself. He was the most audacious of all interpreters and took

---

6. Nietzsche was the first to use *sublimiren* in its specifically modern sense, which is widely associated with Freud. On the history of this interesting term see Kaufmann's *Nietzsche,* Chapter 7, section II.

the whole Socrates only the way one picks a popular tune and folk song from the streets in order to vary it into the infinite and impossible — namely, into all of his own masks and multiplicities. In a jest, Homeric at that: what is the Platonic Socrates after all if not *prosthe Platön opithen te Platön messë te Chimaera.*[7]

191

The ancient theological problem of "faith" and "knowledge" — or, more clearly, of instinct and reason — in other words, the question whether regarding the valuation of things instinct deserves more authority than rationality, which wants us to evaluate and act in accordance with reasons, with a "why?" — in other words, in accordance with expedience and utility — this is still the ancient moral problem that first emerged in the person of Socrates and divided thinking people long before Christianity. Socrates himself, to be sure, with the taste of his talent — that of a superior dialectician — had initially sided with reason; and in fact, what did he do his life long but laugh at the awkward incapacity of noble Athenians who, like all noble men, were men of instinct and never could give sufficient information about the reasons for their actions? In the end, however, privately and secretly, he laughed at himself, too: in himself he found, before his subtle conscience and self-examination, the same difficulty and incapacity. But is that any reason, he encouraged himself, for giving up the instincts? One has to see to it that they as well as reason receive their due — one must follow the instincts but persuade reason to assist them with good reasons. This was the real *falseness* of that great ironic, so rich in secrets; he got his conscience to be satisfied with a kind of self-trickery: at bottom, he had seen through the irrational element in moral judgments.

Plato, more innocent in such matters and lacking the craftiness of the plebeian, wanted to employ all his strength — the greatest strength any philosopher so far has had at his disposal — to prove to himself that reason and instinct of themselves tend toward one goal, the good, "God." And since Plato, all theologians and philosophers are on the same track — that is, in moral matters it has so far been instinct, or what the Christians call "faith," or "the herd," as I put it, that has triumphed. Perhaps Descartes should be excepted, as the father of rationalism (and hence the grandfather of the Revolution) who conceded authority to reason alone: but reason is merely an instrument, and Descartes was superficial.

192

Whoever has traced the history of an individual science finds a clue in its development for understanding the most ancient and common processes of all "knowledge and cognition." There as here it is the rash hypotheses, the fictions, the good dumb will to "believe," the lack of mistrust and patience that are developed first; our senses learn only late, and never learn entirely, to be subtle, faithful, and cautious organs of cognition. Our eye finds it more comfortable to respond to a given stimulus by reproducing once more an image that it has produced many times before, instead of registering what is different and new in an impression. The latter would require more

---

7. "Plato in front and Plato behind, in the middle Chimaera." Cf. *Iliad,* VI:181, where Chimaera is described: "Lion in front and serpent behind, in the middle a goat." For Nietzsche's complex and seemingly contradictory view of Socrates, see Kaufmann's *Nietzsche,* Chapter 13.

strength, more "morality." Hearing something new is embarrassing and difficult for the ear; foreign music we do not hear well. When we hear another language we try involuntarily to form the sounds we hear into words that sound more familiar and more like home to us: thus the German, for example, transformed *arcubalista,* when he heard that, into *Armbrust.*[8] What is new finds our senses, too, hostile and reluctant; and even in the "simplest" processes of sensation the affects dominate, such as fear, love, hatred, including the passive affects of laziness.

Just as little as a reader today reads all of the individual words (let alone syllables) on a page — rather he picks about five words at random out of twenty and "guesses" at the meaning that probably belongs to these five words — just as little do we see a tree exactly and completely with reference to leaves, twigs, color, and form; it is so very much easier for us simply to improvise some approximation of a tree. Even in the midst of the strangest experiences we still do the same: we make up the major part of the experience and can scarcely be forced *not* to contemplate some event as its "inventors." All this means: basically and from time immemorial we are — *accustomed to lying.* Or to put it more virtuously and hypocritically, in short, more pleasantly: one is much more of an artist than one knows.

In an animated conversation I often see the face of the person with whom I am talking so clearly and so subtly determined in accordance with the thought he expresses, or that I believe has been produced in him, that this degree of clarity far surpasses my powers of vision: so the subtle shades of the play of the muscles and the expression of the eyes *must* have been made up by me. Probably the person made an altogether different face, or none at all.

193

Quidquid luce fuit, tenebris agit:[9] but the other way around, too. What we experience in dreams — assuming that we experience it often — belongs in the end just as much to the overall economy of our soul as anything experienced "actually": we are richer or poorer on account of it, have one need more or less, and finally are led a little by the habits of our dreams even in broad daylight and in the most cheerful moments of our wide-awake spirit.

Suppose someone has flown often in his dreams and finally, as soon as he dreams, he is conscious of his power and art of flight as if it were his privilege, also his characteristic and enviable happiness. He believes himself capable of realizing every kind of arc and angle simply with the lightest impulse; he knows the feeling of a certain divine frivolity, an "upward" without tension and constraint, a "downward" without condescension and humiliation — without *gravity!* How could a human being who had had such dream experiences and dream habits fail to find that the word "happiness" had a different color and definition in his waking life, too? How could he fail to — desire happiness differently? "Rising" as described by poets must seem to him, compared with this "flying," too earthbound, muscle-bound, forced, too "grave."

194

The difference among men becomes manifest not only in the difference between their tablets of goods — in the fact that they consider different goods worth striving for and also disagree

---

8. Literally, arm-breast; both words mean crossbow.

9. "What occurred in the light, goes on in the dark."

about what is more and less valuable, about the order of rank of the goods they recognize in common — it becomes manifest even more in what they take for really *having* and *possessing* something good.

Regarding a woman, for example, those men who are more modest consider the mere use of the body and sexual gratification a sufficient and satisfying sign of "having," of possession. Another type, with a more suspicious and demanding thirst for possession, sees the "question mark," the illusory quality of such "having" and wants subtler tests, above all in order to know whether the woman does not only give herself to him but also gives up for his sake what she has or would like to have: only then does she seem to him "possessed." A third type, however, does not reach the end of his mistrust and desire for having even so: he asks himself whether the woman, when she gives up everything for him, does not possibly do this for a phantom of him. He wants to be known deep down, abysmally deep down, before he is capable of being loved at all; he dares to let himself be fathomed. He feels that his beloved is fully in his possession only when she no longer deceives herself about him, when she loves him just as much for his devilry and hidden insatiability as for his graciousness, patience, and spirituality.

One type wants to possess a people — and all the higher arts of a Cagliostro and Catiline suit him to that purpose. Someone else, with a more subtle thirst for possession, says to himself: "One may not deceive where one wants to possess." The idea that a mask of him might command the heart of the people[10] irritates him and makes him impatient: "So I must *let* myself be known, and first must know myself."

Among helpful and charitable people one almost regularly encounters that clumsy ruse which first doctors the person to be helped — as if, for example, he "deserved" help, required just *their* help, and would prove to be profoundly grateful for all help, faithful and submissive. With these fancies they dispose of the needy as of possessions, being charitable and helpful people from a desire for possessions. One finds them jealous if one crosses or anticipates them when they want to help.

Involuntarily, parents turn children into something similar to themselves — they call that "education." Deep in her heart, no mother doubts that the child she has borne is her property; no father contests his own right to subject it to *his* concepts and valuations. Indeed, formerly it seemed fair for fathers (among the ancient Germans, for example) to decide on the life or death of the newborn as they saw fit. And like the father, teachers, classes, priests, and princes still see, even today, in every new human being an unproblematic opportunity for another possession. So it follows ——

195

The Jews — a people "born for slavery," as Tacitus and the whole ancient world say; "the chosen people among the peoples," as they themselves say and believe — the Jews have brought off that miraculous feat of an inversion of values, thanks to which life on earth has acquired a novel and dangerous attraction for a couple of millennia: their prophets have fused "rich," "godless," "evil," "violent," and "sensual" into one and were the first to use the word "world" as an opprobrium. This inversion of values (which includes using the word "poor" as synony-

---

10. This, of course, was what happened to Nietzsche himself after his death.

mous with "holy" and "friend") constitutes the significance of the Jewish people: they mark the beginning of the slave rebellion in morals.[11]

196

Countless dark bodies are to be *inferred* beside the sun — and we shall never see them. Among ourselves, this is a parable; and a psychologist of morals reads the whole writing of the stars only as a parable- and sign-language which can be used to bury much in silence.

197

We misunderstand the beast of prey and the man of prey (for example, Cesare Borgia)[12] thoroughly, we misunderstand "nature," as long as we still look for something "pathological" at the bottom of these healthiest of all tropical monsters and growths, or even for some "hell" that is supposed to be innate in them; yet this is what almost all moralists so far have done. Could it be that moralists harbor a hatred of the primeval forest and the tropics? And that the "tropical man" must be discredited at any price, whether as sickness and degeneration of man or as his own hell and self-torture? Why? In favor of the "temperate zones"? In favor of temperate men? Of those who are "moral"? Who are mediocre? — This for the chapter "Morality as Timidity."

198

All these moralities that address themselves to the individual, for the sake of his "happiness," as one says — what are they but counsels for behavior in relation to the degree of *dangerousness* in which the individual lives with himself; recipes against his passions, his good and bad inclinations insofar as they have the will to power and want to play the master; little and great prudences and artifices that exude the nook odor of old nostrums and of the wisdom of old women; all of them baroque and unreasonable in form — because they address themselves to "all," because they generalize where one must not generalize. All of them speak unconditionally, take themselves for unconditional, all of them flavored with more than one grain of salt and tolerable only — at times even seductive — when they begin to smell over-spiced and dangerous, especially "of the other world." All of it is, measured intellectually, worth very little and not by a long shot "science," much less "wisdom," but rather, to say it once more, three times more, prudence, prudence, prudence, mixed with stupidity, stupidity, stupidity — whether it be that indifference and statue coldness against the hot-headed folly of the affects which the Stoics advised and administered; or that laughing-no-more and weeping-no-more of Spinoza, his so naïvely advocated destruction of the affects through their analysis and vivisection; or that tuning down of the affects to a harmless mean according to which they may be satisfied, the Aristotelianism of morals; even morality as

---

11. But compare section 52 above; also *Human, All-Too-Human*, section 475, and *The Dawn*, section 205 (*Portable Nietzsche*, pp. 61ff.; 86f.); and, above all, sections 248 and 250 below. For a discussion of Nietzsche's image of the Jews and the many pertinent passages in his writings, see Kaufmann, *Nietzsche*, Chapter 10.

12. It has often been alleged that Cesare Borgia was Nietzsche's ideal, but an examination of all of Nietzsche's references to him shows that this is plainly false (Kaufmann, *Nietzsche*, Chapter 7, section III). One can consider a type healthy without admiring it or urging others to emulate it.

enjoyment of the affects in a deliberate thinness and spiritualization by means of the symbolism of art, say, as music, or as love of God and of man for God's sake — for in religion the passions enjoy the rights of citizens again, assuming that —— ; finally even that accommodating and playful surrender to the affects, as Hafiz and Goethe taught it, that bold dropping of the reins, that spiritual-physical *licentia morum*[13] in the exceptional case of wise old owls and sots[14] for whom it "no longer holds much danger." This, too, for the chapter "Morality as Timidity."

199

Inasmuch as at all times, as long as there have been human beings, there have also been herds of men (clans, communities, tribes, peoples, states, churches) and always a great many people who obeyed, compared with the small number of those commanding — considering, then, that nothing has been exercised and cultivated better and longer among men so far than obedience — it may fairly be assumed that the need for it is now innate in the average man, as a kind of *formal conscience* that commands: "thou shalt unconditionally do something, unconditionally not do something else," in short, "thou shalt." This need seeks to satisfy itself and to fill its form with some content. According to its strength, impatience, and tension, it seizes upon things as a rude appetite, rather indiscriminately, and accepts whatever is shouted into its ears by someone who issues commands — parents, teachers, laws, class prejudices, public opinions.

The strange limits of human development, the way it hesitates, takes so long, often turns back, and moves in circles, is due to the fact that the herd instinct of obedience is inherited best, and at the expense of the art of commanding. If we imagine this instinct progressing for once to its ultimate excesses, then those who command and are independent would eventually be lacking altogether; or they would secretly suffer from a bad conscience and would find it necessary to deceive themselves before they could command — as if they, too, merely obeyed. This state is actually encountered in Europe today: I call it the moral hypocrisy of those commanding. They know no other way to protect themselves against their bad conscience than to pose as the executors of more ancient or higher commands (of ancestors, the constitution, of right, the laws, or even of God). Or they even borrow herd maxims from the herd's way of thinking, such as "first servants of their people" or "instruments of the common weal."

On the other side, the herd man in Europe today gives himself the appearance of being the only permissible kind of man, and glorifies his attributes, which make him tame, easy to get along with, and useful to the herd, as if they were the truly human virtues: namely, public spirit, benevolence, consideration, industriousness, moderation, modesty, indulgence, and pity. In those cases, however, where one considers leaders and bellwethers indispensable, people today make one attempt after another to add together clever herd men by way of replacing commanders: all parliamentary constitutions, for example, have this origin. Nevertheless, the appearance of one who commands unconditionally strikes these herd-animal Europeans as an immense comfort and salvation from a gradually intolerable pressure, as was last attested in a major way by the effect of Napoleon's appearance. The history of Napoleon's reception is almost the history of the higher happiness attained by this whole century in its most valuable human beings and moments.

---

13. Moral license.

14. The association of Goethe and Hafiz is suggested by Goethe's great collection of poems, *West-Östlicher Divan* (West-Eastern Divan, 1819), in which he identifies himself with the Persian poet. But the old Goethe, unlike Hafiz, was certainly no sot.

200

A person who lives in an age of disintegration that mixes all the races together, will carry in his body the heritage of his multifarious origins, that is to say, contradictory and often more than merely contradictory standards and instincts that struggle with one another and seldom come to rest. Such a person, in the dimming light of a late culture, will generally be a weak person: his most heartfelt desire is that the war that he *embodies* come to an end. In agreement with a medicine and a mentality that tranquilizes (Epicureanism) or Christianity, for example), he takes happiness to be essentially the happiness of rest, of tranquillity, of satiety, of ultimate oneness, to be the 'Sabbath of Sabbaths',* in the words of the sainted rhetorician Augustine, who was that kind of man himself.

But when the opposition and war in such a nature have the effect of one more charm and incentive of life — and if, moreover, in addition to his powerful and irreconcilable drives, a real mastery and subtlety in waging war against oneself, in other words, self-control, self-outwitting, has been inherited or cultivated, too — then those magical, incomprehensible, and unfathomable ones arise, those enigmatic men predestined for victory and seduction, whose most beautiful expression is found in Alcibiades and Caesar (in whose company I should like to add that *first* European after my taste, the Hohenstaufen Frederick II),[15] and among artists perhaps Leonardo da Vinci. They appear in precisely the same ages when that weaker type with its desire for rest comes to the fore: both types belong together and owe their origin to the same causes.

201

As long as the utility reigning in moral value judgments is solely the utility of the herd, as long as one considers only the preservation of the community, and immorality is sought exactly and exclusively in what seems dangerous to the survival of the community — there can be no morality of "neighbor love." Supposing that even then there was a constant little exercise of consideration, pity, fairness, mildness, reciprocity of assistance; suppose that even in that state of society all those drives are active that later receive the honorary designation of "virtues" and eventually almost coincide with the concept of "morality" — in that period they do not yet at all belong in the realm of moral valuations; they are still *extra-moral*. An act of pity, for example, was not considered either good or bad, moral or immoral, in the best period of the Romans; and even when it was praised, such praise was perfectly compatible with a kind of disgruntled disdain as soon as it was juxtaposed with an action that served the welfare of the whole, of the *res publica*.[16]

In the last analysis, "love of the neighbor" is always something secondary, partly conventional and arbitrary-illusory in relation to *fear of the neighbor*. After the structure of society is fixed on the whole and seems secure against external dangers, it is this fear of the neighbor that again creates new perspectives of moral valuation. Certain strong and dangerous drives, like an enter-

---

15. Medieval German emperor, 1215–50. The members of the Stefan George Circle cultivated "monumentalistic" historiography, in the sense of Nietzsche's second "Untimely Meditation," and penned portraits of great men partly aimed to show the qualities that constitute human greatness. Two of their most celebrated studies are Friedrich Gundolf's *Caesar* (1924) and Ernst Kantorowicz's *Kaiser Friedrich II* (1927). Another such study is Ernst Bertram's *Nietzsche* (1918), whose faults are summed up in the subtitle "Attempt at a Mythology."

16. Commonwealth.

prising spirit, foolhardiness, vengefulness, craftiness, rapacity, and the lust to rule, which had so far not merely been honored insofar as they were socially useful — under different names, to be sure, from those chosen here — but had to be trained and cultivated to make them great (because one constantly needed them in view of the dangers to the whole community, against the enemies of the community), and now experienced as doubly dangerous, since the channels to direct them are lacking, and, step upon step, they are branded as immoral and abandoned to slander.

Now the opposite drives and inclinations receive moral honor; step by step, the herd instinct draws its conclusions. How much or how little is dangerous to the community, dangerous to equality, in an opinion, in a state or affect, in a will, in a talent — that now constitutes the moral perspective: here, too, fear is again the mother of morals.

The highest and strongest drives, when they break out passionately and drive the individual far above the average and the flats of the herd conscience, wreck the self-confidence of the community, its faith in itself, and it is as if its spine snapped. Hence just these drives are branded and slandered most. High and independent spirituality, the will to stand alone, even a powerful reason are experienced as dangers; everything that elevates an individual above the herd and intimidates the neighbor is henceforth called *evil;* and the fair, modest, submissive, conforming mentality, the *mediocrity* of desires attains moral designations and honors. Eventually, under very peaceful conditions, the opportunity and necessity for educating one's feelings to severity and hardness is lacking more and more; and every severity, even in justice, begins to disturb the conscience; any high and hard nobility and self-reliance is almost felt to be an insult and arouses mistrust; the "lamb," even more the "sheep," gains in respect.

There is a point in the history of society when it becomes so pathologically soft and tender that among other things it sides even with those who harm it, criminals, and does this quite seriously and honestly. Punishing somehow seems unfair to it, and it is certain that imagining "punishment" and "being supposed to punish" hurts it, arouses fear in it. "Is it not enough to render him *undangerous*? Why still punish? Punishing itself is terrible." With this question, herd morality, the morality of timidity, draws its ultimate consequence. Supposing that one could altogether abolish danger, the reason for fear, this morality would be abolished, too, *eo ipso:* it would no longer be needed, it would no longer *consider itself* necessary.

Whoever examines the conscience of the European today will have to pull the same imperative out of a thousand moral folds and hideouts — the imperative of herd timidity: "we want that some day there should be *nothing any more to be afraid of*!" Some day — throughout Europe, the will and way to this day is now called "progress."[17]

202

Let us immediately say once more what we have already said a hundred times, for today's ears resist such truths — *our* truths. We know well enough how insulting it sounds when anybody counts man, unadorned and without metaphor, among the animals; but it will be charged against us as almost a *guilt* that precisely for the men of "modern ideas" we constantly employ such expressions as "herd," "herd instincts," and so forth. What can be done about it? We can-

---

17. Cf. F. D. Roosevelt's celebrated demand for "freedom from fear." The idea that much of man's conduct and culture can be explained in terms of fear was first explored extensively by Nietzsche in *The Dawn* (1881). For some discussion and pertinent quotations, see Kaufmann's *Nietzsche,* Chapter 6, section II; for Nietzsche's own opposition to punishment and resentment, *ibid.,* Chapter 12, section V. Nietzsche's critique of one type of opposition to punishment, above, should be compared with *Twilight of the Idols,* section 37.

not do anything else; for here exactly lies our novel insight. We have found that in all major moral judgments Europe is now of one mind, including even the countries dominated by the influence of Europe: plainly, one now *knows* in Europe what Socrates thought he did not know and what that famous old serpent once promised to teach — today one "knows" what is good and evil.[18]

Now it must sound harsh and cannot be heard easily when we keep insisting: that which here believes it knows, that which here glorifies itself with its praises and reproaches, calling itself good, that is the instinct of the herd animal, man, which has scored a breakthrough and attained prevalence and predominance over other instincts — and this development is continuing in accordance with the growing physiological approximation and assimilation of which it is the symptom. *Morality in Europe today is herd animal morality* — in other words, as we understand it, merely *one* type of human morality beside which, before which, and after which many other types, above all *higher* moralities, are, or ought to be, possible. But this morality resists such a "possibility," such an "ought" with all its power: it says stubbornly and inexorably, "I am morality itself, and nothing besides is morality." Indeed, with the help of a religion which indulged and flattered the most sublime herd-animal desires, we have reached the point where we find even in political and social institutions an ever more visible expression of this morality: the *democratic* movement is the heir of the Christian movement.

But there are indications that its tempo is still much too slow and sleepy for the more impatient, for the sick, the sufferers of the instinct mentioned: witness the ever madder howling of the anarchist dogs who are baring their fangs more and more obviously and roam through the alleys of European culture. They seem opposites of the peacefully industrious democrats and ideologists of revolution, and even more so of the doltish philosophasters and brotherhood enthusiasts who call themselves socialists and want a "free society"; but in fact they are at one with the lot in their thorough and instinctive hostility to every other form of society except that of the *autonomous* herd (even to the point of repudiating the very concepts of "master" and "servant" — *ni dieu ni maître*[19] runs a socialist formula). They are at one in their tough resistance to every special claim, every special right and privilege (which means in the last analysis, *every* right: for once all are equal nobody needs "rights" any more). They are at one in their mistrust of punitive justice (as if it were a violation of those who are weaker, a wrong against the *necessary* consequence of all previous society). But they are also at one in the religion of pity, in feeling with all who feel, live, and suffer (down to the animal, up to "God" — the excess of a "pity with God" belongs in a democratic age). They are at one, the lot of them, in the cry and the impatience of pity, in their deadly hatred of suffering generally, in their almost feminine inability to remain spectators, to *let* someone suffer. They are at one in their involuntary plunge into gloom and unmanly tenderness under whose spell Europe seems threatened by a new Buddhism. They are at one in their faith in the morality of *shared* pity, as if that were morality in itself, being the height, the *attained* height of man, the sole hope of the future, the consolation of present man, the great absolution from all former guilt. They are at one, the lot of them, in their faith in the community as the *savior,* in short, in the herd, in "themselves" —

---

18. Cf. *Zarathustra,* "On Old and New Tablets," section 2 (*Portable Nietzsche,* p. 308): "When I came to men I found them sitting on an old conceit: the conceit that they have long known what is good and evil for man . . . whoever wanted to sleep well still talked of good and evil before going to sleep."

And in Shaw's Major Barbara (Act III) Undershaft says: "What! no capacity for business, no knowledge of law, no sympathy with art, no pretension to philosophy; only a simple knowledge of the secret that has puzzled all the philosophers, baffled all the lawyers . . . : the secret of right and wrong. Why, man, you are a genius, a master of masters, a god! At twenty-four, too!"

19. "Neither god nor master"; cf. section 22 above.

203

We have a different faith; to us the democratic movement is not only a form of the decay of political organization but a form of the decay, namely the diminution, of man, making him mediocre and lowering his value. Where, then, must *we* reach with our hopes?

Toward *new philosophers;* there is no choice; toward spirits strong and original enough to provide the stimuli for opposite valuations and to revalue and invert "eternal values"; toward forerunners, toward men of the future who in the present tie the knot and constraint that forces the will of millennia upon *new* tracks. To teach man the future of man as his *will,* as dependent on a human will, and to prepare great ventures and over-all attempts of discipline and cultivation by way of putting an end to that gruesome dominion of nonsense and accident that has so far been called "history" — the nonsense of the "greatest number" is merely its ultimate form: at some time new types of philosophers and commanders will be necessary for that, and whatever has existed on earth of concealed, terrible, and benevolent spirits, will look pale and dwarfed by comparison. It is the image of such leaders that *we* envisage: may I say this out loud, you free spirits? The conditions that one would have partly to create and partly to exploit for their genesis; the probable ways and tests that would enable a soul to grow to such a height and force that it would feel the *compulsion* for such tasks; a revaluation of values under whose new pressure and hammer a conscience would be steeled, a heart turned to bronze, in order to endure the weight of such responsibility; on the other hand, the necessity of such leaders, the frightening danger that they might fail to appear or that they might turn out badly or degenerate — these are *our* real worries and gloom — do you know that, you free spirits? — these are the heavy distant thoughts and storms that pass over the sky of *our* life.

There are few pains as sore as once having seen, guessed, felt how an extraordinary human being strayed from his path and degenerated.[20] But anyone who has the rare eye for the over-all danger that "man" himself *degenerates;* anyone who, like us, has recognized the monstrous fortuity that has so far had its way and play regarding the future of man — a game in which no hand, and not even a finger, of God took part as a player; anyone who fathoms the calamity that lies concealed in the absurd guilelessness and blind confidence of "modern ideas" and even more in the whole Christian-European morality — suffers from an anxiety that is past all comparisons. With a single glance he sees what, given a favorable accumulation and increase of forces and tasks, might yet *be made of man;* he knows with all the knowledge of his conscience how man is still unexhausted for the greatest possibilities and how often the type "man" has already confronted enigmatic decisions and new paths — he knows still better from his most painful memories what wretched things have so far usually broken a being of the highest rank that was in the process of becoming, so that it broke, sank, and became contemptible.

The *over-all degeneration of man* down to what today appears to the socialist dolts and flatheads as their "man of the future" — as their ideal — this degeneration and diminution of man into the perfect herd animal (or, as they say, to the man of the "free society"), this animalization of man into the dwarf animal of equal rights and claims, is *possible,* there is no doubt of it. Anyone who has once thought through this possibility to the end knows one kind of nausea that other men don't know — but perhaps also a new *task!* —

---

20. Perhaps an allusion to Richard Wagner.

Thomas Merton

THE SEVEN-STOREY MOUNTAIN

Introduction by Shelley Baranowski

Thomas Merton (1915–1968), who as a monk and Roman Catholic priest was known as Father Louis, achieved international stature as a religious writer and poet. Born in France to American parents, Merton studied first at the University of Cambridge in England and then at Columbia University in New York, where he earned two degrees in English literature. In 1939 Merton converted to Catholicism while a student at Columbia. This was after a long odyssey in search of the meaning of his life, one that provoked dissatisfaction with various forms of pragmatism and materialism and awakened his spirituality. Two years after his conversion, Merton chose the contemplative life, entering the Trappist monastery of Our Lady of Gethsemane in Kentucky. As heirs to the Benedictines and Cistercians, the Trappists adhere to the Rule of St. Benedict, taking vows of silence, poverty, and obedience in order to emulate the asceticism of early Christianity. In 1949, Merton was ordained a priest, but remained a Trappist monk until his accidental death in Bangkok, Thailand in 1968.

Merton's literary output was prodigious, consisting of eight books and countless shorter pieces. Together, they reveal a striking blend of spiritual and moral commitments, including a strong attraction to mysticism, a deep interest in the religious traditions of Asia (he was attending a Christian-Buddhist conference in Bangkok when he died), and his support of the peace and civil rights movements. Yet Merton's autobiography *The Seven-Storey Mountain,* which was published in 1948, is his best-known work. Like Augustine's *Confessions,* Merton wrote this work after his conversion to Catholicism. As a consequence that most important event of his life colors his reflections on his life prior to his conversion. As a guide for others, Merton seeks to give readers confidence in God's daily intervention in human life. Thus, Merton describes his actions and choices during his youth, even at their most "sinful," as following God's plan for him, the outcome of which was Merton's rescue through conversion.

The selection below opens with Merton enrolled as a Columbia student and wrestling with his attraction to Catholicism that grew in him despite the anti-Catholic prejudices of a surrounding protestant culture and a brief flirtation with communism, which was common during the Depression. Continuous reading and reflection played an important role Merton's self-described transformation, as did the very aspects of Catholicism that secular intellectuals and protestants disparaged. What about Catholic theology and practice specifically did he find so valuable and comforting? Ironically, Merton's developing spirituality owed much to an encounter with a Hindu mystic. What advice from the Hindu reinforced his movement toward

Catholicism? Merton's odyssey forces us to question one of the central claims of the Enlightenment: "revealed" religion (religion that rested on claims about supernatural revelation and intervention), resulted from ignorance and irrationality. Thus, the cultivation of reason through proper education would render human beings more likely to seek rational explanations for natural and cosmological phenomena, and thus less susceptible to the supernatural, mystical or miraculous. Merton's story, however, illustrates the degree to which religion has proven a vital cultural and political force since the eighteenth century, despite the secularizing tendencies of the Enlightenment and its heirs, liberalism and socialism.

I

With a Great Price

There is a paradox that lies in the very heart of human existence. It must be apprehended before any lasting happiness is possible in the soul of a man. The paradox is this: man's nature, by itself, can do little or nothing to settle his most important problems. If we follow nothing but our natures, our own philosophies, our own level of ethics, we will end up in hell.

This would be a depressing thought, if it were not purely abstract. Because in the concrete order of things God gave man a nature that was ordered to a supernatural life. He created man with a soul that was made not to bring itself to perfection in its own order, but to be perfected by Him in an order infinitely beyond the reach of human powers. We were never destined to lead purely natural lives, and therefore we were never destined in God's plan for a purely natural beatitude. Our nature, which is a free gift of God, was given to us to be perfected and enhanced by another free gift that is not due it.

This free gift is "sanctifying grace." It perfects our nature with the gift of a life, an intellection, a love, a mode of existence infinitely above its own level. If a man were to arrive even at the abstract pinnacle of natural perfection, God's work would not even be half done: it would be only about to begin, for the real work is the work of grace and the infused virtues and the gifts of the Holy Ghost.

What is "grace"? It is God's own life, shared by us. God's life is Love. *Deus caritas est.* By grace we are able to share in the infinitely self-less love of Him Who is such pure actuality that He needs nothing and therefore cannot conceivably exploit anything for selfish ends. Indeed, outside of Him there is nothing, and whatever exists exists by His free gift of its being, so that one of the notions that is absolutely contradictory to the perfection of God is selfishness. It is metaphysically impossible for God to be selfish, because the existence of everything that is depends upon His gift, depends upon His unselfishness.

When a ray of light strikes a crystal, it gives a new quality to the crystal. And when God's infinitely disinterested love plays upon a human soul, the same kind of thing takes place. And that is the life called sanctifying grace.

The soul of man, left to its own natural level, is a potentially lucid crystal left in darkness. It is perfect in its own nature, but it lacks something that it can only receive from outside and above itself. But when the light shines in it, it becomes in a manner transformed into light and seems to lose its nature in the splendor of a higher nature, the nature of the light that is in it.

Thomas Merton, *The Seven-Story Mountain* (San Diego/New York/London: Harcourt Brace Jovanovich, 1948/1976), ISBN 0156806797, pp. 169–225.

So the natural goodness of man, his capacity for love which must always be in some sense selfish if it remains in the natural order, becomes transfigured and transformed when the Love of God shines in it. What happens when a man loses himself completely in the Divine Life within him? This perfection is only for those who are called the saints — for those rather who *are* the saints and who live in the light of God alone. For the ones who are called saints by human opinion on earth may very well be devils, and their light may very well be darkness. For as far as the light of God is concerned, we are owls. It blinds us and as soon as it strikes us we are in darkness. People who look like saints to us are very often not so, and those who do not look like saints very often are. And the greatest saints are sometimes the most obscure — Our Lady, St. Joseph.

Christ established His Church, among other reasons, in order that men might lead one another to Him and in the process sanctify themselves and one another. For in this work it is Christ Who draws us to Himself through the action of our fellow men.

We must check the inspirations that come to us in the depths of our own conscience against the revelation that is given to us with divinely certain guarantees by those who have inherited in our midst the place of Christ's Apostles — by those who speak to us in the Name of Christ and as it were in His own Person. *Qui vos audit me audit; qui vos spernit, me spernit.*

When it comes to accepting God's own authority about things that cannot possibly be known in any other way except as revealed by His authority, people consider it insanity to incline their ears and listen. Things that cannot be known in any other way, they will not accept from this source. And yet they will meekly and passively accept the most appalling lies from newspapers when they scarcely need to crane their necks to see the truth in front of them, over the top of the sheet they are holding in their hands.

For example, the very thought of an *imprimatur* on the front of a book — the approbation of a bishop, allowing the book to be printed on the grounds that it contains safe doctrine — is something that drives some people almost out of their minds with indignation.

One day, in the month of February 1937, I happened to have five or ten loose dollars burning a hole in my pocket. I was on Fifth Avenue, for some reason or other, and was attracted by the window of Scribner's bookstore, all full of bright new books.

That year I had signed up for a course in French Medieval Literature. My mind was turning back, in a way, to the things I remembered from the old days in Saint Antonin. The deep, naive, rich simplicity of the twelfth and thirteenth centuries was beginning to speak to me again. I had written a paper on a legend of a "Jongleur de Notre Dame," compared with a story from the Fathers of the Desert, in Migne's *Latin Patrology*. I was being drawn back into the Catholic atmosphere, and I could feel the health of it, even in the merely natural order, working already within me.

Now, in Scribner's window, I saw a book called *The Spirit of Medieval Philosophy*. I went inside, and took it off the shelf, and looked at the table of contents and at the title page which was deceptive, because it said the book was made up of a series of lectures that had been given at the University of Aberdeen. That was no recommendation, to me especially. But it threw me off the track as to the possible identity and character of Etienne Gilson, who wrote the book.

I bought it, then, together with one other book that I have completely forgotten, and on my way home in the Long Island train, I unwrapped the package to gloat over my acquisitions. It was only then that I saw, on the first page of *The Spirit of Medieval Philosophy,* the small print which said: "Nihil Obstat . . . Imprimatur."

The feeling of disgust and deception struck me like a knife in the pit of the stomach. I felt as if I had been cheated! They should have warned me that it was a Catholic book! Then I would never have bought it. As it was, I was tempted to throw the thing out the window at the houses of Woodside — to get rid of it as something dangerous and unclean. Such is the terror that is aroused in the enlightened modern mind by a little innocent Latin and the signature of a priest. It is impossible to communicate, to a Catholic, the number and complexity of fearful associations that a little thing like this can carry with it. It is in Latin — a difficult, ancient and obscure tongue. That implies, to the mind that has roots in Protestantism, all kinds of sinister secrets, which the priests are supposed to cherish and to conceal from common men in this unknown language. Then, the mere fact that they should pass judgement on the character of a book, and permit people to read it: that in itself is fraught with terror. It immediately conjures up all the real and imaginary excesses of the Inquisition.

That is something of what I felt when I opened Gilson's book: for you must understand that while I admired Catholic culture, I had always been afraid of the Catholic Church. That is a rather common position in the world today. After all, I had not bought a book on medieval philosophy without realizing that it would be Catholic philosophy: but the imprimatur told me that what I read would be in full conformity with that fearsome and mysterious thing, Catholic Dogma, and the fact struck me with an impact against which everything in me reacted with repugnance and fear.

Now in the light of all this, I consider that it was surely a real grace that, instead of getting rid of the book, I actually read it. Not all of it, it is true: but more than I used to read of books that deep. When I think of the numbers of books I had on my shelf in the little room at Douglaston that had once been Pop's "den" — books which I had bought and never even read, I am more astounded than ever at the fact that I actually read this one: and what is more, remembered it.

And the one big concept which I got out of its pages was something that was to revolutionize my whole life. It is all contained in one of those dry, outlandish technical compounds that the scholastic philosophers were so prone to use: the word *aseitas*. In this one word, which can be applied to God alone, and which expresses His most characteristic attribute, I discovered an entirely new concept of God — a concept which showed me at once that the belief of Catholics was by no means the vague and rather superstitious hangover from an unscientific age that I had believed it to be. On the contrary, here was a notion of God that was at the same time deep, precise, simple and accurate and, what is more, charged with implications which I could not even begin to appreciate, but which I could at least dimly estimate, even with my own lack of philosophical training.

Aseitas — the English equivalent is a transliteration: aseity — simply means the power of a being to exist absolutely in virtue of itself, not as caused by itself, but as requiring no cause, no other justification for its existence except that its very nature is to exist. There can be only one such Being: that is God. And to say that God exists *a se*, of and by and by reason of Himself, is merely to say that God is Being Itself. *Ego sum qui sum.* And this means that God must enjoy "complete independence not only as regards everything outside but also as regards everything within Himself."

This notion made such a profound impression on me that I made a pencil note at the top of the page: "Aseity of God — God is being *per se*." I observe it now on the page, for I brought the book to the monastery with me, and although I was not sure where it had gone, I found it on the shelves in Father Abbot's room the other day, and I have it here before me.

I marked three other passages, so perhaps the best thing would be to copy them down. Better than anything I could say, they will convey the impact of the book on my mind.

> When God says that He is being [reads the first sentence so marked] and if what He says is to have any intelligible meaning to our minds, it can only mean this: that He is the pure act of existing.

Pure act: therefore excluding all imperfection in the order of existing. Therefore excluding all change, all "becoming," all beginning or end, all limitation. But from this fulness of existence, if I had been capable of considering it deeply enough, I would soon have found that the fulness of all perfection could easily be argued.

But another thing that struck me was an important qualification the author made. He distinguished between the concepts of *ens in genere* — the abstract notion of being in general — and *ens infinitum*, the concrete and real Infinite Being, Who, Himself, transcends all our conceptions. And so I marked the following words, which were to be my first step towards St. John of the Cross:

> Beyond all sensible images, and all conceptual determinations, God affirms Himself as the absolute act of being in its pure actuality. Our concept of God, a mere feeble analogue of a reality which overflows it in every direction, can be made explicit only in the judgement: Being is Being, an absolute positing of that which, lying beyond every object, contains in itself the sufficient reason of objects. And that is why we can rightly say that the very excess of positivity which hides the divine being from our eyes is nevertheless the light which lights up all the rest: *ipsa caligo summa est mentis illuminatio.*

His Latin quotation was from St. Bonaventure's *Itinerarium.*
The third sentence of Gilson's that I marked in those few pages read as follows:

> When St. Jerome says that God is His own origin and the cause of his own substance, he does not mean, as Descartes does, that God in a certain way posits Himself in being by His almighty power as by a cause, but simply that we must not look outside of God for a cause of the existence of God.

I think the reason why these statements, and others like them, made such a profound impression on me, lay deep in my own soul. And it was this: I had never had an adequate notion of what Christians meant by God. I had simply taken it for granted that the God in Whom religious people believed, and to Whom they attributed the creation and government of all things, was a noisy and dramatic and passionate character, a vague, jealous, hidden being, the objectification of all their own desires and strivings and subjective ideals.

The truth is, that the concept of God which I had always entertained, and which I had accused Christians of teaching to the world, was a concept of a being who was simply impossible. He was infinite and yet finite; perfect and imperfect; eternal and yet changing — subject to all the variations of emotion, love, sorrow, hate, revenge, that men are prey to. How could this fatuous, emotional thing be without beginning and without end, the creator of all? I had taken the dead letter of Scripture at its very deadest, and it had killed me, according to the saying of St. Paul: "The letter killeth, but the spirit giveth life!"

I think one cause of my profound satisfaction with what I now read was that God had been vindicated in my own mind. There is in every intellect a natural exigency for a true concept of God: we are born with the thirst to know and to see Him, and therefore it cannot be otherwise.

I know that many people are, or call themselves, "atheists" simply because they are repelled and offended by statements about God made in imaginary and metaphorical terms which they are not able to interpret and comprehend. They refuse these concepts of God not because they despise God, but perhaps because they demand a notion of Him more perfect than they generally find: and because ordinary, figurative concepts of God could not satisfy them, they turn away and think that there are no other: or, worse still, they refuse to listen to philosophy, on the ground that it is nothing but a web of meaningless words spun together for the justification of the same old hopeless falsehoods.

What a relief it was for me, now, to discover not only that no idea of ours, let alone any image, could adequately represent God, but also that we *should not* allow ourselves to be satisfied with any such knowledge of Him.

The result was that I at once acquired an immense respect for Catholic philosophy and for the Catholic faith. And that last thing was the most important of all. I now at least recognized that faith was something that had a very definite meaning and a most cogent necessity.

If this much was a great thing, it was about all that I could do at the moment. I could recognize that those who thought about God had a good way of considering Him, and that those who believed in Him really believed in someone, and their faith was more than a dream. Further than that it seemed I could not go, for the time being.

How many there are in the same situation! They stand in the stacks of libraries and turn over the pages of St. Thomas's *Summa* with a kind of curious reverence. They talk in their seminars about "Thomas" and "Scotus" and "Augustine" and "Bonaventure" and they are familiar with Maritain and Gilson, and they have read all the poems of Hopkins — and indeed they know more about what is best in the Catholic literary and philosophical tradition than most Catholics ever do on this earth. They sometimes go to Mass, and wonder at the dignity and restraint of the old liturgy. They are impressed by the organization of a Church in which everywhere the priests, even the most un-gifted, are able to preach at least something of a tremendous, profound, unified doctrine, and to dispense mysteriously efficacious help to all who come to them with troubles and needs.

In a certain sense, these people have a better appreciation of the Church and of Catholicism than many Catholics have: an appreciation which is detached and intellectual and objective. But they never come into the Church. They stand and starve in the doors of the banquet — the banquet to which they surely realize that they are invited — while those more poor, more stupid, less gifted, less educated, sometimes even less virtuous than they, enter in and are filled at those tremendous tables.

When I had put this book down, and had ceased to think explicitly about its arguments, its effect began to show itself in my life. I began to have a desire to go to church — and a desire more sincere and mature and more deep-seated than I had ever had before. After all, I had never before had so great a need.

The only place I could think of was the Episcopal Church down the road, old Zion Church, among the locust trees, where Father had once played the organ. I think the reason for this was that God wanted me to climb back the way I had fallen down. I had come to despise the Church of England, the "Protestant Episcopal Church," and He wanted me to do away with what there was of pride and self-complacency even in that. He would not let me become a Catholic, having behind me a rejection of another church that was not the right kind of a rejection, but one that was sinful in itself, rooted in pride, and expressed in contumely.

This time I came back to Zion Church, not to judge it, not to condemn the poor minister, but to see if it could not do something to satisfy the obscure need for faith that was beginning to make itself felt in my soul.

It was a nice enough church. It was pleasant to sit there, in the pretty little white building, with the sun pouring through the windows, on Sunday mornings. The choir of surpliced men and women and the hymns we all sang did not exactly send me up into ecstasy: but at least I no longer made fun of them in my heart. And when it came time to say the Apostles' Creed, I stood up and said it, with the rest, hoping within myself that God would give me the grace someday to really believe it.

The minister was called Mr. Riley. Pop had always called him "Dr. Riley" to his great embarrassment. Despite the Irish name, he detested Catholics, like most Protestant ministers. He was always very friendly to me and used to get into conversations about intellectual matters and modern literature, even men like D. H. Lawrence with whom he was thoroughly familiar.

It seems that he counted very much on this sort of thing — considered it an essential part of his ministry to keep up with the latest books, and to be able to talk about them, to maintain contact with people by that means. But that was precisely one of the things that made the experience of going to his church such a sterile one for me. He did not like or understand what was considered most "advanced" in modern literature and, as a matter of fact, one did not expect him to; one did not demand that of him. Yet it was modern literature and politics that he talked about, not religion and God. You felt that the man did not know his vocation, did not know what he was supposed to be. He had taken upon himself some function in society which was not his and which was, indeed, not a necessary function at all.

When he did get around to preaching about some truth of the Christian religion, he practically admitted in the pulpit, as he did in private to anyone who cared to talk about it that he did not believe most of these doctrines, even in the extremely diluted form in which they are handed out to Protestants. The Trinity? What did he want with the Trinity? And as for the strange medieval notions about the Incarnation, well, that was simply too much to ask of a reasonable man.

Once he preached a sermon on "Music at Zion Church" and sent me word that I must be sure to be there, for I would hear him make mention of my father. That is just about typical of Protestant pulpit oratory in the more "liberal" quarters. I went, dutifully, that morning, but before he got around to the part in which I was supposed to be personally interested, I got an attack of my head-spinning and went out into the air. When the sermon was being preached, I was sitting on the church steps in the sun, talking to the black-gowned verger, or whatever he was called. By the time I felt better, the sermon was over.

I cannot say I went to this church very often: but the measure of my zeal may be judged by the fact that I once went even in the middle of the week. I forget what was the occasion: Ash Wednesday or Holy Thursday. There were one or two women in the place, and myself lurking in one of the back benches. We said some prayers. It was soon over. By the time it was, I had worked up courage to take the train into New York and go to Columbia for the day.

ii

Now I come to speak of the real part Columbia seems to have been destined to play in my life in the providential designs of God. Poor Columbia! It was founded by sincere Protestants as a college predominantly religious. The only thing that remains of that is the university motto: *In lumine tuo videbimus lumen* — one of the deepest and most beautiful lines of the psalms. "In Thy light, we shall see light." It is, precisely, about grace. It is a line that might serve as the foundation stone of all Christian and Scholastic learning, and which simply has nothing whatever to do with the standards of education at modern Columbia. It might profitably be changed to *In lumine Randall videbimus Dewey.*

Yet, strangely enough, it was on this big factory of a campus that the Holy Ghost was waiting to show me the light, in His own light. And one of the chief means He used, and through which he operated, was human friendship.

God has willed that we should all depend on one another for our salvation, and all strive together for our own mutual good and our own common salvation. Scripture teaches us that this is especially true in the supernatural order, in the doctrine of the Mystical Body of Christ, which flows necessarily from Christian teaching on grace.

"You are the body of Christ and members one of another. . . . And the eye cannot say to the hand: I need not thy help: nor again the head to the feet, I have no need of you. . . . And if one member suffer anything, all the members suffer with it; and if one member glory all the others rejoice with it."

So now is the time to tell a thing that I could not realize then, but which has become very clear to me: that God brought me and a half a dozen others together at Columbia, and made us friends, in such a way that our friendship would work powerfully to rescue us from the confusion and the misery in which we had come to find ourselves, partly through our own fault, and partly through a complex set of circumstances which might be grouped together under the heading of the "modern world," "modern society." But the qualification "modern" is unnecessary and perhaps unfair. The traditional Gospel term, "the world," will do well enough.

All our salvation begins on the level of common and natural and ordinary things. (That is why the whole economy of the Sacraments, for instance, rests, in its material element, upon plain and ordinary things like bread and wine and water and salt and oil.) And so it was with me. Books and ideas and poems and stories, pictures and music, buildings, cities, places, philosophies were to be the materials on which grace would work. But these things are themselves not enough. The more fundamental instinct of fear for my own preservation came in, in a minor sort of a way, in this strange, half-imaginary sickness which nobody could diagnose completely.

The coming war, and all the uncertainties and confusions and fears that followed necessarily from that, and all the rest of the violence and injustice that were in the world, had a very important part to play. All these things were bound together and fused and vitalized and prepared for the action of grace, both in my own soul and in the souls of at least one or two of my friends, merely by our friendship and association together. And it fermented in our sharing of our own ideas and miseries and headaches and perplexities and fears and difficulties and desires and hangovers and all the rest.

I have already mentioned Mark Van Doren. It would not be exactly true to say that he was a kind of nucleus around whom this concretion of friends formed itself: that would not be accurate. Not all of us took his courses, and those who did, did not do so all at the same time. And yet nevertheless our common respect for Mark's sanity and wisdom did much to make us aware of how much we ourselves had in common.

Perhaps it was for me, personally, more than for the others, that Mark's course worked in this way. I am thinking of one particular incident.

It was the fall of 1936, just at the beginning of the new school year — on one of those first bright, crazy days when everybody is full of ambition. It was the beginning of the year in which Pop was going to die and my own resistance would cave in under the load of pleasures and ambitions I was too weak to carry: the year in which I would be all the time getting dizzy, and in which I learned to fear the Long Island railroad as if it were some kind of a monster, and to shrink from New York as if it were the wide-open mouth of some burning Aztec god.

That day, I did not foresee any of this. My veins were still bursting with the materialistic and political enthusiasms with which I had first come to Columbia and, indeed, in line with their general direction, I had signed up for courses that were more or less sociological and economic and historical. In the obscurity of the strange, half-conscious semi-conversion that had attended my retreat from Cambridge, I had tended more and more to be suspicious of literature, poetry — the things towards which my nature drew me — on the grounds that they might lead to a sort of futile estheticism, a philosophy of "escape."

This had not involved me in any depreciation of people like Mark. However, it had just seemed more important to me that I should take some history course, rather than anything that was still left of his for me to take.

So now I was climbing one of the crowded stairways in Hamilton Hall to the room where I thought this history course was to be given. I looked in to the room. The second row was filled with the unbrushed heads of those who every day at noon sat in the *Jester* editorial offices and threw paper airplanes around the room or drew pictures on the walls.

Taller than them all, and more serious, with a long face, like a horse, and a great mane of black hair on top of it, Bob Lax meditated on some incomprehensible woe, and waited for someone to come in and begin to talk to them. It was when I had taken off my coat and put down my load of books that I found out that this was not the class I was supposed to be taking, but Van Doren's course on Shakespeare.

So I got up to go out. But when I got to the door I turned around again and went back and sat down where I had been, and stayed there. Later I went and changed everything with the registrar, so I remained in that class for the rest of the year.

It was the best course I ever had at college. And it did me the most good, in many different ways. It was the only place where I ever heard anything really sensible said about any of the things that were really fundamental — life, death, time, love, sorrow, fear, wisdom, suffering, eternity. A course in literature should never be a course in economics or philosophy or sociology or psychology: and I have explained how it was one of Mark's great virtues that he did not make it so. Nevertheless, the material of literature and especially of drama is chiefly human acts — that is, free acts, moral acts. And, as a matter of fact, literature, drama, poetry, make certain statements about these acts that can be made in no other way. That is precisely why you will miss all the deepest meaning of Shakespeare, Dante, and the rest if you reduce their vital and creative statements about life and men to the dry, matter-of-fact terms of history, or ethics, or some other science. They belong to a different order.

Nevertheless, the great power of something like *Hamlet, Coriolanus,* or the *Purgatorio* or Donne's *Holy Sonnets* lies precisely in the fact that they are a kind of commentary on ethics and psychology and even metaphysics, even theology. Or, sometimes, it is the other way 'round, and those sciences can serve as a commentary on these other realities, which we call plays, poems.

All that year we were, in fact, talking about the deepest springs of human desire and hope and fear; we were considering all the most important realities, not indeed in terms of something alien to Shakespeare and to poetry, but precisely in his own terms, with occasional intuitions of another order. And, as I have said, Mark's balanced and sensitive and clear way of seeing things, at once simple and yet capable of subtlety, being fundamentally scholastic, though not necessarily and explicitly Christian, presented these things in ways that made them live within us, and with a life that was healthy and permanent and productive. This class was one of the few things that could persuade me to get on the train and go to Columbia at all. It was, that year, my only health, until I came across and read the Gilson book.

It was this year, too, that I began to discover who Bob Lax was, and that in him was a combination of Mark's clarity and my confusion and misery — and a lot more besides that was his own.

To name Robert Lax in another way, he was a kind of combination of Hamlet and Elias. A potential prophet, but without rage. A king, but a Jew too. A mind full of tremendous and subtle intuitions, and every day he found less and less to say about them, and resigned himself to being inarticulate. In his hesitations, though without embarrassment or nervousness at all, he would often curl his long legs all around a chair, in seven different ways, while he was trying to find a word with which to begin. He talked best sitting on the floor.

And the secret of his constant solidity I think has always been a kind of natural, instinctive spirituality, a kind of inborn direction to the living God. Lax has always been afraid he was in a blind alley, and half aware that, after all, it might not be a blind alley, but God, infinity.

He had a mind naturally disposed, from the very cradle, to a kind of affinity for Job and St. John of the Cross. And I now know that he was born so much of a contemplative that he will probably never be able to find out how much.

To sum it up, even the people who have always thought he was "too impractical" have always tended to venerate him — in the way people who value material security unconsciously venerate people who do not fear insecurity.

In those days one of the things we had most in common, although perhaps we did not talk about it so much, was the abyss that walked around in front of our feet everywhere we went; and kept making us dizzy and afraid of trains and high buildings. For some reason, Lax developed an implicit trust in all my notions about what was good and bad for mental and physical health, perhaps because I was always very definite in my likes and dislikes. I am afraid it did not do him too much good, though. For even though I had my imaginary abyss, which broadened immeasurably and became ten times dizzier when I had a hangover, my ideas often tended to some particular place where we would hear this particular band and drink this special drink until the place folded up at four o'clock in the morning.

The months passed by, and most of the time I sat in Douglaston, drawing cartoons for the paper-cup business, and trying to do all the other things I was supposed to do. In the summer, Lax went to Europe, and I continued to sit in Douglaston, writing a long, stupid novel about a college football player who got mixed up in a lot of strikes in a textile mill.

I did not graduate that June, although I nominally belonged to that year's class: I had still one or two courses to take, on account of having entered Columbia in February. In the fall of 1937 I went back to school, then, with my mind a lot freer, since I was not burdened with any more of those ugly and useless jobs on the fourth floor. I could write and do the drawings I felt like doing for *Jester*.

I began to talk more to Lax and to Ed Rice who was now drawing better and funnier pictures than anybody else for the magazine. For the first time I saw Sy Freedgood, who was full of a fierce and complex intellectuality which he sometimes liked to present in the guise of a rather suspicious suavity. He was in love with a far more technical vocabulary than any of the rest of us possessed, and was working at something in the philosophy graduate school. Seymour used consciously to affect a whole set of different kinds of duplicity, of which he was proud, and he had carried the *mendacium jocosum* or "humorous lie" to its utmost extension and frequency. You could sometimes gauge the falsity of his answers by their promptitude: the quicker the falser. The reason for this was, probably, that he was thinking of something else, something very abstruse and far from the sphere of your question, and he could not be bothered to bring his mind all that way back, to think up the real answer.

For Lax and myself and Gibney there was no inconvenience about this, for two reasons. Since Seymour generally gave his false answers only to practical questions of fact, their falsity did not matter: we were all too impractical. Besides his false answers were generally more interesting than the truth. Finally, since we knew they were false anyway, we had the habit of seeing all his statements, in the common factual order by a kind of double standard, instituting a comparison between what he had said and the probable truth, and this cast many interesting and ironical lights upon life as a whole.

In his house at Long Beach, where his whole family lived in a state of turmoil and confusion, there was a large, stupid police dog that got in everybody's way with his bowed head and slapped-down ears and amiable, guilty look. The first time I saw the dog, I asked: "What's his name?"

"Prince," said Seymour, out of the corner of his mouth.

It was a name to which the beast responded gladly. I guess he responded to any name, didn't care what you called him, so flattered was he to be called at all, being as he knew an extremely stupid dog.

So I was out on the boardwalk with the dog, shouting: "Hey, Prince; hey, Prince!"

Seymour's wife, Helen, came along and heard me shouting all this and said nothing, imagining, no doubt, that it was some way I had of making fun of the brute. Later, Seymour or someone told me that "Prince" wasn't the dog's name, but they told me in such a way that I got the idea that his name was really "Rex." So for some time after that I called him: "Hey, Rex; hey, Rex!" Several months later, after many visits to the house, I finally learned that the dog was called nothing like Prince nor Rex, but "Bunky."

Moral theologians say that the *mendacium jocosum* in itself does not exceed a venial sin.

Seymour and Lax were rooming together in one of the dormitories, for Bob Gibney, with whom Lax had roomed the year before, had now graduated, and was sitting in Port Washington with much the same dispositions with which I had been sitting in Douglaston, facing a not too dissimilar blank wall, the end of his own blind-alley. He occasionally came in to town to see Dona Eaton who had a place on 112th Street, but no job, and was more cheerful about her own quandary than the rest of us, because the worst that could happen to her was that she would at last run completely out of money and have to go home to Panama.

Gibney was not what you would call pious. In fact, he had an attitude that would be commonly called impious, only I believe God understood well enough that his violence and sarcasms covered a sense of deep metaphysical dismay — an anguish that was real, though not humble enough to be of much use to his soul. What was materially impiety in him was directed more against common ideas and notions which he saw or considered to be totally inadequate, and maybe it subjectively represented a kind of oblique zeal for the purity of God, this rebellion against the commonplace and trite, against mediocrity, religiosity.

During the year that had passed, I suppose it must have been in the spring of 1937, both Gibney and Lax and Bob Gerdy had all been talking about becoming Catholics. Bob Gerdy was a very smart sophomore with the face of a child and a lot of curly hair on top of it, who took life seriously, and had discovered courses on Scholastic Philosophy in the graduate school, and had taken one of them.

Gibney was interested in Scholastic Philosophy in much the same way as James Joyce was — he respected its intellectuality, particularly that of the Thomists, but there was not enough that was affective about his interest to bring about any kind of a conversion.

For the three or four years that I knew Gibney, he was always holding out for some kind of a "sign," some kind of a sensible and tangible interior jolt from God, to get him started, some mystical experience or other. And while he waited and waited for this to come along, he did all the things that normally exclude and nullify the action of grace. So in those days, none of them became Catholics.

The most serious of them all, in this matter, was Lax: he was the one that had been born with the deepest sense of Who God was. But he would not make a move without the others.

And then there was myself. Having read *The Spirit of Medieval Philosophy* and having discovered that the Catholic conception of God was something tremendously solid, I had not progressed one step beyond this recognition, except that one day I had gone and looked up St. Bernard's *De Diligendo Deo* in the catalogue of the University Library. It was one of the books Gilson had frequently mentioned: but when I found that there was no good copy of it, except in Latin, I did not take it out.

Now it was November 1937. One day, Lax and I were riding downtown on one of those busses you caught at the corner of 110th Street and Broadway. We had skirted the southern edge of Harlem, passing along the top of Central Park, and the dirty lake full of rowboats. Now we were going down Fifth Avenue, under the trees. Lax was telling me about a book he had been reading, which was Aldous Huxley's *Ends and Means*. He told me about it in a way that made me want to read it too.

So I went to Scribner's bookstore and bought it and read it, and wrote an article about it and gave the article to Barry Ulanov who was editor of *Review* by that time. He accepted the article with a big Greek smile and printed it. The smile was on account of the conversion it represented, I mean the conversion in me, as well as in Huxley, although one of the points I tried to make was that perhaps Huxley's conversion should not have been taken as so much of a surprise.

Huxley had been one of my favorite novelists in the days when I had been sixteen and seventeen and had built up a strange, ignorant philosophy of pleasure based on all the stories I was reading. And now everybody was talking about the way Huxley had changed. The chatter was all the more pleasant because of Huxley's agnostic old grandfather — and his biologist brother. Now the man was preaching mysticism.

Huxley was too sharp and intelligent and had too much sense of humor to take any of the missteps that usually make such conversions look ridiculous and oafish. You could not laugh at him, very well — at least not for any one concrete blunder. This was not one of those Oxford Group conversions, complete with a public confession.

On the contrary, he had read widely and deeply and intelligently in all kinds of Christian and Oriental mystical literature, and had come out with the astonishing truth that all this, far from being a mixture of dreams and magic and charlatanism, was very real and very serious.

Not only was there such a thing as a supernatural order, but as a matter of concrete experience, it was accessible, very close at hand, an extremely near, an immediate and most necessary source of moral vitality, and one which could be reached most simply, most readily by prayer, faith, detachment, love.

The point of his title was this: we cannot use evil means to attain a good end. Huxley's chief argument was that we were using the means that precisely made good ends impossible to attain: war, violence, reprisals, rapacity. And he traced our impossibility to use the proper means to the fact that men were immersed in the material and animal urges of an element in their nature which was blind and crude and unspiritual.

The main problem is to fight our way free from subjection to this more or less inferior element, and to reassert the dominance of our mind and will: to vindicate for these faculties, for the spirit as a whole, the freedom of action which it must necessarily have if we are to live like anything but wild beasts, tearing each other to pieces. And the big conclusion from all this was: we must practice prayer and asceticism.

Asceticism! The very thought of such a thing was a complete revolution in my mind. The word had so far stood for a kind of weird and ugly perversion of nature, the masochism of men who had gone crazy in a warped and unjust society. What an idea! To deny the desires of one's flesh, and even to practice certain disciplines that punished and mortified those desires: until this day, these things had never succeeded in giving me anything but goose-flesh. But of course Huxley did not stress the physical angle of mortification and asceticism — and that was right, in so far as he was more interested in striking to the very heart of the matter, and showing the ultimate positive principle underlying the need for detachment.

He showed that this negation was not something absolute, sought for its own sake: but that it was a freeing a vindication of our real selves, a liberation of the spirit from limits and bonds that were intolerable, suicidal — from a servitude to flesh that must ultimately destroy our whole nature and society and the world as well.

Not only that, once the spirit was freed, and returned to its own element, it was not alone there: it could find the absolute and perfect Spirit, God. It could enter into union with Him: and what is more, this union was not something vague and metaphorical, but it was a matter of real experience. What that experience amounted to, according to Huxley, might or might not have been the nirvana of the Buddhists, which is the ultimate negation of all experience and all reality whatever: but anyway, somewhere along the line, he quoted proofs that it was and could be a real and positive experience.

The speculative side of the book — its strongest — was full, no doubt, of strange doctrines by reason of its very eclecticism. And the practical element, which was weak, inspired no confidence, especially when he tried to talk about a concrete social program. Huxley seemed not to be at home with the Christian term "Love" which sounded extraordinarily vague in his contexts — and which must nevertheless be the heart and life of all true mysticism. But out of it all I took these two big concepts of a supernatural, spiritual order, and the possibility of real, experimental contact with God.

Huxley was thought, by some people, to be on the point of entering the Church, but *Ends and Means* was written by a man who was not at ease with Catholicism. He quoted St. John of the Cross and St. Teresa of Avila indiscriminately with less orthodox Christian writers like Meister Eckhart: and on the whole he preferred the Orient. It seems to me that in discarding his family's tradition of materialism he had followed the old Protestant groove back into the heresies that make the material creation evil of itself, although I do not remember enough about him to accuse him of formally holding such a thing. Nevertheless, that would account for his sympathy for Buddhism, and for the nihilistic character which he preferred to give to his mysticism and even to his ethics. This also made him suspicious, as the Albigensians had been, and for the same reason, of the Sacraments and Liturgical life of the Church, and also of doctrines like the Incarnation.

With all that I was not concerned. My hatred of war and my own personal misery in my particular situation and the general crisis of the world made me accept with my whole heart this revelation of the need for a spiritual life, an interior life, including some kind of mortification. I was content to accept the latter truth purely as a matter of theory: or at least, to apply it most vociferously to one passion which was not strong in myself, and did not need to be mortified: that of anger, hatred, while neglecting the ones that really needed to be checked, like gluttony and lust.

But the most important effect of the book on me was to make me start ransacking the university library for books on Oriental mysticism.

I remember those winter days, at the end of 1937 and the beginning of 1938, peaceful days when I sat in the big living room at Douglaston, with the pale sun coming in the window by the piano, where one of my father's water-colors of Bermuda hung on the wall.

The house was very quiet, with Pop and Bonnemaman gone from it, and John Paul away trying to pass his courses at Cornell. I sat for hours, with the big quarto volumes of the Jesuit Father Wieger's French translations of hundreds of strange Oriental texts.

I have forgotten the titles, even the authors, and I never understood a word of what they said in the first place. I had the habit of reading fast, without stopping, or stopping only rarely to take a note, and all these mysteries would require a great deal of thought, even were a man who knew something about them to puzzle them out. And I was completely unfamiliar with anything of the kind. Consequently, the strange great jumble of myths and theories and moral aphorisms and elaborate parables made little or no real impression on my mind, except that I put the books down with the impression that mysticism was something very esoteric and complicated, and that we were all inside some huge Being in whom we were involved and out of whom we evolved, and the thing to do was to involve ourselves back in to him again by a system of elaborate disciplines subject more or less to the control of our own will. The Absolute Being was an infinite, timeless, peaceful, impersonal Nothing.

The only practical thing I got out of it was a system for going to sleep, at night, when you couldn't sleep. You lay flat in bed, without a pillow, your arms at your sides and your legs straight out, and relaxed all your muscles, and you said to yourself:

"Now I have no feet, now I have no feet . . . no feet . . . no legs . . . no knees!"

Sometimes it really worked: you did manage to make it feel as if your feet and legs and the rest of your body had changed into air and vanished away. The only section with which it almost never worked was my head: and if I had not fallen asleep before I got that far, when I tried to wipe out my head, instantly chest and stomach and legs and feet all came back to life with a most exasperating reality and I did not get to sleep for hours. Usually, however, I managed to get to sleep quite quickly by this trick. I suppose it was a variety of auto-suggestion, a kind of hypnotism, or else simply muscular relaxation, with the help of a little work on the part of an active fancy.

Ultimately, I suppose all Oriental mysticism can be reduced to techniques that do the same thing, but in a far more subtle and advanced fashion: and if that is true, it is not mysticism at all. It remains purely in the natural order. That does not make it evil, *per se*, according to Christian standards; but it does not make it good, in relation to the supernatural. It is simply more or less useless, except when it is mixed up with elements that are strictly diabolical: and then of course these dreams and annihilations are designed to wipe out all vital moral activity, while leaving the personality in control of some nefarious principle, either of his own, or from outside himself.

It was with all this in my mind that I went and received my diploma of Bachelor of Arts from one of the windows in the Registrar's office, and immediately afterwards put my name down for some courses in the Graduate School of English.

The experience of the last year, with the sudden collapse of all my physical energy and the diminution of the brash vigor of my worldly ambitions, had meant that I had turned in terror from the idea of anything so active and uncertain as the newspaper business. This registration in the graduate school represented the first remote step of a retreat from the fight for money and fame, from the active and worldly life of conflict and competition. If anything, I would now be a teacher, and live the rest of my life in the relative peace of a college campus, reading and writing books.

That the influence of the Huxley book had not, by any means, lifted me bodily out of the natural order overnight is evident from the fact that I decided to specialize in eighteenth century English Literature, and to choose my subject for a Master of Arts Thesis from somewhere in that century. As a matter of fact, I had already half decided upon a subject, by the time the last pile of dirty snow had melted from the borders of South Field. It was an unknown novelist of the second half of the eighteenth century called Richard Graves. The most important thing he wrote was a novel called the *Spiritual Quixote*, which was in the Fielding tradition, a satire on the more excited kind of Methodists and other sects of religious enthusiasts in England at that time.

I was to work under Professor Tyndall, and this would have been just his kind of a subject. He was an agnostic and rationalist who took a deep and amused interest in all the strange perversions of the religious instinct that our world has seen in the last five hundred years. He was just finishing a book on D. H. Lawrence which discussed, not too kindly, Lawrence's attempt to build up a synthetic, home-made religion of his own out of all the semi-pagan spiritual jetsam that came his way. All Lawrence's friends were very much annoyed by it when it was published. I remember that in that year one of Tyndall's favorite topics of conversation was the miracles of Mother Cabrini, who had just been beatified. He was amused by these, too, because, as for all rationalists, it was for him an article of faith that miracles cannot happen.

I remember with what indecision I went on into the spring, trying to settle the problem of a subject with finality. Yet the thing worked itself out quite suddenly: so suddenly that I do not remember what brought it about. One day I came running down out of the Carpenter Library, and passed along the wire fences by the tennis courts, in the sun, with my mind made up that there was only one possible man in the eighteenth century for me to work on: the one poet who had least to do with his age, and was most in opposition to everything it stood for.

I had just had in my hands the small, neatly printed Nonesuch Press edition of the *Poems of William Blake,* and I now knew what my thesis would probably be. It would take in his poems and some aspect of his religious ideas.

In the Columbia bookstore I bought the same edition of Blake, on credit. (I paid for it two years later.) It had a blue cover, and I suppose it is now hidden somewhere in our monastery library, the part to which nobody has access. And that is all right. I think the ordinary Trappist would be only dangerously bewildered by the "Prophetic Books," and those who still might be able to profit by Blake, have a lot of other things to read that are still better. For my own part I no longer need him. He has done his work for me: and he did it very thoroughly. I hope that I will see him in heaven.

But oh, what a thing it was to live in contact with the genius and the holiness of William Blake that year, that summer, writing the thesis! I had some beginning of an appreciation of his greatness above the other men of his time in England: but from this distance, from the bill where I now stand, looking back I can really appreciate his stature.

To assimilate him to the men of the ending eighteenth century would be absurd. I will not do it: all those conceited and wordy and stuffy little characters! As for the other romantics: how feeble and hysterical their inspirations seem next to the tremendously genuine and spiritual fire of William Blake. Even Coleridge, in the rare moments when his imagination struck the pitch of true creativeness, was still only an artist, an imaginer, not a seer; a maker, but not a prophet.

Perhaps all the great romantics were capable of putting words together more sensibly than Blake, and yet he, with all his mistakes of spelling, turned out the greater poet, because his was the deeper and more solid inspiration. He wrote better poetry when he was twelve than Shelley wrote in his whole life. And it was because at twelve he had already seen, I think, Elias, standing under a tree in the fields south of London.

It was Blake's problem to try and adjust himself to a society that understood neither him nor his kind of faith and love. More than once, smug and inferior minds conceived it to be their duty to take this man Blake in hand and direct and form him, to try and canalize what they recognized as "talent" in some kind of a conventional channel. And always this meant the cold and heartless disparagement of all that was vital and real to him in art and in faith. There were years of all kinds of petty persecution, from many different quarters, until finally Blake parted from his would-be patrons, and gave up all hope of an alliance with a world that thought he was crazy, and went his own way.

It was when he did this, and settled down as an engraver for good, that the Prophetic Books were no longer necessary. In the latter part of his life, having discovered Dante, he came in contact, through him, with Catholicism, which he described as the only religion that really taught the love of God, and his last years were relatively full of peace. He never seems to have felt any desire to hunt out a priest in the England where Catholicism was still practically outlawed: but he died with a blazing face and great songs of joy bursting from his heart.

As Blake worked himself into my system, I became more and more conscious of the necessity of a vital faith, and the total unreality and unsubstantiality of the dead, selfish rationalism which had been freezing my mind and will for the last seven years. By the time the summer was over, I was to become conscious of the fact that the only way to live was to live in a world that was charged with the presence and reality of God.

To say that, is to say a great deal: and I don't want to say it in a way that conveys more than the truth. I will have to limit the statement by saying that it was still, for me, more an intellectual realization than anything else: and it had not yet struck down into the roots of my will. The life of the soul is not knowledge, it is love, since love is the act of the supreme faculty, the will, by which man is formally united to the final end of all his strivings — by which man becomes one with God.

iii

On the door of the room in one of the dormitories, where Lax and Sy Freedgood were living in a state of chaos, was a large grey picture, a lithograph print. Its subject was a man, a Hindu, with wide-open eyes and a rather frightened expression, sitting cross-legged in white garments. I asked about it, and I could not figure out whether the answer was derisive or respectful. Lax said someone had thrown a knife at the picture and the knife had bounced back and nearly cut all their heads off. In other words, he gave me to understand that the picture had something intrinsically holy about it: that accounted for the respect and derision manifested towards it by all my friends. This mixture was their standard acknowledgment of the supernatural, or what was considered to be supernatural. How that picture happened to get on that door in that room is a strange story.

It represented a Hindu messiah, a savior sent to India in our own times, called Jagad-Bondhu. His mission had to do with universal peace and brotherhood. He had died not very long before, and had left a strong following in India. He was, as it were, in the role of a saint who had founded a new religious Order, although he was considered more than a saint: he was the latest incarnation of the godhead, according to the Hindu belief in a multiplicity of incarnations.

In 1932 a big official sort of letter was delivered to one of the monasteries of this new "Order," outside of Calcutta. The letter came from the Chicago World's Fair, which was to be held in the following year. How they ever heard of this monastery, I cannot imagine. The letter was a formal announcement of a "World Congress of Religions." I am writing this all from memory but that is the substance of the story: they invited the abbot of this monastery to send a representative to Congress.

I get this picture of the monastery: it is called Sri Angan, meaning "the Playground." It consists of an enclosure and many huts or "cells," to use an Occidental term. The monks are quiet, simple men. They live what we would call a liturgical life, very closely integrated with the cycle of the seasons and of nature: in fact, the chief characteristic of their worship seems to be this deep, harmonious identification with all living things, in praising God. Their praise itself is expressed in songs, accompanied by drums and primitive instruments, flutes, pipes. There is much ceremonial dancing. In addition to that, there is a profound stress laid on a form of "mental prayer" which is largely contemplative. The monk works himself into it, by softly chanting lyrical aspirations to God and then remains in peaceful absorption in the Absolute.

For the rest, their life is extremely primitive and frugal. It is not so much what we would call austere. I do not think there are any fierce penances or mortifications. But nevertheless, the general level of poverty in Hindu society as a whole imposes on these monks a standard of living which most Occidental religious would probably find unlivable. Their clothes consist of a turban and something thrown around the body and a robe. No shoes. Perhaps the robe is only for travelling. Their food — some rice, a few vegetables, a piece of fruit.

Of all that they do, they attach most importance to prayer, to praising God. They have a well-developed sense of the power and efficacy of prayer, based on a keen realization of the goodness of God. Their whole spirituality is childlike, simple, primitive if you like, close to nature, ingenuous, optimistic, happy. But the point is, although it may be no more than the full flowering of the natural virtue of religion, with the other natural virtues, including a powerful natural charity, still the life of these pagan monks is one of such purity and holiness and peace, in the natural order, that it may put to shame the actual conduct of many Christian religious, in spite of their advantages of constant access to all the means of grace.

So this was the atmosphere into which the letter from Chicago dropped like a heavy stone. The abbot was pleased by the letter. He did not know what the Chicago World's Fair was. He did not understand that all these things were simply schemes for accumulating money. The "World Congress of Religions" appeared to him as something more than the fatuous scheme of a few restless, though probably sincere, minds. He seemed to see in it the first step towards the realization of the hopes of their beloved messiah, Jagad-Bondhu: world peace, universal brotherhood. Perhaps, now, all religions would unite into one great universal religion, and all men would begin to praise God as brothers, instead of tearing each other to pieces.

At any rate, the abbot selected one of his monks and told him that he was to go to Chicago, to the World Congress of Religions.

This was a tremendous assignment. It was something far more terrible than an order given, for instance, to a newly ordained Capuchin to proceed to a mission in India. That would merely be a matter of a trained missionary going off to occupy a place that had been prepared for him. But here was a little man who had been born at the edge of a jungle told to start out from a contemplative monastery and go not only into the world, but into the heart of a civilization the violence and materialism of which he could scarcely evaluate, and which raised gooseflesh on every square inch of his body. What is more, he was told to undertake this journey without money. Not that money was prohibited to him, but they simply did not have any. His abbot managed to raise enough to get him a ticket for a little more than half the distance. After that heaven would have to take care of him.

By the time I met this poor little monk who had come to America without money, he had been living in the country for about five years, and had acquired, of all things, the degree of Doctor of Philosophy from the University of Chicago. So that people referred to him as Doctor Bramachari, although I believe that Bramachari is simply a generic Hindu term for monk — and one that might almost be translated: "Little-Brother-Without-the-Degree-of-Doctor."

How he got through all the red tape that stands between America and the penniless traveller is something that I never quite understood. But it seems that officials, after questioning him, being completely overwhelmed by his simplicity, would either do something dishonest in his favor, or else would give him a tip as to how to beat the various technicalities. Some of them even lent him fairly large sums of money. In any case he landed in America.

The only trouble was that he got to Chicago after the World Congress of Religions was all over.

By that time, one look at the Fair buildings, which were already being torn down, told him all he needed to know about the World Congress of Religions. But once he was there, he did not have much trouble. People would see him standing around in the middle of railway stations waiting for Providence to do something about his plight. They would be intrigued by his turban and white garments (which were partly concealed by a brown overcoat in winter). They observed that he was wearing a pair of sneakers, and perhaps that alone was enough to rouse their curiosity. He was frequently invited to give lectures to religious and social clubs, and to schools and colleges, and he more than once spoke from the pulpits of Protestant churches. In this way he managed to make a living for himself. Besides, he was always being hospitably entertained by people that he met, and he financed the stages of his journey by artlessly leaving his purse lying open on the living room table, at night, before his departure.

The open mouth of the purse spoke eloquently to the hearts of his hosts, saying: "As you see, I am empty," or, perhaps, "As you see, I am down to my last fifteen cents." It was often enough filled up in the morning. He got around.

How did he run into Sy Freedgood? Well, Seymour's wife was studying at Chicago, and she met Bramachari there, and then Seymour met Bramachari, and Bramachari came to Long Beach once or twice, and went out in Seymour's sailboat, and wrote a poem which he gave to Seymour and Helen. He was very happy with Seymour, because he did not have to answer so many stupid questions and, after all, a lot of the people who befriended him were cranks and semi-maniacs and theosophists who thought they had some kind of a claim on him. They wearied him with their eccentricities, although he was a gentle and patient little man. But at Long Beach he was left in peace, although Seymour's ancient grandmother was not easily convinced that he was not the hereditary enemy of the Jewish people. She moved around in the other room, lighting small religious lamps against the intruder.

It was the end of the school year, June 1938, when Lax and Seymour already had a huge box in the middle of the room, which they were beginning to pack with books, when we heard Bramachari was again coming to New York.

I went down to meet him at Grand Central with Seymour, and it was not without a certain suppressed excitement that I did so, for Seymour had me all primed with a superb selection of lies about Bramachari's ability to float in the air and walk on water. It was a long time before we found him in the crowd, although you would think that a Hindu in a turban and a white robe and a pair of Keds would have been a rather memorable sight. But all the people we asked, concerning such a one, had no idea of having seen him.

We had been looking around for ten or fifteen minutes, when a cat came walking cautiously through the crowd, and passed us by with a kind of a look, and disappeared.

"That's him," said Seymour. "He changed himself into a cat. Doesn't like to attract attention. Looking the place over. Now he knows we're here."

Almost at once, while Seymour was asking a porter if he had seen anything like Bramachari, and the porter was saying no, Bramachari came up behind us.

I saw Seymour swing around and say, in his rare, suave manner:

"Ah, Bramachari, how are you!"

There stood a shy little man, very happy, with a huge smile, all teeth, in the midst of his brown face. And on the top of his head was a yellow turban with Hindu prayers written all over it in red. And, on his feet, sure enough: sneakers.

I shook hands with him, still worrying lest he give me some kind of an electric shock. But he didn't. We rode up to Columbia in the subway, with all the people goggling at us, and I was asking Bramachari about all the colleges he had been visiting. Did he like Smith, did he like Harvard? When we were coming out into the air at 116th Street, I asked him which one he liked best, and he told me that they were all the same to him: it had never occurred to him that one might have any special preference in such things.

I lapsed into a reverent silence and pondered on this thought.

I was now twenty-three years old and, indeed, I was more mature than that in some respects. Surely by now it ought to have dawned on me that places did not especially matter. But no, I was very much attached to places, and had very definite likes and dislikes for localities as such, especially colleges, since I was always thinking of finding one that was altogether pleasant to live and teach in.

After that, I became very fond of Bramachari, and he of me. We got along very well together, especially since he sensed that I was trying to feel my way into a settled religious conviction, and into some kind of a life that was centered, as his was, on God.

The thing that strikes me now is that he never attempted to explain his own religious beliefs to me — except some of the externals of the cult, and that was later on. He would no doubt have told me all I wanted to know, if I had asked him, but I was not curious enough. What was most valuable to me was to hear his evaluation of the society and religious beliefs he had come across in America: and to put all that down on paper would require another book.

He was never sarcastic, never ironical or unkind in his criticisms: in fact he did not make many judgements at all, especially adverse ones. He would simply make statements of fact, and then burst out laughing — his laughter was quiet and ingenuous, and it expressed his complete amazement at the very possibility that people should live the way he saw them living all around him.

He was beyond laughing at the noise and violence of American city life and all the obvious lunacies like radio-programs and billboard advertising. It was some of the well-meaning idealisms that he came across that struck him as funny. And one of the things that struck him as funniest of all was the eagerness with which Protestant ministers used to come up and ask him if India was by now nearly converted to Protestantism. He used to tell us how far India was from conversion to Protestantism — or Catholicism for that matter. One of the chief reasons he gave for the failure of any Christian missionaries to really strike deep into the tremendous populations of Asia was the fact that they maintained themselves on a social level that was too far above the natives. The Church of England, indeed, thought they would convert the Indians by maintaining a strict separation — white men in one church, natives in a different church: both of them listening to sermons on brotherly love and unity.

But all Christian missionaries, according to him, suffered from this big drawback: they lived too well, too comfortably. They took care of themselves in a way that simply made it impossible for the Hindus to regard them as holy — let alone the fact that they ate meat, which made them repugnant to the natives.

I don't know anything about missionaries: but I am sure that, by our own standards of living, their life is an arduous and difficult one, and certainly not one that could be regarded as comfortable. And by comparison with life in Europe and America it represents a tremendous sacrifice. Yet I suppose it would literally endanger their lives if they tried to subsist on the standard of living with which the vast majority of Asiatics have to be content. It seems hard to expect them to go around barefoot and sleep on mats and live in huts. But one thing is certain: the pagans have their own notions of holiness, and it is one that includes a prominent element of asceticism. According to Bramachari, the prevailing impression among the Hindus seems to be that Christians don't know what asceticism means. Of course, he was talking principally of Protestant missionaries, but I suppose it would apply to anyone coming to a tropical climate from one of the so-called "civilized" countries.

For my own part, I see no reason for discouragement. Bramachari was simply saying something that has long since been familiar to readers of the Gospels. Unless the grain of wheat, falling in the ground, die, itself remaineth alone: but if it die, it bringeth forth much fruit. The Hindus are not looking for us to send them men who will build schools and hospitals, although those things are good and useful in themselves — and perhaps very badly needed in India: they want to know if we have any saints to send them.

There is no doubt in my mind that plenty of our missionaries are saints: and that they are capable of becoming greater saints too. And that is all that is needed. And, after all, St. Francis Xavier converted hundreds of thousands of Hindus in the sixteenth century and established Christian societies in Asia strong enough to survive for several centuries without any material support from outside the Catholic world.

Bramachari was not telling me anything I did not know about the Church of England, or about the other Protestant sects he had come in contact with. But I was interested to hear his opinion of the Catholics. They, of course, had not invited him to preach in their pulpits: but he had gone into a few Catholic churches out of curiosity. He told me that these were the only ones in which be really felt that people were praying.

It was only there that religion seemed to have achieved any degree of vitality, among us, as far as he could see. It was only to Catholics that the love of God seemed to be a matter of real concern, something that struck deep in their natures, not merely pious speculation and sentiment.

However, when he described his visit to a big Benedictine monastery in the Mid-West he began to grin again. He said they had showed him a lot of workshops and machinery and printing presses and taken him over the whole "plant" as if they were very wrapped up in all their buildings and enterprises. He got the impression that they were more absorbed in printing and writing and teaching than they were in praying.

Bramachari was not the kind of man to be impressed with such statements as: "There's a quarter of a million dollars' worth of stained glass in this church . . . the organ has got six banks of keys and it contains drums, bells and a mechanical nightingale . . . and the retable is a genuine bas-relief by a real live Italian artist."

The people he had the least respect for were all the borderline cases, the strange, eccentric sects, the Christian Scientists, the Oxford Group and all the rest of them. That was, in a sense, very comforting. Not that I was worried about them: but it confirmed me in my respect for him.

He did not generally put his words in the form of advice: but the one counsel he did give me is something that I will not easily forget: "There are many beautiful mystical books written by the Christians. You should read St. Augustine's *Confessions,* and *The Imitation of Christ.*"

Of course I had heard of both of them: but he was speaking as if he took it for granted that most people in America had no idea that such books ever existed. He seemed to feel as if he were in possession of a truth that would come to most Americans as news — as if there was something in their own cultural heritage that they had long since forgotten: and he could remind them of it. He repeated what he had said, not without a certain earnestness:

"Yes, you must read those books."

It was not often that he spoke with this kind of emphasis.

Now that I look back on those days, it seems to me very probable that one of the reasons why God had brought him all the way from India, was that he might say just that.

After all, it is rather ironical that I had turned, spontaneously to the east, in reading about mysticism, as if there were little or nothing in the Christian tradition. I remember that I ploughed through those heavy tomes of Father Wieger's with the feeling that all this represented the highest development of religion on earth. The reason may have been that I came away from Huxley's *Ends and Means* with the prejudice that Christianity was a less pure religion, because it was more "immersed in matter" — that is, because it did not scorn to use a Sacramental liturgy that relied on the appeal of created things to the senses in order to raise the souls of men to higher things.

So now I was told that I ought to turn to the Christian tradition, to St. Augustine — and told by a Hindu monk!

Still, perhaps if he had never given me that piece of advice, I would have ended up in the Fathers of the Church and Scholasticism after all: because a fortunate discovery in the course of my work on my M.A. thesis put me fairly and definitely on that track at last.

That discovery was one book that untied all the knots in the problem which I had set myself to solve by my thesis. it was Jacques Maritain's *Art and Scholasticism*.

iv

The last week of that school year at Columbia had been rather chaotic. Lax and Freedgood had been making futile efforts to get their belongings together and go home. Bramachari was living in their room, perched on top of a pile of books. Lax was trying to finish a novel for Professor Nobbe's course in novel-writing, and all his friends had volunteered to take a section of the book and write it, simultaneously: but in the end the book turned out to be more or less a three-cornered affair — by Lax and me and Dona Eaton. When Nobbe got the thing in his hands he could not figure it out at all, but he gave us a B-minus, with which we were more than satisfied.

Then Lax's mother had come to town to live near him in the last furious weeks before graduation and catch him if he collapsed. He had to take most of his meals in the apartment she had rented in Butler Hall. I sometimes went along and helped him nibble the various health-foods.

At the same time, we were planning to get a ride on an oil barge up the Hudson and the Erie Canal to Buffalo — because Lax's brother-in-law was in the oil business. After that we would go to the town where Lax lived, which was Olean, up in that corner of New York state.

On "Class Day" we leaned out the window of Lax's room and drank a bottle of champagne, looking at the sun on South Field, and watching the people beginning to gather under the trees in front of Hamilton, where we would all presently hear some speeches and shake hands with Nicholas Murray Butler.

It was not my business to graduate that June at all. My graduation was all over when I picked up my degree in the registrar's office last February. However, I borrowed the cap and gown with which Dona Eaton had graduated from Barnard a year before, and went and sat with all the rest, mocking the speeches, with the edge of my sobriety slightly dulled by the celebration that had just taken place with the champagne in Furnald.

Finally we all got up and filed slowly up the rickety wooden steps to the temporary platform to shake hands with all the officials. President Butler was a much smaller man than I had expected. He looked intensely miserable, and murmured something or other to each student, as he shook hands. It was inaudible. I was given to understand that for the past six or seven years people had been in the habit of insulting him, on these occasions, as a kind of a farewell.

I didn't say anything. I just shook his hand, and passed on. The next one I came to was Dean Hawkes who looked up with surprise, from under his bushy white eyebrows, and growled:

"What are *you* doing here, anyway?"

I smiled and passed on.

We did not get the ride on the oil barge, after all, but went to Olean on a train, and for the first time I saw a part of the world in which I was one day going to learn how to be very happy — and that day was not now very far away.

It is the association of that happiness which makes upper New York state seem, in my memory, to be so beautiful. But it is objectively so, there is no doubt of that. Those deep valleys and miles and miles of high, rolling wooded hills: the broad fields, the big red barns, the white farm houses and the peaceful towns: all this looked more and more impressive and fine in the long slanting rays of the sinking sun after we had passed Elmira.

And you began to get some of the feeling of the bigness of America, and to develop a continental sense of the scope of the country and of the vast, clear sky, as the train went on for mile after mile, and hour after hour. And the color, and freshness, and bigness, and richness of the land! The cleanness of it. The wholesomeness. This was new and yet it was old country. It was mellow country. It had been cleared and settled for much more than a hundred years.

When we got out at Olean, we breathed its health and listened to its silence.

I did not stay there for more than a week, being impatient to get back to New York on account of being, as usual, in love.

But one of the things we happened to do was to turn off the main road, one afternoon on the way to the Indian reservation, to look at the plain brick buildings of a college that was run by the Franciscans.

It was called St. Bonaventure's. Lax had a good feeling about the place. And his mother was always taking courses there, in the evenings — courses in literature from the Friars. He was a good friend of the Father Librarian and liked the library. We drove in to the grounds and stopped by one of the buildings.

But when Lax tried to make me get out of the car, I would not.

"Let's get out of here," I said.

"Why? It's a nice place."

"It's O.K., but let's get out of here. Let's go to the Indian reservation."

"Don't you want to see the library?"

"I can see enough of it from here. Let's get going."

I don't know what was the matter. Perhaps I was scared of the thought of nuns and priests being all around me — the elemental fear of the citizen of hell, in the presence of anything that savors of the religious life, religious vows, official dedication to God through Christ. Too many crosses. Too many holy statues. Too much quiet and cheerfulness. Too much pious optimism. It made me very uncomfortable. I had to flee.

When I got back to New York, one of the first things I did was to break away, at last, from the household in Douglaston. The family had really practically dissolved with the death of my grandparents, and I could get a lot more work done if I did not have to spend so much time on subways and the Long Island train.

One rainy day in June, then, I made a bargain with Herb, the colored taximan at Douglaston, and he drove me and all my bags and books and my portable vic and all my hot records and pictures to put on the wall and even a tennis racquet which I never used, uptown to a rooming-house on 114th Street, just behind the Columbia library.

All the way up we discussed the possible reasons for the mysterious death of Rudolph Valentino, once a famous movie star: but it was certainly not what you would call a live issue. Valentino had died at least ten years before.

"This is a nice spot you got here," said Herb, approving of the room I was renting for seven-fifty a week. It was shiny and clean and filled with new furniture and had a big view of a pile of coal, in a yard by the campus tennis courts, with South Field and the steps of the old domed library beyond. The panorama even took in a couple of trees.

"I guess you're going to have a pretty hot time, now you got away from your folks," Herb remarked, as he took his leave.

Whatever else may have happened in that room, it was also there that I started to pray again more or less regularly, and it was there that I added, as Bramachari had suggested, *The Imitation of Christ* to my books, and it was from there that I was eventually to be driven out by an almost physical push, to go and look for a priest.

July came, with its great, misty heats, and Columbia filled with all the thousands of plump, spectacled ladies in pink dresses, from the Middle-West, and all the grey gents in seersucker suits, all the dried-up high-school principals from Indiana and Kansas and Iowa and Tennessee, with their veins shrivelled up with positivism and all the reactions of the behaviorist flickering behind their spectacles as they meditated on the truths they learned in those sweltering halls.

The books piled higher and higher on my desk in the Graduate reading room and in my own lodgings. I was in the thick of my thesis, making hundreds of mistakes that I would not be able to detect for several years to come, because I was far out of my depth. Fortunately, nobody else detected them either. But for my own part, I was fairly happy, and learning many things. The discipline of the work itself was good for me, and helped to cure me, more than anything else did, of the illusion that my health was poor.

And it was in the middle of all this that I discovered Scholastic philosophy.

The subject I had finally chosen was "Nature and Art in William Blake." I did not realize how providential a subject it actually was! What it amounted to, was a study of Blake's reaction against every kind of literalism and naturalism and narrow, classical realism in art, because of his own ideal which was essentially mystical and supernatural. In other words, the topic, if I treated it at all sensibly, could not help but cure me of all the naturalism and materialism in my own philosophy, besides resolving all the inconsistencies and self-contradictions that had persisted in my mind for years, without my being able to explain them.

After all, from my very childhood, I had understood that the artistic experience, at its highest, was actually a natural analogue of mystical experience. It produced a kind of intuitive perception of reality through a sort of affective identification with the object contemplated — the kind of perception that the Thomists call "connatural." This means simply a knowledge that comes about as it were by the identification of natures: in the way that a chaste man understands the nature of chastity because of the very fact that his soul is full of it — it is a part of his own nature, since habit is second nature. Non-connatural knowledge of chastity would be that of a philosopher who, to borrow the language of the *Imitation,* would be able to define it but would not possess it.

I had learned from my own father that it was almost blasphemy to regard the function of art as merely to reproduce some kind of a sensible pleasure or, at best, to stir up the emotions to a transitory thrill. I had always understood that art was contemplation, and that it involved the action of the highest faculties of man.

When I was once able to discover the key to Blake, in his rebellion against literalism and naturalism in art, I saw that his Prophetic Books and the rest of his verse at large represented a rebellion against naturalism in the moral order as well.

What a revelation that was! For at sixteen I had imagined that Blake, like the other romantics, was glorifying passion, natural energy, for their own sake. Far from it! What he was glorifying was the transfiguration of man's natural love, his natural powers, in the refining fires of mystical experience: and that, in itself, implied an arduous and total purification, by faith and love and desire, from all the petty materialistic and commonplace and earthly ideas of his rationalistic friends.

Blake, in his sweeping consistency, had developed a moral insight that cut through all the false distinctions of a worldly and interested morality. That was why he saw that, in the legislation of men, some evils had been set up as standards of right by which other evils were to be condemned: and the norms of pride or greed had been established in the judgement seat, to pronounce a crushing and inhuman indictment against all the normal healthy strivings of human nature. Love was outlawed, and became lust, pity was swallowed up in cruelty, and so Blake knew how:

> The harlot's cry from street to street
> Shall weave old England's winding-sheet.

I had heard that cry and that echo. I had seen that winding sheet. But I had understood nothing of all that. I had tried to resolve it into a matter of sociological laws, of economic forces. If I had been able to listen to Blake in those old days, he would have told me that sociology and economics, divorced from faith and charity, become nothing but the chains of his aged, icy demon Urizen! But now, reading Maritain, in connection with Blake, I saw all these difficulties and contradictions disappear.

I, who had always been anti-naturalistic in art, had been a pure naturalist in the moral order. No wonder my soul was sick and torn apart: but now the bleeding wound was drawn together by the notion of Christian virtue, ordered to the union of the soul with God.

The word virtue: what a fate it has had in the last three hundred years! The fact that it is nowhere near so despised and ridiculed in Latin countries is a testimony to the fact that it suffered mostly from the mangling it underwent at the hands of Calvinists and Puritans. In our own days the word leaves on the lips of cynical high-school children a kind of flippant smear, and it is exploited in theaters for the possibilities it offers for lewd and cheesy sarcasm. Everybody makes fun of virtue, which now has, as its primary meaning, an affectation of prudery practiced by hypocrites and the impotent.

When Maritain — who is by no means bothered by such trivialities — in all simplicity went ahead to use the term in its Scholastic sense, and was able to apply it to art, a "virtue of the practical intellect," the very newness of the context was enough to disinfect my mind of all the miasmas left in it by the ordinary prejudice against "virtue" which, if it was ever strong in anybody, was strong in me. I was never a lover of Puritanism. Now at last I came around to the sane conception of virtue — without which there can be no happiness, because virtues are precisely the powers by which we can come to acquire happiness: without them, there can be no joy, because they are the habits which coordinate and canalize our natural energies and direct them to the harmony and perfection and balance, the unity of our nature with itself and with God, which must, in the end, constitute our everlasting peace.

By the time I was ready to begin the actual writing of my thesis. that is, around the beginning of September 1938, the groundwork of conversion was more or less complete. And how easily and sweetly it had all been done, with all the external graces that had been arranged, along my path, by the kind Providence of God! It had taken little more than a year and a half, counting from the time I read Gilson's *The Spirit of Medieval Philosophy* to bring me up from an "atheist" — as I considered myself — to one who accepted all the full range and possibilities of religious experience right up to the highest degree of glory.

I not only accepted all this, intellectually, but now I began to desire it. And not only did I begin to desire it, but I began to do so efficaciously: I began to want to take the necessary means to achieve this union, this peace. I began to desire to dedicate my life to God, to His service. The notion was still vague and obscure, and it was ludicrously impractical in the sense that I was already dreaming of mystical union when I did not even keep the simplest rudiments of the moral law. But nevertheless I was convinced of the reality of the goal, and confident that it could be achieved: and whatever element of presumption was in this confidence I am sure God excused, in His mercy, because of my stupidity and helplessness, and because I was really beginning to be ready to do whatever I thought He wanted me to do to bring me to Him.

But, oh, how blind and weak and sick I was, although I thought I saw where I was going, and half understood the way! How deluded we sometimes are by the clear notions we get out of books. They make us think that we really understand things of which we have no practical knowledge at all. I remember how learnedly and enthusiastically I could talk for hours about mysticism and the experimental knowledge of God, and all the while I was stoking the fires of the argument with Scotch and soda.

That was the way it turned out that Labor Day, for instance. I went to Philadelphia with Joe Roberts, who had a room in the same house as I, and who had been through all the battles on the Fourth Floor of John Jay for the past four years. He had graduated and was working on some trade magazine about women's hats. All one night we sat, with a friend of his, in a big dark roadhouse outside of Philadelphia, arguing and arguing about mysticism, and smoking more and more cigarettes and gradually getting drunk. Eventually, filled with enthusiasm for the purity of heart which begets the vision of God, I went on with them into the city, after the closing of the bars, to a big speak-easy where we completed the work of getting plastered.

My internal contradictions were resolving themselves out, indeed, but still only on the plane of theory, not of practice: not for lack of good-will, but because I was still so completely chained and fettered by my sins and my attachments.

I think that if there is one truth that people need to learn, in the world, especially today, it is this: the intellect is only theoretically independent of desire and appetite in ordinary, actual practice. It is constantly being blinded and perverted by the ends and aims of passion, and the evidence it presents to us with such a show of impartiality and objectivity is fraught with interest and propaganda. We have become marvelous at self-delusion; all the more so, because we have gone to such trouble to convince ourselves of our own absolute infallibility. The desires of the flesh — and by that I mean not only sinful desires, but even the ordinary, normal appetites for comfort and ease and human respect, are fruitful sources of every kind of error and misjudgement, and because we have these yearnings in us, our intellects (which, if they operated all alone in a vacuum, would indeed, register with pure impartiality what they saw) present to us everything distorted and accommodated to the norms of our desire.

And therefore, even when we are acting with the best of intentions, and imagine that we are doing great good, we may be actually doing tremendous material harm and contradicting all our good intentions. There are ways that seem to men to be good, the end whereof is in the depths of hell.

The only answer to the problem is grace, grace, docility to grace. I was still in the precarious position of being my own guide and my own interpreter of grace. It is a wonder I ever got to the harbor at all!

Sometime in August, I finally answered an impulsion that had been working on me for a long time. Every Sunday I had been going out on Long Island to spend the day with the same girl who had brought me back in such a hurry from Lax's town Olean. But every week, as Sunday came around, I was filled with a growing desire to stay in the city and go to some kind of a church.

At first, I had vaguely thought I might try to find some Quakers, and go and sit with them. There still remained in me something of the favorable notion about Quakers that I had picked up as a child, and which the reading of William Penn had not been able to overcome.

But, naturally enough, with the work I was doing in the library, a stronger drive began to assert itself, and I was drawn much more imperatively to the Catholic Church. Finally the urge became so strong that I could not resist it. I called up my girl and told her that I was not coming out that week-end, and made up my mind to go to Mass for the first time in my life.

The first time in my life! That was true. I had lived for several years on the continent, I had been to Rome, I had been in and out of a thousand Catholic cathedrals and churches, and yet I had never heard Mass. If anything had ever been going on in the churches I visited, I had always fled, in wild Protestant panic.

I will not easily forget how I felt that day. First, there was this sweet strong, gentle, clean urge in me which said: "Go to Mass! Go to Mass!" It was something quite new and strange, this voice that seemed to prompt me, this firm, growing interior conviction of what I needed to do. It had a suavity, a simplicity about it that I could not easily account for. And when I gave in to it, it did not exult over me, and trample me down in its raging haste to land on its prey, but it carried me forward serenely and with purposeful direction.

That does not mean that my emotions yielded to it altogether quietly. I was really still a little afraid to go to a Catholic church, of set purpose, with all the other people, and dispose myself in I pew, and lay myself open to the mysterious perils of that strange and powerful thing they called their "Mass."

God made it a very beautiful Sunday. And since it was the first time I had ever really spent a sober Sunday in New York, I was surprised at the clean, quiet atmosphere of the empty streets uptown. The sun was blazing bright. At the end of the street, as I came out the front door, I could see a burst of green, and the blue river and the hills of Jersey on the other side.

Broadway was empty. A solitary trolley came speeding down in front of Barnard College and past the School of Journalism. Then, from the high, grey, expensive tower of the Rockefeller Church, huge bells began to boom. It served very well for the eleven o'clock Mass at the little brick Church of Corpus Christi, hidden behind Teachers College on 121st Street.

How bright the little building seemed. Indeed, it was quite new. The sun shone on the clean bricks. People were going in the wide open door, into the cool darkness and, all at once, all the churches of Italy and France came back to me. The richness and fulness of the atmosphere of Catholicism that I had not been able to avoid apprehending and loving as a child, came back to me with a rush: but now I was to enter into it fully for the first time. So far, I had known nothing but the outward surface.

It was a gay, clean church, with big plain windows and white columns and pilasters and a well-lighted, simple sanctuary. Its style was a trifle eclectic, but much less perverted with incongruities than the average Catholic church in America. It had a kind of a seventeenth-century, oratorian character about it; though with a sort of American colonial tinge of simplicity. The blend was effective and original: but although all this affected me, without my thinking about it, the thing that impressed me most was that the place was full, absolutely full. It was full not only of old ladies and broken-down gentlemen with one foot in the grave, but of men and women and children young and old — especially young: people of all classes, and all ranks on a solid foundation of workingmen and -women and their families.

I found a place that I hoped would be obscure, over on one side, in the back, and went to it without genuflecting, and knelt down. As I knelt, the first thing I noticed was a young girl, very pretty too, perhaps fifteen or sixteen, kneeling straight up and praying quite seriously. I was very much impressed to see that someone who was young and beautiful could with such simplicity make prayer the real and serious and principal reason for going to church. She was clearly kneeling that way because she meant it, not in order to show off, and she was praying with an absorption which, though not the deep recollection of a saint, was serious enough to show that she was not thinking at all about the other people who were there.

What a revelation it was, to discover so many ordinary people in a place together, more conscious of God than one another; not to fulfil a religious obligation, not a human one. For even those who might have been there for no better motive than that they were obliged to be, were at least free from any of the self-conscious and human constraint which is never absent from a Protestant church where people are definitely gathered together as people, as neighbors, and always have at least half an eye for one another, if not all of both eyes.

Since it was summer time, the eleven o'clock Mass was a Low Mass: but I had not come expecting to hear music. Before I knew it the priest was in the sanctuary with the two altar boys, and was busy at the altar with something or other which I could not see very well, but the people were praying by themselves, and I was engrossed and absorbed in the thing as a whole: the business at the altar and the presence of the people. And still I had not got rid of my fear. Seeing the late-comers hastily genuflecting before entering the pew, I realised my omission, and got the idea that people had spotted me for a pagan and were just waiting for me to miss a few more genuflections before throwing me out or, at least, giving me looks of reproof.

Soon we all stood up. I did not know what it was for. The priest was at the other end of the altar, and, as I afterwards learned, he was reading the Gospel. And then the next thing I knew there was someone in the pulpit.

It was a young priest, perhaps not much over thirty-three or -four years old. His face was rather ascetic and thin, and its asceticism was heightened with a note of intellectuality by his horn-rimmed glasses, although he was only one of the assistants, and he did not consider himself an intellectual, nor did anyone else apparently consider him so. But anyway, that was the impression he made on me: and his sermon, which was simple enough, did not belie it.

It was not long: but to me it was very interesting to hear this young man quietly telling the people in language that was plain, yet tinged with scholastic terminology, about a point in Catholic Doctrine. How clear and solid the doctrine was: for behind those words you felt the full force not only of Scripture but of centuries of a unified and continuous and consistent tradition. And above all, it was a vital tradition: there was nothing studied or antique about it. These words, this terminology, this doctrine, and these convictions fell from the lips of the young priest as something that were most intimately part of his own life. What was more, I sensed that the people were familiar with it all, and that it was also, in due proportion, part of their life also: it was just as much integrated into their spiritual organism as the air they breathed or the food they ate worked in to their blood and flesh.

What was he saying? That Christ was the Son of God. That, in Him, the Second Person of the Holy Trinity, God, had assumed a Human Nature, a Human Body and Soul, and had taken Flesh and dwelt amongst us, full of grace and truth: and that this Man, Whom men called the Christ, was God. He was both Man and God: two Natures hypostatically united in one Person or suppositum, one individual Who was a Divine Person, having assumed to Himself a Human Nature. And His works were the works of God: His acts were the acts of God. He loved us: God, and walked among us: God, and died for us on the Cross, God of God, Light of Light, True God of True God.

Jesus Christ was not simply a man, a good man, a great man, the greatest prophet, a wonderful healer, a saint: He was something that made all such trivial words pale into irrelevance. He was God. But nevertheless He was not merely a spirit without a true body, God hiding under a visionary body: He was also truly a Man, born of the Flesh of the Most Pure Virgin, formed of her Flesh by the Holy Spirit. And what He did, in that Flesh, on earth, He did not only as Man but as God. He loved us as God, He suffered and died for us, God.

And how did we know? Because it was revealed to us in the Scriptures and confirmed by the teaching of the Church and of the powerful unanimity of Catholic Tradition from the First Apostles, from the first Popes and the early Fathers, on down through the Doctors of the Church and the great scholastics, to our own day. *De Fide Divina.* If you believed it, you would receive light to grasp it, to understand it in some measure. If you did not believe it, you would never understand: it would never be anything but scandal or folly.

And no one can believe these things merely by wanting to, of his own volition. Unless he receive grace, an actual light and impulsion of the mind and will from God, he cannot even make an act of living faith. It is God Who gives us faith, and no one cometh to Christ unless the Father draweth him.

I wonder what would have happened in my life if I had been given this grace in the days when I had almost discovered the Divinity of Christ in the ancient mosaics of the churches of Rome. What scores of self-murdering and Christ-murdering sins would have been avoided — all the filth I had plastered upon His image in my soul during those last five years that I had been scourging and crucifying God within me?

It is easy to say, after it all, that God had probably foreseen my infidelities and had never given me the grace in those days because He saw how I would waste and despise it: and perhaps that rejection would have been my ruin. For there is no doubt that one of the reasons why grace is not given to souls is because they have so hardened their wills in greed and cruelty and selfishness that their refusal of it would only harden them more. . . . But now I had been beaten into the semblance of some kind of humility by misery and confusion and perplexity and secret, interior fear, and my ploughed soul was better ground for the reception of good seed.

The sermon was what I most needed to hear that day. When the Mass of the Catechumens was over, I, who was not even a catechumen, but only a blind and deaf and dumb pagan as weak and dirty as anything that ever came out of the darkness of Imperial Rome or Corinth or Ephesus, was not able to understand anything else.

It all became completely mysterious when the attention was refocussed on the altar. When the silence grew more and more profound, and little bells began to ring, I got scared again and, finally, genuflecting hastily on my left knee, I hurried out of the church in the middle of the most important part of the Mass. But it was just as well. In a way, I suppose I was responding to a kind of liturgical instinct that told me I did not belong there for the celebration of the Mysteries as such. I had no idea what took place in them: but the fact was that Christ, God, would be visibly present on the altar in the Sacred Species. And although He was there, yes, for love of me:

He was there in His power and His might, and what was I? What was on my soul? What was I in His sight?

It was liturgically fitting that I should kick myself out at the end of the Mass of the Catechumens, when the ordained *ostiarii* should have been there to do it. Anyway, it was done.

Now I walked leisurely down Broadway in the sun, and my eyes looked about me at a new world. I could not understand what it was that had happened to make me so happy, why I was so much at peace, so content with life for I was not yet used to the clean savor that comes with an actual grace — indeed, there was no impossibility in a person's hearing and believing such a sermon and being justified, that is, receiving sanctifying grace in his soul as a habit, and beginning, from that moment, to live the divine and supernatural life for good and all. But that is something I will not speculate about.

All I know is that I walked in a new world. Even the ugly buildings of Columbia were transfigured in it, and everywhere was peace in these streets designed for violence and noise. Sitting outside the gloomy little Childs restaurant at 111th Street, behind the dirty, boxed bushes, and eating breakfast was like sitting in the Elysian Fields.

v

My reading became more and more Catholic. I became absorbed in the poetry of Hopkins and in his notebooks — that poetry which had only impressed me a little six years before. Now, too, I was deeply interested in Hopkins' life as a Jesuit. What was that life? What did the Jesuits do? What did a priest do? How did he live? I scarcely knew where to begin to find out about all such things: but they had started to exercise a mysterious attraction over me.

And here is a strange thing. I had by now read James Joyce's *Ulysses* twice or three times. Six years before — on one of those winter vacations in Strasbourg — I had tried to read *Portrait of the Artist* and had bogged down in the part about his spiritual crisis. Something about it had discouraged, bored and depressed me. I did not want to read about such a thing: and I finally dropped it in the middle of the "Mission." Strange to say, sometime during this summer — I think it was before the first time I went to Corpus Christi — I reread *Portrait of the Artist* and was fascinated precisely by that part of the book, by the "Mission," by the priest's sermon on hell. What impressed me was not the fear of hell, but the expertness of the sermon. Now, instead of being repelled by the thought of such preaching — which was perhaps the author's intention — I was stimulated and edified by it. The style in which the priest in the book talked, pleased me by its efficiency and solidity and drive: and once again there was something eminently satisfying in the thought that these Catholics knew what they believed, and knew what to teach, and all taught the same thing, and taught it with coordination and purpose and great effect. It was this that struck me first of all, rather than the actual subject matter of their doctrine — until, that is, I heard the sermon at Corpus Christi.

So then I continued to read Joyce, more and more fascinated by the pictures of priests and Catholic life that came up here and there in his books. That, I am sure, will strike many people as a strange thing indeed. I think Joyce himself was only interested in rebuilding the Dublin he had known as objectively and vitally as he could. He was certainly very alive to all the faults in Irish Catholic society, and he had practically no sympathy left for the Church he had abandoned: but in his intense loyalty to the vocation of artist for which he had abandoned it (and the two vocations are not *per se* irreconcilable: they only became so because of peculiar subjective circumstances in Joyce's own case) he meant to be as accurate as he could in rebuilding his world as it truly was.

Therefore, reading Joyce, I was moving in his Dublin, and breathing the air of its physical and spiritual slums: and it was not the most Catholic side of Dublin that he always painted. But in the background was the Church, and its priests, and its devotions, and the Catholic life in all its gradations, from the Jesuits down to those who barely clung to the hem of the Church's garments. And it was this background that fascinated me now, along with the temper of Thomism that had once been in Joyce himself. If he had abandoned St. Thomas, he had not stepped much further down than Aristotle.

Then, of course, I was reading the metaphysical poets once again — especially Crashaw — and studying his life, too, and his conversion. That meant another avenue which led more or less directly to the Jesuits. So in the late August of 1938, and September of that year. my life began to be surrounded, interiorly, by Jesuits. They were the symbols of my new respect for the vitality and coordination of the Catholic Apostolate. Perhaps, in the back of my mind, was my greatest Jesuit hero: the glorious Father Rothschild of Evelyn Waugh's *Vile Bodies*, who plotted with all the diplomats, and rode away into the night on a motorcycle when everybody else was exhausted.

Yet with all this, I was not yet ready to stand beside the font. There was not even any interior debate as to whether I ought to become a Catholic. I was content to stand by and admire. For the rest, I remember one afternoon, when my girl had come in to town to see me, and we were walking around the streets uptown, I subjected her to the rather disappointing entertainment of going to Union Theological Seminary, and asking for a catalogue of their courses which I proceeded to read while we were walking around on Riverside Drive. She was not openly irritated by it: she was a very good and patient girl anyway. But still you could see she was a little bored, walking around with a man who was not sure whether he ought to enter a theological seminary.

There was nothing very attractive in that catalogue. I was to get much more excited by the article on the Jesuits in the *Catholic Encyclopaedia* — breathless with the thought of so many novitiates and tertianships and what not — so much scrutiny, so much training. What monsters of efficiency they must be, these Jesuits, I kept thinking to myself, as I read and reread the article. And perhaps, from time to time, I tried to picture myself with my face sharpened by asceticism, its pallor intensified by contrast with a black cassock, and every line of it proclaiming a Jesuit saint, a Jesuit master-mind. And I think the master-mind element was one of the strongest features of this obscure attraction.

Apart from this foolishness, I came no nearer to the Church, in practice, than adding a "Hail Mary" to my night prayers. I did not even go to Mass again, at once. The following week-end I went to see my girl once again; it was probably after that that I went on the expedition to Philadelphia. It took something that belongs to history to form and vitalize these resolutions that were still only vague and floating entities in my mind and will.

One of those hot evenings at the end of summer the atmosphere of the city suddenly became terribly tense with some news that came out of the radios. Before I knew what the news was, I began to feel the tension. For I was suddenly aware that the quite disparate murmurs of different radios in different houses had imperceptibly merged into one big, ominous unified voice, that moved at you from different directions and followed you down the street, and came to you from another angle as soon as you began to recede from any one of its particular sources.

I heard "Germany — Hitler — at six o'clock this morning the German Army . . . the Nazis . . ." What had they done?

Then Joe Roberts came in and said there was about to be a war. The Germans had occupied Czechoslovakia, and there was bound to be a war.

The city felt as if one of the doors of hell had been half opened, and a blast of its breath had flared out to wither up the spirits of men. And people were loitering around the newsstands in misery.

Joe Roberts and I sat in my room, where there was no radio, until long after midnight, drinking canned beer and smoking cigarettes, and making silly and excited jokes but, within a couple of days, the English Prime Minister had flown in a big hurry to see Hitler and had made a nice new alliance at Munich that cancelled everything that might have caused a war, and returned to England. He alighted at Croydon and came stumbling out of the plane saying "Peace in our time!"

I was very depressed. I was beyond thinking about the intricate and filthy political tangle that underlay the mess. I had given up politics as more or less hopeless, by this time. I was no longer interested in having any opinion about the movement and interplay of forces which were all more or less iniquitous and corrupt, and it was far too laborious and uncertain a business to try and find out some degree of truth and justice in all the loud, artificial claims that were put forward by the various sides.

All I could see was a world in which everybody said they hated war, and in which we were all being rushed into a war with a momentum that was at last getting dizzy enough to affect my stomach. All the internal contradictions of the society in which I lived were at last beginning to converge upon its heart. There could not be much more of a delay in its dismembering. Where would it end? In those days, the future was obscured, blanked out by war as by a dead-end wall. Nobody knew if anyone at all would come out of it alive. Who would be worse off, the civilians or the soldiers? The distinction between their fates was to be abolished. in most countries, by aerial warfare, by all the new planes, by all the marvelous new bombs. What would the end of it be?

I knew that I myself hated war, and all the motives that led to war and were behind wars. But I could see that now my likes or dislikes, beliefs or disbeliefs meant absolutely nothing in the external, political order. I was just an individual, and the individual had ceased to count. I meant nothing, in this world, except that I would probably soon become a number on the list of those to be drafted. I would get a piece of metal with my number on it, to hang around my neck, so as to help out the circulation of red-tape that would necessarily follow the disposal of my remains, and that would be the last eddy of mental activity that would close over my lost identity.

The whole business was so completely unthinkable that my mind, like almost all the other minds that were in the same situation, simply stopped trying to cope with it, and refixed its focus on the ordinary routine of life.

I had my thesis to type out, and a lot of books to read, and I was thinking of preparing an article on Crashaw which perhaps I would send to T. S. Eliot for his *Criterion*. I did not know that *Criterion* had printed its last issue, and that Eliot's reaction to the situation that so depressed me was to fold up his magazine.

The days went on and the radios returned to their separate and individual murmuring, not to be regimented back into their appalling shout for yet another year. September, as I think, must have been more than half gone.

I borrowed Father Leahy's life of Hopkins from the library. It was a rainy day. I had been working in the library in the morning. I had gone to buy a thirty-five-cent lunch at one of those little pious kitchens on Broadway — the one where Professor Gerig, of the graduate school of French, sat daily in silence with his ancient, ailing mother, over a very small table, eating his

Brussels sprouts. Later in the afternoon, perhaps about four, I would have to go down to Central Park West and give a Latin lesson to a youth who was sick in bed, and who ordinarily came to the tutoring school run by my landlord, on the ground floor of the house where I lived.

I walked back to my room. The rain was falling gently on the empty tennis courts across the street, and the huge old domed library stood entrenched in its own dreary greyness, arching a cyclops eyebrow at South Field.

I took up the book about Gerard Manley Hopkins. The chapter told of Hopkins at Balliol, at Oxford. He was thinking of becoming a Catholic. He was writing letters to Cardinal Newman (not yet a cardinal) about becoming a Catholic.

All of a sudden, something began to stir within me, something began to push me, to prompt me. It was a movement that spoke like a voice.

"What are you waiting for?" it said. "Why are you sitting here? Why do you still hesitate? You know what you ought to do? Why don't you do it?"

I stirred in the chair, I lit a cigarette, looked out the window at the rain, tried to shut the voice up. "Don't act on impulses," I thought. "This is crazy. This is not rational. Read your book."

Hopkins was writing to Newman, at Birmingham, about his indecision.

"What are you waiting for?" said the voice within me again. "Why are you sitting there? It is useless to hesitate any longer. Why don't you get up and go?"

I got up and walked restlessly around the room. "It's absurd," I thought. "Anyway, Father Ford would not be there at this time of day. I would only be wasting time."

Hopkins had written to Newman, and Newman had replied to him, telling him to come and see him at Birmingham.

Suddenly, I could bear it no longer. I put down the book, and got into my raincoat, and started down the stairs. I went out into the street. I crossed over, and walked along by the grey wooden fence, towards Broadway, in the light rain.

And then everything inside me began to sing — to sing with peace, to sing with strength and to sing with conviction.

I had nine blocks to walk. Then I turned the corner of 121st Street, and the brick church and presbytery were before me. I stood in the doorway and rang the bell and waited.

When the maid opened the door, I said:

"May I see Father Ford, please?"

"But Father Ford is out."

I thought: well, it is not a waste of time, anyway. And I asked when she expected him back. I would come back later, I thought.

The maid closed the door. I stepped back into the street. And then I saw Father Ford coming around the corner from Broadway. He approached, with his head down, in a rapid, thoughtful walk. I went to meet him and said:

"Father, may I speak to you about something?"

"Yes," he said, looking up, surprised. "Yes, sure, come into the house."

We sat in the little parlor by the door. And I said: "Father, I want to become a Catholic."

vi

I came out of the presbytery with three books under my arm. I had hoped that I could begin taking instructions at once, but the pastor had told me to read these books, and pray and think and see how I felt about it in a week or ten days' time. I did not argue with him: but the hesitation that had been in my mind only an hour or so before seemed to have vanished so completely that I was astonished and a little abashed at this delay. So it was arranged that I should come in the evenings, twice a week.

"Father Moore will be your instructor," said the Pastor.

There were four assistants at Corpus Christi, but I guessed that Father Moore was going to be the one whom I had heard preaching the sermon on the divinity of Christ and, as a matter of fact, he was the one who, in the designs of Providence, had been appointed for this work of my salvation.

If people had more appreciation of what it means to be converted from rank, savage paganism, from the spiritual level of a cannibal or of an ancient Roman, to the living faith and to the Church, they would not think of catechism as something trivial or unimportant. Usually the word suggests the matter-of-course instructions that children have to go through before First Communion and Confirmation. Even where it is a matter-of-course, it is one of the most tremendous things in the world, this planting of the word of God in a soul. It takes a conversion to really bring this home.

I was never bored. I never missed an instruction, even when it cost me the sacrifice of some of my old amusements and attractions, which had such a strong hold over me and, while I had been impatient of delay from the moment I had come to that first sudden decision, I now began to burn with desire for Baptism, and to throw out hints and try to determine when I would be received into the Church.

My desire became much greater still, by the end of October, for I made the Mission with the men of the parish, listening twice a day to sermons by two Paulist Fathers and hearing Mass and kneeling at Benediction before the Christ Who was gradually revealing Himself to me.

When the sermon on hell began, I was naturally making mental comparisons with the one in Joyce's *Portrait of the Artist* and reflecting on it in a kind of detached manner, as if I were a third and separate person watching myself hearing this sermon and seeing how it affected me. As a matter of fact this was the sermon which should have done me the most good and did, in fact, do so.

My opinion is that it is a very extraordinary thing for anyone to be upset by such a topic. Why should anyone be shattered by the thought of hell? It is not compulsory for anyone to go there. Those who do, do so by their own choice, and against the will of God, and they can only get into hell by defying and resisting all the work of Providence and grace. It is their own will that takes them there, not God's. In damning them He is only ratifying their own decision — a decision which He has left entirely to their own choice. Nor will He ever hold our weakness alone responsible for our damnation. Our weakness should not terrify us: it is the source of our strength. *Libenter gloriabor in infirmitatibus meis ut inhabitet in me virtus Christi.* Power is made perfect in infirmity, and our very helplessness is all the more potent a claim on that Divine Mercy Who calls to Himself the poor, the little ones, the heavily burdened.

My reaction to the sermon on hell was, indeed, what spiritual writers call "confusion" — but it was not the hectic, emotional confusion that comes from passion and from self-love. It was a sense of quiet sorrow and patient grief at the thought of these tremendous and terrible sufferings which I deserved and into which I stood a very good chance of entering, in my present condition: but at the same time, the magnitude of the punishment gave me a special and particular understanding of the greatness of the evil of sin. But the final result was a great deepening and awakening of my soul, a real increase in spiritual profundity and an advance in faith and love and confidence in God, to Whom alone I could look for salvation from these things. And therefore I all the more earnestly desired Baptism.

I went to Father Moore after the sermon on hell and said that I hoped he was going to baptize me really soon. He laughed, and said that it would not be much longer. By now, it was the beginning of November.

Meanwhile, there had been another thought, half forming itself in the back of my mind — an obscure desire to become a priest. This was something which I tended to hold separate from the thought of my conversion, and I was doing my best to keep it in the background. I did not mention it either to Father Ford or Father Moore, for the chief reason that in my mind it constituted a kind of admission that I was taking the thought more seriously than I wanted to — it almost amounted to a first step towards application for admission to a seminary.

However, it is a strange thing: there was also in my mind a kind of half-formed conviction that there was one other person I should consult about becoming a priest before I took the matter to the rectory. This man was a layman, and someone I had never yet seen, and it was altogether strange that I should be inclined so spontaneously to put the matter up to him, as if he were the only logical one to give me advice. In the end, he was the one I first consulted — I mean, the one from whom I first seriously asked advice, for I had long been talking about it to my friends, before I came around to him.

This man was Daniel Walsh, about whom I had heard a great deal from Lax and Gerdy. Gerdy had taken his course on St. Thomas Aquinas in the graduate school of Philosophy: and now as the new school year began, my attention centered upon this one course. It had nothing directly to do with my preparation for the exams for the M.A. degree in January. By now degrees and everything else to do with a university career had become very unimportant in comparison with the one big thing that occupied my mind and all my desires.

I registered for the course, and Dan Walsh turned out to be another one of those destined in a providential way to shape and direct my vocation. For it was he who pointed out my way to the place where I now am.

When I was writing about Columbia and its professors, I was not thinking of Dan Walsh: and he really did not belong to Columbia at all. He was on the faculty of the Sacred Heart College at Manhattanville, and came to Columbia twice a week to lecture on St. Thomas and Duns Scotus. His class was a small one and was, as far as Columbia was concerned, pretty much of an academic bypath. And that was in a sense an additional recommendation — it was off that broad and noisy highway of pragmatism which leads between its banks of artificial flowers to the gates of despair.

Walsh himself had nothing of the supercilious self-assurance of the ordinary professor: he did not need this frail and artificial armor for his own insufficiency. He did not need to hide behind tricks and vanities any more than Mark Van Doren did; he never even needed to be brilliant. In his smiling simplicity he used to efface himself entirely in the solid and powerful mind of St. Thomas. Whatever brilliance he allowed himself to show forth in his lectures was all thrown back upon its source, the Angel of the Schools.

Dan Walsh had been a student and collaborator of Gilson's and knew Gilson and Maritain well. In fact, later on he introduced me to Maritain at the Catholic Book Club, where this most saintly philosopher had been giving a talk on Catholic Action. I only spoke a few conventional words to Maritain, but the impression you got from this gentle, stooping Frenchman with much grey hair, was one of tremendous kindness and simplicity and godliness. And that was enough: you did not need to talk to him. I came away feeling very comforted that there was such a person in the world, and confident that he would include me in some way in his prayers.

But Dan himself had caught a tremendous amount of this simplicity and gentleness and godliness too: and perhaps the impression that he made was all the more forceful because his square jaw had a kind of potential toughness about it. Yet no: there he sat, this little, stocky man, who had something of the appearance of a good-natured prize fighter, smiling and talking with the most childlike delight and cherubic simplicity about the *Summa Theologica*.

His voice was low and, as he spoke, he half apologetically searched the faces of his hearers for signs of understanding and, when he found it, he seemed surprised and delighted.

I very quickly made friends with him, and told him all about my thesis and the ideas I was trying to work with, and he was very pleased. And one of the things he sensed at once was something that I was far from being able to realize: but it was that the bent of my mind was essentially "Augustinian." I had not yet followed Bramachari's advice to read St. Augustine and I did not take Dan's evaluation of my ideas as having all the directive force that was potentially in it — for it did not even come clothed in suggestion or advice.

Of course, to be called "Augustinian" by a Thomist might not in every case be a compliment. But coming from Dan Walsh, who was a true Catholic philosopher, it was a compliment indeed.

For he, like Gilson, had the most rare and admirable virtue of being able to rise above the petty differences of schools and systems, and seeing Catholic philosophy in its wholeness, in its variegated unity, and in its true Catholicity. In other words, he was able to study St. Thomas and St. Bonaventure and Duns Scotus side by side, and to see them as complementing and reinforcing one another, as throwing diverse and individual light on the same truths from different points of view, and thus he avoided the evil of narrowing and restricting Catholic philosophy and theology to a single school, to a single attitude, a single system.

I pray to God that there may be raised up more like him in the Church and in our universities, because there is something stifling and intellectually deadening about textbooks that confine themselves to giving a superficial survey of the field of philosophy according to Thomist principles and then discard all the rest in a few controversial objections. Indeed, I think it a great shame and a danger of no small proportions, that Catholic philosophers should be trained in division against one another, and brought up to the bitterness and smallness of controversy: because this is bound to narrow their views and dry up the unction that should vivify all philosophy in their souls.

Therefore, to be called an "Augustinian" by Dan Walsh was a compliment, in spite of the traditional opposition between the Thomist and Augustinian schools, Augustinian being taken not as confined to the philosophers of that religious order, but as embracing all the intellectual descendants of St. Augustine. It is a great compliment to find oneself numbered as part of the same spiritual heritage as St. Anselm, St. Bernard, St. Bonaventure, Hugh and Richard of St. Victor, and Duns Scotus also. And from the tenor of his course, I realized that he meant that my bent was not so much towards the intellectual, dialectical, speculative character of Thomism, as towards the spiritual, mystical, voluntaristic and practical way of St. Augustine and his followers.

His course and his friendship were most valuable in preparing me for the step I was about to take. But as time went on, I decided to leave the notion of becoming a priest out of the way for the time being. So I never even mentioned it to Dan in those days.

As November began, my mind was taken up with this one thought: of getting baptized and entering at last into the supernatural life of the Church. In spite of all my studying and all my reading and all my talking, I was still infinitely poor and wretched in my appreciation of what was about to take place within me. I was about to set foot on the shore at the foot of the high, seven circled mountain of a Purgatory steeper and more arduous than I was able to imagine, and I was not at all aware of the climbing I was about to have to do.

The essential thing was to begin the climb. Baptism was that beginning, and a most generous one, on the part of God. For, although I was baptized conditionally, I hope that His mercy swallowed up all the guilt and temporal punishment of my twenty-three black years of sin in the waters of the font; and allowed me a new start. But my nature, my weakness, and the cast of my evil habits still remained to be fought and overcome.

Towards the end of the first week in November, Father Moore told me I would be baptized on the sixteenth. I walked out of the rectory that evening happier and more contented than I had ever been in my life. I looked at a calendar to see what saint had that day for a feast, and it was marked for St. Gertrude.

It was only in the last days before being liberated from my slavery to death, that I had the grace to feel something of my own weakness and helplessness. It was not a very vivid light that was given to me on the subject: but I was really aware, at last, of what a poor and miserable thing I was. On the night of the fifteenth of November, the eve of my Baptism and First Communion, I lay in my bed awake and timorous for fear that something might go wrong the next day. And to humiliate me still further, as I lay there, fear came over me that I might not be able to keep the eucharistic fast. It only meant going from midnight to ten o'clock without drinking any water or taking any food, yet all of a sudden this little act of self-denial which amounts to no more, in reality, than a sort of an abstract token, a gesture of good-will, grew in my imagination until it seemed to be utterly beyond my strength — as if I were about to go without food and drink for ten days, instead of ten hours. I had enough sense left to realize that this was one of those curious psychological reactions with which our nature, not without help from the devil, tries to confuse us and avoid what reason and our will demand of it, and so I forgot about it all and went to sleep.

In the morning, when I got up, having forgotten to ask Father Moore if washing your teeth was against the eucharistic fast or not, I did not wash them, and, facing a similar problem about cigarettes, I resisted the temptation to smoke.

I went downstairs and out into the street to go to my happy execution and rebirth.

The sky was bright and cold. The river glittered like steel. There was a clean wind in the street. It was one of those fall days full of life and triumph, made for great beginnings, and yet I was not altogether exalted: for there were still in my mind these vague, half animal apprehensions about the externals of what was to happen in the church — would my mouth be so dry that I could not swallow the Host? If that happened, what would I do? I did not know.

Gerdy joined me as I was turning in to Broadway. I do not remember whether Ed Rice caught up with us on Broadway or not. Lax and Seymour came after we were in church.

Ed Rice was my godfather. He was the only Catholic among us — the only Catholic among all my close friends. Lax, Seymour, and Gerdy were Jews. They were very quiet, and so was I. Rice was the only one who was not cowed or embarrassed or shy.

The whole thing was very simple. First of all, I knelt at the altar of Our Lady where Father Moore received my abjuration of heresy and schism. Then we went to the baptistery, in a little dark corner by the main door.

I stood at the threshold.

"Quid Petis ab ecclesia Dei?" asked Father Moore.

"Fidem!"

"Fides quid tibi praestat?"

"Vitam aeternam."

Then the young priest began to pray in Latin, looking earnestly and calmly at the page of the *Rituale* through the lenses of his glasses. And I, who was asking for eternal life, stood and watched him, catching a word of the Latin here and there.

He turned to me:

"Abrenuntias Satanae?"

In a triple vow I renounced Satan and his pomps and his works.

"Dost thou believe in God the Father almighty, Creator of heaven and earth?"

"Credo!"

"Dost thou believe in Jesus Christ His only Son, Who was born, and suffered?"

"Credo!"

"Dost thou believe in the Holy Spirit, in the Holy Catholic Church, the Communion of saints, the remission of sins, the resurrection of the body and eternal life?"

"Credo!"

What mountains were falling from my shoulders! What scales of dark night were peeling off my intellect, to let in the inward vision of God and His truth! But I was absorbed in the liturgy, and waiting for the next ceremony. It had been one of the things that had rather frightened me — or rather, which frightened the legion that had been living in me for twenty-three years.

Now the priest blew into my face. He said: *"Exi ab eo, spiritus immunde:* Depart from him, thou impure spirit, and give place to the Holy Spirit, the Paraclete."

It was the exorcism. I did not see them leaving, but there must have been more than seven of them. I had never been able to count them. Would they ever come back? Would that terrible threat of Christ be fulfilled, that threat about the man whose house was clean and garnished, only to be reoccupied by the first devil and many others worse than himself?

The priest, and Christ in him — for it was Christ that was doing these things through his visible ministry, in the Sacrament of my purification — breathed again into my face.

"Thomas, receive the good Spirit through this breathing, and receive the Blessing of God. Peace be with thee."

Then he began again to pray, and sign me with Crosses, and presently came the salt which he put on my tongue — the salt of wisdom, that I might have the savor of divine things, and finally he poured the water on my head, and named me Thomas, "if thou be not already baptized."

After that, I went into the confessional, where one of the other assistants was waiting for me. I knelt in the shadows. Through the dark, close-meshed wire of the grille between us, I saw Father McGough, his head bowed, and resting on his hand, inclining his ear towards me. "Poor man," I thought. He seemed very young and he had always looked so innocent to me that I wondered how he was going to identify and understand the things I was about to tell him.

But one by one, that is, species by species, as best I could, I tore out all those sins by their roots, like teeth. Some of them were hard, but I did it quickly, doing the best I could to approximate the number of times all these things had happened — there was no counting them, only guessing.

I did not have any time to feel how relieved I was when I came stumbling out, as I had to go down to the front of the church where Father Moore would see me and come out to begin his — and my — Mass. But ever since that day, I have loved confessionals.

Now he was at the altar, in his white vestments, opening the book. I was kneeling right at the altar rail. The bright sanctuary was all mine. I could hear the murmur of the priest's voice, and the responses of the server, and it did not matter that I had no one to look at so that I could

tell when to stand up and kneel down again, for I was still not very sure of these ordinary ceremonies. But when the little bells were rung I knew what was happening. And I saw the raised
Host — the silence and simplicity with which Christ once again triumphed, raised up, drawing
all things to Himself — drawing me to Himself.

Presently the priest's voice was louder, saying the *Pater Noster*. Then, soon, the server was
running through the *Confiteor* in a rapid murmur. That was for me. Father Moore turned around
and made a big cross in absolution, and held up the little Host.

"Behold the Lamb of God: behold Him Who taketh away the sins of the world."

And my First Communion began to come towards me, down the steps. I was the only one at
the altar rail. Heaven was entirely mine — that Heaven in which sharing makes no division or
diminution. But this solitariness was a kind of reminder of the singleness with which this
Christ, hidden in the small Host, was giving Himself for me, and to me, and, with Himself, the
entire Godhead and Trinity — a great new increase of the power and grasp of their indwelling
that had begun only a few minutes before at the font.

I left the altar rail and went back to the pew where the others were kneeling like four shadows, four unrealities, and I hid my face in my hands.

In the Temple of God that I had just become, the One Eternal and Pure Sacrifice was
offered up to the God dwelling in me: the sacrifice of God to God, and me sacrificed together
with God, incorporated in His Incarnation. Christ born in me, a new Bethlehem, and sacrificed
in me, His new Calvary, and risen in me: offering me to the Father, in Himself, asking the
Father, my Father and His, to receive me into His infinite and special love — not the love He
has for all things that exist — for mere existence is a token of God's love, but the love of those
creatures who are drawn to Him in and with the power of His own love for Himself.

For now I had entered into the everlasting movement of that gravitation which is the very
life and spirit of God: God's own gravitation towards the depths of His own infinite nature, His
goodness without end. And God, that center Who is everywhere, and whose circumference is
nowhere, finding me, through incorporation with Christ, incorporated into this immense and
tremendous gravitational movement which is love, which is the Holy Spirit, loved me.

And He called out to me from His own immense depths.

Albert Camus

"THE GUEST"

Introduction by Charles Pfeiffer

Albert Camus (1913–1960) was born in Mondovi, Algeria of impoverished parents. His father, of Alsatian origin, died before Albert reached his first birthday. His mother moved to Algiers where Albert attended public schools and took a degree in philosophy at the University of Algeria. Before entering the university he had a bout with tuberculosis that interfered with his passion for playing soccer, and during his studies he held a number of odd jobs to support himself including working in an auto parts shop. From 1937–1941, Camus practiced journalism, traveled through Europe, wrote three of his most important works, *The Stranger* (a novel), *The Myth of Sisyphus* (an essay), and *Caligula* (a play), and taught at a private school in Oran. In 1942, he went to Paris to edit the newspaper, *Combat,* the voice of the French resistance in Nazi occupied France. After the war Camus remained in Paris and dedicated himself to writing. In 1957, he published a book of short stories, *Exile and the Kingdom,* in which "The Guest" appeared. In that same year he received the Nobel Prize for Literature.

Camus laid no claim to being an existentialist philosopher. He even sharply divided with Jean-Paul Sartre over some key issues. However, his ideas and manner of expression are very much embedded in the existentialist view which strongly influenced the inter-war and post WWII years. The key concept in Camus' thought is the notion of absurdity, the fact that there is no order, logic, or meaning discernable in the events of human existence. In fact, the more life is scrutinized, the more absurd life appears. Camus' notion of absurdity might be more easily understood by using the current expression *random*. Statements such as "I met this random person at this party" or "I just picked up some random book and was leafing through it..." could easily be interpreted as vague or unarticulated feelings that all the pieces in life's puzzle don't neatly fit. Camus thought that reflection on everyday experience, war, injustice, inequality, and especially the suffering of children, would make it clear that not only do the pieces not fit, but the only reasonable judgment that can be rendered is that human existence is absurd. On the other hand, Camus also recognized an inner, deep-seated desire on the part of humans to understand, make sense of, and impose an order on the events of life. That, according to Camus, is what produces meaning in life. Meaning is the refusal to accept randomness and absurdity; it is the refusal to give in or give up. Meaning occurs when the desire for order and purpose rebel against absurdity and rises above it to affirm human existence as being worthy and worth the effort.

Another central concept for existentialism is freedom of choice. Not only can choices be made, but they must be made. They cannot be pushed off onto someone else. The individual must take responsibility with no way of knowing what the correct choices are, and this radical individuality can give rise to feelings of isolation and insecurity. Sartre went so far as to say that "we are condemned to [exercise] our freedom." These choices are important and lead to consequences. These consequences lead to new situations that require another whole set of choices. For Camus, however, the consequences of choices are not the most important elements; consequences may turn out to be completely unexpected and increase life's absurdity and randomness. The meaningful element here is the continual rising to the challenge of making choices and attempting to create order and purpose against the absurdity of the random and chance events that human beings encounter daily.

By giving us a glimpse into the life of his main character in "The Guest," Camus allows us to see the whole human condition. Consideration of a few questions can throw this into bold relief. How does the setting of the story reflect the existentialist view? Does Camus give evidence that Daru experiences his situation as absurd and random? What measures does Daru take to rebel against the contradictory situation that he is thrust into? What sort of choices does Daru have to make (It might be good simply to make a list.), and what sort of tensions pull him in one direction or the other? Once Daru has made certain choices, what are the consequences? What does Daru's new situation demand of him? In wrestling with these questions it becomes apparent what Robert Frost meant when he wrote, "how way leads on to way," in "The Road Not Taken."

Camus' analysis of the human condition was tragically borne out in his own life. He preferred to travel by rail and disliked cars. One evening in January 1960, when he and his publisher were ready to return to Paris, Camus asked for a lift to the station. His publisher persuaded him to drive back to Paris with him. Their car crashed on the way, and Camus was killed. The unused portion of his rail ticket was found on his body — indeed, a random absurdity.

The Guest

The schoolmaster was watching the two men climb toward him. One was on horseback, the other on foot. They had not yet tackled the abrupt rise leading to the schoolhouse built on the hillside. They were toiling onward, making slow progress in the snow, among the stones, on the vast expanse of the high, deserted plateau. From time to time the horse stumbled. Without hearing anything yet, he could see the breath issuing from the horse's nostrils. One of the men, at least, knew the region. They were following the trail although it had disappeared days ago under a layer of dirty white snow. The schoolmaster calculated that it would take them half an hour to get onto the hill. It was cold; he went back into the school to get a sweater.

He crossed the empty, frigid classroom. On the blackboard the four rivers of France, drawn with four different colored chalks, had been flowing toward their estuaries for the past three days. Snow had suddenly fallen in mid-October after eight months of drought without the transition of rain, and the twenty pupils, more or less, who lived in the villages scattered over the plateau had stopped coming. With fair weather they would return. Daru now heated only the single room that was his lodging, adjoining the classroom and giving also onto the plateau to the east. Like the classroom windows, his window looked to the south too. On that side the school was a few kilometers from the point where the plateau began to slope toward the south. In clear weather could be seen the purple mass of the mountain range where the gap opened onto the desert.

Somewhat warmed, Daru returned to the window from which he had first seen the two men. They were no longer visible. Hence they must have tackled the rise. The sky was not so dark, for the snow had stopped falling during the night. The morning had opened with a dirty light which had scarcely become brighter as the ceiling of clouds lifted. At two in the afternoon it seemed as if the day were merely beginning. But still this was better than those three days when the thick snow was falling amidst unbroken darkness with little gusts of wind that rattled the double door of the classroom. Then Daru had spent long hours in his room, leaving it only to go to the shed and feed the chickens or get some coal. Fortunately the delivery truck from Tadjid, the nearest village to the north, had brought his supplies two days before the blizzard. It would return in forty-eight hours.

Besides, he had enough to resist a siege, for the little room was cluttered with bags of wheat that the administration left as a stock to distribute to those of his pupils whose families had suffered from the drought. Actually they had all been victims because they were all poor. Every day Daru would distribute a ration to the children. They had missed it, he knew, during these

Albert Camus, "The Guest," from Raymond Harris, ed., *Best Short Stories,* (Chicago: Jamestown, 1990), ISBN 0890617015, pp. 201–213.

bad days. Possibly one of the fathers or big brothers would come this afternoon and he could supply them with grain. It was just a matter of carrying them over to the next harvest. Now shiploads of wheat were arriving from France and the worst was over. But it would be hard to forget that poverty, that army of ragged ghosts wandering in the sunlight, the plateaus burned to a cinder month after month, the earth shriveled up little by little, literally scorched, every stone bursting into dust under one's foot. The sheep had died then by thousands and even a few men, here and there, sometimes without anyone's knowing.

In contrast with such poverty, he who lived almost like a monk in his remote schoolhouse, nonetheless satisfied with the little he had and with the rough life, had felt like a lord with his white-washed walls, his narrow couch, his unpainted shelves, his well, and his weekly provision of water and food. And suddenly this snow, without warning, without the foretaste of rain. This is the way the region was, cruel to live in, even without men — who didn't help matters either. But Daru had been born here. Everywhere else, he felt exiled.

He stepped out onto the terrace in front of the schoolhouse. The two men were now halfway up the slope. He recognized the horseman as Balducci, the old gendarme he had known for a long time. Balducci was holding on the end of a rope an Arab who was walking behind him with hands bound and head lowered. The gendarme waved a greeting to which Daru did not reply, lost as he was in contemplation of the Arab dressed in a faded blue jellaba, his feet in sandals but covered with socks of heavy raw wool, his head surmounted by a narrow, short *chèche*. They were approaching. Balducci was holding back his horse in order not to hurt the Arab, and the group was advancing slowly.

Within earshot, Balducci shouted: "One hour to do the three kilometers from El Ameur!" Daru did not answer. Short and square in his thick sweater, he watched them climb. Not once had the Arab raised his head. "Hello," said Daru when they got up onto the terrace. "Come in and warm up." Balducci painfully got down from his horse without letting go of the rope. From under his bristling mustache he smiled at the schoolmaster. His little dark eyes, deep-set under a tanned forehead, and his mouth surrounded with wrinkles made him look attentive and studious. Daru took the bridle, led the horse to the shed, and came back to the two men, who were now waiting for him in the school. He led them into his room. "I am going to heat up the classroom," he said. "We'll be more comfortable there." When he entered the room again, Balducci was on the couch. He had undone the rope tying him to the Arab, who had squatted near the stove. His hands still bound, the *chèche* pushed back on his head, he was looking toward the window. At first Daru noticed only his huge lips, fat, smooth, almost Negroid; yet his nose was straight, his eyes were dark and full of fever. The *chèche* revealed an obstinate forehead and, under the weathered skin now rather discolored by the cold, the whole face had a restless and rebellious look that struck Daru when the Arab, turning his face toward him, looked him straight in the eyes. "Go into the other room," said the schoolmaster, "and I'll make you some mint tea." "Thanks," Balducci said. "What a chore! How I long for retirement." And addressing his prisoner in Arabic: "Come on, you." The Arab got up and, slowly, holding his bound wrists in front of him, went into the classroom.

With the tea, Daru brought a chair. But Balducci was already enthroned on the nearest pupil's desk and the Arab had squatted against the teacher's platform facing the stove, which stood between the desk and the window. When he held out the glass of tea to the prisoner, Daru hesitated at the sight of his bound hands. "He might perhaps be untied." "Sure," said Balducci. "That was for the trip." He started to get to his feet. But Daru, setting the glass on the floor, had knelt beside the Arab. Without saying anything, the Arab watched him with his feverish eyes.

Once his hands were free, he rubbed his swollen wrists against each other, took the glass of tea, and sucked up the burning liquid in swift little sips.

"Good," said Daru. "And where are you headed?"

Balducci withdrew his mustache from the tea. "Here, son."

"Odd pupils! And you're spending the night?"

"No. I'm going back to El Ameur. And you will deliver this fellow to Tinguit. He is expected at police headquarters."

Balducci was looking at Daru with a friendly little smile.

"What's this story?" asked the schoolmaster. "Are you pulling my leg?"

"No, son. Those are the orders."

"The orders? I'm not . . ." Daru hesitated, not wanting to hurt the old Corsican. "I mean, that's not my job."

"What! What's the meaning of that? In wartime people do all kinds of jobs."

"Then I'll wait for the declaration of war!"

Balducci nodded.

"O.K. But the orders exist and they concern you too. Things are brewing, it appears. There is talk of a forthcoming revolt. We are mobilized, in a way."

Daru still had his obstinate look.

"Listen, son," Balducci said. "I like you and you must understand. There's only a dozen of us at El Ameur to patrol throughout the whole territory of a small department and I must get back in a hurry. I was told to hand this guy over to you and return without delay. He couldn't be kept there. His village was beginning to stir; they wanted to take him back. You must take him to Tinguit tomorrow before the day is over. Twenty kilometers shouldn't faze a husky fellow like you. After that, all will be over. You'll come back to your pupils and your comfortable life."

Behind the wall the horse could be heard snorting and pawing the earth. Daru was looking out the window. Decidedly, the weather was clearing and the light was increasing over the snowy plateau. When all the snow was melted, the sun would take over again and once more would burn the fields of stone. For days, still, the unchanging sky would shed its dry light on the solitary expanse where nothing had any connection with man.

"After all," he said, turning around toward Balducci, "what did he do?" And, before the gendarme had opened his mouth, he asked: "Does he speak French?"

"No, not a word. We had been looking for him for a month, but they were hiding him. He killed his cousin."

"Is he against us?"

"I don't think so. But you can never be sure."

"Why did he kill?"

"A family squabble, I think. One owed the other grain, it seems. It's not at all clear. In short, he killed his cousin with a billhook. You know, like a sheep, *kreezk*!"

Balducci made the gesture of drawing a blade across his throat and the Arab, his attention attracted, watched him with a sort of anxiety. Daru felt a sudden wrath against the man, against all men with their rotten spite, their tireless hates, their blood lust.

But the kettle was singing on the stove. He served Balducci more tea, hesitated, then served the Arab again, who, a second time, drank avidly. His raised arms made the jellaba fall open and the schoolmaster saw his thin, muscular chest.

"Thanks, kid," Balducci said. "And now, I'm off."

He got up and went toward the Arab, taking a small rope from his pocket.

"What are you doing?" Daru asked dryly.

Balducci, disconcerted, showed him the rope.

"Don't bother."

The old gendarme hesitated. "It's up to you. Of course, you are armed?"

"I have my shotgun."

"Where?"

"In the trunk."

"You ought to have it near your bed."

"Why? I have nothing to fear."

"You're crazy, son. If there's an uprising, no one is safe, we're all in the same boat."

"I'll defend myself. I'll have time to see them coming."

Balducci began to laugh, then suddenly the mustache covered the white teeth. "You'll have time? O.K. That's just what I was saying. You have always been a little cracked. That's why I like you, my son was like that."

At the same time he took out his revolver and put it on the desk.

"Keep it I don't need two weapons from here to El Ameur."

The revolver shone against the black paint of the table. When the gendarme turned toward him, the schoolmaster caught the smell of leather and horseflesh.

"Listen, Balducci," Daru said suddenly, "every bit of this disgusts me, and first of all your fellow here. But I won't hand him over. Fight, yes, if I have to. But not that."

The old gendarme stood in front of him and looked at him severely.

"You're being a fool," he said slowly. "I don't like it either. You don't get used to putting a rope on a man even after years of it, and you're even ashamed — yes, ashamed. But you can't let them have their way."

"I won't hand him over," Daru said again.

"It's an order, son, and I repeat it."

"That's right. Repeat to them what I've said to you: I won't hand him over."

Balducci made a visible effort to reflect, He looked at the Arab and at Daru. At last he decided.

"No, I won't tell them anything. If you want to drop us, go ahead; I'll not denounce you. I have an order to deliver the prisoner and I'm doing so. And now you'll just sign this paper for me."

"There's no need. I'll not deny that you left him with me."

"Don't be mean with me. I know you'll tell the truth. You're from hereabouts and you are a man. But you must sign, that's the rule."

Daru opened his drawer, took out a little square bottle of purple ink, the red wooden penholder with the "sergeant-major" pen he used for making models of penmanship, and signed. The gendarme carefully folded the paper and put it into his wallet. Then he moved toward the door.

"I'll see you off," Daru said.

"No," said Balducci. "There's no use being polite. You insulted me."

He looked at the Arab, motionless in the same spot, sniffed peevishly, and turned away toward the door. "Good-by, son," he said. The door shut behind him. Balducci appeared suddenly outside the window and then disappeared. His footsteps were muffled by the snow. The horse stirred on the other side of the wall and several chickens fluttered in fright. A moment later Balducci reappeared outside the window leading the horse by the bridle. He walked toward the little rise without turning around and disappeared from sight with the horse following him. A big stone could be heard bouncing down. Daru walked back toward the prisoner, who, without stirring, never took his eyes off him. "Wait," the schoolmaster said in Arabic and went toward the bedroom. As he was going through the door, he had a second thought, went to the desk, took the revolver, and stuck it in his pocket. Then, without looking back, he went into his room.

For some time he lay on his couch watching the sky gradually close over, listening to the silence. It was this silence that had seemed painful to him during the first days here, after the war. He had requested a post in the little town at the base of the foothills separating the upper plateaus from the desert. There, rocky walls, green and black to the north, pink and lavender to the south, marked the frontier of eternal summer. He had been named to a post farther north, on the plateau itself. In the beginning, the solitude and the silence had been hard for him on these wastelands peopled only by stones. Occasionally, furrows suggested cultivation, but they had been dug to uncover a certain kind of stone good for building. The only plowing here was to harvest rocks. Elsewhere a thin layer of soil accumulated in the hollows would be scraped out to enrich paltry village gardens. This is the way it was: bare rock covered three quarters of the region. Towns sprang up, flourished, then disappeared; men came by, loved one another or fought bitterly, then died. No one in this desert, neither he nor his guest, mattered. And yet, outside this desert neither of them, Daru knew, could have really lived.

When he got up, no noise came from the classroom. He was amazed at the unmixed joy he derived from the mere thought that the Arab might have fled and that he would be alone with no decision to make. But the prisoner was there. He had merely stretched out between the stove and the desk. With eyes open, he was staring at the ceiling. In that position, his thick lips were particularly noticeable, giving him a pouting look. "Come," said Daru. The Arab got up and followed him. In the bedroom, the schoolmaster pointed to a chair near the table under the window. The Arab sat down without taking his eyes off Daru.

"Are you hungry?"

"Yes," the prisoner said.

Daru set the table for two. He took flour and oil, shaped a cake in a frying-pan, and lighted the little stove that functioned on bottled gas. While the cake was cooking, he went out to the shed to get cheese, eggs, dates, and condensed milk. When the cake was done he set it on the window sill to cool, heated some condensed milk diluted with water, and beat up the eggs into an omelette. In one of his motions he knocked against the revolver stuck in his right pocket. He set the bowl down, went into the classroom, and put the revolver in his desk drawer. When he came back to the room, night was falling. He put on the light and served the Arab. "Eat," he said. The Arab took a piece of the cake, lifted it eagerly to his mouth, and stopped short.

"And you?" he asked.

"After you. I'll eat too."

The thick lips opened slightly. The Arab hesitated, then bit into the cake determinedly.

The meal over, the Arab looked at the schoolmaster. "Are you the judge?"

"No, I'm simply keeping you until tomorrow."

"Why do you eat with me?"

"I'm hungry."

The Arab fell silent. Daru got up and went out. He brought back a folding bed from the shed, set it up between the table and the stove, perpendicular to his own bed. From a large suitcase which, upright in a corner, served as a shelf for papers, he took two blankets and arranged them on the camp bed. Then he stopped, felt useless, and sat down on his bed. There was nothing more to do or to get ready. He had to look at this man. He looked at him, therefore, trying to imagine his face bursting with rage. He couldn't do so. He could see nothing but the dark yet shining eyes and the animal mouth.

"Why did you kill him?" he asked in a voice whose hostile tone surprised him.

The Arab looked away. "He ran away. I ran after him."

He raised his eyes to Daru again and they were full of a sort of woeful interrogation. "Now what will they do to me?"

"Are you afraid?"

He stiffened, turning his eyes away.

"Are you sorry?"

The Arab stared at him openmouthed. Obviously he did not understand. Daru's annoyance was growing. At the same time he felt awkward and self-conscious with his big body wedged between the two beds.

"Lie down there," he said impatiently. "That's your bed."

The Arab didn't move. He called to Daru:

"Tell me!"

The schoolmaster looked at him.

"Is the gendarme coming back tomorrow?"

"I don't know."

'Are you coming with us?"

"I don't know. Why?"

The prisoner got up and stretched out on top of the blankets, his feet toward the window. The light from the electric bulb shone straight into his eyes and he closed them at once.

"Why?" Daru repeated, standing beside the bed.

The Arab opened his eyes under the blinding light and looked at him, trying not to blink.

"Come with us," he said.

In the middle of the night, Daru was still not asleep. He had gone to bed after undressing completely; he generally slept naked. But when he suddenly realized that he had nothing on, he hesitated. He felt vulnerable and the temptation came to him to put his clothes back on. Then he shrugged his shoulders; after all, he wasn't a child and, if need be, he could break his adversary in two. From his bed he could observe him, lying on his back, still motionless with his eyes closed under the harsh light. When Daru turned out the light, the darkness seemed to coagulate all of a sudden. Little by little, the night came back to life in the window where the starless sky was stirring gently. The schoolmaster soon made out the body lying at his feet. The Arab still did not move, but his eyes seemed open. A faint wind was prowling around the schoolhouse. Perhaps it would drive away the clouds and the sun would reappear.

During the night the wind increased, The hens fluttered a little and then were silent, The Arab turned over on his side with his back to Daru, who thought he heard him moan, Then he listened for his guest's breathing, become heavier and more regular. He listened to that breath so close to him and mused without being able to go to sleep. In this room where he had been sleeping alone for a year, this presence bothered him. But it bothered him also by imposing on him a sort of brotherhood he knew well but refused to accept in the present circumstances. Men who share the same rooms, soldiers or prisoners, develop a strange alliance as if, having cast off their armor with their clothing, they fraternized every evening, over and above their differences, in the ancient community of dream and fatigue. But Daru shook himself; he didn't like such musings, and it was essential to sleep.

A little later, however, when the Arab stirred slightly, the schoolmaster was still not asleep. When the prisoner made a second move, he stiffened, on the alert. The Arab was lifting himself slowly on his arms with almost the motion of a sleepwalker. Seated upright in bed, he waited motionless without turning his head toward Daru, as if he were listening attentively. Daru did not stir, it had just occurred to him that the revolver was still in the drawer of his desk. It was better to act at once. Yet he continued to observe the prisoner, who, with the same slithery motion, put his feet on the ground, waited again, then began to stand up slowly. Daru was about to call out to him when the Arab began to walk, in a quite natural but extraordinarily silent way. He was heading toward the door at the end of the room that opened into the shed. He lifted the latch with precaution and went out, pushing the door behind him but without shutting it. Daru had not stirred. "He is running away," he merely thought. "Good riddance!" Yet he listened attentively. The hens were not fluttering; the guest must be on the plateau. A faint sound of water reached him, and he didn't know what it was until the Arab again stood framed in the doorway, closed the door carefully, and came back to bed without a sound. Then Daru turned his back on him and fell asleep. Still later he seemed, from the depths of his sleep, to hear furtive steps around the schoolhouse. "I'm dreaming! I'm dreaming!" he repeated to himself. And he went on sleeping.

When he awoke, the sky was clear; the loose window let in a cold, pure air. The Arab was asleep, hunched up under the blankets now, his mouth open, utterly relaxed. But when Daru shook him, he started dreadfully, staring at Daru with wild eyes as if he had never seen him and such a frightened expression that the schoolmaster stepped back. "Don't be afraid. It's me. You must eat." The Arab nodded his head and said yes. Calm had returned to his face, but his expression was vacant and listless.

The coffee was ready. They drank it seated together on the folding bed as they munched their pieces of the cake. Then Daru led the Arab under the shed and showed him the faucet where he washed. He went back into the room, folded the blankets and the bed, made his own bed and put the room in order. Then he went through the classroom and out onto the terrace. The sun was already rising in the blue sky; a soft, bright light was bathing the deserted plateau. On the ridge the snow was melting in spots. The stones were about to reappear. Crouched on the edge of the plateau, the schoolmaster looked at the deserted expanse. He thought of Balducci. He had hurt him, for he had sent him off in a way as if he didn't want to be associated with him. He could still hear the gendarme's farewell and, without knowing why, he felt strangely empty and vulnerable. At that moment, from the other side of the schoolhouse, the prisoner coughed. Daru listened to him almost despite himself and then, furious, threw a pebble that whistled through the air before sinking into the snow. That man's stupid crime revolted him, but to hand him over was contrary to honor. Merely thinking of it made him smart with humiliation. And he cursed at one and the same time his own people who had sent him this Arab and the Arab too who had dared to kill and not managed to get away. Daru got up, walked in a circle on the terrace, waited motionless, and then went back into the schoolhouse.

The Arab, leaning over the cement floor of the shed, was washing his teeth with two fingers. Daru looked at him and said: "Come." He went back into the room ahead of the prisoner. He slipped a hunting-jacket on over his sweater and put on walking-shoes. Standing, he waited until the Arab had put on his *chèche* and sandals. They went into the classroom and the schoolmaster pointed to the exit, saying: "Go ahead." The fellow didn't budge. "I'm coming," said Daru. The Arab went out. Daru went back into the room and made a package of pieces of rusk, dates, and sugar. In the classroom, before going out, he hesitated a second in front of his desk, then crossed the threshold and locked the door. "That's the way," he said. He started toward the east, followed by the prisoner. But, a short distance from the schoolhouse, he thought he heard a slight sound behind them. He retraced his steps and examined the surroundings of the house; there was no one there. The Arab watched him without seeming to understand. "Come on," said Daru.

They walked for an hour and rested beside a sharp peak of limestone. The snow was melting faster and faster and the sun was drinking up the puddles at once, rapidly cleaning the plateau, which gradually dried and vibrated like the air itself. When they resumed walking, the ground rang under their feet. From time to time a bird rent the space in front of them with a joyful cry. Daru breathed in deeply the fresh morning light. He felt a sort of rapture before the vast familiar expanse, now almost entirely yellow under its dome of blue sky. They walked an hour more, descending toward the south. They reached a level height made up of crumbly rocks. From there on, the plateau sloped down, eastward toward a low plain where there were a few spindly trees and, to the south, toward outcroppings of rock that gave the landscape a chaotic look.

Daru surveyed the two directions. There was nothing but the sky on the horizon. Not a man could be seen. He turned toward the Arab, who was looking at him blankly. Daru held out the package to him. "Take it," he said. "There are dates, bread, and sugar. You can hold out for two days. Here are a thousand francs too." The Arab took the package and the money but kept his full hands at chest level as if he didn't know what to do with what was being given him. "Now look," the schoolmaster said as he pointed in the direction of the east, "there's the way to Tinguit. You have a two-hour walk. At Tinguit you'll find the administration and the police. They are expecting you." The Arab looked toward the east, still holding the package and the money against his chest. Daru took his elbow and turned him rather roughly toward the south. At the foot of the height on which they stood could be seen a faint path. "That's the trail across the plateau. In a day's walk from here you'll find pasturelands and the first nomads. They'll take you in and shelter you according to their law." The Arab had now turned toward Daru and a sort of panic was visible in his expression. "Listen," he said. Daru shook his head: "No, be quiet. Now I'm leaving you." He turned his back on him, took two long steps in the direction of the school, looked hesitantly at the motionless Arab, and started off again. For a few minutes he heard nothing but his own step resounding on the cold ground and did not turn his head. A moment later, however, he turned around. The Arab was still there on the edge of the hill, his arms hanging now, and he was looking at the schoolmaster. Daru felt something rise in his throat. But he swore with impatience, waved vaguely, and started off again. He had already gone some distance when he again stopped and looked. There was no longer anyone on the hill.

Daru hesitated. The sun was now rather high in the sky and was beginning to beat down on his head. The schoolmaster retraced his steps, at first somewhat uncertainly, then with decision. When he reached the little hill, he was bathed in sweat. He climbed it as fast as he could and stopped, out of breath, at the top. The rock-fields to the south stood out sharply against the blue sky, but on the plain to the east a steamy heat was already rising. And in that slight haze, Daru, with heavy heart, made out the Arab walking slowly on the road to prison.

A little later, standing before the window of the classroom, the schoolmaster was watching the clear light bathing the whole surface of the plateau, but he harldy saw it. Behind him on the blackboard, among the winding French rivers, sprawled the clumsily chalked-up words he had just read: "You handed over our brother. You will pay for this." Daru looked at the sky, the plateau, and, beyond, the invisible lands stretching all the way to the sea. In this vast landscape he had loved so much, he was alone.

Michel Foucault

DISCIPLINE AND PUNISH

Introduction by Shelley Baranowski

The French philosopher Michel Foucault (1926–84) was one of the foremost theorists of postmodernism, a movement that has had a profound impact on the fine arts, social sciences, and humanities since the nineteen seventies. Born in Poitiers, France, Foucault taught philosophy in several French universities, as well as in Tunis, Uppsala, and Warsaw before being elected to the prestigious College de France in 1970. His international reputation grew rapidly in the years before his death in 1984 and has continued to flourish since.

Foucault challenged the concept of the self that had been in place since Descartes. Descartes' famous maxim, "I think, therefore I am," implied that the self was not only a stable entity but also the source of knowledge. By contrast, Foucault maintained that the self or "subject" was subject to change and influenced over time by historical events, impersonal forces such as capitalism, and powerful social institutions such as the police, public health and welfare, the medical establishment, and the church. Following Nietzsche's belief that traditional values had lost their power over individuals, Foucault maintained that truth itself was not absolute. Rather, the systems of knowledge (which include academic disciplines) and social institutions in place at a given historical moment define what is "true" or "false." The relationship between the self on the one hand and Western society and the state on the other constituted Foucault's career-long preoccupation.

Foucault's link with postmodernism lies in his skepticism toward the Enlightenment, especially its "humane" reformism and its doctrine of "progress" that became so influential during the nineteenth century. Again influenced by Nietzsche, Foucault maintained that the will to power motivated human behavior either directly through individuals or indirectly through the sciences and social sciences and the institutions dependent on them. Foucault focused particularly on the "micropolitics" of power. Instead of investigating the obvious instruments of government (the executive or the national legislature, for example), he probed the diffusion of power through public institutions such as the legal system and prison, mental hospital, and military barracks. In his last years, he undertook a detailed study of the emergence of modern Western concepts of sexuality and the body and their relationship to issues of power. Foucault questioned whether modern Western therapeutic institutions were really as humane as the Enlightenment conceived of them, raising the possibility that their primary purpose was to discipline the body and shape individual identities to conform to the requirements of the modern state and capitalism. Always attentive to the socially marginalized, be they asylum patients, prisoners, or non-Europeans, Foucault further questioned whether the Enlightenment's emphasis on reason as the key to human emancipation had really turned into an instrument of domination and repression.

The reading below is drawn from *Discipline and Punish* (1975), Foucault's study of the emergence of modern Western penal systems. Beginning with the early modern period, in which the church and the personality of the sovereign underwrote very public and gruesome tortures and executions, Foucault identifies increasingly impersonal, rational, measured, and less public means of punishing criminals, who were incarcerated behind the walls of penitentiaries as the nineteenth century progressed. The British liberal Jeremy Bentham contributed significantly to that development with his design of the prison as "panopticon," which increased the surveillance capability of penal officers over prisoners. How, according to Foucault, does the prison claim to function as opposed to how it actually functions? What disciplines have contributed to the penal system? Is the modern penitentiary and legal system "humane" as the Italian Enlightenment thinker Caesere Beccaria suggested it would be? Often Foucault is interpreted as suggesting that Western culture, far from being "progressive" or "humane," has more often than not disciplined, excluded, and repressed those whom Western culture does not consider "normal." Drawing on his work on prisons, do you agree?

Complete and Austere Institutions

(from Discipline and Punish)

It would not be true to say that the prison was born with the new codes. The prison form ante-dates its systematic use in the penal system. It had already been constituted outside the legal apparatus when, throughout the social body, procedures were being elaborated for distributing individuals; fixing them in space; classifying them; extracting from them the maximum in time and forces; training their bodies; coding their continuous behavior; maintaining them in perfect visibility; forming around them an apparatus of observation, registration, and recording; consti-tuting on them a body of knowledge that is accumulated and centralized. The general form of an apparatus intended to render individuals docile and useful, by means of precise work upon their bodies, indicated the prison institution, before the law ever defined it as the penalty *par excel-lence*. At the turn of the eighteenth and nineteenth centuries, there was, it is true, a penality of detention; and it was a new thing. But it was really the opening up of penality to mechanisms of coercion already elaborated elsewhere. The "models" of penal detention — Ghent, Gloucester, Walnut Street — marked the first visible points of this transition, rather than innovations or points of departure. The prison, an essential element in the punitive panoply, certainly marks an important moment in the history of penal justice: its access to "humanity." But it is also an important moment in the history of those disciplinary mechanisms that the new class power was developing: that in which they colonized the legal institution. At the turn of the century, a new legislation defined the power to punish as a general function of society that was exercised in the same manner over all its members, and in which each individual was equally represented: but in making detention the penalty *par excellence,* it introduced procedures of domination characteristic of a particular type of power. A justice that is supposed to be "equal," a legal machinery that is supposed to be "autonomous," but contains all the asymmetries of disciplinary subjection, this conjunction marked the birth of the prison, "the penalty of civilized societies."[1]

One can understand the self-evident character that prison punishment very soon assumed. In the first years of the nineteenth century, people were still aware of its novelty; and yet it appeared so bound up, and at such a deep level, with the very functioning of society that it ban-ished into oblivion all the other punishments that the eighteenth-century reformers had imag-ined. It seemed to have no alternative, as if carried along by the very movement of history: "It is not chance, it is not the whim of the legislator that have made imprisonment the base and almost the entire edifice of our present penal scale: it is the progress of ideas and the improvement in morals."[2] And, although, in a little over a century, this self-evident character has become trans-formed, it has not disappeared. We are aware of all the inconveniences of prison, and that it is dangerous when it is not useless. And yet one cannot "see" how to replace it. It is the detestable solution, which one seems unable to do without.

This "self-evident" character of the prison, which we find so difficult to abandon, is based first of all on the simple form of "deprivation of liberty." How could prison not be the penalty

---

The Foucault Reader, ed. Paul Rabinow (New York: Pantheon, 1984), pp. 214–225.

1. P. Rossi, *Traité de droit pénal,* III (1829), p. 169.
2. P. Van Meenan, "Congrès pénitentiaire de Bruxelles," *Annales de la Charité* (1847), pp. 529–30.

par excellence in a society in which liberty is a good that belongs to all in the same way and to which each individual is attached, as Duport put it, by a "universal and constant" feeling? Its loss has therefore the same value for all; unlike the fine, it is an "egalitarian" punishment. The prison is the clearest, simplest, most equitable of penalties. Moreover, it makes it possible to quantify the penalty exactly according to the variable of time. There is a wages-form of imprisonment that constitutes, in industrial societies, its economic "self-evidence" — and enables it to appear as a reparation. By levying on the time of the prisoner, the prison seems to express in concrete terms the idea that the offense has injured, beyond the victim, society as a whole. There is an economico-moral self-evidence of a penality that metes out punishments in days, months, and years and draws up quantitative equivalences between offenses and durations. Hence the expression, so frequently heard, so consistent with the functioning of punishments, though contrary to the strict theory of penal law, that one is in prison in order to "pay one's debt." The prison is "natural," just as the use of time to measure exchanges is "natural" in our society.[3]

But the self-evidence of the prison is also based on its role, supposed or demanded, as an apparatus for transforming individuals. How could the prison not be immediately accepted when, by locking up, retraining, and rendering docile, it merely reproduces, with a little more emphasis, all the mechanisms that are to be found in the social body? The prison is like a rather disciplined barracks, a strict school, a dark workshop, but not qualitatively different. This double foundation — juridico-economic on the one hand, technico-disciplinary on the other — made the prison seem the most immediate and civilized form of all penalties. And it is this double functioning that immediately gave it its solidity. One thing is clear: the prison was not at first a deprivation of liberty to which a technical function of correction was later added; it was from the outset a form of "legal detention" entrusted with an additional corrective task, or an enterprise for reforming individuals that the deprivation of liberty allowed to function in the legal system. In short, penal imprisonment, from the beginning of the nineteenth century, covered both the deprivation of liberty and the technical transformation of individuals. . . .

The prison, the place where the penalty is carried out, is also the place of observation of punished individuals. This takes two forms: surveillance, of course, but also knowledge of each inmate, of his behavior, his deeper states of mind, his gradual improvement; the prisons must be conceived as places for the formation of clinical knowledge about the convicts; "the penitentiary system cannot be an *a priori* conception; it is an induction of the social state. There are moral diseases, as well as breakdowns in health, where the treatment depends on the site and direction of the illness."[4] This involves two essential mechanisms. It must be possible to hold the prisoner under permanent observation; every report that can be made about him must be recorded and computed. The theme of the panopticon — at once surveillance and observation, security and knowledge, individualization and totalization, isolation and transparency — found in the prison its privileged locus of realization. Although the panoptic procedures, as concrete forms of the exercise of power, have become extremely widespread, at least in their less concentrated forms, it was really only in the penitentiary institutions that Bentham's utopia could be fully expressed in a material form. In the 1830s, the panopticon became the architectural program of most prison

---

3. The play between the two "natures" of the prison still continues. A few days ago [summer 1974] the head of state recalled the "principle" that detention ought to be no more than a "deprivation of liberty" — the pure essence of imprisonment, freed of the reality of prison; and added that the prison could be justified only by its "corrective" or rehabilitating effects.

4. L. Faucher, *De la réforme des prisons* (1838), p. 6.

projects. It was the most direct way of expressing "the intelligence of discipline in stone";[5] of making architecture transparent to the administration of power;[6] of making it possible to substitute for force or other violent constraints the gentle efficiency of total surveillance; of ordering space according to the recent humanization of the codes and the new penitentiary theory: "The authorities, on the one hand, and the architect, on the other, must know, therefore, whether the prisons are to be based on the principle of milder penalties or on a system of reforming convicts, in accordance with legislation which, by getting to the root cause of the people's vices, becomes a principle that will regenerate the virtues that they must practice."[7]

In short, its task was to constitute a prison-machine with a cell of visibility in which the inmate will find himself caught as "in the glass house of the Greek philosopher"[9] and a central point from which a permanent gaze may control prisoners and staff. Around these two requirements, several variations were possible: the Benthamite panopticon in its strict form, the semicircle, the cross-plan, the star shape. In the midst of all these discussions, the Minister of the Interior in 1841 sums up the fundamental principles: "The central inspection hall is the pivot of the system. Without a central point of inspection, surveillance ceases to be guaranteed, continuous, and general; for it is impossible to have complete trust in the activity, zeal, and intelligence of the warder who immediately supervises the cells. . . .The architect must therefore bring all his attention to bear on this object; it is a question both of discipline and economy. The more accurate and easy the surveillance, the less need will there be to seek in the strength of the building guarantees against attempted escape and communication between the inmates. But surveillance will be perfect if from a central hall the director or head-warder sees, without moving and without being seen, not only the entrances of all the cells and even the inside of most of them when the unglazed door is open, but also the warders guarding the prisoners on every floor. . . . With the formula of circular or semicircular prisons, it would be possible to see from a single center all the prisoners in their cells and the warders in the inspection galleries."[10]

But the penitentiary panopticon was also a system of individualizing and permanent documentation. The same year in which variants of the Benthamite schema were recommended for the building of prisons, the system of "moral accounting" was made compulsory: and individual report of a uniform kind in every prison, on which the governor or head-warder, the chaplain, and the instructor had to fill in their observations on each inmate: "It is in a way the *vade mecum* of prison administration, making it possible to assess each case, each circumstance and, consequently, to know what treatment to apply to each prisoner individually."[11] Many other, much more complete systems of recording were planned or tried out.[12] The overall aim was to make the prison a place for the constitution of a body of knowledge that would regulate the exercise of penitentiary practice. The prison has not only to know the decision of the judges and

5. C. Lucas, *De la réforme des prisons*, I (1836), p. 69.

6. "If one treats of the administrative question by abstracting the question of buildings, one runs the risk of drawing up principles that are based on no reality; whereas, with a sufficient knowledge of administrative needs, an architect may accept a particular system of imprisonment that theory may have dismissed as utopian" (Abel Bouet, *Projet des prisons cellulaires* [1843], p. 1).

7. L. Baltard, *Architectonographie des prisons* (1829), pp. 4–5.

8. "The English reveal their genius for mechanics in everything they do . . . and they want their buildings to function as a machine subject to the action of a single motor" (Ibid., p. 18).

9. N. P. Harou-Romain, *Projet de pénitencier* (1840), p. 8.

10. Ducatel, *Instruction pour la construction des maisons d'arrêt* (1841), p. 9.

11. E. Ducpétiaux, *De la réforme pénitentiaire*, III (1837), pp. 56–7.

12. See, for example, G. de Grégory, *Projet de Code pénal universel* (1832), p. 199ff; and Grellet-Wammy, *Manuel des prisons*, II (1839), pp. 23–5, 199–203.

to apply it in terms of the established regulations; it has to extract unceasingly from the inmate a body of knowledge that will make it possible to transform the penal measure into a penitentiary operation, which will make of the penalty required by the offense a modification of the inmate that will be of use to society. The autonomy of the carceral regime and the knowledge that it creates make it possible to increase the utility of the penalty, which the code had made the very principle of its punitive philosophy: "The governor must not lose sight of a single inmate, because in whatever part of the prison the inmate is to be found, whether he is entering or leaving, or whether he is staying there, the governor must also justify the motives for his staying in a particular classification or for his movement from one to another. He is a veritable accountant. Each inmate is for him, in the sphere of individual education, a capital invested with penitentiary interest."[13] As a highly efficient technology, penitentiary practice produces a return on the capital invested in the penal system and in the building of heavy prisons.

Similarly, the offender becomes an individual to know. This demand for knowledge was not, in the first instance, inserted into the legislation itself, in order to provide substance for the sentence and to determine the true degree of guilt. It is as a convict, as a point of application for punitive mechanisms, that the offender is constituted himself as the object of possible knowledge.

But this implies that the penitentiary apparatus, with the whole technological program that accompanies it, brings about a curious substitution: from the hands of justice, it certainly receives a convicted person; but what it must apply itself to is not, of course, the offense, nor even exactly the offender, but a rather different object, one defined by variables which at the outset at least were not taken into account in the sentence, for they were relevant only for a corrective technology. This other character, whom the penitentiary apparatus substitutes for the convicted offender, is the *delinquent*.

The delinquent is to be distinguished from the offender by the fact that it is not so much his act as his life that is relevant in characterizing him. The penitentiary operation, if it is to be a genuine reeducation, must become the sum total existence of the delinquent, making of the prison a sort of artificial and coercive theater in which his life will be examined from top to bottom. The legal punishment bears on an act, the punitive technique on a life; it falls to this punitive technique, therefore, to reconstitute all the sordid detail of a life in the form of knowledge, to fill in the gaps of that knowledge, and to act upon it by a practice of compulsion. It is a biographical knowledge and a technique for correcting individual lives. The observation of the delinquent "should go back not only to the circumstances, but also to the causes of his crime; they must be sought in the story of his life, from the triple point of view of psychology, social position, and upbringing, in order to discover the dangerous proclivities of the first, the harmful predispositions of the second, and the bad antecedents of the third. This biographical investigation is an essential part of the preliminary investigation for the classification of penalties before it becomes a condition for the classification of moralities in the penitentiary system. It must accompany the convict from the court to the prison, where the governor's task is not only to receive it, but also to complete, supervise, and rectify its various factors during the period of detention."[14] Behind the offender, to whom the investigation of the facts may attribute responsibility for an offense, stands the delinquent, whose slow formation is shown in a biographical investigation. The introduction of the "biographical" is important in the history of penality. Because it establishes the "criminal" as existing before the crime and even outside it. And, for this reason, a psychological causality, duplicating the juridical attribution of responsibility, con-

---

13. Lucas, *De la réforme des prisons*, II, pp. 449–50.
14. Ibid., pp. 440–2.

fuses its effects. At this point one enters the "criminological" labyrinth from which we have
certainly not yet emerged: any determining cause, because it reduces responsibility, marks the
author of the offense with a criminality all the more formidable and demands penitentiary
measures that are all the stricter. As the biography of the criminal duplicates in penal practice
the analysis of circumstances used in gauging the crime, so one sees penal discourse and psychiatric discourse crossing each other's frontiers; and there, at their point of junction, is formed
the notion of the "dangerous" individual, which makes it possible to draw up a network of
causality in terms of an entire biography and to present a verdict of punishment-correction.[15]

The delinquent is also to be distinguished from the offender in that he is not only the author
of his acts (the author responsible in terms of certain criteria of free, conscious will), but is
linked to his offense by a whole bundle of complex threads (instincts, drives, tendencies, character). The penitentiary technique bears not on the relation between author and crime, but on
the criminal's affinity with his crime. The delinquent, the strange manifestation of an overall
phenomenon of criminality, is to be found in quasi-natural classes, each endowed with its own
characteristics and requiring a specific treatment, what Marquet-Wasselot called in 1841 the
"ethnography of the prisons"; "The convicts are . . . another people within the same people;
with its own habits, instincts, morals."[16] We are still very close here to the "picturesque"
descriptions of the world of the malefactors — an old tradition that goes back a long way and
gained a new vigor in the early nineteenth century, at a time when the perception of another
form of life was being articulated on that of another class and another human species. A zoology
of social subspecies and an ethnology of the civilizations of malefactors, with their own rites
and language, were beginning to emerge in a parody form. But an attempt was also being made
to constitute a new objectivity in which the criminal belongs to a typology that is both natural
and deviant. Delinquency, a pathological gap in the human species, may be analyzed as morbid
syndromes or as great teratological forms. With Ferrus's classification, we probably have one of
the first conversions of the old "ethnography" of crime into a systematic typology of delinquents. The analysis is slender, certainly, but it reveals quite clearly the principle that delinquency must be specified in terms not so much of the law as of the norm. There are three types
of convict; there are those who are endowed "with intellectual resources above the average of
intelligence that we have established," but who have been perverted either by the "tendencies of
their organization" and a "native predisposition," or by "pernicious logic," an "iniquitous
morality," a "dangerous attitude to social duties." Those that belong to this category require isolation day and night, solitary exercise, and, when one is forced to bring them into contact with
the others, they should wear "a light mask made of metal netting, of the kind used for stone-cut-
ting or fencing." The second category is made up of "vicious, stupid or passive convicts, who
have been led into evil by indifference to either shame or honour, through cowardice, that is to
say, laziness, and because of a lack of resistance to bad incitements"; the regime suitable to
them is not so much that of punishment as of education, and if possible of mutual education:

---

15. One should study how the practice of biography became widespread at about the same time as the constitution of
the individual delinquent in the punitive mechanisms: the biography or autobiography of prisoners in Appert; the
drawing up of biographical files on the psychiatric model; the use of biography in the defense of accused persons. On
the last point one might compare the great justificatory memoirs of the late eighteenth century written for the three
men condemned to the wheel, or for Jeanne Salmon — and the defenses of criminals in the period of Louis Philippe.
Chaix d'Est-Ange pleaded for La Roncière: "If long before the crime, long before the charge is laid, you can scruti-
nize the defendant's life, penetrate into his heart, find its most hidden corners, lay bare all his thoughts, his entire soul"
(*Discours et plaidoyers*, III, p. 166).

16. J. J. Marquet-Wasselot, *L'Ethnographie des prisons* (1841), p. 9.

isolation at night, work in common during the day, conversations permitted provided they are conducted aloud, reading in common, followed by mutual questioning, for which rewards may be given. Lastly, there are the "inept or incapable convicts," who are "rendered incapable, by an incomplete organization, of any occupation requiring considered effort and consistent will, and who are therefore incapable of competing in work with intelligent workers and who, having neither enough education to know their social duties, nor enough intelligence to understand this fact or to struggle against their personal instincts, are led to evil by their very incapacity. For these, solitude would merely encourage their inertia; they must therefore live in common, but in such a way as to form small groups, constantly stimulated by collective operations, and subjected to rigid surveillance."[17] Thus a "positive" knowledge of the delinquents and their species, very different from the juridical definition of offenses and their circumstances, is gradually established; but this knowledge is also distinct from the medical knowledge that makes it possible to introduce the insanity of the individual and, consequently, to efface the criminal character of the act. Ferrus states the principle quite clearly: "Considered as a whole, criminals are nothing less than madmen; it would be unjust to the latter to confuse them with consciously perverted men." The task of this new knowledge is to define the act "scientifically" *qua* offense and above all the individual *qua* delinquent. Criminology is thus made possible.

The correlative of penal justice may well be the offender, but the correlative of the penitentiary apparatus is someone other; this is the delinquent, a biographical unity, a kernel of danger, representing a type of anomaly. And, although it is true that to a detention that deprives of liberty, as defined by law, the prison added the additional element of the penitentiary, this penitentiary element introduced in turn a third character who slipped between the individual condemned by the law and the individual who carries out this law. At the point that marked the disappearance of the branded, dismembered, burnt, annihilated body of the tortured criminal, there appeared the body of the prisoner, duplicated by the individuality of the "delinquent," by the little soul of the criminal, which the very apparatus of punishment fabricated as a point of application of the power to punish and as the object of what is still called today penitentiary science. It is said that the prison fabricated delinquents; it is true that it brings back, almost inevitably, before the courts those who have been sent there. But it also fabricates them in the sense that it has introduced into the operation of the law and the offense, the judge and the offender, the condemned man and the executioner, the noncorporal reality of the delinquency that links them together and, for a century and a half, has caught them in the same trap.

The penitentiary technique and the delinquent are in a sense twin brothers. It is not true that it was the discovery of the delinquent through a scientific rationality that introduced into our old prisons the refinement of penitentiary techniques. Nor is it true that the internal elaboration of penitentiary methods has finally brought to light the "objective" existence of a delinquency that the abstraction and rigidity of the law were unable to perceive. They appeared together, the one extending from the other, as a technological ensemble that forms and fragments the object to which it applies its instruments. And it is this delinquency, formed in the foundations of the judicial apparatus, among the "*basses œuvres*," the servile tasks, from which justice averts its gaze, out of the shame it feels in punishing those it condemns, it is this delinquency that now comes to haunt the untroubled courts and the majesty of the laws; it is this delinquency that

---

17. G. Ferrus, Des prisonniers (1850), pp. 182ff, 278ff.

must be known, assessed, measured, diagnosed, treated when sentences are passed. It is now this delinquency, this anomaly, this deviation, this potential danger, this illness, this form of existence, that must be taken into account when the codes are rewritten. Delinquency is the vengeance of the prison on justice. It is a revenge formidable enough to leave the judge speechless. It is at this point that the criminologists raise their voices.

But we must not forget that the prison, that concentrated and austere figure of all the disciplines, is not an endogenous element in the penal system as defined at the turn of the eighteenth and nineteenth centuries. The theme of a punitive society and of a general semio-technique of punishment that has sustained the "ideological" codes — Beccarian or Benthamite — did not itself give rise to the universal use of the prison. This prison came from elsewhere — from the mechanisms proper to a disciplinary power. Now, despite this heterogeneity, the mechanisms and effects of the prison have spread right through modern criminal justice; delinquency and the delinquents have become parasites on it through and through. One must seek the reason for this formidable "efficiency" of the prison. But one thing may be noted at the outset: the penal justice defined in the eighteenth century by the reformers traced two possible but divergent lines of objectification of the criminal: the first was the series of "monsters," moral or political, who had fallen outside the social pact; the second was that of the juridical subject rehabilitated by punishment. Now the "delinquent" makes it possible to join the two lines and to constitute under the authority of medicine, psychology, or criminology, an individual in whom the offender of the law and the object of a scientific technique are superimposed — or almost — one upon the other. That the grip of the prison on the penal system should not have led to a violent reaction of rejection is no doubt due to many reasons. One of these is that, in fabricating delinquency, it gave to criminal justice a unitary field of objects, authenticated by the "sciences," and thus enabled it to function on a general horizon of "truth."

The prison, that darkest region in the apparatus of justice, is the place where the power to punish, which no longer dares to manifest itself openly, silently organizes a field of objectivity in which punishment will be able to function openly as treatment and the sentence be inscribed among the discourses of knowledge. It is understandable that justice should have adopted so easily a prison that was not the offspring of its own thoughts. Justice certainly owed the prison this recognition.